# Rethinking Trinitarian Theology

# Rethinking Trinitarian Theology

## Disputed Questions and Contemporary Issues in Trinitarian Theology

*Edited by*

*Giulio Maspero*

*and*

*Robert J. Woźniak*

t&t clark

**Published by T&T Clark International**
*A Continuum Imprint*
The Tower Building, 11 York Road, London SE1 7NX
80 Maiden Lane, Suite 704, New York, NY 10038

www.continuumbooks.com

**British Library Cataloguing-in-Publication Data**
A catalogue record for this book is available from the British Library

ISBN 13: 978–0–567–60381–4 (hardback)
ISBN 13: 978–0–567–22546–7 (paperback)

Typeset by Fakenham Prepress Solutions, Fakenham, Norfolk NR21 8NN
Printed on acid-free paper in Great Britain

# CONTENTS

# INTRODUCTION

*Fides omnium christianorum in Trinitate consistit* – 'the faith of all Christians rests on the Trinity'.[1] After a long period of theoretical and practical negligence this statment attains once again its fundamental truth in the present moment of Christian theology and in a Christian theological worldview.[2] It is due to the huge work which was done in the last decades of theological thinking. This work brought a strong revival of Trinitarian interest in Christianity. Such a revival was not only the resuscitation of a somehow already dead tradition from the past. Mostly it was a new impulse which has produced a real broadening of the horizon: in this process new areas of investigation were added to the classical thinking and the mystery started to be seen from new perspectives. Trinity became a key to the whole spectrum of theological problems and the true heart of different theological disciplines. As a result, it is a kind of theological *faux pas* to omit the Trinity in the process of writing and talking about Christian theology today. The revival we are considering was of such a nature and strength that some of the authors speak even about a Trinitarian Renaissance in theology.[3]

The collection of essays gathered here shows the vitality of Trinitarian theology at the centre of Christian theology. There are still a lot of disputed questions in this field. Ultimately, they all are connected to the problem of human self-understanding. The Christian doctrine of a Triune God is the matrix of the Christian vision of man (anthropology). In other words, there is a specific hermeneutical circle between theology and anthropology: in the Trinitarian doctrine the full meaning of man and his world is disclosed. The essays presented here inscribe the Trinity in the heart of the reality of man and his knowledge about himself and his human world.

The new vision and understanding of Trinitarian theology that we are adressing is possible mainly because of *ressourcement* which took place in Christian theology in the first half of the twentieth century. The twentieth

---

[1] Caesarius of Arles, *Sermo 9, Exp. Symb.*, (CCL 103), p. 47.
[2] Cf. B. D. Marshall, *Trinity*, in G. Jones (ed.), *The Blackwell Companion to Modern Theology*, Oxford: Blackwell 2007, pp. 183–203.
[3] Ch. Schwöbel, 'Die Trinitätslehre als Rahmentheorie des christlischen Glaubens. Vier Thesen zur Bedeutung der Trinität in den christlischen Dogmatik', in idem., *Gott in Beziehung: Studien zur Dogmatik*, Tübingen: Mohr Siebeck 2002, p. 27.

century has proved itself to be a very fruitful and almost revolutionary time for theology, due to a rediscovery of the Scriptural, Liturgical and Patristic sources. The perception of a lack of Trinitarian understanding was one of the main motives for these movements. For that reason, it is interesting, at the end of the first decade of the twenty-first century, to verify in dialogue with scholars from different theological and cultural traditions, how the overcoming of the old hermeneutics is paving the way to a deeper understanding of Trinitarian mystery from historical, ecumenical and philosophical perspectives.

Theology was stirred in the twentieth century by fierce tides that brought a deep rethinking of its very methodology: the importance of Scriptural, Patristic and Liturgical sources was rediscovered together with the contribution of contemporary philosophy[4]. The Trinitarian doctrine was at the centre of this movement, since it is at the centre of Christian thought.[5] That fact spurs many scholars to try to show the connections of the different branches of theology with its core.

Theology became at that time a thoroughly historical enteprise. Theologians started to search for historical materials shaped in pre-modernity. The focus of their interest was especially on ancient and medieval theology. A joint venture of historical, linguistic and philosophical methods applied to the theological text allowed scholars to see old documents of faith in new way. First of all, they were read once again according to hermeneutical principles in their entirety and taking into account their different native contexts. The great theology of the Fathers and medieval ecclesiastical writers ceased to be used only as marginal neo-scholastic 'proof from the tradition'.[6] Instead of looking for adequate quotations, historians of theology and theologians devoted themselves to the very proufond and detailed studies of main topics and entire treatises of different writers from the past. It opened the way to more consistent and integral understanding of the origins of the doctrinal dimension of Christian faith and illuminated the true roots and original shapes of hitherto neglected reality. The new awareness of real content and shape of doctrine helped with undertaking the job of renovation of the dogmatic treatise on God (*De Deo Uno et Trino*).

---

[4] Cf. Th. H. McCall, *Which Trinity? Whose Monotheism? Philosophical and Systematic Theologians on the Metaphysics of Trinitarian Theology*, Grand Rapids: Eerdmans 2010 and Th. McCall and M. C. Rea (eds), *Philosophical and Theological Essays on the Trinity*, Oxford: Oxford University Press 2010.

[5] Cf. O. H. Pesch, *Katholische Dogmatik aus ökumenischer Erfahrung*, I/2, *Die Geschichte der Menschen mit Gott*, Ostfildern: Matthias Grünewald 2008, pp. 707–10. A kind of panoramic view on the recent development in the field of Trinitarian theology can be found in: G. Emery, *Bulletin de théologie trinitaire* and *Chronique de théologie trinitaire*, both in various issues of *Revue Thomiste*.

[6] R. Del Colle, *Neo-Scholasticism*, in D. A. Fergusson, *The Blackwell Companion to Nineteenth-Century Theology*, Oxford: Blackwell-Wiley 2010, pp. 375–94.

This brought a deeper understanding of the unity of theology, and of the concept of unity itself, seen now in its theological, i.e. Trinitarian, and not only philosophical content, which includes the dialogical dimension. The new light swept away some old hermeneutic paradigms, both at the historical and at the systematic level that hindered Ecumenism and the plain discussion of many topics. For example, the European and the American schools of theology are getting in touch, comparing and sharing their results.

At the present moment, one can see many fruits of this work: some paradigms have been revised[7] and new theological movements have appeared (e.g. Radical Orthodoxy). It seems that something is happening and that it is time to offer a tool that can help scholars and students in theology, philosophy and history of the Church to approach the bulk of the new results.

One of the fundamental discoveries of this theological-archaeological work was the consideration of the crucial role played by the reality and notion of the history of salvation in ancient and medieval Christian theology. This notion proved immediately its basic Trinitarian character. Salvation history which was marginalized by the theology of the school was discovered to be a Trinitarian concept. At the same time Trinitarian theology was understood once again as a salvific and existential mystery.[8] It is not strange that from such a perspective theology started to become more and more aware of its Trinitarian nature. It is enough to mention here the two greatest protagonists of contemporary Trinitarian theology, namely Barth and Rahner, whose work transmitted achievements of historical inquiries into the very heart of systematics.

If the narration mentioned above is true, one can admit that Trinitarian revival in contemporary theology was nurtured by the rise of historical theology. The present book intends humbly to witness to the Trinitarian revival which happened in our time by pointing out its first fruits and, sometimes, the premature effects and postulates. It means that this is the work in historical theology in its scope to testify to a concrete historical moment in the history of the development of Trinitarian theology.

---

[7] The good example of such historical revision made for systematic theology is L. Ayres, *Nicaea and its Legacy: an Approach to Fourth-Century Trinitarian Theology*, Oxford: Oxford University Press 2004 (see esp. pp. 384–435); ibid. (with A. Radde-Gallwitz), 'Doctrine of God', in S. Ashbrook and D. G. Hunter (eds), *Oxford Handbook of Early Christian Studies*, Oxford: Oxford University Press 2008, pp. 864–85. See as well K. Anatolios, 'Discourse on the Trinity', in W. Löhr and F. Norris (eds), *Cambridge History of Christianity*, II, *Constantine to 600*, Cambridge: Cambridge University Press 2007, pp. 431–59 and his forthcoming *Retrieving Nicaea: The Development and Meaning of Trinitarian Doctrine*, Grand Rapids: Baker Academic 2011. Cf. interesting discussion on Ayres' *Nicea and its Legacy* in special issue of *Harvard Theological Review* 100:2 (2007) 125–75.

[8] A. Cozzi, *Manuale di dottrina trinitaria*, (Nuovo corso di teologia sistematica, 4), Brescia: Queriniana 2009, pp. 10–32.

But there is at least one reason more to allow us to describe our project as historical. In order to grasp it, one has to take into account the very nature of theology as such. Theology is already always a historical project not because it has to draw by definition on the tradition: the historical nature of theology consists in its never ending task to talk (*logos*) about the holy and awe-inspiring mystery of Trinity. This task has to be received constantly from the beginning. Time is the horizon of theology. Time gives to theology its always contemporary character and importance. To do theology requires the ability both to think from the tradition and to look into the depth of the present in order to propose some solutions to the ancient and modern problems for the future. The revival of Trinitarian theology has to be repeated constantly for each coming generation.

What we mean by the title of the book – *Rethinking Trinitarian Theology* – is located between those two poles of the historical nature of theology: a historical search for the true shape of past formulations, and constructive theological work (always in direct relation to the historical theology). To *rethink* Trinitarian theology does not mean a liberal and revolutionary breaking with tradition, but indicates the need to think it once again in the context of the present time. Such a resolution to think about the Trinity once again does not intend to give it a totally new meaning. Rather, it aims at a more profound and fuller understanding of God's own primordial mystery of life and love. The changing horizon of time seems to be of help in such an endeavour. It gives a new opportunity to understand old traditions by scrupulously analyzing its *Wirkungsgeschichte* and it allows us to apply to the traditional topics new sensitivity. This is why the essays gathered in the present volume intend to maintain a balance between historical perspective and new approaches. The main goal of the publication is not only a description of what happened to Trinitarian theology in the modern age; it is rather to indicate the typically modern specificity of the Trinitarian debate and – first of all – to encourage development in the main areas and issues of this subject.

The book aims at showing the most important topics and paradigms in modern Trinitarian theology. It is supposed to be both a comprehensive guide to the many traces of development of Trinitarian faith and a guideline for serious future research in the field. As such it is thought to systematize the variety of contemporary approaches to the field of Trinitarian theology in the present philosophical-cultural context. The important feature of the proposed publication is its ecumenical perspective: ecumenism is the 'to be or not to be' of Christian theology as a whole. From a methodological point of view, this present book aims to bring together scholars characterized by different approaches, geographical origins, confessions and ages, assigning to each of them a specific topic, in order to cover the main developments of the last years.

The following papers are grouped into five parts: the first one intends to show what is going on today from the perspective of historical theology; the second one presents the main key concepts, whose historical understanding is under revision (e.g. person, substance, freedom, perichoresis); a third part is focused on the ontological and epistemological dimensions of Trinitarian faith; the fourth part shows some fundamental dimensions of the anthropological paradigm in Trinitarian theology that have come into play recently (community, becoming a person, social Trinitarianism, spirituality, etc.); the fifth and last one aims to suggest possible theological ideas which can help to prove in the future a systematic dimension of Trinitarian faith as a real centre of a whole theological worldview.

We would like to express our gratitude and appreciation to all the contributors of the present volume. Theology (especially Trinitarian theology) is always a work of community. As theologians we do not work for ourselves. Theology is not our private job. According to this principle, the 'Rethinking Trinitarian Theology' project is a fruit of collaboration and friendship. It is a kind of 'theological banquet' and 'theological symphony' in which the dialogue and exchange of thoughts are crucial and vital. As this book was born out of dialogue we hope it will lead to new dialogues on the most important issue in Christianity's self-understanding. *Sit maneat quaestio!*

In a very special way we would like to express our gratitude to Thomas Kraft from Continuum Publishing House for his great care and expertise. His friendship, love for theology and editing professionalism are remarkable and outstanding. Without his help the publication of this book would not have been possible at all.

Letting this work enter into theological circulation we share with Saint Augustine his sincere desire and wish: 'For God Himself, whom we seek, will, as I hope, help our labours, that they may not be unfruitful, and that we may understand how it is said in the holy Psalm, "Let the heart of them rejoice that seek the Lord. Seek the Lord, and be strengthened: seek His face evermore." For that which is always being sought seems as though it were never found; and how then will the heart of them that seek rejoice, and not rather be made sad, if they cannot find what they seek? For it is not said, the heart shall rejoice of them that find, but of them that seek the Lord. And yet the prophet Isaiah testifies, that the Lord God can be found when He is sought, when he says: "Seek the Lord; and as soon as you have found Him, call upon Him: and when He has drawn near to you, let the wicked man forsake his ways, and the unrighteous man his thoughts." If, then, when sought, He can be found, why is it said, "Seek ye His face evermore?" Is He perhaps to be sought even when found? For things incomprehensible must so be investigated, so that no one may think he has found nothing, when he has been able to find how incomprehensible that is which he was seeking. Why then does he so seek, if he comprehends that which he seeks to be incomprehensible, unless because he may not give over seeking so long as he makes progress in the inquiry itself into things incomprehensible, and becomes ever better and better while seeking so great a good, which is both sought in order to be found, and found in order to be sought? For it is both sought in order that it may be found more sweetly, and found in order that it may be sought more eagerly'.[9]

Giulio Maspero
Robert J. Woźniak
Rome (Italy) – Kraków (Poland)
Feast of the Transfiguration
8 January 2010

---

[9] Aurelius Augustinus, *De Trinitate*, XV, II. 2, (CCL 50), p. 461.

# PART ONE

# Historical perspectives: what can and should we learn from history?

# 1

# Into the Cloud of Witnesses: Catholic Trinitarian Theology Beyond and Before its Modern 'Revivals'[1]

## Lewis Ayres

In one still very common narrative of Trinitarian theology, Latin theology over time wandered far from authentic Trinitarianism, and has only called back to its true path in the past few decades.[2] This theological 'fall' was either the work of Augustine himself, or the result of a trajectory initiated by him and coming to fruition in the centuries that followed.[3] In such narratives Latin Trinitarian theology stumbled by forgetting that Trinitarian doctrine moves us beyond any ultimate philosophical monism. Embracing such monism, Latin theology has spawned a variety of errors: treating God

---

[1] This paper was presented to a conference of the Centre for Catholic Studies at Durham University in November 2009. I am particularly grateful to all those who responded and commented, especially David Burrell, Karen Kilby, Mark McIntosh, Paul Murray and David Tracy.
[2] Throughout I have used 'Latin' as a term for theologies for whom Latin is either the language of expression or the tradition of ultimate origin.
[3] Occasionally the narrative suggests that the real failure begins with Nicaea itself; see e.g. Catherine Mowry LaCugna, *God for Us*, San Francisco: Harper Collins, 1993, pp. 41–4.

as fundamentally one mind or person; failing to grasp the wide metaphysical significance of relationship in the Godhead; forgetting that in the narrative and dynamic interactions of God's actions in Christ (and in the Spirit-filled body of the Church), we see the nature of God reflected. In all of these errors a monistic theology of God *in se* is assumed as a reality prior to the 'economic' Trinity.[4] At times Latin Trinitarianism's wandering from the path of righteousness is even taken partially to have prepared the way for both the anti-Trinitarian movements in the sixteenth and seventeenth centuries, as well as Enlightenment and post-Enlightenment philosophical attacks on Christianity.

Those who hold to some version of this narrative do so as part of a commitment to one version or other of a 'revival' in Trinitarian theology, a re-articulation of Trinitarian thought that will reverse Latin theology's 'fall'. Interestingly, these 'revivalists' rarely offer any dense account of their proximate philosophical sources. In particular, while many of those who count themselves as 'revivalists' over the past three or four decades point to particular Biblical or Patristic themes as sources, it is rare for any who do so openly to embrace the strains of *modern* thought that have shaped their appropriation of pre-modern resources. It was not always so. There have, in fact, been a series of 'revivals' in Trinitarian theology stretching back to the early nineteenth century, and many of those revivalists acknowledged that their efforts depended on the achievement of particular philosophical traditions. These earlier revivalists do not share the same story of separation between Greek and Latin, or (at least universally) the same story of a peculiarly western failure, even if they do point to a consistent failure of Christians to grasp the heart of the doctrine; but they do share a set of philosophical inspirations. Hegel, his legacy, and various kinds of personalism used to similar ends are a constant presence.

The argument of this paper travels along a path marked on the one side by the undermining of the narratives on which the most recent revivalists depend and, on the other, by increasing recognition that the broader post-Hegelian revivalist project has depended on philosophical and theological trajectories that are not the only or perhaps even the most suitable resources for articulating Trinitarian theology, at least Trinitarian theology that embraces Nicene orthodoxy. While there were always figures who refused the idea of Latin Trinitarianism's fall, recent decades have seen a considerable body of revisionist historical scholarship on the major figures of the Latin tradition that has undercut many of the pivotal assumptions of the narrative discussed in the first paragraph of this paper, scholarship that has

---

[4] 'Economic' is in quotation marks to remind us that the term itself is a product of the post-Hegelian accounts that undergird the revivalist project. The distinction between the 'economic' and the 'immanent' Trinity is probably one first stated clearly by F. A. Staudenmeier.

increasingly followed the modern historiographical trend to place texts in proximate contexts, to avoid reading terminology in the light of its later development, and to be wary of assuming that texts which later become 'classics' for a tradition originally had the unitary focus and summative qualities with which tradition invests them. It is also noteworthy that in the case of, for example, Augustine and Thomas, while this revisionist scholarship has opened new debates about the meaning of each figure and the relationship between the two, it has not met with any scholarly attempt to defend the older readings that are taken to enable the 'fall' narrative.

My intention in this paper is not, however, to argue further against the narrative described above, but the more positive one of indicating some new conversations that are now emerging within Latin traditions and to suggest that in these conversations we will find the most appropriate and generative source of Catholic Trinitarian theology in the next few years. The contours of these new conversations remain unclear, and thus I have not tried to offer a typology but sought only to offer as examples three very personal conversations that have emerged from my own work on Augustine and some of his Latin and Greek contemporaries over the past few years. This personal reflection should be taken as an indication that many more conversations remain to be uncovered.

Two general features of these new conversations demand mention. First, when I suggest that these debates in historical scholarship should serve as the points of departure for good Trinitarian theology my intent could fairly be described as tactical; as interventions in current Trinitarian discussion these conversations have the effect of de-centring some of the questions and dynamics that the revivalists take to be normative. I do not necessarily think that these conversations answer all the concerns of the revivalists, but they do suggest a range of rather different questions. But second, and more strategically, part of my intention in focusing on these conversations is to argue for a different conception of good practice in Trinitarian theology.

## Hegelian Revivalists

As a backdrop to the new conversations I want to highlight, it is important that I give a little more density to my comments about the significance of Hegel for the modern 'revivalist' projects in Trinitarian theology. How may Hegel be described as their fountainhead? Most importantly, of course, Hegel sees himself as 'reviving' the doctrine by revealing its true philosophical content. By describing dialectical difference as partly constitutive of *Geist* and thus drawing together the history of our world and the being of God, Hegel fashioned a powerful account of the doctrine's utility – whatever its relationship to classical Christianity![5] The attempts of Protestant theologians and philosophers, even of many who resisted Hegel's particular way of conceiving the relationship between God and world, to make use of the resources he offered, constitutes the first of the modern 'revivals'. Writing in the late 1870s, Isaac Dorner congratulates the followers of Hegel for keeping alive the doctrine in what had seemed otherwise dark days. Dorner prefers other strands of Idealist thought in his own attempts at reconstructing the doctrine, but he could recognize the common work of reconstruction at which he and his opponents all aimed.[6]

But if we are to understand the character of the revival that Hegel offers, we must make brief mention of his own sources. One of the most interesting recent attempts at placing Hegel's Trinitarian vision in broader context is that of Cyril O'Regan. Whether or not one buys into O'Regan's account of the return of a theological grammar that can be termed 'Gnostic', his account of the relationship between Jacob Boehme's seventeenth-century overturning of some classical Trinitarian fundamentals remains highly illuminating. O'Regan's account depends on distinguishing the 'narrative of divine manifestation' one find in Boehme from that found in late medieval exponents of 'negative theology', such as Eckhart.[7] For O'Regan, one must read Eckhart within the tradition of Latin Neoplatonic Christian thought, and against this context, Eckhartian emphasis on the divine as process and becoming occurs against the background of an equally fundamental emphasis on the divine unity and overflowing plenitude. At the same time, Eckhart sustains the Pseudo-Dionysian division between the 'super-essential Godhead' who is known only in unknowing and the Trinity of manifestation, revelation and faith; the latter draws us to the former and is only formally distinct. Nevertheless, Eckhart, for O'Regan, points toward Boehme in his talk of a divine birth, the eternal speaking of the Word which

---

[5] For a fundamental statement of his position see the 1827 version of his lectures on the topic, G. W. F. Hegel, *Lectures on the Philosophy of Religion*, III, *The Consummate Religion*, Peter Hodgson (ed.), Berkeley: University of California Press 1985, pp. 271–4 (in summary), 275–347 (*in extenso*). On Hegel's views of his own project in relation to that of 'the theologians' see e.g. pp. 258–62. For a good basic introduction to Hegel's Trinitarian project see Samuel L. Powell, *The Trinity in German Thought*, Cambridge: Cambridge University Press 2001, pp. 104–41.

[6] E.g. I. A. Dorner, System der christlichen Glaubenslehre, Vol I Berlin: Hertz, 1879, p. 199ff.

[7] C. O'Regan, *Gnostic Apocalypse: Jacob Boehme's Haunted Narrative*, New York: SUNY Press 2002, esp. here the summary at pp. 69ff. For O'Regan's justification of terming certain modern movements 'Gnostic' see his *Gnostic Return in Modernity*, New York: SUNY Press 2001. See also the excellent summary account in Cyril O'Regan, 'The Trinity in Kant, Hegel, and Schelling,' in Gilles – Emery and Matthew Levering (eds), *The Oxford Handbook of the Trinity* Oxford: Oxford University Press, 2011, pp. 254–66.

moves the divine – some narrative language is here possible – into manifestation, into self-consciousness.[8]

Eckhart's Christian, Trinitarian insistence that God is also eternally thus enables (as it had for many others before him in different ways) this adaptation of the Neoplatonic principle of divine self-diffusion – an adaptation that, of course, must offer an account of God's non-discursive knowing as not incompatible with God's status as the ground of all. Boehme, however, first follows Luther's insistence that the real mystery lies in the manifestation, in the divine communication that occurs in Christ and then, second, focuses on the divine will as that which inaugurates the divine process of self-manifestation and self-constitution. The divine will's expression through the production of the Word – and ultimately through the creative act – is not the beginning of the divine as such; it is the beginning of manifestation from impenetrable hidden depths. While the role of the divine will in Boehme has been previously noted, O'Regan draws attention to Boehme's presentation of the will as the actualization of divine potential. Placing the will centre stage, O'Regan argues, is genuinely new, but projects on to the divine a privative condition only overcome through the divine manifestation, the realization of the divine will as the completion of the divine joy and love.

Boehme sees this movement as one that necessarily involves sudden change and dialectical reversal, not simply evolutionary progress. Further detail about how Boehme construes this movement is not necessary for our purposes. All that need be noted here is that to understand Hegel's Trinitarian vision we must recognize that he stands in a tradition which ultimately depends on a modification – or even corruption – of late medieval classical Trinitarianism, a Trinitarian tradition infused with Platonic principles that enabled the conception of a divine movement that was also rest and fullness. The modification, or corruption, of this tradition in Boehme and then Hegel itself draws on Lutheran accounts of the divine disclosure and thus suggests a possible account of the divine self-determination through Trinitarian community and exchange. It is this account, modified in Hegelian thought, that becomes the motivating force behind many of the 'revivals' of the nineteenth and twentieth centuries – appearing, of course, in forms more or less obviously Hegelian, more or less intentionally still aiming to preserve the principles of prior Trinitarian orthodoxy. Although, like all significant theological developments, the shifts here are multi-dimensional, at their heart lies a transformation, misunderstanding or outright rejection of the

---

[8] On Eckhart and other uses of Neoplatonic themes to articulate divine rest and movement in this period, see Rik Van Nieuwenhove and Jan van Ruusbroec, *Mystical Theologian of the Trinity*, Notre Dame: University of Notre Dame Press 2003, pp. 77–99 and his 'In the Image of God: The Trinitarian Anthropology of St Bonaventure, St Thomas Aquinas and the Blessed Jan van Ruusbroec' in *Irish Theological Quarterly* 66 (2001) 109–123 & 227–37.

ways in which the classical Trinitarian tradition describes divine activity and 'movement' against the background of an account of divine fullness and transcendence owing much to adaptation of Neoplatonic dynamics. As we shall see, this Neoplatonist influence takes diverse forms (and often involved adaptations that non-Christian Neoplatonists would have found unconvincing), but was a constant shaping force behind subtly different visions in the Latin Trinitarian tradition.[9]

# Revivalist Diversity

But mention of Hegel, his transformations of Trinitarian doctrine, and his debts to prior thinkers, does not suffice as even a sketch of the proximate sources of the various Triniatrian 'revivalists'. During the nineteenth century a variety of other revivalist styles appear, styles less obviously 'Hegelian' in the manner I have so far described, but dependent in different ways on the legacy of German idealism. Various forms of personalism provide key resources for a wide variety of theologians, but usually alongside a fundamental strategy of revitalizing by injecting a supposed dynamism into the divine life. 'Personalism' covers a broad range of traditions, some owing to Hegel directly some developed in opposition to many forms of idealism, Hegelian as well as Kantian.[10] Schelling's 'opposition' to Hegel and his resulting personalist emphases are a particularly revealing example. Schelling's sense of the quasi-modalist dynamic of prior Trinitarian traditions pushes him toward a notion of tripersonal agency complemented with a still Hegelian account of the manner in which that agency shapes the divine being and communion. A number of nineteenth- and twentieth-century figures (philosophers as well as theologians) make use of the same traditions in order to emphasize the divine as *one* supreme person (Feuerbach provides an excellent example); others, especially in the twentieth century, make

---

[9] Allow me to record three provisos. 1) The same tradition of thought was also extremely influential on Greek theological traditions, again in a variety of ways. I return to this briefly later; here it needs to be mentioned only against the perception that Latins alone engaged this tradition. 2) Neoplatonic themes in rather different ways were also influential on some of the sixteenth–seventeenth-century anti-Trinitarians, and on various forms of idealism. But against those, such as Werner Beierwalters and Wayne Hankey, who tend to read many versions of idealism as the simple inheritors of Neoplatonic tradition, I would argue that in the case of Trinitarian theology the rejection of the classical notion of divine fullness indicates a significant break. 3) Throughout, I do not prejudge the use of Neoplatonic themes by Christian authors as an indication that their Christianity has been corrupted.

[10] For an introduction to the diverse notion of Personalism see Thomas D. Williams & Jan Olof Bengtsson, 'Personalism', in *The Stanford Encyclopedia of Philosophy*, plato/stanford. edu/entries/personalism (accessed January 2011).

use of personalist themes as a way of supposedly revitalizing Trinitarian doctrine by injecting a certain perceived dynamism to the divine relationships. Avowed social Trinitarians and such figures as Walter Kasper and John Zizioulas make quite different use of personalist themes, but they share an instinct that these themes enable an enhanced attention to the language of personal interaction and drama in the divine life. This is so even while both Kasper and Zizioulas are far more attentive to the fundamental principles of classical Trinitarianism.[11] Thus however far distant personalism and Hegelian idealism often were and are, in Trinitarian contexts they often serve similar goals, and goals whose value was determined by Hegel's vision.[12]

Recent feminist reconstructions of Trinitrian doctrine fit, for the most part, within these same post-Hegelian revivalist traditions. While, for example, Elizabeth Johnson rejects much earlier Trinitarian theology for its Patriarchalism (and has little space for the Father's *monarchia*), her attempt at retrieving an alternative from within western tradition depends upon a version of the persons in inter-relationship that is heir to many of the personalist and social Trinitarian moves of earlier twentieth-century revivals.[13] Her critique of Patriarchalism shapes her rejection of virtually any Trinitarian order, but what might seem a radical difference from the work of Kasper and Zizioulas masks a common set of philosophical resources used towards a common vision of what must be involved in Trinitarian 'revival'.

Obviously my aim here is not to provide a typology of modern Trinitarian theology, only to suggest that a surprising number of its constitutive movements depend more or less openly on some similar historical assumptions and philosophical dynamics. Later in the paper I will offer some remarks about the engagement between Latin and Greek Trinitarian theology.[14] Here let me only remark that those who have advocated the 'eastward turn' that has become so fundamental a part of recent Trinitarian thinking are frequently implicated in many of the same dynamics I have sought to identify. Many of these theologians assume that in Greek Trinitarian theologies one finds an account of personal differentiation in the godhead that has none of the unitarian tendency apparent in the west; many

---

[11] See e.g. W. Kasper, *The God of Jesus Christ*, London: SCM 1983, pp. 288–90 and J. Zizioulas, *Being as Communion*, Crestwood: SVS Press 1985, pp. 27–49 & 105-7.

[12] Neither Kapser nor Zizioulas can be tarred with the brush of ultimate theological failure without hyperbole, even if we can locate them, as I have done here, and raise questions about the way in which they use personalist themes. We can, however, suggest that they cut themselves off from resources that would help them articulate the Classical Trinitarian principles they so strongly espouse.

[13] E. Johnson, *She Who Is*, New York: Crossroad 1992.

[14] I use 'Greek' as a term for theologies whose original language of expression is Greek or who find in Greek theology a clear point of origin.

assume that in Greek thought we find the Father's *monarchia* preserved in a way that is both more 'biblical' and more able to preserve the irreducibility of the persons. In making these assumptions such theologians tend not only to read Latin theology as inherently corrupt, but they also implicitly foist onto Greek theology all the dynamics of modern post-Hegelian revivalism. My own suspicion is that such an account does little to foster sensitive evaluation of the continuities between Greek and Latin theology, or of the internal diversity and history of Greek theology.

The previous paragraphs have interwoven references to Protestant and Catholic figures without any comment on the history of Trinitarian theology in different Christian communions. In part this follows from the lack of an extended history of Catholic Trinitarian theology in the modern period. But I suspect that were such a history to be written it would show interesting diversity. Certainly from the late nineteenth century through into the twentieth, Catholic theology sustained a variety of historical narratives about the development of the doctrine. Not surprisingly, while some of these celebrated the achievement of Greek theology, understood as a distinct tradition, few offered any account of Latin failure.[15] It should similarly not be surprising that such narratives tended also to present Latin theology as moving by stages toward a Thomist synthesis. The increasing prominence of Patristic *ressourcement*, combined with a variety of attempts to revitalize Catholic thought laid the groundwork for Catholic theologians to adopt varieties of the emphases I have sketched. However, throughout the twentieth century, it is noteworthy that many Catholic writers sought to revitalize without denigrating their own tradition: thus, for example, Congar's work on pneumatology and Mühlen's attempts to revitalize western accounts of the Spirit as joining Father and Son in love through the use of a philosophy of communication. At the same time, the Thomist tradition has not simply survived within Catholic thought, but has undergone something of a renaissance in recent years, a renaissance that has seen much significant work attempting to recover with historical sensitivity Thomas' own doctrinal vision and resources for modern Catholic thought. These specifically Catholic developments can, I will suggest, help to provide the foundations for the development of a new understanding of the shape of Latin Trinitarian discussion. Nevertheless, there has been, by some Catholic theologians, a far more wholesale adoption of the dynamics I have identified as those of the modern 'revivalists', and some relevant figures I have already noted.

Of course, any attempt to summarize in just a few paragraphs the dynamics of such a diverse movement as the post-Hegelian Trinitarian revivals will

---

[15] One might compare in this regard the very different narratives of De Régnon and Garrigou-Lagrange. For a further sketch of the possibilities to be found in nineteenth century Catholic Trinitarianism see Aiden Nichols, 'Catholic Theology of the Trinity in the Nineteenth Century', in Emery and Levering (eds), Oxford Handbook of the Trinity, pp. 281–93.

leave out significant exceptions and fail to capture their full diversity. At the same time, it is important to make clear that while these common themes are sometimes used in ways that take their authors far beyond the pale of Trinitarian orthodoxy, in other writers they are carefully hedged round with the boundaries of that orthodoxy. Yet, all too easily, the mere presence of those resources – and especially the narratives that now accompany them – draws theologians away from fruitful and generative exploration of classical Trinitarian conversations. These themes and narratives have tended to infuse revivalist Trinitarian theologies with what one might term a hermeneutic of forgetfulness concerning the Latin theologians they demonize.

But a growing body of scholarship on a range of Latin theologians has begun to open new possibilities, and it is here that my own argument begins. It has, I think, become increasingly well known that this scholarship has undercut many of the central narrative assumptions that have been taken to justify both the rejection of earlier Latin theology and the necessity of a Trinitarian 'revival' relying on the dynamics I have sketched in the first parts of this paper. But this scholarship does not only refute standard assumptions, it also suggests new conversations *within* Latin tradition. One of the distinctive features not only in anti-Latin narratives, but even in the narratives of those who have continued to cherish the Latin tradition, has been an assumption of linear and cumulative progress in Latin theology. Latin tradition certainly involved a constant appropriation and adaptation of previous tradition, but recent historical scholarship has also emphasized the change involved in any act of appropriation and adaptation, such that we can now be more attentive to the different visions that emerge as traditions are appropriated in the light of changing intellectual contexts. Not surprisingly, I see those conversations that explore continuity and change between Patristic and medieval figures to be of particular importance; I offer some reflections on why and how in the conclusion to the paper. In the following sections I sketch three conversations that I hope will give a sense of the texture of many others that are emerging.

## Persons and Nature

Each of the three conversations I will explore come from working on Augustine over the past few years, and they are thus each personal conversations; I hope they have universal relevance, but part of my point through them is that current forms of scholarship are giving rise to many other such conversations. The first concerns the manner in which we envisage the divine three, Father, Son and Spirit, as individuals in communion. Let me begin by sketching some of the themes in Augustine that have prompted this conversation. One of the most interesting aspects of Augustine's Trinitarian thought is his rejection of the explanatory force of genus- and species-type terminologies. He is simply not convinced that the terminology of nature and person can provide a philosophically sustainable resource for imagining the relationships between the divine three. Along with a number of other recent commentators, I see this rejection as intentional and coherent. In short, and following logical principles learnt from Porphyry's *Isagoge*, Augustine does not think that any of the normal rules of genus, species and individual predication can apply in the case of the Trinity, and thus all such terminologies fail to be useful other than as a basic ecclesiastical terminology for our confession.[16]

What does Augustine say instead? He first presents the generation of the Son, in rather traditional Nicene manner, as the generation of one from the Father's substance or essence, a generation in which the Father shares all that he is with the Son, the one who is God from God. This generation must be understood within what we can say of the divine simplicity; divine life as perfect Wisdom and the source of all must be one and undivided. And yet the Father gives rise to one who is perfect Wisdom – as the Son must be if he is truly God. But if we can imagine so far then it must be that paradoxically the Son must be both fully Wisdom itself and yet never divided from the one simple Wisdom that is God.[17] Genus and species terminologies cannot, for Augustine, comprehend this relationship.

Augustine moves beyond his Latin (and Greek) predecessors when he attempts to understand the consequences of the Son being born from the Father's substance. He finds it a matter of simple logic, for example, to state that each of the divine three is 'true God', despite the exegetical problems that such a claim presents around texts such as John 17:3.[18] Augustine's willingness to accord each of the divine three titles such as the *solus verus Deus* of this text in part reflects the fact that he inherits the results of the fourth-century Trinitarian controversies. He certainly expends much energy arguing against the enemies of Nicaea (and these enemies were a real force in his day), but the faith that he defends comes to him embedded within a long tradition of articulation and development. At times he feels the need to stretch this tradition, facing head on topics that have received insufficient deep consideration, and offering alternative solutions where those currently available do not seem to satisfy. Thus in doing so he is part of a shift in Nicene tradition (in the Greek world Cyril of Alexandria is a parallel

---

[16] See my *Augustine and the Trinity*, Cambridge: Cambridge University Press 2010, pp. 211–20; for Augustine's initial famous scepticism see *Trin.*, 5, 8, 9–9, 10, and for his argued rejection of their logical coherence see *Trin.*, 7, 4, 7 and 7, 6, 11. I have found particularly helpful for the argument of Richard Cross, 'Quid tres? On What Precisely Augustine Professes not to Understand in De Trinitate V and VII,' *Harvard Theological Review* 100 (2007), 215–32.
[17] See Augustine and the Trinity, pp. 221–7. Augustine presents his argument most clearly at *Trin.*, 7, 1, 2–2, 3.
[18] See Ayres, *Augustine and the Trinity*, pp. 100–3.

figure[19]), taking the principles of Nicene Trinitarian faith as a given, not only arguing for those principles, but also arguing *from* them, finding in them a generative resource.

In his mature work Augustine's account of the Son's generation is completed by arguing that any act Scripture predicates of the Son towards the Father is identical with His being and also with His eternal generation. Thus, for example, the Son's seeing of the Father in John 5:19 is constitutive of His being and is identical to His being born. The Son is constituted by his seeing of the Father, and for the Son to be generated is for Him to be constituted as the one who sees the Father.[20] In this picture the Son's individual existence as Wisdom itself and Life itself is grasped as an eternal act, and Scriptural terms for the Son become newly the focus of our attempts to describe the relationship between the persons.

This account of the Son is complemented by an account of the Spirit. Building in part on a common Latin problematic in which Spirit is understood to be a name both for divinity as such and for the Holy Spirit, Augustine develops his famous account of the Spirit as 'something common' to Father and Son.[21] I start with the phrase 'something common' to indicate that while Augustine shows a distinct preference for describing the Spirit as love, he is also clear that our knowledge allows us little certainty here. Most importantly, however, the concept of the Spirit as love and gift is used to argue for the Spirit as also eternally act or in act. In a striking exegesis of Acts 4:32, Augustine argues that just as the Spirit draws Christians into unity, so is the Spirit eternally breathed by the Father as the one who loves Father, Son and Spirit into their unity of substance.[22] As the Spirit of the Father and the Spirit of the Son, the Spirit is, one might almost say, their essence.[23] Such terminologies are frequently misleading, but perhaps there is some virtue in thinking of Augustine as espousing an apophatic personalism: a personalism because of the growing focus on each of the divine three as the fullness of the divine life and as each identical to the acts that Scripture predicates of them; apophatic because Augustine conditions what he positively says about the acts and being of each with the insistence we have already seen on the failure of individual and species terminologies

---

[19] A similar observation about Trinitarian theology in Greek tradition beginning with Cyril of Alexandria is made by Andrew Louth in his 'Later Greek Theology' in Emery and Levering (eds), *The Oxford Handbook of the Trinity*, pp. 138–51.

[20] Ayres, *Augustine and the Trinity*, pp. 233–50.

[21] See e.g. *Trin.*, 6. 5–7.

[22] Ayres, *Augustine and the Trinity*, pp. 256–8.

[23] Ayres, *Augustine and the Trinity*, pp. 251–6. I argue there that the 'Spirit of' texts (such as Gal. 4:6 & Rom. 8:9–11) become central in Augustine's mature pneumatology because they point to the Spirit's relationship to both Father and Son.

such as person and nature. But this terminology is not Augustine's and it is important to note the tentative quality of his expositions.[24]

In the light of this reading of Augustine, the question has arisen for me of how one can relate the bishop of Hippo's account to those found in later western tradition. If we recognize the force with which Augustine rejects so much philosophical terminology, and the manner in which he explores alternative scriptural modes of exposition, then we should be wary of treating him as an inchoate Thomas, waiting only for the latter to define with clarity the *relatio subsistens*. Even if we confine ourselves to the relationship between these two points of reference, we must first ask ourselves about the similarities and differences between them, and then ask what developments in terminology make those later accounts possible. This question depends in part on our understanding of how figures beginning with Boethius developed an extensive account of the very language Augustine rejected, even as they also treat him as a significant authority. In part, we need also to ask how Augustine's Trinitarianism itself was immediately received: while many of his arguments and exegeses are taken up in later tradition, my suspicion is that his wholesale rejection of person and nature language is not. Thus, when later writers attempt to develop a detailed account of how that language may be used of the Trinity, they do not do so against Augustine; but their doing so certainly creates an important conversation within Latin tradition, even if it is one that we are far more able than they to articulate.

When we think directly about the relationship between Augustine and Thomas, we find both similarities and differences.[25] On the one hand, and here I owe much to the work of Gilles Emery, because Thomas develops his account as a way of mediating between different ways of linking person and essence without making either a secondary feature, his account is intended as much to name the uniqueness of the idea of a divine relation expressed as a *hypostasis* as it is to offer a fully comprehensible account of a particular sort of individual.[26] Elsewhere Thomas clearly maintains the difficulties of using any such language in a Trinitarian context, and thus there are clear similarities between the two theologians.[27] But on

---

[24] Ayres, *Augustine and the Trinity*, pp. 258–62.

[25] Another question to pursue would be that suggested by Russell L. Friedman, *Medieval Trinitarian Thought from Aquinas to Ockham*, Cambridge: Cambridge University Press 2010.

[26] G. Emery, *The Trinitarian Theology of St. Thomas Aquinas*, Oxford: Oxford University Press 2007, pp. 114–19; see also his 'Essentialism or Personalism in the Treatise on God in St. Thomas Aquinas?', in *The Thomist* 64 (2000) 521–63 [and in his *Trinity in Aquinas*, Ypsilanti: Ave Maria Press, 2003, pp. 165–208].

[27] For discussion see the essay by Richard Cross in this volume and his earlier 'Duns Scotus on Divine Substance and the Trinity,' *Medieval Philosophy and Theology* II (2003) pp. 181–201. Cross and I differ over how far the rejection of such terminology is intristic to Latin Trinitarianism.

the other hand, in his *Lectura in Iohannem*, Thomas seems not quite to grasp Augustine's reading of John 5:19. He first links Augustine's reading to those of Hilary and Chrysostom (which I would argue are actually rather different because of their reliance on the consequences of nature language). Then Thomas argues that Augustine's account exemplifies his own reading in which the Son's 'seeing' is a mode of receiving knowledge. The Son thus proceeds from the Father by an 'intellectual procession' which simultaneously involves him in 'seeing' the Father.[28] This reading shows us both Thomas' (unsurprising) commitment to the logical/philo-sophical language of western Trinitarianism, *and* it shows us a little of the great explanatory force that a model of intellectual procession has for him. But this latter is not simply a feature of his 'Augustinianism': I have argued that while Augustine indeed has much to say about the illustrative usefulness of the *verbum interior* when discussing the *Verbum Dei*, he emphasizes strongly its ultimate failure as an illustration and he makes little use of the relationship between love and knowledge to explore the relationship between Son and Spirit.[29] The emergence of Thomas' account of the interrelationship between intellect and will is a story to be traced through attention to post-Augustinian developments, and through attention to developments away from (even if in the wake of) Augustine's own project.

This first conversation thus refutes some common assumptions of the post-Hegelian revivalists and de-centres some of the questions that have often pre-occupied modern Trinitarian theology. It refutes then, most obviously, in its demonstration of a deep concern to present the individual divine 'persons' as distinct and as each possessing the fullness of life. And yet this conversation does not only refute particular assumptions, it also de-centres discussion. Take for instance the discussion of 'person': one set of modern theologians has focused on the suitability of the term and the possibility of using some other; another has been perfectly happy with the use of the term 'person' and assumed that it may best be filled out by the use of various personalist and existentialist dynamics. Both sets have assumed the centrality of 'person' to Latin Trinitarianism and that we can narrate the term's sense fairly easily. Both approaches are de-centred once we realize that Latin theology itself demonstrates a long-running conver-sation about whether 'person' itself is adequate and offers a variety of ways of using and filling the term. The more we become aware of the range of ways in which person has been discussed and used within Latin tradition, the more it should become clear that attention to this history may well turn

---

[28] See *Ioan.*, 5, lect. 3, n. 747–53.
[29] For a summary see Ayres, *Augustine and the Trinity*, pp. 319–25. For the *verbum interior* in Augustine see pp. 194–6, 290–3.

out to be the best source of creative and faithful thinking in the present circumstances.

In such observations it might be thought that I am simply following the trajectory of the ever more particular historian whose concern is always with the distinctions between positions. This focus on the distinctive qualities of texts and people that were once easily placed within a unitary narrative certainly disrupts some ways of relating to figures, especially those which seek primarily to view the shape and character of an idea in earlier thinking from the perspective of a later author in whom one finds what is taken to be a flowering or fullness of the given idea. But there are ways in which such disruption is also opportunity. In this case, such an act of disruption creates an opportunity for theologians to think again about the boundaries and discussions that constitute Latin tradition – and, I would hope, about the ways in which these different moments within the tradition succeed in drawing the theologian's attention to the mystery of which these texts attempt to speak.

The theologian receptive to this way of viewing Latin tradition need not (and should not) abandon the idea of a cumulative narrative. Catholic theologians (and those of many other communions) are beholden to accept a story in which the mysteries of faith are increasingly clearly articulated in the foundational period of creedal articulation, and are also committed to recognizing the gradual unfolding of technical conversations (in changing philosophical contexts) about ways in which one might resolve or explore questions to which Patristic theological developments inevitably gave rise. But at the same time there are many ways of understanding the trajectory of this story; one can (and, I would argue, should) read this story of elaboration as (at its best) an entirely appropriate Christian exploration of the speculative mysteries into which revelation invites us (inviting us, thus, into a constant philosophical and exegetical exploration of those mysteries). But one need not read that story of elaboration and increasing sophistication as simply one of progress. Rather, one should read it in two directions at once: in one direction the story points forward (at least to the competing visions of the high medieval period); in another, the story invites always a balance, invites the theologian to be attentive to the fundamental principles amid the diverse possible paths for elucidation and exploration. Thus while the particular conversations constitutive of western tradition to which I point are only examples, the first two (at least) also exhibit a general principle of some importance; conversations between Patristic texts and medieval particularly involve a reflection on what principles are fundamental, and what exploratory. I return to this point in my conclusion.

# 'Even as we are one'

My second example, again reflecting a very personal interest, concerns the character of analogy in Latin theological tradition and especially the so-called 'psychological analogy'. One of the features of Augustine's theology that I have found myself struggling to interpret over the years has been his use of the language of memory, intelligence and will in the *De trinitate*.

In the first place, I have argued in a number of contexts that in *De trinitate* 8–10 and 14 Augustine is not drawing on an independent psychological analysis of three mental faculties or even a standard psychological analogy that one can find elsewhere in his work. In psychological terms Augustine operates with a basically twofold division of the soul into higher and lower parts and never gives any clear sense that he sees the higher part divided into distinct faculties. Although there is much talk of the role of the memory and the will in Augustine's work, extended discussion of the interrelationship between these three terms is *only* a feature of the *De trinitate*.[30] When Augustine speaks of these three in that work, he is exploring the highest part of the soul as the locus of the *imago Dei* by reading a threefold process *out of* the life that for him constitutes intellectual, loving existence. He makes use of three terms that find their origin in Latin rhetorical tradition (possibly interpreted in the light of Neoplatonic discussion of virtue), three features which must be appropriately present and co-ordinated if the human being is to learn prudence.[31] But *at the same time*, Augustine makes use of the language of Nicene Trinitarian tradition to explore and read that to which he attends: the three are distinct and yet inseparable because our faith demands that they be so. Thus the language of faith guides as much as it is understood by means of the investigation.[32] The exercise as a whole is one that takes its place as the most developed of the mature Augustine's attempts to adapt to Christian intellectual reflection the traditions of dialectical reasoning that he inherited from the 'liberal arts' tradition.[33] At the same time, the very labelling of this triad as an 'analogy' is problematic: Augustine consciously eschews the term (which he under-

---

[30] For my fullest treatment see Ayres, *Augustine and the Trinity*, pp. 275–318. For the different ways in which Augustine divides the soul see Gerard O'Daly, *Augustine's Philosophy of Mind*, London: Duckworth 1987, pp. 11–15. For some good comparative discussion of the use of noetic triads, see also David Manchester, 'The Noetic Triad in Plotinus, Marius Victorinus and Augustine'. in Richard T. Wallis (ed.), *Neoplatonism and Gnosticism*, Albany: SUNY Press 1992, pp. 207–22.

[31] See Ayres, *Augustine and the Trinity*, pp. 308–15.

[32] See Ayres, *Augustine and the Trinity*, pp. 288–9.

[33] For Augustine's engagement with the 'liberal arts' see see Ayres, *Augustine and the Trinity*, pp. 121–70.

stands to imply a comprehensible proportion between two terms) in favour of the far broader *similitudo*.[34]

Augustine's use of this triad thus does not implicate him in treating divine existence and human existence as exemplifying the same intellectual life, or as treating the divine as one instance of such life. This is so in part because he combines a description of intellectual life and judgment as the highest form of existence, and the point at which we see how we are in the image of the Trinity, with a thoroughgoing analysis of the ways in which the divine life transcends that which is a constitutive feature of our intellect, the progress from lack toward fullness. At the same time, Augustine argues that each of the divine three possesses the fullness of the divine being and life, each thus being the one divine source of all, even as the Trinity is that one source. Thus for both basic philosophical and more advanced theological reasons, Augustine's use of a model of intellectual existence focuses attention on the transcendence of the divine and its unique Trinitarian mode of life. Augustine's usage reveals also the ontological foundations of these patterns of speech: a raft of diverse themes adapted from Neoplatonic traditions (Christian and non-Christian) concerning the character of the source of all – its peculiar unity, omnipresence and transcendence – is one key source not of Augustine's quasi-modalism or univocal naming of existence, but of the manner in which he *escapes* them.[35]

If these theses are correct, then, once again, it is not simply that some persistent views of what Augustine is about are shown to be false (although they certainly are), but that new questions emerge for anyone exploring the character of Latin Trinitarianism. It is increasingly clear that anyone seeking to understand the character of any exploration of a likeness in the created order must be carefully attentive to the purpose envisaged for such exploration – the vision of exercising of the intellect and of the function of such thought for the Christian as thinker, pray-er and teacher – and the extent to which that exploration is taken to be governed by the principles of Trinitarian orthodoxy.

In the case of Augustine I have argued (as have many others) that the practice of reflection he displays through the *De trinitate* is dependent on his adaptation of themes from the ancient 'liberal arts' tradition.[36] One of

---

[34] See my '"Remember that you are Catholic" (*serm.* 52.2): Augustine on the Unity of the Triune God,' in *Journal of Early Christian Studies* 8 (2000) 39–82.

[35] In stating Augustine's partially parasitical relationship to this tradition I do not assume a model of Christianity's relationship to classical non-Christian traditions in which Christianity is either free from external influence or in thrall to external authority. Rather, I primarily conceive of the relationship exegetically: early Christian thinkers' use of philosophical themes needs to be judged theologically on an ad hoc basis, and in so far as those themes enabled persuasive exegesis of contested texts.

[36] See Ayres, *Augustine and the Trinity,* pp. 121–41.

the most important features of this adaptation is the development of what I have called a 'Christological epistemology', an account of how the Christian ascends in thought and desire towards understanding that follows in reverse order the route laid out by the Word's humble assumption of humanity. At the core of this ascent lies a growth in appreciation for moral and intellectual humility, the need for grace and the imagining of ways in which, when it speaks of God, the text of Scripture invites us to think towards the intelligible and away from the sensible language and imagery used for our sake.[37] Although this process of intellectual and spiritual transformation certainly begins now, Augustine also maintains a strong distinction between faith and knowledge, the latter being fulfilled only eschatalogically.[38] This set of themes is the context within which Augustine undertakes his exploration of illustrative sites in the created order, and this context must be taken into account if we are to interpret well the role he accords those explorations. How is this paralleled or not in later cultural contexts?; how is this perspective received and/or modified when Latin theologians begin to adapt Pseudo-Dionysian accounts of kataphasis, apophasis and the symbolic into their theology? Only in the light of approaching such questions as these can we begin to talk usefully about how the 'Latin tradition' approaches 'analogical' discussion of the Trinity.

It will be of particular importance within any emerging conversation on this theme to examine how and when the language of love and knowledge (and especially their interaction as a model for the relationship between Son and Spirit) achieves prominence, and how understanding of that language shifts. Assumptions about the supposedly necessary consequences of using an account of intellectual life to explore aspects of Trinitarian doctrine has, in the revivalist context, hampered dense reflection on the various different accounts of the relationship between love and knowledge in western tradition, and led to that language being used extensively now only within a few Catholic contexts.[39] Lack of awareness of the multiplicity of ways in which such language may be used thus, once again, closes off many modern interpreters from potential resources in Latin tradition.[40]

---

[37] See Ayres, *Augustine and the Trinity*, pp. 142–73.

[38] On this theme see especially M. R. Barnes, 'The Visible Christ and the Invisible Trinity: Mt 5:8 in Augustine's Trinitarian Theology of 400', in *Modern Theology* 19 (2003) 329–55.

[39] It may perhaps be that Rahner's idealist adaptation of a Thomist version of the relationship between love and knowledge has particlaly enabled its positive use in Catholic circles beyond the avowedly Thomist.

[40] For another example of the interrelationship between discussing unity and diversity in God and discussion of how far the Trinity may be known by reason, see Gilles Emery's analysis of this relationship in the twelfth to fourteenth centuries: 'The Threeness and Oneness of God in Twelfth- to Fourteenth- Century Scholasticism', *Trinity in Aquinas*, 1–32.

# Monarchia

On at least one occasion where I have presented an argument of this form, the following question has been asked: 'If part of your argument is that Latin theologians need no longer turn east in order to find the themes that De Régnon told them they would find there, are you then arguing that Latin Trinitarianism is self-sufficient, that the dialogue with Greek theology is no longer paramount?' This is a very good question, one that can lead us to a third possible conversation, one that I do not think has yet emerged, but should.

Let me begin by noting one key factor that makes any discussion of the relationship between Latin and Greek theologies a complex engagement. Perhaps obviously enough, I do not think that a dialogue between Latin theology and Greek (or Russian) theology can any longer be understood as one between two distinct traditions known in their essences by particular and secure tokens. If we are to think about the engagement between Greek and Latin theology, we must always ask ourselves about the origins of any particular unitary vision of Greek tradition, and we must be careful to offer precision about which text or theologian or particular part of Greek tradition we seek to bring into dialogue. This is particularly so because the strong emphasis on Patristic sources and the attempt to present a unified vision of the Greek Patristic tradition within modern Orthodox Trinitarian theology is itself the product of a conscious revival of the Patristic heritage. The emergence in Russia and then in Russian exilic contexts of a consciously Patristic approach to Trinitarian exposition occurred in large part against the perceived bad influence of western and specifically idealist thought in nineteenth-century Russia, and against what was perceived as centuries of dependence on western thought forms.[41] This is not to say that such re-appropriation is mistaken, or even that there was no such thing as a distorting indebtedness to Latin theology in earlier Orthodox tradition, but it is to say that it is important to ask how that context shapes the themes celebrated as foundational. In a manner parallel to my emphases in the case of Latin theology, we

---

[41] For essays which advocate a 'Neopatristic' turn against inappropriate western influence on Orthodox thought see especially Georges Florovsky, 'Western Influences in Russian Theology' and 'The Ways of Russian Theology', in *Aspects of Church History*, (Collected Works of Georges Florovsky, 4), Vaduz: Büchervertriebsanstalt 1987, pp. 157–82 & 183–209. One of the most helpful discussions of Florovsky's vision remains the biography (by the editor) and interpretative essay (by George Williams) in Andrew Blane (ed.), *Georges Florovsky: Russian Intellectual and Orthodox Churchman*, Crestwood: SVS Press 1997. P. Valliere, *Modern Russian Theology. Bukharev, Soloviev, Bulgakov. Orthodox Theology in a New Key*, Grand Rapids: Eerdmans 2000, offers a far more sympathetic account of the tradition in modern Russian theology influenced by such thinkers as Schelling.

also need to ask whether and in what ways the attempt to synthesize a tradition centuries long involves the smoothing out of debates in favour of clear lines of evolution: most controversially in debate with Latin theology, how far can the Palamite distinction between 'essence' and 'energy' be used as a hermeneutic for viewing Patristic tradition? At the same time, a number of figures in contemporary Orthodox thought have been significantly influenced by the same revivalist dynamics (especially personalist dynamics) that have motivated many Latin theologians since the 1960s.

Nevertheless, Latin theology must engage with Greek, and three reasons come immediately to mind. First, to understand Latin theology as an enclosed tradition would be to deny the realities of its history. At key points Latin theology has found its voice partly through an engagement with Greek: whether we speak of the influence of Greek theology on Latin Trinitarianism in the late fourth century, whether we speak of the influence of John Damascene on Thomas, or whether we speak of the ways in which argument with Orthodox theologians in the period from the Council of Bari in 1098, to Florence in the 1430s and on into the work of the great seventeenth-century Jesuit Dionysius Petavius was deeply generative. Second, Latin theology developed out of the common faith of the early Church and if Patristic thought has anything like the foundational role for Catholic theology that I allege here, then there could be no justification for not thinking about the broad field of that thought world and the other orthodox traditions which developed from the same root. Third, and specifically in the Catholic context, Latin theology exists alongside a variety of traditions founded very much in Greek thought in the same ecclesial communion. Ignoring the traditions on which those communities draw would be an act of theological hubris.

But, then, how will the conversation between Greek and Latin theology proceed? Just as I have suggested that our conversations about the content of Latin tradition must proceed by noticing and engaging the plurality of conversations that should follow new work in historical theology, we must also see how new conversations may consequently emerge between Greek and Latin theologians. An example may make my point clearer. One of the themes of my own work has been to emphasize the centrality of the Father in Augustine's Trinitarian theology. Augustine consistently (and not surprisingly against the background of preceding Latin tradition) presents *Deus* as most naturally the Father. Son and Spirit may also be termed *Deus* because of the Father's eternal act in constituting them as being fully divine. Augustine then presents the missions of Son and Spirit as intended to reveal that Son and Spirit are from the Father in a manner that saves, a manner that draws us to participation in the life of God. The Son and Spirit are sent, he tells us, to reveal the 'hidden eternity' that is the Father.[42] Similarly, in his mature account of inseparable operation, Augustine presents all divine acts as occurring in an order (through Son and in Spirit) established in eternity by the Father. But, as we saw earlier in this paper, Augustine is striking, when read against his predecessors, for the thoroughgoing nature of his insistence that those two who are God from God not only share in the fullness of the divine nature but that the character of the divine life is constituted by the eternal interpersonal acts of the divine three. Thus we see very clearly a vision of the Father's giving himself that combines the Father's role as source of the two with an account of the Father's eternal establishment of the divine unity as a communion of three who are equal in all save the dependence of Son and Spirit on the Father.

This perspective on the Father's role suggests the possibility of mining Latin tradition to uncover conversations about how one balances the ordering role of the Father without turning to a voluntarist position in which the true character of the Father's eternal gift is hidden. But the same account of Augustine also suggests the need for a new exploration *between* Greek and Latin theologians, not about the bare principle of the Father's *monarchia*, but about how the different ways in which that principle is envisaged within and between different traditions. The discovery of our common faith releases us from the idea that Latins must 'borrow' or 'learn' this principle from Greeks, but it should also release us into the possibility of a new and much more complex conversation about how we envisage that *monarchia*.

One significant theological problem shaping the ways in which we present the Father's status as source dates from Patristic attempts to articulate the doctrine of 'inseparable operation' without according each of the divine three a separate part or role within every divine action and thus contravening Nicene principles of the unity of the divine will, power and nature. Emphasis on the Father's status as source of the Trinitarian life, and yet as an atemporal and immutable source who is eternally one with Son and Spirit, demands that the theologian recognize that the Father's person is revealed as mystery, and in a manner that necessarily generates fruitful tensions in human speech. Returning for a moment to the conversations opening within Latin tradition, I have already observed (following Cyril O'Regan) that the line of development running from Luther through Boehme to Hegel involves a transformation of the ways in which some high and late medieval trends conceived of movement and rest in the divine life against the background of asserting the eternal divine fullness – an account of movement and rest that owes to Neoplatonic tradition. When we recognize the diverse ways in which Neoplatonic tradition has shaped

---

[42] Trin., [ref.] See Ayres, *Augustine and the Trinity,* pp. 177–98.

Latin theology, we may see emerging from the fog of an overly unified vision of Latin tradition a complex conversation about how movement and rest may be predicated on the Triune life. Such a conversation is, in part, one about how we envisage the role of the Father as the source of that 'movement'. At the same time, some of the same themes (from the same philosophical sources) are latent within Greek tradition – and apparent, for example, in Maximus the Confessor's discussions of Gregory Nazianzen's reference to movement within the Godhead. But – and detailed exploration might prove me wrong – Greek theologians are generally even more reticent about using such dynamics of the divine life than Latin theologians. For those concerned with the Father's place in the Trinitarian order there is here a great resource, and yet another in which we must ask whether Patristic reticence to speak should be read as a boundary marker for our speculation, or as an invitation towards a multiplicity of explorations.

## Theology's Speculative Moment

I have argued, then, that the emphases of recent historical scholarship are beginning to shape conversations among different parts of Latin theological tradition. These conversations do not serve only to refute the assumptions that partly undergird the post-Hegelian revivalists, nor do they serve merely to defend fixed positions or developing trajectories in Latin theology that are well known. Rather, these conversations provide us with new points of departure for considering the dynamics of, distinctions within and development of Latin theology, and in these conversations we may find the best resources for the articulation of Trinitarian orthodoxy.

It may be helpful to reiterate my earlier point that the three conversations I outlined all stem from my own work on Augustine. Were this paper written by a scholar of Thomas or of another significant post-Patristic figure within Latin tradition, quite different conversations might have been highlighted. Nevertheless, it is important to ask whether attention to Patristic authors has a special place and significance for the future of Catholic Trinitarian theology. The category of 'the Fathers' is necessarily a complex one for the Catholic tradition. It is difficult to identify a particular chronological period as that of the 'Fathers' in any precise sense, simply because of the importance Catholic theology places on the development of dogma and doctrine under the inspiration of the Spirit. In 1968 the then Father Ratzinger offered a useful reflection on the question, ultimately arguing that although we cannot speak with certainty of an age of 'the Fathers' with precise chronological boundaries, we can identify the Fathers theologically as those who first witness to the articles of faith in the concrete

dogmatic and liturgical forms that become normative for later tradition.[43]
The Fathers are those who, under the inspiration of the Spirit of Christ,
give answer – or, better, speak again – the word spoken in the Scriptures.
If something like this account may be sustained, conversations that emerge
in the light of modern historical concerns between Patristic and later
aspects of Latin tradition may exercise a number of unique and theologically important functions. Such conversations should aid the theologian in
identifying the baseline and heart of the fundamental dogmatic mysteries
of Christian faith and focus attention on those central mysteries. While
from one perspective clarity about such fundamentals relativizes the importance of later and competing doctrinal elucidations, we must be careful
not to think of this relativizing as a rendering unimportant. Rather, it is
to locate those later speculations as amplifications and speculations that
may well be appropriate and even invited by the Scriptural witness to any
given article of faith (and here I use the term 'speculation' in the sense of
an invited intellectual gazing towards the rim of what may be grasped by
the human intellect). This particular notion of 'relativizing' may even be
aided by the gradual shift in accounts of doctrinal development from those
which present development as organic, seamless and cumulative, towards
those which open up the more differentiated and conversational model of
tradition that I have indicated in this paper.

I have elsewhere suggested that Catholic doctrinal theology in our age
needs to conceive of itself as an ineluctably historical enterprise, and that
the manner in which we have tended to distinguish the systematic and
the historical has been an unhelpful response to the epistemological and
historicist challenges of modern thought. Other ways of engaging these
modern concerns are possible.[44] This paper may be read as suggesting that,
at least at the tactical and operational level, fostering good Trinitarian
theology will require of us not merely new narratives of tradition that can
be incorporated into the 'constructive' work of the systematician, but much
careful thought about how theology's speculative moment is frequently to
be found in the opening of historical conversations, allowing 'newness' to
arise without assuming that we need consciously to 'construct' it.

In May 2010 many – with I hope appropriate despair at what human
beings make of the world – will have noted the seventieth anniversary
of the German crossing of the Meuse in May 1940 and their subsequent
advance to the Channel coast. This event came as a body blow to the French
and English high commands, and a surprise to many of their German

---

[43] J. Ratzinger, 'Die Bedeutung der Väter für die gegenwätige Theologie', in *Theologisch
Quartalschrift* 148 (1968) 257–82; tr. in *Principles of Catholic Theology. Building Stones for
a Fundamental Theology*, San Francisco: Ignatius, 1987, pp. 133–52.
[44] See my *Nicaea and Its Legacy: An Approach to Fourth-Century Trinitarian Theology*,
Oxford: Oxford University Press 2004, pp. 384–429.

counterparts. But, as recent research has shown, it was not a victory won simply by a strategic vision of the way in which German armour would carry all before it, but by a careful revival of the stormtrooper tactics *Auftragstaktik* developed in 1918 by which at the tactical and operational level small groups would infiltrate the enemy front, bypassing obstacles and points of defence wherever possible, creating a dislocation and confusion that could cause whole fronts to collapse and new strategic realities to appear.[45] What we see with the emergence of the new conversations in Latin theology that I have celebrated here is a tactical advance and infiltration that I hope will not only push back some of the odder themes of the Trinitarian revivalists, but will ultimately lead to a rethinking of the Latin tradition and of how good Trinitarian theology should proceed.

---

[45] See K. H. Freiser, *The Blitzkrieg Legend*, Annapolis: Naval Academy Press 2005.

# 2

# Medieval Trinitarianism and Modern Theology

## Richard Cross

Perhaps the main stumbling block in the Christian doctrine of the Trinity is the view that three persons could nevertheless be one God and one substance. Attempted solutions to this problem in recent years have by and large taken two different and incompatible routes. Some focus on the concept of *person*. Such views tend to see persons as psychological subjects. There being three divine persons thus amounts to there being three divine psychological subjects. This view is often labelled 'social Trinitarianism', and it can be spelled out in various ways. For example, some accounts stress the status of the persons as subjects; others, unhappy with the implied Cartesianism of such accounts, focus on the fact that such subjects require relations to other such subjects in order to count as persons in any full sense of the word. (I do not think that these relational views of personhood involve denying that persons are psychological subjects, or, more loosely, minds; the difference is one of emphasis. I return to this in section two below.) The second approach to the doctrine of the Trinity tends to focus on the concept of *substance*. Such views stress the numerical identity of the substance in all three persons, and in consequence tend to reject the view that persons count as psychological subjects, or that the presence of three persons entails the presence of three psychological subjects. This view has been labelled, somewhat misleadingly, 'Latin Trinitarianism'.[1] Clearly,

---

[1] See Brian Leftow, 'A Latin Trinity', in *Faith and Philosophy* 21 (2004) 304–34. I criticize the terminology in my 'Latin Trinitarianism: Some Conceptual and Historical Considerations', in T. McCall and M. C. Rea (eds), *Philosophical and Theological Essays on the Trinity*, Oxford: Oxford University Press 2009.

the problem for the social view – if there is one – is explaining precisely how tritheism is false; the problem for the 'Latin' view is explaining how modalism is false.

Medieval views of the Trinity are all clearly in the so-called 'Latin' camp. Curiously, this does not mean that they have nothing to offer social views, and I will try to bring out various relevant features as I proceed. In fact, I will tend to focus on this – partly because it seems to me that much recent Trinitarian thought is indeed social in nature. I will not be too specific here: I am going to assume a working knowledge of recent Trinitarian theology, and not relate what I say to particular modern theologians. The trajectories that I am going to follow are, I think, clear enough. I begin by considering the question of the divine substance; and I go on to examine some of what the medievals say about the so-called 'personal properties' – those features of a person that distinguish that person from the other two persons.

# The Divine Substance

As just suggested, the classic Trinitarian problem is this: how is it coherent to suppose that there are three divine persons but nevertheless just one God? At heart, the problem is metaphysical: how can there be three divine persons, but yet only one divine substance? One obvious answer to the second question would be to maintain that the divine substance is a *universal*: something co-ordinatively shared by all three persons. In what follows, I shall explore this option, with the help of two medieval theologians, Henry of Ghent and John Duns Scotus, both of whom develop something like this thought. Note that in itself this solution does not of itself answer the first question, since on standard views of universals, three exemplifications of a universal – say *horseness* – count as three things – in this case, three horses. So three exemplifications of the divine nature would on the face of it count as three Gods. So once I have sketched the metaphysics, I return to the question of tritheism. Basically, the solution will involve distinguishing the metaphysics of the divine case from the metaphysics of all other cases, and then making some appropriate semantic rules to govern the use of the term 'God'.

As it happens, Latin views generally involve the rejection of the claim that the divine substance could be a universal. Aquinas expresses the matter definitively:

> Universal and particular cannot be in God. Four reasons can be given for this. First, because according to Avicenna wherever there is genus and species, it is necessary for a quiddity to differ from its being (*esse*) … and this does not apply in God; secondly, because a universal essence is not

numerically the same in things beneath it other than according to reason, whereas the divine essence is numerically the same in many persons; thirdly, because a universal requires multiplicity in those things which are contained under it, whether actually or potentially ...; fourthly, because the particular is always related to a universal by addition. But in God, on account of maximal simplicity, no addition is possible, and therefore [there is] neither universal nor particular.[2]

The first of these reasons relates specifically to Aquinas' metaphysics, and I ignore it here. But the remaining ones could be affirmed by many theologians in the medieval Latin tradition. The second is crucial. According to many medieval thinkers who count as realists on the question of universals, extramental universals – usually called 'common natures' – are somehow numerically *divided* into the particulars that instantiate them. Although humanity, for example, in Socrates and Plato has some kind of reality and identity, this identity is not numerical: Socrates's humanity and Plato's humanity are numerically distinct from each other. (In what follows, I use 'common nature' as a technical term for such *divisible* universals.) But, Aquinas maintains, the *concept* of humanity really is one and the same concept, even though humanity itself – the common nature – lacks this kind of identity. The third argument seems to amount to much the same. The final one notes that the humanity of Socrates (for example) differs from the humanity of Plato by virtue of an individuating feature – one in Socrates and one in Plato – that is distinct both from the humanity of Socrates and from the humanity of Plato. God's maximal simplicity prevents there being some such individuating feature in a divine person. (I return to this last issue in the next section.)

Universals, in this view, are numerically many in their instantiations; the divine essence is supposed to be numerically identity in the three persons. In some sense, this refusal to countenance the view that the divine essence could be a universal is simply a terminological matter. For example, recent realists on the question of universals tend to affirm the view that extramental universals do indeed have numerical identity. David Armstrong, for example, comments on medieval views about the non-numerical identity of common natures as follows:

> For myself, I cannot understand what this second, lesser, sort of identity is. Partial identity, as when two things overlap but do no more than overlap, or when two things have some but not all the same properties so that their nature 'overlaps', can be understood readily enough. But

---

[2] Aquinas, *Scriptum super Libros Sententiarum*, 1.19.4.2 (ed. P. Mandonnet and M. F. Moos, 4 vols.), Paris: Lethielleux, 1929–1947, I, p. 483.

identity is just identity.... I take it that the Realist [on the question of universals] ought to allow that two 'numerically diverse' particulars which have the same property are *not* wholly diverse. They are partially identical in nature and so are partially identical.[3]

Even among medieval writers, there was some sense that we might think of the divine essence as a certain sort of universal – not the same sort of universal as we find in the creaturely domain, to be sure, but for all that a sort of universal: specifically, something like an Armstrong-style universal. Henry of Ghent introduces the idea and develops it more fully than any else (as far as I know). Henry more or less agrees with the kind of line we have just seen Aquinas take on the question of creaturely essences, and for this reason denies that, on the usual understanding of the term, the divine essence could be a universal. But he allows that there is clearly an intelligible sense in which the divine essence is a universal. In the passage which follows, Henry talks of a universal part: he means by this an instantiation of a common nature; and when he denies that there are such instantiations in God, he also means to deny that there are instantiated common natures in God:

> Speaking of a universal properly speaking, it is true that there is no universal part in God. But speaking improperly about the universal, a universal is really common, and is a form common to many by the commonness of one singular thing existing in them, and whole in each of them, though under diverse features by which they are distinguished from each other, or at least in the way in which divine persons are distinguished by the notional features of the personal properties.[4]

---

[3] D. M. Armstrong, *Nominalism and Realism*, Cambridge: Cambridge University Press 1978, p. 112.

[4] Henry of Ghent, *Summa quaestionum ordinariarum*, [= *SQ*] 75.6 ad 1, 2 vols, Paris, 1520, II, fo. 310rN. I am grateful to Scott Williams for drawing my attention to this passage. In my 'Duns Scotus on Divine Substance and the Trinity', in *Medieval Philosophy and Theology* 11 (2003) 181–201, I show how Scotus adopts – if less explicitly – a very similar teaching. When I wrote that article, I did not know of the presence of the view in Henry. For Henry's teaching on the common nature, see *SQ* 43.2 (*Opera Omnia*, ed. R. Macken, Ancient and Medieval Philosophy, De Wulf-Mansion Centre, Series 2, Leuven University Press, Leuven; Brill Leiden, 1979–), XXIX, pp. 52, l. 31–54, l. 71). Henry's Trinitarian theology is the subject of an Oxford doctoral dissertation currently in progress: Scott Williams, 'Henry of Ghent on the Trinity: Metaphysics and Philosophical Psychology', which, on the topics it examines, fleshes out the more introductory material in J. C. Flores, *Henry of Ghent: Metaphysics and the Trinity*, (Ancient and Medieval Philosophy, De Wulf-Mansion Centre, Series I, 36), Leuven: Leuven University Press 2006. See too S. Williams, 'Augustine, Thomas Aquinas, Henry of Ghent, and John Duns Scotus: On the Theology of the Father's Intellectual Generation of the Word', in *Recherches de théologie et philosophie médiévales* 77 (2010) pp. 35–81.

The idea is that the divine essence is numerically identical in all three persons – the three persons are, in Armstrong's phrase, 'partially identical'. Henry here does not specify the features which distinguish the persons – he calls them 'notional features of the personal properties' (I assume this is an objective genitive). I return to this issue in the next section.

The usefulness of a move like this is obvious. In effect, Henry appeals to two different kinds of universal – divisible natures in the case of creatures, and an indivisible nature in the case of God – and this allows him to distinguish between creaturely cases – as many natures of a given kind as there are instantiations of the nature – and the divine one – one nature common to all exemplifications of it. And in this case we have a powerful way of drawing a metaphysical distinction between the two cases – just the thing that is needed as a first stage in any Trinitarian investigation. Indeed, if we just focus on what Henry has achieved thus far, it seems that the divine case is, if anything, easier to understand than the creaturely case, and for much the same reasons outlined by Armstrong in his reaction to medieval theories of the common nature. It is easy enough to imagine overlapping or partially identical persons; it is very hard indeed to imagine the kind of non-numerical identity that medieval theories of the common nature seem to entail.

But by itself this does not provide a means for avoiding tritheism; neither does it give any reason for supposing that the views are true. On the second issue here, one reason why realists have historically favoured divisible common natures over indivisible universals is that they believe positing indivisible universals to be incoherent. Thus Scotus, for example:

> The universal is numerically one object of the intellect, and is understood by numerically one intellection, such that the intellect, in attributing [the universal] to diverse singulars, attributes numerically the same object, conceived many times, to diverse subjects, in stating 'this is this'. But it seems impossible that something real is numerically the same intelligible thing and yet be predicated in this way of diverse [subjects].[5]

The idea seems to be that the relation between a common nature – say humanity – and an instantiation of it – say Plato – must be such that it can make (say) the statement 'Plato is a man' true; and Scotus does not see how it could do this if Plato's humanity is identical to Socrates's humanity, since (he reasons) humanity as such is finite: Plato's humanity is somehow 'exhausted' by being Plato's, and Socrates' by being Socrates'.

---

[5] Duns Scotus, *Quaestiones super libros Metaphysicorum Aristotelis*, 7.18, n. 21 (ed. G. J. Etzkorn and others (eds), (Opera Philosophica, IV), St Bonaventure, N.Y.: The Franciscan Institute, 1997–2006, p. 343.

If the humanity of Socrates is identical to the humanity of Plato, Socrates and Plato must themselves be identical. But, Scotus claims, the situtation is different in the case of the divine essence: the divine essence is infinite, and belonging to (say) the Father no more exhausts it than does belonging to Son or Spirit.[6]

Equally, other arguments Scotus has against the existence, in the creaturely realm, of extramental universals really identical in their exemplifications turn out not to be generalizable to the divine.[7] For example:

> This opinion posits that that one substance [namely the universal], under many accidents, will be the whole substance of all individuals, and then it will be both singular and this substance of this thing [$x$], and in another thing [$y$] than this thing [$x$]. It will also follow that the same thing will simultaneously possess many quantitative dimensions of the same kind; and it will do this naturally, since numerically one and the same substance is under these [namely $x$'s] dimensions and other [namely $y$'s] dimensions.[8]

The argument is that accepting Armstrong-style universals entails that every exemplification of the same universal has all the same features, since universals are natures, and the accidental features of things inhere in their natures. Socrates and Plato have different accidents on the grounds that Socrates' accidents inhere in Socrates' humanity, and Plato's in Plato's humanity, and Socrates' humanity is non-identical with Plato's. Clearly, this argument need have no application in the case of God, since it may be that we do not believe God to have accidents; or if God does have accidents, it may be that all three persons have exactly the same accidents. I return to this argument later, because it seems to me that we may end up wanting to deny the claim that accidents inhere in natures. For now, the point I wish to make is that there may be reasons for supposing that Armstrong-style realism is coherent, but that there may be reasons for supposing that it cannot obtain in the case of creaturely natures. And if this were the case, we would have principled reasons for supposing that the divine case is significantly different, from a metaphysical point of view, from creaturely cases.

This approach provides a way of giving an account of the question of the perichoresis or interpenetration of the three divine persons. For suppose that the divine essence is the only essence such that it is numerically identical

---

[6] Duns Scotus, *Ordinatio*, [= *Ord.*] 1.2.2.1–4, n. 385 (Vatican, II, p. 348).

[7] On these, see section 3 of my 'Divisibility, Communicability, and Predicability in Duns Scotus's Theories of the Common Nature', in *Medieval Philosophy and Theology* 11 (2003) 43–63.

[8] Scotus, *Reportatio Parisiensis*, 2.12.5, n. 3 (Opera omnia, XI), Lyon 1639, p. 326b).

in all of its exemplifications. The divine essence is the overlap of the three persons. And three overlapping persons could certainly be said to exist *perichoretically* in a way that non-overlapping persons – human persons, for instance – do not. Again, Henry of Ghent makes this point most explicitly:

> In God, one person exists in another ... through something belonging to it that it has in common with that [person] in which it exists.[9]

And Henry draws attention to a further kind of perichoretic relation too:

> The Father is in the Son because the Son is from him, and the Son in the Father because the Son is not from anyone else; the only-begotten is in the unbegotten because the only-begotten is from the unbegotten.... They are in each other since nativity can only be from the Father.[10]

The second perichoretic relation amounts to the mutual dependence of the three persons. (Note that these questions of ontological perichoresis are independent of any further kind of perichoretic relation: for example, shared agency or mental life.) Henry explicitly traces both of these ideas back to passages from Hilary of Poitiers quoted by Peter Lombard,[11] though it is clear that Henry has added a lot of (necessary) formal metaphysics to Hilary's inchoate suggestions.

What about the tritheism question? Here things become, to my mind, rather trickier. Tritheism is the claim that there are three Gods, so one way to avoid tritheism is simply to stipulate that the reference of the term 'God' is restricted to the divine substance. Scotus, for example, believes that numerical terms properly track sortal terms, and sortal terms properly refer to concrete substances: if there is just one divine substance, then there is just one God. Scotus spells out his principles on this when discussing the claim that the Holy Spirit proceeds from the Father and the Son – the so-called '*Filioque*'. Scotus holds that the divine persons share intellect and will, and he holds that this shared mentality entails shared agency.[12] In the case of spiration, the Father and Son count as one agent.[13] And there is a sortal

---

[9] Henry of Ghent, *SQ* 53.10 (Paris, II, fo. 74vT).

[10] Henry of Ghent, *SQ* 53.10 (Paris, II, fo. 74vV).

[11] See Henry of Ghent, *SQ* 53.10 (Paris, II, fo. 74vV). On the first, see Hilary, *De trinitate,* [=*De trin.*] 3.4, ll. 13–14 (CCSL 62, I), Turnhout: Brepols 1979, p. 75), quoted at Peter Lombard, *Sententiae,* [=*Sent.*] 1.19,4, n. 2, (2 vols, 3rd edition, Spicilegium Bonaventurianum), 4–5, Grottaferrata: Editiones collegii S. Bonaventurae 1971–81, I, p. 162, ll. 10–11); on the second, see Hilary, *De trin.* 7.39, ll. 31–33 (I, p. 307): see Lombard, *Sent.* 1.19.4, n. 3 (I, p. 162).

[12] Scotus, *Quodlibet,* [=*Quod.*] 8, n. 6 (Wadding, XII, p. 205).

[13] See e.g. Scotus, *Ord.*, 1.11.1, n. 18 (Vatican, V, pp. 6–7); *Ord.* 1.12.1, nn. 49–51 (Vatican, V, pp. 53–55); and *Ord.*, 3.1.2.un., n. 216 (Vatican, IX, pp. 96–97).

term applied to things that spirate – namely, 'spirator'. Given that sortal terms refer to substances, and given that there is just one divine substance, there is just one spirator:

> When a numerical term is added to a substantive, as if we say 'two spirators', the adjectival numerical term [namely 'two'] immediately has a substantive on which it depends, since an adjective determines that on which it depends. Therefore the significate of its substantive is denoted to be [plurally] numbered.[14]

Since there are not two substances here, but only one, Father and Son are just one spirator. Thus the general rule is that, when we count substances, we do just that: we do not count persons as such. (Of course, created human natures standardly coincide with persons.)[15] Still, there are two persons, and Scotus thinks that we can talk about two 'spirating ones' (*spirantes*). Now, Latin allows the substantival use of participles in a way that English tends not to. But Scotus treats the participle gramatically here simply as an adjective that lacks a substantive for it to modify. He takes there to be an implied substantive, but this substantive is wholly unspecified – 'ones', or 'somethings' or 'persons' (recall that 'person' is not the name of a natural kind in Aristotelian metaphysics). And since, on this priniciple, '*spirans*' does not necessarily refer to a substance, we can indeed say two *spirantes*:

> The [plural] enumeration of a determinable form [in the case of a deter-minable adjectival term and not of a substantival one is] on account of [the adjectival term's] association with a *suppositum*. When [an adjective numerical term – e.g. 'two'] is added to a [determinable] adjective, as when we say 'two *spirantes*', both [terms] … are dependent on a third on which they depend and which is determined by them. In the case at hand, this is 'someones' or 'persons', as if we were to say 'Three creating "someones"', or 'three [creating] persons'.[16]

So according to Scotus, there are two divine persons spirating the Holy Spirit, and we can thus talk about two *spirantes*. But 'two Gods' (for example) would refer to numerically two divine substances, and 'two human beings' to numerically two human substances. Factually, there are (at least) two human beings; so 'two human beings' has a genuine reference. But there is necessarily only one divine substance; so 'two Gods'

---

[14] Duns Scotus, *Ord.*, 1.12.1, n. 46 (Vatican, V, p. 51).
[15] I say 'standardly' since the Incarnation provides a theological counterexample.
[16] Duns Scotus, *Ord.*, 1.12.1, nn. 45–6 (Vatican, V, p. 51).

can never refer to anything. I return to all this in the next section, where I consider the question of the distinctions between the divine persons. I will suggest that medieval discussions of these issues force us to focus on certain metaphysical issues about the reality of the features that distinguish persons from each other, and in doing so I will consider again the context-dependent senses of the word 'God'.

If all this is right, it gives a way of affirming Trinitarianism without *ipso facto* being committed to tritheism. It is not the only way, of course, of doing so. Many social Trinitarians, for example, hold that tritheism is false on the grounds that the persons require each other for their existence in ways that human persons, for example, do not. Richard Swinburne, for example, explicitly appeals to this requirement:

> What in denying tritheism, the view that there are three Gods, were the Councils trying to rule out? I suggest that they were denying that there were three *independent* divine beings, any of which could exist without the other; or which could act independently of each other.
>
> … The three divine individuals taken together would form a collective source of the being of all other things; the members would be totally mutually dependent and necessarily jointly behind each other's acts. This collective would be indivisible in its being for logical reasons – that is, the kind of being that it would be is such that each of its members is necessarily everlasting, and would not have existed unless it had brought about or been brought about by the others.
>
> … The claim that 'there is only one God' is to be read as the claim that the source of being of all other things has to it this kind of indivisible unity.[17]

At any rate, it seems to me that social Trinitarians, as much as 'Latin' ones, could if so minded make use of the kind of analysis offered by Henry of Ghent and his followers. The analysis also has the advantage of placing Latin views much closer to the kinds of views that we find in the Greek theological tradition from Gregory of Nyssa onwards.[18] Gregory holds that the divine essence is a universal, numerically identical in each divine person – just as in the view that Henry defends. But Gregory makes the theory of universals fully general: creaturely natures, as much as the divine nature, are numerically identical in each exemplification, and on the principle that substance-sortals refer to natures, Gregory concludes not only that there is

---

[17] R. Swinburne, *The Christian God*, Oxford: Clarendon Press 1994, pp. 180–1.
[18] But on the thought that the differences between Greek and Latin theologies turn out to be more semantic than substantive, see my 'Two Models of the Trinity?', in *Heythrop Journal* 43 (2002) 275–94, reprinted in M. C. Rea (ed.), *Oxford Readings in Philosophical Theology*, vol. 1, *Trinity, Incarnation, Atonement*, Oxford: Oxford University Press 2009, pp. 107–26.

only one God but also that there is only one man.[19] Gregory consequently appeals to considerations other than theories of universals to explain divine unity: his principle is unity of activity,[20] something that is developed at greater length and in greater detail by some of the Latin theories of the personal properties which I consider in the next section.

# Relations

In the previous section, I spoke occasionally of the so-called 'personal properties' – those features of the divine persons that distinguish them from each other. It was a commonplace of the history of the doctrine of the Trinity after Gregory of Nazianzus that the only such features were the *relations* between the persons. There are a couple of ways in which this thought can be developed. Social Trinitarians, for example, sometimes claim that the presence of such relations is necessary for the distinction of persons given that tritheism needs to be avoided: the relations secure the radical *inseparability* of the persons – as in the passages from Swinburne just quoted. But such theologians would generally not claim that the relations are the only features that the persons do not share. Social trinitarians would generally affirm that the persons are three minds, not one, and that mental properties are intrinsic to the persons in ways that relations are not.[21] But Latin Trinitarians might accept that the only possible personal properties are relations, for something like the reason given by Aquinas in the very first quotation above: whatever distinguishes the persons, it cannot be anything real added to the essence, or that makes composition with it. And relations seem to fit this description: relations between two substances can change in virtue of a real change merely in one of the substances (so-called 'merely Cambridge changes'). Considerations of divine simplicity, in other words, seem to drive the account.

Writers are not always very clear on this, slipping between the view that causal relations between the persons are what distinguish them and the view that all personhood is fundamentally relational. Thus Alistair I. McFadyen:

> The terms of personal identity within the Trinity identify not just unique individuals but the form of relation peculiar to them. Father,

---

[19] Gregory of Nyssa, *Ad ablabium,* [=*Abl.*], (GNO III/1) 40, 8–9.
[20] Gregory of Nyssa, *Abl.,* 44, l. 7; 53, l. 3.
[21] I do not want to get into the vexed philosophical problem of the distinction between intrinsic and relational properties, not least because it is very hard to give a completely coherent account of the distinction in the case that the relations are *necessary* features of the persons that have them.

for instance, denotes both a specific individual and the form of relation existing between Him and the other persons. Or, rather, it identifies that specific individual through an implicit (metaphorical) reference to his unique relational form (Fatherhood or origin) and, thereby, to the other persons.[22]

... The unique subjectivities of each person are formed through the unique intersubjectivity which pertains to them. Like all living things they are neither fully open nor fully closed systems. It is their radical openness to and for one another (in which Personal closure still retains a place) which constitutes their existence in this unique community.[23]

The first paragraph here sounds fully 'Latin': the only things which the persons do not share in common are their relations of origin. The second, contrariwise, seems fully Social: the divine persons are capable of 'intersubjective' relations – something that suggests they are three minds or subjects of psychological properties. And McFadyen is happy to refer to them as 'three individuals of a common divine nature'[24] – again suggesting that his view is at some distance from the Latin view from which he seems to start. Thinking of the persons as defined not by their relations of origin (as in typical Latin views) but by their intersubjective relationships raises a further problem that has been nicely highlighted and criticized by Harriet A. Harris.[25] It is fashionable to talk about a relational ontology – the view that persons, and substances more generally, are fundamentally relations. Now, this claim needs to be understood carefully: it is not that substances are just relations, or are simply *reducible* to relations, but that the identity of a substance is parasitic on its relations. But substances undergo constant relational changes, and this view of what a person is seems to suggest that there is no continuous personal existence at all.[26] Rather, as Harris argues, substances 'are ontologically prior to relations'.[27] It cannot be the case that relations, not substances, are basic: relations do not 'precede' substances.[28]

So the question is not whether persons are constituted by relations, but whether they possess any non-shared monadic or non-relational properties – a claim that I take to be endorsed by social Trinitarians but not by Latin ones. In the rest of this section, I will consider an argument from Henry

---

[22] A. I. McFadyen, *The Call to Personhood: A Christian Theory of the Individual in Social Relationships*, Cambridge: Cambridge University Press 1990, p. 27.

[23] McFadyen, *The Call to Personhood*, p. 29.

[24] McFadyen, *The Call to Personhood*, p. 28.

[25] H. Harris 'Should We Say that Personhood is Relational', in *Scottish Journal of Theology* 51 (1998) 214–34. McFadyen's account is one of Harris's main targets.

[26] Harris, 'Should We Say that Personhood is Relational', pp. 217–19.

[27] Harris, 'Should We Say that Personhood is Relational', p. 227.

[28] Harris, 'Should We Say that Personhood is Relational', p. 228.

of Ghent to the effect that the *only* possible features that the persons do not share are relations, and then Scotus' attempt to rebut it. The truth of Scotus' view, which entails weakening some of the classical restraints on divine simplicity, is a necessary condition for social Trinitarianism – even though this is not a theory that Scotus himself would have been happy with. Finally, I will consider questions of divine simplicity in the light of the Scotist discussion of the personal properties – showing in particular how he would respond to the fourth of Aquinas' arguments outlined in the very first passage quoted above.

Henry develops Aquinas' argument to show that the personal properties must be relations to persons – specifically, what are known as 'relations of origin': *being the Father of, being the Son of* and *being spirated by Father and Son.* If the personal properties are non-relational, Henry supposes, they will involve some real addition to the essence, and he holds that one and the same essence could not be a constituent of three different things in the case that each thing includes something real over and above the essence. So any case of essence + non-relational property amounts to an instantiation of the essence: Socrates' humanity, distinct from Plato's humanity, for example. In God, a non-relational account of the personal properties would result in three deities, and thus three Gods:

> If there is a *suppositum* in God, it is necessary that it is constituted by a respective *ratio* founded in the essence, which does not bring about any determination of the thing considered in itself (because it [namely the relation] does not determine the essence), but [brings about the determination] only of the thing compared to another according to relative opposition, which is [a determination] of the related thing, which is itself constituted as it were from essence and relation, and itself determined and distinct.[29]

Underlying this is a strong commitment to divine simplicity, just as in Aquinas' account. According to both Henry and Aquinas, relations, unlike monadic properties, do not count as *things*. (I began to discuss this view above, mentioning merely Cambridge changes as evidence for this sort of view.) Hence essence + relation is no more composite than essence alone. Aquinas, for example, makes the point that the lack of a distinction in terms of any real entity by no means entails the lack of a distinction *simpliciter*:

> In God, the essence is not really distinct from the persons (*non sit aliud essentia quam persona secundum rem*), but nevertheless the persons are really distinguinguished from each other.... When the relation [namely:

---

[29] Henry, *SQ* 53.6 (Paris, II, fo. 68rH).

the personal property] is compared to the essence, it differs not really but merely rationally; but when compared to the opposed relation, it has, in virtue of the opposition, real distinction.[30]

The idea is that relations are not real entities or things in the world, and thus are not robust enough to create a distinction in terms of real entity between a thing $x$ on the one hand and $x$ + a relation on the other. The trick is supposed to be that, despite this fact, the relations are robust enough to distinguish related real things: e.g. it is possible for two items – $x$ + relation$_1$ and $x$ + relation$_2$ – to be distinct, even though neither of the relations is a real thing in the world, and thus even though in terms of all real entity there is *no* distinction between the two items.

Henry makes a similar point, by contrasting relations – *modes* of things – with fully-fledged things such as substances, qualities and quantities. Relations do not count as things because they are intrinsically parasitic on *other* features of the world, where such features are both necessary and sufficient for the reality of the relations. Henry's argument relies on a key Aristotelian text that he himself quotes: 'There is no *per se* motion or mutation in respect of relation.'[31] What both Aristotle and Henry are getting at is that there can be no change that is *merely* in the category of relation: a relation between two or more objects cannot change unless something intrinsic to one or more of the objects itself changes:

> [A relation] is not factible in itself, and ... it is in no way factible *per se*: neither in itself, nor in another: for it can be the end term of an action neither in itself nor in another.[32]

Presumably what Henry has in mind is that things are the kinds of items that can be made (by God) independently of other things ('in itself ... *per se* ... [not] in another'); relations are not like this, and so are not things. On this account, substance, and the two non-relational accidents, qualities and quantity, are the only items that count as things.[33] According to Henry, if two or more things are united to form (in some way or another) a further thing really composed of thing-like components, this composition requires there to be real relations (of inherence and of being-inhered-in, or informing and being informed) between the various things thus united. And this gives a further argument, derived from Avicenna, against the thing-like status of relations. If a relation were a thing, then it would require a relation (of

---

[30] Aquinas, STh., I. a.39. q.1 c.
[31] Henry, *Quod.*, 7.1–2 (Paris, fo. 255$^r$N), quoting Aristotle, *Ph.*, 5.1 (225b11–13).
[32] Henry, *Quod.*, 7.1–2 (Paris, fo. 257rY).
[33] On this, see M. G. Henninger, *Relations: Medieval Theories 1250–1325*, Oxford: Clarendon Press 1989, pp. 48–52.

inherence) in order for it to belong to a subject. And on the assumption that all relations are things, this requirement quickly generates an infinite regress, since relations of inherence would themselves require further relations of inherence, and so on.[34] This argument is, then, that relations are not things because things united to each other do so in a way that requires some real composition (here, relations of inherence), and relations cannot be so united. In fact, crucially for the Trinitarian argument here, as Henry sees it, really distinct items united to each other compose an *individual existent*.[35] Essence + non-relational property compose an individual substance; essence + (say) three non-relational properties compose three individual substances, at least in the case that the non-relational property is non-accidental: in the case, that is, that it is an individuating feature.

Scotus disagrees with these relation theories. His worry is that if there is no distinction between the divine essence and a personal property, each person will be identical (Leibniz-style) with the divine essence, and thus modalism will be true. In this text, he talks about the divine essence as 'communicable', and the personal property as 'incommunicable':

> Here there remains a further difficulty. Unless some distinction is posited between the notion of essence and the notion of *suppositum*, it does not seem intelligible that the essence is numerically one while the *supposita* are many.... I say without asserting it, and without prejudice to some better opinion, that the notion by which a *suppositum* is incommunicable (let it be 'a') and the notion of essence as essence (let it be 'b') have some distinction prior to every act of intellect, whether created or uncreated. I prove it thus: The first *suppositum* [namely the Father] formally possesses communicable entity [namely the divine essence], otherwise he could not communicate it; and he really possesses incommunicable entity too, otherwise he could not positively be a *suppositum* in real entity.[36]

As Scotus later points out, he holds that the divine essence and the personal property are equally *real*, as it were: if they were not, the personal properties would not be sufficiently robust to distinguish the persons from each other:

---

[34] For the argument see Henry, *Quod.*, 3.4 (Paris, fo. 51rN).

[35] Henry, *Quod.*, 10.7 (Leuven, XIV, 164). I discuss all of this at length in my 'Relations and the Trinity: The Case of Henry of Ghent and Duns Scotus', in *Documenti e studi sulla tradizione filosofica medievale* 16 (2005) 1–21.

[36] Scotus, *Ord.*, 1.2.2.1–4, nn. 388–90 (Vatican, II, pp. 349–350); see too *Ord.*, 1.11.2, n. 52 (Vatican, V, pp. 23–4); *Ord.*, 1.26.un., n. 31 (Vatican, VI, pp. 9–10). I discuss this issue further in my *Duns Scotus on God*, (Ashgate Studies in the History of Philosophical Theology), Aldershot: Ashgate 2005, pp. 235–40.

The relation constitutes the person only as compared to the essence. But it does not constitute a person other than as a thing, otherwise the person, as formally constituted, would not be a thing; therefore the relation, as compared to the essence, is a thing.[37]

Given this, Scotus holds that any account of the personal properties, whether they be relations or non-relational properties, requires weakening the simplicity requirement that motivates Aquinas and Henry. Aquinas' worry is that a non-relational personal property would be *added* to the essence, and Henry's that it would entail that a person is *composed* of two things, essence and property. The composition worry seems to me a local, medieval kind of worry, since standard medieval Aristotelianism involves the claim that, in any case of composition, one component is *potential* and the other *actual* (think matter and form, or substance and accident), and the medievals held that God cannot include potentiality. There seem to me reasons for rejecting the view that God cannot include potentiality, but I do not need to explore this right now. Scotus' move is simply to reject standard Aristotelianism here: he supposes that essence and property could be, as it were, co-ordinate features of a divine person, tied to each other in a way that does not require potentiality and actuality.[38] And this seems a reasonable move: we now do not generally suppose that all cases of property-possession need to be analyzed in the Aristotelian way. But Henry's view involves a further move too, namely that distinct items united to each other compose a discrete individual existent, at least in the case that neither of the two items is an accident of the other. And Scotus rejects this move:

I say that if we posit that the persons are relational, it is necessary to posit that they are truly subsistents and that the same undivided nature is in them. This cannot be posited on account of some imperfection of the persons in [their manner of] subsisting, for they are posited to be as truly subsistent as they would be if they were absolute. Therefore it must be posited on account of the infinity of the essence which is in the subsistents. But the infinity of the essence would be the same if the persons were absolute. Therefore it would not be necessary for the nature to be divided in that case, just as now the [relational personal] property does not [divide the nature]. Therefore let this be proved: 'Every nature, common to absolute *supposita*, is distinguished in them.' For this is true in creatures, but in the case at hand it begs the principal conclusion.[39]

---

[37] Scotus, *Quod.*, 3, n. 4 (Wadding, XII, p. 70). I discuss this issue further in my *Duns Scotus on God*, pp. 240–4.

[38] On this, see my *Duns Scotus on God*, pp. 111–13.

[39] Scotus, *Ord.*, 1.26.un., n. 82 (Vatican, VI, p. 37).

The relevant requirement of orthodoxy is that tritheism is false: that is, as Scotus sees it, that 'the same undivided nature is in' all three persons. Scotus does not see that satisfying this principle requires positing that the persons are distinct by relations, since it could just as well be the case that the same undivided nature were in all three persons on the assumption that what distinguishes the persons is some non-relational feature. As Scotus sees it, it is the infinity of the essence that entails its being numerically the same in all three persons. This does not mean that the persons might not also have necessary causal relations to each other – e.g. to satisfy the inseparability requirement. The aim is merely to show that it is possible for the persons to have non-relational individual properties too.

If Henry's argument is unsound, it follows that the persons can possess distinct non-relational properties. And the unsoundness of Henry's argument is thus required for any view that maintains that the persons have distinct psychological properties. And social Trinitarian views require this, since they are generally spelt out in terms of the psychological relations between the persons, such that the three persons must be (or have) three minds – as I noted above. In this case, then, a medieval debate has a direct bearing on modern debates: indeed, social Trinitarians need to be able to answer Henry's objection, and one way of doing this is indeed to follow Duns Scotus – albeit that Scotus himself does not want to apply this argument to psychological properties, since he believes on Augustinian grounds that the three divine persons must indeed have shared mentality – since as Scotus sees it this is the only way of supporting Augustine's claim that 'Father, Son, and Holy Spirit ... operate inseparably.'[40] It is not clear to me that Augustine's claim is true here, and thus not at all clear to me that it gives grounds for supposing that the divine persons have shared mentality. Certainly, this is rejected by social Trinitarians, as just noted.

Scotus' view here looks preferable, since it is not at all clear to me that three persons can be distinct *merely* by relations in the absence of any distinctive non-relational properties, especially if we deny that relations are real things. The opposing view seems unavoidably modalistic. A natural development of the view that the divine essence is merely the overlap of the persons, and that what distinguish the persons must be further real intrinsic features of the persons, is to hold that each person counts as a God. This is the line taken by Swinburne, on the grounds that denying it entails modalism (each person is identical with God, i.e. with the divine substance).[41] As noted above, Swinburne maintains that we should nevertheless affirm one God,

---

[40] Augustine, *De trinitate,* [=*Trin.*] 1.4.7 (CCSL 50), Turnhout: Brepols 1968, p. 36; see too e.g. Augustine, *Trin.,* 2.2.3 (p. 83); *Trin.,* 5.14.15 (p. 223), which last Scotus cites at *Quod.,* 8, n. 3 (Wadding, XII, p. 205). For Scotus's argument in favour of Augustinianism here, see in particular Scotus, *Quod.,* 8, n. 6 (Wadding, XII, p. 205).

[41] Swinburne, *The Christian God,* p. 181.

not three, on the grounds that 'God' refers most naturally to the inseparable collective of persons. Scotus, as I pointed out earlier, holds that sortal terms track substances, not persons. But he allows too the claim that each person is (a) God on the grounds that each person is nevertheless an exemplification of the divine essence.[42] What grounds this context-dependent use of the term 'God' is the non-identity (in Leibnizian terms) of each person with the divine essence: that the divine essence is God allows the predication to piggy-back onto each use of a person term (such as 'Father').[43] And grounding this fact is the further one that sortal terms fundamentally track substance terms. The move is reminiscent of Gregory of Nyssa's view, but allows sortal terms derivatively to track person terms without requiring that what grounds this derivation is anything like unity of action.

These are deep metaphysical matters, and what I refer to as 'context-dependent' uses of terms entail that such uses are in some sense bound to be *ad hoc*. My point here is simply that there are various ways of dealing with these issues, open to both social and Latin Trinitarians, and that there is guidance for some of them that can be found in the medieval theologians. And all Trinitarian theologians require some way of dealing with these issues. Positions such as those affirmed by Swinburne and Scotus open the way for the persons to possess distinct accidental properties. I noted above Scotus' denial of this possibility – for reasons other than those connected with the distinction of the persons from each other. But Scotus' argument on this point seems to be mistaken: properties inhere in persons, not shared substances – shared substances (i.e. in this context universals) are, after all, most naturally thought of as *properties* of persons. And if persons are subjects of properties – whether or not psychological properties – there is no reason in principle why one or more person might not be the subject of accidental properties. The medievals were unhappy with this thought for the local Aristotelian reasons mentioned above: namely, that the inherence of accidents requires an analysis in terms of potentiality and actuality, and God was thought of as pure act. But the doctrine of the Incarnation seems to require that at least one divine person was the subject of a set of properties accidental to that person: namely, the human properties that the person had contingently and temporarily. Again, there is a lot that might be said about this, but doing so would require consideration of matters beyond the scope of a discussion of issues connected merely with Trinitarian doctrine, and thus beyond the scope of the current volume.[44]

---

[42] Scotus, *Ord.*, 1.4.2.un., n. 10 (Vatican, IV, p. 4).

[43] Scotus, *Ord.*, 1.4.2.un., n. 11 (Vatican, IV, pp. 5–6).

[44] For some of it, see my discussion of Scotus in *The Metaphysics of the Incarnation: Thomas Aquinas to Duns Scotus*, Oxford: Oxford University Press 2002, pp. 34–6, 124–8.

\* \* \*

The relation between medieval views and modern ones is complex, not least because of the variety of positions held in both periods. I have tried to show two things. First, that medieval accounts of universals might provide ways for both Latin and social Trinitarians to account for the shared nature of the divine essence, and secondly that there are medieval arguments from the nature of the personal properties that challenge social Trinitarians, and that medieval responses to such arguments help social Trinitarians defend their position. Thus far I have said nothing about the relative desirability of Latin and social views. But it seems to me that if Latin views are construed as entailing that the only feature that one person can possess uniquely is a relation (to the other persons), then Latin Trinitarianism must be false. My reason for holding this is that the only obvious rationale for accepting Trinitarianism is the Christian doctrine of the Incarnation, and this doctrine seems to entail that at least one person possesses a set of properties – i.e. human properties – that the other persons do not possess. But, again, that is a story for another time.

# 3

# Rethinking Trinitarian Theology: Theology since the Reformation

## Samuel M. Powell

## The Reformation's Medieval Heritage

The Reformers inherited a creedal tradition stretching back to Nicea and a history of Trinitarian thought whose major exponent was Augustine.

The council of Florence (begun in 1431) represents the status of the doctrine of the Trinity at the end of the Middle Ages. With respect to the Trinity, the council's main purpose was to establish doctrinal unity with churches of the east. Practically speaking, this meant securing their agreement on the validity of the *Filioque* clause of the creed of Constantinople – the affirmation that the Spirit proceeds from the Father and from the Son. In this respect, the council was a success.[1] One effect of the council was to reinforce the Latin church's endorsement of Augustine's understanding of the Trinity, particularly his emphasis on the unity of the Trinity. Although both the eastern and the western churches affirmed this unity, it was characteristic of the Augustinian tradition to insist that Father, Son and Spirit differ from each other in nothing except in their relations – the Father begetting, the Son being begotten, and the Spirit proceeding. This tradition also affirmed that, in relation to the created world, the Father, Son

---

[1] See the statements of the sixth, eighth, and eleventh sessions of the council. The council's goal of achieving real unity with the eastern churches ultimately failed.

and Spirit are a single principle of action – that there is a single divine action towards the world, in which the three persons act jointly and inseparably. This is the Trinitarian theology that underlies the statements of the council of Florence, especially in its eleventh session. The Trinitarian theology of the Reformers was written within the doctrinal space created by the creedal tradition from Nicea to Florence, a tradition that embodied the Augustinian understanding of the Trinity.

# The Trinity in the Reformation

There are two main points to keep in mind when trying to understand the doctrine of the Trinity in the Reformation. One is the Reformers' embrace of the creedal tradition. The other is their dispute with the medieval church over the issues of authority and scriptural interpretation. The first point accounts for the doctrinal conservatism of the Reformers; the second explains their endeavour to expound the doctrine strictly on the basis of biblical texts.

## Martin Luther and the Lutheran Tradition

Martin Luther (1483–1546) exemplifies the task that Protestants felt. On the one hand, he endorsed the early Trinitarian creeds, at no point doubted the validity of the doctrine of the Trinity, and expressly condemned the ancient Trinitarian heresies.[2] On the other hand, Luther would not acknowledge the creeds as authorities in their own right. Their authority and truth were, he argued, strictly dependent on their relation to the Bible. He considered them authoritative because they summarized the Bible's teaching. And while he accepted the traditional language of Trinitarian missions and appropriations, he eschewed the equally traditional and Augustinian attempt to make sense of the Trinity by means of analogies, insisting instead that the Bible's teaching, especially its Christology, is the sole ground of our knowledge of the Trinity.[3]

---

[2] Accordingly, the Augsburg Confession expressly endorsed the Nicene-Constantinopolitan creed.

[3] For Luther's view of the Trinity see Ch. Helmer, *The Trinity and Martin Luther: A Study on the Relationship between Genre, Language, and the Trinity in Luther's Works (1523–1546)*, Mainz: Verlag Philipp von Zabern 1999; R. Jansen, *Studien zu Luthers Trinitätslehre*, (Basler und Berner Studien zur historischen und systematischen Theologie, 26), Bern: Herbert Lang/ Frankfurt a. M.: Peter Lang 1976; R. Prenter, *Spiritus Creator*, Philadelphia: Muhlenberg Press 1953; S. M. Powell, *The Trinity in German Thought*, Cambridge: Cambridge University Press 2001, pp. 12–30.

Luther's contribution to the doctrine of the Trinity lay not in the development of the doctrine *per se*, but in showing the doctrine's Christological and soteriological roots. To use later terms, Luther's Trinitarian theology proceeds from the economic Trinity to the eternal Trinity. Of course, Luther began with a commitment to the church's doctrine of the eternal Trinity.[4] To say that he began with the economic Trinity is not to say that he somehow deduced the eternal Trinity from the economic, but only that his controlling interest in the doctrine of the Trinity was its soteriological role.

For Luther, there is a fundamental distinction between God revealed and God hidden. God is hidden to unaided human reason; however, in Jesus Christ the hidden God has become manifest. The Bible's account of Jesus, disclosing Trinitarian relations and processions, is a true and full revelation of God's being. The revelation of God is, accordingly, not a guise or mere appearance of God. The revealed God is simply the hidden God who has shown us the divine essence. Although this essence remains incomprehensible and transcendent, the revelation of the essence is a true disclosure. We do not understand how God is three persons in one substance. Further, our speech is wholly inadequate to the task of communicating about God. We stammer when we use words such as 'Trinity' and Luther did not insist on technical terms such as 'homoousios'. Nonetheless, we know that the revealed Trinity of Father, Son and Spirit truly is God's eternal essence.

To say that the Trinity is the revealed God is to say that God has come into the world for us. In this revelation God has become our God. Reason can apprehend God as the governor of the world or as the law-giver, but only revelation shows us God as the one who turns towards us and comes to us in grace. The revelation of the Father, Son and Spirit is thus God's act of salvation.

The revelation of the Trinity is given to us in the words of the Bible. Luther thus identified proof-texts, such as Psalm 2:7 and Galatians 4:4, which prove that the Father and Son are distinct persons. He likewise adduced Joel 2:28 to show that the Spirit is distinct from the Father and the Son. At the same time, the revelation of the Trinity has a strongly Christological character, for in revelation God gives God's self to us and we behold this self-giving most concretely in Jesus Christ.

Luther's associate, Philipp Melanchthon[5] (1497–1560) wrote an influential textbook of Lutheran theology, the *Loci Communes*.[6] In its first

---

[4] On Luther's affirmation of the eternal Trinity see Ch. Helmer, 'God from Eternity to Eternity: Luther's Trinitarian Understanding', in *Harvard Theological Review* 96 (2003) 127–46.

[5] E. P. Meijering, *Melanchthon and Patristic Thought: The Doctrines of Christ and Grace, the Trinity and the Creation*, (Studies in the History of Christian Thought), Leiden: Brill 1983; Powell, *The Trinity in German Thought*, pp. 12–30.

[6] There is an English translation of the first edition: 'Loci Communes' in W. Pauck (ed.), *Melanchthon and Bucer*, (The Library of Christian Classics, 19), London: SCM Press 1969.

edition Melanchthon advocated a strictly biblical theology and wrote rather stridently about the vain speculations of the scholastic theologians. The divine mysteries, he averred, were better adored than investigated and he therefore focused attention on overtly soteriological topics, hurrying past the Trinity and other seemingly speculative topics. By the final editions of *Loci Communes*, however, he had revised his approach, having come into contact with anti-Trinitarian movements. He accordingly felt the need to expound the doctrine of the Trinity more substantially, referring directly to technical Trinitarian terms and to use Augustinian-style analogies for purposes of exposition. In this way, Melanchthon exhibited the tendency of later Protestants to adopt a friendlier attitude towards scholastic theology.

## The Theology of the Radical Reformation

The Reformation introduced into Western theology the idea that the Bible alone is the source and norm of Christian doctrine. For Luther and other magisterial reformers, this idea caused no difficulty with respect to the doctrine of the Trinity; for them, the ecumenical creeds and Patristic writers had faithfully expounded the Bible's witness to God's Trinitarian nature. The principle of *sola scriptura* did not signal discontinuity with the early church's doctrinal consensus. The radical reformation, however, was a movement with little concern with the Patristic era and its creeds. The radical reformers were, like the magisterial reformers, concerned only to be faithful to the Bible; however, unlike the magisterial reformers, they did not feel the need to demonstrate continuity with earlier, post-biblical times.

As a result, early radical reformers could craft a confession of faith (the Schleitheim confession of 1527) that made no mention of the Trinity at all. It wasn't that they denied this doctrine; it was simply not a theological problem that, in their estimation, required comment. Later, as the movement matured, the Dordrecht confession (1632) did offer a simple affirmation of faith 'in one eternal, almighty, and incomprehensible God, the Father, Son, and Holy Ghost'.[7] Initially, however, practical matters of ethics and church order prevailed.

The Trinitarian theology of the radical reformers, then, is notable for the way in which they framed their affirmations and for what they omitted from these affirmations. They happily confessed the doctrine of the Trinity but typically did so in exclusively biblical terms, eschewing the technical language that theologians had developed over the centuries. Their

---

There is also a translation of a later edition: *Melanchthon on Christian Doctrine: Loci Communes 1555*, (Library of Protestant Thought), New York: Oxford University Press 1965.
[7] Available at: www.mcusa-archives.org/library/resolutions/dordrecht/index.html.

affirmations, in other words, tend to be collections of scriptural references.[8] This occasionally led to difficulty with other Protestants, who were troubled by their reluctance to use terms such as *person*.[9] The issue for Protestants was whether confession of the orthodox faith required use of the traditional terms or whether framing affirmations in exclusively biblical terms sufficiently preserved the orthodox teaching. In a situation of doctrinal and hermeneutical uncertainty, Protestants had reason to wonder whether ancient heresies might lie concealed in Anabaptist theology.

## John Calvin and the Reformed Tradition

John Calvin's Trinitarian teaching fits solidly within the Augustinian tradition.[10] The trintarian persons are subsistent (1.13.6) and the term *God* properly refers not to the Father, but to the divine essence (1.13.24). What is notable in his theology is therefore not any innovative teachings but instead the framework in which he presented the doctrine of the Trinity.

First, like Luther, Calvin insisted on the soteriological character of Christian doctrine. What is critical is not a speculative knowledge of the divine nature but instead knowledge, joined with devotion, of God's works (1.5.9; 1.2.2).[11] The doctrine of the Trinity is important for the Christian because it tells us who and what sort of God the revealed God is and thus distinguishes God from the idolatrous creations of human imagination 1.13.1).

Second, like Luther, Calvin departed from medieval attempts to support the doctrine by means of analogies. On the contrary, for Calvin there is only one ground of our knowledge of the Trinity: the Bible. His exposition of the Trinity (1.13) appeals only to scripture and expressly declines the use of analogies (1.13.18). At the same time, Calvin had to confront the fact that the traditional doctrine uses non-scriptural terms such as *person* and *homoousios*. The fact that such terms have no express biblical warrant was clearly a problem for Calvin. His Bible-centred method might have inclined him to adopt the Anabaptist approach, which was to restrict Christian

---

[8] See P. Rideman, *Account of Our Religion*, Rifton, NY: Plough Publishing House 1974, pp. 22–4 and *The Writings of Pilgram Marpeck*, (Classics of the Radical Reformation, 2), Kitchener, Ontario: Herald Press 1978, pp. 508–9.

[9] J. Yoder, 'The Frankenthal Disputation: Part II Outcome, Issues, Debating Methods', in *Mennonite Quarterly Review* 36 (1962) 116–17, 132.

[10] T. F. Torrance, 'Calvin's Doctrine of the Trinity', in *Calvin Theological Journal* 25/2 (1990) 165–93. See also 'Pro G. Farello et Collegis Ejus Adversus Petri Caroli Calumnias' (Ioannis Calvini Opera Quae Supersunt Omnia, 7), Braunschweig 1863–1900, pp. 289–340 for evidence of Calvin's concern for maintaining continuity with the Patristic tradition.

[11] References to Calvin are taken from John Calvin, *Institutes of the Christian Religion*, (Library of Christian Classics), Philadelphia: The Westminster Press 1960.

doctrine to biblical modes of expression. Calvin, however, argued for the propriety of technical, non-biblical terms as a legitimate means of defending the doctrine. Although having no special commitment to any particular term, Calvin saw no harm in using technical terms pragmatically in so far as they express the truth in some way (1.13.5). This is in keeping with his view that, although church councils and their creeds must be judged by their agreement with the Bible (4.9.8), the most ancient creeds are reliable expressions of the Bible's teaching.[12]

Accordingly, Calvin publicly opposed the anti-Trinitarian thinkers of his day who believed that the creeds differed from the teaching of the Bible. His refutation consisted in a biblical argument for the Trinity. In doing so, he firmly established a cornerstone of Reformation teaching – that although the Bible is the church's only doctrinal norm, the principle of *sola scriptura* does not lead to doctrinal aberration. With the Reformation's elevation of the Bible as the only norm, the question arose of whether the Bible's teaching was truly in agreement with the church's doctrinal tradition. Calvin's goal was to justify a position between the medieval church and the anti-Trinitarians. Against the latter he uncompromisingly affirmed the traditional doctrine's agreement with the Bible. But he also felt that medieval modes of argumentation were overly speculative. His task was to expound and defend the traditional doctrine on the basis of scripture alone.

Not surprisingly, Reformed creeds enshrine these same themes. Both the Belgic confession of 1561 (article 8) and the Second Helvetic confession of 1566 (chapter 3) support the doctrine with strictly scriptural arguments and expressly condemn ancient Trinitarian heresies. The Belgic confession also affirmed the Nicene and Athanasian creeds.

## Richard Hooker and the Church of England

Like Continental Protestant traditions, Anglican affirmations about the Trinity reproduced the language of Nicea and Constantinople, affirming the full divinity of the Son and Spirit and that the Trinitarian persons are of one and the same substance and eternity.

However, Richard Hooker (1554–1600) distinguished himself from some Continental Protestants by acknowledging that the Bible does not give us the doctrine of the Trinity 'by express literal mention'. Instead, he claimed, the doctrine must be deduced from the Bible 'by collection', i.e. by logical inference. Although confident that the Bible contains the doctrine, Hooker believed that 'contains' does not mean that the Bible sets forth the doctrine in plain terms'. On the contrary, discovering the doctrine requires the use of

---

[12] S. Reynolds, 'Calvin's View of the Athanasian and Nicene Creeds' in *Westminster Theological Journal* 23 (1960) 33–7.

human reason to draw conclusions from Scripture.[13] Protestants varied in the extent to which they thought the Bible expressly and plainly states the doctrine; however, few were interested in inserting human reason into the interpretative process, preferring to see the doctrine as an immediate implication of Scriptural affirmations. Hooker thus gave the Anglican tradition a distinctive approach to the doctrine.

# Anti-Trinitarian Movements in the Sixteenth and Seventeenth Centuries

The new situation created by the Reformation created an opportunity for novel ideas of all sorts to proliferate. With the role of authority and respect for ecclesiastical traditional diminished and with the rules governing biblical interpretation open to dispute, doctrinal diversity reigned.

For the doctrine of the Trinity this meant, besides the radical reformers' disdain for technical terms, the overt rejection of the doctrine by some thinkers. In various places – Poland, Hungary, Italy – movements arose that rejected the doctrine, often on the grounds that it was not attested in the Bible.

Michael Servetus (1511–1553) was one of the most prominent of the anti-Trinitarians. His critique of the doctrine was extensive and rested on several bases.[14] He argued that the doctrine does not take Christ's humanity seriously (1.15), that it amounts to belief in three gods (1.31), and that it commits the believer to an inconceivable belief (1.45). He understood the Word of John's gospel to be, not a divine hypostasis, but the act of God speaking (2.4–5). Christ was the incarnate Word, not because of a hypostatic union, as in the creed of Chalcedon, but because he reveals the Father's will (3.16; 2.5). The *Son* is not a being, a supposed second person of the Trinity, but is instead Jesus Christ. The Son is therefore a creature (2.9). To affirm that Jesus Christ is God is to say that he exercises the authority that God gave to him (1.25). The Holy Spirit similarly is not a divine hypostasis, but is a term designating God acting within humans in a spiritual way (4.2–4.3).

What is notable about Servetus' theology is his claim that the doctrine of the Trinity is not a properly biblical doctrine and instead rests on

---

[13] R. Hooker, *Laws of Ecclesiastical Polity*, I, 14. See also L. W. Gibbs, 'Richard Hooker's Via Media Doctrine of Scripture and Tradition', in *The Harvard Theological Review* 95/2 (2002) 230–1.

[14] All references to Servetus are from his 'On The Errors of the Trinity' in *The Two Treatises of Servetus on the Trinity*, (Harvard Theological Studies, 16), New York: Kraus Reprint Co., 1969.

metaphysical modes of thought that are foreign to the Bible.[15] The Bible, he argued, describes the way in which God appears and acts, not God's nature, which is a metaphysical category (1.51) The use of terms such as *ousia* is likewise an illegitimate application of alien concepts to the biblical text.

Servetus thus represented an unintended consequence of Reformation theology. Having rejected the authority of creeds and councils, the Reformers found the church's sole authority in the Bible, with the understanding that the early creeds fitly expressed the Bible's doctrine of God and Christ. However, this rejection opened the door for thinkers of all sorts who questioned the reliability of the creeds to offer alternative interpretations of the Bible's teaching. Servetus and other anti-Trinitarians could thus claim to be rejecting the doctrine on biblical grounds, believing that they had discovered the true meaning of the Bible. From the perspective of both Catholics and Protestants, radicals such as Servetus were simply rationalists who refused to accept the clear teaching of revelation. From their own perspective, however, they were peeling back layers of misunderstanding with which the Bible had been surrounded for centuries. Of course, by arguing that the traditional doctrine was irredeemably tainted with metaphysical concepts, Servetus and others overlooked their own metaphysical commitments or simply identified them with the ideas of the Bible. Nonetheless, by distinguishing the Bible from the post-biblical tradition of doctrine, and by distinguishing the Bible's rather Hebraic conceptual world from the later church's use of Hellenistic philosophies, anti-Trinitarians such as Servetus anticipated important themes in modern theology and biblical studies.[16]

Similar developments took place in England in the seventeenth century.[17] Here the concept of person became problematic. Whereas traditionally the term *person* designated the Father, Son and Spirit and thus had a distinctively theological meaning, in the seventeenth century it increasingly came to be equated with consciousness. As a result, the doctrine of the Trinity looked more and more like a doctrine about three divine beings. Further, the century saw a growing desire for precision in language and a growing impatience with both scholastic subtleties and mystical tendencies. As a result, the doctrine of the Trinity was increasingly regarded not as a vital

---

[15] It should be added that, later in life, Servetus' thought took on a more Neoplatonic character and he came to a greater appreciation of philosophy.

[16] See also *The Racovian Catechism with Notes and Illustrations*, London 1818. This document represents the Polish tradition of anti-Trinitarianism. Like Servetus' theology, this document offers a mix of biblical argument and critical analysis of concepts such as *person*.

[17] See P. Dixon, *Nice and Hot Disputes: The Doctrine of the Trinity in the Seventeenth Century*, London: T & T Clark 2003 and Jason E. Vickers, *Invocation and Assent: The Making and Remaking of Trinitarian Theology*, Grand Rapids, MI: Eerdmans, 2008.

basis of the Christian life, but instead as a technical problem requiring a solution. Further, theologians came to regard God's unity and attributes as matters of relative clarity, in contrast to the Trinity, which seemed highly obscure. In an intellectual climate impressed with René Descartes' emphasis on clear and distinct ideas and John Locke's theory of ideas, and in which Latitudinarian skepticism about theological proprieties abounded, the difference in clarity between God's being and the Trinity proved disastrous for the doctrine of the Trinity. The 1690s thus saw an active controversy about the Trinity in which the leading voices of Deism argued, like Servetus, against the doctrine in favour of what they took to be a more biblical approach to the idea of God.[18]

# The Trinity in the Eighteenth Century

## Orthodox Theological Schools[19]

The doctrinal history of the eighteenth century is the story of a three-way contest between the schools of orthodox Protestant and Catholic theology, Pietistic influences, and the growing tide of rationalistic approaches to theology. Although at the beginning of the century there were severe tensions between the orthodox schools and Pietists, by the end of the century the two had begun to join forces to combat the threat posed by rationalistic tendencies.[20]

With respect to the doctrine of the Trinity, orthodox theology was characterized by four features. First, it regarded the Bible as a storehouse of revealed truth, waiting to be systematically assembled into doctrines by theologians. For Johann Albert Bengel (1687–1752), the Biblical writers showed exact knowledge of truth, expressed themselves with unsurpassable precision and provided biblical doctrine with systematic arrangement. The entire Bible, he argued, was a complete and perfect system.[21]

Second, and consequently, they used the proof-text method of

---

[18] See G. Reedy, 'Socinians, John Toland, and the Anglican Rationalists' in *Harvard Theological Review* 70 (1977) 285–304.

[19] For a characterization of Protestant scholastic theology see M. I. Klauber, 'Reason, Revelation and Cartesianism: Louis Tronchin and Enlightened Orthodoxy in Late Seventeenth-Century Geneva' in *Church History* 59 (1990) 326–39 and 'The Drive toward Protestant Union in Early Eighteenth-Century Geneva: Jean-Alphonse Turrettini on the 'Fundamental Articles' of the Faith', in *Church History* 61 (1992) 334–49. See also R. A. Muller, 'Scholasticism Protestant and Catholic: Francis Turretin on the Object and Principles of Theology', in *Church History* 55 (1986) 193–205.

[20] See Powell, *The Trinity in German Thought*, chapters 2 and 3.

[21] J. A. Bengel, *Gnomon of the New Testament*, I, 5–6, 42, Edinburgh: T & T Clark, n.d.

argumentation. The doctrine was, especially among Protestants, supported by an array of biblical texts that proved God's unity and the distinction and deity of the Trinitarian persons. This method is used abundantly in Johann Reinbeck's (1683–1741) theology. He made the standard appeal to Genesis 1:26 ('Let us make man in *our* image'), the baptismal formula of Matthew 28:19 and 1 John 5:8 to prove a plurality of persons in God.[22]

Third, they employed the concept of mystery. The Trinity is a revealed but incomprehensible truth. Although not contradicting reason, it cannot be discovered or proved by reason. It can only be accepted on the basis of revelation's authority.[23]

Finally, orthodox theologians contended for the doctrine against its critics, notably the Socinians. Reinbeck's apologetic strategy was to show that the doctrine has a sound scriptural basis and that there is nothing in the doctrine that is logically contradictory. To this end he used analogies drawn from natural phenomena to prepare the unprejudiced mind to consider the Biblical teaching about the Trinity and to show that the doctrine of the Trinity is not self-contradictory.[24]

# The Theology of Pietism

Pietism was a departure, not from orthodox doctrine, but from the driving concerns of orthodox schools. Conceptual precision, polemics, clear distinctions between Catholic, Reformed and Lutheran beliefs – none of these characteristics of orthodox schools appealed to Pietists. Although embracing confessional doctrines, their interests lay elsewhere, especially in the practice of the Christian life.

This emphasis on practical matters might have constituted a problem for Pietists' affirmation of the Trinity. This doctrine, after all, was commonly regarded as an incomprehensible, revealed mystery. However, Pietists of all sorts not only vigorously affirmed the doctrine but saw in it an important doctrinal support for their deepest convictions.

Take John Wesley (1703–1791), for example. Wesley was a staunch defender of the orthodox doctrine of the Trinity, consciously contending for it against Socinian criticisms.[25] But the focus of his (and his brother Charles') interest in the Trinity was its soteriological and doxological

---

[22] J. Reinbeck, *Betrachtungen über die in der auspurgischen Confession enthaltene und damit verknupfte göttliche Wahrheiten*, Berlin 1740) §16 & §19.

[23] Ch. Wolff, *Gesammelte Werke*, I. Abteilung, (Gesammelte Kleine Philosophische Schriften, 21.5), Hildesheim: Georg Olms Verlag 1981, 21.5:341–2 and 375.

[24] Reinbeck, *Betrachtungen*, §13.

[25] J. Wesley, Sermon 55, 'On the Trinity', §15, (The Bicentennial Edition of the Works of John Wesley, vol. 2: Sermons II), Nashville: Abingdon Press 1985. See H. D. Rack, 'Early Methodist Visions of the Trinity', in *Proceedings of the Wesleyan Historical Society* 46 (1987) 65–7.

importance. The idea of the Trinity, in other words, was much more than an object of doctrinal belief. It was an existential truth deeply connected to the experience of salvation.[26]

Like Wesley, Nicolaus Ludwig von Zinzendorf (1700–1760) was doctrinally orthodox and affirmed the Augsburg Confession's article on the Trinity.[27] However, he also criticized that article for its lack of connection to soteriology.[28] He thus marked a considerable departure from the theology of the orthodox schools, for he reverted to the spirit Melanchthon's early theology, with its exclusive emphasis on the practical benefits of religious knowledge. Zinzendorf swore abstinence from all forms of metaphysics, natural theology and the contamination of theology by philosophy.[29] He rejected all speculative prying into divine matters and insisted that Christian theology has to do only with God as God is revealed to us.[30] Consequently, he paid comparatively little attention to what modern theologians have called the ontological or essential Trinity. The impetus for Zinzendorf's innovation lay in his Lutheran conviction that theology should confine itself to expounding revelation, eschewing all speculations into God's inner being. Revelation, in turn, was for him not the Bible but instead Jesus Christ. His epistemology, accordingly, was radically Christocentric, not bibliocentric.

## Rationalistic Theology

Rationalism in the eighteenth century came in several varieties. Some types were simply attempts to defend traditional Christian doctrine with rational arguments. Others were more radical and simply rejected Christian doctrine, seeking to re-fashion theology in overtly non-Christian ways.

Of the radical types, some expended their critical energies through biblical criticism. Herman Samuel Reimarus (1694–1768) is the outstanding example of this type. Reimarus insisted that the New Testament was to be read as a document of first-century Judaism, not as a cache of revealed truth to be mined for doctrinal content. Terms such as *Son of God*[31]

---

[26] B. E. Bryant, 'Trinity and Hymnody: The Doctrine of the Trinity in the Hymns of Charles Wesley', in *Wesleyan Theological Journal* 25/2 (1990) 64–73.

[27] N. L. von Zinzendorf, 'Ein und zwanzig Discurse über die augspurgische Confession', (Hauptschriften, 6) Hildesheim: Georg Olms Verlagsbuchhandlung 1963, pp. 4–5, 67–8.

[28] Zinzendorf, 'Ein und zwanzig Discurse ...', pp. 60–2.

[29] H. Ruh, *Die christologische Begründung des ersten Artikels bei Zinzendorf,* Zürich: EVZ-Verlag 1963, pp. 55–6; E. Beyreuther, 'Christozentrismus und Trinitätsauffassung', in *Studien zur Theologie Zinzendorfs: Gesammelte Aufsätze,* Neukirchener Verlag 1962, pp. 23–4.

[30] Ruh, *Die christologische Begründung*, p. 100 and Beyreuther, 'Christozentrismus und Trinitätsauffassung', p. 22.

[31] H. S. Reimarus, *Reimarus: Fragments*, Philadelphia: Fortress Press 1970, pp. 76–84.

and *Holy Spirit*[32], accordingly, had vastly different meanings from those assumed by the orthodox tradition. More broadly, Reimarus believed that Jesus had no intention of creating a new religion; his mission was not to reveal mysteries.[33] Christianity as a new religion of revealed mystery was, he argued, the creation of Jesus' disciples who, with evil motives, distorted Jesus' teaching.[34]

The other type of radical theology was more philosophically inclined. Immanuel Kant (1724–1804) illustrates this type. Kant was adamant that the idea of the Trinity could not be regarded as a mystery of revelation to which human reason must submit, for any such mystery could have no moral value. He was therefore deeply suspicious of the traditional doctrine of the Trinity, for it seemed to him to be an attempt at describing the being of God in itself, quite apart from any moral relation to us. Kant expressly denied that the Trinitarian terminology describes God in some direct way. In fact, he asserted, God is a single being, not a Trinity of truly distinct persons.[35] The most he would concede is that God's three-fold moral relation to us (holiness, benevolence and justice) must presuppose some 'three-fold original principle of activity' in God.[36] For Kant, then, the doctrine of the Trinity is a way of expressing God's moral relation to humanity.

 # The Trinity in the Nineteenth Century[37]

## Friedrich Schleiermacher and Liberal Theology

Friedrich Schleiermacher (1768–1834) marks a watershed in theology and in the doctrine of the Trinity. He saw that the assumptions of traditional orthodox theology were not up to the task of responding to the critique posed by rationalism. He perceived that the Bible could no longer be

---

[32] Reimarus, *Reimarus: Fragments*, pp. 89–91.

[33] Reimarus, *Reimarus: Fragments*, pp. 65–71.

[34] Reimarus, *Reimarus: Fragments*, pp. 240–8.

[35] I. Kant, *Religion Within the Bounds of Religion Alone*, New York: Harper Torchbooks, Harper & Row Publishers, 1960, pp. 130, 133, 137.

[36] Kants gesammelte Schriften, 3e Abteilung: Handschriftlicher Nachlaß, Bd. 18, Berlin: Walter de Gruyter 1928, p. 449.

[37] See S. M. Powell, '19th Century Protestant Doctrines of the Trinity' in G. Emery and M. Levering (eds), *Oxford Handbook of the Trinity*, (Oxford: Oxford University Press 2011, pp. 267–80). A good account of the development of Trinitarian thought in America in this period is B. M. Stephens, *God's Last Metaphor: The Doctrine of the Trinity in New England Theology*, (American Academy of Religion Studies in Religion, 24), Chico, CA: Scholars Press 1981. See also Sam Powell, 'The Doctrine of the Trinity in 19th Century American Wesleyan Theology', in *Wesleyan Theological Journal* 18 (1983) 33–55.

employed as a treasure trove of revealed truths and that revelation could no longer be thought of as the communication of mysteries.[38]

Schleiermacher responded to the theology of the Enlightenment by presenting a new understanding of revelation and doctrine. In particular, he advanced (1) a novel way of thinking about humankind's knowledge of God and (2) a novel account of the relation of language to doctrine.

For Schleiermacher, our knowledge of God is not primarily cognitive (in contrast to orthodox and rationalistic theologies) or moral (in contrast to Kant and Deists). It is instead affective – a matter of 'feeling', defined by Schleiermacher as a pre-conscious, pre-verbal state. Feeling is, in the language of later philosophy, the state of being prior to the emergence of subject and object in consciousness. It is in this pre-conscious feeling that our being is united with the infinite being of God.[39]

The knowledge of God inevitably manifests itself in acts of communication, especially speech.[40] Shared feeling expressed in language is thus the basis of religious communities.[41] So, although revelation is not verbal, our knowledge of God in the form of feeling comes to be verbalized. The Bible is the result of such verbalization. It is not a written transcript of God's thoughts but is instead the expression of the early church's feeling-knowledge of God.[42] Consequently, the Bible is not, as orthodox theologians believed, an immediate source of information about the Trinity or an infallibly inspired collection of truths. Schleiermacher believed that an authentic account of the Trinity must be founded in the Bible, but not it would not be found by assembling scriptural texts into a systematic doctrine.

Schleiermacher was sharply critical of the traditional doctrine of the Trinity. It was, he argued, an unacceptably speculative theory of the being of God. It speaks of eternal distinctions in God, which bear no relation to our actual experience of God.[43] The notion that the Son and Spirit proceed from the Father destroys the intended equality of the persons.[44] Further, the doctrine inevitably vacillates between a Platonic view of the divine essence (in which the essence is more real than the persons) and a nominalistic view, in which the three persons are in effect three separate

---

[38] See Powell, *Trinity in German Thought*, pp. 87–101 and F. Schüssler Fiorenza, 'Schleiermacher's Understanding of God as Triune', in Jacqueline Mariña (ed.), *The Cambridge Companion to Friedrich Schleiermacher*, Cambridge: Cambridge University Press 2005, pp. 171–88.
[39] F. Schleiermacher, *The Christian Faith*, Philadelphia: Fortress Press 1976, p. 131.
[40] Schleiermacher, *The Christian Faith*, pp. 76–7.
[41] Schleiermacher, *The Christian Faith*, p. 27.
[42] Schleiermacher, *The Christian Faith*, p. 363.
[43] Schleiermacher, *The Christian Faith*, pp. 739–40.
[44] Schleiermacher, *The Christian Faith*, pp. 479–80.

beings.[45] More important for Schleiermacher, in the traditional order of theological doctrines, the Trinitarian persons are introduced before the historical revelation of Jesus Christ and the Holy Spirit.[46] The doctrine, in other words, is overly abstract, presenting the Trinity as an account of God's eternal being without consideration of the fact that this doctrine is grounded in the experience of salvation. That is why Schleiermacher placed the doctrine of the Trinity at the end of his *Christian Faith* – this doctrine presupposes the concrete facts of Christology, salvation and the church.

For Schleiermacher, the fundamental affirmation of the doctrine is that the divine essence has united with human nature.[47] In Jesus Christ this union is person-forming. God was in Christ in such a way as to constitute him, from the beginning of his existence, as an individual person.[48] The Holy Spirit is the union of the divine essence with collective human nature. The result of this union is not a person, but the church.[49] Curiously, Schleiermacher's *Christian Faith* has no section on the Father; however, we may infer that the symbol of Father points to the union of the divine essence with the created world as a whole.

For Schleiermacher, then, the doctrine of the Trinity is not about eternal, personal distinctions within God. It is instead about the progressive unions between God and the world, especially in the person of Jesus Christ and then in the Holy Spirit, which is the common spirit of the church. However, it is important to note that he did not think of Jesus as merely a human being and the Holy Spirit as just a name for the church's fellowship. On the contrary, the divine union that creates Jesus Christ and the church is an expression of God's creative and causal activity. The Trinity is thus a doctrine about God's causal intervention in the world for the purpose of salvation.

The theologians of the Ritschlian school (Albrecht Ritschl [1822–1889] and his students, notably Wilhelm Hermann [1846–1922] and Adolf von Harnack [1851–1930]) accepted Schleiermacher's critique of the traditional doctrine of the Trinity; however, they were not interested in taking up his suggestion that the doctrine be reconstructed in terms of the progressive union of the divine essence with human nature. As a result, their remarks about the Trinity are almost wholly critical.[50]

These liberal theologians were especially convinced that the traditional

---

[45] Schleiermacher, *The Christian Faith*, pp. 740–1.
[46] Schleiermacher, *The Christian Faith*, pp. 746–7.
[47] Schleiermacher, *The Christian Faith*, pp. 738–9.
[48] Schleiermacher, *The Christian Faith*, pp. 399–407.
[49] Schleiermacher, *The Christian Faith*, p. 569.
[50] Powell, *The Trinity in German Thought*, pp. 142–72. For the impact of Ritschl's theology on British theology, see For an understanding of developments in British theology, see T. A.

doctrine violated Luther's thesis that all authentic knowledge of God is knowledge of God as revealed. The doctrine, they believed, was an attempt to describe God apart from revelation. They held as well that the traditional doctrine was overly philosophical, lacking a clear connection with soteriological concerns. At the same time, for them the fundamental concept for understanding God was *person*. With this emphasis, there was little chance that the traditional notion of Trinitarian persons would find much affinity with the liberals' basic notion of God. Finally, with the advantage of progress in historical research and biblical scholarship, they were more attuned to differences between the Bible and post-biblical doctrinal development than was Schleiermacher. They accordingly saw the early creeds as alien to the spirit of the Bible. The increasing dominance of Ritschl's theology meant that by the early decades of the twentieth century the doctrine of the Trinity was widely perceived as having nothing to contribute to theological discourse.

# Idealist Philosophy[51]

The principal German idealists with an interest in the Trinity were Georg Wilhelm Friedrich Hegel (1770–1831) and Friedrich Wilhelm Joseph Schelling (1775–1854). The idealists accepted Kant's critique of reason; however, they remained unsatisfied with the results of this critique and in response embraced the ancient *logos* doctrine of Greek philosophy. In effect, they represented reason as the universal principle of all reality. This understanding opened the door to a robust doctrine of the Trinity.

For idealists, the key to advancing beyond Kant was to see that reality itself, as a whole and in its parts, has a conceptual, rational form. This made metaphysics once again possible after the brief Kantian sceptical interlude. As a result, the idea of God was again regarded as something thinkable and rational. The doctrine of the Trinity was, they held, the ecclesiastical form of the rational idea of God.

The idealistic philosophers thus represented a significant departure from the eighteenth-century tradition of rationalism and deism. Against the opinions of radical Deists like Reimarus, they accepted the validity

---

Langford, *In Search of Foundations: English Theology 1900–1920*, Nashville: Abingdon Press 1969, pp. 217–33.

[51] For an analysis of German idealist philosophy on Roman Catholic theology, see T. F. O'Meara, *Romantic Idealism and Roman Catholicism: Schelling and the Theologians*, Notre Dame: University of Notre Dame Press 1982. W. L. Fehr's *The Birth of the Catholic Tübingen School: The Dogmatics of Johann Sebastian Drey*, (American Academy of Religion Series, 37), Chico, CA: Scholars Press 1981, pp. 182–98 describes the way in which idealist philosophy affected one theologian's understanding of the Trinity. For the impact of idealism on British theology, see Langford, *In Search of Foundations*, pp. 55–87.

of historical Christianity and its doctrines, although they were sensitive to standard rationalist criticisms of the doctrine. They hoped thereby to preserve the essence of the doctrine from the inadequate form in which it had historically been cast.

The key to understanding Hegel's view of the Trinity is to grasp his distinction between religious thought (*Vorstellung*) and philosophical thought (*Begreifen*). The former thinks about God with images; the latter thinks with rigorous concepts. The former portrays God using a familial image (father and son); the latter interprets the Trinity as a way of speaking about the ultimately real, the absolute idea.[52]

For Hegel, the doctrine of the Trinity is the religious way of thinking about the absolute idea (*Idee*) as it appears in the domain of spirit. The absolute idea is the unity of thought and reality. In the domain of spirit (which embraces religion), the idea is portrayed as God (or gods). Christianity is the consummate religion because in it the idea is for the first time portrayed adequately (although within the limitations of religious language, with its use of images). Adequate means that in Christianity God is thought of according to the logic of the concept (*Begriff*). The concept is a movement of thought that embraces three logical moments: (1) the abstract universality and simple identity of the objects of thought; (2) the particularity of real things, which are thus *different* from the objects of thought; and (3) the unity of thought and reality in concrete universality. The doctrine of the Trinity is the truth about God (in the form of religious thought). In it the first moment of the concept (universality and identity) is portrayed in the image of the Father, the second moment (particularity and difference) is portrayed in the image of the Son, and the third moment (concrete universality) is portrayed as the Holy Spirit. In Jesus Christ, the second moment assumes the form of a particular individual in history; this moment of difference achieves a peak in the death of Jesus, which is in reality the death of God – the reality of difference and otherness in the absolute idea. In the Holy Spirit, religious thought passes beyond the particularity of Jesus to the universality of the Holy Spirit, in which all is reconciled: God and the world, universality and particularity, identity and difference.[53]

Schelling's view of the Trinity differs in important respects from Hegel's. Above all, Schelling felt that Hegel had described only God's necessary nature. For Schelling, the three moments of the concept that Hegel

---

[52] See D. Schlitt, *Hegel's Trinitarian Claim: A Critical Reflection*, Leiden: Brill 1984. J. Splett, *Die Trinitätslehre G. W. F. Hegels*, (Symposon: Philosophische Schriftenreihe, 20), Freiburg: Verlag Karl Alber 1965). Powell, *The Trinity in German Thought*, pp. 104–41.

[53] The best place to find Hegel's account of the Trinity is in G. W. F. Hegel, *Lectures on the Philosophy of Religion*, 3, *The Consummate Religion*, Berkeley: University of California Press 1984.

portrayed operate by a logic of necessity. There is, he agreed, a necessary aspect of God – God's nature; but there is additionally in God a primordial act of freedom.[54] For Schelling, God's necessary nature consists in a triad of potencies (as he called them); however, these potencies do not correlate with the persons of the Trinity.[55]

In an act of freedom, God allows the potencies to pass outside of God. This is the creation of the world, which is thus constituted by the same realities that constitute God's nature.[56] However, the potencies, which eternally co-exist in God, appear sequentially in the world. The history of the world is thus the history of the potencies, each in a way succeeding the previous. In particular, the second potency strives to gain control over the first potency. This is the metaphysical account of the rise of spirit out of matter and the attempt of spirit to attain freedom from its material constraints. The second potency's history culminates in Jesus Christ. In Christ, the second potency attains the form of a personal divine being.[57]

Within world history, the Holy Spirit initially subsists in a potential state, not as a fully actual person. Like the Son, the Spirit is initially a 'demiurgic' power, one that works through nature as a final cause. But when the second potency restores harmony to the potencies (i.e. with the appearance of Jesus Christ), the Spirit becomes actual as a divine person. The Spirit's personality and full divinity are thus made possible by the activity of the Son.[58] Similarly, the Father emerges as a personal divine being only as the end of history and as a result of the Son's work of restoring harmony. Until then, the Father is, in Schelling's words, invisible – active, but not actual. As in the case of the Holy Spirit, it is the mediating activity of the Son (in overcoming the first potency) that brings the Father to full actualization as a divine person.[59]

Schelling in this way emphasized the plurality of Trinitarian persons;

---

[54] F. W. J. Schelling, *The Ages of the World*, (Columbia Studies in Philosophy, 3), New York: Morningside Heights 1942, pp. 96, 103, 188, 194 (hereafter cited as *Ages*); H. Fuhrmans, 'Der Gottesbegriff der Schellingschen postiven Philosophie', in A. M. Koktanek (ed.), *Schelling Studien*, FS Manfred Schröter zum 85. Geburtstag, München-Wien: R. Oldenbourg 1965, pp. 33–4; and W. Schulz, *Die Vollendung des Deutschen Idealismus in der Spätphilosophie Schellings*, Pfullingen: Verlag Günter Neske 1975, p. 246.

[55] See E. A. Beach, *The Potencies of God(s): Schelling's Philosophy of Mythology*, (SUNY Series in Philosophy and SUNY Series in Hegelian Studies), Albany, N.Y.: State University of New York Press 1994 for an analysis of Schelling's theory of the potencies.

[56] Schelling, *Ages*, pp. 188–200.

[57] F. W. J. Schelling, Ausgewählte Werke, 10 Bände, vols. 1–2, *Philosophie der Mythologie*, vols. 3–4, *Philosophie der Offenbarung*, Darmstadt: Wissenschaftliche Buchgesellschaft 1983, 4:58–9, 78–9 and 82. Hereafter cited as *Werke*.

[58] Schelling, *Werke*, 3:334–5.

[59] Schelling, *Werke*, 3:335–6.

as a result, he could not give whole-hearted support to the Augustinian tradition, which emphasized the unity of the divine nature over the plurality of persons. Schelling emphasized the plurality because of the essential historicity of the persons. Like Schleiermacher, he understood the Trinitarian persons to be developments of the being of God in the temporal course of natural and human history. So, with both Schleiermacher and Schelling, there is an observable shifting of the Trinity from eternity to history. For both, the doctrine of the Trinity expresses not the eternal being of God, but instead the historical relation of God with the world.

# The Trinity in the Twentieth Century[60]

## Continuity with the Nineteenth Century

Two trajectories from the nineteenth century continued on into the twentieth century. On the one hand, the idealist tradition lived on in the theology of Paul Tillich (1886–1965). Although informed by phenomenology and existentialism, Tillich was nonetheless public about his commitment to the idealist view of God and its importance for interpreting the doctrine of the Trinity.[61] On the other hand, liberal theology's critique of the doctrine continued with full force in such writers as G. W. H. Lampe, who argued that the meaning of the Bible's Trinitarian terms differs from the meaning of those terms in the post-biblical tradition of doctrinal development.[62]

## The Trinity and Revelation

By far the most important development in Trinitarian thought in the twentieth century was the emphasis on revelation. In response to liberal theology, Karl Barth (1886–1968) argued that theology must be based on revelation.[63] However, Barth had assimilated at least some of the results of modern theology. In particular, he did not think of the Bible as revelation and did not regard revelation as the communication of mysterious truths. On the contrary, for Barth revelation is primarily Jesus Christ. Revelation

---

[60] See J. Thompson, *Modern Trinitarian Perspectives*, New York: Oxford University Press, 1994 for an overview of twentieth century Trinitarian thought.
[61] Powell, *The Trinity in German Thought*, pp. 180–3, 211–16, 240–3.
[62] G. W. H. Lampe, *God as Spirit*, Oxford, Clarendon Press 1977.
[63] Powell, *The Trinity in German Theology*, pp. 183–93. Barth discussed the connection between the Trinity and revelation in *Church Dogmatics*, I/1, *The Doctrine of the Word of God*, Edinburgh: T & T Clark 1963, chapter 2 (hereafter cited as *CD, I/1*)

has, moreover, a Trinitarian structure; the doctrine of the Trinity is in fact an explication of the fact that God reveals.

Jesus Christ, for Barth, is the incarnate Word of God and at the same time the historical person Jesus of Nazareth. Revelation is thus identical with a particular event in history. But this event is no ordinary event: it is the union of the divine and the human in this man, Jesus. Indeed, the event of this union is itself the moment of revelation, for here God is disclosed to us precisely in the particulars of this man's history.

Barth felt it was important to note that God's eternal being corresponds to the revealed Trinity. There is, he argued, no divine nature that remains hidden behind the revealed Trinity. God is eternally, therefore, exactly what God is in the event of revelation. The revelation of the divine Trinity is a true disclosure of what God is, and not a mere appearance of God. At the same time, revelation is a free act of God. God's being is not exhausted in this historical revelation, as though God did not possess eternal being. Even though God is fully disclosed in revelation and is identical with revelation, God exists beyond the event of revelation.[64]

Although revelation is the event of Jesus Christ, this event is available for us today. It is mediated by the Bible and by preaching (which are thus secondary forms of the Word of God); however, without the work of the Holy Spirit, Bible and preaching remain merely human words. The Holy Spirit, called by Barth the subjective possibility and reality of revelation, takes these human words and uses them to bring us into the event of revelation. As the subjective possibility of revelation, the Holy Spirit makes it possible for us to receive revelation. As the subjective reality of revelation, the Spirit is the event of revelation *now*. When revelation takes place now, it occurs in and through the Spirit.[65]

Revelation thus has a Trinitarian structure. The Father is the God who speaks and reveals; Jesus Christ is revelation in its objectivity; the Holy Spirit is the event of revelation as it is mediated to and received by human beings.[66]

Most theologians following Barth have appreciated his renewed emphasis on revelation; however, Wolfhart Pannenberg (b. 1928) criticized Barth for equating revelation with Jesus Christ. Instead, he argued, revelation is the totality of history as the field of divine action. This is because revelation is about God's rule – God's kingdom. Jesus is the revealer because in him God's rule is actualized; however, the full measure of the kingdom becomes a reality only at the end of history. Only at the end is it true that God is lord. The whole of history seen from its eschatological end, therefore, constitutes

---

[64] Barth, *CD* I/1, p. 548.
[65] Barth, *CD* I/1, pp. 514–15.
[66] Barth, *CD* I/1, pp. 339–43.

the revelation of God. But like Barth, Pannenberg argued that the God revealed in history is the Trinity: Jesus the revealer, the Father whom he revealed, and the Spirit whom Jesus sent and in whose power he conducted his ministry.[67]

## The Trinity and Soteriology

Another important theme in twentieth-century Trinitarian thought is the connection between the Trinity and soteriology. Although many theologians have developed this theme, it is especially associated with Karl Rahner (1904–1984) and Catherine LaCugna (1952–1997).[68]

Rahner's treatment of the Trinity arose from the observation that, in the tradition of dogmatic treatises about the Trinity, this doctrine was always located near the beginning of the dogmatic system and far from soteriological doctrines. The traditional treatises thus gave the impression that the Trinity is a wholly speculative doctrine, i.e. a doctrine that pertains first and foremost to the eternal being of God. Only later in the dogmatic system was the Trinity's importance for soteriology made clear. The problem is that such a treatment suggests that we know about the Trinity through a purely formal and verbal revelation in the Bible and not through the experience of salvation. This sort of treatment also drove an unnecessary wedge between the eternal Trinity (the ontological or essential Trinity) and the Trinity in its historical revelation (the economic Trinity). Located in widely separated parts of the dogmatic system, the discussions of the eternal and historical Trinities seemed unconnected to each other.

Rahner's solution was to assert the identity of the eternal and historical Trinities as a methodological point. By this Rahner meant to insist that the doctrine of the Trinity should be treated first of all from the perspective of soteriology. The Trinity is known in and through the experience of salvation, and its doctrinal significance is completely tied to its soteriological function. So influential has Rahner's solution been that it has been dubbed 'Rahner's Rule' and simplified into the assertion that the ontological Trinity is the economic Trinity.

Catherine LaCugna began her work on the Trinity with an affirmation of Rahner's theology but wished to draw out the implications of Rahner's Rule further than Rahner himself did. For LaCugna, it is not enough to assert the identity of the ontological and economic Trinities as a methodological point. It is necessary as well to see that the economic Trinity is the

---

[67] W. Pannenberg, *Systematic Theology*, Grand Rapids, MI: William B. Eerdmans Publishing Co., 1991, 1:193–227; 2:23–30.

[68] K. Rahner, *The Trinity*, New York: Herder and Herder 1970; C. Mowry LaCugna, *God for Us: The Trinity and Christian Life*, New York: HarperCollins 1993.

continuation into history of the movement of God that begins in eternity. LaCugna, in other words, felt that Rahner's theology still preserved an overwrought distinction between God's eternal Trinitarian being and the Trinitarian revelation of God in history. LaCugna proposed that we think of the Trinity as a movement from the Father to the Son and then to the Spirit. This movement is eternal but it continues into history. The revelation of the Trinitarian God in history is therefore not arbitrary; on the contrary, this revelation is in a way natural to God. The Trinitarian revelation in history is continuous with God's eternal being.[69] With the economic Trinity connected to the ontological Trinity even more closely than in Rahner's theology, LaCugna was able to assert the absolute centrality of the Trinity to Christian life and practice. In particular, she argued that the Trinity, as a communion of co-equal persons, is the norm and source of Christian life in the church.[70]

## The Trinity and Relationality

LaCugna's belief in the Trinity as a communion of co-equal persons is closely related to another major theme of twentieth-century theology, the relational understanding of persons, which is associated most notably with John Zizioulas (b. 1931).[71] The basic insight is that theology has long laboured under the consequences of an inadequate concept of person. In the Western theological tradition, Boethius' definition held sway: a person is an individual substance of a rational nature. This view accords poorly with a Trinitarian conception of person, according to which the persons exist only in relation to each other. Augustine thus argued that the Father is the Father only in relation to the Son.[72] This was formalized by Thomas Aquinas, who defined the Trinitarian persons as subsisting relation.[73] To the extent that the emphasis in Boethius' definition falls on 'individual substance', this definition is misleading.

Contemporary theologians such as Zizioulas and LaCugna are interested in seeing the Trinity as a model for human life. But, they argue, for this to happen we must begin to regard even human persons in relational terms and not as individual, non-related substances. For Zizioulas, to be is to be in communion. The proper definition of substance thus includes relationality.

---

[69] LaCugna, *God for Us*, chapter 7.

[70] LaCugna, *God for Us*, chapter 8.

[71] J. D. Zizioulas, *Being as Communion: Studies in Personhood and the Church*, (Contemporary Greek Theologians, 4), Crestwood, NY: St Vladimir's Seminary Press 1997, chapter 2.

[72] Augustine, *On the Trinity*, VII, 2.

[73] Thomas Aquinas, STh, 1.q. 29, a. 4.

To the extent that we think of persons relationally, we have a basis for a correct understanding of human community.

For Jürgen Moltmann (b. 1926), seeing persons in relational terms and regarding the Trinity as a model of human community has definite implications for the church, especially in overcoming latent hierarchical tendencies. Additionally, a church modelled on the Trinity will be a 'kenotic community' in which each members is emptied out in relation to others and enjoys a unity that mirrors the perichoretic unity of the Father, Son and Spirit.[74] The doctrine of the Trinity, in other words, is a prescription for the church's life.

## The Trinity and Feminist Thought

Trinitarian thought has been influenced by feminist theology.[75] One aspect of this influence is the way in which feminist theologians have raised anew the question of theological language. From its beginning, Christian theology has taken note of the unusual character of words as they are applied to God. In Western theology, it is customary to see such language as analogical. Language about God is used neither literally nor equivocally, but instead analogically. It points to real features of God's being without doing so in a direct and literal way.

Feminist theologians have recently challenged this view, calling attention to the fact that theological language consists of images that are the result of human thought and which reflect the social and political location of the dominant members of the communities in which they are developed.[76] Not surprisingly, they argue, symbols used in theological discourse are overwhelmingly male. Worse, such symbols are incorporated into a social-theological system that has systematically suppressed female voices and experience from theological discourse.[77]

Because theological language is a human construct, it is changeable. The project of feminist theology is accordingly to allow women's experience of God to find expression and to be incorporated into theology. For Elizabeth

---

[74] J. Moltmann, 'Perichoresis: An Old Magic Word for a New Trinitarian Theology' in M. Douglas Meeks (ed.), *Trinity, Community, Power: Mapping Trajectories in Wesleyan Theology*, Nashville: Kingswood Books 2000, pp. 69–83.

[75] See the remarks of J. Moltmann in '"I Believe in God the Father": Patriarchal or Non-patriarchal Talk of God?' in Id., *History and the Triune God: Contributions to Trinitarian Theology*, New York: The Crossroad Publishing Co., 1992, pp. 1–18.

[76] For an articulation of the view that language about God is constituted by images, see S. McFague, *Metaphorical Theology: Models of God in Religious Language*, Philadelphia: Fortress Press 1982.

[77] E. A. Johnson, *She Who Is: The Mystery of God in Feminist Theological Discourse*, New York: The Crossroad Publishing Co., 1999, chapter 1.

Johnson (b. 1941), this means speaking about the Trinity in terms of God's relatedness to the world in acts of creation and redemption. The Trinity is not so much about a mystery of eternal being as it is about the love shared among the Trinitarian persons and the world. The doctrine of the Trinity is not simply a theory about God but, as a model of human social relations, is also a prescription with political implications. Finally, because theological language consists of images that humans construct and apply, it is perfectly appropriate to speak of God using distinctively feminine images such as *sophia*.[78]

## The Social Analogy of the Trinity

Another feature of twentieth-century Trinitarian thought is the growing popularity of the social analogy for the Trinity. This analogy goes back at least as far as Richard of St Victor (died 1173), who expounded the Trinity in terms of mutual love. If God is truly love, then we can think about God only as a plurality of persons who love each other.[79] This approach contrasts with the dominant Western view that God is best thought of as a single being characterized by self-love. Richard's view and those like it are classified as social analogies of the Trinity, since they represent the Trinity as a society of persons.

The dominant Western tradition received strong support from Karl Barth, whose Trinitarian theology in the first volume of the *Church Dogmatics* presented God as a single subject existing in three modes of being.[80] The Anglican theologian Leonard Hodgson (1889–1969) was thus swimming against the current when he proposed a revival of the social analogy. Hodgson argued that the early church struggled to fit a Trinitarian concept of God onto an unsuitable concept of divine unity. This view of unity necessarily pointed toward subordinationism, for the only way to think of the unity of the three Trinitarian persons was to represent one of the persons as the source of the others. For Hodgson, the truth is that God's unity is the dynamic unity of three persons. The persons are not modes of

---

[78] Johnson, *She Who Is*, chapter 10.

[79] The critical edition of Richard's book on the Trinity is Jean Ribaillier, *De Trinitate: Texte Critique*, (Textes Philosophiques du Moyen Age, 6), Paris: Vrin 1958). A translation of book 3 can be found in G. A. Zinn, *Richard of St. Victor: the Twelve Patriarchs; the Mystical Ark; Book Three of the Trinity*, (The Classics of Western Spirituality), New York: Paulist Press 1979. A translation of book 1 is available at pvspade.com/Logic/docs/StVictor.pdf.

[80] *CD*, I/1, pp. 402–7. However, Barth modified his view of the Trinity in *CD*, IV/1, where he presented a more dialectical picture of the relation between the Father and the Son. In this picture, both persons appears as agents. See pp. 163–205.

being (as Barth argued) but are instead full-fledged personal beings, united in a thoroughly dynamic and relational way.[81]

Unexpectedly, the mainstream of Trinitarian thought has begun to depart from Barth's single-subject view of the Trinity. This departure occurred through the influence of Wolfhart Pannenberg and Jürgen Moltmann, both of whom sharply criticized Barth for misrepresenting the Trinitarian persons.[82] For Moltmann, the history of revelation is not the history of a single subject. Thinking in this way presents the doctrine of God as a type of monotheism, which, Moltmann argued, is associated with hierarchical and patriarchal modes of thinking and social organization.[83] It is instead the history of the dynamic interaction between the Father, the Son and the Spirit.[84] The emphasis, for Moltmann, should fall on the reciprocal relations among the persons. The Father sends the Son, and the Son reveals the Father. Jesus is sent in the power of the Spirit and then sends the Spirit upon the disciples.[85] Consequently, the plurality of persons attested in history is, for Moltmann, theology's point of departure. The task is to account for the unity, a task that Moltmann addresses in a way similar to Hodgson.

# A Few Conclusions

There are a few conclusions to be drawn from this narrative of modern Trinitarian thought:

First, despite the tumultuous history of Trinitarian thought in the modern era, in one sense very little has changed. Except for the development of the Unitarian Church and the emergence of marginal Christian groups such as the Watchtower Society, Christian churches continue to affirm the doctrine of the Trinity and the ancient creeds that express it. Additionally, there continues to be a deep reservoir of theologians in the churches who give assent to the doctrine, even if for some of them it does not become thematically important. The doctrine of the Trinity remains, at least formally, a foundational doctrine of the Christian tradition.

Second, Protestant churches have had an especially difficult time with Trinitarian theology. This is because, by insisting that every doctrine must

---

[81] L. Hodgson, *The Doctrine of the Trinity*, New York: Charles Scribner's Sons 1944, especially pp. 85–112.

[82] See W. Pannenberg, 'Die Subjektivität Gottes und die Trinitätslehre' in *Kerygma und Dogma* 23 (1977) 25–40; J. Moltmann, *The Trinity and the Kingdom: The Doctrine of God*, San Francisco: Harper & Row 1981, pp. 52–3, 63–4, 139–44.

[83] Moltmann, *The Trinity and the Kingdom*, pp. 129–32, 191–202.

[84] Moltmann, *The Trinity and the Kingdom*, pp. 63–4.

[85] Moltmann, *The Trinity and the Kingdom*, pp. 72–4.

have an express scriptural warrant, they forced generations of theologians and scholars to find the doctrine of the Trinity in the Bible by highly questionable exegetical practices. At the same time, they inadvertently encouraged the rise of anti-Trinitarian movements whose adherents, believing that the doctrine is not clearly stated in Scripture, concluded that the doctrine is wholly illegitimate. This insistence on clear Scriptural warrants has been the source of much unnecessary tension and argument in the theological community. Karl Barth's grounding of the doctrine in the idea of revelation and the subsequent emphasis on the economic Trinity represents a notable improvement in Protestant theology.

Third, the modern era illustrates the difference between the doctrine and the various ways in which the doctrine is understood. Considered as a dogma, there has been no development of the doctrine of the Trinity since the late middle ages and no significant development since the creeds of the Patristic era. However, there is more to doctrine than its dogmatic formulation. There is also the way in which a doctrine is understood. In this respect there has been considerable development. The social analogy, for instance, almost completely unknown before the twentieth century, has lately become a leading way of understanding the Trinity. Similarly, the thesis that our knowledge of the Trinity begins with the economic Trinity of history, scarcely mentioned until the nineteenth century, is today almost an axiom for many theologians. The dogma of the Trinity, in short, is capable of sustaining a rich and dynamic history of varying interpretations.

# 4

# The Paternity of the Father and the Procession of the Holy Spirit: Some Historical Remarks on the Ecumenical Problem

## Lucas Francisco Mateo-Seco

The 'question' of the *Filioque* has been preferentially treated in the Trinitarian theology of recent years, particularly in ecumenical circles. The *Clarification* of the Pontifical Council for the Promotion of Christian Unity is a good example, not only because of the attention it has received, but also because of the 'openness' with which it sought to pose the 'question' of the *Filioque* and the search for a convergence of the venerable Pneumatological traditions of the Orient and Occident[1]. The *Clarification* attempted to find

---

[1] Pontifical Council for the Promotion of Christian Unity, 'The Procession of the Holy Spirit in Greek and Latin Traditions', in *L'Osservatore Romano*, 13.IX.1995. Among the commentaries on this document, cf. J-M. Garrigues, 'La Clarification sur la procession du Saint-Esprit', in *Irenikon* 68 (1995) 501–6; Id., 'À la suite de la clarification romaine: Le *Filioque* affranchi

this convergence outside of the strict question of the 'procession' of the Spirit, expanding its consideration to the entirety of the Trinitarian mystery. Certain phrases have no other scope than this: 'In the same way that the Father is characterized as Father by the Son whom He generates, the Spirit – who has his origin from the Father – characterizes Him in a Trinitarian manner in his relation to the Son, and characterizes the Son in a Trinitarian manner in his relation to the Father: In the fullness of the Trinitarian mystery, they are Father and Son in the Holy Spirit'.

In the light of the respectful reception of the *Clarification*, the numerous objections that were raised to it[2] manifest that, in order to progress on this question, is not enough to use dialectics, but that it is also necessary to consider the procession of the Spirit in the greater context of the totality of the mystery of the Trinity, particularly in the light of the fontality of the Father's Person and, more concretely, in the light of the relation of the Father with the Son. As is well known, this thought is not new in the history of theology, and we find it explicitly formulated from the medieval period, particularly in Thomas Aquinas.

We do not propose to turn to the question of the *Filioque* in order, in the best of cases, to add another variant to the various propositions for resolving the divergence between Greeks and Latins, but to focus attention on the theology of the Father, in order to show the great richness it entails, the variety of approaches that are found in different authors, and the existing convergence between Greeks and Latins. At first glance, it seems odd to affirm that there are 'irreconcilable' differences between both traditions in reference to the procession of the Spirit, while in the theology of the Father – who is the fontal principle of the Spirit – there does not appear to be any 'irreconcilable' difference. Precisely because the variety of positions on the theology of the Father are found in both traditions, it would seem prudent to think that there must be a much greater convergence than is sometimes admitted regarding the procession of the Spirit as well.

---

du filioquisme', in *Irenikon* 69 (1996) 188–212; B. Bobrinskoy, 'Vers une vision commune du Mystère trinitaire', in BSS, 22.XI.1995; Fr. Ph. Jobert, 'A propos du *Filioque*', in *La Documentation Catholique* (26.IX.1995), 601–3; G. Ferraro, 'L'origine dello Spirito Santo nella Trinità secondo le tradizioni greca e latina', in *La Civiltà Cattolica*, I (1996) 222–31.

[2] For an overview of these reactions, cf. J. Y. Brachet and E. Durand, 'La réception de la "Clarification" de 1995 sur le "*Filioque*"' in *Irénikon* 78 (2005) 47–109. Cf. also L. F. Mateo Seco, *Teología Trinitaria: Dios Espíritu Santo*, Madrid: Rialp 2005, pp. 146–203.

# Ordo Orignis and the Equality of the Three Divine Persons

Both the *equality* of the divine Persons and the *order of origin* have been explicitly present in the Church's proclamation of faith from the beginning. Some good witnesses to this are e.g. the missionary mandate (cf. Mt 28.19) or the discourse of Saint Peter on the day of Pentecost (Acts 2.22–36). The Father, Son and Holy Spirit are already explicitly mentioned, always with the same order, and always in equal dignity.

This is also universally manifested in the celebration of Baptism and the Eucharist, and in the various Creeds. In respect to baptism, the well known text of the *Didache* is paradigmatic (ca. 90/100)[3]; while with respect to the Eucharist, the celebrated passage of the *First Apology of Saint Justin* (+ 163/167)[4] is eloquent, so that one can affirm that the God of the Christian liturgy is God the Trinity[5]. Christian liturgy is directed to the Father, as the ultimate recipient of the praise and thanksgiving that are made through the Son, in the unity of the Holy Spirit[6].

The ample presence of Old Testament texts in Christian celebration keeps the prominent attributes of God from the Old Testament continually present, so that when one speaks of the Father, one thinks of the only creator who is transcendent to all things, as well as the merciful Father, that is, the God of the Covenant whom Jesus of Nazareth called his Father[7]. Together with this, liturgy continually recalls in an explicit manner that the God who revealed himself in the Old Testament in the unicity of his nature revealed himself as Trinity of Persons in the last times (cf., e.g., Ro 15. 6; 2 Cor 1.3, 11.31; Eph 1.3). It is this same liturgy that, with its movement of *exitus-reditus*, already explicates an essential 'theology of the Father': Everything comes from the Father, through the Son, and in the Holy Spirit.

---

[3] 'Concerning Baptism, baptize thus: after having taught all that precedes, baptize in the name of the Father and of the Son and of the Holy Spirit.' (*Didache* 7, 1, 3).

[4] 'The brothers bring bread and a chalice with water and wine to the presider, and he, after having taken them, directs a prayer of praise and glorification to the Father of the entire universe and in the name of the Son and the Holy Spirit, and then he offers a long thanksgiving for the gifts that have been received.' (Saint Justin, *First Apology*, 65).

[5] Cf. C. Vagaggini, *El sentido teológico de la liturgia*, Madrid 1959, 201.

[6] Cf. E. Lodi, *Il Padre di Gesù Cristo nella liturgia*, Bologna: Dehoniane 1998, esp. 95–102; G. Bonaccorso, 'Il "ritorno" dell'uomo al Padre nella celebrazione', in *Rivista liturgica* 82 (1995) 45–62.

[7] It is enough to recall the famous article of K. Rahner, 'Gott als erste trinitarische Person im Neuen Testament', in *Zeitschrift für katholische Theologie* 66 (1942) 71–88. Cf. also A. García Suárez, 'La primera persona trinitaria y la filiación adoptiva', in Id., *Eclesiología, catequesis, espiritualidad*, Pamplona: Eunsa 1998, 575–627; F. Ocáriz, *Hijos de Dios en Cristo: Introducción a una teología de la participación sobrenatural*, Pamplona: Eunsa 1972.

Everything returns to the Father through the Son in the sanctification of the Holy Spirit.

As is well known, this is the structure of the earliest Christian prayers known to us, such as that found in the Martyrdom of Saint Polycarp[8]. These venerable texts speak above all of the fontality of God the Father: Everything proceeds from Him and everything returns to Him, in both intra-Trinitarian life and in creation and the work of salvation. That which theology specifies as the *ordo Trinitarius* already appears clearly in these texts: In the Trinity the Father has priority in so far as He is the real source of the Son and the Holy Spirit. In this sense one must say that the Father is *greater*, because the two other divine Persons proceed from Him. Denying this means denying that the Father truly engenders and spirates. All that the Son has He receives from the Father. The same is true of the Holy Spirit. The Father is the *first* Person, the Son is the *second*, and the Holy Spirit is the *third*, and this order cannot be changed.

Saint Irenaeus' (ca. 202) witness is particularly valuable due to his authority, his influence and because he takes the time to explicate the relation of each of the divine Persons with the history of salvation, relations that are in harmony with the internal *ordo trinitarius*[9].

## The Creed of the First Council of Nicaea

The affirmations on God the Father contained in the Nicene Creed gather all of this teaching and are undoubtedly the foundation of that which the Creed of the First Council of Constantinople affirmed regarding the Person

---

[8] 'Lord, Almighty God, Father of your beloved Son Jesus Christ, through whom we have received knowledge of your name, God of the angels and powers and of all creation, and of all the generations of saints who live in your presence, I bless you for having judged me worthy to take part, among your martyrs, of the chalice of your Christ, through the resurrection of eternal life for the soul and the body, in the incorruptibility of the Holy Spirit. I praise you and bless you and glorify you through the heavenly and eternal High Priest, your most beloved Son ...'. (*Martyrdom of Polycarp*, 14, in Th. Camelot (ed.), Ignace d'Antioche, Polycarpe de Smyrne, *Lettres, Martyre de Polycarpe*, (SCh 10), París: Cerf 1968, pp. 226–8.

[9] 'For this reason, our new birth – Baptism – occurs by these three articles, which bring us the grace of the new birth in God the Father, through his Son in the Holy Spirit. For those who receive the Spirit of God are led to the Word, that is, to the Son. But the Son presents them to the Father, and the Father gives them incorruptibility. Thus without the Spirit it is impossible to see the Son of God, and without the Son nobody can approach the Father, because the Son is the knowledge of the Father, and the knowledge of the Son is made by means of the Holy Spirit.' (*Demonstration of the Apostolic Faith*, 7). Froideveaux, in his edition of this work, offers a vast panorama of the parallel loci and the Trinitarian tradition in which this text is inserted (Cf. Irénée de Lyon, *Démonstration de la Prédication apostolique*, (L. M. Froideveaux, ed.), SCh 62, París: Cerf 1958, pp. 41–4).

of the Father and his relation with the Person of the Son and the Person of the Holy Spirit[10].

The Creed begins with the confession of 'one God, the Father almighty, Maker of heaven and earth'. This formula summarizes the revelation of the Old and New Testaments on divine unicity. Ortiz de Urbina observes that, in the Creed's phrases, the unicity of God is not immediately referred to the divine *substance*, but to God-Person, and concretely to God the Father as source of everything that exists. This genetic conception of the divinity initiates everything in the Father to have it all flow from Him to the Son and the Spirit, and, at another level, to give being to all creation[11].

The theology of the Father, and in particular his fontality as it is understood by the Fathers between 325 and 381, is very important to situate in its proper perspective the doctrine of the First Council of Constantinople about the procession of the Spirit, since this is to speak of the source from which the Spirit proceeds. The paternity of the Father is in turn marked by his relation to the Son, because Father is a relative name. The manner in which Our Lord calls God his Father is presented in these authors with a high degree of precision and with great theological fecundity.

## The Testimony of Athanasius

In this regard the thought of Saint Athanasius is of great interest, not only because he was witness to the Council of Nicaea, but also because of the acuity and depth of his doctrine on the Father-Son relation, and consequently of his entire theology of the Father. Widdicombe has studied this paternity in a recently published book on the paternity of God from Origen to Athanasius[12]. The reader will find sound (and in my opinion important) reflections in this book, both on the place that God the Father has in Athanasian thought[13], as well as on the different perspectives in which the

---

[10] We will not enter into the questions of the relations that might exist between the Creed of I Constantinople and that of the Council of Nicaea. It is clear that the fathers of Chalcedon thought that Constantinople confirmed Nicaea, and this is sufficient for the present study. On this aspect, see the important works of A. M. Ritter, *Das Konzil von Konstantinopel und sein Symbol*, Göttingen: Vandenhoeck und Ruprecht 1965; I. Ortiz de Urbina, *Nicea y Constantinopla*, Victoria: Eset 1969; L. Abramowski, 'Was hat das Nicaeno-Constantinopolitanum mit dem Konzil Konstantinopel zu tun?', in *Theologie und Philosophie* 67 (1992) 481–513; B. Sesboüé and J. Wolinski, *Historia de los dogmas*, I, *El Dios de la salvación*, Salamanca: Secretariado Trinitario 1995, pp. esp. 188–221.

[11] Cf. I. Ortiz de Urbina, *Nicea y Constantinopla*, p. 75.

[12] P. Widdicombe, *The Fatherhood of God from Origen to Athanasius*, Oxford: Clarendon Press 2000, pp. 159–62 are especially interesting for our study.

[13] 'The word Father in Athanasius' theology is the word that identifies God's being as fruitful, inherently generative, relational and dynamic; it is the word that indicates that the divine being exists first as the relation of Father and Son.' (P. Widdicombe, *The Fatherhood of God*, p. 159).

Arian objections and Saint Athanasius' responses were situated[14]: while the question of the Son is not tied to the question of the Father for the Arians, for Athanasius, the question of the Son is above all a question of the Father, and definitively, a question on God's fecundity or infecundity, that is, on his fontality.

The objection made by the Arians, according to Athanasius' summary[15], can be reduced to three fairly simple affirmations or negations: (1) The Word belongs to the creaturely realm, and not the realm of the strictly divine; (2) There was a time in which the Word did not exist; (3) God is therefore not eternally Father, but He became father by having a son. These are fundamentally three aspects of one question, the equality of the Son with the Father, which, as we shall see, becomes in Athanasius the question of the perfection and fecundity of God the Father.

## Citations of Sacred Scripture

In his responses to Arian questions, Athanasius gives the teaching of Scripture on the Father-Son relation great importance, providing an ample list of texts similar to the manner he does so in the *Letters to Serapion* on the divinity of the Holy Spirit. In *Contra Arianos*, the list of Scriptural texts, although not attempting to be exhaustive, is substantial, and above all it gives sufficient indicators to see how Saint Athanasius understands the Father-Son relation, because it does not argue using easy dialectics, but from his faith, and thus from his understanding of the revealed texts.

Jn 1.1 stands out from among these texts, where not only is the co-eternity of the Father and Son accentuated, but it is also stressed that the Son is eternally *in* the Father[16]. This text is related to Ap 1.4 – *He who is, who was, and is to come* – in order to clarify the eternity of the Word joined to the Father. The Word belongs to the Father so intimately that Athanasius takes the radical affirmations of our Lord, where He says that

---

[14] 'While the most obvious threat that Arianism posed was to the Son's status as divine, Athanasius considered that this threat was necessarily also a direct threat to God's status as Father, and ultimately to a proper conception of the nature of divinity itself.' (*The Fatherhood of God*, p. 159).

[15] It is obviously not the time to enter into the question of whether Athanasius properly understood Arian thought. On this, cf. C. Kannengiesser, *Athanase d'Alexandrie évêque et écrivain. Une lecture des traités contre les Ariens*, Paris: Beauchesne 1983. What interests us here is the theology of God the Father contained in Athanasius' responses to the questions he understands the Arians pose. In the light of his manner of arguing with the Pneumatomachists, I think that Athanasius shows a good understanding of the Arian errors.

[16] Cf. *Contra arianos*, I, 11, (PG 26, 33 C-D; Opitz, 120) (*Athanasius Werke. Herausgegeben im Auftrage des Kirchenväter-Kommission der Preussischen Akademie den Wissenschaften von Han-Georg Opitz*, (*Contra Arianos* I and II: *Die Dogmatischen Schriften* I, 1, Lfrg. 2; *Contra Arianos* III, *Die Dogmatischen Schriften* I, 1, Lfrg. 3), Berlin-New York, 1934–2007.

He is the *Truth*[17] and the *Life* (Jn 14.6)[18], in their strongest sense, along with the sayings of Saint Paul who qualifies Christ as the *power* and *wisdom* of God (cf. 1 Cor 1.24), *the resplendence of his glory and the figure of his substance* (He 1.3)[19]. These texts recall the teaching of the Nicene Creed to Athanasius – *God of God, Light of Light* – with recourse to the image of light and its resplendence as an expression of the light: 'resplendence is proper to light and without resplendence, light ceases to be light.'[20]

Athanasius joins the citation of Jn 1.1–3 to 1 Cor 8.6: 'There is but one God: the Father from whom everything proceeds, and the Son through whom all things are'[21]. The echoes of chapters 6 and 7 of Irenaeus' *Epideixis* are clear: everything comes from the Father and reaches us through the Son in the Holy Spirit.

In this list, two texts of critical importance are repeated in reference to the equality and union – without any identification – of the Father and the Son: *only the Father knows the Son, and only the Son knows the Father* (cf. Mt 11.27) and Jesus' response to Philip during the Last Supper: *Whoever has seen Me has seen the Father* (Jn 14.9).

Athanasius also cites Jn 14.28: *The Father is greater than Me*, and understands it of the Word precisely because 'the Father is the source from which the Son springs forth, the light of which the Son is the resplendence'[22], that is, the Father is greater than the Son only in the sense that He is his 'cause' and source.

Athanasius reserves a particular importance for the words of the theophany of the Transfiguration: The Father says, This is my beloved Son (cf. Mt 17.5). For this reason, Athanasius comments, the Son can 'properly' call God his Father[23]. Athanasius often uses the adjective of 'proper' (ἴδιος) to emphasize the difference between the Son and creatures, and thus to manifest the especially intimate relation that exists between the Father and the Son. Their unity is so tight that whoever does not honour the Son does not honour the Father (cf. Jn 5.23)[24].

Athanasius sometimes repeatedly joins texts that show the unity between the Father and the Son, as if they were texts that He has heavily meditated:

---

[17] Cf. *Contra arianos*, I, 20 (PG 26, 53 C; Opitz, 130).

[18] Cf. *Contra arianos* I, 19 (PG 26, 52 A; Opitz, 128).

[19] Cf. *Contra arianos*, I, 12 (PG 26, 37 A; Ibid. 24: PG 26, 61 B–C; Ibid. 32: PG 26, 77 A–C); *Contra arianos* III, 59 PG 26, 448–B–C); *Contra arianos* III, (PG 460 A–B; Opitz, 121–2; 134; 141–2; 372; 377–8).

[20] *Contra arianos*, I, 12 y 13 (PG 26, 37 A and 40 A; Opitz, 121 and 123).

[21] *Contra arianos*, I, 19 (PG 26, 52 B–C; Opitz, 129).

[22] *Contra arianos*, I, 13 (PG 26, 37 C; Opitz, 122).

[23] *Contra arianos*, I, 15 (PG 26, 44 C); *Contra arianos* III, 59 (PG 26,448 B–C; Ibid., 65, 461 B. Opitz, 125; 371–2; 379–80).

[24] *Contra arianos*, I, 33 (PG 26, 80 C; Opitz, 143).

*I am in the Father and the Father in Me* (Jn 14.10), *He who has seen Me has seen the Father* (Jn 14.9), and *I and the Father are one* (Jn 10.30)[25].

Finally, Athanasius considers the love of the Father for the Son as quite important, not only citing the theophany of the Transfiguration, but also basing himself in a text that will be paradigmatic of the Athanasian vision of the relation of the Father with the Son: *The Father loves the Son, and has given all things into his hand* (Jn 3.35)[26]. This means that love is present in the Son's generation.

## Fundamental Themes in the Theology of the Father

The *list* of scriptural texts used by Athanasius sheds a fair amount of light on his theology of God the Father. In the first place, for Athanasius, the Son is God from God and Light from Light. From here, there is no doubt as to the *equality* and *co-eternity* that exists between the Father and the Son.

The Arians who argued against *co-eternity* said that if the Father and the Son were co-eternal, they would be brothers, to which Athanasius responds by underscoring the realism of generation, and thus the Father's fontality[27]. The reason for their distinction is found here, Athanasius insists: 'They are co-eternal, but one is Father and the other is the Word of the Father. How can the Word be called the brother of Him whose Word He is?'[28]. The Athanasian expression alerts us not only to the co-eternity of the Father and the Son, but also of the fontal relationship between Them, as well as to the intimacy and inseparability with which They are united. The Word is the wisdom, word and resplendence of the Father: Without the Word, the Father would be without wisdom and would be a light without resplendence, that is, He would be neither light nor Father.

In his struggle against the Arians, Athanasius has recourse to concepts and arguments that would be quite successful in later theology, simply because they correspond to the truth of things: the Father and the Son were not engendered by a principle that was anterior to Them, but the Father is the principle and generator of the Son, while He has not been

---

[25] *Contra arianos*, I, 34 (PG 26, 81 B–C); *Contra arianos* III (PG 26, 328 B; Ibid., 5–6: PG 26, 332 B–333 C; Ibid., 64: PG 26, 460 A; Opitz, 143–4; 309; 311–12; 377–8).

[26] *Contra arianos* III, 66 (PG 26, 461 C; Opitz, 379).

[27] 'If however, while calling Him eternal we confess that He proceeds from the Father, How can He who is engendered be called the Son of the One who engenders Him? And if our faith is directed to the Father and the Son, What brotherhood can exist between Them? How can the Logos be called the brother of Him of Whom He is Logos?' (*Contra arianos* I, 14 (PG 26, 41 A; Opitz, 123–4).

[28] *Contra arianos*, I, 14 (PG 26, 41 A–C; Opitz, 123).

engendered by anyone. The Father is father and was never a son, and none can be considered the brother of the Father[29]. Co-eternity is required for other fundamental theological reasons as well: the nature of the Father was never imperfect, so that it never lacked a Son that was 'properly' his, that is, something that pertains to the intimacy and perfection of his Person[30], nor could the Son be later than the Father, because He is not engendered as men are engendered, but He is most perfectly engendered. The Son is eternal because 'the nature of God was always most perfect.'[31] To say that there was a time in which the Son did not exist is the same as saying that there was a time in which the source was 'arid, without life, and without wisdom'[32].

Athanasius emphasises that this argument is valid only for the Father-Son relationship, and not for that of Creator-creature. The Creator is not imperfect because He has not yet created; while the Father would be lacking in his 'proper' perfection if there had been a time when He did not have a Son. This observation is quite important for the theology of the Father, because it allows us to understand how Athanasius strongly stresses that the Son is not among the things 'outside' the Father, but that He belongs to the 'intimacy' of the Father, since He is not made, but engendered[33]. The 'Image' of the Father is not something 'exterior' to the Father, but interior[34].

Recourse to the 'interiority' of the 'image' in which the Father contemplates himself is one more way of founding the co-eternity of the Father and the Son, but at the same time it shows how profoundly the Son belongs to the Person of the Father. In presenting this argument, Athanasius offers an interesting description of the Father's characteristics:

The Father is eternal, immortal, powerful, Light, King, all-powerful, God, Lord, Creator and Maker. This must all be present in the image as well, so that He who sees the Son truly sees the Father (cf. Jn 14.9)[35].

The Arians objected that if the Son were equal to the Father, He should also engender in turn. Athanasius' response introduces us into one of the most important aspects of his theology of the Father: the Father does

---

[29] *Contra arianos*, I, 14 (PG 26, 41 A–B; Opitz, 123, 124).

[30] For a detailed study of the Athanasian concept of the Son as the 'proper' Son of the Father, cf. P. Widdicombe. *The Fatherhood*, pp. 193–9.

[31] *Contra arianos*, I, 14 (PG 26, 41 B–C; Opitz, 124).

[32] *Contra arianos*, I, 19 (PG 26, 52 A–B; Opitz, 128–9).

[33] *Contra arianos*, I, 13 (PG 26, 40 B–C; Opitz, 123).

[34] 'Since the image of God is not something painted on the exterior, but God himself is his generator, [and He is One] in whom He delights, seeing himself (Pr 8, 30) (...) But when did the Father not contemplate himself in his own Image, or when did He not delight in Him, so that some have dared to say that the Image is made from nothing, and that the Father did not delight in Him before the Image was born' (*Contra arianos*, I, 20, PG 26, 53 B–C; Opitz, 129).

[35] *Contra arianos*, I, 21 (PG 26, 56 A; Opitz, 130).

not proceed from any Father, because He is only and completely Father;
while the Son in turn is only and completely Son, and not Father. For this
reason, the Father and the Son are not 'interchangeable'. Athanasius repeats
that the Father is always Father, and the Son is always Son, and that neither
can the Father be the son of another father, nor can the Son be a father of
another son[36]. This is equivalent to affirming that the Father is unbegotten
and therefore Father (and not the reverse), and that the Son, to be the image
of the Father, must be immutable like He is, that is, that He must be always
Son and cannot become Father in turn[37].

Negating the eternity of the Son will then entail conceiving of Him as
something outside (ἔξωθεν) the Father, and not someone engendered of the
same nature as the Father[38]. The Father did not engender the Son in the
way that someone makes a tool for doing other things, but He engendered
Him from (ἐκ) himself, not as something outside, but as something that is
proper (ἴδιος) to Him, that is, as something belonging to his own nature or
substance (οὐσία). Thus, Athanasius notes, 'things that are extrinsic, such as
a house one buys, are possessions that pass from one to another. The Son
however is something proper and intimate that proceeds from one's own
nature, in such a way that the Father is in the Son, while remaining what He
himself is. For this reason the Father is in the Son and the Son in the Father.
The Father eternally exists in the Son, and the Son eternally remains in the
Father.'[39]

While speaking of the generation of the Word, Athanasius keeps
constantly present two divine attributes, simplicity and immutability.
Simplicity leads him to affirm that the Father is *completely* in the Son,
while eternity leads him to say that neither the Son nor the Father began to
be son or father, and that this relation between Them will never end[40], i.e.
that paternity and filiation exist without any change. This is then a unique
and incomparable relation. The equality between the Father and the Son
is perfect: since God was not made, neither are his Image, his Word and

---

[36] *Contra arianos*, I, 22 (PG 26, 57 A–B; Opitz, 132).

[37] 'And if the Father is immutable and perpetually remains that which He is, it is also necessary
that He who is the Image of the Father remains that Image which He is and that He does
not change. Since the Son is engendered by the Father, He cannot become anything but that
which is proper to the Father's nature.' (*Contra arianos*, I, 22: PG 26, 57 B; Opitz, 132). The
argument is clear: the Son does not have any being other than to be the immutable Image of
the Father, and thus He will not engender another son who would be in his likeness. In citing
Eph 3.15, Athanasius notes that human paternity is not the exemplar of divine paternity, but
the reverse: It is from the Father that all other paternity takes its name (*Contra arianos* III, 67:
PG 26, 465, B; Opitz, 381).

[38] *Contra arianos*, I, 25 (PG 26, 64 C; Opitz, 135).

[39] *Contra arianos*, I, 27 (PG 26, 68 B–C; Opitz, 137).

[40] Cf. *Contra arianos*, I, 28–9 (PG 26, 69 A–73 A; Opitz, 137–9). Athanasius continues, emphasizing that the Son is the 'proper' of the Father.

Wisdom, made[41]. This is a complete intimacy: The wisdom of God is innate to the Father and exists conjoined with Him[42].

This intimacy is so great that it leads Athanasius to state that, in mentioning the Father, one mentions the Son at the same time[43]. It is from this that, for Athanasius, the name of Father indicates more precisely what God is than the name of unbegotten, and, consequently, much more than All-Powerful or Creator. 'It is very telling – says Athanasius – that God is called Father in Scripture, but on the other hand He is not called unbegotten. For this reason it is more in conformity with the truth to call God Father because of his Son. This name is relative to the Son and signifies the Son in itself. Further, it is the name that our Lord Jesus Christ himself gives to God. He did not instruct us to address God by calling Him unbegotten, but Father.'[44] Baptism is also not administered in the name of the Creator, but in the name of the Father, the Son and the Holy Spirit[45]. And we, who belong to created things, by Baptism are made sons of God and call Him Father. In this name we recognize the filiation of the Word, and that He is in the Father[46].

For Athanasius, the fact that the Father is in the Son and the Son in the Father means, further, that one must attribute the same things to the Son as are attributed to the Father. For this reason the Lord says that He and the Father are one (cf. Jn 10.30) and that He is in the Father and the Father in Him (cf. Jn 10.38). 'This intimacy can only be founded', Athanasius concludes, 'because the Son is truly engendered by the Father.'[47]

In the entire *Contra Arianos* one hears the echoes of the 'begotten not made' of the Nicene Creed, and one senses the essential distinction between created and uncreated. For this reason, Athanasius emphasizes that the generation of the Son is not a work that proceeds from the Father's liberty: the Son proceeds by the Father's nature, and cannot therefore be confused with creatures, which are freely created[48]. The Word is not made but engendered, not by will, but by nature[49]. This certainly does not mean that there

---

[41] *Contra arianos*, I, 31 (PG 26, 75 C; Opitz, 141).

[42] *Contra arianos*, I, 32 (PG 26, 77 A–B; Opitz, 142).

[43] Ὁ δὲ τὸν θεὸν Πατέρα καλῶν, εὐθὺς τὸν Υἱὸν καὶ θεωρεῖ (*Contra arianos*, I, 33: PG 26, 80 B; Opitz, 143).

[44] *Contra arianos*, I, 34 (PG 26, 81 A–B; Opitz, 143–4).

[45] Cf. *Contra arianos*, I, 34 (PG 26, 81 B–84–A; Opitz, 143–4).

[46] Cf. *Contra arianos*, I, 34 (PG 26, 81 C–84–A; Opitz, 144).

[47] *Contra arianos* III, 5 (PG 26, 329 B–C; Opitz, 310–11).

[48] 'We know that liberty and desire come before things that are made, since there was a time in which they did not exist.' (*Contra arianos* III, 60: PG 26, 449 A; Opitz, 372–3. Cf. also ibid. 61–2: PG 26, 452–3; Opitz 373–5).

[49] Athanasius' language is clear from the context. The Son is not a creature that proceeds from the Father's free will, but He proceeds from his nature, as the radiance – which is light itself in so far as it is shining – does not come from the light's liberty, but from its very nature. There

is any 'necessity' in God. God is good by nature and exists by nature. It is in this same sense that it is said that the Son proceeds by nature from the Father, and not by his will[50].

Here we reach one of Athanasius' accentuations, which becomes highly important for the theology of the Father: the Son does not proceed by the will of the Father, but He is engendered by love. He is the Son of his good pleasure (Mt 3.17). He is engendered by love and He rests in the Father's love. These are Athanasius' words:

> One should not call the Son a work of the will (θελήματος δημιούργημα) [...] Although the Son does not have his origin from the Father's will, He does not exist outside the Father's will or intelligence. As well as the Father loves his own hypostasis, also the Son who is of the same substance is desired and loved by the Father. For this reason all will piously not think that God does not desire [Him], but that He does desire [Him]. Since the Son loves the Father with the same will with which He loves Him, He loves the Father, He loves and honours Him, and it is the same will that exists in the proceeding Son and the Father, so that, for this reason, the Son is in the Father and the Father is contemplated in the Son[51].

What Athanasius wishes to clarify is that the Son is not the work of the Father's will as is the creation of the world, but in doing this, he has given us one of the best texts on the manner in which he conceives the relation between the Father and the Son: It is a relation of mutual love. What follows is one of the most eloquent Athanasian texts on the love that exists in the generation of the Son and the mutual love between Father and Son:

> The Father loves and desires Him because He is his 'proper' Son by nature. For to say, 'of will he came to be', in the first place implies that once He was not. Further, the will has the power to incline in one way or another, as has already been said, and one could thus think that the Father could have not desired the Son. From this, it is a great impiety and temerity to say that the Son could have not been, and it is something that damages the very nature of the Father, as if that which is proper to Him [the Father] could have not existed. It is the same as saying that the Father could have been not good. But in the same way in which the

---

is a phrase that expresses his thought clearly: 'The things that we engender are not the work of the will, but are like us. We do not become fathers by prior deliberation, but engendering is proper to nature, and it is for this reason that we also are images of our fathers.' (*Contra arianos* III, 66: PG 26, 461 A–B; Opitz 378–9).

[50] *Contra arianos*, 64 (PG 26, 457–60; Opitz, 376–7).

[51] *Contra arianos* III, 66 (PG 26, 464 A; Opitz, 379–80).

Father is always good by nature, so is He engendering by nature. Thus the manner of speaking as 'the Father desires the Son and the Son desires the Father' does not signify an antecedent will, but the equality of nature, essential property and likeness. In the same way one can say radiance of the light, as radiance is not willed in antecedent light, but is its natural offspring (γέννημα), and the light desires that which is engendered, not by voluntary deliberation, but by nature and truth. Thus in all truth one can say of the Father and the Son: The Father loves the Son, and the Son loves the Father[52].

The theological richness of the images of the Nicene Creed is evident: light and its radiance are inseparable, since light shines in its radiance, and is light by its radiance. Both are inseparably united by nature because there is no light without radiance. The Father is Father by the Son. The end of the argument is as follows:

Since the Son is all the things that belong to the Father, there is nothing in the Father that is anterior to the Word; but there is also will in the Word, and through Him are made all things that belong to the will, as we say for Sacred Scripture[53].

For Athanasius, the relation between the Father and Son is the foundation of the divine perfection and of everything that exists. Widdicombe's observation that follows could seem audacious, but one can also say that it is correct:

To receive the Spirit of the Word into one's heart is simultaneously to receive the Father. The fatherhood of God cannot be an object of perception over against the attributes of God, however superior it may be, because *as* Father and Son the divine being is the ground and source of those attributes and their expression[54].

## God the Father in Saint Basil

One can say that Saint Basil's theology of the Father is marked by three fundamental points: the influence of Saint Athanasius, his defence of the divinity of the Holy Spirit, and the polemic with Eunomius, which leads him to defend the primacy of the name of Father over that of unbegotten, as well as to accentuate, more than previous fathers, the divine transcendence

---

[52] *Contra arianos* III, 66 (PG 26, 464 A–B; Opitz, ibid).
[53] *Contra arianos* III, 67 (PG 26, 465 A; Opitz, 380–1).
[54] Widdicombe, *The Fatherhood of God*, p. 251.

above every word and concept. Basil frequently cites Athanasius, and uses the same texts of Sacred Scripture that we saw in his works, particularly those that speak of the co-eternity of the Word with the Father (cf. e.g. Jn 1.1), of the equality and residing of one in the other – which will later be called *perichoresis* (cf. Jn 9.14–11) – and those that speak of an authentic generation, that is, of a real procession of the Son by means of generation (cf. Mt 11.25–30).

## Father and Ubegotten

As is known, the questions on *agennesía* and divine *ineffability* guide *Contra Eunomium* I as a direct response to the Eunomians. Basil put special emphasis on the fact that the term *agénnetos* is not found in Scripture, while Father is found, which has the same meaning as *agénnetos*, but implying the notion of Son, because it is *relative* to it[55]. The notion of the Father shows the essential 'relativity' of the Person of the Father in reference to the Person of the Son, which is not the case with the concept of unbegotten.

This observation contains two highly important affirmations for Basil's Trinitarian theology, and the theology of the Father in particular: On the one hand, he identifies Father and unbegotten; and on the other, he gives primacy to the name of Father. The identification of unbegotten and Father is not a 'dialectical' argument in response to Eunomius, but rather a consideration that marks Basil's theology of the Father. Basil frequently repeats that each divine Person is essentially and unlimitedly that which He is: the Father is Father and only Father. Consequently He cannot be the son of anyone, and thus cannot be engendered by another, and must be unbegotten. He uses the same argument for the Son: The Son cannot be father of anyone, because his entire being is essentially and completely filiation. Basil's words are totally unambiguous:

> Since He is truly Father and only this, He does not have his origin in another, and not to come from another is the same as being unbegotten. So then we do not need to prefer the name of unbegotten over that of Father, unless we wish to be wiser than the teaching of the Saviour who

---

[55] As B. Sesboüé notes, Basil developed his understanding of relative names in *Contra Eunomium* II, 9, 11–27 and 24, 1–29. 36, which constitutes one of his most important contributions to the theological elaboration of the doctrine of the Trinity. The importance of the Person's *relativity* would be adopted by Saint Augustine (Cf. Basile de Césarée, *Contre Eunome* I, ed. B. Sesboüé, (SCh 299), París 1982, p. 176, nt. 1).

says: *Go ... baptizing ... in the name of the Father and of the Son and of the Holy Spirit* (Mt 28.19)[56].

Basil considers that the name of Father is the first name to be attributed to the first Person. This is his most proper name. Paternity – it is worth repeating – is the essential nucleus of the concept of Father. It is from Paternity that any other 'property' (ἰδιότης) by which the Father is distinguished from the other two Persons is derived. According to this perspective, the Father is not Father in order to be unbegotten, but He is unbegotten in order to be Father. Further – and Basil considers this argument quite important – 'Father' is the name with which He is called by our Lord. This underscores the importance that the Father-Son relation has for Basil. One understands how it was easy for Basil to take the word unbegotten simply as something negative, that is, as the simple absence of passive generation by the Father, and not as something positive:

> In the same way that incorruptible means that there is no corruption in God, and invisible means that He transcends any sensing by means of the eyes, and incorporeal means that his substance is not three dimensional, and immortal means that there is not and never will be any corruption in Him, in the same way we say that unbegotten means that there is no generation in Him[57].

There follow, as is well known, the texts where Basil underscores the transcendence of God and the fact that *agennesía* does not designate the divine substance, but the manner in which the Person of the Father exists. In the same way – he argues – that the name *unbegotten* applied to Adam does not designate his substance, but the mode in which this substance received being, *agennesía* does not say what God is, but how He is[58]. It should be added that the divine substance is above any created knowledge, only the Son and the Spirit know Him, and this knowledge is proper to Them alone. Basil says this referring to Mt 11.27 and 1 Cor 2.10–11, thus accentuating the equality that exists between the Three of the Trinity.

# The Truthfulness of Generation in God

Eunomius denies the divinity of the Son, basing himself above all in the concept of human generation. According to him, the Father could not

---

[56] Basil of Caesarea, *Contra Eunomium* I, 5 (SCh 299, 176).
[57] Basil of Caesarea, *Contra Eunomium* I, 9 (SCh 299, 202).
[58] Basil of Caesarea, *Contra Eunomium* I, 11–15 (SCh 299, 208–28).

communicate his nature to the Son – something essential to generation – because the Father's nature is to be unbegotten, and a son is engendered by definition. In order to refute Eunomius, Basil bases himself exclusively on the names given to God in Scripture, and above all in Jn 14.9 and Jn 12.45: *He who sees the Son sees the Father.* Following Athanasius, Basil insists on the fact that the Son is *sealed* by the Father (cf. Jn 6.27) and is the *Image of the invisible God* (cf. Col 1.15), *the radiance and image of his substance* (cf. He 1.3). He is a perfect image, and for this reason, Basil stresses, He must be a living image:

> Not an inanimate image, nor made by hand nor the work of technique or concept, but a living image, or better, an image that is life itself, maintaining intact the absence of any difference, it is not a superficial likeness, but in the substance itself[59].

The importance of this Basilian argument comes from the fact that only generation can give rise to an absolutely perfect image of the Father. The term 'radiance' again evokes Nicaea's 'light of light'. The perfection of the Image leads us to admit the truthfulness of generation in God, and vice versa: the divine generation leads us to admit the perfect equality of the Father and Son.

From this, Basil deduces the necessity for the generation of the Word to be eternal, and consequently, that order in the Trinity is not to be taken as a before and after, but as an order that comes from 'causality': the Father and Son are co-eternal, but the Father is the first Person, because He truly engenders the Son, and the Son is the second Person, because He is truly engendered by the Father. Basil calls this 'natural concatenation' (ἀκολουθία), because it arises from the causal relation in which the Father and Son are united[60]. In this context, the words of Jesus where He affirms that the Father is greater than Him (cf. Jn 14.28) are applied to the Word and not to the humanity of the Lord, and they are referred to the truth of his generation by the Father:

> Since the Son has his principle (ἀρχή) in the Father, for this reason He calls the Father greater in so far as cause and principle (ὡς αἴτιος καὶ ἀρχή)[61].

That is, the Father is greater than the Son because He is his fontal principle. In *Contra Eunomium* II, Basil insists on the characteristics proper to

---

[59] Basil of Caesarea, *Contra Eunomium* I, 18 (SCh 299, 234–6).
[60] Basil of Caesarea, *Contra Eunomium* I, 20 (SCh 299, 246).
[61] Basil of Caesarea, *Contra Eunomium* I, 125 (SCh 299, 262).

generation in God. Since to be Father is a perfection, the Father has to have always been a Father, and thus generation in God is eternal[62]. His paternity (πατρότης) 'is co-extensive with his own eternity'[63], and 'the concept of Son enters immediately into the concept of Father.'[64] There is nothing – no interval (διάστημα) – that separates the Father from the Son, so that our thought moves from the Son to the Father without moving through any interval[65]. He who sees the Son sees the Father in Him immediately, as is said using a text of the New Testament that is dear to Athanasius (Jn 14.9).

Basil describes the characteristics of this generation in four terms: The Father engenders the Son with a generation that is 'without passion, without division, without separation, and without time'[66]. This is a spiritual generation. Basil again uses the image of radiance, which is inseparable from light, as well as the pages of Scripture that speak of the immanence of the Father and Son, and that the Father has left his mark, his seal, in the Son[67].

In any case, Basil firmly bases himself on the fact that our Lord called God his Father, and also instructed us to call Him our Father, even if in a different sense: the Son is the natural Son, and we are sons by adoption; He belongs to the divinity, we were adopted as sons[68]. He is the light of the light, that is, 'engendered light of unbegotten light', 'the vivifying source that proceeds from essential life'[69].

A little further on, Basil, basing himself on Jn 17.10 – *all mine are thine, and thine are mine* – refutes Eunomius' affirmation on the procession of the Spirit. Eunomius stated that the Spirit was a creature of the Son, while Basil primarily affirms that the Spirit proceeds from the Father:

Is there anyone in the world who does not see in all clarity that no activity of the Son is found separated from the Father, and there is nothing in the realm of being that belongs to the Son without belonging to the Father? [...] Why does he attribute the cause of the Spirit to the Only Begotten alone and does use it to attack his [the Spirit's] nature by the production of this second?[70]

---

[62] Basil of Caesarea, *Contra Eunomium* II, 12 (SCh 305, 44).
[63] Basil of Caesarea, *Contra Eunomium* II, 12 (SCh 305, 46).
[64] The Greek text is of exquisite clarity: καὶ εὐθὺς τῇ τοῦ Πατρὸς ἐννοίᾳ ἡ τοῦ Υἱοῦ συνέρχεται, With the conception of the Father, the conception of the Son immediately enters.
[65] Basil of Caesarea, *Contra Eunomium* II, 12 (SCh 305, 46).
[66] 'ἀπαθῆ, ἀμέριστον, ἀδιαίρετον, ἄχρονον' (Basil of Caesarea, *Contra Eunomium* II, 16, SCh 305, 64).
[67] Basil of Caesarea, *Contra Eunomium* II, 16 (SCh 305, 64–6).
[68] Basil of Caesarea, *Contra Eunomium* II, 23 (SCh 305, 94).
[69] Basil of Caesarea, *Contra Eunomium* II, 27 (SCh 305, 114).
[70] Basil of Caesarea, *Contra Eunomium* II, 34 (SCh 305, 140).

Following the text of Jn 17.10, the unity of the Father and the Son in being and activity seem to be interchangeable in Basil's argument. Although everything has been done by the Word – Basil insists – the 'God of the Universe', i.e. the Father, is the cause of everything.

## The Treatise on the Holy Spirit

What Basil says on the paternity of the Father and his original fontality is already completely contained within the books of *Contra Eunomium*, which were written much earlier than the treatise on the Holy Spirit[71]. This is his last work, and appears as a spiritual testament in that Basil 'makes his confession of faith in the Trinity and affirms the certainty of man's vocation to divinization in the "sacrament" of the Church'[72].

The theology of the Father endures unaltered, but the perspective in which it is situated now is quite different: it is that of emphasizing the divinity of the Holy Spirit, which proceeds from the Father, not by generation, but in a distinct manner. The key chapter of the treatise, in which this question is explicitly developed, is chapter 18, dedicated to the confession of the three hypostases while maintaining 'the pious doctrine of the monarchy'. It deals with why the three Persons are 'connumerated' and with the refutation of those who say that They are 'subnumerated', because the three Persons have equal dignity.

Basil's starting point is the missionary mandate (Mt 28.19), where the Lord sends his disciples to baptize in the name of the Three. 'One God and Father, one Only Begotten Son, and one Holy Spirit' Basil says, in a language that echoes the use of Θεός in the New Testament. In the confession of Trinitarian faith, it is necessary to maintain the 'monarchy' at the same time that one maintains the distinction of the three hypostases:

> When one adores a God who proceeds from God, we also confess that which is proper (ἰδιάζον) to the hypostases and we remain in the 'monarchy' without disregarding 'theology', because, in God the Father and in God the Only Begotten, we contemplate, so to speak, a unique form that is reflected in the immutable divinity. For the Son is in the Father and the Father in the Son (...) and They are one. Thus, according

---

[71] The work of *Contra Eunomium* is from between 360–6, while the composition of the treatise on the Holy Spirit is from 375 (cf. B. Sesboüé *Introduction* in SCh 299, p. 44).

[72] G. Azzali Bernardelli, *Introducción*, in Basil of Caesarea, *El Espíritu Santo*, Madrid: Ciudad Nueva 1996, p. 5.

to the property (ἰδιότης) of the Persons, They are one and one, but in regard to the community of nature, both are only one[73].

The doctrine of monarchy means that the Father is the principle of the entire divinity. Together with this, Basil underscores the immanence that exists between the Father and the Son, implicitly citing Jn 10.38 and the perfect equality of the Image. The only difference between Them stems from the fact that the Son is the Image, and the Father is the exemplar that is reflected in the image. The same thing is to be said for the Holy Spirit, in reference to both distinction and unity: He is as united to the Father and the Son 'as unity is united to unity'[74].

# The Procession of the Spirit

This unity has origin in that the Spirit also proceeds from the Father, not as something external, that is, as a creature, but as something internal, something 'proper' to the Father:

> It is said that He is from God (ἐκ τοῦ Θεοῦ εἶναι), not as all things proceed from God, but as He who proceeds (προελθόν) from God, without being engendered as the Son, but as the 'spirit' of his mouth. It is understood that mouth is not a member, nor the breath a breeze that fades, but 'mouth' is to be understood in a manner worthy of God, and 'breath' as a living substance, ruling over sanctification. This is the reason for his 'community' [with the Father and the Son], but the mode of his existence remains ineffable[75].

The Spirit's belonging to the realm of the divinity has its foundation in his procession from the Father. Basil is quite interested in stating that the Spirit does not proceed by generation, but that it is undoubtedly a true procession from the Father. The use of θεοῦ indicates, without giving rise to doubts, that Basil is thinking of the Father. The description of this second procession as the 'breath from God's mouth', beyond its relation to known passages of Sacred Scripture, is classic in the fourth century[76],

---

[73] Basil, *On the Holy Spirit*, 18, 45, ed. B. Pruche, (SC 17 bis), Paris: Cerf 1968, pp. 404–6. B. Pruche comments that the expression of 'the proper of the hypostasis (τὸ ἰδιάζον τῶν ὑποστάσεων)' is not identical to the expression of 'the property' (ἰδιότης) of each person: the proper of the hypostasis is that two of them come from one, while the property of the persons resides in the fact that one is Father, another Son and the other the Holy Spirit (p. 405, nt. 8).
[74] Basil, *On the Holy Spirit*, 18, 46 (SCh 17 bis, 408).
[75] Basil, *On the Holy Spirit*, 46: (SCh 17 bis, 408).
[76] Cf., e.g., Gregory of Nyssa, *Oratio catechetica magna*, 1.

and permits Basil to speak of its ineffability and to distinguish it from generation.

The illuminating and sanctifying action of the Spirit at the same time shows that He belongs to the divine realm, and that He remains united with the Father and the Son 'as unity is united to unity'[77]. The itinerary that Basil follows, both ascending and descending as it is, is identical to that followed by Irenaeus[78]. The spirit shows the truth of God in himself. He does not show it 'from outside', but 'from inside' the divine intimacy to which He pertains and in which He is:

> The path of knowledge of God goes from the only Spirit, but by means of the only Son, to the only Father. And inversely, substantial goodness, sanctity by nature and supreme dignity flow from the Father, by the Only Begotten to the Spirit. Thus one confesses the hypostases without harming the pious doctrine of the monarchy[79].

The confession of the monarchy is compatible with this order in the divine actuality, already so firmly proposed by Saint Irenaeus. Everything proceeds from the Father, by the Son and reaches the Spirit. For this reason, knowledge of God occurs in the Spirit, by the Son and reaches the Father. This is so because the Spirit's procession makes of Him God of God and Light of Light as well. In this sense, the affirmations contained in n. 47 of this chapter are of the greatest interest, since they summarize an approach that is dear to Saint Basil[80]: with the Spirit's illuminating powers, we fix our eyes on the Image of God, and we see the Archetype in Him. Basil insistently repeats here that the Spirit contains *in himself* the power to contemplate the Truth, which is *in Him himself* – and not from outside – and it is in this way that He gives knowledge of the Truth, i.e. the Word. In speaking of the Spirit showing the Word in himself, Basil is suggesting an analogy between the reason for which the Father is manifested in the Word and the Word is manifested in the Spirit.

All of this – unity and distinction – is founded in the monarchy of the Father, who is the source from which the Son and the Spirit proceed. Saint Basil also considers this problem from the perspective of personal 'properties', focusing his attention on the notes that distinguish the Persons from each other. Questions of particular theological importance can be found in *Letter* 38. These questions represent developments in relation to what we have henceforth seen in Basil. There is a debate as to whether

---

[77] Basil, *On the Holy Spirit*, 18, 45 (SCh 17 bis, 408).
[78] Irenaeus, *Epideixis*, 6 and 7.
[79] Basil, *On the Holy Spirit*, 18, 46 (SCh 17 bis, 412).
[80] We find in a passage of *Letter* 226: 'Our spirit, illuminated by the Spirit, regards the Son, and in Him, as in an Image, it contemplates the Father.' (PG 32, 849 A).

*Letter* 38 is by Basil or his brother Gregory[81]. In either case, we are in the domain of Basil's Trinitarian theology, so that, as V. H. Drecoll observes, 'If one nevertheless desires to insist on Gregorian provenance, one must underscore Gregory's strong dependency on Basil in both language and content.'[82]

*Letter* 38 states that the 'God who is over all' (the Father) has as characteristic of his hypostasis 'to be Father and to exist without any cause: by this sign one recognizes what is proper to Him'; the Son, 'who for himself and with himself gives us knowledge of the Spirit who proceeds from the Father, and is the only one who burns as the radiance of the unbegotten light'; the Spirit has the following sign as the property of his hypostasis: 'to be known from and with the Son and to subsist from the Father (ἐκ τοῦ Πατρὸς ὑφεστάναι')[83].

Father and unbegotten are the notes that distinguish the Father, but being *agénnetos* is derived from the fact of his paternity; the Son is distinguished by his filiation, and being the 'radiance of the unbegotten light'; the characteristics of the Spirit are his reception of his subsistence from the Father and the fact that He cannot be known except in union with the Son: His procession from the Father and ineffable union with the Son are thus clear.

At the end of the *Letter*, Basil turns again to the Father-Son relation, basing himself in the same texts of Scripture as those in which Saint Athanasius based himself: Jn 14.9, Col 1.15, Wi 7.26, Jn 16.15 and Jn 14.10. These are texts where, as is known, the unity between the Father and Son and their perfect likeness are supported. All of the Father is in the Son, who is the image and seal of the Father, 'the light engendered by the unbegotten light'. In this context, Basil encapsulates his thought on the Father's 'relativity' in a phrase with deep theological consequences: 'since it is impossible, when referring to the Son, not to think of the Father in the same thought, because the Father is rightly manifest in the form of this relation'[84].

---

[81] Cf. Basil of Caesarea, *Le lettere* (M. Forlin Patrucco, ed.), Turin 1983, 84, 22–3. On possible authorship by Gregory of Nyssa, cf. pp. 407–8. Cf. also H. Hübner, 'Gregor von Nyssa als Verfasser der sogenannten Epist. 38 des Basilius,' in J. Fontaine and C. Kannengiesser (eds), *Epektasis. Mélanges patristiques offerts au Cardinal Jean Daniélou*, Paris: Beauchesne 1972, pp. 463–90; P. J. Fedwick, *A Commentary of Gregory of Nyssa on the 38th Letter of Basil of Caesarea*, in *Orientalia Christiana Periodica* 44 (1978) 31–51. Cf. also V. H. Drecoll, 'Diff Ess Hyp (Ep. 38 or Ad Petrum fratrem),' in L. F. Mateo-Seco and G. Maspero (eds), *The Brill Dictionary of Gregory of Nyssa*, Leiden: Bril 2010, pp. 233–6; L. F. Mateo-Seco, 'Epist.', in *The Brill Dictionary of Gregory of Nyssa*, pp. 271–2. For a detailed study of the Cappadocians' pneumatology, see M. Brugarolas, *El Espíritu Santo de la divinidad a la procesión*, Pamplona: Eunsa, forthcoming.

[82] V. H. Drecoll, 'Ep. 38', in *The Brill Dictionary of Gregory of Nyssa*, 344.

[83] Basil, *Letter* 38, 4 (PG 32, 329 C–332 A), Cf. Basil of Caesarea, *Le lettere* (M. Forlin Patrucco, ed.), Turin 1983, pp. 84, 22–3.

[84] Basil, *Letter* 38, 7–8 (ed. M. Forlin Patrucco, pp. 38–40).

# Saint Gregory of Nazianzus

The teaching of Gregory of Nazianzus on God the Father has the same fundamental traits as that of Saint Basil. Gregory is only distinguished from him by a greater depth in Trinitarian doctrine – perhaps marked by a greater perfection in his formulations – and by a clear progress regarding the procession of the Holy Spirit and his clarity in speaking of the Spirit's divinity. His teaching on God the Father is principally found in the *Theological Carmens* and in *Theological Orations* 29 and 31, on the Son and the Spirit respectively[85].

# The Theological Orations

The generation of the Son is treated extensively in *Oration* 29, and with it the characteristics of the Father's paternity are also treated. Gregory primarily accentuates the eternity of the three Persons, including the Holy Spirit, and clearly distinguishes the procession of the Spirit from the generation of the Son to the point of declaring that the Son does not proceed (οὐκ ἐκπεπορεύεται) from the Father, but is engendered by Him before time[86]. This is then an eternal generation, as we have seen Saint Basil note many times.

The Three of the Trinity are eternal, Gregory continues, but only the Father is without principle: the Son and the Spirit are eternal, but also have their principle in the Father. The linguistic precision is important: He who has no principle is eternal – Gregory explains – but not all that is eternal is without principle. The Son and the Spirit are not without cause since They really proceed from the Father, but the cause (the Father) is not anterior to Them, because it must be said that They have no beginning. A little further on, Gregory states: being engendered does not necessarily entail having a beginning through generation[87].

Who is this Father who never began being a Father? Gregory asks. The

---

[85] The first three *Theological Carmens* are expressly dedicated to the Trinity and each of the divine persons (cf. PG 37, 397–445; cf. P. Gallay, *Grégoire de Nazianze, Poémes et letters chosis*, Paris 1941). For a commentary on the pneumatological kontent of this *Carmens*, cf. M. Brugaroles, 'San Gregorio Nacianceno: la unidad de los Tres', in: *Excerpta e dissertationibus in Sacra Theologia 58* (Universidad de Navarra, 2011) 130–139. The *Orations* are also edited by P. Gallay (*Grégoire de Nazianze, Discours 27–31*, [SCh 250], Paris; Cerf 1978).

[86] Gregory of Nazianzus, *Theological Oration* 29, 3 (SCh 250, 180–2). Note the clarity with which Gregory distinguishes the two Trinitarian processions based on concrete signification of the verb ἐκπορεύω, while stressing that the Son 'does not proceed, but is engendered' (οὐκ ἐκπεπορεύται, ἀλλὰ γεγενέται). He opposes 'ἐκπορεύσις' to generation.

[87] Gregory of Nazianzus, *Theological Oration* 29, 5 (SCh 250, 185–6).

response engages a model that is quite important for the theology of the Father:

> He did not begin to be, while those who began to be also began to be fathers. He was not Father a little later, because He had no beginning. Further: He is Father in the proper sense, because He is not son in any way. In the same way, the Son is Son in the proper sense, because He is not also Father[88].

This entire *Discourse* is full of similar affirmations, which evoke that which we have already cited of Saint Basil. In Gregory there is perhaps a better formulation of his thought, but it is in the same line as Basil. The Father is father in the proper sense, because He is only Father and this includes with it not receiving his being from another, i.e. being unbegotten[89]. He cannot be father and son at the same time.

Gregory's intellectual *iter* seems clear: being unbegotten derives from being Father. Father and unbegotten are the notes that characterize the Father; paternity is however the first one, and the key characteristic for his entire Person; it is also the first that we know of Him. Father is, above all, the name that the Lord taught us. A little further on, Gregory will state, while recalling Eunomius' position, that being 'unbegotten' is proper to the Person of the Father, and not the divine substance. Unbegotten does not refer to the substance, but to the 'mode' in which this substance possesses being[90].

Gregory stresses the fact that the Father's paternity is without beginning or passion. It is thus outside of our categories of voluntariness and liberty. Gregory follows Basil to the letter on this: Is the Father God – he asks the Eunomians – because He wanted to be so? Is it the case that God wanted to be God before being so? Affirming this would be the same as saying that God chose to have goodness as his substance. The reality is completely the reverse: God is goodness by nature[91]. In fact, generation in God, and consequently paternity, is a great mystery that must be honoured by our silence[92]. In any case, it is clear that the name of Father is not a name that designates the divine substance or divine action, but a name of the relation of the first Person with the Son[93].

---

[88] Gregory of Nazianzus, *Theological Oration* 29, 5 (SCh 250, 184).

[89] Paternity and Agennesía are hypostatic properties (ἰδιότης) of the Father (cf. Saint Gregory of Nazianzus, *Theological Oration* 29, 12 (SCh 250, 201, nt. 2).

[90] Cf. Gregory of Nazianzus, *Theological Oration* 29, 10–12 (SCh 250, 196–202).

[91] Gregory of Nazianzus, *Theological Oration* 29, 6 (SCh 250, 186–8).

[92] 'Θεοῦ γέννησις σιωπῇ τιμάσθω' (Saint Gregory of Nazianzus, *Theological Oration* 29, 7 (SCh 250, 192).

[93] Gregory of Nazianzus, *Theological Oration* 29, 16 (SCh 250, 210).

As can bee seen from *Oration* 31, 4[94], the Three are inseparably related, since They are one God in substance, and Three due to the 'properties'. There is a deeply insightful formula here: 'The Three are One in the divinity, and One is three in reference to the properties (ἰδιότησιν).'[95]

## The Theological Carmens

The *Poemata Theologica* I-III make a good summary of Gregory's Trinitarian theology, expressed in a pedagogical manner[96]. The doctrine, as can be expected, is perfectly in accord with what we have seen in the teachings of Gregory, Basil and Athanasius. It is enough to quote the most auspicious expressions that refer to God the Father. In the verses dedicated to God the Father, he describes Him thus: there is only one God, without principle or cause (ἄναρχος καὶ ἀναίτιος) (v. 5), infinite and eternal, 'great Father of the great Only Begotten', who is also another (ἄλλος) (vv. 29–30) God, but not other in the divinity, but as Word of God, the living seal of the Father, who is the only one without principle; and only one Spirit, God who proceeds from (ἐξ) (v. 35) the good God.

The verses dedicated to the Son insist on the same fundamental formulations regarding the Father: nothing exists before the Father, because He has everything in himself. There is none greater than Him. The Word of the great God is engendered by the Father. There was no time before the Word, whose Father is without time and who receives 'a beginning without time' (ἄχρονον ἀρχήν) (v. 21). There is no interval between Them. Nothing separates Them, neither time nor voluntariness, Gregory writes, recalling what he says in his *Orations* on the fact that the Father is Father, not by choice, but by nature (vv. 26–30).

We also sing the glory of the Spirit. One cannot separate with one's words that which nature has not separated (v. 2). We have known God by the Spirit: He is God and makes me God. He proceeds from the Father (Πατρόθεν ἐρχόμενον) (v. 7)[97], he is not the Son (there is only one good Son

---

[94] 'If there were a time in which the Father was not, there would be a time in which the Son was not. If there were a time in which the Son was not, there would have been a time in which there was no Spirit either. If one of Them was *from the beginning* (1 Jn 1.1), then the three were.' (Gregory of Nazianzus, *Theological Oration* 31, 4 (SCh 250, 280–2). This simultaneity of existence of the three divine Persons also entails keeping the simultaneity of their *relations* in the foreground.

[95] Gregory of Nazianzus, *Theological Oration* 31, 9 (SCh 250, 292).

[96] Gregory of Nazianzus, *Poemata Theologica*, I–III (PG 37, 397 A–415 A). There is an excellent critical edition of these poems: St. Gregory of Nazianzus, *Poemata arcana*, (Edited with a Textual Introduction by C. Moreschini. Introduction, Translation and Commentary by D. A. Sykes), Oxford 2007.

[97] Sykes notes: 'Again, a technical term of the Niceno-Constantinopolitan Creed is excluded by

who is the Best), but He is not outside the divinity, and receives the same glory (ὁμόδοξον) as the Father and the Son (v. 9).

At the end of the verses, once the 'properties' of each Person have been enumerated, Gregory returns to the union of Trinity and Unity, using an image that is well loved by the Cappadocians: the Three are three suns that are so united as to give but one light:

> 'There is one God in three splendours, who governs the world.' (verse 43). 'The Trinity proceeds from unity (μόναδος) and unity (μονὰς) comes from the Trinity.' (verse 60) 'Each one is God when we speak of One. And there is again only One, from which all the riches of the Divinity come.' (verses 75–76).

Unity and Trinity spring forth from the Person of the Father. As C. A. Beeley comments, 'for Gregory the monarchy of the Father and the coequality and consubstantiality of the three persons not only belong together, but necessarily do so and in fact amount to the same thing. The priority of the Father within the Trinity does not conflict with the divine unity and equality, but is rather what causes and enables them'[98]. 'One God in three splendours', M. Brugarolas suggest that this expression may serve very well as a recapitulation of Gregory of Nazianzus' pneumatology. An idea that points the continuity between the Trinitarian theology of Gregory of Nazianzus, Gregory of Nyssa and John Damascene.[99]

# Latin Theology

The Trinitarian perspective in Latin theology has an essential reference point in Saint Augustine and finds its most prominent expression in Saint Bonaventure and Saint Thomas Aquinas. We will focus on them as the most

---

metre, for ἐκπορευόμενον cannot be fitted into a hexameter.' (o.c., 120). This position is no longer pertinent, as Sykes notes in the same place.

[98] C. A. Beeley, *Gregory of Nazianzus on the Trinity and knowledge of God*, Oxford: Oxford University Press 2008, pp. 209–10. A few pages earlier, in describing the 'properties' of the Person of the Father, Beeley writes: 'As Gregory elaborates, it is the special property of the Father to be both the source of himself – in the sense that he is self-existent divinity, being unbegotten, uncaused, and without source – and the source of the Son and the Holy Spirit, and thus the cause and source of the Trinity as a whole.' (ibid. 205). Although it is clear what this phrase means in the domain of occidental theology, it is possible that this does not precisely express the manner in which Gregory thinks of *agennesía*. As can be seen from the cited texts, it seems logical to think that Gregory would never accept the affirmation that the 'Father is source of himself'.

[99] Cf. M. Brugarolas, 'San Gregorio Nacianceno: la unidad de los Tres', 138–139.

important and significant milestones. The positions of these authors in the manner of conceptualizing the paternity of the Father have a considerable degree of diversity, particularly in reference to the concepts of *primitas* and *ingenitus*. Undoubtedly, both Saint Bonaventure and Saint Thomas are fit fully in the Augustinian tradition.

## The Augustinian Heritage

In the Eunomian controversy, the term *agénnetos* was reserved for the person of the Father as his proper name, but at the same time another question arose. Should *agennesía* be understood in a negative sense – as only signifying that the Father does not have an origin – or in a positive sense, as a name that, inside its negative expression, designates a positive property of the Father?

For Saint Augustine as well, who in this corresponds with the Cappadocian Fathers[100], the term of *ingenitus* must be taken in a negative sense: it simply signifies that the Father does not proceed from anyone. He writes at the end of the *De Trinitate*:

> Pater enim solus non est de alio, ideo solus apellatur ingenitus, non quidem in Scripturis, sed in consuetudine disputantium.[101]

Augustine warns that the term *ingenitus* is not Scriptural, but that it is fruitfully used by those who consider the Trinitarian mystery since it corresponds to the reality. The Father does not proceed from any person in the Trinity, and this characteristic is proper to Him alone, distinguishing Him from the other Persons. Only the Father is *ingenitus*. For this reason, the name of *ingenitus* is proper to Him. Augustine's position is clear, as can be seen in the consequences that follow when he must ask the why (according to our way of speaking) of the Father's paternity. *Innascibility* is not used as a reason for paternity (as *plenitudo fontalis*) but only as a negation of the fact that the Father proceeds from another.

> Ingenitus porro quid est, nisi non genitus? (…) quia sicut filius ad patrem et non filius ad non patrem, ita genitus ad genitorem, et non genitus ad non genitorem referatur necesse est.[102]

---

[100] Cf. V. H. Drecoll, 'Agennesía', in *The Brill Dictionary of Gregory of Nyssa*, pp. 9–11.

[101] Augustine, *De Trinitate*, XV, 26, 47. and in *Letter* 238, 1, 6: '*Patrem* in illis libris nusquam ingenitum legimus, et tamen dicendum esse defenditur.'

[102] Augustine, *De Trinitate*, V, 7, 8.

This text is from the chapter of *De Trinitate* that Augustine dedicates to the relative names, in order to demonstrate that negation does not change the nature of the predicate. Engendered is a relative name, because it refers to Him who engenders. Consequently, *unbegotten* is also a relative name, referring to another person who, in the case of un-begotten, does not exist.

> At si quantum valet quod dicitur filius, tantumdem valet quod dicitur non filius. Relative autem negamus dicendo non filius; relative ergo negamus dicendo non genitus.[103]

The conclusion is logical, and one can see that the Eunomian position is taken into account. Augustine concludes that the name of *unbegotten* does not designate the divine substance, but relativity, that is, the Person of the Father. Thus the Person of the Father, and consequently *paternitas*, occupies the centre of the Trinitarian system. It is the reason for the Father's fontality, that is, that He is the first principle of all things. It is here that we also encounter the root of the divergence with those who deny the *Filioque*: for Augustine, the Father's perfect paternity requires the perfect equality of the Son with the Father, and consequently that the Father gives all that he is to the Son, except, of course, paternity.

Following earlier tradition, this paternity is conceived along the lines of the mental word, i.e. paternity consists in the Father expressing himself in his Word. The following aphorism of Augustine is both proverbial and rich with theological consequences: 'Eo quippe Filius quo Verbum; et eo Verbum quo Filius.'[104]

There is a perfect correlativity that expresses the essential nucleus of the Father's paternity: the Son is Word in that the Father expresses himself perfectly, i.e. *He says himself* to himself. There are numerous Augustinian texts in this sense. It is enough to recall *De Trinitate* XV, 14, where Augustine insists on the perfect equality between the Father and the Son, precisely because the Father's paternity is perfectly expressed in the Son:

> Et ideo Patri, sicut esse non est a Filio, ita nec nosse. Proinde tanquam se ipsum dicens Pater genuit Verbum sibi aequale per omnia. Non enim se ipsum integre perfecteque dixisset, si aliquid minus aut amplius esset in eius Verbo quam in ipso.[105]

The Father does not receive his being from the Son, and thus He does not receive knowledge either, since it is He who eternally engenders the Word

---

[103] Augustine, *De Trinitate*, V, 7, 8.
[104] Augustine, *De Trinitate*, VII, 2.
[105] Augustine, *De Trinitate*, XV, 14.

precisely in expressing himself to himself. This is perfect generation, and thus perfect self-expression. This thought leads Augustine to emphasize the complete equality between the Word and the Father, not only to defend the divinity of the Son, but also to clarify the infinite perfection of the Father's paternity: in this paternity, the Father expresses himself 'integrally and perfectly' in an eternal today:

> Novit itaque omnia Deus Pater in se ipso, novit in Filio: sed in se ipso tanquam seipsum, in Filio tanquam Verbum suum, quod est de his omnibus quae sunt in se ipso (...) Sciunt ergo invicem Pater et Filius: sed ille gignendo, iste nascendo. Et omnia quae sunt in eorum scientia, in eorum sapientia, in eorum essentia, unusquisque eorum simul videt.[106]

Saint Augustine's formulation uses the identity that exists between knowledge and being in God as a guide: the Father and Son mutually know each other. The Father knows as engendering, while the Son knows in being engendered. This perspective implies that, according to our mode of understanding, the Father's fontality as principle and source of the entire Trinity must situate paternity in harmony with the fact of understanding *ingenitus* as a purely negative concept.

Undoubtedly, there is a strong current within Augustinian tradition that interprets *innascibilitas* in a positive sense, and consequently thinks that the Father is Father because He is innascible. This position is present in Richard of St Victor (1173), Alexander of Hales (between 1231 and 1237) and Saint Bonaventure (1274)[107]. The term *unbegotten* will however have the advantage of underscoring the Father's monarchy. This can be seen with particular force in the theology of Saint Bonaventure.

## Primitas et Plenitudo in Saint Bonaventure

Saint Bonaventure is the most typical and vigorous Latin proponent of understanding the term *ingenitus* with a positive sense that is the reason underpinning paternity. The Father's *innascibilitas* is, according to him, the reason of his fontal fullness, i.e. of his intra-Trinitarian fecundity and his creative power. We will therefore find ourselves facing not only a strong accentuation of the Father's *monarchy*, but also a conceptualization of the Trinitarian mystery that is based in the *emanations* or *gifts* of the Father to each of the divine Persons because of his *fontal fullness*, and we ultimately reach the conviction that the good is self-diffusive.

---

[106] Augustine, *De Trinitate*, XV, 23.
[107] Cf. Richard of St Victor, *De Trinitate*, 5, 6 (SCh 63, 318); Saint Bonaventure, *In Sent.*, I, d. 27, p. 1., q. 2, ad 3.

There have been important studies devoted to this subject in recent years which are indispensable and accessible. There is a notable agreement between them. It is also true that Saint Bonaventure's texts are quite clear and do not require a great exegetical labour. Among these studies, some prominent ones are the books of G. Émery, especially *La théologie trinitaire de saint Thomas d'Aquin*[108], the doctoral thesis of Robert Józef Woźniak titled *Primitas et plenitudo*[109], and articles of E. Durand[110].

# The Good as Self-Diffusive

Saint Bonaventure's arguments for the existence of persons in God are quite similar to those of Richard of St Victor[111], although the perspective is different. The Bonaventurian perspective is that diffusion is essential to the good, and that consequently, if God did not communicate himself in a perfect manner, i.e. if He did not communicate his entire substance in a perfect diffusion, He could not be considered the highest good.

Saint Bonaventure is logically thinking of God the Father as the source and origin of the entire Trinity. His fontality comes precisely from the fact of his being unbegotten, since this characteristic signifies his full possession of his being, and consequently of the fullness of goodness. The theme is extensively treated in *De mysterio Trinitatis*. He dedicates question eight on whether '*summa primitas*' can co-exist with '*trinitas*'. The first objection situates the problem in an argument that is usually used to speak of God's unicity: Bonaventure reminds that '*primitas in essentia*' 'necessarily excludes any other essence'. The absolutely first essence necessarily excludes equality with another, because otherwise neither of them would be first.

Bonaventure's conclusion is of great intellectual audacity: 'Primitas non solum non excludit trinitatem, verum etiam eam includit'[112]. Primacy not only does not require solitariness in the first principle, but

---

[108] G. Émery, *La théologie trinitaire de saint Thomas d'Aquin*, Paris Cerf 2004.

[109] R. J.Woźniak, *Primitas et plenitudo. Dios Padre en la teología trinitaria de san Buenaventura*, Pamplona: Eunsa 2007.

[110] E. Durand, 'L'innascibilité et les relations du Père sous le signe de sa primauté, dans la théologie trinitaire de Bonaventure', in *Revue Thomiste* 106 (2006) 531–63; ibid., 'Généalogie de la typologie médiévale sur l'innascibilité du Père. Pierre Lombard, Guillaume d'Auxerre et Alexandre de Halès', in *Archives d'histoire doctrinale et littéraire du Moyen Âge* 74 (2007). For an overview, cf. L. F. Ladaria, 'La fede in Dio Padre nella tradizione cattolica', in *Lateranum* 66 (2000) 755–88.

[111] Bonaventure, I *Sent* d. 2, a. un, q. 2; I *Sent* d. 27, p. 1, a un., q. 2, a 3; *Quaestiones disputatae de mysterio Trinitatis*, qq. 1–8; *Hexaemeron*, XI, 11; *Itinerarium mentis in Deum*, cp. 6.

[112] Bonaventure, *De mysterio Trinitatis*, q. 8.

it includes the plurality of persons. The reason that the Father's fontality includes the plurality of persons in itself is found in the fact that the production of the first principle is a fully perfect production, according to the consideration that the diffusion of the first good must be a full and perfect diffusion. We see in the Bonaventurian texts:

> Primitas summa in summo et altissimo principio ponit summam actualitatem, summam fontalitatem et summam fecunditatem. Primum enim principium, hoc ipso quod primum, est perfectissimum in producendo, fontalissimum in emanando, fecundissimum in pullulando (...) Et quia perfectissima productio non est nisi respectu aequalium, fontalissima emanatio non est nisi respectu coaeternalium, fecundissima pullulatio non est nisi respectu consubstantialium[113].

The fontal perfection of the first principle does not exclude the Trinity of persons, but instead requires complete equality between Them. This is due to the perfect fecundity that the first principle possesses. It can be said in a formulation of R. Woźniak, 'The mystery of the Father includes the entire Trinitarian mystery in itself. The logic and dynamics of the divine life as a whole is found in it.'[114] J. Zizioulas uses similar expressions: 'If God exists, He exists because the Father exists, that is, He who out of love freely begets the Son and brings forth the Spirit. Thus God as person – as the hypostasis of the Father – makes the one divine substance to be that which it is: the one God. This point is absolutely crucial.'[115]

This perspective is in fact crucial, and it marks an unmistakable structure at the time of presenting the Trinitarian mystery in view of its theological systematization. R. J. Woźniak underscores the fact that, according to Saint Bonaventure, the negativity of the Father's *innascibilitas* is a 'sign of something very positive, which is in fact a properly paternal reality, i.e. his primacy in the *intra-Trinitarian life*: the Father is absolutely first. Primacy is understood here as a 'quintessentially ontological value', i.e. as highest good and highest fecundity'. This interpretation, Woźniak concludes, 'situates Bonaventure quite close to the vision of Basil the Great, who placed the concepts of innascibility and paternity together in his time.'[116] He is not without reason. As can be seen above, Basil's orientation regarding the theology of God the Father has an orientation similar to that of Bonaventure.

In any case, it is clear that, in applying that which Bonaventure says

---

[113] Bonaventure, *De mysterio Trinitatis*, q. 8.
[114] Woźniak, *Primitas et plenitudo*, p. 89.
[115] J. Zizioulas, *Being as communion*, Crestwood: St Vladimir's Press 1997, p. 41 (cited by Woźniak, Primitas et plenitudo, p. 89, nt. 1).
[116] Woźniak, *Primitas et plenitudo*, p. 97.

about *perfectissima productio* to the generation of the Son, he stresses the necessity that there be no greater difference between the Father and the Son than that found between the Exemplar and his perfect Image: the necessity that the Son is not distinguished from the Father by anything other than being Son, i.e. in his reciprocal and opposed relation. This is what we saw in Saint Augustine as well, reinforced by the affirmation that '*Eo quippe Filius quo Verbum; et eo Verbum quo Filius.*'[117] The Father expresses himself most perfectly in his Word with a most perfect fecundity.

## The First Principle in Saint Thomas Aquinas

Saint Thomas' position on the theology of the Father is well known[118], and is in great continuity with his perspective on the definition of person in God as *relatio subsistens*. From this, his perspective is quite different from that of Saint Bonaventure in regard to the reason for the Father's fontality. According to Saint Thomas, the Person of the Father is constituted (according to our way of speaking) by his relation of opposition to the Son and the Spirit. In the *Summa Theologiae*, Saint Thomas directly treats *innascibilitas* in the article dedicated to the question as to whether being unbegotten is a property of the Father. His response is as follows:

> Pater innotescit quidem paternitate et communi spiratione, per respectum ad personas ab eo procedentes: inquantum autem est principium non de principio, innotescit per hoc, quod non est ab alio: quod pertinet ad proprietatem innascibilitatis, quam significat hoc nomen ingenitus[119].

The Father is the principle without principle. He is the principle of the Life that God has in himself. The Father possesses this life in communion with the Son and the Spirit, who are consubstantial with Him, because He eternally gives Them, in the today of eternity, his own indivisible substance. The vital flow of intelligence and love that is given between the three divine Persons, and which constitutes God in an ineffable interpersonal communion, springs forth from the Father and returns to the Person who is the principle without principle. This fontality however arises from his paternity.

According to Thomas Aquinas, *innascibilitas* is to be understood in a negative sense, i.e. as the simple absence of origin. Saint Thomas knows of

---

[117] Augustine, *De Trinitate*, VII, 2.
[118] Thomas' Trinitarian doctrine, as is to be expected, is the object of frequent reflection and study. Among the most recent and important studies, cf. G. Émery, *La théologie trinitaire de Thomas d'Aquin*, pp. esp. 185–212 and E. Durand, 'Le Père en sa relation constitutive au Fils selon Thomas d'Aquin', in *Revue Thomiste* 107 (2007) 47–72.
[119] Thomas Aquinas, STh I, q. 33, a. 4, in c.

the Bonaventurian position, as can be seen in the responses to objections in the current article: some say that the name of innascibility, he writes, is not only said in a negative manner, 'but that it implies two things: that the Father does not proceed from anyone, and that He is the principle of others', but this 'does not appear to be true'[120].

In the solution to the third objection, he stresses that the name of unbegotten applied to God the Father does not refer to the substance, but is a name in reference to the relative, 'like negation is reduced to the genus of affirmation'. To say unbegotten only means that the Father is without any relation that would include being engendered, and nothing else. Saint Thomas refers to the line of thought that culminates in Saint Bonaventure in using the generic 'some', and insists that his position corresponds to that of Saint Augustine, who he cites explicitly (*De Trinitate*, V, 10).

G. Emery and E. Durand have wisely emphasized the divergence between these two great medieval theologians in their understanding of the Father's *innascibilitas*: Thomas, Durand comments, could not adhere to Bonaventure because, for Bonaventure, the hypostasis of the Father, due to his *primitas* and *innascibilitas*, can be considered to be already included before considering his relation of paternity, while according to Thomas' perspective, it is paternity as subsisting and distinguishing relation that constitutes the hypostasis of the Father[121].

We find diverging thought on *innascibilitas* in Saint Bonaventure and in Saint Thomas. This is not a subtle difference, but one that has important consequences for structuring the treatise on the triune God. Both are aware that, in this difference, they are representatives of the rich traditions that have preceded them. As was known, and then underscored by Émery, Woźniak and Durand, Saint Bonaventure is situated in the line of Richard of St Victor, while Saint Thomas substantially follows that of his teacher, Saint Albert the Great[122]. These are two diverging traditions in the conception of the Father's paternity, but which are both within the Christian faith. At the same time, it does not appear that they manifest serious divergencies from the teachings of the Greek fathers, but that they are witnesses to the same faith. Both authors readily cite Saint Athanasius, Saint Basil, Saint John Damascene, or Pseudo-Dionysius.

In any case, both traditions, understood as theological reflections inside the one faith, have, in their divergence itself, contributed to the avoidance of unilaterality that is always dangerous when speaking of the Trinity. Concretely, the Thomasian accentuation of the importance of relation avoided the consideration of the Father constituted in himself in

[120] Ibid., ad 1.
[121] Durand, 'Le Père en sa relation constitutive', p. 72.
[122] Émery, *La Théologie trinitaire*, pp. 206–9

abstraction from the other Persons of whom He is principle. Also avoids the consideration of the Father as *principium non de principio* like the principle of all created things, as necessarily anterior to that of which He is principle. Saint Thomas already emphasizes this difference in his commentary on the Sentences, in a passage that recalls both Saint Augustine and Pseudo-Dionysius:

> Respondeo dicendum, quod, secundum Augustinum (*De Trinitate*, IV, 20, 29) Pater est principium totius divinitatis; unde etiam Dionysius (*De divinis nominibus*, II, 5 and 7) dicit quod in Padre est fontana deitas. Unde si in divinis personis esset qui poneret prius et posterius, Pater esset primum principium. Sed quia ibi non est talis ordo, loco eius quod est primum, dicimus principio non de principio[123].

One must never think of the Father's *primitas* separated from the other divine Persons of whom He is the principle and Origin. For this reason, He is not the first principle, but the *principium non de principio*.

In revealing the mystery of the Trinity to us, the Lord made us participants in his *Abba* directed to the Father. All of Christian tradition, including Latin tradition, as we saw in citing Augustine, has accentuated the perfect paternity of the Father, noting that it has no before or after, that it is eternal, that the Father expresses himself perfectly in the Son, and that the Son is the perfect Image of the Father. God, the *Catechism of the Catholic Church* teaches following 1 Jn 4.8 and 16, 'is an eternal exchange of love'[124]. This is an exchange of knowledge and love that has its origin in the Father. It is to this origin and source that one must always look to contemplate the Trinity, as Saint Irenaeus already did in his *Epideixis*:

> Baptism gives us the grace of the new birth from God the Father by means of his Son in the Holy Spirit. Thus those who receive the Spirit of God are led to the Word, that is, to the Son. The Son presents them to the Father and the Father gives them incorruptibility[125]

## Ecumenical Perspectives

We have stopped at the important landmarks of the history of the theology of God the Father with the conviction that the questions that are raised regarding the procession of the Spirit, and specifically those relative to the *Filioque*, are best contextualized for a proper response within the global

---

[123] Thomas, *In I Sent.*, dist. 28, q. 1, a. 1 resp.
[124] CEC, n. 221.
[125] Irenaeus of Lyon, *Demonstration of the Apostolic Faith*, 7.

consideration of the Trinitarian mystery, and especially in the theology of the Father as the *fons et origo totius Trinitatis*.

Here, in the theology of the Father, there is a great convergence of the Orient and Occident. There are also different perspectives within Western theology – in theology and not in faith – especially between Saint Bonaventure and Saint Thomas. These variations mean that they both coincide, although in different ways, with the Oriental tradition and the different perspectives that are also found in it regarding the theology of the Father, and specifically regarding the Father's *agennesía* and the reason for his *primitas* and *plenitudo*. This outline of the history of the theology of the Father ended with the suggestion of always considering the questions regarding one divine Person – and the Holy Spirit in particular – in the entirety of the Trinitarian mystery.

Constantinople I, before the Pneumatomachists, attempted to dispel all doubt as to the divinity of the Holy Spirit. The question of the *Filioque* was not within the scope of the Council Fathers' preoccupations[126]. One can see this from something that clearly appears in many of the Fathers who were present at the Council: the Spirit is inseparable from the Son; He is the Spirit of the Son, in such a way that one can say that the Spirit proceeds from the Father by means of the Son[127]. This had already been written before the Council of Constantinople I by Gregory of Naziance and Gregory of Nyssa, whose presence was so decisive in the Council. As A. de Halleux has written, it would be abusive to consider the definition of Constantinople I as a solemn definition of *monopatrism* when the Cappadocians themselves admit the δι' υἱοῦ, through the Son[128].

Today, the teaching of the Council of Constantinople I is still an expression of the one common faith of the Church and of all Christianity. This Creed must be the locus where we all meet. The line maintained by Thomas Aquinas, according to which, if one profoundly affirms that the Spirit proceeds from the Father, one is affirming his procession from the Son at the same time, is highly consistent, because, in reference to spiration, the Father is not opposed to the Son[129] and the Son is not understood as a co-principle of spiration.

---

[126] Cf. B. Sesboüé, J. Wolinski, *El Dios de la salvación*, in B. Sesboüé (ed.), *Historia de los Dogmas*, I, p. 219.

[127] The formulation of this thought by J. D. Zizioulas is pertinent here: 'If, therefore, we are allowed to interpret *I Const.* in the light of Cappadocian Theology, we must conclude that the phrase *ek tou Patros*: a) does not exclude a mediating role of the Son in the procession of the Spirit; b) does not allow for the Son to acquire the role of *aition* by being a mediator' (J. D. Zizioulas, 'The Teaching of the 2nd Ecumenical Council on the Holy Spirit in Historical and Ecumenical Perspective', in J. Saraiva Martins (ed.), Credo in Spiritum Sanctum, I, *Libreria Editrice Vaticana*, Vaticano 1983, p. 44).

[128] A. de Halleux, 'La profession de l'Esprit Saint dans le Symbole de Constantinople', in Id., *Patrologie et oecumenisme*, Leuven: Peeters 1990; pp. 334–5.

[129] Thomas Aquinas, STh I, q. 36, a. 2, ad 2.

# PART TWO

# Modern Analytical Perspectives

# 5

# The Trinitarian Concept of Person

## Ángel Cordovilla Pérez

The classical concepts that we use to speak about God in theology, such as terms like mission, procession, relation, person or perichoresis, attempt to express something of the nature of the being and internal life of God, starting from the doctrine of analogy, in order to affirm the three central mysteries of Christianity: the Trinity, the Incarnation of God and the divinization of man. These concepts help us to understand better what it means to say that God is love, relation, communion and the fullness of life, and that, for this reason, He can enter into history without ceasing to be God. He can integrate it into himself without being emptied of his content and properties, thus raising it to his fullness[1]. The entire conceptual effort of Trinitarian theology throughout history to develop these categories was not a rhetorical exercise or a sterile conceptual pastime, neither was it an attempt to appropriate the reality of God with reason, nor a Hellenisation of the original message expressed in the New Testament, but rather the concrete expression of the desire to receive the revelation of the God of Jesus Christ in all of its truth and originality, as witnessed to in Sacred Scripture and confessed in the creeds of the ancient Church. The faithfulness and truth of this revelation, that is witnessed to in the Scriptures, presupposed an authentic revolution in the

---

[1] K. Rahner, 'Über den Begriff des Geheimnisses in der katholischen Theologie', in ibid., *Menschsein und Menschwerdung Gottes*, (Sämtliche Werke, 12), Freiburg-Basel-Wien: Herder 2005, pp. 132–6; ibid., 'Geheimnis II. Theologisch', (Sämtliche Werke, 12), pp. 238–9; ibid., *Grundkurs des Glaubens*, (Sämtliche Werke, 26), Freiburg-Basel-Wien: Herder 1999, pp. 135–6.

vision of God (theology), implied a transformation in the understanding of the human being (anthropology), and a decisive change in the ultimate perception of reality (metaphysics).

Beyond the precise etymological sense of the concept of person and its proper application in Trinitarian theology, the ultimate foundation of the value and dignity of the human being, as well as the ultimate understanding of reality, stands or falls with the Trinitarian concept of person. The German theologian Walter Kasper expressed himself clearly in this sense, in one of the best theological manuals of the twentieth century: 'Neither the ancient substance nor the modern subject are ultimate and decisive, but it is relation as the basic category of reality. The affirmation that the persons are relations is an affirmation of the Trinity of God, but from this comes something decisive about man as the image and likeness of God. Man is neither a self-sufficient "being in himself" (substance) nor an autonomous, individual, "being for himself" (subject), but a being that comes from God and goes to Him, who comes from men and goes to them. Man only truly lives humanly in the relations of I, you and us. *Love appears as the path of being*.'[2] This understanding of the persons in God represents a true challenge for the understanding of God's being itself: as love, relation, communion, fullness of life, internal fecundity, alterity, life, etc.; in the understanding of being as gift and love; and in the understanding of human being as constitutive gift and relation. The existing man has a dilemma before him: to understand himself from the Son[3] or from the animal[4]. In this matter the Trinitarian concept of person is decisive. It constitutes, as the Spanish philosopher Julián Marías has seen, the great contribution of Christianity to the history of the human spirit. It is its radical innovation and the distinctive element of the *Christian perspective*: 'There can certainly be *theological* difficulties in thinking of the mystery of the Trinity, above all if theology aligns itself with concepts that are foreign to Christianity, and it gets caught up in them. One cannot think of God as the "Supreme Being" that is barely personal as in the deist perspective. It is necessary to think of God *personally*, with all of the resources at our disposal. If one looks closely, some of them are very recent, and this is not a sufficient motive to renounce them. The incorporation of that which is *personal* into the Christian perspective is necessary.'[5]

---

[2] W. Kasper, *El Dios de Jesucristo*, Salamanca: Sigueme [4]1994, p. 330 (Orig. *Der Gott Jesu Christi*, Mainz 1982). Italics mine.

[3] Cf. M. Henry, *C'est moi la vérité. Pour une philosophie du christianisme*, Paris: Seuil 1996.

[4] Cf. P. Singer, *Unsanctifying Human Life: Essays on Ethics*, (H. Kuhse, ed.), Oxford: Blackwell 2001.

[5] J. Marías, *La perspectiva cristiana*, Madrid: Alianza 1999, p. 47. Author's italics.

# The Recovery of Analogy

One of the major acquisitions of contemporary Trinitarian theology is the recovery of the doctrine of analogy, as was magisterially expressed in the fourth Lateran Council (1215), which affirmed, in response to the Trinitarian theology of Joachim of Fiore, that the likeness that exists between the Creator and the creature is always to be expressed in the light of a greater dissimilitude[6]. As the larger Christian tradition has always known, the term *person* expresses an analogous concept, which requires at least three essential differences in its applications: a) when we speak of God and man; b) when we speak of God as personal being and when we refer to the divine persons; and c) when we speak of the concrete form of each of the divine persons: Father, Son and Holy Spirit. When we use the concept of person we must be aware that it does not have the same meaning if we are using it to refer to God and man; to Christology or Trinitarian studies; to the affirmation of a personal God or to each one of the divine persons – to the Father, the Son, or the Holy Spirit. However, in placing these three domains in relation through analogy, we do not only take the difference or dissimilitude into account, but also affinity and likeness. Although they are distinct domains that require different applications of the concept of person, they are profoundly related. They are related to the point that the use of the term person to speak of the being of God and his intra-divine life (Father-Son-Holy Spirit) becomes the guarantee of the affirmation of the personal character of God, and thus makes possible the affirmation of a God that is distinct from the world (transcendent), that can really enter into relation with it (immanence) and be the ultimate foundation of the personal character of every human being, created in the image and likeness of God. In this sense, to abandon the use of the term person in Trinitarian discourse to speak of the Father, the Son and the Holy Spirit would have numerous extremely negative consequences for understanding the manner in which Christianity thinks of the relation between God and the world, and the value that it accords to each and every human being.

The recovery of analogy requires us to think of this concept from another perspective. In speaking of person we seek to manifest a negative and affirmative theology at the same time. I am in full agreement with Gisbert Greshake when he maintains that the use of the concept of person in Trinitarian theology is a clear example of the interrelationship of apophatic and cataphatic theology, that is, it is a limiting concept for *negatively* stating that there is difference in God, and to say *positively*

---

[6] DH, 806: 'Inter creatorem et creatura non potest tanta similitudo notari, quin inter eos maior sit dissimilitudo notanda.'

that the content of this difference is relation, gift and communion[7]. From here we can situate the primary differences in contemporary Trinitarian theology: those who follow the classic affirmation of Augustine maintain that the concept of person does not tell us anything real about the being of God, but that it is used exclusively to show what is distinct in God, including for those who argue why it would be better to abandon it; and those who make this concept the principal centre of Trinitarian doctrine, in order to move from a theology centred in essence and unity to one that is centred in communion and alterity. This second group is aware that it must have a positive understanding of the concept of person, since it is not only a limiting or negative concept, but it itself 'signals a specific direction'. This direction is common, but the concrete content is lightly variegated: person is relation (C. E. Gunton; Ch. Schwöbel), communion (I. Zizioulas), reciprocity (W. Pannenberg, G. Greshake) or gift (H. U. von Balthasar; L. F. Ladaria). If the Trinitarian and anthropological concepts of person have been centred around the axis of incommunicability (I) throughout the centuries, it is now understood from that of relation (other). In a highly synthetic manner we can say that we have passed from identity to alterity. This displacement can be verified in the manner in which contemporary theology reads and recovers its own history (history of thought), confronts the difficult question of God's personal character (in the context of theological agnosticism and interreligious dialogue), and the concrete developments of contemporary Trinitarian theology centred in a renewed concept of person (relation, communion, reciprocity and gift).

# Questions Regarding the History of the Concept

Behind the modern concept of person, there are three classical terms with different connotations: Latin *persona*, Greek *prosopon* and Greek *hypostasis*. Before they were technical concepts referring to God, Christ and man, they were common terms with distinct, although not necessarily mutually exclusive, meanings[8]. While *persona* and *prosopon* are comparable terms, *hypostasis* in some manner breaks form with this similarity. The first terms refer to *vision* and the *form that appears before* others, while *hypostasis* refers to the concrete reality that *sustains* us and makes a reality be precisely what it is. The history of the concept of person is well known.

---

[7] G. Greshake, *El Dios uno y Trino. Una teología de la Trinidad*, Barcelona: Herder 2000, p. 85 (Orig. *Der dreieine Gott: eine trinitarische Theologie*, Freiburg-Basel-Wien: Herder 1997).
[8] B. Meunier (ed.), *La personne et le christianisme ancien*, Paris: Cerf 2006, p. 9.

Nevertheless, its interpretation and actuality is object of debate. We will briefly review the fundamental milestones of its history as well as certain more important aspects that are the object of a profound revision today.

# Etymological Reflections

Contemporary literature dedicated to the study of the etymological origin of the concept of *person* has posed two questions: Whether it comes from the world of theatre and whether its fundamental sense as applied to man is a Christian development. All the authors that have studied the etymological origin of the concept have encountered difficulty in determining its origin and its exact signification. Andrea Milano expressed it clearly when he spoke of an 'etymological enigma'[9], and Bernard Meunier recently did the same in referring to the 'obscure etymology of the concept'[10]. The Latin term signified a variety of things: role or character in theatre (Plautus, Terence); the person of the verb in grammar (Varro); or individual in a social sense (Cicero). The Greek term *prosopon* is already witnessed to in Homer with the meaning of 'face', comes to mean 'to gaze', then 'that which is seen', and will finish tied into the world of theatre in the Hellenistic period. Finally, the meaning of *hypostasis* is determined by its etymology. Composed of *hypo-* (under) and the root *sta* (to hold oneself), it originally had a common meaning of foundation, base, cement or point of departure for an expedition. It will be from the first century AD that the term will begin to have the abstract signification of existence, which will then quickly become the common meaning of the term[11]. Ancient Christian literature will adopt this second, more abstract, meaning.

Beyond its strict original meaning and its later development, it is clear that *prosopon* was immediately tied into the world of theatre, something that is used by various theologians with a specifically theological intention. Thus John Zizioulas, Henri de Lubac and Hans Urs von Balthasar have developed and explored the theological and anthropological consequences of this 'fabulous' or 'legendary' connection. For the Greek Orthodox theologian this relation is so close because 'it is in [Greek] theatre that man struggled to be a person, to raise himself against the harmonious unity that oppresses him (cosmos) as a rational and moral necessity. It is there that he struggled with the gods and with his destiny ... This same man, thanks to

---

[9] A. Milano, *Persona in teología. Alle origini del significato di persona nel cristianesimo antico*, Bologna: Dehoniane ²1996, pp. 63–6.

[10] B. Meunier, '"Persona" en latin classique', in Meunier, *La personne et le christianisme ancien*, pp. 23–8; here p. 23.

[11] Cf. ibid., '"Hupostasis" en grec clasique et hellénistique', in Meunier *La personne et le christianisme ancien*, pp. 163–9.

the same mask, also tasted the bitter consequences of his rebellion. Thanks to the mask, nevertheless, he became a person, even if he was thus for but a short time, and he learned what it means to live as a free, unique and unrepeatable being. The mask is in relation to the person, but this relation is tragic.'[12] The Swiss theologian Hans Urs von Balthasar used this tie to explain better the sense of his dramatic anthropology. Every human being, as a spiritual subject, is called by Christ to take up a vocation and to realize the mission entrusted to him by God in the world. Human life is an exercise of representation in the strong sense of the term: 'Greek *prosopon* originally meant "mask", and from this, the (fixed) "role" in the piece; and from this, one's role in life.'[13] This etymology permitted placing the categories of mission and drama at the centre of the understanding of person (Calderón de la Barca, H. de Lubac, Balthasar), so that person is the spiritual subject that presents a drama before God in the great theatre of the world in order to begin to be person in the full sense of the term; in this manner one moves from spiritual subject to the proper concept of personal being. 'To be a person is always to have a role, according to its ancient original meaning, that is however internalized – it is essentially to enter into relation with others to contribute to a Whole. The call to a personal life is a vocation, that is, it is a call to have an eternal role.'[14]

The second question regards the Christian specificity of prosopon. The term is not a Christian invention, since it exists in classical antiquity, as is witnessed to by pre-Christian sources. Christianity will adopt the term, but in its application to God and Christ this will not be without some difficulties, and only after recourse to analogy. Later, in its application to man created in God's image, the term will be given a new meaning[15]. It will permit a turn from thought that is centred in the cosmos and nature to one that is centred in the person, in the singular and unrepeatable individual. This will become the basis of law and the State in modern society, as well as the ultimate foundation, even if implicit, of the declaration of human rights[16]. In this sense one must listen to the radical and provocative expression of the Greek Orthodox theologian John Zizioulas when he affirms that 'the concept of person with its ontological, absolute content was historically

---

[12] I. Zizioulas, *El ser eclesial. Persona, comunión, Iglesia*, Salamanca: Sigueme 2003, pp. 46–7 (orig., *L'Être ecclésial*, Paris: Labor et Fides 1981).

[13] H. Urs von Balthasar, *Theodramatik*, II/2, *Die Personen des Spiels: Die Personen in Christus*, Einsiedeln: Johannes Verlag ²1998, p. 194.

[14] H. de Lubac, *Catolicismo. Aspectos sociales del dogma*, Madrid 1988, 233 (orig. *Catholicisme, les aspects sociaux du dogme*, Paris: Cerf 1938).

[15] Cf. I. Zizioulas, *El ser eclesial*, pp. 49–63.

[16] Cf. H. U. von Balthasar, *Theologik*, III, *Der Geist der Wahrheit*, Einsiedeln: Johannes Verlag 1987, p. 238: 'Society and State ultimately rest on the reciprocal recognition of personal dignity and rights. This is a thought that was introduced into history only by Christianity. It is on this that the entire Hegelian philosophy of law is founded.'

born from the Church's project of giving ontological expression to its faith in the Triune God.'[17] We can say that there is a certain consensus today in affirming that although the concept of person was not an *ex novo* creation of Christianity, the contribution made by Christianity in its elaboration was both decisive and fundamental for its understanding. Since it was capable of uniting (Greek) *hypostasis* and *prosopon* as well as (Latin) *individuo* and *persona*, it made possible and developed a new understanding of God, of man and of the world that is centred in personalism, in love and in relation.

# The Technical Understanding of the Christological and Trinitarian Controversies of the Third and Fourth Centuries

The Greek term *prosopon*, although already found in Justin and prosopographical exegesis[18], is used for the first time by Hippolytus in a strictly Trinitarian sense to indicate the individual subsistence of the Father and Son[19]. Before Noetus' Monarchism, while commenting on the celebrated passage of Jn 10.30, 'I and the Father are One', Hippolytus defends the personal duality of the Father and Son without affirming two principles of activity, or two gods, for this reason (*due prosopa, mia dynamis*)[20]. The Latin term *persona* was introduced into theological writings by Tertullian, in his treatise *Adversus Praxean*, in part because it was a term to which the Monarchians were opposed[21]. For Tertullian, *persona* primary expresses a *speaking subject* (*Ad Prax* 5) that is manifested in its *responsible action* (*Ad Prax* 12, 3). The term person designates plurality, number and distinction in God (*distinctio trinitatis, Ad Prax* 11, 4). Although the technical theological sense that will be found in the fourth century begins to be sketched, the term is nevertheless used in its then current, concrete sense[22]. Although Tertullian does not naturally use the expression *three persons and one substance*[23], he does however set the foundations for the formula: 'one unique substance

---

[17] I. Zizioulas, *El ser eclesial*, p. 49.

[18] Justin, *Dialogus* 88; 1 *Apologia* 36.

[19] Cf. M. Simonetti, 'Commento 7,1', in Hippolytus, *Contro Noeto*, edited by Manlio Simonetti, Bologna 2000, pp. 217–18.

[20] Hippolytus, *Contra Noetum*, 7, 1: '"We are" is not said of one, but it gave knowledge of two persons, but only one power.' Cf. *CN* 14,3: 'The Father is only one, but the persons are two, because also the Son exists and as a third there is also the Holy Spirit.'

[21] B. Studer, 'Persona', in *Diccionario Patrístico de la Antigüedad Cristiana* II, Salamanca: Sígueme 1998, pp. 1768–9; ibid., 'Der Person-Begriff in der frühen kirchenamtlichen Trinitätslehre', in *Theologie und Philosophie* 57 (1982) 168–77.

[22] G. Scarpat, 'Introduzione', in Tertullian, *Contro Prassea*, Critical Edition by G. Scarpat, Turin 1985, 7–122, esp. pp. 84–5.

[23] An expression that is fairly present in his work *De pudicitia* 21, 16: 'The Church itself is

in three that remain joined' (*Ad Prax* 12, 7). Despite this, Tertullian takes a decisive step for the use of this concept for the Son in order to explain that He is, while proceeding from the Father, before Him as 'a subsisting reality in virtue of the property of the substance, in such a way that He can be considered a thing and in some way a person.' (*Ad Prax* 7, 5)[24]. Origen, for his part, gives theological significance to the term *hypostasis* while speaking of the Father, the Son and the Holy Spirit. In his Commentary on the Gospel of John, he speaks for the first time of *three hypostases*, 'three subsisting realities, the Father, the Son, and the Spirit'[25]. In this manner, we have three concepts for the term person: two Greek ones, *hypostasis* and *prosopon*, and a Latin one, *persona*. In Greek theology the term *hypostasis* will triumph, partially by contrasting it with the idea included in *prosopon*. Latin theology will use the term *persona* (which was normally used with the sense of *prosopon*), understood here in the sense of *hypostasis*.

In the fourth century, among their Trinitarian controversies, will be found one of the most important events for theology and, through it, for human thought in general. This event is the union of the concepts of hypostasis and persona[26]. With Basil of Caesarea the terms of *hypostasis* and *prosopon* emerge as technical concepts of Trinitarian theology[27]. Before Marcellus of Ancyra, who is considered to be a new Sabellius, Basil will defend the confession of *tria prosopa* in order to express plurality in God, without however mentioning the term hypostasis[28]. Later on, he will feel the need to use the term *hypostasis* in the same sense, distinguishing it from the term *ousia* in reaction to the modalist position of Marcellus of Ancyra, who identified *ousia* and *hypostasis*, as well as to the ambiguity of certain of the extreme defenders of the faith of Nicaea such as Paul of Antioch[29].

---

properly the Spirit itself in which there is the Trinity of a unique Divinity (*trinitas unius divinitatis*), The Father, the Son, and the Holy Spirit.'

[24] Cf. G. Uríbarri, *La emergencia de la Trinidad inmanente. Hipólito y Tertuliano*, Madrid: Universidad Comillas 1999, p. 131: 'The word "person" first of all designates a reality capable of breaking God's solitude, and is thus with a certain individuality. It was already perceived that this individuality, properly understood, could exhibit those characteristics that are compatible with monotheism, even if this is not what occurs with the Valentinian Gnostics. Later on, in *Adversus Praxean*, Tertullian will make more precise his concept of person, considering it, and specifically for the case of the Son, as the quality of substantiality, and understanding it as a "res substantiva" (Ad Prax 7, 5) that is really capable of producing an authentic duality.'

[25] Origen, *Commentary on St John* I, Book II, X, 75; also in *De principiis* I, 2, 6, 168; *Contra Celsum* VIII,12; Cf. C. Blanc, 'Apéndice IX', Origen, *Commenaire sur S Jean* I, Texte critique par Céline Blanc, SCh 120 bis, Paris: Cerf 1996, 406.

[26] I. Zizioulas, *El ser eclesial*, p. 50.

[27] Cf. S. M. Hildebrandt, *The Trinitarian Theology of Basil of Caesarea. A Synthesis of Greek Thought and Biblical Truth*, Washington: CUA Press 2007, pp. 82–92.

[28] Hildebrandt, *The Trinitarian Theology of Basil of Caesarea*, pp. 83–4. The author's basis is Basil's Homily 24, composed circa 372.

[29] Hildebrandt, *The Trinitarian Theology of Basil of Caesarea*, p. 84. Basil mentions this error

In *Epistle* 214, Basil clearly expresses the inconsistency of Paul's position, and recommends using the content of the concept of *hypostasis* in order to understand the precise meaning of the term *prosopon*, in this distinguishing *hypostasis* from the term *ousia*. A person (*prosopon*) without subsistence (*anhypostatica*) would be an absurdity. The persons must subsist in a true personality (*hypostasis*)[30]. While *hypostasis* presents the true sense of the word *prosopon*, the first term is to be understood as the combination of *ousia* and *idioma*, that is, being and personal property[31].

At the risk of falling into generalities, we can say that *hypostasis* is a term closer to substance, as it expresses the concrete subsistence of a reality, while *prosopon* refers to its external aspect, its mode of appearance. *Hypostasis* literally signifies the reality that is beneath, sustaining a reality so that it is this and not that; while *prosopon*, composed of the preposition '*pros*' which means towards and '*upon*' which means that which is seen, will then derive a meaning of external aspect, role and mask[32]. From this the strong metaphysical connotation of the concept of hypostasis will be reciprocally melded with the idea of visibility and manifestation that is linked to the concept of prosopon. The possibility of a modalist derivation from the term of *prosopon* is avoided by the bestowal of an ontological and metaphysical density to it through the term *hypostasis*. In this way, Trinitarian theology of the fourth century avoided, at least terminologically, the possibility of a tritheistic or modalist derivation. However, the decisive importance of that which we have henceforth presented is not only to be found in the domain of Trinitarian theology; it has further influence. This identification implies two fundamental affirmations for the understanding of God, and of all reality from Him: in the first place, person is not an addendum to being, rather, it is the hypostasis of being itself; in second place, the person is converted into being itself. Person is the constitutive element of beings. Beings do not owe their being to (abstract) being, but to person, which is that which constitutes being[33].

From these developments of Trinitarian theology the foundations will be laid for a new understanding of reality centred in what is personal, in front of a world that until then had been centred on *physis* and the rule of necessity[34]. The ontology or metaphysics of the person will become

---

in Ep. 125.

[30] Hildebrandt, *The Trinitarian Theology of Basil of Caesarea*, pp. 88–9.

[31] Hildebrandt, *The Trinitarian Theology of Basil of Caesarea*, p. 91.

[32] N. Tanner, 'Greek Metaphysics and the Early Church', in *Gregorianum* 90 (2009) 51–7; esp. 55.

[33] Zizioulas, *El ser eclesial*, p. 50.

[34] Cf. S. Álvarez Turienzo, 'El Cristianismo y la formación del concepto de persona', in: *Homenaje a X. Zubiri* I, Madrid 1971, 42–77; esp. 45–51; G. Amengual, *Antropología filosófica*, Madrid 2007, 210–11.

the keystone of the understanding of reality, as was already understood by one of the best synthetic minds of the Patristic era, Maximus the Confessor, even if the centre of his thought is more Christological than Trinitarian, since it is centred in the Chalcedonian synthesis[35]. After having contributed by improving the systematization of the concepts of *physis* and *hypostasis*, bestowing on them a range of technical senses in Trinitarian and Christological language, Maximus' contribution was decisive for the step that will be made by the medieval period and finalized in the modern period: the passage from the ontological understanding of person to the psychological one, centred in being, self-awareness and liberty[36].

## The Definitions of the Medieval Period

Following the use of person in Trinitarian theology and Christology, attempts at terminological clarification were born. We will briefly recall the three most significant definitions found in the theology of the medieval period (Boethius, Richard of St Victor and Thomas Aquinas) from the perspectives made possible by the latest studies that cast a new light on this period, which is so fruitful and rich for theology, thanks to the more balanced vision of medieval theology that has been developed in recent years.

In the first place, we must take into account the definition developed by *Boethius*, who followed the language and method of Aristotle's book of the *Categories* and Porphyry's *Isagogue*[37]. It is not the only definition. We could speak of variations around a concept[38]. There is however no doubt that this definition found in his *Theological Treatise against the Doctrine of Eutyches and Nestorius* is the most important due to the history of its effects, particularly through the critical reception that it received by authors such as Richard of St Victor and Thomas Aquinas in order to use it as a Trinitarian concept. It reads: 'If person is only in substances, and only in those that are rational, and if substance is a nature that is not in the universal but is found in the individual, the definition of person has

---

[35] Cf. H. U. von Balthasar, *Kosmische Liturgie. Das Weltbild Maximus des Bekenners*, Einsiedeln: Johannes Verlag ³1988, pp. 47–67; A. Cordovilla, *Gramática de la encarnación. La creación en Cristo en la teología de K. Rahner y H. U. von Balthasar*, Madrid: Universidad Comillas 2004, pp. 232–41.

[36] Milano, *Persona in teologia*, pp. 190–210; esp. 192.

[37] Cf. C. Schlapkohl, *Persona est naturae rationabilis individua substantiva. Boethius und die Debatte über den Personbegriff*, Marburg 1999, pp. 199–217; J. Marenbon, *Boethius*, Oxford: Oxford University Press 2003, pp. 70–6; J. Marenbon (ed.), *The Cambridge Companion to Boethius*, Cambridge: Cambridge University Press 2009, esp. pp. 105–78.

[38] M. Nedoncelle, 'Les Variations de Boèce sur la personne', in *Revue des sciences réligieuses* 29 (1955) 201–38.

been found: "individual substance of a rational nature."[39] We find the definition in a short Christological treatise that aims to discuss the validity, from a philosophical perspective, of the Church's solution of two natures and one person in Christ, by analysing the concepts of nature and person. Nevertheless, we cannot forget that Boethius offers his definition for the person of Christ in both the Nestorian and Monophysite controversies, and particularly against Nestorius, who does not correctly distinguish nature and person[40].

What, however, is the context in which we find this famous definition? Boethius first confronts the definition of the concept of nature, of which he offers us three definitions: '*natura est earum rerum quae, cum sint, quoquo modo intellectu capi posunt*' (OSV, 1,67–8); '*natura est vel quod facere vel quod pati possit*' (OSV, 1,81–2); '*natura est motus principium per se non per accidens*' (OSV, 1,99–100). None of these definitions is useful for his definition of person. He therefore offers us another one, which will be a base for his definition: '*natura est unam quamque rem informans specifica differentia*' (OSV, 1,111–12)[41]. In the second chapter, he begins his argumentation for the definition of the concept of person using the Aristotelian system as found in Porphyry's version (tree) of the classification of *species* and *genus*. According to the Aristotelian-Porphyrian system, things are categorized according to whether or not they belong to the primary categories, and whether they are individual or universal. In this view, Boethius understands person as an individual substance. This is to say that it belongs to the order of primary categories, and to those that are individual. Person is thus an individual substance. Our author however immediately adds something more. This is its specific difference. *Difference* belongs to species, among which there are two fundamental groups: corporeal and incorporeal. There are corporeal rational substances, e.g. man, and incorporeal rational

---

[39] Boethius, *Opuscula theologica*, V, *Contra Eutychen et Nestorium* 3, 168–72 (OSV, 3, pp. 168–72): 'Quocirca si persona in solis substantiis est atque in his rationabilibus, substantiaque omnis natura est nec in universalibus sed in individuis constat, reperta personae est definition: "naturae rationabilis individua substantia"', ed. C. Moreschini, *De consolatione philosophie. Opuscula theologica*, (Bibliotheca Teubneriana), Munich ²2005, p. 214. English translation in Boethius, *Theological Tractates*, London–Cambridge 1973, pp. 84–5: 'Wherefore if person belongs to substance alone, and these rational, and if every substance is a nature, and exists not in universals but in individuals, we have found the definition of person: "The individual substance of a rational nature."'

[40] Boethius uses the term person 96 times: 89 in the *Treatise Against Eutyches*, four in *Utrum Pater*, one in the *De Trinitate* treatise and twice in *De fide catholica*. Cf. M.-É. Bély, '"Persona" dans le traité théologique "Contra Eutiquès et Nestorius" de Boèce', in Meunier, *La personne et le Christianisme ancien*, pp. 245–78; esp. p. 277.

[41] 1. 'Nature belong to those things which, since they exist, can in some way be apprehended by the intellect' (79); 2. 'Nature is either that which can act or that which can be acted' (79); 3. 'Nature is the principle of movement, per se and not accidental' (81); 4. 'Nature is the specific difference that gives form to anything' (81).

substances, e.g. God and the angels. These all belong to the definition of person, so that Boethius seeks a definition that can include God, man and the angels. The great advantage of this definition is precisely that it can be applied to God and men, although it will be undoubtedly necessary to pay a high price, since it implies that the persons of the Trinity, like men, belong to the primary categories, and in some way should be classified inside the Aristotelian categories. Nevertheless, Boethius will attempt to show how this definition of person can be applied to God without it requiring to insert Him into the primary Aristotelian categories or to understand Him as some likeness of them[42]. After giving the definition of person, he offers us a series of etymological meanings of the word person and its equivalents in Greek, in which he makes the following equations: *ousia=essentia*; *ousiosis=subsistentia*; *hypostasis=substantia*; *prosopon=persona* (OSV 3, 243–50). Applied to God, Boethius will say that God is essence, since He is of the special form because the being of all things proceeds from Him; He is subsisting, because He subsists in absolute independence; He is one essence (*ousia*) and three substances (*hypostasis*) 'One essence of the Trinity, three substances and three persons' (OSV 3, 255–8).

Going beyond the immediate context in which Boethius developed this definition, there is currently a consensus that we encounter there three essential characteristics: substantiality, individuality and rationality. He defines the person from an ontological perspective, but this does not mean he does it from the essence or nature. Person is the 'always singular, total and undivided, immediate and unsubstitutable act, the reality or existence of a spiritual nature. This reality is the fact of possessing oneself in oneself, and thus to have one's end in oneself. It is the form of reality that presents the liberty of a spiritual being, in which its intangible dignity is founded'[43]; it 'is characterized by the existence for self (subsistence), an irreducible and absolutely singular manner (individual), with the liberty of action that corresponds to it essentially (intellectual nature)'[44]. For Boethius, the distinctive aspect of person is its singularity and irreducibility. We could say in a somewhat anachronistic manner that, for him, person is an absolute in itself. It is not far from Kant's anthropological vision when, in underscoring the autonomy of the subject, he affirms that every man, by the simple fact of being one, is an end in himself, although the root from which this is affirmed is radically different. I believe that it is from this point of view that his definition should be evaluated, along with the history of its consequences in medieval theology and philosophy.

---

[42] Marenbon, *Boethius*, pp. 71–2.
[43] M. Müller, 'Person', in K. Rahner (ed.), *Sacramentum Mundi 5*, Barcelona 1985, pp. 444–56; esp. pp. 444–5.
[44] G. Emery, *La théologie trinitaire de saint Thomas d'Aquin*, Paris: Cerf 2004, p. 133.

This evaluation does not prevent us from being conscious of its limitations, which originate from its foundation in the Aristotelian philosophical system. It is not capable of giving an importance to relation, a central category for the definition of person in Trinitarian theology, as we will later see with Thomas Aquinas, and as was anticipated by the Cappadocian fathers in the Christian Orient and by Augustine in the Occident. Nevertheless, Boethius is not oblivious to the need to describe a certain plurality, alterity and relation in God, as he affirms in his short treatise *De Trinitate* 'For the principle of plurality is otherness; for apart from otherness plurality is unintelligible.'[45] This plurality does not include multiplying the divine essence to constitute three gods, and there is no multiplicity in it that comes from the accidents either[46]. Our author both knows and uses the term of *relatio* to speak of the Trinity, so that he can say that while substance contains unity, relation forms the Trinity (*'substantia continet unitatem, relatio multiplicat trinitaten'*)[47]. This is certainly a context in which he uses the term of person[48].

It is however noteworthy that our author does not give this category a larger role in his definition of person[49]. Unfortunately, when Boethius speaks of person, he does not use relation in more decisive manner, and when he speaks of relation, the concept of person does not appear clearly. In fact, the use of the concept of *relatio* for the Trinitarian persons is more logical than ontological. It is in this sense that some have spoken of an 'unfortunate and decisive reduction'[50] in his definition that led to an excess of individualism and intellectualism, which, although not directly tied to Boethius' definition, has been tied to his followers' application of it[51]. If Boethius primarily understands and explains person as an individuality, he is in fact defining it more for the 'what' than the 'who', two realities that are closely related but that cannot be confused. The who of the person needs to integrate the what of individuality and nature, but the what cannot specify

---

[45] Boethius, *Opuscula theologica* I, 1, 15: 'Principium enim pluralitatis alteritas est; praeter alteritatem enim nec pluralitas quid sit intellegi potest.'

[46] Boethius, *Opuscula theological* I, 3.

[47] Boethius, *Opuscula theologica* I, 6, 339. Section 5 of this treatise is dedicated to the analysis of the concept of relation taken from Augustine's *De Trinitate*.

[48] Boethius, *Opuscula theologica* I, 5,

[49] Book V of Augustine's *De Trinitate* is one of the texts that Boethius studies with most attention and care, as can be appreciated in *Opuscula theologica* I (*De Trinitate*) and II (*Utrum Pater et Filius*). The latter is a synthesis of one aspect of this teaching of Augustine, as well as a development of the Bishop of Hippo's doctrine. Cf. Marenbon, *Boethius*, pp. 77–8; 82–7.

[50] J. Ratzinger, 'Zum Personenverständnis in der Theologie', in *Theologie und Verkündigung*, München-Freiburg 1973, 225. Cf. R. Spaemann, *Personen. Versuche über den Unterschied zwischen 'etwas' und 'jemanden', Menschen und ihre Identität*, Stuttgart: Klett-Cotta 1996.

[51] C. E. Gunton, *The Promise of Trinitarian Theology*, Edinburgh: T&t Clark 1991, p. 92: 'The syndrome of intellectualism and individualism found in Boethius'.

and determine the sense of the who. This is true above all of relation[52]. We can thus say that the unfortunate and decisive reduction to which Ratzinger referred is the reduction of the person to their individuality, without taking into account their relative and ecstatic dimension, as well as the reduction to its rational capacity, without taking into account other elements that are substantial for the personal being, even though rationality cannot be reduced to the capacity of the intellect, but is to be understood as the faculty of intellectual knowledge and spiritual life. Nevertheless, the element of individuality and incommunicability, which is clearly affirmed in the definition, cannot be denied. For all of our emphasis on relation in the definition of person, without an affirmation of substantiality, however it is understood, the understanding of person runs the risk of losing itself by opening into a pure actualism[53].

In conclusion, for Boethius 'person is characterized by existence for itself (subsistence), in an irreducible and absolutely singular manner (individual), with the liberty of action that corresponds to it by nature (intellectual nature). All of these characteristics found the dignity of the person. When it is applied to God, this definition will guarantee the divinity of the three persons (divine intellectual nature) against Arianism, as well as their proper subsistence (individual substance) against Sabellianism, and will also found its activity (individual intelligent and free substance).'[54]

Secondly, Richard of St Victor knows Boethius' definition and uses it as a foundation of his thought, but he transforms it on the basis of his own Trinitarian theology, because this definition for him runs the risk of 'conceiving the divine substance as a person'[55]. He places the affirmation of 1 Jn 4.8, 16 'God is love' at the centre of his theological reflection. For Richard, if God is the Good in its greatest fullness and consummation, He is also the fullness and consummation of love. This is a love that can only be understood from the reality of dialogue, and ultimately of Trinity. That is to say, for the Augustinian Regular Canon, love in itself is not the full face of love. This is found only through the relation with a you (Gregory the Great: 'There is no *caritas* between less than two'[56]). For this reason, divine love requires that there be two divine persons in order to be considered love in fullness: 'The fullness of love only exists when there are more persons in God.' (*De Trin.* III, 2). We must however add that Richard's dialogical understanding of love is not the model of the fullness of love. For this to be a fullness, the presence of a third who is loved in the communion of the two is required, and the inclination of the two sides must unite in the flame

---

[52] J. L. Ruiz de la Peña, *Antropología teológica*, Santander: Sal Terrae 1988, p. 165.
[53] Ruiz de la Peña, *Antropología teológica*, p. 164.
[54] Emery, *La théologie trinitaire de saint Thomas d'Aquin*, p. 133.
[55] Emery, *La théologie trinitaire de saint Thomas d'Aquin*, p. 137.
[56] Gregory the Great, *Homiliae in Evangelium*, 17,1.

of love for the third (*De Trin.* III, 19). It is only in a third understood as *condilectus* (conjoint love) that the fulfilment of love is reached (*consummatio caritatis*)[57].

How does our author explain the logic and dialectic of love in the intra-Trinitarian life? In the first place, in order to avoid falling into a tritheism, one must transform the concept of person transmitted by the Boethian tradition[58]. According to Richard's understanding of God from the logic of love, if one applies the definition as it is, there is the risk of affirming three distinct substances, that is, three gods. His new definition reads: '*persona divina sit divinae naturae incomunicabilis exsistentia.*'[59] Persons are no longer nature (*aliquid*), but the manner of having nature, its origin (*aliquis*). In order to underscore this *who* of the personal nature, Richard performs a series of significant changes to Boethius' definition. In the first place, he substitutes the adjective *rational* with *divine*. While Boethius' definition could seem to be attributable analogously from man to God, Richard's refers exclusively to divine persons. In the second place, he changes the expression of *individua* for *incommunicabilitas*, accentuating the principle of individuation that distinguishes the persons, that is, *exsistere*, which is incommunicable in turn. Although that which Boethius wishes to say with individual substance is the same as that which Richard says with the incommunicability of persons, the latter attempts to underscore the singular, irreducible and non-transferable character of each of the persons[60]. Precisely for this reason, in the third place, Richard substitutes the term *substantia* by *existentia*, introducing the relative character of person directly into the definition itself by the substitution of substance for *exsistentia,* which implicates the substantial reality (*sistentia*) in its origin (*ex*). Following the traditional perspective, Richard affirms that person is a substantial reality which is determined by its incommunicability, that is, by the unique and non-transferable (*incomunicabilis*) form that each one is, and possesses the common nature (*sistentia*) from a common origin (*ex*). The person is not formally a nature, a what, without a who, but is defined by the manner of being this nature[61].

---

[57] F. Courth, 'Trinität in der Scholastik', in *Handbuch der Dogmengeschichte* II/1b, Freiburg 1985, 61–7; M. Schniertschauer, *Consummatio Caritatis. Eine Untersuchung zu Richard von St Victors De Trinitate*, Tübingen 1995; P. Cacciapuoti, '*Deus existentia amoris*'. *Teologia della carità e teologia della Trinità negli scritti di Ricardo di Vittore*, Paris-Turnhout: Brepols 1997; M. Mühling-Schlapkohl, *Gott ist Liebe: Studien zum Verständnis der Liebe als Modell des trinitarischen Redens von Gott*, Marburg 2000.

[58] Richard of St Victor, *De Trinitate* IV, 21 (SChr 63, 279–81).

[59] Ibid., *De Trinitate* IV, 22 (SChr 63, 280). Cf. N. den Bok, *Communicating the Most High. A Systematic Study of Person and Trinity in the Theology of Richard of St Victor*, Paris-Turnhout: Brepols 1996.

[60] G. Emery, *La théologie trinitaire de saint Thomas d'Aquin*, pp. 137–8.

[61] Cf. G. Salet, 'Notes complémentaires', in Richard de Saint-Victor, *La trinité*, Paris 1999, pp. 487–9.

In addition, from this definition, Richard of St Victor will be able to affirm in book V, when he studies the processions, that each divine person is distinguished by its manner of loving, that each person is identical to its love, and that *each person is its love*[62]. Thus the *Father* is the origin without origin of the intra-divine love. He is pure love that gives itself. The *Son* is love that receives and also gives and offers. The *Spirit* is pure love that only receives. The Father is love as pure gift, the Son is love as reception and gift, and the Spirit is love as pure reception[63]. God is charity, and 'this love is realized in three different manners in God: the Father as original and purely gratuitous love, the Son as received love that expands, and the Spirit as simply received love. In this mystery of mutual love it must be affirmed that everything is common to the persons, since each of them offers that which it has to the others. Without a doubt, they are each distinct: only the Father is pure giver (origin), only the Spirit is simply received, and only the Son is in the centre, as He who receives and offers at once.'[64] We owe this beautiful formula to Richard, which makes it possible to think at once of unity, plurality and consummation in God: *'In Padre origo unitatis, in Filio inchoatio pluralitatis, in Spiritu Sancto completio trinitatis.'*[65]

This was one of the changes most underscored by later theology, as well as most commented in contemporary theology, since it accentuates the perspectives of *relation* and *communion in love* in order to understand the divine persons. If Richard's theology was overlooked in theological thinking due to the influence of Augustinian-Thomistic Trinitarian theology, it then took on a central place in contemporary theologies that attempt to understand the Trinity as interpersonal communion. Two items must however be noted in respect to this conception of the Augustinian Canon, in order to avoid falling into 'a premature modernization of Richard's thought'[66]. In the first place, Richard does not use the concept of relation more than once. It is therefore not a term with a central and separate position as it is now. His influence is therefore more inspirational than mimetic. In second place, if one admits that, without using the concept, Richard moved from a more ontological concept of the person to a more relative one, he does not give it exactly the same signification as is currently underscored in this dimension of relativity, since Richard clearly refers to relations of origin, while today

---

[62] Richard of St Victor, *De Trinitate* V, XX: 'Ipsum persona sua quod dilecto sua. [...] Quoniam ergo quaelibet persona est idem quod amor suus' (SChr 63, 352).
[63] Courth, *Trinität in der Scholastik*, 67.
[64] X. Pikaza, 'La Trinidad como misterio de Dios', in O. González de Cardedal (ed.), *Introducción al cristianismo*, Madrid 1994, 257.
[65] Richard of St Victor, *De tribus appropiatis personis in Trinitate*, in *Opuscules théologiques*, ed. J. Ribaillier, Paris 1967, 184.
[66] G. Emery, *La théologie trinitaire de saint Thomas d'Aquin*, p. 137, note 2. He supports himself in this study by N. den Bok, who is cited in note 58.

those authors who support this perspective do it precisely in order to surpass this type of archaeological-relative understanding (processions) for one that is relative-communional (perichoresis).

Finally, Thomas Aquinas knows the definitions of Boethius and Richard. While he is aware of the difficulties of the theologians of the twelfth century in respect of the definition of the first, Aquinas opts to use the definition of the Roman theologian as the starting point for his reflection on the divine persons. On this point he distances himself from Albert the Great and Bonaventure, who accept both Richard's criticism and his definition. Thomas Aquinas 'holds that Boethius' definition, as long as it is understood correctly, is fitting for God.'[67]

Why should he prefer Boethius' definition to Richard's? This is because while Boethius' definition can be used to speak of God and man (in analogy), Richard's is only applicable to God. After analysing Trinitarian language and establishing the necessary equivalences between the Greek and Latin terms, Thomas confesses and recognizes with the Councils of the Church that in God there are three distinct subsistent Ones in the unity of the divine substance. In order to describe these three subsistent Ones, the Church used the terms *hypostasis* and *persona*. What does this expression mean when we apply it to God? In order to respond to this question, Thomas develops his doctrine of *subsisting relation*, which has been rightfully considered 'the synthesis of his speculative Trinitarian theology'[68]. Thomas' synthesis is found in *quaestio* 29 of the first part of the *Summa Theologiae*[69]: 'The divine person thus signifies relation as subsisting. And this is to signify relation in the manner of the substance that is the subsisting hypostasis in the divine nature; although the subsistor in the divine nature is nothing other than the divine nature.'[70] And later: 'The divine persons are the subsisting relations themselves.'[71] Without renouncing the ontological perspective in the definition of person, Thomas resolves the aporia that had been a stumbling block for Augustine and subsequent medieval theology. Moving beyond the essentialist position of Augustine and his followers, he will follow the path opened by William of Auxerre, who affirmed that person principally signifies relation, and indirectly the divine essence. Relation is not an accident, but is the divine essence itself, and for this reason is subsisting, as the divine essence subsists. The divine person is relation insofar as this relation subsists. Both Boethius' individual substance and Richard's incommunicable existence are understood as relation insofar as subsisting. That which is incommunicable and non-transferable consti-

---

[67] Emery, *La théologie trinitaire de saint Thomas d'Aquin*, p. 138.
[68] Emery, *La théologie trinitaire de saint Thomas d'Aquin*, p. 142.
[69] Cf. Emery, *La théologie trinitaire de saint Thomas d'Aquin*, pp. 141–56.
[70] Thomas Aquinas, STh I, q. 29, a. 4.
[71] STh I, 40, 2.

tutes the persons, and this is identified with the *relations*, which are relations of origin. The persons are not prior to the relations. The persons are constituted by the relations. There is not a pre-existing substrate for gift and relation. They are in so far as they are reciprocally relative. Relation unites and distinguishes at the same time. The unity of God is not that of a solitary, but that of a perfect communion. The being of God is identified with relation, and is an eternal exchange of love: relation, in so far as it is a divine reality, is the essence itself. God's being is love. This presupposes a co-dignity of the three persons; a same love that is possessed in a different manner by each of them; it also presupposes distinction. With Thomas Aquinas it is absolutely clear that there is no pre-existing substrate of the Father, the Son and the Holy Spirit, whose being is reciprocal gift or communion in love.

The rereading of medieval Trinitarian theology realized in the current investigation gives us the results of the rehabilitation of Boethius' definition, understanding it in its proper perspective, with its possibilities and its limits. It assumes the term person without problems, and converts it into a concept that is essentially synthetic, giving it a new semantic value with an accentuation of the value of individuality, which opens a path for its use in theological anthropology. Its greatest originality has been understood from the perspective that 'it developed for the first time a systematic theory of the equivalence of the terms hypostasis = persona = substantia = prosopon.'[72] Secondly, it attributes the proper role to the theology of Richard of St Victor, from the actualization of his theology of interpersonal love in order to understand the Trinity and the importance of relation in the definition of person, although some authors rightfully warn us to avoid prematurely *modernizing* his theology and contributions. Finally, although nobody has lost sight of this locus, the studies of the Trinitarian theology of Thomas Aquinas that follow show the genius of the Dominican theologian. Although the Trinitarian doctrine in the Summa of Theology turns around the concept of substance, Thomas' great contribution is the definition of the Trinitarian persons as subsisting relations, thus placing the foundations for what will henceforth be called a relational ontology centred in the person. A good synthesis of this positive side of medieval theology, integrating the richness and multiplicity of models that we find in various authors, can be found in the definition offered by L. Oening-Hanhoff: '*Persona est modus existendi rationalis essentiae ad alium et in alio.*'[73] This definition of the Trinitarian concept of person recapitulates, in a balanced manner, the

---

[72] Bély, '"Persona" dans le traité théologique'. 'Contra Eutiquès et Nestorius' de Boèce', p. 277.
[73] L. Oening-Hanhoff, 'Trinitarische Ontologie und Metaphysik der Person', in W. Breuning (Hrsg.), *Trinität. Aktuelle Perspektiven der Theologie*, (QD), Freiburg: Herder 1984, pp. 143–82, esp. p. 162. Cf. the commentary of E. Salmann, *Neuzeit und Offenbarung. Studien zur trinitarischen Analogik des Christentums*, Rome 1986, pp. 307–8.

fluctuating history of the interpretation of this concept, underscoring at once the importance of essence, rationality, reflexivity, incommunicability and relation as essential characteristics of the Trinitarian persons.

# The Psychological Turn of Modern Philosophy

Modernity includes a decisive change for Trinitarian doctrine. In this epoch, there was a fundamental shift that would be the cause of a loss of vitality in Trinitarian doctrine. From this period, in general, it would be considered an incomprehensible enigma (Goethe), a useless doctrine for the sphere of human life and action (Kant), or a theological metaphysics without any clear salvific value. The seventeenth century marks the decisive turn for the understanding of this doctrine. It was a century obsessed with the reality of God, but also tempted to domesticate his transcendence[74]. What are the causes of this progressive marginalization and irrelevance of Trinitarian doctrine? In the first place, it was the loss of the *meaning of analogy*, to the profit of a univocality in discussion of God. However, since the Trinity cannot be adequately expressed in univocal language, this recognition was converted into something difficult and obscure. The materialism that reigned in the theory of knowledge (Thomas Hobbes) would accentuate this problem. Secondly, we must understand which concept of person is being used. The so-called anthropological turn of modern philosophy supposes a lack of continuity in reflection on the concept of person since 'it stops being an ontological greatness to be reduced to a psychological datum.'[75]

'With Descartes a path to a new concept begins to open up: it is no longer defined in respect to autonomy in being, but in reference to self-knowledge.'[76] This will be a challenge and a problem for the application of the concept of person to God. Although the concept in its deepest sense, as we saw above, was born in the Trinitarian debate, and from there was extended to Christology and finally to the domain of anthropology, it is now philosophical anthropology that decides the meaning of this concept and presents it to theological reflection. However, this return of the concept of person to Trinitarian theology will be extremely complicated. At this point it will move from being understood as a metaphysical term (*hypostasis*) to a subject of action and responsibility as knowing individual (subject). Person begins to be understood as knowledge of self. For John Locke, the concept of substance does not belong to the definition of person, since it

---

[74] Ph. Dixon, *Nice and Hot Disputes. The Doctrine of the Trinity in the Seventeenth Century*, London–New York: Continuum 2003, p. 5; W. Placher, *The Domestication of Trascendence*, Louisville: Westminster Press 1996.

[75] Ruiz de la Peña, *Antropología teológica*, p. 161.

[76] G. Amengual, *Antropología filosófica*, Madrid: BAC 2009, p. 218.

is defined by the awareness of self. Person is a thinking conscious self and personal identity consists not in the identity of substance, but in the identity of consciousness[77]. Although this definition belongs to the human person, it will eventually directly affect Trinitarian theology, making its use incomprehensible in this domain and provoking what will be called the splendid marginalization of Trinitarian theology.

In this sense, the rehabilitation of the doctrine of analogy and the concept of person from relation are two good symptoms of the recovery of the greater tradition in Trinitarian theology. Is is not perhaps again the time for Trinitarian theology to offer the depth and profundity contained in the theological concept of person to philosophical reflection, in order to found the anthropological conception which is in doubt today?

# The Contemporary Debate: Between Mono-Subjectivity and Inter-Personality

The debate on the concept of person applied to the Trinity was re-opened in the theology of the twentieth century by Karl Barth and Karl Rahner. Regarding the psychological concept of person, first Barth and then Rahner thought that if it were applied as such, Trinitarian doctrine would be dangerously approaching tritheism. Beginning from the modern reduction of person to an individual or subject that is conscious, free and responsible for its acts, it is rather difficult to apply this terminology to God; if one affirmed God as three persons, three self aware subjects, one would be implicitly affirming a crude tritheism. For this reason both Barth and Rahner proposed returning to the original meaning of the concept of hypostasis, while exchanging the concept of person for 'modes of being' (*Seinsweisen*) and 'modes of subsistence' (*Subsistenzweisen*). In God there is a unity of being and consciousness that subsists in three different modes of being and subsisting. Both of these theological positions were accused of being modalist (Moltmann)[78]. This judgement appears exaggerated and unjustified[79]. It is however true that the proposition has not had much success, and what is more obvious, it has not been followed in contem-

---

[77] Cf. J. Locke, *Essay Concerning Human Understanding*, II, 27, 11 and 19.

[78] J. Moltmann, *Trinidad y Reino de Dios*, Salamanca: Sígueme 161, n. 41 (Orig. *Trinität und Reich Gottes*, München 1980); 165: 'Rahner's idealist modalism'. G. Greshake, M. Striet and G. Essen prefer to speak of monosubjectivism.

[79] Cf. R. Miggelbrink, '*Latens Deitas*. Das Gottesdenken in der Theologie Karl Rahners', in R. Siebenrock (ed.), *Karl Rahner in der Diskussion*, Innsbruck–Vienna: Tyrolia 2001, pp. 99–129; esp. 128–9; ibid., 'Modalismusvorwurf und Personbegriff in der trinitätstheologischen Diskussion', in A. R. Batlogg, M. Delgado and R. A. Siebenrock (Hrsg.), *Was den Glauben in Bewegung bringt. Fundamentaltheologie in der Spur Jesu Christi*. Festschrift für K. H. Neufeld SJ, Freiburg-Basel-Wien 2004, pp. 279–96.

porary theology, which is more given to accentuating the dialogical and tripersonal perspective of God.

Although we cannot overlook the warnings of these two great theologians, who return Trinitarian theology to the centre of theology, it is to be recognized that both expressions are excessively formal and do not clearly manifest the importance of reciprocity (you) and love (us) in the signification of the concept of person, be it in Trinitarian theology or the domain of anthropology. Further, because the expressions do not pretend to be anything other than the recovery of the ontological understanding of person sketched by Patristic and medieval theology[80], their reception was further limited. Contemporary theology has preferred to follow the lead of dialogical and personalistic philosophy, by thinking of the persons from the perspective of relation. Nevertheless, the debate on this question is not over. The various theological positions, accusing each other of tritheism and modalism according to the application of the concept of person in Trinitarian theology, have come to produce a fierce debate in German theology between Herbert Vorgrimler and Gisbert Greshake, who is currently one of the most important theologians in the German language. If one's self-awareness and free self-determination belong to the concept of person today, can we still apply it to God according to the formula of *'una substantia – tres personae'*? While from Rahner's viewpoint we should avoid a concept of person that implies the sense of three self-aware divine centres, from the second perspective the real difference of the divine persons cannot be maintained before the moment of self-aware subjectivity and free determination, making it possible to speak of three 'I's or centres of self-awareness in God[81]. The first position has been called monopersonal Trinitarianism and the second has been called social Trinitarianism[82].

There are two questions behind this polarization that are fundamentally unresolvable if they are made in a unilateral manner. In the first place, we can contemplate the history of the concept of person as a permanent fluctuation between the two fundamental and absolutely necessary pillars that form part of its understanding: on the one hand, identity and subsistence (self-being) and on the other hand alterity, relation and gift of self (self-giving). For this reason, it would be good to consider that 'the persons in God are realities that are as autonomous as they are, at the same time, dialogical and relative, who cannot be conceived in a manner that is independent of

---

[80] Both the expression of modes of being and that of modes of subsistence refer to the expression of Athanasius of Alexandria (one essence in three modes of existing) and that of Thomas Aquinas (persons as subsisting relations).

[81] H. Hoping, 'Deus Trinitas. Zur Hermeneutik trinitarischer Gottesrede', in M. Striet (Hrsg.), *Monotheismus Israel und christlicher Trinitätsglaube*, (QD), Freiburg-Basel-Wien: Herder 2004, 128–54; esp. 128–9.

[82] de Bok, *Communicating the Most High*, pp. 17–52.

the others with whom they are permanently in relation.'[83] Current debate is largely polarized on these two perspectives. One can desire to understand the person as 'radical relativity' as well as 'absolute being-by-oneself'[84]. In the second place, it is necessary to 'remember that the decisive question that is object of discussion is nothing but the possibility of convincingly understanding Trinitarian monotheism, that is, how to articulate adequately the divine unity and Trinity as equally originating realities'[85]. This can be done through an understanding of the concepts of person and divine substance that equally reinforces each pole.

# The Personal God or the De-Personalization of God

Together with this theological problem there is the eternal question of whether we can refer the concept of person to God, that is, whether God is a personal being – whether this ultimate reality, the founding foundation that we have named with the name of God, is a personal being or not[86]. Can we apply a concept that implies limitation and alterity to the infinite and incomprehensible reality? This question appears to be tied to Fitche and the famous controversy on atheism. Even if it appeared to have been superseded, it turned out to be fully actual due to a series of circumstances, among which we can note the conjoined influence of a neo-Oriental current in the Occident that accentuated the ineffability and incomprehensibility of the mystery, to the point that any possibility of personal description or identity becomes impossible. This is the case in certain postmodern philosophers who perceive a threat in the affirmation of a personal God to both true alterity and reality of the completely Other, as well as to man's liberty. The personal character of God is questioned anew today among various new currents that we can call in a general manner deism, esoterism and agnosticism.

In Christian tradition, the person who really begins this process that can be called the de-personalization of God is Pseudo-Dionysius, by proposing

---

[83] Greshake, *El Dios uno y Trino*, p. 215.

[84] G. Essen, 'Person – ein philosophisch-theologischer Schlüsselbegriff in der dogmatischen Diskussion', in *Theologische Revue* 94 (1998) 243–54; esp. 245.

[85] S. del Cura Elena, 'Contribución del Cristianismo al concepto de persona: reflexiones de actualidad', in I. Murillo (ed.), *Religión y Persona. 5 Jornadas de Diálogo Filosófico*, Colmenar Viejo 2006, pp. 17–45; esp. 42–3.

[86] Cf. J. Werbick, *Gott verbindlich. Eine theologische Gotteslehre*, Freiburg-Basel-Wien: Herder 2007, pp. 583–95; K. Müller, *Streit um Gott. Politik, Poetik und Philosophie im Ringen um das wahre Gottesbild*, Regensburg: Pustet 2006, pp. 97–104.

a jump from the *name* of God to the unnameable, who in being thus can have many names, since He is definitively above all names. This is the search to move from the name of God (limitation) to the divinity (incomprehensible infinity). Heidegger needs to be situated in this line of thought when he promotes placing God above the most original and fecund reality of the sacred[87], as well as what we can call the current mystical and apophatic tendency which, before the personal God of classical theism, proposes a personal monism as an alternative.

One should be aware of two things in this debate. This tendency in fact begins with the presupposition and even the prejudgement that naming or personal being is a limitation. Yet God can have no limits (as Fichte)[88]. On the other hand, it does not take into account that a negation of God's personality (liberty, will, etc.) is limiting to God himself. It is clear that when we speak of God's personality or of God as a personal being, we are not attempting to state that God is person in the same way as a human person. The use of this concept to speak of God is always made within the doctrine of analogy. In this sense we cannot fall into anthropomorphism. Likeness is underpinned by greater dissimilitude. At the same time however, we must consider whether the anthropomorphic revelation of God as it is found in sacred Scripture is a rustic anthropomorphism, that is, a projection of the best or worst that is found in the human soul, or whether the revelation God expressed in human form is of a personal God, who can be invoked by a name, whose face can be sought, who can be asked something, be sung of, who can be both listened to and obeyed. If God is not a personal being, whether one can speak of a word of God, a revelation or an incarnation comes into question. All of these realities on which Christian faith is based would be nothing more than mythological forms for speaking of fundamental realities of the human being, but not a revelation of God strictly speaking.

Some authors who defend this theory call on the commandment that prohibits making any image of God to justify their position. However, in response to this we can say that the prohibition of making images of God is a prohibition against static images of God that seek to 'appropriate' his reality. God is experienced in a theo-drama, that is, in so far as God and man are involved and engaged in the history of a relation, which we call history of salvation and revelation. It is only from this point that it is

---

[87] O. González de Cardedal, *Dios*, Salamanca: Sígueme 2006, p. 110: 'With this second passage made by Pseudo-Dionysius, from God to the divinity, the equivalent of which is Heidegger's claim of placing God in being or the sacred in the divinity, from here identifying them in a second moment, we have entered into a deadly process that I will call "de-figuration", "de-sacralization", "de-historization" or "de-personalization" of God.'

[88] Cf. J. G. Fichte, 'Über den Grund unseres Glaubens an eine göttliche Weltregierung', in *Fichtes Werke 5*, Berlin: de Gruyter 1971, pp. 175–89.

legitimate to speak of God specifically as a personal being, who is capable of speaking and entering into relation[89]; who is capable of love and fidelity to their utmost extremes; who is the subject of a free will. In this way we can say that the prohibition of making an image of God that appears in Scripture is in view of a defence of God's personality and the conviction that man is the only true image of God – in man's capacity of speaking and entering into relation, in his creativity, in his capacity to pardon and the capacity of feeling joy. In this manner, as Klaus Berger has underscored very well, the concept of person in Scripture is not determined so much by the concept of subjectivity and interior life as by its condition of being an open reality, for its *Öffentlichkeit*. From this fundamental characteristic, Trinitarian doctrine is understood not as an interference of Greek thought or of ecclesial dogma with the original content of Scripture, but within the understanding of the only God who opens up in search of man's divinization[90].

# New Perspectives in Trinitarian Theology

As we mentioned at the beginning of this study, current Trinitarian theology, in taking the history of salvation as its starting point, has again centred theological discussion on the divine persons. It is important to remember this historical perspective, since an excessively formal conception of the term person will eventually turn against the fecundity of Trinitarian doctrine and theology as a whole[91]. Trinitarian theology centred in the personal, in the intimate life of God, can only be maintained if its starting point and its horizon are the understanding of the history of revelation and salvation witnessed to in Sacred Scripture and actualized in the liturgical and sacramental life of the Church. It is therefore not so important to reach a formal definition of the concept of person as it is to fill in the content of how each of the divine persons, Father, Son and Holy Spirit, exists. Since we cannot forget that, whenever we use a unique concept that is equal for all of them, it is equal also in that which differentiates them. The Father is person in a distinct manner from how the Son or the Spirit is, and vice versa. From here, we can think in a more abstract manner of the term person, but as a

---

[89] It was the prosopographical root of the concept of person that designated the speaker in grammar. Cf. e.g. Tertullian, *Ad. Prax* 5–7.

[90] K. Berger, *Ist Gott Person? Ein Weg zum Verstehen des christlichen Gottesbildes*, Gütersloh 2004; esp. pp. 197–206.

[91] This is sometimes insisted upon by C. E. Gunton in reference to current Trinitarian theology, using Irenaeus' Trinitarian theology as an example. This historical foundation does not hinder reflection on the immanent Trinity, but instead requires it. This reflection on Trinitarian ontology must however respect and base itself in historical-salvific revelation.

second concept which remains provisional. This tying of Trinitarian doctrine to the concrete affirmations of the New Testament and the liturgical life of the Church means that any concept of person from which we desire to work must take into account, on the one hand, the *concrete person of Jesus before God, his Father*, showing that he is an individual consciousness (I) who, *in* the liberty of the Holy Spirit orients himself to the Father as a real you, in difference and reciprocity of consciousness and love (as Gisbert Greshake, Magnus Striet, Georg Essen). On the other hand, however, one must take into account that this person is not constituted in himself as another God before God, but as *his* Son, as *his* Word, as *his* Image; that is to say, in virtue of its faithfulness itself, Trinitarian theology, with its central concept of person, should show its continuity with biblical and liturgical monotheism that begins from the awareness that, when it is oriented to the Father by the Son in the Spirit, it does this *to the only God*, not to three gods that form a communion (as Helmut Hoping, Josef Wohlmuth, Jürgen Werbick)[92]. Therefore one can accept neither a concept of person that breaks Trinitarian monotheism, thus in fact falling into tritheism, nor an abdication of the concept of person due to the difficulties that modern philosophy has introduced, which ends in implicitly affirming a new modalism. The current controversy around the concept of person is related to the controversy that has always existed in Trinitarian theology between those who are driven to accentuate monotheism (unity) or the Trinity (plurality).

From this affirmation on principles, I would like to present four perspectives that are profoundly related to each other, and which attempt to manifest the centrality of the concept of person, not only for Trinitarian theology, but also for anthropology (understanding of man) and metaphysics (understanding of reality). Without denying the pole of singularity and individuality that classical theology has accentuated in its ontological definition, Trinitarian theology today underscores that person is relation (C. E. Gunton; Ch. Schwöbel), communion (I. Zizioulas), reciprocity (W. Pannenberg, G. Greshake) and gift (Hans Urs von Balthasar, L. Ladaria).

---

[92] This is the reasonable and balanced position manifested by H. Hoping, *Deus Trinitas. Zur Hermeneutik trinitarischer Gottesrede*, pp. 143–5, inside the fierce debates currently under way in German theology, although he ultimately takes a position with Trinitarian theology that underscores monotheism in opposition to the possibility of speaking of three centres of self-awareness, of an exchange of divine liberties of an intra-Trinitarian dialogue. The subsistence of the divine persons is not personal in the sense that there are three 'I's or three centres of self-awareness and liberty in God. The exclusion of a pluralization of the divine essence excludes, in turn, excessive speculation on the legitimate difference of the Trinitarian persons and their reciprocal relations (p. 148).

# Person is Relation

Many authors could be studied here to show this form of conceiving of person, both in its perspective of Trinitarian theology and in its anthropological dimension. It has already been noted that the dialogue of twentieth-century theology with philosophy with Jewish roots, and personalism born in the Christian tradition, led to a significant attention to this pole of the definition of person. Two authors stand out in this position: The Anglo-Saxon author Colin E. Gunton and the German Christoph Schwöbel, who have fruitfully collaborated on various common projects.

Colin E. Gunton gets his fundamental model from the Trinitarian theology of Irenaeus of Lyon[93]. The reason for this is that all reflection on the immanent Trinity is tied to the revelation of God in history, and from it the fundamental problems of human life which man has always thought about can be illuminated. From this Irenaean theology we can understand perfectly one of the definitions that Gunton offers us of Trinitarian theology: 'The doctrine of the Trinity is the doctrine that attempts to do just that: to identify the God who comes among us in the way that He does; to enable us to see as much as we need of the nature of our God.'[94] Trinitarian doctrine is therefore not a distant speculation on life, but to speak and think of the Trinity is to speak and think about life. 'The Trinity is about life, life before God, with one another and in the world.'[95] In this manner, on the one hand, it is impossible to realize an essentialist Trinitarian ontology (which he, in a manner that is sometimes a little unfair, ties to Occidental Trinitarian theology derived from the Augustinian synthesis) and, on the other hand, he theologically founds the importance of the personal (in a world where the impersonal reigns) and the materiality of the world (in an Occidental theology marked by an excessive dualism and a modernity incapable of living in the body)[96]. In this way the author has sought to create a dialogue with modernity and its passion for liberty, not in order to negate it, but to assume it and place it in its authentic and true perspective, one where the affirmations of subjectivity, individuality, universality and unity are not made at the cost of alterity, communion, particularity and plurality[97].

---

[93] The reference to Irenaeus is obvious in all of his works, particularly in relation to Christology and Trinitarian theology. Cf. his latest work on the Trinity, *Father, Son and Holy Spirit. Essays Toward a Fully Trinitarian Theology*, London-New York: Continuum 2003, pp. 8–11.

[94] Gunton, *Father, Son and Holy Spirit*, p. 12.

[95] Gunton, *Father, Son and Holy Spirit*, p. 11.

[96] Gunton, *Father, Son and Holy Spirit*, p. 10.

[97] C. E. Gunton, *The One, the Three and the Many. God, Creation and the Culture of Modernity*, Cambridge: Cambridge University Press 1993.

There are four fundamental categories of Trinitarian theology for Gunton: person, relation, alterity and liberty. Of these, the central one is undoubtedly person. The theologians of classical Christian antiquity had to conceive what is implicated in what we call personal being in an entirely new way. The Trinitarian concept of person is therefore, for this author, the keystone of all Trinitarian doctrine, even though he recognizes that it is the category that is the most difficult to understand. Nevertheless, he also finds one of the greatest possibilities for current Trinitarian theology in it. On the one hand, it is impossible to define, since its reality is irreducible to other categories or entities that include the personal reality, in some form or another. For this author, the central aspect for understanding person is that which distinguishes it from the individual, in the sense that person, according to modern understanding, is to be defined in terms of separation from other individuals. It is however rather the contrary that is true. Person is defined in terms of relation with other persons, who are not only an extension of my own person, but who really constitute a distinct person, in alterity, with whom I choose to enter into relation in full liberty: 'To think of *persons* is to think in terms of relations: Father, Son and Spirit are the particular persons they are by virtue of their relations with each other. That, too, enables us to understand what is meant by *relation*. A relation is first of all to be conceived as the way by which persons are mutually constituted, made what they are. But we cannot understand relation satisfactorily unless we also realize that to be a person is to be related as an *other*. One person is not the tool or extension of another, or if he is, his personhood is violated. Personal relations are those which constitute the other person as other, as truly particular. And, finally, persons are those whose relations with others are – or should be, for it is the nature of fallenness to distort our being – *free* relations.'[98]

These four concepts (person, relation, alterity and liberty) can be finally summarized in that of love. 'The relations of the three are summarized in the concept of love, which involves a dynamic of both living and receiving. The persons are what they are by virtue of what they give to and receive from each other. God's being is a being in relation, without remainder relational.'[99] It is clear that this definition is thinking of the human person, as is clear in the definition that he offers us: 'To be is not to be an individual; it is not to be isolated from others, cut off from them by the body that is a tomb, but in some way to be bound up with another in relationship. Being a person is about being from and for and with the other.... Persons are beings who exist only in relation – in relation to God, to others and to the world from which they come.' There is however no doubt that for Gunton

98 C. E. Gunton, *The Promise of Trinitarian Theology*, Edinburgh: T&T Clark 1991, p. 11.
99 Gunton, *The Promise of Trinitarian Theology*, p. 143.

the ultimate foundation of this definition is the Trinitarian doctrine of the divine persons: 'Trinity is this view of persons as being from and for and with one another.... The Trinity is that in God the three persons are such that they receive from and give to each other their unique particularity. They have their being in relation to one another. The Son is not the Father, but receives his being from him; the Father cannot be the Father without the Son; and so on. Being in communion is being that belongs together, but not at the expense of the particular existence of members. The Father, Son and Spirit are *persons* because they enable each other to be truly what the other is... There are not three gods, but one, because in the divine being a person is one whose being is so bound up with the being of the other two, that together they make up the one God.'[100]

This relational ontology that is understood from the persons (as well as understanding the persons from the relations) that are constituted in a mutual giving and reception, and which Gunton has sometimes bravely and suggestively called *sacrificial ontology*[101], has been deepened by his colleague Christoph Schwöbel in a book that is entitled *God in Relation*[102]. The category of relation that has its roots in Trinitarian theology is used as a grammar for the fundamental content of theology. The author begins from this affirmation of principle: 'The affirmation "God is love" cannot be understood only as predicated of a property, an action or a disposition of God's being. It can also be understood as an *ontological affirmation of the understanding of God's personal being in relation*, and thus love can also be understood from an ontological perspective, interpreted in a highly relational sense.'[103] The starting point to understand the Christian God is thus his personal being, which is defined by relationality, and this in turn is understood by love. In some manner we can say that the author is situated in the great Christian tradition which, like Maximus the Confessor, Bernard of Clairvaux and Richard of St Victor, perceives that the Biblical expression *God is love* does not only constitute a predicate of a property of God, but that one must also give this expression an ontological range in order to think of the *being* of God, his personal reality in itself. The author responds succinctly to the actual question on the personal nature of God. The Christian God is a personal being,

---

[100] Gunton, *Father, Son and Holy Spirit*, p. 16.
[101] Gunton, *The promise of Trinitarian Theology*, pp. 174–5: 'That is a "sacrificial" ontology of God as three persons constituted by their relations of reciprocal giving and receiving. Sacrifice is also a way of understanding the end for which the world is made: to echo the mutual giving and receiving of Father, Son and Spirit within the dynamics of space and time, as sacrifice of praise. Thus creation can be understood as the sheer gift of God, the free giving of shape in otherness to that which echoes eternal giving and receiving of Father, Son and Spirit.'
[102] Ch. Schwöbel, *Gott in Beziehung*, Tübingen: Mohr Siebeck 2002.
[103] Schwöbel, *Gott in Beziehung*, p. 277. Italics mine.

and this personal character is defined by love. This is a love which is definitively personal relation between the Trinitarian persons of Father, Son, and Holy Spirit. This means that God is relation in himself, and that this is the necessary condition for the possibility of Him entering into relation with the world. The being of God and the foundation of his free and loving action in the world is the relation between the persons, or, as the author says, the *hypostatic identities*: 'the intra-Trinitarian relations constitute the hypostatic identity of the Father, of the Son and of the Holy Spirit. In this way the essence of the one God is not behind the hypostatic identities of the Father, of the Son and of the Spirit, but the unity of God is constituted *through* the Trinitarian relations.'[104] This hypostatic identity is embedded in the Father as the inexhaustible and total source of being and love for the Son in liberty and gratuity; in the Son as the personal object of his love, who is the principle of alterity and difference in God; and in the Spirit, the principle of communion in the Trinity, through which the Father and the Son give and receive his communion in liberty and love: 'God is not only free in relation to that which is not God, but He is also free in the personal communion that He is. God does not only love that which He has created and is the object of his love, but God also *is* love in the relation that He is.'[105]

## Person is Communion

Both Colin E. Gunton and Christoph Schwöbel have had as interlocutor the Greek Orthodox theologian Iohannes Zizioulas, who has rehabilitated the contribution of the Cappadocian theologians to Trinitarian theology more than any other contemporary author. His understanding of the divine persons can be clearly understood from the titles of the two books in which the author has considered the various contributions being made on the theme: *Being as communion* and *Communion and Otherness*. We can synthesize the thesis of this author in the expression of *the being of God as love and communion*, from the understanding of the mystery of the Father as origin and source of the divinity and of all reality. Love (as gift and offering) is thus discovered as the fundamental dimension of the Father's being, and in Him and from Him, of the entire Trinity. This is the ultimate reason for which Zizioulas, in deciding to think of the being of God as communion, follows faithfully in the Greek tradition that sees the origin of the Trinity and the source of communion in the Father[106]. The Father as

---

[104] Schwöbel, *Gott in Beziehung*, p. 47.
[105] Schwöbel, *Gott in Beziehung*, p. 171.
[106] I. Zizioulas, *Being as Communion: Studies in Personhood and the Church* (Contemporary Greek Theologians Series, No 4), Crestwood: St Vladimir Seminary Press 1997.

cause is a person that generates alterity from his being that is identified with liberty and love[107].

For the Orthodox theologian, contemporary Trinitarian theology must assume the revolutionary doctrine of the Cappadocian Fathers in order to confer a substantial character to person and to make of it, beginning from the person of the Father, the starting point for the understanding of the mystery of the Trinity. One must start from person, and not from a generic and abstract concept of being or even of communion. The centre of both Trinitarian and ontological reflection is the person and not the substance. Beginning from the person of the Father to think of the Trinitarian God means introducing personal liberty and love into ontology. The absolute liberty of self gift and the personal love of the Father both generate the Son and spirate the eternal Spirit. 'By making the Father origin of the Trinity, the Cappadocians introduced liberty into ontology, because the Father as person, and not as substance, can alone exist in liberty and in relation with the other persons.'[108] The Father is the personal and ontological origin, in the sense that his causality is found 'before and outside of time', at a hypostatic or personal level that presupposes liberty and love[109]. Liberty is ontological, as the Father is the initiator of both the personal being and the ontological alterity of the Trinity[110]. In this sense, in God 'alterity is constitutive of unity, and is not its consequence. God is not first one and then three, but is both one and triune at once. His unicity and unity are not protected for the unity of substance, but for the *monarchy* of the Father. He himself is one in the Trinity.' Likewise, 'Unity is expressed through the indissoluble *koinonia* that exists between the three persons, in such a way that alterity does not limit unity, but is instead its *conditio sine qua non*.'[111]

This primacy of the Father as source of the Trinitarian persons does not indicate an ontological superiority of the Father in respect to the Son and the Spirit, because alterity is constitutive of this personal communion. None of the divine persons 'possesses' the divine nature with an anteriority of the others. 'The co-emergence of the divine nature with Trinitarian existence initiated by the Father implies that He also "acquires" divinity only in so far as the Son and the Spirit exist: He is incomprehensible as Father without them, that is, only "when" the divine nature is "possessed" by all three.'[112] The Orthodox author concludes with clarity: 'The Trinitarian

---

[107] Zizioulas, *Comunión y alteridad. Persona e Iglesia*, Salamanca: Sígueme 2009, pp. 147–96 (Orig. *Communion & Otherness: Further Studies in Personhood and the Church*, London–New York: Comtinuum 2007).
[108] Zizioulas, *Comunión y alteridad*, p. 155.
[109] Zizioulas, *Comunión y alteridad*, p. 155.
[110] Zizioulas, *Comunión y alteridad*, p. 157.
[111] Zizioulas, *Comunión y alteridad*, p. 18.
[112] Zizioulas, *Comunión y alteridad*, p. 179.

order and causality protect (and do not reduce) the equality and fullness of the divinity of each person.'[113] If the relation were symmetrical to the point of permitting the Father to be caused as person by the Son and the Spirit, monotheism would be in danger[114]. 'The Cappadocian Fathers avoided this problem by introducing the principle of ontological precedence, and by making the Father the "cause" of Trinitarian existence.'[115] In this manner, in the opinion of the Greek Orthodox theologian, they managed to eliminate any logical contradiction between monotheism and Trinity, as well as to harmonize Christian monotheism with the biblical identification of God and the Father[116].

## 4.3 Person is Reciprocity

Zizioulas has recovered an ontology of the person for Trinitarian theology that raises us to understand the being of God as communion and alterity. However, by introducing the concepts of cause (*aitia*) and origin (*arché*) into the divinity in reference to the person of the Father, is he not running the risk that this ontology of communion be subsumed and suppressed by a cosmological category of causality?[117] On the other hand, does not this accentuation of the monarchy of the Father imply a subordination of the other divine persons? By understanding the Father as source and origin of the divinity, he gives the impression that the Father's personal being is not constituted by relation but by himself, something that could lead to the error of thinking of the Father as an *absolute person*[118]. For this reason, certain contemporary theologians have criticized this dependence of the current Trinitarian discourse on the processions of origin in its favouring the person of the Father to the prejudice of the other two. In this way justice is not done to the reciprocity of relations that exist in the salvific economy between Father – Son – Holy Spirit. If the being of God is communion, one would do better to think of the divine persons and the Trinity from reciprocal interpersonal relations. The German theologians Wolfhart Pannenberg and Gisbert Greshake have emphasized this reciprocity of the divine persons, in order to support their equality. The different and distinct relations of Jesus

---

[113] Zizioulas, *Comunión y alteridad*, p. 179.

[114] Zizioulas, *Comunión y alteridad*, p. 190.

[115] Zizioulas, *Comunión y alteridad*, p. 191.

[116] Zizioulas, *Comunión y alteridad*, p. 191.

[117] A. J. Torrance, *Persons in Communion. Trinitarian Description and Human Participation*, Edinburgh: T&T Clark 1996, pp. 283–306; Gunton, *The Promise of Trinitarian Theology*, xxiii–xiv. Zizioulas took account of these criticisms and responded in chapter 3, 'The Father as Cause. The Person that Generates Alterity', of his book *Comunión y alteridad*, 147–96.

[118] Cf. L. Ladaria, 'Dios Padre. Algunos aspectos de la teología sistemática reciente', in *La Trinidad, misterio de comunión*, Salamanca: Secretariado Trinitario 2002, pp. 157–71.

in regard to his Father and to the Spirit must be the starting point and the foundation of Trinitarian theology, rather than the classical doctrine of missions that reach an understanding of immanent relations of origin, in that the Father is situated above the Son and the Spirit, thus justifying a latent Patrocentrism.

Pannenberg understands Trinitarian theology as 'the interpretation of Jesus' relation with the Father and with the Spirit'[119]. This must be the starting point of Trinitarian doctrine[120]. This relation and alterity of Jesus before the Father is understood as autodifferentiation, a key word of the German author's Trinitarian theology: 'Self-differentiating himself from the Father, submitting himself as his creature to his will and thus making it the place of his divinity, what is equally required of all of his predications on the Kingdom of God is precisely the manner in which Jesus shows himself as the Son of God, one with the Father who sent Him.'[121] This historical salvific perspective on the relation of Jesus Christ with the Father in the context of the Kingdom of God opens us to the immanent Trinity. The difference in the salvific economy is understood as reciprocal autodifferentiation at the heart of the Trinity. The persons, for Pannenberg, unlike the view in traditional theology, cannot be identified with the relations of origin (paternity, generation and spiration), but their personal identity and the communion between them is constituted by that which the author calls *active relations*. All these relations are what constitute the peculiar diversities of the three persons. The persons are the relations, the reality that distinguishes them in their particularity and also makes them able to enter into communion. Up to this point the German theologian follows traditional theology[122]. He separates from it, however, by introducing into this relation not only the relations of origin, but also a wider understanding of divine relations: 'The reciprocal autodifferentiation by which the relations of the three persons are defined does not permit that these relations be reduced to relations of origin, in the sense of traditional terminology: the Father does not only "engender" the Son, but also offers Him his Kingdom to receive it from Him anew. The Son is not only engendered, but is "obedient" to the Father, "glorifying" Him as the only God. The Spirit is not only spirated, but "fills" the Son, "descends" on Him and glorifies Him in his obedience to the Father, thus glorifying the Father at the same time. It is He who in this way leads us to the full truth (Jn 16.13) and who knows the depths of

[119] W. Pannenberg, *Teología Sistemática*, I, Madrid 1992, p. 331 (Orig. *Systematische Theologie*, Göttingen 1988).

[120] Cf. Pannenberg, *Teología Sistemática*, p. 283nn.; 325–31.

[121] Pannenberg, *Teología Sistemática*, 336.

[122] I wrote a critical evaluation of W. Pannenberg's position, later supported with nuances by G. Greshake, in 'Reino de Dios y teología trinitaria: influencia de este concepto en la renovación de la teología trinitaria', *Estudios Trinitarios* 43 (2009) 213–56; esp. 249–52.

the divinity (1 Cor 2.10 ff.).'[123] 'The kingdom of the Father, his monarchy, is inserted into creation through the work of the Son, and is perfected through the work of the Spirit.'[124]

The pressing question at this point is that of the divine monarchy. Is the monarchy of the Father and the unity of the Trinity compromised by thinking of the divine persons with active relations? The monarchy of the Father should not be thought of outside the personal mediation of the Son and the Holy Spirit. The Father is the final end of the history of salvation, but He is only the end through the Son, who will offer the Kingdom to the Father so that God be all in all (cf. 1 Cor 15.28). The Father offers 'all' to the Son. This all is to be understood from the perspective of his divinity, to the point that his Kingdom comes to depend on the Son. In turn however, the Son 'returns it to the Father', because 'the Reign of the Son consists in nothing more than announcing the Kingdom of the Father, in giving Him glory and in subjugating everything to Him. It is for this reason that the Reign of the Son will not end (Lk 1.33) when He returns his power to the Father. On the contrary, it reaches its fullest plenitude at the moment in which He submits it to the Fathers Reign, when all creation glorifies Him as the only God.'[125]. This reciprocity between the divine persons, in mutual autodistinction, does not imply a destruction of the Father's monarchy. 'On the contrary, the Kingdom of the Father, his monarchy, is infixed in creation through the work of the Son, and is perfected through the work of the Spirit.... Without the Son however, the Father does not possess his Kingdom. It is only through the Son and the Spirit that He has his monarchy.'[126] The monarchy of the Father, until now the starting point for the understanding of the unity of God and the origin of the other divine persons, is mediated by the Trinitarian relations. The monarchy 'is *the result of the conjoined action of the three persons. It is the seal of its unity.*'[127] 'Since the monarchy of the Father and knowledge of it are conditioned by the Son, it is essential to include the economy of the divine relations with the world in the question of the essential unity of God. That is, the idea of the unity of God is not fully clarified by saying that its content is the monarchy of the Father. If the monarchy of the Father is not realized directly as such, but only mediated by the Son and the Spirit, the essence of the unity of the Kingdom of God will also be in this mediation. In no case can the mediation of the Son and the Spirit be something extrinsic to the Father's monarchy.'[128]

---

[123] Pannenberg, *Teología Sistemática*, p. 347.
[124] Pannenberg, *Teología Sistemática*, p. 351.
[125] Pannenberg, *Teología Sistemática*, p. 339.
[126] Pannenberg, *Teología Sistemática*, p. 351.
[127] Pannenberg, *Teología Sistemática*, p. 353.
[128] Pannenberg, *Teología Sistemática*, p. 354.

For the German theologian, Gisbert Greshake, the discovery of the person provides new access to a deeper understanding of the mystery of the Trinity. The history of the concept of person has permitted Trinitarian theology to consider that the personal differences in God are found on the same level, and have the same importance, as unity – better, they are identified with the essence of God. In the second place, the persons in God are realities that are both autonomous and relational, and they cannot be conceived of independently. The one God is a network of relations of three different personal hypostases[129]. For this reason, the traditional form of understanding the unity of God, and from it the Trinity or persons, is a serious obstacle for understanding the Trinity as communion and the divine unity as in relation and communion in love. Rather than starting from a common essence (Occidental tradition) or the fontality of the person of the Father (Oriental tradition), one should 'take the differentiation of the persons rather from the reciprocal relation of *communio* as it is found in the history of salvation, holding the testimony of Scripture as the principle of knowledge, and using the analogy of the phenomenology of interpersonal behaviour[130]. Both forms of approaching Trinitarian theology up to this point must be surpassed by the paradigm of *communio*, which is the reciprocal mediation of unity and plurality *from oneself.*'[131] 'There is no divine essence that could even be thought of independently of the relational network of the divine persons, and there is no divine person that could be independent of the relational network that ties it to the other persons. Better yet, the one divine essence *is* mediation: an eternal and constitutive *one-with-the-other* of the three persons in a *one-from-the-other* and a *one-towards-the-other*, in an inseparable conjunction of auto-unification with the auto-differentiation in respect to the others, just as with union and relation with Them.'[132]

For this author 'the divine persons are characterized by a one-being-towards-the-other that is so intimate that it is present in and actuates the other. This being-in-the-other of a relational kind shows that God, according to his essence, is communion.'[133] Greshake does not confront the distinction and properties of each person, from the classical doctrine of processions,

---

[129] Greshake, *El Dios uno y Trino*, p. 215.

[130] Greshake, *El Dios uno y Trino*, p. 255.

[131] Greshake, *El Dios uno y Trino*, p. 227. Author's italics.

[132] Greshake, *El Dios uno y Trino*, p. 228. Author's italics. Greshake's position is quite close to Pannenberg, as he himself states in pp. 235–36. The difference is found in the different analogies that they employ to speak of the reciprocal relations of the persons in this simultaneous movement of auto-differentiation and auto-unification: the modern field theory of M. Faraday (Pannenberg) and the theory of play (Greshake) used by H. Rombach, *Strukturanthropologie*, Munich 1993, 61. Cf. K. Hemmerle, *Thesen zur Trinitarischen Ontologie*, Einsiedeln: Johannes 1992, 44–8.

[133] Greshake, *El Dios uno y Trino*, 124.

nor in the relations themselves, but this differentiation must be thought of from the reciprocal realization of *communio*[134]. From these foundations, Greshake understands the *Father*, in the rhythm of love, as the *original gift*, in that his being consists in that it is given and is permanently exiting itself. The Father is continuously towards the other so that He can obtain his identity from Them. The Father, inside the Trinity, is – as in any human community – the base and foundation of *communio*, the crystallizing point for the entire community. The Father is completely oriented, as pure gift, to the Son and the Spirit, and is constituted in this being in relation[135]. The *Son* is defined, following von Balthasar, as *receptive existence*[136]. He is however reception of gift in such a way as to recognize the gift as such and in this way to return it, or better, He returns it by passing it on. Insofar as gift reaches its objective in its reception, reception is not only its reflection, but gift acquires figure and expression in reception, becoming truly the other within God. We could say that the Son is the principle of alterity in God, However, at the same time, He is not only being in reception but also being in transmission to the Spirit, and in this sense is the principle of manifestation and communication. The Son is completely relation to the Father and from the Father, but at the same time is before Him, both of Them united in the Spirit[137]. The Holy Spirit is pure reception on one hand, in so far as He receives the gift of the Father, and, in another way, from the Son, turning Himself towards Them in love, gratitude and glorification, while at the same time being the bond of communion between Them. The Spirit is received as love between the Father and the Son, as common gift, at once the result of both and a distinct third that makes possible and guarantees the relation between Them[138].

# 5. Person is Gift

If one finally had to choose a definition of person that could be analogously applied to God, to Christ and to man, thus becoming the key and centre for understanding reality, it could be stated that person signifies *to be oneself, in order to give oneself,* or *to be as self giving.* Paraphrasing the title of one of the books of the French philosopher J. L. Marion, we can say that

---

[134] Greshake, *El Dios uno y Trino*, p. 255.
[135] Greshake, *El Dios uno y Trino*, p. 262.
[136] Cf. H. U. von Balthasar, *Theologie der Geschichte. Ein Grundriss*, Einsiedeln: Johannes Verlag 1959, pp. 23–30.
[137] Greshake, *El Dios uno y Trino*, p. 262.
[138] Greshake, *El Dios uno y Trino*, p. 262.

person is *being giving itself, being in gift*[139]. I am aware that this does not sound particularly elegant, but it has the advantages of conciseness and the integration of the two necessary poles for a definition of person: the I (consciousness of being) and relation (gift); consciousness and liberty; the classical metaphysical dimension and modern psychology. Karl Rahner, in a passage that is rarely cited in this context, presents a definition of the human being that can be reworked for a definition of person: 'The Incarnation of God is, in itself, the unrepeatably supreme case of the essential realization of human reality. This realization consists in that *man is in so far as he gives himself.*'[140] Such a definition is ultimately possible only because of the Trinitarian God. Man is self-giving, in the image of God whose being is permanent gift and offering in love. The divine person is person, not by being in and for itself, but in being in and for the other. Without being able to identify completely the human person with the divine, we can think that the image of God can be found in this radical manner of being person. In God, being and gift is simultaneous, and in Him man gives himself as a vocation, since he first is and finally reaches the fullness of his being in giving himself.

The understanding of the divine person (and the human in his image and likeness) as gift and giving was one of the great contributions of Hans Urs von Balthasar's theology. For the Swiss theologian, the starting point of Trinitarian reflection is the paschal mystery. It is there that the Trinitarian mystery was fully revealed to us, and, concretely, the persons as pure relations from pure and disinterested love[141]. The depth of the love manifested in the paschal mystery reveals the Trinitarian relations to us as the expression of absolute gratuity in the gifted gift (Father: gift of himself) and in the received gift (Son: existence in reception), capable of establishing a dialogical relation that does not terminate in totality as the destruction of the other, but in mutual glorification (Holy Spirit). From this point, our author understands that the mystery of God and the mystery of the Father come to be equivalent in so far as the Father is, in his original gift, the only source and origin of the divinity[142]. This gift is the foundation of the divine mystery. With this it is clear that the divine essence is determined through the hypostases or persons, and not through the abstract substance[143]. 'The

---

[139] J. L. Marion, *Etant donée*, Paris: PUF 2001.

[140] K. Rahner, Zur Theologie der Menschwerdung', (*Menschsein und Menschwerdung Gottes, Sämtliche Werke 12)*, Freiburg-Basel-Vienna: Herder 2005, pp. 309–22; esp. p. 312.

[141] H. U. von Balthasar, *Theologie der Drei Tage*, Einsiedeln: Johannes Verlag 1990, pp. 32–3. The original work titled *Mysterium Paschale* of 1969 is integrated into the collective work of *Mysterium Salutis* III/2, Einsiedeln 1970, pp. 133–26.

[142] Cf. H. U. von Balthasar, *Theologik II, Wahrheit Gottes*, Einsiedeln: Johannes Verlag, pp. 137–8.

[143] Cf. Ladaria, *La trinidad misterio de comunión*, p. 119.

Trinity of God is not a penultimate reality, through which an unfathomable essence would be concealed, which would be inaccessible to any creature. Instead, God the Father, in engendering the Son and in the giving of Him to the world, has engendered everything in its totality (Ro 8.32), in such a way that with the rejection of all this, He has nothing else to offer (cf. He 6.4–8, 10.26).'[144]

There is nothing prior to relation, and definitively to his person. The Father is, in so far as He is total relation and gift: 'In no case does the Father "send" in order to be origin, so that the Son and the Spirit would be his executors, so to speak, through their obedience. The equal eternity of the procession of the Son and the Spirit reflects on the origin without eliminating the order of origin.'[145] The Father is origin in order to be total capacity of gift without reserving anything for himself. That He communicates everything except paternity is nothing but the expression that there is true alterity in God, understood not as something negative, but as a positive reality. That the Son does not become the Father, although this last communicates all that He is and has, is the necessary condition so that there can be a relation between God and creatures, in that these last can share the very divine nature, without losing their proper state. 'In the immanent Trinity the Father gives everything to the Son except paternity. This undoubtedly does not mean that the Father reserves something for himself. Likewise, the Trinitarian God does not reserve something for himself when He permits creatures "to participate in the divine nature" (2 Pe 1.4) without them becoming the God who gives. We thus encounter the axiom of the positive character of the other.'[146]

In a study on the Trinitarian concept of person, one cannot interrogate as to the formal content of the concept. Instead, from it, one must show how *each of the divine persons is a person*, and then, as we have said, how each of them is person is a different way. For this reason, the fundamental question of Trinitarian theology is not so much that of a formal definition of person that can be applied to God in order to affirm unity and Trinity, but rather: how are the Father, the Son and the Holy Spirit persons? In the Trinitarian mystery, the Father is origin and source of the divinity and by it, of all reality and of the history of salvation, because his being consists in being Father, that is, in being pure offering and radical gift. True love cannot have any foundation other than love itself. In the Trinity, this receives the name of Father. He is the love without foundation that in turn founds everything[147]. The Father is God by being only Father, that is,

---

[144] von Balthasar, *Theologik*, II, pp. 137–8.
[145] von Balthasar, *Theologik*, II, p. 137.
[146] von Balthasar, *Theologik*, II, p. 138.
[147] H. Urs von Balthasar, *Theologik*, III, *Der Geist der Wahrheit*, Einsiedeln: Johannes Verlag 1987, p. 405.

complete gift and original offering. He does not keep the divine being to himself, but communicates all of it to his Son, and they both communicate it to the Spirit. It is in this self-giving to the Son and the Spirit, communicating his being to Them to the point that They are equal in essence and dignity with Him, that his fontality, authority and primacy consist. All these realities must be understood from that being that consists in being pure gift for the other, establishing that the other exists and will exist with the same dignity in alterity and relation, which are equally radical. In the Christian tradition – in both Greek and Latin theology – the Father has been considered as the source of the Trinity and the principle of unity. He is the origin without origin, and the principle of the Son and the Holy Spirit, who are God like Him in turn. This implies neither a diminution of his person nor a subordination of the other two, because He is principle in such a way as to not diminish by sharing his being and because He shares it in such a way (completely) that the One to whom He is origin is not less than Him. His being is total gift. The Father is pure capacity to give, of total giving, without reserving anything for himself. In this way we can say that He is Father in the sense that, in offering his own life, He offers life and being in such a way as to elicit the full communion of love. Love (as gift and offering) is thus discovered as the fundamental dimension of the Father's being, and in Him and through Him of the entire Trinity. From this perspective, we can and should understand the Father as the original gift, in that his being and his identity consist in that He gives himself and is ever exiting himself. The Father is entirely towards the other so that He obtains his identity from the two others. For this reason, situating God the Father as the source and principle of the Trinity, according to all of Christian tradition, does not imply a devaluation of the other two divine persons, nor does it consider the Father as an absolute person, since He is only Father in the Son and from the Spirit.

From this perspective, important aspects of human life and the organization of society, paternity and authority, are illuminated for the man of today. These are realities that are in some way suspect in this period. Without a doubt, these realities are profoundly transformed in light of the Trinitarian mystery. The paternity of God is transformed into the source, foundation and model of human and spiritual paternity. Authority does not consist in the despotic use of force, but in the capacity of creating and constituting a reality that is distinct from oneself, and in communion with oneself, to which one can give oneself. At the root of communion is love that offers and gives oneself, that places one's life as the foundation of being and existence for others. To be a father is to give life, to engender a new life, to make possible a radically new beginning. This is possible in the measure that one's being is itself absolute gift, pure self-gift to the other.

If, in the logic of God's personal love, the Father is being as total gift, that is to say that his being Father consists in giving himself in such a way that it constitutes the Son as Son, the Son, within this same logic, is being understood as welcoming and receptive, i.e. the Son is pro-existence in reception. The Father gives himself and the Son receives and welcomes. However, with the identification of his being with the pure reception of the Father's being, this true reception, in its turn, consists in being transmission and gift of his being to others (proexistence). The Son is not understood in himself, from himself, but from his capacity to receive. His welcoming is, however, all the greater in its manifestation and communication of the Father's being (pure gift) that He has previously welcomed, from that which He is (reception and gift). This is a way of expressing the historical life of Jesus narrated in the New Testament. It was entirely determined by two realities which, without being completely identified, become inseparable in Him and in his person, life and destiny. These are God (Abba) and Kingdom (Basilea). Jesus did not announce himself to himself. We can say that his message is theocentric and soteriological. His entire life and mission (his person) were oriented on the one hand towards the Kingdom, whose coming He announced as immanent, and which constituted its centre and *entelekeia*[148], and on the other hand towards the Father, to Him whom He called Abba (Mk 14.34). He invited his disciples to find the courage to call on Him in the same way in his same Spirit (Lk 10.2, Gal 4.4 ff., Ro 8.16). This relational aspect of Jesus' person is what is behind the Christological titles that have had a central importance in the development of Trinitarian theology: Word (Jn 1), Image (Col 1) and Son (Eph 1). In the texts where these titles appear, the pre-existence of Christ with God is clearly spoken of. This implies, although the New Testament does not explicitly reflect on it, that there is a relation in God, an alterity, a dialogue, a space. God is unique, but He is not solitary[149]. In Him there is communication, participation and relation, and for this reason He can integrate the world into himself. If paternity and authority are illuminated from the person of the Father, liberty and autonomy acquire their true value and consistency from the person of the Son. From this theology, the Son would cause human life to be understood as filiation[150] and the full liberty and autonomy of the creature as a grace that is welcomed and offered. Man is existence in reception (Balthasar) and man is self-offering (Rahner). Man's adventure in modernity is correct in reclaiming liberty and autonomy before any alien or heteronymous power. They are a sign of his true humanity formed in the image of the Son. The only equivocation was understanding this liberty

---

[148] H. Schürmann, *El destino de Jesús: su vida y su muerte*, Salamanca: Sígueme 2003, p. 21 (Orig. *Gottes Reich – Jesu Geschick. Jesu ureigener Tod im Licht seiner Basileia-Verkündigung*. Freiburg-Basel-Wien: Herder 1983).

[149] Cf. Hippolytus, *Contra Noetum* 10, 1–2; Tertullian, *Adversus Praxean* 5, 2; G. Uríbarri, *La emergencia de la teología trinitaria: Hipólito y Tertuliano*, Madrid 1999, pp. 59–62.

[150] Cf. M. Henry, *C'est moi la vérité*, pp. 120–91.

and autonomy as realities that man could maintain by appropriating them and negating any possible relation with the world, with men and with God. The negation of relation as the constituting element of liberty finished in a negation of liberty itself[151].

Although Scripture does not explicitly affirm that the Holy Spirit is a distinct person from God (from the Father), it states in all clarity that He belongs to the divine realm. The affirmation of his personal being as pertaining to the divinity with the same rank and honour as the Father and the Son was affirmed in the Council of Constantinople of 381. Sacred Scripture uses a great richness of expressions and images to speak of the Spirit in relation to God and his Christ (breath of YHWH, Spirit of God, Spirit of Christ, Spirit of Truth, Paraclete) and of his action in the world (fluttering, blowing, liberating, groaning, resurrecting, guiding, communicating, praying, etc.). He appears tied to wind, fire, water, law, desire, heart, life, love, the gift of God, first fruits, deposit, glory, etc. This richness is the expression of the unfathomable richness of the gift of God and his inscrutable ways for those who seek Him – He guides and leads men to his definitive salvation. Nevertheless, in this great variety and plurality, there is a common denominator: the Spirit comes from God and leads to Him. He is present in the life of the world, of man and of the Church, but He goes beyond them. He is both immanent and transcendent. This is however a transcendence that must be understood as superabundance rather than in negative terms. The Spirit is the excess of God in his love for men. He is the revelation of God's superabundance, of his *magis*, of *Deus semper maior*.

The Spirit is pure relation and reference to the Father and Son whom He makes known, and to men, whom He makes enter into divine communion. The Spirit is the being for the other, working the communion with the other. He is pure referentiality tending to disappear in his 'personal contours' in order to realize his work of personalization in man in his relation to God. Certain authors have seen a sort of *kenosis* here (Boulgakov, Balthasar, Congar). The Spirit sustains, breathes, causes to be and appear, personalizes, remaining hidden, silent, revealing himself indirectly through the work of the Son and of men. His personal being consists in this. If the ultimate sense of paternity and authority is illuminated by the person of the Father, and the sense of liberty and autonomy is illuminated from the person of the Son, the difficult and perennial question of the adequate articulation of the relation between unity and diversity is illuminated from the person of the Spirit. The Spirit makes the greatest thinkable unity possible, without losing or lessening the differences of each of the members that make up a

---

[151] Cf. C. E. Gunton, *Unidad, Trinidad y pluralidad. Dios, la creación y la cultura de la modernidad*, Salamanca: Sígueme 2005, pp. 13–54.

society[152]. It is in this that his being in the Trinity consists in what concerns of the relations between the Father and the Son, and this is his mission in the economy of salvation in the Church and in the world.

---

[152] Cf. Gunton, *Unidad, Trinidad y pluralidad*, pp. 207–37.

# 6

# The Trinitarian Concept of Essence and Substance

## Michael Schulz

The publishers of this volume wanted an overview of the debate about the concept of the essence and substance of Trinitarian theology, as some newer approaches would like to dispense with the concept of essence completely. Has it become superfluous? Or does a meaningful and necessary use for the concept still emerge? A few but nonetheless significant approaches to Trinitarian theology from the German-speaking world will be sketched out and their use of the concept of essence will be examined in what follows.

The subject is introduced with reference to Hegel's Trinitarian philosophy, as it places the concept of substance within the context of subject theory, which becomes significant for the understanding of the Trinity. It also provides the building blocks for a theology of a social Trinity, with the help of which one would, however, like to overcome a conception of the Trinity which is oriented towards the notion of subject.

Recent works on Trinitarian theology have sympathized with Hegel's subject-theoretical Trinitarian philosophy. Why? A discussion of a Trinitarian concept of essence which aims at a convergence of the approaches forms the end of the article.

# Hegel's transformation of Substance into the Subject

For Georg Wilhelm Friedrich Hegel (1779–1831) doing justice to philosophy and its ability to know within the conditions of modernity depends on '… grasping and expressing the ultimate truth not as substance but as subject as well.'[1] Since René Descartes (1595–1650), modernity had built its truths on the rock of the certainty of the subject. For Hegel, the concept of subject (*Subjektbegriff*) combines with the idea of continuous self-determination (*Selbstbestimmung*), which takes as its starting point an ineluctable point which ought to guarantee certainty and truth. This point is the subject itself in its own pre-reflexive immediacy (*Unmittelbarkeit*) and the immediate unity (*unmittelbare Einheit*) with everything, with everything objective. In *Science of Logic*, Hegel calls this immediacy being (*Sein*) without any definition.[2] From this point all other terms are to be developed, for example subjectivity and objectivity, but above all the whole system of science. The concept of subject equally comprehends the absolute that religion calls God. The concept of subject identifies with an absolute or infinite structure which already defines the human 'I'. The 'I' represents a pure self-reference and is in this sense not dependent on anything else, only on itself. Finitude, by contrast, implies dependence on something else. In so far as 'I' in its self-reference is independent on everything else, it represents an infinite greatness; it is something that is unlimited, the presence of the absolute self-reference, the divine in the finite.[3]

The concept of the subject also forms the building block of Hegel's philosophy of religion. With its help, Hegel evaluates the figure of truth of a religion (*Wahrheitsgestalt*). Religion comes closest to the truth, and is that which acknowledges and honours the absolute as the subject, which at the same time is to be found in the human I. The verisimilitude of a religion can be grasped by religion and exalted when it is transposed into the appropriate form for truth: in the form of self-determining subjectivity, a form that Hegel also describes with the term concept (*Begriff*).[4]

---

[1] G. W. F. Hegel, *Phänomenologie des Geistes*, (Werke in zwanzig Bänden, Bd 3), Suhrkamp: Frankfurt am Main 1982, p. 23. C. M. Schulz, *Sein und Trinität*, St Ottilien: Eos Verlag, 1997, pp. 301–422.

[2] Cf. G. W. F. Hegel, *Wissenschaft der Logik*, I, (Werke, Bd 5), p. 82f.

[3] Cf. G. W. F. Hegel, *Enzyklopädie der philosophischen Wissenschaften*, (Werke, Bd 8), § 28; 94ff.

[4] In this context, the term concept (*Begriff*) does not limit itself to the meaning of representing an element of human knowledge; rather, Hegel understands *Begriff* in terms of subject theory: it is the logical form for the understanding of oneself (*Sich-selbst-Begreifen*) or for the conscious self-to-self behaviour which unequivocally characterizes subjectivity (both human and divine).

When therefore the Christian tradition uses the expressions essence, nature and substance in order to describe the absoluteness and unsurpassable greatness of God[5] (which according to Christianity's understanding of self is also philosophically recognizable), and to establish the unity, as well as the egalitarian divinity of the persons of Father, Son and Spirit in Trinitarian teaching, then these concepts which are often used synonymously under the conditions of modernity must be transformed into subjective-philosophy; in other words, Christianity and the Christian concept of God are to be developed along the lines of the absolute subjectivity (*absolute Subjektivität*).

In *Phenomenology of Spirit* Hegel identifies the historical emergence of the Christian incarnational belief with a shift from a paradigm of substance to one of the subject, because the historical presence of God in Jesus of Nazareth is of a subjective, personal nature.[6] Hegel links this evolutionary interpretation of Christianity with the notion that God's Essence or Substance is self-defined. The divine attributes, formulated by man, are the result of divine self-definition, which become revealed to man through his knowledge of God (*Gotteserkenntis*); these are not characteristics that man assigns to God, originating from himself, as he would to an object. God's self-definition does not only constitute human recognition of the divine but also religion and cult. According to Hegel the religious relationship of man to God is to be understood as a critical form of salvation-historical, economic self-relation of God. Only for this reason, religion and knowledge of God (*Gotteserkenntnis*) are really connected to God.

In the *Lectures on the Philosophy of Religion*, Hegel presents Christianity as an absolute and 'consummated religion'[7] because the Trinitarian dogma offers the best religious Representation of the Absolute. According to the philosophical concept, the absolute is to be understood as that absolute subjectivity which mediates itself triadically to its own grasped identity,

---

[5] Anselm's concept of God, according to which God is to be understood as *aliquid quo maius nihil cogitari potest* (*Proslogion*, 2) as well as he who exceeds our thinking (*maius quam cogitari possit*, *Proslogion*, 15), contains a rational criterion for the philosophical and theological statements that can be made about God's essence. Anselm's proof for the existence of God brings its uniqueness to the fore: in contrast to the finite essence, God's essence (nature, substance) is pure, unlimited reality and is not characterized by the difference between essence and being.

[6] The subjective presence of God is anticipated in the Greek statues of Greek gods which gives rise to the peculiar religious-historical twist that it was the Greek religion that paved the way for the Epiphany of God in Jesus, and not Judaism. When God becomes man then God no longer stands in opposition to mankind; instead he is much more subjectively represented in a man and therefore in a structural parallel to his own absolute subjectivity, cf. Hegel *Phänomenologie des Geistes*, pp. 495–574.

[7] G. W. F. Hegel, *Vorlesungen über die Philosophie der Religion*, Teil 3: *Die vollendete Religion*, Meiner: Hamburg 1984, p. 179 (pp. 177–269).

out of the addressed immediacy (*angesprochene Unmittelbarkeit*) through difference (*Differenz*) and mediation (*Vermittlung*). This self-mediation of the absolute is also described through other known terms like the unity of subject (concept, idea) and object (reality, nature). Father, Son and Spirit respectively stand for subject (immediacy, being, identity, concept, universality) and object (mediation, nothing, difference, particularity) and the unity of both (mediated immediacy, becoming, unity of identity and difference, singularity). The self-differentiation of the absolute also takes place 'to the outside'. To it belong all the forms of the non-absolute that mean the forms (*Gestalten*) of the finite. Christianity expresses the external form of the self-mediation (*Selbstvermittlung*) of the absolute through the representation (*Vorstellung*) of creation and salvation history in consummate form: the death of God on the cross underlies this logic. From the difference of the crucifixion arises God's spiritual existence as community.[8]

In *Science of Logic,* Hegel offers the logical distillation of the transition from the category of substance to the logical form, which underlies the subject, to the category of the concept.[9] This logical shift characterizes the transition in intellectual history from medieval to modern thought; it authenticates the reasonableness and truth of the Trinitarian concept of God. Hegel deduces the emergence of the concept out of the relationships, which are tied to the term substance. One substance which defines itself exclusively to its accidents according to Aristotelian-Scholastic understanding, or rather manifests and determines itself in them, must transcend the sum of its accidents and must represent itself in equal greatness in something truly other. This other must equally be substance. Consequently, the substance in the second substance draws on itself. A self-relationship (*Selbstverhältnis*) becomes apparent, represented in the concept. The substance has become concept, subject. This self-relationship can in turn open up vis-a-vis others, thereby allowing for revelation. A religion of revelation must therefore follow the logical structure of the concept, or rather, subjectivity. With that it equally follows another category, which became important in the theological reception, namely the true infinity (*wahre Unendlichkeit*). This true infinity incorporates the distinction from what is finite and does not only define itself against the finite. Alternatively, should the infinite be excluded from the finite and it would therefore be limited on its part; a limited infinite, however, represents something limited and finite. The truly infinite therefore positions itself beyond the abstract border between the infinite and finite.[10]

---

[8] Cf. Hegel, *Die vollendete Religion*, pp. 249nn, 254: 'God existing as community'.
[9] Cf. Hegel, *Wissenschaft der Logik*, II, (Werke, Bd. 6), pp. 217–301.
[10] Cf. Hegel, *Wissenschaft der Logik*, I, pp. 150–73.

The justificational importance of criteria for logical categories established in *Science of Logic* shows that Hegel defines and justifies religion in its truth from a philosophical perspective. While philosophy, with its conceptual thinking, offers the truth in an adequate form, religion with its theology operates on the plane of representation (*Vorstellung*). Hegel understands *Vorstellung* as that which the German word *Vor-stellung* implies: that one places (*stellen*) truth as an object, as something opposite and discrete, in front of (*vor*) oneself. Religious *Vorstellung* makes God, or the unity of God and man in Christ, into an object which is separated from humanity, which is, according to Hegel, incompatible with the incarnational character of Christianity, namely the unity of God and man.[11] In [the practice of] a cult, in the mystical unity of the God-man Christ, this unity is at least partially consummated.

Hegel's epistemic relativization of religion does not necessarily discredit it. For him it guides man towards knowing of the truth. Therefore Hegel does not neglect religion, but offers to it supporting arguments on the plane of representation, for example in causa Trinity.

With the help of reference to the sociality of the human person, Hegel invalidates the suggestion that the dogmatically demanded talk of three divine persons necessarily implied a rationally unacceptable tri-theism, he respectively demands an absurd equation of one with three and vice versa. Hegel argues that this criticism operates with an understanding of person which orients itself entirely from the idea of the isolated individual. If, however, the person only becomes a person through the gift of self to others (*Hingabe*), argues Hegel, then God's three-personality becomes easier to understand: the divine persons are God's personality in an act of reciprocal transfer of self. Hegel therefore offers a two-pronged line of argument. He secures Trinitarian dogma both on the formally relative plane of truth, tied to representation, as well as on the higher plane of the philosophical concept. Trinitarian belief must above all flee into the concept in order to escape the criticism of the Enlightenment on the Trinity.[12]

It is evident that Hegel's Trinitarian-philosophical initiative found a great theological echo, both in the nineteenth and also in the twentieth century. Approval and rejection have gone hand in hand, which is unlikely to change in the future. The subject-theoretical understanding of the divine appears to tie itself successfully to the decisive Augustinan-Thomistic conception of Trinitarian theology under the conditions of modernity which found its beginnings with René Descartes. Hegel's reference to the feeling of love and an intersubjective profile of the concept of person inspire the development

---

[11] On *Vorstellung* and *Begriff*, cf. Schulz, *Sein und Trinität*, pp. 306–22.
[12] Cf. Hegel, *Die vollendete Religion*: 'That is the position of philosophy, that the content flees into the concept and receives its justification through thinking.'

of the concept of social Trinity, of which Richard of St Victor (1110–1173) is regarded a proponent and which found its continuation in the Franciscan intellectual tradition. These two traditions,[13] which were widely seen as competing schools of thought, appear to have been equally taken up by Hegel and used argumentatively, even if on different epistemic planes and with a differing claim on Truth. Because of the difference between these epistemic planes, Hegel does not offer to combine the content of the two traditions, which would allow God's essence to be understood as at once 'at one with himself' (*Beisichsein* self-possession, subjectivity) and as being love (*Liebesein*). In recent decades, a renewal of Trinitarian theology after the latter inter-personal model has found by far the greatest approval. The concept of Essence is thereby wholly integrated into the personal dimension. And yet approaches which are theoretically close to Hegel's Trinitarian philosophy are also gaining consensus, so that God's substance is again being thought of in terms of 'at one with himself' and subject.

# Jürgen Moltmann: God's Substance as Community

Jürgen Moltmann (b. 1926) follows Hegel's references to social Trinitarian teachings. In addition, he approves the Trinitarian-theological concept of essence and with it the concept of absolute subject. Against the unity of the persons in the divine essence, he invokes the 'unity of the three persons among one another';[14] 'their eternal perichoresis'.[15] Regarding the salvation-historical self-revelation of God, he speaks of 'three different subjects in a living unity'.[16] Augustine's (354–430) concept of relationship serves Moltmann as an aid to the understanding of the being of the persons.[17] But Augustine comes under Moltmann's criticism for making the concept of substance the basis for the concept of person. Despite distancing himself from Hegel, Moltmann's understanding of God is reminiscent of Hegel's concept of the absolute, that is to say, the spirit. According to Moltmann the expression 'immanent Trinity' does not describe God's being-in-self, but

---

[13] This schematization is not without its problems, like the classification of the Western and Eastern approach: in the metaphysical unity of the divine essence or in the biblically witnessed economy of salvation of the divine persons.

[14] Jürgen Moltmann, *Trinität und Gottes Reich. Zur Gotteslehre*, München: Gütersloher (2) 1986, p. 167.

[15] Moltmann, *Trinität und Gottes Reich*, p. 174.

[16] Moltmann, *In der Geschichte des dreieinigen Gottes. Beiträge zur trinitarischen Theologie*, München: Gütersloher 1991, p. 238.

[17] Moltmann, *Trinität und Gottes Reich*, p. 190.

rather the salvation-historical-eschatological consummation of God's being for mankind. It is the Trinitarian God of relation, who unveils himself in his radical otherness, out of love to mankind, in transience and death. In this crisis, the unity of the persons of Father and Son would threaten to break, Moltmann suggests pithily, if the spirit of love ruling in the person of the Holy Spirit were not stronger than sin and death.[18] A Trinitarian metaphysics of essence, which would exclusively stress the inviolable unity of God, could not according to Moltmann's evaluation overtake this biblical perspective. It is not by accident that the theologian from Tübingen does not connect any philosophical ambitions with his Trinitarian-theological concept. The temptation to describe God philosophically as substance and subject, which could only entail a Trinitarian modalism or historically-insensitive essentialism, is too close to home. In his otherness the biblical God of faith challenges philosophy's concept of God. According to Moltmann, the God indicated by the Bible should promote a new logic of love and inter-personality.[19] Moltmann explains his sympathy for the so called eastern Trinitarian teaching and its personal approach according to this new inter-personal logic. This preference does not, however, hinder Moltmann from anchoring God's one-ness as the original entity in the monarchy of the Father.[20] Elsewhere, Moltmann says that a monarchical model of the Trinity mistakenly leads to the idea of a monarchical papal Church in contrast to a favoured synodal church as an image of the otherwise preferable social consensual Trinity.[21]

In summary, Moltmann's sometimes disparate Trinitarian terminology[22] does not instil confidence in his call to think of the one-ness of God exclusively as the unity of the persons and relinquish the notion of a divine substance.[23] The rejection of Hegel's subject-Trinity lacks a convincing alternative. The Trinitarian concept of essence must naturally conform to Moltmann's concern of making God's commitment in history imaginable;

---

[18] Cf. Moltmann, *Trinität und Gottes Reich*, pp. 97–9. 'Here [in the passion] the innermost life of the Trinity is at stake' (p. 97); 'Father and Son are so divided on the cross that their relationship breaks off' (p. 98); The thus separated are connected by the spirit of self-giving, the Holy Spirity ibid.', p. 141.

[19] Moltmann, *Trinität und Gottes Reich*, pp. 26–31.

[20] Moltmann, *Trinität und Gottes Reich*, p. 216n.

[21] Moltmann, *Trinität und Gottes Reich*, pp. 217–20.

[22] For a discussion of Moltmann's Trinitarian theology, cf. Gisbert Greshake, *Der dreieine Gott. Eine trinitarische Theologie*, Freiburg-Basel-Wien: Herder 1997, pp. 168–71, who recognizes the 'danger of a certain tri-theism' (p. 171) in Moltmann's approach and makes the renunciation of a concept of the unity of essence of God responsible (footnote 456).

[23] The Fourth Lateran Council (1215) argued against a Trinity of social unity on the basis of the concept of substance, as one saw conceived too much according to the analogy of a human-moral unity. How far the position of Joachim de Fiore (+1202) is rebutted must be left for personal consideration (DH 803).

with this idea, Hegel's category of true infinity (*wahre Unendlichkeit*) must be realised theologically. However, objections can be raised against Moltmann's notion of God's historical self-becoming through the crisis of the cross, for the consummation of the divine love which grows on resistance supports its essential dependence on sin and death, which cannot be the case if God must overcome both. At least Moltmann makes one consider that God is interesting for his own sake and should be loved for his own sake.[24] This statement can also be understood in such a way that God's being-in-self and essence for itself are already absolutely consummate, not just thanks to a crisis that has been overcome. Moltmann's induced Trinitarian suspicion of projection, that the western model of the Trinity leads to a hierarchical papal Church, or rather is supported by it, quickly collapses if the preference of synodal ecclesiology is to find its original apotheosis in a social teaching of the Trinity. If theology is to be more than knowledge-leading interests projected into the heavens, one must think through potential Trinitarian analogies more thoroughly.

# 3. Woflhart Pannenberg: God's substance as spirit-field

Wolfhart Pannenberg (b. 1928)[25] euphorically celebrated Hegel's agapeological notion of the Trinity on the basis of the possibility arising out of it, namely to identify the one-ness of God with the reciprocal surrender of the divine persons.[26] Hegel's Trinitarian-subjectivity, on the other hand, is rejected.[27] Pannenberg strikes another note in his *Systematic Theology*. That which is retroactive and tri-theistic in the divine unity resulting from the reciprocal gift of self motivates the Lutheran theologian to rehabilitate the concept of essence. But he does not return to Hegel's approach but rather turns to physical field theory.[28] Pannenberg understands the Godhead as a sort of field which appears in the divine persons similar to a universal force field, which has no need of a subject of inhesion (*Inhäsionssubjekt*)

---

[24] Cf. Moltmann, *Trinität und Gottes Reich*, p. 170.

[25] Gunther Wenz gives an excellent overview of Pannenberg's Systematic Theology in *Wolfhart Pannenberg. Ein einführender Bericht*, Göttingen: Vandenhoeck 2003. On the Trinity, cf. pp. 71–122.

[26] W. Pannenberg, 'Die Subjektivität Gottes und die Trinitätslehre. Ein Beitrag zur Beziehung zwischen Karl Barth und der Philosophie Hegels', in W. Pannenberg, *Grundfragen systematischer Theologie. Gesammelte Aufsätze*, II, Göttingen: Vandenhoeck 1980, pp. 96–111, here p. 108; Pannenberg, *Grundzüge der Christologie,* München: Gütersloher 1964, p. 7.

[27] W. Pannenberg, 'Person und Subjekt', in *Grundfragen,* II, pp. 80–95, here pp. 86ff.

[28] Cf. W. Pannenberg, *Systematische Theologie*, Band I, Göttingen: Vandenhoeck 1988, p. 414n.

because of its autonomy, but still manifests itself in certain material or energetic manifestation. He calls the persons [of the Trinity] 'manifestations and forms ... of the divine essence' (*Manifestationen und Gestalten ... des einen göttlichen Wesens*). These are 'modes of being of the one divine life' (*Daseinsweisen des einen göttlichen Lebens*)[29] and 'centres of activity' (*Aktzentren*)[30] or 'centres of life of the all-encompassing and permeating movement of the divine Spirit' (*Lebenszentren der sie alle umfassenden und durchdringenden Bewegung des göttlichen Geistes*).[31]

Starting with the social-psychological approach of George Herbert Mead (1863–1931) Pannenberg deepens his concept of the Trinity in a way which brings him close to Hegel's way of thinking. Not only in an anthropological sense, but also in the context of Trinitarian theology, he construes the Trinitarian person as unity of (present) I and (future) self. Pannenberg identifies the divine essence with this self, with which every divine person, in comparison to the human, has ever been totally identical, so that the 'I' of the divine person brings being God into the present. The substantial self is the divine person, only however accessible through the personal agency of the respective other persons: only in relation to them is the divine person itself and present of the divine essence. Pannenberg even formulates '... the self-distinction of God [is] constitutive for the Trinitarian Persons and for their own divinity' (*die Selbstunterscheidung von Gott [ist] konstitutiv für die trinitarischen Personen und für ihre eigene Gottheit*).'[32]

Both, Trinitarian field theory and the subjective interpretation of divine essence as self raise questions. The physical quality of the field, which supposedly exists without a subject of inhesion (*Inhäsionssubjekt*), stands in mental tension with the pneumatic interpretation of the field, as spirit (*Geist*) is difficult to imagine without a subjective structure. The interpretation of essence as self is then at hand. But does not the essence of God therefore win an independent sphere of reality as distinct to the persons, especially when it is said that the divine persons must be distinct from God (who is meant by this now?) in order to constitute themselves in their divinity?

The personalization of the distinction between essence and person obscures the concept of essence as a subjectless unity of the persons.[33] It remains unmistakably established that divine essence and persons are really identical. With reference to Pannenberg's thesis of the reciprocal constitution

---

[29] Pannenberg, *Systematische Theologie*, I, p. 417; cf. p. 388.

[30] Pannenberg, *Systematische Theologie*, I, p. 347.

[31] Pannenberg, *Systematische Theologie*, I, p. 417; cf. p. 464.

[32] W. Pannenberg, 'Der Gott der Geschichte', in *Grundfragen*, II, pp. 112–28, here p. 24.

[33] Cf. this notation by Elmar Salmman, 'Wer ist Gott? Zur Frage nach dem Verhältnis von Person und Natur in der Trinitätslehre', in *Münchener Theologische Zeitschrift* 35 (1984) 245–61.

of the divine persons, which should overcome any Subordinationism,[34] one must be aware that it cannot result in dissolution of the order which marks the intra-divine procession. Otherwise it would be difficult to explain in what way the persons can even distinguish themselves in terms of immanent Trinity. In the end only one property of essence, like love, for example, would be able to create the distinction. But it would remain unclear why one ought to speak of Father, Son and Spirit. That said, Pannenberg doubts the possibility of a derivation of the Trinity out of one quality of the divine essence; this would lead to Modalism – the essence generates the persons – or Subordinationism because one person in possession of the essence primarily deals with the other persons. This Subordinationism also marks the agapeological approach of Richard of St Victor.[35] The intra-divine and salvation-historical dependence (*Abhängigkeit*) of the Father on the working of the Son (and Spirit), which Pannenberg expounds to counter this, does not, of course, imply a second begetting (*Zeugung*), but instead seeks to hold on to the scripturally attested dependence of the Father on the working of Jesus. Yet one must note: the reciprocal dependence comes from the surrender of one person to another, neither from the motive, nor by relativizing the existing precedence/superiority of one person, like the precedence which seems to belong to the beginningless Father. The consubstantiality (*Wesensgleichheit*) of the persons of the Trinity, the classical meaning of the statement in the Nicene Creed (325), already weakens Subordinationism on an essential plane. A consequent belief of the person-shaping function of the relations supports this: the property of unbegottenness does not constitute the Father, but rather his fatherhood does.

Unlike Moltmann, Pannenberg recognizes the crucial relevance of philosophical reflection for theology. Philosophy is able to establish framing concepts which guarantee the rationality of theological propositions. In this sense, Pannenberg demands that the relationship of God to creation, operating divine attributes (*operative Gottesattribute*) and the identity of an immanent and economic Trinity,[36] be conceived after the example of Hegel's concept of true infinity (*wahren Unendlichkeit*).[37] For Pannenberg the category of true infinity even holds a clue about a difference in God, because otherwise God, in his multiplicity (*Vielheit*), would stand one-sidedly in the face of the finite.[38]

---

[34] Cf. Pannenberg, *Systematische Theologie*, I, pp. 335–47.

[35] Cf. Pannenberg, *Systematische Theologie*, I, pp. 311n., 323, 325.

[36] Cf. also Pannenberg's epistemologically developed notion of God as the all-deciding reality, which redeems the category of the true infinity: as an omnipotence separated from the finite, God would only rule himself, but not the totality of reality 'external' to him. Cf. W. Pannenberg, *Wissenschaftstheorie und Theologie*, Suhrkamp: Frankfurt 1987, p. 304.

[37] Cf. Pannenberg, *Systematische Theologie*, I, pp. 192nn., 430nn., 441., 476nn.

[38] Cf. W. Pannenberg, 'Die Bedeutung der Kategorien "Teil" und "Ganzes" für die

Pannenberg considers the notion of the infinite as a significant concept of a philosophical theology, because only against the horizon of the infinite can the finite be recognized as such, while the infinite will also always be implicitly recognized alongside it.[39] In an intellectual link with the theology of the late Middle Ages (J. Duns Scotus, b. 1308), Pannenberg describes the infinite as the determination of God's essence which ties philosophy and theology to each other.[40] From God's essence he distinguishes God's *Dasein* (being), to which he attributes all the appearances of God in history.[41]

In summary – the philosophical and theological notion of the divine – infinite – essence fulfils a significant epistemological and criterological function according to Pannenberg: he builds up the internal rationality of Trinitarian theology and brings a philosophical approach to it. God's essence and being (*Dasein*) correspond to the category of true infinity (*wahre Unendlichkeit*), which, however, means that vis-a-vis Hegel the being (*Dasein*) of God in salvation history is a manifestation of divine liberty. Because God's essence is identical to God's freedom, God can determine to be governed by the course of history, whose fate decides equally over God's divinity. Unlike Moltman, however, this does not mean for Panneberg that God only can only reach consummation through history. In terms of Trinitarian theology, personalizing the difference between the planes of essence and person proved problematic. The real identity (*Realidentität*) of divine essence and divine persons must be established first. The difference between the concepts essence (*Wesen*) and person (*Person*) is defined by the *rationes* of both notions: essential Absoluteness (*wesenhafte Absolutheit*) and personal relativity/relationality (*personale Relativität/Relationalität*). The difference between essence and person can only be of a theoretical nature, with objectively logical reference, of course, in so far as the real identity (*Realidentität*) between essence and person/s does not break down the disjunction between absolute – relational/relative, but rather assumes it. If one understands God's essence not only as self and spirit, but at the same time as being love (*Liebe-Sein*), then it becomes evident that the absolute essence can truly be in relational-relative personal relationships. Pannenberg combines the Western approach to the personalistic approach. What remains open for discussion is how far the persons can be described as their own centres of activity (*Aktzentren*) without sounding tri-theistic.

---

Wissenschaftstheorie der Theologie', in *Theologie und Philosophie* 53 (1978) 481–95, here p. 491.

[39] With Friederich Schleiermacher, Pannenberg formulates that the finite is to be understood, to a certain extent, as 'coming forth' from the infinite. Cf. Pannenberg, *Systematische Theologie,* I, p. 154.

[40] Cf. Pannenberg, *Systematische Theologie,* I, pp. 128–32, pp. 429–33.

[41] Cf. Pannenberg, *Systematische Theologie,* I, pp. 376–89.

# Eberhard Jüngel: God's substance as self-mediation to consummate love

Despite a strict adherence to a theology of Revelation along the lines of Karl Barth which at the same time absorbs Hegel's Trinitarian philosophy, Eberhard Jüngel's (b. 1934) approach backs the need to reflect on the concept of essence both philosophically and in terms of Trinitarian theology. Hegel's theocentric understanding of religion is reflected in Jüngel's theology of faith; man does not move towards God from the finite, with analogous concepts and transcendental laws of causality, in order to determine his essence, but rather God defines himself through his revelation in history, in the language of faith (*Glaubenssprache*) and in the knowledge of faith (*Glaubenserkenntnis*). Not only does Jüngel reject any philosophical deduction of the divine persons out of the essence of God, but he also rejects every natural or philosophical theology, which made him a significant opponent of Pannenberg in German Evangelic circles. Jüngel sees his theology of faith confirmed in terms of temporal diagnosis (*zeitdiagnostisch*). For Jüngel, the notion of God as the highest substance and untouchable essence *supra nos nihil ad nos* which was developed under the conditions of modernity leads to atheism for the sake of mankind, because man, in his freedom, does not want to be dependent on an unknown absolute essence. The only way to avoid a philosophical theism and atheism, Jüngel claims, is a theology which sets out with the revelation of God in Jesus, the crucified one, and proceeds in a strictly Trinitarian way, in that it raises God's existence as resistance to nothingness, sin and death in favour of being (*Sein*), reconciliation and life. The rejection of philosophy as an approach to faith and theology does not however stop Jüngel from moving intellectually close to Hegel's philosophy of Christianity. So the concept of the transformation of divine substance into an absolute subject finds an echo in Jüngel's phrasing. He says that God 'fulfils his being subject in a Trinitarian way (*sein Subjektsein trinitarisch vollzieht*)'[42] and that 'God [is] the unconditional subject of himself' (*Gott … unbedingtes Subjekt seiner selbst*).[43] 'Modes of being'(*Seinsweisen*)[44] is what Jüngel – like Karl Barth – calls the divine persons, without further reflecting on this Trinitarian concept of person. The expression mode of being (*Seinsweise*) fits with the phrase 'God is his own mediation' (*Gott ist sich selber Vermittlung*).[45] Although Jüngel denies aiming for absolute spiritual subject (*Geistsubjekt*)[46] in terms

---

[42] E. Jüngel, *Gott als Geheimnis der Welt. Zur Begründung der Theologie des Gekreuzigten im Streit zwischen Theismus und Atheismus*, Tübingen: Mohr (8)2010, p. 433.

[43] Jüngel, *Gott als Geheimnis der Welt*, p. 212.

[44] Jüngel, *Gott als Geheimnis der Welt*, pp. 527, 532.

[45] Jüngel, *Gott als Geheimnis der Welt*, p. 521.

[46] Cf. Eberhard Jüngel, 'Nihil divinitatis, ubi non fides. Ist christliche Dogmatik in rein

of Trinitarian theology, contrary assumptions are unsurprising.[47] Something similar applies to the Trinitarian phrase God comes 'from God to God as God'.[48] What is meant with this phrase is that the divine essence cannot be abstracted in a way that isolates it 'from the unfolding of the triune existence' (*von dem Geschehen des dreifaltigen Daseins Gottes*).[49] This event is, however, thought out along the lines of subjective self-mediation: as a unique event,[50] not, as in Pannenberg's approach, as a reciprocal constitution of persons. Although Jüngel presents his Trinitarian theology as an inter-pretation of the Johannine definition of God as love, the intra-Trinitarian event in his main work *God As the Mystery of the World*, is only weakly outlined; the thought of perichoresis, for example, does not play a special role. It is different in Jüngel's paraphrase of Karl-Barth, 'God's being is in becoming' (*Gottes Sein ist im Werden*).[51] But even here closer explanation of the immanent Trinity is omitted in favour of the question of the action of the three modes of being (*Seinsweisen*) *ad extra* and the question of the corresponding appropriations.[52] It is clear that the preferred pattern of the Trinitarian persons and their perichoretic unity towards economy is dictated by the fear that once again a metaphysical God *supra nos* might be established.[53] Linked with this, then, it is not surprising that Jüngel develops thoughts about a self-consummation of God through history as the reali-zation of divine being-love along the lines of Hegel. According to Jüngel's evaluation, God would remain the 'most sublime egoist' (*sublimste Egoist*) if God did not also give himself to humankind.[54] Even the generation of the Son and the proceeding of the Spirit are first conceived of as finalized into Creation.

In summary: Jüngel's desire to represent God's philanthropy in theological terms bases itself on the idea that this can only be a God who perfects himself in his selflessness over the course of history. This

---

theoretischer Perspektive möglich? Bemerkungen zu einem theologischen Entwurf von Rang', in *Zeitschrift für Theologie und Kirche* 86 (1989) 204–35, here pp. 219n.

[47] Cf. Wolfhart Panneberg, 'Understanding and grasping faith itself. An Answer' in *Zeitschrift für Theologie und Kirche* 86 (1989) 355–70, 365n; 'even after re-reading' *God as Mystery of the World* the impression remains that the 'domininace of a divine I' presides in Jüngel's explanation of the Trinitarian being-love.

[48] Jüngel, *Gott als Geheimnis der Welt*, p. 522.

[49] E. Jüngel, 'Das Verhältnis von „ökonomischer" und 'immanenter' Trinität, in E. Jüngel, *Entsprechungen. Theologische Erörterungen*, Bd II, Tübingen: Mohr 1980, pp. 265–75, here p. 274.

[50] According to F. Meessen, *Unveränderlichkeit und Menschwerdung Gottes. Eine theologie-geschichtlich-systematische Untersuchung*, Freiburg-Basel-Wien: Herder 1989, p. 319.

[51] Cf. E. Jüngel, *Gottes Sein ist im Werden. Verantwortliche Rede vom Sein Gottes bei Karl Barth. Eine Paraphrase*, Tübingen: Mohr (4)1986, p. 43ff.

[52] Cf. Jüngel, *Gottes Sein ist im Werden*, pp. 41–53.

[53] Cf. Jüngel, *Gottes Sein ist im Werden*, p. 45f.

[54] Jüngel, *Gott als Geheimnis der Welt*, p. 513.

notion can be contradicted thanks to the idea of the completeness (*Vollkommenheit*) of the divine essence which arises out of itself. Jüngel's tone, steeped in subject-theory, conversely illustrates a problem arising from the thinking of Moltmann and Pannenberg: the fading of the profile of the divine persons, which can only be brought sharply into relief through salvation-history. This idea of the divine person's completeness (*Vollkomenheit*) demands that the intra-divine evocation (*Beziehungsreichtum*) also unfolds inherently (*an sich*), not only *ad extra*. Otherwise, as Pannenberg observes very clearly, there can be no discussion of God's *self*-revelation (*Selbstoffenbarung*). A philosophical theology which already thinks of God's essence as openness (*Offenheit*) for creation and history – as true infinity – does not impose a God on humanity who threatens freedom, but rather one who serves the rationality of revelation theology.

# Karl Rahner: God's Substance as Self-Possession

Even Karl Rahner's (1904–1984) Trinitarian theology uses a vocabulary coloured with idealism, in order to carry on the faith under the conditions of modernity. In comparison with Moltmann and Jüngel, this approach includes a philosophical demonstration of the divine (*Gottesaufweis*). Rahner demands to find an imprint in the human spirit, even for the Trinity, so that after the ensuing revelation, the truth of the dogma of the Trinity can conveniently be presented in the highest measure, even for philosophical reason. At the same time, Rahner's Trinitarian theology stays in line with the Scholastic tradition, according to which the consummation of God's essence by means of creation and salvation history is unthinkable. And yet Rahner does very little to develop the immanent Trinity. In contrast to Moltmann and Pannenberg, Rahner does not take up Hegel's agapeologic-personalist notion of Trinity; he prefers instead the subject-theoretical line of thought as a structure on which to mount ontology and the doctrine of God (*Gotteslehre*): 'All conduct and action, from the simply material to the internal life of the triune God are only variations of this one metaphysical theme, self-possession'.[55] Johann Baptist Metz (b. 1928) added the word 'subjectivity' in his edition of this thesis which had been approved by Rahner,[56] thus strengthening the idealistic tone of this thesis. Rahner adopts

---

[55] K. Rahner, *Hörer des Wortes*, (Sämtliche Werke Bd 4), Freiburg-Basel-Wien: Herder 1997, p. 76.
[56] Rahner, *Hörer des Wortes*, p. 77.

Hegel's shift from substance to subject. It is rather fitting that Rahner, therefore, clearly rejects the social, interpersonal blueprint for Trinitarian teaching,[57] despite his criticism of the so-called psychological Trinitarian theology of St Augustine and his concerns about oblivion of the Trinity (*Trinitätsvergessenheit*) in both the practice of faith and theology. Talk of three persons in God leads to tritheism because of modern notions of person as the result of the identification of the individual and person, in other words consciousness of self.

The uniqueness of generation *(Zeugung)* and its speculative identification with the knowing, productive 'saying' *(Sagen)* of the eternal Logos through the Father are the reasons why Rahner cannot reconcile himself with the thesis of the reciprocal intra-Trinitarian 'you', because, given the premise of psychological Trinitarian teaching, accepting the reciprocal 'you' would ultimately amount to the idea of three-fold generation. Rahner keeps a very formal understanding of the immanent Trinity, not least in order not to lay unnecessary strain on the interreligious dialogue with Judaism and Islam. It is therefore unsurprising that his manner of speaking is once again reminiscent of Barth and Jüngel when it comes to the subject of the three distinct modes of subsistence, of the one self-owning (subjective) divine substance, provoking the accusation of Modalism; for example, Moltmann raised this objection.[58] Piet Schoonenberg's (1911–1999) adoption of Rahner's terminology contributed to the suspicions of Modalism in Rahner's work, by giving it a modalistic edge and only assigning a personal profile to the modes of subsistence within the realm of Salvation history.[59] Other things, however, can also be found in Rahner. In order to make the expression 'distinct mode of subsistence' (*distinkte Subsistenzweise*) comprehensible, Rahner explained the expression subsistence (*Subsistenz*) with reference to the experience of human indefensibility (*Unvertretbarkeit*).[60] Nothing else gets to the heart of the Trinitarian notion of person. Rahner appreciates Richard of St Victor's 'personalistic concept'.[61] With a lot of emphasis, Rahner also stresses that the three modes of subsistence (persons) are not three types of the same genus but instead different forms of existence of God, so that it becomes clear why only the Son took on a human nature, and not the Father or the Holy Spirit. The divine pneuma substantiates its

---

[57] Cf. K. Rahner, 'Der dreifaltige Gott als transzendenter Urgrund der Heilsgeschichte' in J. Feiner and M. Löhrer (eds), *Mysterium Salutis*, II, Zürich: Benzinger (3)1978, pp. 317–401.

[58] Cf. Moltmann, *Trinität und Gottes Reich*, pp. 161–6.

[59] Cf. Piet Schoonenberg, 'Trinität – der vollendete Bund. These zur Lehre vom dreipersönlichen Gott' in *Orientierung* 37 (1973) 115–17, here p. 116: 'In economic terms the distinction in God is to be called personal, but on an inner-divine level, at most, modal'.

[60] Cf. Rahner, 'Der dreifaltige Gott', p. 385.

[61] Cf. Karl Rahner, 'Einzigkeit und Dreifaltigkeit Gottes im Gespräch mit dem Islam', in K. Rahner, *Schriften zur Theologie*, 13, pp. 129–47, here p. 147.

own explicit relation between sanctification (*Heiligung*) and the gifts of grace (*Gnadengaben*) for the Christian. Rahner also wants to emphasize the unique relationship of every divine person *ad intra*.

With his reflections to specific and not just appropriated relationships between the divine persons *ad extra*, he aims to justify even the talk of a historical revelation of the Trinity. Nevertheless, Rahner conveys these personalistic statements, which owe their existence to salvation history, without the centre of gravity (*Gravitationszentrums*) of his subject-philosophical approach, so that the impression of a faintly contoured immanent Trinity is dissolved.

Rahner's understanding of the essence of God is wholly in line with Augustinian Trinitarian theology, but applies a transcendental-theological (*transzendentaltheologische*) tone to it. A God revealed to humankind must enter into the matrix of truth and love, the basic precepts of the human spirit, which offer a guide to deducing a preconception of the economic Trinity.[62] Since it is to be understood as the historical form of revelation of the immanent Trinity, it also yields the Trinitarian interpretation of God's basic precepts: the proceeding of the word of truth (*Wahrheitswortes*) and the spirit of love. Given the above, Rahner qualifies this thought as a transcendental theological one; this means he does not claim to present an actual proof of the Trinity but rather – *Trinitate posita* – to prove its truth. Rahner's requirement of proof *(Beweisanspruch)* therefore does not match up to Hegel's. For Hegel it is not surprising that the Church's Trinitarian representation does not reach the plane of proof of the concept. For Rahner, that which is subsequent (*nachträglich*) in the argument corresponds to the philosophical underivability of the salvation-historical event through which the Trinity is revealed.

In summary: in his approach Rahner does not undermine the absoluteness and perfection of God implicit in the Trinitarian concept of essence. The divine persons do not serve towards the consummation of a 'self-explanation of the divine essence' (*Selbstexplikation des göttlichen Wesens*) which would otherwise remain incomplete. God's perfection during salvation history grows just as little. The subject-theoretical reading of the divine essence allows the autonomy of the divine persons to fade on a terminological plane. An intellectual counterweight to this is formed by the reflections to the specific (not-appropriated) relations of the persons *ad extra*; the singularity ('individuality') of each person is thereby exposed. These reflections of Rahner's are crucial: they prove that an approach oriented along the lines of Augustine does not necessarily mask the distinctiveness of the persons, even if Rahner's transformation of the divine substance to subject can appear to have given that impression. Even more, however, Rahner's thoughts on

---

[62] Cf. Rahner, 'Der dreifaltige Gott', pp. 370–82.

the respective singularity of the divine persons form the criterion for other personalistic conceptions, which allow the distinctions between the persons to pale because they shift the concept of person close to a generic term.

# Hans Urs von Balthasar: God's Substance as Being-love

Hans Urs von Balthasar (1905–1988) developed his theo-dramatic concept 'eye to eye' with Hegel.[63] He views the two lines of tradition running together in Hegel as complementary, even converging, approaches to the Trinitarian mystery that has still not allowed itself to be brought to a smooth simple concept.[64] The Swiss theologian favours a rapprochement to the secret of the Trinity by means of a multitude of metaphors, symbols, representational complexes (*Vorstellungskomplexen*) and analogies, which lead to a controversial assessment of the approach: tritheism and Gnostic understanding of divine things were attested to among other things.[65] Balthasar's thinking circles around God's love which was made apparent through the Christ-event (*Christusereignis*); Balthasar assigns it the property of the 'that which we cannot think of in advance (*Unvordenklich*), through which it wins its credibility (*Glaubwürdigkeit*)'. This love does not allow itself to be harnessed to any deductive system of derivation. Its own logic which rules over all human reason and logic is worth considering.[66] The epistemic difference from Hegel but also from Pannenberg and Rahner is apparent. Nevertheless, Balthasar did not swing to the position of a philosophically abstinent theology of faith, as roughly developed by Karl Barth, Emil Brunner (1889–1966) or Eberhard Jüngel.

Balthasar's judgement of the actual historical service of philosophical reason lies at the root of the sceptical evaluation of philosophical reason, before and independent of the emergence of Christianity. Accordingly it is certain that not even the personality of God was comprehensible before

---

[63] This is the opinion of Balthasar's cousin Peter Henrici in '*Zur Philosophie Balthasars*', in K. Lehmann and W. Kasper (eds), *Hans Urs von Balthasar. Gestalt und Werk*, Köln: Communio 1989, pp. 237–59, here p. 247.

[64] Cf. H. Urs von Balthasar, *Theologik*, II, Einsiedeln: Johannes 1985, p. 35.

[65] C. Kappes, *Freiheit und Erlösung. Überlegungen zu den Grundlagen der Soteriologie in den Entwürfen von Hans Urs von Balthasar, Karl Rahner und Jürgen Moltmann*, Bielefeld 1986, p. 39f., p. 139n. H. Vorgrimler, *Gott Vater, Sohn und Heiliger Geist*, Paderborn: Aschendorff 2003, pp. 113–22, recognizes a threat to the belief in a triune God in the defenders of social Trinitarian theology, among whom he also counts Balthasar as well as Moltmann and Greshake.

[66] Cf. paradigmatic H. Urs von Balthasar, *Glaubhaft ist nur Liebe*, Einsiedeln: Johannes Verlag (6) 2000.

Christ. The divine personality, which first enables a relationship between God and man, was understood in the polytheistic myths and was not identified with the philosophical notion of the absolute by reason. The God of Aristotle has no relation to mankind. Without the inspiration of Judaism, Christianity and Islam, the personality of God as well as that of men remained hidden, and comes to its perfection in community with the divine. According to Balthasar, even Hegel's philosophical demand, to develop and read the absolute in terms of the Trinity, owes itself in every regard to the Christian context. Philosophy which opens itself to religion comes to central inspirations and can change its concepts in innovative ways, while still very much following reason.[67]

That the philosophical realization of the essence of God – for example, Aristotle's unmoved mover – can experience a conceptual modification and deepening through Revelation, just as with ontology and anthropology, becomes the foundation for Balthasar in the analogy of being (*Analogie des Seins*). The not 'surpassing being-ness' (*überseinshafte*) Revelation of the divine mystery reveals further aspects of reality.[68]

Balthasar develops these hermeneutical co-ordinates in order to formulate a different answer from that of Jüngel and Moltmann, for example, with a view on the debate about Hellenisation. Through it he can combine the Aristotelian concept of God as the unmoved and unmovable mover with the God of Revelation of inexaustible love that he assigns divine love these quailties. This means the love of God requires neither an external stimulus nor an internal motivator in order to reach perfection. Rather, it is already real in fullness and is enough motive in itself. As the fullness of reality (*actuality*), God's essence is an eternal spiritual liveliness. Balthasar sets this thought of fullness of essence (*Wesensfülle*) as a challenge to Hegel. Because Hegel's absolute is not in itself fullness, it requires both internal and external development. The action (*Handeln*) of God therefore always follows internal need and is not really free. Even the love of the absolute, who makes the death on the cross the predicate of the absolute is more likely to follow the 'cunning' of reason, to reach itself, as the motive for the surrender for the sake of the other.[69]

Greek philosophy was convinced of the lack of suffering (*Leidlosigkeit*) of the divine. In Balthasar's reinterpretation: as a passive experience the suffering of God's being (*Sein*) can in fact be ruled out, but as an expression of his actuality (*Aktualität*) and love it is attributable to God. The cross

---

[67] Cf. H. Urs von Balthasar, *Das Ganze im Fragment*, Einsiedeln: Johannes (2)1990, pp. 61–74.
[68] Cf. H. Urs von Balthasar, *Herrlichkeit*, Vol. III/1: *Im Raum der Metaphysik*, Einsiedeln: Johannes 1965, pp. 943–83.
[69] Cf. H. Urs von Balthasar, *Apokalypse der deutschen Seele*, I, *Der Deutsche Idealismus*, (1937/1947), Freiburg: Johannes (3)1998, pp. 611–19.

does not contradict the divine essence; as being love is capable of sym-pathy (*Sym-pathie*).[70]

Balthasar thinks of the divine entirely from the perspective of the persons and their missions (*Sendungen*). Balthasar rules out God's substance in each independent existence which does not depend on the persons. Only in personal implementation (*Vollzug*) does the essence of God have a fruitful nature, an abundance, an overflow, movement, a 'the more, the bigger'.[71] The divine substance is God's unity, but which is only really there as it personally shares and receives unity, not as a fourth factor, which unifies the three persons existing from him.[72] In order to underline the dependence of the essence towards the persons, Balthasar rejects the thesis of an absolute subsistence of the divine essence, which tradition would have known: for example, Francisco Suárez (1548–1617).[73] The distinguishing mark of concrete subsistence is only awarded to individual persons, not even to a general concept of person. The essence, by contrast, is several essences (*Wesen, verbaliter*). It is the pure 'whereby' (*Wodurch*) of the divine life (*principium quo*), whether subject or proceedings or the divine action *ad extra*. The Father (*principium quod*) generates the force of the essence; by virtue of the essence the Son Man and the Holy Spirit are sent.[74]

But Balthasar does not define God's essence as anonymous working or energy field. Close in thought to Hegel and Rahner, he calls it the 'in itself formed self-possession' (*in sich gefasster Selbst-besitz*),[75] yes, Balthasar speaks of a 'spiritual-personal centre of activity of the absolute spirit' (*geistig-personalen Aktzentrum des absoluten Geistes*). The persons can be described by him as the three modes (*drei Weisen*)[76] of this centre, which again reminds us of the terminology of Barth, Jüngel und Rahner. This manner of expression is unusual for Balthasar, and stands against the backdrop of his critique of latently tri-theistic Trinitarian theologies. Back in the mainstream of his own Trinitarian statements, Balthasar emphasizes that one may not conceive the generation (*die Zeugung*) as emanating from a subjective divine substance (*Gottsubstanz*) of the Father, but rather that one must think of the generation as beginning with the Father and his divine substance;[77] in

---

[70] Cf. the excellent study on the subject by T. Krenski, *Passio Caritatis. Trinitarische Passiologie im Werk Hans Urs von Balthasars*, Einsiedeln Johannes 1990, pp. 187–91.

[71] Cf. H. Urs von Balthasar, *Theodramatik*, IV: *Das Endspiel*, Einsiedeln: Johannes 1983, p. 68.

[72] Balthasar, *Theodramatik*, IV: *Das Endspiel*, p. 57.

[73] Cf. the exceptional study of T. Marschler, *Die spekulative Trinitätslehre des Francisco Suárez SJ in ihrem philosophisch-theologischem Kontext*, Paderborn: Aschendorff 2007, pp. 245–59, pp. 717–24.

[74] Cf. Balthasar, *Theologik*, II, p. 122.

[75] Hans Urs von Balthasar, *Spiritus Creator. Skizzen zur Theologie,* III, Einsiedeln: Johannes (3)1999, p. 97.

[76] Balthasar, *Spiritus Creator*, p. 117.

[77] Cf. Balthasar, *Theologik*, II, p. 120, pp. 122f., pp. 163f.

the Father, the spiritual nature (*Geistsubstanz*) is always already real in a fatherly way. God's essence is not only coextensive (*koextensiv*) in the proceedings (*Hervorgängen*) but also, determined (*mitbestimmt*) through the 'each unique participation' (*je-einmalige Teilnahme*) of the person.[78] The essential recognition (*Erkennen*) (self-ownership, spiritual centre) in the Father can only be a real, notional and productive knowing (*Erkennen*) in that the essential knowing is carried and consummated by the Father, so that with Augustine the Son can be understood as *notia* or *verbum* of this knowing. Starting with the idea of essential 'being-love' Balthasar emphasizes that the productive recognition of the Father is to be understood as love, wherein the selflessness of the recognition and its productivity stand as the centre point, and not the self-reference (*Selbstbezug*) of the Father, who would only find himself through the generation (*Zeugung*) as the knower (*Erkenner*). Otherwise, the Son who proceeds out of the knowing of the Father would make the Father whole in his divinity (*Gottsein*); without the Son, the Father would be blind. The unity of divinity would have been dissolved. Balthasar deepens and completes the speculative Trinitarian doctrine of Augustinian provenance with agapeological reflections. Also the Son and the Spirit are knowers (*Erkennende*) as a result of their divinity, but not in the way in which their person is constituted. According to Balthasar, the qualities of the divine essence which are always the same are real according to different personal properties: the Son recognizes himself and the Father as his source, and recognizes his recognition as an original 'being recognized' (*Erkanntwerden*). In this way the Son is the archetype of creaturely knowing. His person contains, together with that of the Father, the evidence that the essential knowing which represents the unity of the act-of-knowing (*Erkenntnisaktivität*) and – passivity/receptivity. God's substance encompasses the unity of activity and passivity, of loving and being loved, wanting and being wanted. Only therefore can God truly be loved by man, i.e. something according to God's essence can be bestowed on God.[79]

Balthasar famously defines that loving, productive knowing of the Father as the *ur-kenosis*, as a radical self-emptying, which becomes apparent in the historical gift of self (*Dahingabe*) of the Son through the Father. The Son reveals his identity in his kenosis and self-giving; it is the answer to the Father. The essential recognition and loving is immanent to the Spirit, which makes it easy to understand that he functions economically as light, in which the crucified is recognized as the Son, and the glory of the Father is revealed and recognized. The spirit is a gift of God which allows God's love. God-internally he is neither an active recognizer

---

[78] Balthasar, *Theologik*, II, p. 127.
[79] Cf. Balthasar, *Theologik*, II, pp. 162–70.

nor a passive recognizee, but rather the essential recognition and loving in person.[80] As distinct from Hegel, Balthasar thinks the passive in God is not something that still needs development, but rather something highly active, which belongs to the essence of love; without receiving, it remains unreal.[81] The order of the proceedings, after which the Spirit represents pure reception (*Empfangen, spiratio passiva*), can therefore, according to Balthasar, not be dissolved.[82] Not only does Balthasar's notion of the perfection of the divine essence stand up against Hegel's concept of a historical explicating and gaining absolute; but he also emphasizes on the personal level: no difference, whether it is sin or death enlarges or fulfils the personal differences in God. On the other hand, Balthasar says: God can have something from the world, namely himself, through the people this does not augment but rather reveals their qualities, to be an eternal evermore (*je Mehr*) of relationship and love, for which it is essential not only to give but also to receive from others.[83]

In summary: Balthasar's Trinitarian theology documents without a doubt the sense and the need to speak of a divine essence. The often metaphorical manner of speaking and the transfer of individual aspects of the economy of salvation in the immanent Trinity and the talk of the intra-divine kenosis (over-death, parting) have given rise to criticism, which finds fault in a tritheism and is reminiscent of the criticism levelled against Moltmann.

Balthasar thinks of God's essence as fullness as well as an openness for the other which goes beyond Aristotle, overtaking Hegel, as a free agency in history and as far as the interior of man is thought – also in the sense, of true infinity. Balthasar calls the divine essence 'being love', that is really in the persons. The reception of metaphysical divine attributes, changelessness (*Unveränderlichkeit*) and immobility (*Unbeweglichkeit*) prevent us from construing this love with human yardsticks, i.e. in need of consummation. Balthasar offers important clues with his agapeological reflections on God's essence and the basic precepts for an Augustinian-spiritual metaphysical Trinitarian theology. Generation as a word-productive knowing must be subject to a matrix of selfless Love. In this manner, Balthasar's concept of convergence succeeds: the essence is imaginable as self-possession and at the same time as being-love. The persons, which are definitely thought of as subject, are the concrete existence and subsistence of the divine essence. When Balthasar retains the term subsistence of the persons, this is not to

---

[80] Cf. H. Urs von Balthasar, *Theologik*, III: *Der Geist der Wahrheit*, Einsiedeln: Johannes 1987, pp. 180–8, pp. 207–30.

[81] Cf. H. Urs von Balthasar, *Theodramatik*, III: *Die Handlung*, Einsiedeln: Johannes 1980, pp. 297–305.

[82] Cf. Balthasar, *Theologik I*, p. 127; III: pp. 129f.

[83] Cf. Balthasar, *Theodramatik III*, p. 297, pp. 302–9; *Theodramatik, IV: Das Endspiel*, Einsiedeln: Johannes 1983, pp. 463–76.

deny the essence of God's existence or to demote it to simple power, but rather to emphasize that the divine substance is concretely real only when it is made up of three persons, and that the persons carry the divine essence metaphysically, not that the essence realizes the persons (allows them to subsist) as his properties.

# Trinitarian theology without direction?

The further development of Trinitarian theology swings between the marked poles and attempts to arbitrate between them. However, this does not mean that Trinitarian theology is without direction; rather, it shows its complexity, which must be understood as a warning against superficial answers. For example, Magnus Street (b. 1964) promises the most from an understanding of the Trinity (*Trinitätsverständnis*) in which the constitution of the divine persons can be seen to imply a reciprocal freedom event (*Freiheitsgeschehen*); every essentialism would be turned off by it. This event (*Geschehen*) of the three freedoms might even demand it to be entered into God's eternal timeliness (*Zeitlichkeit*).[84]

The Trinitarian concept of essence that is completely absorbed by the interpersonal event of course no longer functions criteriologically in order to secure the absoluteness of the persons in their Godhead and bring to the fore the dissimilarities of infinite Freedom and finite freedom. To the ontological 'concentration' (*Konzentration*) of the divine being belongs the immediate unity of self-constitution and self-realization. Even God's resolution to creation, which is unnecessary and therefore contingent, bears no temporal chronology in God's reality, as God has forever wanted the unnecessary and contingent with his unchanging will, not just at one point in time. The aliveness (*Lebendigkeit*) of the divine implementation of freedom (*Freiheitsvollzugs*) is no longer dependent on a stretched, strewn temporality: it differs from the view of Paul Tillich, 1886–1965. Much more, God is constant simultaneously unlimited aliveness and consummation of his freedom; agreement with himself. To the absoluteness of God, which as he explains can only be God's absolute love in Christian understanding, belongs, as described, openness to the temporal, the finite and even an active soteriological ability to show mercy in favour of a contingent freedom in order to complete their time in eternity. In the generation, one can, like Balthasar, recognise an archetype (*Urbild*) about origin and future:

---

[84] Cf. Magnus Striet, *Offenbares Geheimnis*, Regensburg: Pustet 2003, pp. 231–64; 'Spekulative Verfremdung? Trinitätstheologie in der Diskussion', in *Herder-Korrespondenz* 56 (2002) pp. 202–7. Cf. also H. Vorgrimler, 'Randständiges Dasein des dreieinigen Gottes? Zur praktischen und spirituellen Dimension der Trinitätslehre', in *Stimmen der Zeit* 220 (2002) 545–52.

the Father describes the Son's provenance, the Son the future of the Father. The Spirit is both now – in God and externally.[85]

After Gisbert Greshake's (b. 1933) impressive blueprint for a Trinitarian-communial theology with a focus on the total reality (*Gesamtwirklichkeit*),[86] it looked as though the social theoretical direction would decide the future. Magnus Striet's approach delivered a further example. The undeniable deficiency of social Trinitarian theology became the reason for a renaissance of spiritual metaphysical approaches, which understand the divine persons as instances, hypostases, modes of being in the spiritual nature of God, but does not think of them as subjects of freedom.

# Roland Kandy: God's substance as self-knowledge – Augustine's discovery

Roland Kany (b. 1958) is almost showman-like when he presents the positions outlined above in his profound study on Augustine's Trinitarian thought.[87] First their partially clichéd criticism is exposed, and then it is shown that even a common adversary does not unify them as systematic congruence. Far from it, contradistinctions convulse their own anti-Augustinian position. To counter it, Kany praises Augustine's Trinitarian thought. Kany was able to bring Augustine's brilliance to the fore thanks to his meticulous investigations. He notes the subject-theoretical insight that the original self-knowledge (*Selbstwissen*) which precedes all intentional acts – including self-awareness (*Selbsterkenntniss*) and, connected with it, self-objectification (*Selbstverobjektivierung*) – is as an actual discovery of Augustine's.[88] The initial self-presence (*Selbstgegenwart*) distinguishes itself accordingly from every kind of objective knowledge (*Erkenntnis*), even from the self-objectification in self-awareness. This non-objective self-presence of the spirit manifests itself in the self-reflexive forms (*Gestalten*) *memoria, intellegentia* and *voluntas*, where each in itself is identical with the spirit and represents its life. As the human is unable either to catch up with or to set the starting point of his self-reference (*Selbstbezug*), he knows himself as creature (*Geschöpf*) and in so far as image of God. God is the archetypal absolute self-presence, whose *memoria* remembers its beginningless beginning, the Father, and comprehends itself expressly in the knowledge-Word (*Erkenntnis-Wort*). By virtue of the spirit affirming

---

[85] Cf. Balthasar, Theodramatik, IV, pp. 80–3, 88–90.
[86] Cf. Greshake, *Der dreieine Gott*, p. 199.
[87] Cf. R. Kany, *Augustins Trinitätsdenken*, Tübingen: Mohr 2007, pp. 369–92.
[88] Cf. Kany, *Augustins Trinitätsdenken*, pp. 507–34.

the divine self-insight (*Selbst-einsicht*), beginning (*Ursprung*) and Word are willingly tied together. Referring to Plotinus (205–270), Augustine discovers a unity in the self-presence of the spirit that can be applied before Subject-Object (*Subjekt-Objekt-Differenz*) become distinct, and is therefore compatible with a primal unity (*Ureinen*). Plotinus excludes difference between subject and object of self-awareness from the *hen*, so that the Trinity, according to this philosophical yardstick, is not thought of as an unsurpassable absolute greatness but rather is only understood on the second plane of the *nous*. Augustine's Trinitarian theology therefore first ensures the rationally demonstrable absoluteness of the Trinity. Kany likewise builds a bridge to Idealism, to Johann Gottlieb Fichte's (1762–1814) original insight into the nature of the original self-consciousness (*Selbstbewusstsein*) before intentional actions.[89] In *Science of Logic*, Hegel positions the immediacy of thought before every differentiation in subject and object parallel to it. Reflexive knowledge arises from original immediacy (*Unmittelbarkeit*).

In summary, Augustine offers a concept of the divine essence that makes the supra-objective transcendental unity of the Trinity rationally conceivable, thereby ensuring its absoluteness and myth-free divinity. God is not represented as an object (*Gegenstand*) of human recognition, as Hegel would say – in other words separated from people as any other object – but rather as a transcendent foundation/reason (*Grund*) present at the centre of the human spirit, which gives self-presence and can be understood as the basis for this self-presence. In his self-presence, man allows participation in God's spirituality and self-presence. Their internal complexity can be thought about without harming their unity. The insights into Augustine's Trinitarian thought conveyed by Kany do not of course solve the systematic question after the own profile of the divine persons. Kany's reconstruction of Augustinian Trinitarian thought could once more allow Islam's criticism of Christian Trinitarian doctrine to arrive at the conviction that the discussion of three divine persons only represents clumsy Christian attempts to represent the living spirituality of God. The systematic Trinitarian models of which Kany is critical have at least taken on this problem.

---

[89] Kany, *Augustins Trinitätsdenken*, pp. 531n. On intersubjectivity in Fichte, cf. R. Lauth, *Transzendentale Entwicklungslinien von Descartes bis zu Marx und Dostojewski*, Hamburg: Meiner 1989, pp. 180–95.

# Thomas Schärtl: God's substance as instantive self-mediation

Thomas Schärtl's (b. 1969) investigations in linguistic philosophy concerning the intelligibility, i.e. the logic of a discussion, of a Trinitarian God,[90] mark the location (*Ort*) of the discussion initially in reference to Hegel and western Tradition: as God-appropriate (*Gott entsprechend*) human speech, it cannot be externally applied to God; rather God encompasses the final standing point (which was made manifest in the Incarnation) as true infinity and as spirit, and from that point enables pneumatically to divine speech (*Gottesrede*). As is recognizable in Pannenberg and also Rahner to a certain extent, Schärtl is no less interested in moving forward the philosophical knowledge of God through Trinitarian theology. This does not take place by calling on *rationes necessariae* (Anselm), but rather by using 'weaker' arguments of convenience which take into account the contingency of salvation history. Through this, philosophical aporiae of the knowledge of God are to be overcome, by addressing the ontological question about the finite multiplicity out of divine one-ness or the epistemic question about the possibility of addressing God's one-ness of essence with a multiplicity of attributes. Only a God differentiated in himself, who is also Word and who doesn't stand in an abstract in him-ending contrast to the plurality of the finite, allows the human address, which aims towards divinity out of the multiplicity of the finite. Corresponding to Hegel's notion which is guaranteed absolute truth in the present, Schärtl speaks of a co-presence of God, which allows for religious and theological discussion of God in the now.

As a regulative principle of the divine attributes (*Gottesprädikate*) Schärtl introduces the concept of perfection (*Vollkommenheitsbegriff*), which connotes vitality, in other words, self-mediation. With it he rejects a historical consummation (*Vervollkommnung*) of God, without however, as can be seen, taking God's essence out of history. Instead, in the generation (*Zeugung*) and spiration, he sees an intra-divine approach to the openness of God for the finite and the relationship with the creator. The operative qualities of God as creator, Lord, redeemer and consummator Schärtl calls a new essentiality of God (*neue Wesentlichkeit Gottes*). With this expression he signals, like Hegel and Pannenberg, that God reveals his real essence in his acts, and therefore it is to be assumed that God has decided and determined to his acting *ad extra* from eternity. With this statement Schärtl draws the general consequences from the incarnationally uncontested insight that

---

[90] Cf. T. Schärtl, *Theo-Grammatik. Zur Logik der Rede vom trinitarischen Gott*, Regensburg: Pustet 2003.

the concrete, true God will no longer be conceivable without the human nature taken on by the Logos, and through it, makes every reference of man to God possible.

The essence of God qua self-mediation (*Selbstvermittlung*) Schärtl understands as subject. Hegel's category of the absolute idea (which is anticipated in the concept (*Begriff*) offers a paradigmatic insight into the triadic process of self-mediation: immediate given-ess (*Gegebensein*), difference-establishing reflexion and synthesizing spirituality. Like Rahner and also Helmut Hoping (b. 1956), Schärtl problematizes the concepts like subject, freedom and awareness used by the representatives of social Trinitarian doctrine to identify the divine persons because of its almost uncircumventable tri-theism.[91] In addition, the description of the persons' subsisting relations without a specification of the relata – so once again the persons – represents an aporia. Under the assumption that Trinitarian terminology does not offer a pictorial representation of the Trinity (*Dreieingkeit*), Schärtl uses a grammatical and indexical system for the concept of subject. The object-reference (*Sachreferenz*) for this lies in the three, assumed irreducible instances of the self-mediation of God. These instances should be understood as hypostases or modes of being (*Seinsweisen*) of the essentially existing God. Origin (*Herkünftigkeit*), self-possession (*Selbstbesitz*, (Truth) and self-affirmation (Goodness) mark all these instances in their reciprocity. Schärtl conceives of the Trinity in a way which is reminiscent of Peter Abelard (1079–1142): divine attributes (Abelard: Omnipotence, Wisdom, Goodness) become the marks of the three personal instances in the process of divine self-mediation. The parallels to the teaching of appropriation are equally unmistakable.

In summary, from Hegel to Schärtl, Trinitarian theology has come full circle, to put it succinctly. God's substance becomes subject, thereafter social tri-personality, and finally back to subject. In other words: does nothing remain but swinging between Modalism and Tritheism? Or is pluralism in Trinitarian theology simply legitimate? Is God himself the author of this multiplicity if the human point of view is to be encompassed and underpinned by the divine (incarnationally and pneumatically)? Or are there convergences of the approaches, as Balthasar suggests?

---

[91] Cf. H. Hoping, 'Göttliche und menschliche Person', in *Theologie und Glaube* 41 (1998) 162–74, here pp. 168n; Schärtl, *Theo-Grammatik*, pp. 473n.

# Summary: God's substance as Trinitarian self-knowledge and love

The following perspectives, where the Trinitarian concepts of essence and substance are concerned, are opened up: the Trinitarian concept of essences links Trinitarian doctrine with a philosophical approach to the concept of the divine. In connection with the philosophical notion of God, the concept of essences provides a rational unfolding of Trinitarian doctrine, regardless of whether it conceived from spirit theory (*geisttheoretisch*) or social theory. The concept of essence expresses God's absoluteness or true infinity (*aliquid quo maius nihil cogitari potest*) as well as God's closeness to humans (*deus interior intimo meo*). Based on this concept it is clear that neither the historical engagement of God nor his personality, which is thereby assumed, are understood in terms of myth.

The concept of essence expresses God's natural, substantial one-ness. That this essential unity can be itself differentiated persons, and not serve as the fourth factor which unifies people, is demonstrated in the reconstruction of the Augustinian approach. In the pre-reflexive self-present of the human spirit, a dimension becomes visible into which differences are enclosed, but which are not set up as such. What is suggested here about the human spirit and its unity must be all the more acceptable to God. God's essence is spirit in the consummation of one unity, whose inner differences lie beyond the difference-unity of subject and object as well as the dialectic of unity. The Trinitarian structure of the human self-present becomes visible according to Kany with the explanation of the self-present, the difference of the knower and the known is not just bound through knowledge. This differentiation must always already be real in the divine spirit. Kany and Schärtl elucidate how this self-presence (*memoria, Selbstgegenwart*) is volitional: the difference of the knower and the known is not just bound through knowledge but through an *An-Erkenntnis*, or acknowledgement, through self-affirmation. The being-spirit (*Geistsein*) is *intelligentia* and *voluntas*.

Balthasar's agapeological considerations of a productive knowledge rightly underline that God's spirit-performances (*Geistvollzüge*) form an essential unity, and do not represent separate faculties of the substantial spirit; and above all the generating knowledge (*zeugende Erkenntnis*) in God should be considered through the characteristic of revelation: as surrender in terms of the truth of the other in his otherness. With his deliberations over productive knowledge (*productive Erkenntnis*), Balthasar offers an insight which intellectually can be placed close to the thoughts of Emmanuel Levinas (1906–1995), who demands a correction of the concepts of knowledge and subject, in order to exclude any possessive form of knowing. It is important to remember, therefore, that God's essence must be first thought of as being-love (*Liebe-sein*) (Jüngel, Pannenberg, Balthasar);

this is the point from which the spirit-metaphysical consequences and implications are to be developed: God's self-presence and self-possession (Rahner, Balthasar, Schärtl).

If God's essence is thought of as love, then the revelation of God as a free occurrence (*Geschehen*) is compatible with the essential unchangingness of the divine reality (Balthasar). God's engagement is not motivated by overcoming egoism (Jüngel), but it remains unclear where the measure for the actuation in love originates, which is clearly not identical to God. With Balthasar the thought of the unchanging but receptive divine love can be developed in regard to the world in its relationship to God. From the world, God receives himself as creator, redeemer and consummator of the world, without becoming more perfect. Because the divine persons respectively receive from one another in different ways in that they communicate and receive the divine essence – in other words each in his own way completes it – it is appropriate to God's being (*Sein*) to receive himself in terms of salvation history. It is only with the doctrine of the Trinity that it becomes clear that essential being-love (*Liebe-sein*) is not just outpouring (*bonum diffusivum sui*), but also reception.

In the light of the divine essence being defined as love, there is a lot in favour of the already heralded personalistic manner of speaking. It fits, not least, with biblical and liturgical evidence. He who connects or identifies the Logos with the 'I' Jesus that speaks to the Father also has to comprehend the Logos as a personal other of the Father. This seems clearly to convey more than the statement of the first mode of consummation or the first instance of divine mediation. Something similar is relevant to the multiplicity of the Holy Spirit's activities, who is considered to be their subject. With this biblical evidence, the social Trinitarian teaching has its legitimate starting point.

In order not to expose teaching about the social Trinity to a naive game with interpersonal relationships and projections, it must be brought closer to the level of reflection that Kany suggests. Therefore it is necessary to show that the presence of fellow human beings belongs to pre-reflexive self-presence (*Selbstgegenwart*) of the human spirit, like a common spirit, in which the self-presence of the one is real with the other. When it is initially said, with reference to man, that the knowing self-familiarity (*Selbstvertrautheit*) does not set its own starting point, but rather owes itself to some inconceivable transcendental reason, then it must be added that this reason conveys itself through fellow human beings. In terms of the theory of consciousness, it means that self-presence (*Selbstgegenwart*) qua self-consciousness (*Selbstbewusstsein*) is neither given through intentional positing (*Setzung*) nor out of itself through solitary self-familiarity, but rather through a pre-reflexive relatedness (*Bezogensein*) to other (*anderes*), which only with itself allows for familiarity (*vertraut sein*). This other cannot be exhausted in a direct object (*Sachobjekt*), because a relational consciousness is structurally foreign to it; it cannot become familiar with itself and so therefore cannot develop into consciousness.

This other cannot be exhausted in a direct object, as a consciousness cannot become familiar with itself, in other words, cannot realise itself as consciousness, in reference to something that is structurally alien to it. In order to arrive at oneself while coming from the other, the other must be an other (*Anderes*); it must be another consciousness, which, as Johann Gottlieb Fichte (1762–1814) says, 'calls to' (*anruft*) the (first) consciousness. The second consciousness makes possible the defining of the first consciousness through a delimiting distinction from the second one, in unity with him. Coming from the other consciousness, consciousness is pre-reflexive self-consciousness; it is self-presence.

What is set out with it is likewise not a posited but rather a pre-given unity, which imparts relatedness from consciousness to consciousness. Once again, it is important to emphasize the non-intentional, intuitive-immediate or pre-reflexive character of this Triad. If one were to insist that the factors mentioned (*Größen*) and relations *(Bezüge)* are constituted of an intentional positing (*intentionale Setzung*), then one would yet again obscure the subject-theoretical discoveries of Augustine and Fichte – the immediate knowledge of self (*Sichwissen*) as condition of over intentional relation (*intentionalen Bezug*).

We add the following thought: the immediate self-knowledge comes from the other towards it, is a given, granted self-familiarity (*Selbstvertrautheit*). The infinity of the 'I' of which Hegel speaks is only true infinity if it includes the you and the us. The ultimate basis of the self-given, self-receiving human knowledge of self (*Sichwissen*) is the three-personed God who possesses in himself an analogous spirit structure (*Geiststruktur*). With this, we argued that the relationality of the human self-present is not exclusively an indicator of limitation (*Begrenztheit*) and contingency (*Kontingenz*), but rather primarily indicates something quite positive, the reality of spirit and love. In other words the divine persons do not only dispose of themselves, but they are also not themselves as persons without the respective others. As concrete realities of the one essential self-presence of God, they show this self-presence as one which is not given without reference to otherness (*Andersheit*) or without the unity of self-presence and otherness. Augustinian Trinitarian teaching now says this in exactly the same way as interpersonal teaching. The reality of the interpersonal reality of the divine self-presence does not demand a plural representation (*Darstellung*) through unique individuals, but rather it is really in and of itself the one indivisible divine essence. In the human case the third does not even necessarily represent a third person; it deals with the together (*Beisammen*) and the between (*Zwischen*), the sociality of man, which can, according to Hegel be grasped as an objective spirit. In

God, the third is the 'We' personified, as Heribert Mühlen (1927–2006) claims.[92] In the three-personhood of the one God, the divine essence is not a neutral primordial cause (*Urgrund*), not its own subject, but rather spirit which does not only fulfil itself triadically but is also a real Trinity in the framework of the persons.

Paradoxically the persons are both relata and relations. The Thomistic Trinitarian theology speaks more precisely of a logical priority of the person-shaping relations, and in so doing the persons before the processes (*Hervorgängen*), in order to demonstrate that all the dealings of God are also the dealings of the persons, and the persons are therefore not to be seen as mere products of the processes; otherwise one would have once again declared the essence to be the actual subject of the productivity of the divine persons. For this reason it is always the Father who generates; the Father is not the Father because he generates.[93]

Names and 'locations' (*Orte*) of the persons in God are to be originally taken out the Scriptural evidence. For this reason, speculation about the Trinity cannot neutralise the original person of the Father. If the Trinity is thought of as Love, then there is no problem of dominance and subordination with the primacy of the Father. What does become problematic is when, for the sake of the equality of the persons, one thinks that all persons must be conceived in the same way. Through it their difference (*Unterschiedlichkeit*) becomes unclear. The divine persons cannot change their 'places' in God. Their constitutive personal quality (*Personeneigenschaft*) is not communicable (Richard of St Victor), only the divine essence. The incommunicableness (*Nichtmitteilbarkeit*) or untenablity (*Unvertretbarkeit*) of the persons first becomes thinkable when God's essence is understood as love and communication. One would hardly be able to ascribe to the divine persons a consciousness (*Bewusstsein*) of their own singularity in their interconnection (Verbund), without immediately conjuring tritheism. Because of the unsoundness (*Unvertretbarkeit*) of the divine persons, Balthasar even dares to speak of the secret in God (*Geheimnis in Gott*). The Father can never be the Son (just as knowing – *Erkennen* – is not the same as volition, *Wollen*): what is implied in being the Son is opened to the Father only from the son and so on. The essential self-presence of God enfolds this being-from-and-of-the-others (*Von-Anderen-Her-Sein*) in itself. It is only from the three-personality of God that this dimension of the self-presence of God becomes visible. It is not a flat understanding (*Durchblicken*) or seeing through (*Durchschauen*), it is not a mere knowing about (*Bescheidwissen*),

---

[92] Cf. H. Mühlen, *Der Heilige Geist als Person. In der Trinität bei der Inkarnation und im Gnadenbund: Ich-Du-Wir*, Münster: Aschendorff (4) 1980.
[93] Cf. STh. I, 40, 4.

but rather a being-self-illumined (*Selbstgelichtetsein*), productive knowing, openness and reception. It is therefore greater than a subjectivity which is 'short-circuited'; it converges with love.

# 7

# Perichoresis: A Key Concept for Balancing Trinitarian Theology

## Emmanuel Durand O.P.

The 'perichoresis' or 'circumincession' of the three divine Persons, a concept of Patristic origin, has acquired today a growing and varied audience, to the point that the delineation of its theological relevance has become a pressing matter.[1] In order to develop the necessary detail required for study of this concept, it will be treated here beginning from the precise meaning established by the Greek Fathers, i.e. the mutual immanence of Father, Son and Holy Spirit. Attention to this foundation favours a true and proper actualization of the concept, through a theology of reciprocity and communion among the divine persons.

There are two primary aspects that invigorate the current interest elicited by the concept of perichoresis: renewal of an understanding of divine unity, and promotion of ecumenical dialogue on the origin of the Holy Spirit.

Nowadays perichoresis is often invoked, however, without an in-depth analysis of the concept, as an alternative to other expressions of Trinitarian faith, e.g. consubstantiality or unity of essence, the monarchy of the Father, or the order of the three hypostases. Perichoresis is thus firmly situated as a primary or foundational concept in Trinitarian theology, as one of its explanatory keys. It is worth analyzing this position in order to determine

---

[1] See E. Durand, *La périchorèse des personnes divines. Immanence mutuelle, réciprocité et communion*, (Cogitatio Fidei, 243), Paris: Cerf 2005.

whether perichoresis should fill the role of a foundational concept, or whether it should instead be understood as a concept which balances and recapitulates Trinitarian theology.

In contemporary ecumenical discussion, oriental and occidental theologians have looked to elements of Trinitarian perichoresis to make progress in the domain of Pneumatology. Perichoresis, understood as inseparability or reciprocity, can in fact have a 'correcting' role in reference to the so called occidental 'filioquist' tendencies to a certain subordination of the Spirit in relation to the Father and Son. This view of the role of the concept of perichoresis is certainly stimulating and promising, but it as of yet lacks a solid speculative basis, one rigorously constructed on a well-defined concept.

In order to make progress towards such a concept, one must look to a decisive moment in the intellectual history of perichoresis, situated between John Damascene and contemporary theologies. Following a translation of Damascene's *De Fide Orthodoxa* in the middle of the twelfth century, the thirteenth century brought forth a variety of manners in which the concept was received, as well as a constructive reflection on the aspects of the mystery it relates to. This led to models of understanding that can still serve today in our rediscovery of the perichoresis of the divine Persons. Bonaventure is known to have given pride of place to *circumincessio*. His interpretation is in fact fundamental in recognizing that perichoresis is a concept that integrates unity of essence and personal distinction. This opens the path to developments of perichoresis as a form of communion that is at once consubstantial and interpersonal. However, in order to develop a theology of perichoretic communion of the divine Persons, it is useful to explore certain relatively unknown intuitions of Thomas Aquinas, and particularly his original presentation of the mutual immanence of the Three Persons. The *aporia* of a certain subordination of the relation of the Father and Son to the Spirit in relationship to the relation of the Father to the Son nevertheless remains in Thomasian theology. In order to overcome this difficulty, a theology of perichoresis should be founded on a hermeneutic study of the Johannine verses that witness to the mutual immanence of Jesus and his Father.[2] From this perspective, and in dialogue with theological tradition, a speculative proposal for redefining the concept of Trinitarian perichoresis becomes possible, one that understands it in the light of the connection of the intra-divine processions and the reciprocity of Trinitarian relations. This gives us a better understanding of divine paternity, and permits an ecumenical approach to the origin of the Spirit.

---

[2] See Jn 10.37–38, 14.10–11, 17.21–23.

# Tradition and Contemporary Theology

Trinitarian perichoresis has become fashionable these days, and for this we owe a debt to certain pioneers in the field of what has been called 'positive' theology, notably D. Petau in the seventeenth century and T. de Régnon at the end of the nineteenth century. Trinitarian *perichoresis* is, however, a late Patristic notion. The verb *perichorein* was first used in Christology by Gregory Nazianzen, and later by Maximus the Confessor, to signify the communication of idioms (human or divine properties) in the unique person of Christ. The transposition to Trinitarian theology occurs thanks to John Damascene's *De Fide Orthodoxa*.[3] We can note revealing changes in prepositions, however, in this shift from Christology to Trinitarian theology: whereas the verb is constructed with the preposition *eis* + accusative in Christology, it is constructed with *en* + dative when applied to Trinitarian theology. We have gone from the idea of *exchange* or *permutation* of the properties of the natures of Christ to the evocation of a reciprocal *indwelling* of the Trinitarian hypostases – each in the two others.

In the second half of the twelfth century the term *circumincessio* entered the West through a Latin translation of *De Fide Orthodoxa*. Whereas Alexander of Hales and Bonaventure took the meaning of *circumincessio* as their own, Albert the Great and Thomas Aquinas contented themselves with the Johannine statements concerning the mutual indwelling between Jesus and his Father. In his commentary of I *Sent.*, d. 19, a. 1, q. 3, Bonaventure understands *circumincessio* to be the reunion of personal distinction and unity of essence in a single concept. In *Summa theologiae* Ia, q. 42, a. 5, Thomas Aquinas explains the mutual indwelling between the Father and the Son with three considerations: 1) unity of essence; 2) correlativity of persons; and 3) the modes of the origins of the Son as Word and of the Holy Spirit as Love. Only this last consideration is proper to the Aquinate, and it depends on the precision with which he represented the generation of the Son by analogy with our conception of an immanent and relative word (i.e.

---

[3] See V. Conticello, 'Pseudo-Cyril's "De SS. Trinitate": A Compilation of Joseph the Philosopher', in *Orientalia Christiana Periodica* 61 (1995) 117–29; J. P. Egan, 'Primal Cause and Trinitarian Perichoresis in Gregory Nazianzen's Oration 31.14', in *Studia Patristica* XXVII (1991) 21–8; V. Harrison, 'Perichoresis in the Greek Fathers', in *St Vladimir's Theological Quarterly* 35 (1991) 53–65; J. P. Egan, 'Toward Trinitarian Perichoresis: Saint Gregory the Theologian, *Oration* 31.41', in *Greek Orthodox Theological Review* 39 (1994) 83–93; D. F. Stramara, 'Gregory of Nyssa's Terminology for Trinitarian Perichoresis', in *Vigiliae christianae* 52 (1998) 257–63; G. D. Dragas, 'Exchange of Properties and Deification: Antidosis or Communicatio Idiomatum and Theosis', in *The Greek Orthodox Theological Review* 43/1–4 (1998) 377–99; R. Cross, 'Perichoresis, Deification, and Christological Predication in John of Damascus', in *Mediaeval Studies* 62 (2000) 69–124 (unfortunately unaware of Conticello's demonstration); L. F. Mateo-Seco, 'Perichoresis y circuminsessio', in *Scripta theologica*, 35/2 (2003) 507–15.

concept), and the procession of the Spirit by analogy with our production of an immanent and relative term in the operation of loving. This second image relies on the experience of carrying a beloved person in one's heart. The immanence of the beloved within the will of the lover is then described as a kind of affective impression or imprint (*impressio*). Following this created image, the Holy Spirit can be understood as the Love from the Father that rests on the Son, and returns from the Son to the Father.

The analysis of Aquinas' third explication of the mutual indwelling of Father and Son, combined with a facet of his Pneumatology that regards the Spirit as mutual love, brings us to the development of a contemporary thesis: following the example of Jn 17.21 ('that they may all be one, even as you Father, are in me and I in you'), Trinitarian perichoresis has a similar development and renewal in the concept of an interpersonal communion of love. This idea is broadly adhered to today, but rarely with the speculative support that it requires.

Moltmann is one contemporary who was strongly influenced by the concept of perichoresis, enough to make it the starting point of his conception of Trinitarian Unity.[4] From our point of view, however, perichoresis cannot be an initial 'given' in Trinitarian theology, but it must rather play the role of regulating other concepts, in particular the order of origin of the Divine Persons, the Monarchy of the Father and the *Filioque*. What is interesting in Moltmann's proposition is his desire to conceive of Trinitarian Unity as welcoming and capable of integration. This vein of thought was explored by Boff, who considered that Trinitarian perichoresis can inspire a model for society, akin to a humanizing utopia.[5] However, before both Moltmann and Boff, Mühlen had already envisaged perichoresis as the Trinitarian origin of the Church in a persuasive way.[6] During the last two decades, the list of publications dealing with Trinitarian perichoresis has notably increased, with authors exploring various implications of this doctrine in many fields of theology.[7]

---

[4] See J. Moltmann, 'Perichoresis: An Old Magic Word for a New Trinitarian Theology', in M. D. Meeks (ed.), *Trinity, Community, and Power*, Nashville: Kingswood, 2000, pp. 111–25; 'God in the World – The World in God: Perichoresis in Trinity and Eschatology', in R. Bauckham, C. Mosser (eds), *The Gospel of John and Christian Theology*, Grand Rapids: Eerdmans, 2008, pp. 369–81; *Trinity and the Kingdom: The Doctrine of God*, San Francisco, 1981.
[5] See L. Boff, *Trinity and Society*, Maryknoll NY: Orbis 1988.
[6] See H. Mühlen, *Una mystica persona. Eine Person in vielen Personen*, Paderborn: Schöningh 1964.
[7] See R. L. Kress, 'Unity in Diversity and Diversity in Unity: toward an ecumenical perichoresic kenotic trinitarian ontology', in *Dialogue et Alliance* 4 (1990) 66–70; T. Hart, 'Person & Prerogative in Perichoretic Perspective – an ongoing dispute in trinitarian ontology observed', in *Irish Theological Quarterly* 58 (1992) 46–57; M. G. Lawler, 'Perichoresis: New Theological Wine in an Old Theological Wineskin', in *Horizons* 22/1 (1995) 49–66; L. Thunberg, 'Circumincession once more: Trinitarian and Christological Implications in an

# Fundamental Proposal

We shall now present our own development of the doctrine of perichoresis. The concept fundamentally signifies the mutual immanence between the Father and Christ, but fortunately it has been extended to refer to the three divine Persons. This leads to a considerable enrichment of the initial content of the theme. The mutual immanence of the three Persons is understood as a consequence of their inseparability, because, since they are all in one other, the mention or presence of one of the three Persons is accompanied by that of the two others as well. Such a perichoresis can be seen, on the one hand, in the intrinsic connection between generation and procession, and on the other hand, in the effective reciprocity of the Trinitarian relations. Trinitarian perichoresis can thus be formulated according to two blueprints: one, of the immanent acts of the divine life, and the other, of the Trinitarian relations expressed by these acts. For neither the two immanent acts (generation of the Son and procession of the Holy Spirit) nor the two pairs of reciprocal relations (Father – Son and Father & Son – Holy Spirit) are external to each other.

Following the third Johannine formulation of the mutual immanence of the Father and Christ (Jn 17:21), Trinitarian perichoresis takes on a sense of a communion of love. In this manner the fully personal signification of perichoresis can be seen. By the recapitulation of the unity of essence and the distinction of Persons, it supports an interpersonal interpretation of the Trinity. This reading is in harmony with the Johannine verses that indicated the Patristic developments of perichoresis. Another characteristic of this mystery of communion is that it finalizes the other aspects of the concept, thereby clarifying their meanings.

We are now able to situate the role that perichoresis can and should have in a complete exposition of Trinitarian doctrine. Perichoresis is not a primary or foundational concept that can replace consubstantiality or Trinitarian order, but this should not lead us to reduce it to a simple, almost superfluous, corollary concept. Beyond the fact that it is a recapitulative

---

Age of Religious Pluralism', in *Studia Patristica* XXIX (1997) 364–72; C. Sorč, 'Die pericho-retischen Beziehungen im Leben der Trinität und in der Gemeinschaft der Menschen', in *Evangelische Theologie* 58 (1998) 100–19; J.-P. Batut, 'Monarchie du Père, ordre des processions, périchorèse', in *Communio* XXIV/5–6 (1999) 17–29; M. Kotiranta, 'The Palamite Idea of Perichoresis of the Persons of the Trinity in the light of Contemporary neo-Palamite Analysis', in *Byzantium and the North – Acta Byzantina Fennica* 9 (1999) 59–69; K. Kilby, 'Perichoresis and Projection: Problems with Social Doctrines of the Trinity', in *New Blackfriars* 81/956 (2000) 432–45; R. E. Otto, 'The Use and Abuse of Perichoresis in Recent Theology', in *Scottish Journal of Theology* 54/3 (2001) 366–84; O. D. Crisp, 'Problems with Perichoresis", in *Tyndale Bulletin* 56 (2005) 119–40; D. G. Attfield, 'I in you and you in me: Perichoresis and Salvation', in *Theology* 109/852 (2006) 421–9.

concept enriched through numerous harmonizing factors, perichoresis can also have a central moderating role throughout the entire Trinitarian study. This shows that the pertinence of perichoresis in Trinitarian theology is not to be limited to only the descriptive level (sometimes even the imaginative level, e.g., when one speaks of an intra-divine dance), but that it has a function on the analytical level itself.

# The Role of Perichoresis in Trinitarian Theology

How should the concept of perichoresis intervene throughout a presentation of the Trinitarian mystery? First, perichoresis, as we have defined and worked with it, affirms the immanence of generation and the reciprocity of the relation between the Father and the Son. In fact, the Johannine formulations of mutual immanence that refer to Jesus and the Father are at the beginning of the development of the concept of perichoresis. However, following the Johannine prologue, they also qualify, by means of the economy of the Only Begotten in the flesh, the eternal relationship of the Logos to his Father (*pros ton Theon / pros ton Patera*). The Son is not external to the Father who engenders Him, but He dwells in Him. Reciprocally, the Father is completely present in the Son. This is the most simple formulation of the mutual immanence proper to divine generation.

In order to understand this reciprocity (not only does the Son dwell in his Father as in his origin, but the Father is also in the Son), we can refer to two examples developed by Augustine in his *De Trinitate* (VIII, 14 and IX, 1 f.): the analogy of self-knowledge and self-love (*mens, notitia, amor*), according to which the Father begets the Son in knowing himself, and is thus completely understood by his Word; and the analogy of mutual love between two lovers (*amans, amatum, amor*), according to which the Father enjoys and reposes in his Son through the eternal Love that He bears for Him, and that He receives from Him in return. Since this love is reciprocal, the immanence between the Son and the Father is thus understood as being mutual. This reciprocity is a property of the relation between the Father and the Son. Although the act of generation is not reciprocal, because it establishes a real distinction according to the order of origin, the relation that it expresses is fully reciprocal. This is clear in a very simple manner in the very names of Father and Son, which are relative names. This particularity of (revealed) language shows more deeply that, in their very existence, the Father and the Son are correlative. This neither means that they are in some way interchangeable, nor does it mean that the order of origin between them can be reversed. It simply means that the personal existence of each one is tied to that of the other. The Father alone is principle in the eternal generation of the Son, however; although He does not receive his being from the Son, the Father is entirely relative to Him. The personal perfection of the Father can be neither completed nor considered without his relation to the Son. Hilary of Poitiers stated as much: *Patrem consummat Filius*.[8] It will be necessary to say as much in reference to the relation between the Father and the Spirit.

Second, the help in specifying the immanence and reciprocity between the Father and the Son disposes one for a better understanding of the procession of the Holy Spirit. Whatever analogy is chosen to speak of this must respect that the proceeding Spirit must fill the double requirement, in regard to his principle, of immanence and reciprocity established in regard to the Son. From this appears the delimitation of a 'non-filioquist' perspective on the Spirit as the third Person of the Trinity. The manner in which the Spirit is understood needs to be verified through the mutual immanence of the Father and the Holy Spirit, as well as by the reciprocity of their relation. A conception of the Spirit as that of the Love that comes forth from the Father satisfies these criteria. On one hand, the Father loves the Son and is completely present in his Love, which is the Spirit. Reciprocally, the Spirit that is Love dwells in his paternal origin. On the other hand, not only is the Spirit relative to the Father, but the Father is also relative to the Spirit. The personal existence of the Father is really co-determined by his relation to the Holy Spirit, just as it is by his relation to the Son. We will return to this in the next section.

Third, once the processions and relations have been considered in light of perichoresis, one must explicate, at the end of an exposition on the Trinity, the fact that the order of origin established among the three Persons in this way is free from any form of subordination (anteriority-posteriority, superiority-inferiority). This can be realized in the first place through the conception of perichoresis as the connection between generation and procession, and then according to the conception of perichoresis as the reciprocity of relations. Divine generation cannot be fully understood without its intrinsic connection to the procession of the Spirit as the Love of the Father for the Son. Thus even if an order between generation and procession exists, it is free of all posteriority or subordination, and in no way represents a juxtaposition of two independent acts in the divine life. From the general concept of order, one should only conserve the aspect of the relation to a principle in reference to the Trinity, without transposing any idea of degradation to God.

Other than this first adjustment of the understanding of Trinitarian order, the reciprocity of relations between the Father and the Son, like

---

[8] See Hilary of Poitiers, *De Trinitate*, VII, 31; L. F. Ladaria, '... *Patrem consummat Filius. Un aspecto inédito de la teología trinitaria de Hilario de Poitiers*', in *Gregorianum* 81/4 (2000) 775–88.

those between the Father and the Spirit, also bring a valuable correction. If Trinitarian order is first of all understood according to the analogy of Trinitarian life found in a linear model of immanent emanations (the Latin *processio* in a general sense, including both generation of the Son and procession of the Spirit), it falls to the model of relations to perfect a proper understanding of order – as long as this second model is applied with an affirmation of the full perichoresis of the relations. One must then demonstrate that the relation of the Father to the Spirit is neither posterior nor in any way subordinate to the relation of the Father to the Son.

Fourth, at the end of a treatise on the Trinity, the concept of perichoresis can advantageously fill the role of a concept that integrates both unity and distinction. This was the original intuition of Bonaventure in regard to *circumincessio*. Perichoresis is in fact a manner of affirming unity after the consideration of distinction. In itself, if it is understood as a foundational concept as Moltmann does, perichoresis explains neither unity of origin nor unity of essence. Perichoresis, however, offers a possibility of understanding unity while integrating distinction under the form of communion. If one returns to the formulation and context of Jn 17.21–26, mutual immanence takes on the sense of an interpersonal communion of love, one that presupposes the unity of essence while giving it its true significance.

## Perichoretic Interpretation of the Person of the Father

Let us now briefly reflect on the benefits of the regulating of Trinitarian studies through perichoresis in reference to the Persons of the Father and the Holy Spirit. Our perspective on the Father, inspired by Aquinas, is distinguished from the Bonaventurian (and Oriental) one, in so far as we seek first to characterize the hypostasis of the Father, not by a negative path (as principle without principle, or unbegotten, etc.), but in a positive, relative manner.[9] The hypostasis of the Father can be negatively characterized, as He who has no origin, or positively, by his acts and relations. If one takes the perichoresis of the three divine Persons into account, it is not relevant to begin by situating the Father independently from his relation to the Son and his relation to the Spirit in a negative manner. We should adopt, even for the Father, a relative concept of Person, in conformity with the Thomistic doctrine of the Trinitarian Person understood as subsisting relation. However, in order to provide a content for the paternal relations, it is necessary first of all to consider the acts of his interior life.

---

[9] See E. Durand, *Le Père Alpha et Oméga de la vie trinitaire*, (Cogitatio Fidei, 267), Paris: Cerf 2008.

The Father eternally begets his *Only Begotten Son*, who is also designated as the *Word*. The understanding of generation would be incomplete without taking into account the love that accompanies it in every father worthy of the name. As Athanasius of Alexandria has shown,[10] even if the generation of the Son, like the procession of the Spirit, is an act whose formal principle is the divine nature in such a way that it is completely communicated, love cannot be external to this eminently paternal act. One could say that this love is 'concomitant' to generation.

This can be put together with another suggestive approach to generation, which consists in conceiving it as a *gift* of the divine goodness by the Father to the Son. This gift is certainly imprinted with love, even if it arises, formally speaking, from the divine nature that is entirely communicated in its essential goodness. This understanding of generation can be superimposed on the image of the good that is communicated in the divine life following the order of origin (*bonum diffusivum sui*). This likeness, privileged by Bonaventure, permits a proper understanding of the analogy of knowledge and love of self (*mens, notitia, amor*). For, if one establishes that procession by way of love is intrinsically connected to generation by way of knowledge, the gift of divine goodness included in generation naturally implicates this same love.

This has the added benefit of verifying the importance of the analogical *intellectus fidei* of the procession of the Holy Spirit as hypostatic Love. Connected to the very act of generation that eternally places the Son as the Beloved of the Father, the Spirit proceeds as precisely this love of the Father for the Son. Without being principle of the Son in any way, the Holy Spirit is nevertheless eternally present in the very 'place' of his eternal birth (*in sinu Patris*), as the paternal Love that eternally 'hypostates' itself in its reposing on the Son. The Son is himself fully Son in the very fact that He returns this same Love to the Father in eternal thanksgiving. This returning of a received, filial Love to its paternal Source achieves the Trinitarian cycle of eternal life.

If one can formulate a first form of Trinitarian reciprocity as the return of Love given to the Father by the Son, this perspective remains nevertheless limited to the level of emanation, and the relative model remains indispensable in order to express Trinitarian faith. The concept of relation is easily interlinked with the immanent acts of generation and procession, in so far as they naturally express two pairs of reciprocal relations, between the Father and the Son and the Father and the Holy Spirit respectively.

The two immanent acts of the divine life, of which the hypostasis of the Father is the personal principle, express the fact that the Father himself is relative to the Son *and* to the Spirit. Even if the name of Father does not

---

[10] See Athanasius of Alexandria, *Contra arianos*, III, 62–6.

formally and directly consignify more than the Son, the hypostasis of the Father is no less relative to the Spirit than to the Son. This double relativity characterizes the Father in his eternal personal perfection. Since the Son is engendered and the Holy Spirit proceeds, it is easy to conceive of both of them as relative to the paternal principle. On the other hand, given that the Father is the principle of the communication of his divine nature to the Son and the Spirit, it is less spontaneous to conceive of Him as relative to the two hypostases that come from Him. This is not however contradictory if one has established the distinction between the constitutive *correlativity* of the Persons and the *dependence* that follows the order of origin.

It is also worth distinguishing hypostasis from person. Hypostasis designates the metaphysical subject (Latin *suppositum*) in its concreteness, something that is presupposed to the acts that come from it in our manner of understanding. Person today has come to synthesize the existential fullness of the subject considered in the richness of its relations. This contemporary re-definition of person is not without basis in the Thomistic foundation of Trinitarian Person as subsisting relation. One should however avoid univocity, and remain conscious of the re-interpretation that has been made. The Father, person in the full sense of the term, is not only source of the entire Trinitarian life, but is also characterized as Father by both his relation to the Son and by his relation to the Spirit, as well as by their reciprocal relations. Once the real distinctions that come from a theological analysis of the Trinity have been made, it is worthwhile to explicate the personal fullness of the divine life, which can be expressed as gift and gratitude, according to the reciprocity of relations.

We have thus attempted to respect a proper understanding of the monarchy of the Father and a relative characterization of his Person. Within this view, it remains to examine the influence of perichoresis on the origin of the Holy Spirit.

# Perichoretic Interpretation of the Origin of the Holy Spirit

Beyond the unsolvable alternatives of the procession of the Spirit from the Father alone (monopatrism) or the subordination of the Spirit in relationship to the Father and the Son (filioquism), one can characterize the origin of the Spirit according to the two relations that express and extend the divine paternity. The Father is certainly the only 'fontal' principle on which depends the full communication of the divine nature to the Spirit, as to the Son. However, one should not isolate the Father-Son relation from the Father-Spirit relation, nor isolate the Father-Spirit relation from the Father-Son relation. On the one hand, considering the Father-Son relation as completed in itself leads to a subordination of the Spirit in reference to the Father-Son pair. This is the major failure of the Occidental 'filioquist' current. On the other hand, considering the Father-Spirit relation independently from the Father-Son relation leads to obscuring the fullness of the personal character of the Father in his communion with the Son in the origin of the Spirit. This is the limitation of monopatrism in the controversy.

Without making the Son a principle that is extrinsic to the Father in the procession of the Spirit, the paternal origin of the Spirit will only be honoured in its fullness if one does not abstract the Father-Son relation from this origin. The procession of the Spirit thus assuredly has the Father as its principle, but this Father does not exist, in the reality of the Trinitarian mystery, other than as Father of the Son. If the Father in his communion with the Son is, in reference to his Person itself, fully characterized by the Spirit's proper mode of subsistence, He is no less characterized by the Son's proper mode of subsistence in his relations at the origin of the Spirit.

We should here specify the difference between the concepts of relation and communion. When our analysis of the Trinitarian mystery is following the order of origin, the paternity-filiation relation appears to be constitutive of the Persons of the Father and the Son, even before the consideration of the relation of the Father to the Holy Spirit. Nevertheless, the paternal-filial relation cannot completely express the Persons of the Father and the Son in their Trinitarian perfection without the implication of the proper relativity of the Spirit. In order to highlight this, we can accentuate the communion of the Father and Son as the ultimate perfection of their relation in the Trinitarian mystery, something that excludes any subordination of the Holy Spirit.

What the concept of communion brings to that of relation invites another development: in a manner analogous to the concept of order (*taxis*), can one, without excessive inadequacies, purify that of end (*telos*) in such a way that it expresses the perfection in communion of the Father-Son relation in the very relation of the Father to the Spirit? At first glance, the concepts of order or origin appear inadequate for the divine nature, in which there exists no change. The divine simplicity requires one to exclude all composition in God, and in particular that of potentiality and act. It follows that, properly speaking, there is no movement or passage to act in God. However, following the Fathers, medieval authors managed to eliminate any connotation of anteriority-posteriority or superiority-inferiority from the concept of order, to keep from origin only the relationship of that which has a principle to its principle.

In an analogous and complementary manner, it appears possible to separate the concept of *end* (with the ambivalence of finality and termination) from any change or becoming, in order to reach a likeness that permits a rational approach, as much as is possible, to another aspect of the Trinitarian mystery. We can thus keep the concept of real *perfection* from finality, which, in the Trinity, implies the relativity of communion of the Father and Son to the Spirit, without however implying a relationship of final causality. In the relationship between the Father-Son relation and the Father of the Son-Holy Spirit relation, it becomes thus possible to consider the Spirit, following Cyril of Alexandria, as the 'culmination of the Trinity' (*sumplèrôma*),[11] in the sense that the perfection of communion of the Father-Son relation is expressed in it. In regard to this fullness, the Father-Son relation appears as the condition of the relation of communion from the Spirit to the Father. Reciprocally, the relation of the Spirit to the Father appears as the ultimate perfection of the paternal-filial relation.

In this view, recognizing 'one principle' of the procession of the Spirit will simply be to consider the Father as the origin of Spirit, without abstractly isolating the Father from the Son. In this we follow the reinterpretation of the expression *tanquam ex uno principio* from the Council of Lyon as proposed by the Roman Clarification on the *Filioque* in light of the Catechism of the Catholic Church.[12] The Father is not Father except as Father of his Son, and as loving Him. Because of their communion, the Son is inseparable from the Father, even in so far as the Father is principle of the procession of the Holy Spirit, since it unfailingly belongs to the very Person of the Father to love his Son as the proper object of his good pleasure.

In return, the procession of the Spirit manifests the property of the paternal-filial relation. As Thomas affirms in a suggestive manner: 'as the Father loves himself and his Son with one love, and reciprocally [the Son loves himself and his Father with one love], in the Holy Spirit himself, as Love, the relation of the Father to the Son is implicated, and recipro-cally [that of the Son to the Father], as [the relation of] the lover to the beloved'.[13] Put another way, the paternal-filial relation, which implies the love that characterizes its origin, is manifested in the Holy Spirit himself.

This can be developed according to the relationship that love has with the sharing that founds it. The generation of the Son is characterized by the relationship of perfect natural likeness that exists between the Father and the Son. In this respect, the Son is called the Image of the Father in a proper manner. However, the property of likeness in the Father-Son relation is not fully characterized if it is not understood as a basis for a communion

---

[11] See M.-O. Boulnois, *Le paradoxe trinitaire chez Cyrille d'Alexandrie*, Paris: Études Augustiniennes 1994, pp. 437–42.

[12] See *Catechism of the Catholic Church*, n. 248; Pontifical Council for the Promotion of Christian Unity, 'Greek and Latin Traditions Regarding the Procession of the Holy Spirit', in *Osservatore Romano English Edition*, 20 Sept. 1995; J.-M. Garrigues, 'La réciprocité trinitaire de l'Esprit par rapport au Père et au Fils selon saint Thomas d'Aquin', in *Revue thomiste* 98 (1998) 266–81; J.-Y. Branchet and E. Durand, 'La réception de la *Clarification* romaine de 1995 sur le *Filioque*', in *Irénikon* 78/1–2 (2005) 47–109.

[13] Thomas Aquinas, STh Ia, q. 37, a. 1, ad 3: 'cum Pater amet unica dilectione se et Filium, et e converso, importatur in Spiritu Sancto, prout est Amor, habitudo Patris ad Filium, et e converso, ut amantis ad amatum.'

of love. It is only in the Son that the Father recognizes the perfect (filial) image of his (paternal) goodness. This is accompanied by a love that is the measure of this unique likeness. The Spirit comes forth from this love. The object of the mutual love of the Father and the Son is the goodness of the divine essence, which alone is capable of adequately determining the divine will. This first goodness, communicated by the Father to the Word in generation, is however marked by this act of generation and gift. In the Father, the divine goodness is in the form of a principle, it is 'fontal', while it is identical in the Word, although received and 'filial'. The Spirit is like the hypostatic sign of the sharing between the Father and the Son, in so far as the Spirit proceeds from their mutual love. The quality of his paternal and filial origin appears in the Spirit, the Person who proceeds from the love of the Father and the Son. The likeness that is characteristic of the relation of image between the Father and the Son manifests its true property in the Spirit. This is to be at the origin (not as principle, but as condition) of the love that accompanies generation as gift.

In this perspective, it is possible to reinterpret the Occidental doctrine of the property of spiration at the origin of the Spirit, considered common to the Father and the Son. While its common character is counterbalanced in Aquinas by the communion of love that unites the two spirating subjects, the scholastic tradition largely retained the aspect of undifferentiated property in a unilateral manner, thus exposing itself to the reproach of essentialism.[14] The common spirative *virtus* is important in the perspective of the *Filioque*, since it avoids conceiving of the implication of the Son in the procession of the Spirit as simply an instrumental role, something that would lead to an unacceptable subordination of the Son. We can however understand this in a nuanced manner. The common property in fact covers the Father's loving inclination to and satisfaction with his Son, as well as the returning love of the Son to the Father from whom He receives everything. To summarize, as Bolotov has already taught,[15] the regulating of perichoresis leads to honouring the inseparability of the Father and the Son at the origin of the Spirit, without however misunderstanding the monarchy of the Father: the Father, from whom the Spirit proceeds, is inseparably the Father of the Son, who is himself constituted by his relation to the Father and his relation to the Spirit.

---

[14] See V. Lossky, 'La procession du Saint-Esprit dans la doctrine trinitaire orthodoxe' (1948), in *À l'image et à la ressemblance de Dieu*, Paris: Cerf, 1967, 67–93.

[15] See B. Bolotov, 'Thèses sur le *Filioque*', in *Revue Internationale de Théologie* VI/24 (1898) 681–712; Klingenthal Memorandum 'The *Filioque* Clause in Ecumenical Perspective' (1979) in: L. Vischer (ed.), *Spirit of God, Spirit of Christ: Ecumenical Reflections on the Filioque Controversy*, (Faith and Order Paper, 103), Geneva: WCC 1981.

# Implications: Ecclesial and Sacramental Communion

Let us now examine how Trinitarian perichoresis might offer a model and end for ecclesial, anthropological and social communion. First, we will place ourselves on the level of the relation between ecclesial communion and Trinitarian perichoresis (interpreted in an interpersonal way). With the help of *Mystici Corporis* 67 and *Gaudium et Spes* 24, we will then show the form under which ecclesial participation in Trinitarian communion is mediated by the two missions of Christ and the Holy Spirit.

Ecclesial participation in the communion of the Trinity has rightly been a permanent aspect of Ecclesiology ever since Vatican II. However, with his Encyclical *Mystici Corporis* of 1943, Pius XII had already made the traditional expression *una mystica persona* his own, clarifying its meaning by use of the established comparison in Jn 17.21–23 between the mutual indwelling of the Father and the Son, and the unity of believers: '[...] the unbroken tradition of the Fathers from the earliest times teaches that the Divine Redeemer and the Society which is his Body form but one mystical person (*cum sociali corpore unam* [...] *mysticam personam*), that is to say, to quote Augustine, the whole Christ (*Christum totum*). Our Saviour himself in his priestly prayer did not hesitate to liken this union (*coagmentationem*) to that wonderful unity by which the Son is in the Father, and the Father in the Son (*miranda illa unitate, qua Filius est in Patre et Pater in Filio*).'[16] The unity of the disciples is compared to the divine unity here, as witnessed to by the mutual indwelling of the Father and the Son, but only in the measure that the disciples are united to Christ. In other words, it is quite clear that the mission of Christ is the key which institutes the effective analogy between ecclesial communion and Trinitarian communion.

It is not enough, therefore, to affirm a kind of formal resemblance between the union or mutual indwelling of the Father and the Son and the communion of the children of God in the mystery of the Church. It is necessary to show the way that this likeness becomes effective participation. In this respect, the Johannine text of Jn 17.20–26 gives certain indications concerning the effective mediation of Christ for the participation of the disciples in the union of the Father and the Son. The linking of v. 23 is significant: 'I in them and You in Me, that they may become perfectly one.' The role of Christ here presents Him as the one who is an intermediary link between the disciples and the Father: the Father dwells in Jesus and Jesus dwells in the disciples, and in this way Jesus brings to his disciples

---

[16] *Mystici Corporis* n. 67, in *Acta Apostolicae Sedis* 1943, p. 226; see *Gaudium et Spes* n. 24, *Denzinger* 4324.

the perfection of unity that the Father wants to grant them. Christ's 'I in them' concerning his disciples returns in v. 26: 'I made known to them your name, and I will make it known, so that the love with which You have loved Me may be in them, and I in them.' One notes that the presence of Christ in his disciples accompanies the fact that the love of the Father for Him is extended to include them. If we interpret this verse through a developed Pneumatology, the Spirit allows himself to be recognized in this love from 'before the foundation of the world' that the Father bears for the Son and which the Son then communicates to his disciples.

Translated into theological terms, the effective participation in the communion of the Father and of the Son proves to be founded directly on the missions of the Son and the Spirit, which are interconnected. The Paschal economy of the manifestation of the Name by Christ is finalized by the gift that He makes of the love of the Father, that is, by the effusion of the Spirit. The glorification of Christ frees this gift in its fullness for mankind. The unity of the Church has no other meaning than to witness to the mission of Christ and the gift of the Love of the Father: 'that they may become perfectly one, so that the world may know that You have sent Me and have loved them as You have loved Me' (v. 23).

If the Eucharist is the sacrament of this ecclesial unity in communion, it is so not only because it grants the disciples the beneficial effects of the Paschal mystery, but above all because it introduces them into the relation of Christ with his Father. Johannine theology clearly connects the gift of the Eucharist to the gift of Christ's flesh on the Cross, itself an offering founded on the gift of the Son to the world by the Father. This appears in the structure of Jn 6. In v. 32, Jesus indicates the original gift that comes from the Father: 'my Father gives you the true bread from heaven. For the bread of God is that which comes down from heaven, and gives life to the world.' (Jn 6.32–3). But a little further on in v. 51, Jesus reveals another gift, that of his own flesh on the cross, which extends his descent from the Father: 'I am the living bread which comes down from heaven [i.e. *given by the Father*]; if any one eats of this bread he will live for ever; and *the bread which I shall give* for the life of the world is my flesh.' (Jn 6.51). In verses 53–4 however, another change in vocabulary occurs, this time from 'to eat' (*phagein*) the flesh and drink the blood, to 'to chew' (*trôgein*) the flesh and drink the blood. This shift indicates a passage from communion by faith to sacramental communion. In this development of Johannine theology, the bread can therefore signify successively: 1) the Son given by the Father who sends Him; 2) the Son who offers himself on the Cross; and 3) the Son who gives himself in the Eucharist. These are all in the same perspective however, in so far as these mysteries extend, and are developed, one from another. Jn 6 reveals, moreover, that the Eucharist accomplishes a reciprocal 'dwelling with' between Christ and us, so that we discover the sacramental 'how' of the 'I in them and You in Me' of Jn 17.23. In fact, Eucharistic communion in the mystery of Christ makes us live of the very life that He himself receives from the Father: 'He who eats my flesh and drinks my blood abides in Me, and I in him. As (*kathôs*) the living Father sent Me, and I live because of (or for) the Father, so he who eats me will live because of (or for) Me.' (Jn 6.56–7). Here again, the Johannine *kathôs* means a real participation: to live by and for Christ is to live, with Him, his relation to the Father.

According to Johannine theology, it is therefore very much within the mystery of the Church that participation in Trinitarian communion is most proper. All the same, from this point our perspective can be widened. The anthropological dimensions of communion appear as if finalized by an ecclesial assumption, even if, in many cases, this will not be clear until eternal life begins.

Ecclesial communion therefore proves to be entirely relative to Trinitarian perichoresis which, as both its model and final cause, is mediated by the closely related missions of Christ and the Holy Spirit. However, in the light of Revelation, some true human realizations of communion may appear as places of 'potential ecclesiality', where God makes his grace available to each person. The woundedness of creation, especially when aspiring to communion, means that we need an eschatological vision of the Kingdom of God. Without this divine end, our yearning for communion would only be an aspiration without guarantee, a projection, a vague desire, a utopia. On the contrary, however, Trinitarian communion provides a realism to our faith by revealing itself as the end on which the realization of the Kingdom of God principally depends. This Kingdom will be the definitive participation of human beings in the divine Trinitarian perichoresis.

# 8

# Trinitarian Freedom: is God Free in Trinitarian Life?

## by Metropolitan John Zizioulas

### Introduction

The question of divine freedom has permeated Christian theology from the very beginning. This was due to the insistence of Biblical religion on God's absolute transcendence.[1] According to the Old Testament God is absolutely free to act as He wills and is not constrained by anyone or anything in his freedom. The same principle is to be found also in the New Testament: God is free to raise children of Abraham even from stones (Luke 3,8), everything is possible for God (Mt 19,26), and none can interrogate God why He did this rather than that (Rom. 9:20). One could say that the borderline between Biblical and pagan religion is drawn by the idea of absolute and totally unrestrained divine freedom. Any theological position implying, even to the smallest degree, a conditioning of God's absolute freedom would automatically introduce a departure from the Biblical conception of God.

This absolute freedom of God would especially apply to the idea of creation. In classical Greek thought the world was believed to be eternal, and therefore without beginning. Plato in his *Timaeus* spoke of a creator of the world who created it 'willingly' (*thelēsei*), and yet a careful study of

---

[1] See among others W. Eichrodt, *Theology of the Old Testament*, I, London: SCM Press 1961, pp. 408f. and vol. II, 1967, pp. 31f., 74f., 310f.

this work reveals that god's freedom was restricted in several fundamental ways: he had to create out of pre-existing matter, on the model of eternally preconceived ideas, and within a given space (*chora*).[2]

Christian theology wrestled with this problem from the beginning of Patristic thought. After several unsuccessful attempts which were marked with a considerable degree of Platonic influence (e.g. Justin and Origen),[3] the Biblical idea of God's absolute and unrestricted freedom was finally imposed on the doctrine of creation in the form of *creatio ex nihilo*: God was not restricted by any condition whatsoever in creating the world; neither ideas nor matter or space existed before creation: the world was in no way connected with the being of God, being the product of His will alone. This distinction between what pertains to God's being and what is a result of His will played the decisive role during the Arian controversy. One could describe this controversy as a discussion of the subject of divine freedom. It was during this controversy that Patristic thought was led to the formulation of the distinction between *created* and *uncreated* being, a principle that has dominated Patristic theology ever since.

# The Emergence of the Problem of Trinitarian Freedom

Up to the time of the Arian controversy, Christian theology was preoccupied with God's freedom in relation to the world. The problem, however, was to be inevitably transferred also to the inner life of God. This came as a result of the distinction made by Athanasius and Nicaea between *substance* and *will* in God. That the world was created out of the will and not the substance of God safeguarded God's freedom vis-a-vis the world, but at the same time gave rise to the question of God's freedom in the begetting of the Son: if the Son is born not of the will of God but of his substance, as was taught by the Fathers of Nicaea, does this mean that there is no freedom in Trinitarian life? If substance is to be contrasted with will, would this imply an 'un-willed' and unfree Trinitarian life?

This question was in fact put to the Orthodox by the Arians. Athanasius' reply showed that the concern for safeguarding God's freedom in all cases, including Trinitarian life, was still as strong at that time as ever before. Challenged by the Arians to accept or deny divine freedom in relation to the begetting of the Son, Athanasius would have betrayed the Biblical idea

---

[2] Plato, *Timaeus* 48a, 50b–d, 49a etc.
[3] Justin, *Apol.*, I, 20; *Dial.*, 5; Origen, *In Ioan.*, I, 22; XIX, 5. Cf. G. Florovsky, *Creation and Redemption*, (Collected Works, 3), Belmont: Nordland 1976, p. 52 ff.

of an absolutely free God if he replied that the Son's generation from God's substance was unfree. He therefore immediately replied that although the generation of the Son was not, as the creation of the world was, from the will of God, it was not 'unwilled'.[4] But how is this to be understood and to make sense?

If the difference between the generation of the Son and the creation of the world lies in the fact that the latter came from the will of God, whereas the former did not come from His will, how can the generation be 'willed' without the Son falling into the category of creaturehood? Athanasius did not develop his reply any further. It was left to Cyril of Alexandria and mainly to the Cappadocians to work out an explanation of this apparently contradictory position. Cyril of Alexandria spoke of the divine will as 'concurrent' (*sundromos*) with divine substance.[5] By that he wanted to exclude the priority of the will in the generation of the Son. The Son is not generated unwillingly (*athelētos*), but unlike what applies to the creation of the world, in the case of the Son the will did not precede the generation. By being 'concurrent' with divine substance the divine will made the generation of the Son willed, without making it an outcome of the will, as if the will somehow preceded or intervened with the generation. By being 'concurrent' with divine substance the divine will was common to all three persons of the Trinity, all of them possessing the same will.[6]

Translated in terms of freedom this would mean that divine freedom is not independent of, or prior to, God's being, but coincides with it. It would, therefore, be inappropriate to speak of God's being as a *necessary being*.[7] For the Greek Fathers, freedom is a quality of God's very substance. Or, to put it differently, divine freedom is an *ontological* category. God's substance and His freedom 'concur' and coincide.

By making divine will 'concurrent' with divine substance, Cyril of Alexandria safeguarded divine freedom in the free generation of the Son from the substance of the Father. The Trinity is constituted freely because the substance which the three Persons share is 'concurrent' with divine will, i.e. it is a *free substance*. This seems to be the Cyrilian position.

However, the attachment of freedom to the substance of God would not prove to be satisfactory in view of Eunomius' identification of divine substance with the person of the Father. In response to the Eunomian challenge the Cappadocian Fathers have made a clear distinction between the level of substance and that of the Trinity. The generation of the Son and the procession of the Spirit should not be referred to the substance

---

[4] Athanasius, *Contra arianos*, 3, 66.

[5] Cyril Alex., *De Trin.*, 2.

[6] Cf. Maximus, Conf., *Amb.*, (PG 91, 1264B).

[7] For an understanding of divine being as a 'necessary being', see E. Gilson, *L'esprit de la philosophie médiévale*, Paris: Vrin 1932, pp. 45–66.

of God but to the level of His personal or hypostatic existence: it was not the substance of God but the person of the Father that 'caused' the Trinitarian existence.[8] By insisting on this the Cappadocian Fathers transferred the question of divine freedom from the level of substance to that of personhood: it is not the freedom of divine substance but the freedom *of the Father* that accounts for Trinitarian freedom.

This is evident from the way Gregory Nazianzen treats the question of freedom in the generation of the Son. Unlike Cyril of Alexandria, he does not refer it to the substance of God but to the Father. In his third Theological Oration (6–7) he refutes the Arian accusations that by denying the generation of the Son from the will of the Father the Orthodox introduce necessity into God's being. His argument includes the following:

> 'And yet I think that the Person who wills is distinct from the act of willing; He who begets from the act of begetting; the speaker from the speech, or else we are all stupid. On the one side we have the mover, and on the other that which is, so to speak, the motion. Thus the thing willed is not the child of that will, for it does not always result therefrom; nor is that which is begotten the child of generation ... but *of the Person who willed*, or begot ...' (6)

It is clear from this passage that for Gregory the question of divine freedom is not a matter of linking freedom with divine substance but with the Person of the Father. Gregory solves the problem of how Trinitarian existence, unlike that of creation, can be free or unwilled without coming from the *will* of God, by making a distinction between the 'will' and the 'willing one'. The Son is not generated unwillingly, because he is born *of the Father*, who as a Person and not substance is the 'willing one'. Trinitarian Freedom is due to a Person, the Father. Gregory would apply this also to the hypostasis of the Father himself: the Father constitutes freely not only the hypostases of the Son and the Spirit, but also of himself. Without being the 'child of will' (since one part of Him cannot be will and another the object of will, for this would make him 'divisible'), He exists willingly, since he would not have been God if something or someone compelled him to exist. This is the argument in paragraph seven of the third Theological Oration. As Athanasius had already put it, the Father is the willing one (*theletēs*) of his own hypostasis.[9]

---

[8] Basil, *Epist.*, 361 and 362; *Contra Eunomium*, 1, 14–15; Gregory Naz., *Theol. Or.*, 3, 2; 15. More on this in my *Communion and Otherness*, London-New York: Continuum 2006, pp. 128f.

[9] Athanasius, *Contra arianos*, 3, 66.

# Trinitarian Freedom as Personal Freedom

The association of divine freedom not with divine substance but with divine personhood raises immediately the question of the relationship between substance and personhood in God. Under the influence of modern existentialist thought, one may be inclined to identify substance with necessity and to regard personhood as *freedom from substance*. Such an understanding of personhood as freedom *from* nature may be applied to the human condition in which nature is a 'given' to the person: humans are born as a result of given natural laws. But in the case of God there is no antinomy between nature and person precisely because the divine persons do not derive from divine nature but from a divine person (the Father), and also because each person bears divine substance in its totality and not partially. Therefore personhood in God cannot indicate freedom *from* nature, as modern existentialist thought would suggest.

However, this does not undermine the importance of attaching freedom in God to the divine persons and not to the divine nature. For even in God, in whom there is no conflict between substance and personhood, it is the divine persons that safeguard and express divine freedom. Had it not been for the Trinity, God would have been a necessary being, a monad enslaved to its essence, a being incapable of going out of itself. It is the Trinity that makes God free from the necessity of his essence; had it not been for the Trinity God would require an eternal creation in order to be free to reach beyond his essence, and then he would bind himself necessarily and eternally to creation. By transferring divine freedom from the level of substance to that of personhood, the Fathers rescued theology from eternally binding God to his creation, a danger inherent in pagan religions and to a great extent also in ancient philosophical thought.

The essence of Trinitarian freedom, therefore, lies in God's capacity to be *ek-static* not in relation to something other than God, but *in himself*. If this ek-static character of divine being is understood as corresponding to what we call *love*, then the statement 'God is love' (I John 4,8) can be applied primarily to God in his immanent being, and only by extension to his relation with the world. By being love in himself eternally as Trinity, God realizes his freedom as a perpetual exodus from the self, not in order to meet an already existing 'other' (individualism) but to affirm the 'other' as a unique Being. Freedom, therefore, in its Trinitarian sense is not a freedom *from* but a freedom *for* the other to the point of raising the other to the status of absolute uniqueness irreducible[10] to the sameness of nature. Owing to its ontological character Trinitarian freedom is not simply ek-static but

---

[10] The expression belongs to V. Lossky, *In the Image and Likeness of God*, Crestwood: St Vladimir's Seminary Press 1974, p. 120.

in being ek-static it is also *hypostatic*, as it produces ontological otherness, i.e. unique personal identities (*hypostaseis*).

The ek-static character of Trinitarian personhood has led certain theologians, particularly on the Orthodox side, to speak of Trinitarian freedom as *kenotic*. According to this view, there is in Trinitarian existence a constant movement of self-denial, of each person's 'emptying' itself in order to 'make room' for the other persons to 'co-inhere' (*perichorēsis*). This understanding of the Cappadocian idea of *perichorēsis*, attractive as it may be at first sight, is not without serious difficulties. The idea of *kenosis* is borrowed from Christology (Phil. 2,7) and although basic to that particular doctrine, it becomes problematic when it is transferred to the immanent Trinity.

In the first place, even at the level of the economic Trinity, it is only *one* person of the Trinity (the Son) that empties himself of his glory, as it is only this person that becomes incarnate. Vladimir Lossky has also spoken of the 'economy of the Spirit', but this idea raises great difficulties.[11] Even if we accept the view that the Spirit also 'empties' himself in the economy, what about the Father's *kenosis*? And if not all three divine persons 'empty' themselves in the economy, how can we transfer the idea of *kenosis* to the level of the immanent Trinity, i.e. to all three divine persons? We shall see later how the logical movement from the economic to the immanent Trinity affects divine freedom. For the moment let us note the following difficulties.

If the idea of *kenosis* is not to be understood psychologically but ontologically, it must be taken to mean that each person of the Trinity 'empties' itself of its own *being*;[12] it reaches the point of non-being, of 'death'. This is what we encounter on the Cross, but is it legitimate to transfer this to the immanent Trinity? Can we speak of non-being in God? Can God be truly free if he is faced with the possibility of non-being?

The answer to this question may be that in God the non-being implied in *kenosis* is *automatically* overcome by being through his love. But even so the implication remains that there is in God's existence a sort of Manichean conflict between good and evil, being and non-being. This can be hardly reconciled with an absolutely free God.

But perhaps the greatest difficulty with applying the notion of *kenosis* to the immanent Trinity arises with regard to the relational ontology of the Trinity. The idea of *kenosis* presupposes that the persons of the Trinity exist as entities first and then 'empty' themselves of their being. This could make sense in an individualistic conception of personhood in which one first exists as an entity and then relates to other entities. But how can we speak

---

[11] See my *Being as Communion*, Crestwood: St Vladimir's Seminary Press, 1985, ch. 2.
[12] An idea reminiscent of Hegel, *Lectures on the Philosophy of Religion*, III, p. 125: 'love consists in giving up one's personality, all that is his own ... [it is] the supreme surrender in the other.'

of one 'emptying' one's self of a being one does not possess until one relates to another?

There is only one way to avoid these difficulties, and that is to understand the ek-static and the hypostatic aspects of the Trinity as simultaneous. In God there is no freedom *from* – not even from self (*kenosis*), for there is no such thing as selfhood in him. There is only freedom *for*, an ek-static movement of love as pure affirmation, a constant 'yes' (II Cor. I, 19–20).

All this means that freedom in God coincides with *love*. Love in this case is not a feeling, a psychological state, but a relationship which affirms other beings granting them otherness. Divine freedom, particularly in its Trinitarian manifestation, is not a psychological but an *ontological* freedom, as it grants identity to other beings through relating them with one another. When the Father says to the Son 'You *are* my Son', and the Son replies 'You *are* my Father', a relationship is established and affirmed which involves the affirmation of otherness. Thus a particular identity is established as other, an identity that is free to be itself. Being other and being free in an ontological sense, that is in the sense of being free to be yourself, and not someone or something else – this is what Trinitarian freedom amounts to.

The freedom to be and to be other is what Trinitarian freedom is about. We reserve for later the discussion of the significance of this for human freedom. We can only state now that this kind of freedom is far more important for humanity than a freedom of choice, i.e. moral freedom. For the moment let us stick to the observation that this ontological freedom is the only kind of freedom applicable to God.

# Freedom and Causation

The Cappadocian idea of Trinitarian causation has been met with criticism precisely in connection with the problem of Trinitarian freedom: if the Father is the cause of the Son's and the Spirit's existence, how free are the last two to exist as persons? As one of the critics puts it with clarity, if the Father is the cause of the existence of the Son and the Spirit, 'then the Father has a type of freedom which the Son and the Spirit do not possess. The Son and the Spirit do not possess the freedom to constitute their existence as communion. They may possess the freedom to confirm this existence of communion, but not to constitute it in the way that the Father – as the exclusive causal principle – is able to. If freedom is defined by the person of the Father as freedom from the given, then freedom which the Son and the Spirit possess is qualitatively different, since they are faced eternally with the given of the Father. If freedom from the given is the mark of true

personhood, then the Son and the Spirit are not persons in the true sense.'[13]
Another critic would also argue that making the Father the cause of the
existence of the other two persons of the Trinity would not only make 'the
freedom of the Father ... *qualitatively* (emphasis in the original) distinct
from that of the Son and the Spirit', but would also 'parallel the cosmological freedom of the Father vis-à-vis the created order as a whole'.[14]

These critical views illustrate well the problem of Trinitarian freedom in
its ontological content. How can we understand the position we defended
earlier that Trinitarian freedom is not moral but ontological, i.e. the
freedom to be and be other, if the otherness of the Trinitarian persons is
'caused' by one of them, namely the Father? Are we not obliged either to
drop altogether the idea of causality as incompatible with the notion of
freedom or, if we keep it, to apply it equally to all three persons of the
Trinity, making each divine person cause the personal otherness of the other
two?[15]

The reason why the Cappadocian Fathers introduced the idea of
causation into Trinitarian theology was precisely in order to safeguard
freedom in the emergence of the Trinitarian persons. As Gregory Nazianzen
argued, Trinitarian life must not be understood as the natural overflowing
of a crater; it should be attributed to personal freedom.[16] Only if personal
existence is due to a person – and not some impersonal natural factor – can
it be free. We cannot, therefore, drop the idea of causality in Trinitarian life
without risking the loss of freedom in Trinitarian existence. Thus we are left
with two alternatives: a) it is the Father that causes Trinitarian otherness, or
b) it is the persons of the Trinity that cause one another's personhood.

The Cappadocian Fathers clearly opted for the faith that it is only the
Father that is the cause of Trinitarian existence, the other two divine persons
being 'of the cause'. This is what came to be known as the *monarchia* of the
Father, meaning that the Father is the 'source' (*pēgē*) or 'origin' (*archē*) of
the Trinity. This they did for reasons that cannot be ignored or overlooked
in any decision we make as to whether we might replace the faith that the
Father is the cause of the Trinity with the view that all three divine persons
cause each other's personal existence.

As the discussions concerning the *Filioque* in the early Church have
shown, the Eastern theologians, beginning with Photius and reaching the

---

[13] A. Papanikolaou, *Being with God*, Notre Dame: Notre Dame University Press 2006, p. 150f.
[14] A. J. Torrance, *Persons in Communion*, Edinburg: T&T Clark 1996, p. 292. Cf. Papanikolaou, *Being with God*, p. 203, n. 93.
[15] Papanikolaou's suggestion, *Being with God*, pp. 151f.
[16] Gregory Naz., *Theol. Or.*, 3,2 f: we regard the Father as the *monas* from which the other two came, because we want to avoid what 'some Greek philosophizing (= Plato, *Tim.*, 41 D) dared to say concerning the first and second cause by likening God to an overflowing (with love) crater' in order 'not to introduce a necessary (*akousion*) generation'.

debates of the thirteenth and the fourteenth centuries, argued that unless the Father is understood as the *only* cause of Trinitarian existence monotheism would immediately collapse. This is because in the East it was the Father and not divine substance that guaranteed the oneness of God. The debate about the *Filioque* demonstrated the personalistic approach to monotheism, which characterized the Trinitarian theology of the Greek theologians. Two 'causes' would mean two Gods. The one substance would not be sufficient to protect monotheism in Trinitarian theology, since the one God was for the Greek Patristic tradition, as it was for the Bible too, the person of the Father.

The suggestion, therefore, that in order to safeguard full ontological freedom for all three persons of the Trinity we might speak of the three divine persons as causing each other's existence would imply that causation would either be irrelevant to the question of the oneness of God, in which case we should seek the divine unity in divine substance (or in some kind of triunity),[17] or, if relevant, would lead to tritheism (three causes equals three 'sources' or 'principles'). In introducing the language of 'cause' and applying it exclusively to the Father the Cappadocians did nothing more than paraphrase the Nicene *ek tou Patros*, recognizing in it a personalist meaning[18] and precluding any interpretation that would make substance the source of the Trinity.

Having stated the reasons why the idea of 'cause' could not be applied equally to all three persons of the Trinity – it is not accidental that such an application is novel and was never suggested in the theological tradition of the past – we can now consider the objections raised with regard to Trinitarian freedom. Are the other two persons equally free with the Father ontologically, if the Father is a 'given' to them which they have to accept? I suggest that these objections derive from false assumptions that are totally foreign to divine being. Let us consider them.

I have already argued earlier on that givenness and choice are notions inapplicable to God for the following reasons:

a) Givenness and choice presuppose some kind of *time*, i.e. a movement from the earlier to the later, as Aristotle defined time.[19] The 'given' ontologically precedes the one of whom it is 'given'. But in the case of God nothing can be said to precede or be preceded. Givenness implies time and cannot be applied to the Trinity. Causation in the case of the Trinity is timeless and

---

[17] An expression used by Barth, A. J. Torrance and others.

[18] It deserves particular attention that the Fathers of the Second Ecumenical Council in Constantinople 381 A.D. changed the phrasing of the Creed of Nicaea and made it read '*ek tou Patros*' instead of '*ek tēs ousias tou Patros*' ('from the Father', instead of 'from the ousia of the Father'). They made it clear in this way that the origin of the Son is a person rather than substance.

[19] Aristotle, *Physics*, IV 10–11, 218a 30ff.

for this reason inconceivable in terms of givenness. By being the 'cause' of the Son and the Spirit, the Father cannot be regarded as a 'given' to them.

b) Givenness and choice presuppose *individuality*. An individual, as opposed to a person, is an entity established prior to its relationship with someone or something. It first exists and then relates. In the case of God, no person of the Trinity is established ontologically prior to its relationship with the other two persons, the Father included. In speaking of causation, therefore, we must not allow for any assumption that the Father exists as Father prior to his relationship with the Son (and the Spirit). There is no such an entity as a person prior – and therefore given – to the Son and the Spirit, since the Father himself emerges in and through his relationship (communion) with them.

If these basic truths are taken into account, causation ceases to be a threat to freedom. For indeed, wherever there is givenness and individuality, there cannot be freedom in the absolute ontological sense of the term, as the given constitutes the most serious provocation to one's freedom. Had any person of the Trinity been presented with a given, i.e. with an entity established prior to this person and 'given' to it, this person would be automatically faced with a provocation to its freedom.

Now, if the Father cannot be spoken of as an entity established prior – and therefore given – to the Son and the Spirit, how can he be said to *cause* their personal existence? Can there be a cause which is not established as an entity prior to its relationship with that of which it is a cause? If we try to answer this question from our experience of fragmented time in which we creatures exist, the answer cannot but be a negative one: there is no cause which is not established prior (chronologically and logically) to what it causes. It is this experienced existence that interferes, consciously or unconsciously, with the reasoning of those who assume that, in being the cause of the Son and the Spirit, the Father threatens their freedom with the givenness of his own person. But in a being such as that of the Trinity, in which no entity can be established prior to or independently from its relationships, there is no givenness that can constitute a threat to freedom.

If, therefore, we wish to avoid the anthropomorphic reasoning which would transfer our own fragmented existence to the Trinity, we must seek to understand causation as something respecting fully the conditions of Trinitarian being: the cause is not established as a personal entity prior to that of which it is a cause, but in and through its relationship with it. In what sense, then, is there a first, a second and a third in the Trinity? In what sense can we justify the use of the idea of cause in Trinitarian existence?

The priority of the Father as the 'first one', the *Theos*, is a statement of the Bible with which Christian theology had to operate from its inception. Trinitarian theology had to respect this in developing its Trinitarianism. The Father must always remain 'greater' than the Son (John 14, 28) and the Spirit without any undermining of their equality in terms of divine nature, the hierarchical sequence being left only to the level of personhood. Was that arbitrary or accidental?

The idea of causation was introduced by the Cappadocian Fathers precisely in that context. They were absolutely clear: equality of nature, hierarchy of persons. Nature must be undifferentiated, for it is by definition common to all divine persons, but persons being *idia*, also by definition, must differ, not in their natural properties but their hypostatic-personal ones. These latter were from the beginning defined ontologically: the Father is *agennētos*, the Son *gennētos* and the Spirit *exporeuton*. In these ontological differentiations there is inherent not simply a sequence and hierarchy but also a causation: the one who generates causes the generation of the one who is generated etc.; the latter owes its existence to the former. The generating is first, for it cannot be logically placed after the generated one, albeit not in the sense of a 'given' entity, since it is established in relationship with the generated (and the spirated) one, but only because of the difference of their hypostatic properties (generator, generated, spirated).

Trinitarian hierarchy (first-second-third) is therefore not to be understood as an order of individuals ontologically established in that particular *taxis*[20], but as an order implied in their distinct hypostatic properties: *agennētos, gennētos, ekporeutos*. These properties should not be confused with the Persons as such; they are properties *of* the Persons, not the Persons themselves who are established as such in relation to each other. When we say, therefore, that the Father is 'first' (and 'cause'), we do not imply by that that he is established as a person as a 'given' to the other two persons, but that within the nexus of the divine relations, in which he establishes himself as a person, he possesses a hypostatic property (Generator) which makes him 'first' (and 'cause'): the Generated one derives from the ungenerated Generator (*ek tou Patros* – Creed of Nicaea/Constantinople), hence the order of causation. There is thus no danger of subordinationism[21] in this sort of hierarchy or *taxis*, since all the persons in the Trinity exist in relation to one another, the order implied in causation occurring within the nexus of this relationship and referring to their distinct hypostatic properties.[22]

---

[20] The idea of *taxis* (order) in the immanent Trinity is fundamental to Patristic theology. See: Iustin, I *Apol.*, 13,3; Basil, *C. Eun.*, 3,1; 1,20; Gregory Naz., *Or.*, 42,15; Gregory Nys., *Quod non sint* ... (PG 45, 133). It is wrong, therefore, to limit the order of Trinitarian persons to the economic Trinity, as V. Lossky and others seem to do. Thus, V. Lossky, *In the Image and Likeness of God*, p. 92f.; T. F. Torrance, *Trinitarian Perspectives*, Edinburg: T&T Clark 1994, p. 32; C. Gunton, *The Promise of Trinitarian Theology*, Edinburgh: T&T Clark 1991, p. 196f.

[21] Of which certain theologians speak in relation to the Cappadocian idea of causation in the immanent Trinity.

[22] The distinction between the person as such and its hypostatic (personal) properties is crucial not only for the purpose of understanding causation in the Trinity, but for Trinitarian theology in general. Calling God *Father* is a name denoting his person, while calling him 'unoriginate' or *agennētos* is a name denoting not his person but a property of his person. This subtle

# Trinitarian Freedom and the Economy

The axiom proposed by Rahner and accepted by many theologians[23] that the immanent Trinity is the economic Trinity and vice versa raises the problem of Trinitarian freedom in an acute way. This axiom is based on the logic that whatever the Trinity represents in the economy must correspond to what the Trinity is in its true eternal being, for otherwise God would undergo in the economy an ontological change which would be improper to apply to the divine being. After all, the argument would go, it is only through the economic Trinity that we know God, and unless the economic Trinity coincides fully with the immanent one, God would not have given us his true and full involvement in our life.

The implications of this axiom for the question of Trinitarian freedom are extremely important. They appear, for example, in their acuteness when we consider statements such as that of Pannenberg, who writes that 'revelation cannot be viewed as extraneous to (God's) deity' and we must 'constantly link the trinity in the eternal essence of God to his historical revelation'.[24] Similar views are expressed by Moltmann[25] for whom the economic Trinity 'is nothing other than the eternal perichoresis of Father, Son and Holy Spirit in their dispensation of salvation'.[26] This leads to the idea of an eternally 'suffering' God, for if God is truly love, then the self-giving that marks the Trinity of history cannot be an arbitrarily chosen deed but must arise directly out of the essence of God.[27]

If these views are considered from the angle of Trinitarian freedom, the conclusion would be that whatever happens in the economy is logically determined by what God is in his essence and vice versa. Thus, God would not be free *not* to reveal himself, being eternally in a state of self-revelation, and in revealing himself he cannot but do so as the second person of the Trinity who is defined precisely as God's eternal self-revelation.[28] Similar reasoning is applied to the Holy Spirit, who on the basis of the Augustinian

---

distinction is repeatedly used by the Fathers in their argument against the Arians. See, for example, Athanasius, *C. Ar.*, 1,34 (we do not pray to the 'unoriginate' but to the Father); Basil, *C. Eun.*, 1,5 (we are not baptized in the name of the *agennētos* but of the Father); Gregory Naz., *Or.*, 31, 23 etc.

[23] K. Rahner, *The Trinity*, New York: Herder and Herder 1997, p. 22; J. Moltmann, *The Trinity and the Kingdom*, Minneapolis: Fortress Press 1981; E. Jüngel, *God as the Mystery of the Word*, Grand Rapids: Eerdmans 1983; C. M. LaCugna, *God for Us*, New York: HarperOne 1991, et al.

[24] W. Pannenberg, *Systematic Theology*, I, Grand Rapids: Eerdmans 1993, p. 328.

[25] Moltmann, *The Trinity and the Kingdom*, p. 57–8.

[26] Moltmann, *The Trinity and the Kingdom*, p. 157.

[27] Moltmann, *The Trinity and the Kingdom*, pp. 90 and 160.

[28] Cf. K. Barth's portrayal of the eternal life of the Trinity as a sort of self-revelation of God within the eternal being of God. Cf. *Church Dogmatics*, I/1, London-New York: Continuum

tradition is defined as God's love: it is in the form of the Spirit that God reveals himself in history as love, and it is because the Spirit reveals God in history in this particular way that the Spirit is eternally love.

Such views compromise Trinitarian freedom because they tend to identify act with being in God. This is a tendency characterizing western theology throughout its history.[29] The way God acts does not correspond to the way God is in the Eastern tradition. By identifying the persons of the Trinity with a particular way of acting (revealing, loving etc.) one binds God's hypostatic properties to certain activities which thus become ontological. Just as the Son cannot but be generated and the Spirit spirated, in the same way the Son is in his exclusive hypostatic property God's self-revelation and the Spirit God's love. This would mean that the Father and the Son cannot be love but for the existence of the Spirit[30] and the Spirit cannot reveal God except as a sort of Son's 'assistant'. The Greek Fathers would never place divine activities on the level of personal properties, regarding all activities as common to all three persons of the Trinity (unity of *opera ad intra*). There are certainly specific activities attached to each Trinitarian person *in the economy*, but these do not correspond to the ontological properties of that particular person. These activities *ad extra* were freely undertaken and applied by the Trinitarian persons and not dictated by their ontological 'mode of being'.

The immanent Trinity is indeed the economic Trinity and the economic Trinity is indeed the immanent Trinity, for otherwise the world would not be in communion with the life of the Triune God which is the ultimate purpose of the salvation offered in Christ. This identification of the two Trinities manifests the *ek-static* character of God, i.e. his freedom to reach beyond himself, being *ek-static* both within himself and outside himself. But the way he reaches beyond himself is dictated by the special conditions of those he wishes to reach (creation and humanity), as condescensions for their sake, and not by any inner logical or ontological necessity. Revelation, *kenosis*, suffering, death, etc. are *freely* undertaken by God for our sake, precisely because they are not his natural condition, being extraneous to him. The economy manifests God's freedom precisely by showing that God

---

2010, p. 349, 411, 439. Rahner also speaks of the Son as the eternal self-revelation of God, cf. *The Trinity*, p. 29.

[29] The equation of God's being with God's activity is characteristic particularly of medieval theology. See Gilson's *L'esprit de la philosophie médiévale*, pp. 89, 94: 'être, c'est agir et agir, c'est l'être.' This survives in modern theologies, such as that of Karl Barth, R. W. Jenson etc.

[30] Thus we read in R. W. Jenson, *Systematic Theology*, I, Oxford: Oxford University Press 2001, p. 153, that a binetarian ontology leads to a dyadic struggle in which freedom and personhood cannot be maintained, and that it is the Holy Spirit that liberates the Father and the Son from any determination in order to be both subject and object of the other. By being the love in the Trinity, the Spirit frees the Father and the Son to become true persons for each other and thus becomes the divine future 'into which all things will at last be brought'.

is free to become what he is not rather than what he is in his own being. By projecting what God has done for our sake in the economy into what he is eternally in his Trinitarian being we implicitly undermine his freedom to become what he eternally is not.

# Trinitarian Freedom and Human Freedom

Humans as creatures are by definition faced with a 'given' (or an infinite number of 'givens'). Their freedom consists in their ability to choose from among these 'givens', which means that decision (deliberation as to what is preferable) and choice are fundamental presuppositions for the exercise of human freedom. This is what we normally call freedom of the will.

Trinitarian freedom, we have argued here, is not based on similar presuppositions. God, by definition, is not faced with any 'given', being himself the author of all that exists, and for this reason we cannot speak of him as 'deciding' or 'choosing', as theologians often do.[31] This applies also to the Trinity. The Trinitarian persons are not to be understood as subjects of consciousness, since they possess but one will, mind etc. both *ad intra* and *ad extra*, according to Patristic thought. Trinitarian relations cannot be spoken of in terms of givenness, decision, choice etc. since everything that pertains to the Trinity refers to the uncreated God who is not bound by the condition of time[32], a condition existentially attached to givenness, decision and choice.

Trinitarian freedom is, negatively speaking, freedom from the given and, positively, the capacity to be other while existing in relationship and in unity of nature. In as much, therefore, as unity of nature provides sameness and wholeness, Trinitarian freedom, as the capacity to be other, can be spoken of as freedom from sameness. And in as much as otherness provides particularity, Trinitarian freedom can be spoken of as freedom from selfhood and individuality. How do these characteristics relate to human freedom?

---

[31] We have already noted the reason why the language of choice cannot be used in the case of Trinitarian freedom. The understanding of divine freedom in terms of decision is found in many modern theologians, including Barth, Jüngel and others. This would also be difficult to accept, particularly if presented in connection with the idea of election as is the case with Barth. Decision presupposes an act of deliberation and finally opting for a certain possibility. The same implication is to be found also in the idea of election: someone or something is being 'rejected'. This may compromise divine freedom through the assumption of a metaphysical 'given' confronting God.

[32] It is not accidental that Barth, Jenson and others, who operate with the idea of election, decision, act, etc. in connection with the immanent Trinity are in the end forced to introduce time somehow into God's Trinitarian existence.

Human beings appear to be very often content with the freedom of will, i.e. the ability to choose from among given possibilities, and sometimes they boast of that.[33] And yet deep in their hearts there lies a thirst for something more than that. It is the desire to be free from the given, including the given *par excellence* that is God. The rejection of God, whether in the form of Adam's fall or that of modern atheism, is a proof of the fact that the human being wishes to be free from the given. Divine freedom is therefore the kind of freedom that the human being aspires to.

On another level, human beings thirst for Trinitarian freedom, as each of them strives to secure their particularity and otherness, being faced with the sameness of natural laws (particularly decay and death) or with various forms of uniformity in their social life. The history of humanity in its entirety is a struggle to reconcile the one and the many, to be one and many at the same time. It is a struggle to obtain Trinitarian freedom in human life.

It lies beyond the scope of this paper to discuss whether or how Trinitarian freedom can become a reality also for the human being. Certainly this, and maybe only this, constitutes the essence of the Christian Gospel and the purpose of the Church. What can be said here as a conclusion is that Trinitarian freedom and human freedom are not two different kinds of freedom, as they appear to be at first sight. If human freedom is to be true freedom it can only be modelled after the freedom of Trinitarian life.

The purpose of the divine economy is precisely to lead humanity and through it the entire creation 'from the slavery of corruption to the freedom of the glory of the children of God' (Rom. 8.21) through our 'sonship' (*ibid.* 23), i.e. our reception by grace in the Spirit into the very life and freedom of the Triune God.

---

[33] It is usually overlooked that animals too possess such a kind of freedom.

# PART THREE

# New Readings

# 9

# Patristic Trinitarian Ontology

## Giulio Maspero

### Why Trinitarian Ontology?

Trinitarian Ontology is an expression that can be understood in various ways. In general it indicates the metaphysical reinterpretation founded in Trinitarian revelation. This is one of the principal elements that appeared in the second half of the twentieth century. It was validated by the *Thesen* of Hemmerle, which were addressed in the form of philosophical letters to von Balthasar,[1] who in turn treated the question in his *Theodramatik*.[2] The theme clearly touches the relationship between theology and philosophy, as well as the rethinking of this relationship.

What occurs when one takes seriously the revealed truth that the *archê* is actually one Substance in three Persons? This is expressed well by Daniélou, who wrote in 1968: 'We thus touch the depths of Christian Trinitarian ontology. This is one of the points in which the Trinitarian mystery best illuminates human situations. It shows us that the very foundation of existence, the foundation of reality, the form of everything because it is its origin, is love, in the sense of interpersonal community. The foundation of being is a community of persons. Some say the foundation of being is

---

[1] Cf. K. Hemmerle, *Thesen zu einer trinitarischen Ontologie*, Einsiedeln: Johannes Verlag 1976.

[2] H. U. Von Balthasar., *Welt aus Trinität*, in *Theodramatik* IV, Einsiedeln: Johannes-Verlag 1983, pp. 53–95. See also L. Oening-Hanhoff, *Trinitarische Ontologie und Metaphysik der Person*, in W. Breuning (ed.), *Trinität: Aktuelle Perspektiven der Theologie*, Freiburg: Herder 1984, pp. 143–82.

matter, others that it is spirit, others that it is the one: they are all wrong. The foundation of being is communion.'[3] It is significant that Daniélou was one of the most important experts of Gregory of Nyssa. In fact, it was in the works of the Fathers of the Church that the first authentic Trinitarian ontology has been recognized to exist *in nuce*.[4]

In the light of this, one can delineate, in a somewhat schematic manner, two primary lines of development in historical-dogmatic studies on this subject in the final thirty years of last century:[5] a more occidental one, in the Augustinian tradition, focused on the concept of relation and developing its relationship with substance; and a more oriental one, which, beginning from the great theology of the Greek Fathers, primarily worked with the concept of person, showing its antecedence in relation to philosophical substance.

Ratzinger works in the first perspective, having shown in 1968 the revolutionary scope of Trinitarian doctrine from a metaphysical perspective, in particular with the new ontological status that it recognizes for relation.[6] His reflections were obviously founded on the study of Augustine, in whose thought can be found a true and proper Trinitarian ontology.[7] Once elected to the See of Peter, Ratzinger accentuated the importance of developing this dimension, in a certain sense instigating in philosophers and theologians a development of the metaphysics of relation.[8] The fruits of this research have also been echoed in the domain of Thomistic philosophy with the studies of W. Norris Clarke and his understanding of being as substance-in-relation.[9]

The second perspective has John Zizioulas, the Metropolitan of Pergamus, as its principal representative. In *Being as Communion*, the first edition of which was published in 1985, he develops the reformulation of metaphysics from the personal principle and concretely from the monarchy of the Father.[10] The doctrine of the Greek Fathers of the fourth century marks a fundamental shift in the development of ontology, as they placed the Person of the Father as the source of all Being, both intra-divine and participated

---

[3] J. Daniélou, *La Trinité et le mystère de l'existence*, Paris: Desclée de Brouwer 1968, pp. 52–3.

[4] G. Greshake, *Der dreieine Gott*, Freiburg i.Br.: Herder 1997, p. 454.

[5] For an overview, see: L. Žák, *Premessa: Verso un'ontologia trinitaria*, in P. Coda and L. Žák, *Abitando la Trinità*, Rome: Città Nuova 1998, pp. 5–25.

[6] Cf. J. Ratzinger, *Einführung in das Christentum*, Munich: Kösel Verlag 1968. [Eng. trans. *Introduction to Christianity*, San Francisco: Ignatius Press 1990, pp. 130–2.]

[7] Cf. K. Kienzler, *Zu den Anfängen einer 'trinitarischen Ontologie'. Augustinus' 'Bekenntnisse'*, in M. Albus, R. Göllner et. al. (eds), *Der dreieine Gott und die eine Menschheit*, Freiburg i.Br.: Herder 1989, pp. 45–60.

[8] Benedict VI, *Caritas in veritate*, 53–4.

[9] Cf. W. N. Clarke, *Explorations in Metaphysics*, Notre Dame: University of Notre Dame Press 1994, and *Person and Being*, Milwaukee: Marquette University Press 1993.

[10] J. D. Zizioulas, *Being as Communion*, Crestwood: St Vladimir's Seminary Press 1985.

in the economy. This shows that the personal dimension is the fundamental one on the metaphysical level.

The two perspectives seem to move on different planes, as Levering[11] has shown: the first works on the pair of substance-relation, in a context that attempts to harmonize classical philosophy and theology through the simple fact of using metaphysical categories; the second is based on the purely theological category of monarchy, affirming the priority of the Person of the Father over substance. In this way, it manifests the discontinuity between Greek philosophical reflection and Patristic reflection to a greater extent.[12]

The goal of this contribution is to show a possible harmonization of these two readings from a reconstruction of the historical-dogmatic development of fourth century Greek Patristics, particularly if, together with the reflections of Basil the Great, one uses the reflections of his younger brother, Gregory of Nyssa, and his insistence on the co-relativity of the divine Persons. This co-relativity is the element that might permit a reconciliation of the two readings, in so far as it expresses personal communion in terms of relation, and thus in terms of relationship to substance.

We wish to offer a contribution to the neopatristic synthesis promoted by John Zizioulas in *Being as Communion*,[13] in the hope that it may be useful for dialogue between the various Christian confessions.[14]

# Logos and the Trinity

In order to see how co-relativity emerged in the theology of the Greek Fathers, it is necessary to begin with the concept of *logos*, which, from the philosophical signification of necessary relationship will move, through Christian revelation, to that of free and reciprocal relation, which expresses divine filiation and founds Trinitarian *koinonia* itself.

*Logos* is an essential element of ancient metaphysical conceptualization. It has the fundamental signification of measure or law of necessary proportion, and is inevitably tied to a role of mediation and unification

---

[11] Cf. M. Levering, *Scripture and Metaphysics: Aquinas and the Renewal of Trinitarian Theology*, Oxford: Blackwell 2004, pp. 202–10.

[12] 'Thus God as person – as the hypostasis of the Father – makes the one divine substance to be that which it is: the one God. This point is absolutely crucial.' (Zizioulas, *Being as Communion*, p. 41)

[13] Zizioulas, *Being as Communion*, p. 26.

[14] The ecumenical importance of reflection on Trinitarian ontology has been accentuated e.g. in: J. Y. Lacoste, 'Being', in ibid., *Encyclopedia of Christian Theology*, I, New York: Routledge 2005, p. 193.

of that which is multiple and subject to movement. It is thus a concept of linking and boundaries.

From Heraclitus[15] to Plato,[16] *logos* is considered the measure according to which the elements are combined and the dynamics of the cosmos are guided. This is all founded in a metaphysical vision of a limited world that is eternal and necessary, tied to the first principle by an ontological ladder that man can follow with his thought. *Logos* is thus the relationship between the beings and the ideas by which the Platonic Demiurge forged first matter. It is also the relationship between the various Aristotelian motors which unite the world to the First Mover in a continuous and necessary manner. *Logos* thus represents the fixed relationship between the rungs of the ontological ladder, which was extended between the two ontological principles of the One, on the one hand, and negative and eternal matter or pure potentiality on the other, which together constituted ancient ontological dualism. Everything was held together by the tension between the multiple and the One, whose perfection was based precisely in its being free of all relation. This necessary *logos*, which was defended by Plato and Socrates against Sophist relativism, is also at the root of the tragic dimension that is inherent in the Greek world as the manifestation of the impossibility of reconciling the requirements of the absolute law with those of the individual.

There was an essential development in the passage to Neoplatonism: the opposition between the multiple and the One was resolved, thanks to the contributions of Philo and the Neopythagoreans, in the unicity of the Neoplatonic first principle.[17] The condition for reaching this was, however, the linking of multiplicity to the degradation of the various ontological levels, which, in a continuously decreasing ladder, united the One and the world in a necessary manner. In this vision, *logos* was still understood as a law of fixed proportion that governed this degradation from the One to the multiple. *Logos* was thus necessary and source of necessity. This understanding of *logos* implied that relation was marked with imperfection,[18] as was already implicit in the Platonic conception of the image as a degradation in respect to the prototype and in the categorization of the Aristotelian *pros ti* on the accidental level.

The Jewish conception was quite different, in so far as the *logos* was immediately tied to the Word of God who enters into relation with his chosen people. The God of Israel speaks, chooses, becomes angry and saves. The very being of the people, its identity, is constituted by its relation with

---

[15] Cf. Heraclitus, *Fragments* DK 1; DK 72; DK 31.

[16] Cf. Plato, *Timeus*, 32bc.

[17] Cf. G. Maspero, 'Logos e ontologia trinitaria: il percorso di Gregorio di Nissa', in R. Radice, A. Valvo, *Dal logos dei Greci e dei Romani al logos di Dio*, Milan: Vita e Pensiero 2010, pp. 317–37.

[18] Cf. e.g. Porphyry, *Comm. in Platonis Parm.*, III, 32–IV, 4.

this God who reunited diverse nomadic tribes and made a great nation of them. The key to this conceptualization is creation. While everything is eternal and necessary in the Greek world, in the Jewish world everything was created freely by God. There is thus an infinite metaphysical hiatus between the creature and the Creator, an ontological gap that can only be traversed by the will of God. The *logos* of Hellenistic, Greek-speaking Judaism was therefore tied to the will of God, who entered into relation with his people as a person. God speaks to man, God enters into relation with man, revealing himself as person and not only as power, or life, or unmoved mover. The continuous ontological ladder is broken in such a way that the Jew is conscious that none can know God if He does not reveal himself, if He does not want it. In this manner, the personal *logos* of a God who is person and desires to reveal himself and enter into relation by creating and saving substitutes the necessary *logos* that corresponds to ontological necessity. The Jewish *logos* is then already a descending and free relation: the God of Israel is Person and has relations.

The next step could only be completed through New Testament revelation, which reached a God who is not only personal, but who is three Persons. In this manner the *logos* will move from the role of divine activity that reveals the personality of YHWH to that of the Person of the Son, whose identity is founded on his reciprocal relation with the Father. In this perspective one discovers not only that God has relations, but that He is Relations. This requires a further revolution in ontological conceptualization.

In fact there can be no intermediate degree between God and the world, but in Christ – the *Logos* himself who is God – that which is inside the *archê* enters into history because He wishes to, out of love. In this way, divinity and humanity are united forever in Christ, not by nature, but by grace. The source of unity of everything is always the *Logos*, which is however now outside the world, and comes from the uncreated dimension that belongs to the Trinity alone.

Comparison to Neoplatonism is inevitable, in so far as it was the philosophical *koinê* of the fourth century. Arianism itself is a reduction of revealed truths to the previous understanding of a descending ontology of the *logos* of necessary relationship, which could lead to nothing in theology other than Trinitarian subordinationism, as in the Neopythagorean doctrine of three gods and that of the three hypostases.[19]

The orthodox response, from Athanasius to the Cappadocians, thus had to be on the metaphysical level, through the creation of a new ontology that facilitated expression of the Trinitarian Mystery, thus presenting it for adoration without blemishing its ineffable depth. As Zizioulas rightly

---

[19] Cf. C. H. Kahn, *Pythagoras and the Pythagoreans. A Brief History*, Indianapolis: Hackett PC 2001, pp. 98–9.

observes, an essential passage of this process was that of tracing the divinity to the hypostasis of the Father, in such a way that the *archê* was no longer the anonymous and necessary substance of Greek philosophy, but the infinite mystery of the First Person of the Trinity. The Metropolitan of Pergamus is attentive to the fact that the origin of the Son and the Holy Spirit should not be understood only as substantial communication, according to a schema that is more philosophical than theological: 'It is only when divine nature is somehow confused with the person of the Father, and personal causation with a process of *imparting of divine nature* by the Father to the other two persons, that the equality of the Trinitarian persons as fully divine is put at risk ... Divine nature does not exist prior to the divine persons, as a sort of possession of the Father who grants it to the other persons ... Divine nature exists only when and as the Trinity emerges, and it is for this reason that it is not 'possessed' by any person in advance'.[20] In this manner the concept of *relation*, was elevated, according to the Trinitarian grammar that emerged during the difficult discussions that followed the Council of Nicaea and led to that of Constantinople, as a metaphysical principle equal to that of essence.

In the thought of Gregory of Nyssa, this passage is realized in continuity with the theology of Athanasius and of Gregory's brother Basil. His proper characteristic is that of extending the co-relative interpretation of the Father and the Son to the relationship with the Holy Spirit. The *Logos* is fully understood in its dimension of perfect, reciprocal and eternal relation only when it is considered together with the Holy Spirit, the Giver of Life. Athanasius had succeeded in recovering the concept of *Logos* as fixed proportion, purifying it thanks to the 'theology of natures'. Justin, Clement of Alexandria and Origen had used the philosophical concept of *logos* in order to present the history of salvation in unison with the history of man and the search for God. However, this operation left their flank exposed to subordinationism, because the divine *Logos*, although eternal, could not be considered in its being independently from creation: it was the thought of creation that was eternally conceived by God. For this reason, Athanasius, faithful to the inspiration of the first verse of the Johannine prologue, re-expressed the relationship between God and the world in terms of natures, identifying the Trinity with the unique eternal and uncreated nature, while every other being is a creature and has a different nature.

In this manner the *Logos* and the *Pneuma* ceased to be mediating figures, in order to be inserted into the immanence of the unique first principle, *inside* God. Proportion no longer applied to the relationship between God and the world, as the Arians understood it, but it characterized the very

---

[20] Cf. J. D. Zizioulas, *Communion & Otherness: Further Studies in personhood and Church*, London: T & T Clark 2006, p. 140.

being of God, in so far as the eternal *Logos* was the image of the Father, just as the Spirit was the image of the Son;[21] the Son was to the Father as the Spirit was to the Son. The second Person of the Trinity was thus the proportional middle that maintained the unity of the Trinity itself. Being image was no longer understood as a degradation, but as perfection in relation, which includes the Son and the Spirit in the heart of the First Principle of the *archê*. This reading was clearly relational, in so far as the Father is Father only because He has a Son, and the Son is Son only because He has a Father. The weak point of this initial magnificent construction was the lack of a principle of distinction between the first and second procession. This left the door open for the criticisms of the Tropists, that was the Father the grandfather of the Spirit. Proportionality still borrowed too much from its physical conceptualization: the relation is eternal, but still too vertical and necessary. There is not yet a perfect co-relativity of the divine Persons.

In order to overcome this difficulty, Gregory of Nyssa developed the reflection on the relationship between the *Logos* and the Spirit in their origin from the Father. He then developed the relationship between the two processions, co-relationally reinterpreting both the relationship between the Father and the Son as well as that between the Holy Spirit and the two first Persons. His specific contribution was the inclusion of the Spirit in the understanding of the relationship between the Father and the *Logos*, showing that subordinationism could only be overcome by moving from a conception of the *Logos* as *ratio* to one of the *Logos* as *relatio*. This was only possible by understanding the processions in the sense of a free gift, and thus by developing the role of the Spirit in the eternal generation of the Son.

Gregory turned to the biblical categories of the Kingdom and Glory for this, reinterpreting these in a relational sense. The Kingdom was understood as the reason for which the Son is King, i.e. the perfect – and not not deficient as in Neoplatonism – image of the Father, while Glory was understood as the eternal gift that the Father and Son exchange. The reinterpretation of the third Person in the sense of the eternal relation permits reinterpreting the relation between the Father and his *Logos* in the sense of liberty, so that They are One in the Other, and One through the Other. Trinitarian conceptualization becomes ever more dynamic, and the *Logos* itself is interpreted in a purely relational sense, as the Son of the Father's Love.

This study focuses on the essential fact that the Persons proceed from the Persons. For this reason the freedom of gift that constitutes the processions is accentuated. Nevertheless, one should note that, as generation was purified of the limits that characterize it on the creaturely level in order to

---

[21] Cf. Athanasius, *Letters to Serapion*, III, 1, 2.

be predicated of God, so too liberty, when it is applied to the intra-divine processions, must be freed of any connection to contingency. For man, liberty is tied to the ability to not be, in such a way that if a reality is free, it cannot be necessary. But one cannot say that the Absolute is not necessary. Thus, the processions are free, but are eternal at the same time, i.e. they cannot not be.[22] We are before the limits of man's expressive capacities in its contact with the extreme depths of being. When one applies the concept of liberty to God's inner life, one does it in a manner that is radically different from when, for example, one speaks of God's liberty in the act of creation. The world is contingent, while this is not the case of God's inner life, as the Cappadocian Fathers always stressed: the Son and the Spirit are eternal and cannot *not* exist.

For this reason, in his reformulation of ontology, Gregory begins by identifying the Son with the *principle*, using the theology of nature:

> The Father is principle (ἀρχή) of all things. But it is proclaimed that the Son is also in this principle, since he is by nature that which the principle is. In fact, God is principle and the Word that is in the principle is God.[23]

Faithful to the theology of the Johannine prologue, Gregory of Nyssa introduces the *Logos* into the principle, identifying it with the principle itself. This operation implies an ontological shift, in so far as the *Logos* cannot be a mediating figure between God and the world. His identification with the Son pushes reflection in the line of a perfect relation that does not subordinate. The Christian *Logos* is thus doubly tied to a conceptualization of filiation that is radically original in comparison with the Greek world. One key for understanding its importance is the connection that Gregory presents with the idea of *image*:

> The Son is in the Father, as the beauty of the image is in the form of the model (ἐν τῇ ἀρχετύπῳ μορφῇ), and the Father is in the Son, as the exemplary beauty (τὸ πρωτότυπον κάλλος) is in its own image. While with the images made by the hand of man, there is always a temporal distance between communicated image and model, in this case, however, the one cannot be separated from the other.[24]

---

[22] See the beautiful text of C. Schönborn: 'En vérité, ce que le Fils nous a lui-même révélé est profondément paradoxal, à savoir: qu'il est à la fois obéissant en tout au Père et uni en tout à Lui. En Dieu il n'y a pas de domination du supérieur sur l'inférieur: l'obéissance est identique à la liberté, le don total de soi est identique à la pleine possesion de soi.' (Ch. Schönborn, *L'icône du Christ*, Paris: Cerf 1986, p. 53.)

[23] *Contra Eunomium* III, (GNO II), 193, 23–6.

[24] *Contra Eunomium* I, (GNO I) 209, 8–14.

The text clearly refers to divine immanence, i.e. the being of God, in order to affirm a manner of being image that is essentially different from Platonic conceptualizations, which read it as a degradation – as a material corruption of the ideal prototype, a reading that is at the root of subordinationist theology.[25] With the words of J. Daniélou: 'It [the term *eikôn*] designates a true community of nature. It nevertheless implies a certain number of distinctions that were not provided for by the non-Christian uses of the term. Applied to *logos*, as is already found in Saint Paul (Col 1.15, cf. Wi 7.26), the term *eikôn* does not designate a deficient participation, but the pure relation of origin in perfect equality of nature. This is a new sense, tied to Trinitarian dogma.'[26] One thus reaches the surprising affirmation that not only does the Son possess all that the Father possesses, but the Son possesses the Father himself.[27] Further, the name of Father refers to two Persons, because the idea of Son spontaneously follows that of Father: in saying Father, our faith pushes us to think of the Father with the Son.[28] Everything is read in terms of co-relativity, in an effort of purification of the concept of filiation, which ceases to be subject to the temporal and material limits that are characteristic of human generation.

# Relationship and the Holy Spirit

Generation is therefore no longer to be read as necessary degradation, but as self gift of the Father to the Son. However, this is only understandable to the extent to which the relationship between the *Logos* and the Spirit is developed. This is the most specific and important contribution on Gregory's part in comparison to Basil and Athanasius. First of all, the name of Christ is interpreted as a direct reference to the Holy Spirit, in so far as the Anointed cannot be without the Anointing:

> How will one who does not recognize the Chrism along with the Anointed One confess Christ? *God anointed this man*, he says, *in the Holy Spirit* (Act 10.38).[29]

Thus, to think of Christ is necessarily to think of the Holy Spirit, in the same way as thinking of the Father leads one to think of the Son. This

---

[25] For an overview of this concept in Gregory of Nyssa's thought, cf. G. Maspero, 'Image', in L.-F. Mateo-Seco and G. Maspero (eds), *The Brill Dictionary of Gregory of Nyssa*, Leiden: Brill 2010, pp. 411–15.

[26] J. Daniélou, *Platonisme et théologie mystique*, Paris: Aubier 1944, p. 48

[27] Cf. *Contra Eunomium* II, (GNO I) 288, 19–23.

[28] Cf. *Contra Eunomium* III, (GNO II) 81, 3–4 and *Eun* II, (GNO I) 208, 11–14.

[29] *Adversus Macedonianos*, (GNO III/1) 102, 14–16.

characteristic relation of Christ is based in his eternal being, as can be seen in the rest of the text:

> So if the Son is king by nature, and the chrism is a symbol of his kingship, then what does the logic of the reasoning mean to you? That the chrism is not something foreign to the natural king, and we do not classify the Spirit with the Holy Trinity as a stranger and someone with a different nature. Indeed the Son is king. But the Holy Spirit is the living, substantial and subsistent kingship (ζῶσα καὶ οὐσιώδης καὶ ἐνυπόστατος). Since he has been anointed with this kingship, the only-begotten Christ is also king of all existing things. So if the Father is king and the Only-begotten is king and the Holy Spirit is kingship, the reason for kingship in the case of the Trinity is absolutely the same.[30]

The reason that the Son is the perfect image of the Father, in a radically original manner compared to how it was understood by Greek philosophy, and in a more perfect manner than in Athanasius and Basil, can be found precisely in the third Person. For the Spirit is the eternal Kingdom, thanks to which the Son, like the Father, is King.[31] The personal property of the third Person is reinterpreted in co-relative terms, in respect to both the Father and the Son. This is an original idea that Gregory founds exegetically by putting together *Your Kingdom come* of Mt 6.10 and the variant of Lk 11.2 *May your Spirit come upon us and purify us*.[32] Gregory is one of the witnesses to this variant[33] that is characteristic of the Syriac tradition, and is possibly tied to a liturgical invocation that accompanied the pre-baptismal anointing, as is witnessed to in the *Acts of Thomas*.[34] The equivalence of the two verses permits Gregory to identify the Spirit and the Kingdom, and to individuate the personal property of the third Person in the uniting of the first two. This pushes him to reinterpret their relationship in terms of gift, understood as free self-gift. The Father eternally generates the Son in giving Him his Spirit, and thus his Kingdom. The *Logos* is born of Love and not necessity. Thus Gregory writes:

---

[30] *Adversus Macedonianos*, (GNO III/1) 102, 22–31.

[31] One notes a decisive progress here in comparison to Basil, who limited himself to affirming the Spirit's participation in the Kingdom, cf. Basil, *De Spiritu Sancto*, 20, 51, 49–50, (SCh 17bis), pp. 428–30).

[32] *Oratio dominica*, (GNO VII/1) 39, 15–19.

[33] See M. Alexandre, 'La variante de Lc 11, 2 dans la Troisème Homélie sur l'Oraison Dominicale de Grégoire de Nysse et la controverse avec les pneumatomaques', in M. Cassin et al. (eds), *Grégoire de Nysse: La Bible dans la construction de son discours*. Actes du colloque de Paris, 9–10 février 2007, (Études augustiniennes), Paris: Brepols 2008, pp. 163–89.

[34] Alexandre, *La variante de Lc 11, 2*, p. 168–9.

There is no difference in any way between calling the Only Begotten God the *Son of God* or the *Son of his Love* (υἱὸν τῆς ἀγάπης αὐτοῦ).[35]

Love is placed here as the very foundation of being, since it is presented in a highly ontological sense, and not only a psychological one. Absolute gift is in fact only thinkable in this new ontology, which does not admit any *meson* that can be interposed between (*metaxy*) the Father and the Son, so that the union between the first two Persons is also immediate (*adiastatos*):

> Reason recognizes nothing intermediary (μέσον), so that some special border (μεθορίῳ) nature be thought to exist between (μεταξὺ) the created and the uncreated, in such a way it partakes of both and is neither perfectly.[36]

The language is clearly metaphysical and directly denies the foundations of Platonic ontology, which are recalled in the terminology that is used, in order to affirm that the Spirit is not an intermediary being between God and the world. The Spirit is rather the One in the Trinity who unites the Father and the Son. Without inverting Trinitarian order, Gregory affirms that the intermediary between the Father and the Son must be of their same nature, and thus that due to divine simplicity He must be of a unique nature with Them.

This is the final step in the theological effort to overcome the Neoplatonic and Gnostic conception of an ontological ladder that unites God and the world. The first movement of this surpassing was the modification of the philosophical concept of *logos* as the mediator between Heaven and earth. The Johannine prologue required inserting the *logos* itself into the divinity, i.e. into the *archê*. The debates with the Arians specifically touched on this point. The next step was to exclude completely the possibility that the Spirit could occupy a mediating position between the Creator and the created, as the Pneumatomachists wished. Placing the *Pneuma* in the divine *archê* itself meant reinterpreting both the mediation of the Son and that of the Spirit in purely immanent terms. Gregory accomplished this by developing the reciprocal relationships between the two processions. This result is the fruit of Gregory's intellectual itinerary, as can be demonstrated by a diachronic study of his interpretation of Jn 17.5 and the concept of glory as applied to the third Person.

In *Ad Eustathium*, Gregory already outlines the themes of Kingdom and

---

[35] *In Cantica Canticorum*, (GNO VI) 213, 15–17.
[36] *Adversus Macedonianos*, (GNO III/1) 104, 8–12.

Glory, precisely when he explains that chrism refers to the dignity of the third Person. The text is reminiscent of Basil's *De Spiritu Sancto*:[37]

> The Holy Spirit shares (κοινωνεῖ) the glory and kingship of the only-begotten Son of God.[38]

Later, in *Adversus Macedonianos*, the relationship between the Spirit and the Kingdom becomes one of identification, even if *doxa* appears without the article,[39] because the affirmation is about consubstantiality. And yet the exegesis of Jn 17.5 points directly to the identification of glory and the Spirit. This is clear in *Antirrheticus*:

> And the glory that is contemplated before the world and all creation and all the ages, in which the Only-Begotten God is glorified, is nothing other than the glory of the Spirit (τὴν δόξαν τοῦ πνεύματος), according to our thought. In fact, the doctrine of piety teaches that only the Holy Trinity is eternal. *He who exists from before the ages* (Ps 54.20) gives the prophecy of the Father; and the Apostle says in reference to the Son: *Through Him were made the ages* (He 1.2). The glory before the ages, contemplated in the Only-Begotten God, is the Holy Spirit.[40]

In *In Canticum Canticorum*, at the height of his theological maturity, Gregory will present the Spirit as the Glory that the Father and Son eternally exchange:[41]

> It is better to quote textually the divine words of the Gospel: *So that all be one. As You Father, are in Me and I in You, that they be also one in Us* (Jn 17.21). And the bond of this unity is the glory (τὸ δὲ συνδετικὸν τῆς ἑνότητος ταύτης ἡ δόξα ἐστίν). But no prudent person could oppose the fact that the Spirit is called 'glory', if the words of the Lord are considered. For He says: *The glory that You gave Me I gave to them* (Jn 17.22). He gave, in fact, that glory to the disciples, saying to them *Receive the Holy Spirit* (Jn 20.22). Having embraced human nature, He received this glory that He already possessed forever, from before the world was made (cf. Jn 17.5). And, since this human nature was glorified by the Spirit, the communication of the glory of the Spirit happens to all who belong to the same nature (ἐπὶ πᾶν τὸ συγγενὲς), starting with the disciples. For this He says: *And the glory that You gave Me, I gave to*

---

[37] Cf. Basil, *De Spiritu Sancto*, 20, 51, 50.
[38] *Ad Eustathium*, (GNO III/1) 16, 6–7.
[39] Cf. *Adversus Macedonianos*, (GNO III/1) 108, 33–109, 2.
[40] *Antirrheticus*, (GNO III/1) 222, 11–19.
[41] The theme is already present in *Tunc et ipse*, (GNO III/2) 21, 17–22, 14.

*them, so that they be one like Us. I in them and You in Me, so that they be perfect in unity* (Jn 17.22–3).*

In order for the disciples to be one like the Father and the Son, it is necessary that they receive the Spirit, who is the bond of this union. The Spirit is thus not a necessary bond, but *syndetikon* in his being the Person who is the relationship itself of the first two Persons.

Glory and the Spirit are recognized as the intra-Trinitarian bond in which the unity that is communicated outside the Trinity is founded. The theology of glory illuminates that of the Kingdom here, showing how Gregory's conception of immanent relations deepened and developed. The foundation of unity is placed within the Trinity, in the free and reciprocal eternal gift that constitutes the relation between the Father and the Son. Once the divinity of the Son has been accepted, Gregory can respond to the Pneumatomachists by inserting the Spirit between the first two divine Persons, without blemishing the Trinitarian order of course, by positing the third Person as the bond that unites Them. In this manner it is completely clear that the Father, in engendering the Son, does not simply give Him something, but that He gives himself in the Holy Spirit.

Thanks to this development of the personal character of the Spirit, the relationship between the Father and the Son is read in terms of free gift, and thus as relationship, and not as necessary relation. Generation is perfect thanks to the Spirit, the Kingdom and Glory of the Father who is eternally gifted to the Son as constitutive of his being Son, i.e. as perfect image of the Father. Each of the three Persons is co-relative to the other two. This co-relationality thus becomes an expression of communion. For, as Zizioulas states, it is 'impossible to make the Father ontologically ultimate without, at the same time, making communion primordial', in such a way that one cannot speak of the Father without also speaking of the Son and the Spirit.[42]

This identification permits us to take up the metaphysical discourse once more, in so far as the divine substance is identified with the three Persons, and thus with the eternal relations that constitute *koinonia*. Reference to substance is reference to the ultimate ontological reality, which, in the case of God, is communion of Persons that are each themselves in their free relation of gift with the other two. In the Trinity, each One is himself through the Other: The Father is himself in the Son whom He engenders in giving Him his Glory and his Kingdom, i.e. the Spirit. The Son is himself in being engendered by the Father, i.e. in receiving from and giving anew to

---

[42] Zizioulas, *Communion and Otherness*, p. 126.

the Father his Kingdom and Glory. The Holy Spirit is himself in being given and received as the *syndetikon* that leads to the unity of the Trinity.[43]

# Apophatic Theology and the Icon

This new ontological understanding naturally transformed into a new understanding of knowledge: there is a Trinitarian gnoseology that corresponds to a Trinitarian ontology. In fact, in relation to the *logos* of classical philosophy understood as necessary relationship, there was a theology that corresponded to it, and was identified with the *ontology of thought*, according to the definition offered by E. Berti for Aristotelian doctrine.[44] However, the passage to the Trinitarian *Logos*, understood as a free and eternal relation of filiation, implicates a theology that is not only an ontology of thought, but an ontology of thought and liberty, i.e. of the will, of gift and of love. For the Father generates the Son, not from a pre-existing essence, but in giving himself freely, in the Glory that is his Spirit, who in turn is freely returned to the Father by the Son.

This implication of the will and liberty means that man can only know that which God reveals, that only divine action is the source of knowledge for man. Man cannot raise himself alone to the understanding of the divine immanence. Man's thought can approach the mystery only through the love with which God gives himself. This seems to distance man from God, but it in fact brings him closer, because God's action no longer has intermediaries, and the world, in so far as created, is desired and loved by God. Man's world is the fruit of the Creator's will[45]. Man can thus know the One and Triune God only through a free, personal relationship with Him.

Apophatism, i.e. the affirmation that God remains beyond any human capacity of understanding, is thus the gnoseological expression of the centrality of relation and Person. Once the ontological ladder that connected the world and the divine in Greek philosophy has been broken, knowledge is only possible through gift. If the *logos* as necessary proportion is substituted by the Trinitarian *Logos*, knowledge itself becomes an act of filial communion. This is however possible only by renouncing its possession, and humbly recognizing the greatness of the divine:

---

[43] Basil states that the Holy Spirit leads the Trinity to completion (*sumplêroun*) (cf. Basil, *De Spiritu Sancto*, 18, 45, 24–7, (SCh 17bis, 408)

[44] Berti, E. 'Per i viventi l'essere è il vivere' (Aristotele, De anima 415.b.13)", in M. Sánchez Sorondo (ed.), *La vita*, Rome: Lateran University Press 1998, p. 30.

[45] Cf., *Contra Eunomium* II, (GNO I) 293, 28–30. See also *De Anima et resurrectione*, (PG 46, 124B) and *Apologia in Hexaemeron*, (PG 44, 69A); *Tunc et ipse*, (GNO III/2) 11, 4–6.

Thus this concept was explained by the master, thanks to which it is possible that those who have not been obscured by the veil of heresy can clearly discern that the divine, as for that which regards nature, is unfathomable (ἀνέπαφον) and inconceivable (ἀκατανόητον) and superior to every understanding based on reasoning. But the human mind, engaging itself in inquiry and research as far as is possible for reasoning, extends and reaches to touch (ἐπορέγεται καὶ θιγγάνει)[46] the inaccessible and sublime nature. It has not such an acute sight as to see the invisible clearly, nor is it absolutely excluded from every possibility of approximation, in such a manner as not to be able to reach any representation (εἰκασίαν) of that which is searched out. But on the one hand, it conjectures (ἐστοχάσατο) something of that which is searched out through contact (ἐπαφῆς) of reasoning, and on the other, it has knowledge of that which is searched out in a certain way (κατενόησεν) by the very fact of being unable to contemplate it (κατιδεῖν), forming so to say a clear knowledge (γνῶσιν) of the fact that what is sought is above every knowledge (γνῶσιν).[47]

The condition that permits the human reason to reach the point of touching the divine nature is the acceptance of apophatism itself, which in this way becomes the bastion of orthodoxy, by guaranteeing that the level of thought is not confused with that of the essence, thus opening the path to relational reflection. Before Eunomius who held that the human *logos* is capable of understanding and expressing the divine essence, the Cappadocian Fathers distinguished the plan of being from that of being expressed.[48]

God always remains a mystery, something that remains inviolate even in his self-gift to man, due to the very liberty with which He gives himself and his infinite being. The human *logos*, in its filial roots, can access this mystery only in humility and by beginning from the initiative of the Trinity that gives itself. One can thus know only from the divine liberty and will that acts in the world, in so far as God himself, in acting, impresses the Trinitarian and relational dimension in being:

But every activity (ἐνέργεια), which from God is propagated to creation and is called according to the various conceptions, has origin from (ἐκ) the Father, continues (πρόεισι) by means of (διὰ) the Son and is accomplished in (ἐν) the Holy Spirit.[49]

---

[46] As in a contest where he who touches first wins.
[47] *Contra Eunomium* II, (GNO I) 265, 23–266, 6.
[48] Cf. *Contra Eunomium* II, (GNO I) 271, 30 and 272, 8–10.
[49] *Ad Ablabium*, (GNO III/1) 47, 24–48, 2.

In this manner the ultimate fundamental element of Gregory's Trinitarian ontology is *energeia, activity*, which is critical for understanding the relationship of distinction without separation of being and language. This is a technical term that unites immanence and economy, the being and action of God. Thus, knowledge through *energeia* is something quite similar to the experience of the child who, in hearing the voice of his father, recognizes him and says 'it's daddy', or the lover who recognizes the presence of the beloved. Once one has entered into relation with the three Persons, it is possible to recognize Them in the unity of the divine action, in which each One intervenes according to their own personal characteristic, i.e. in reciprocal relationship with the Others. The Father is always the ultimate origin of every action, the Son receives the paternal will and identifies himself with it in making it his own, so that everything is accomplished in the Spirit, i.e. in the unity of the Father and the Son.

The cognitive act, in light of revelation, is recognized to be essentially filial, and inseparable from love. We only truly know as sons in the Son, by recognizing the gift of the Father in the splendour of his goodness, i.e. in the Spirit who unites the Father and the Son. Knowledge is only possible in relation, because being itself is relation in its depths, and to know is to recognize this relation.

In this manner however, once man has become aware of the infinite distance that separates him from God, the dynamics of the eternal relations, known through the self-gift that the Trinity offers to man, permit a knowledge of the divine Persons that is identified with praise:

> Do you see the cyclical revolution of glory through the same actions? The Son is glorified by (ὑπό) the Spirit. The Father is glorified by (ὑπό) the Son. Again, the Son has glory from (παρά) the Father, and the only-begotten becomes the glory of the Spirit. In what will the Father be glorified if not in the true glory of the Only-begotten One? In what again will the Son be glorified if not in the grandeur of the Spirit? So, entering this circular movement, reason (ὁ λόγος) glorifies the Son through (διά) the Spirit, and the Father through (διά) the Son.[50]

This text suggests that Trinitarian ontology essentially consists of 'applying prepositions to being', i.e. it consists of reinterpreting being from the perspective of relation, in a properly dynamic view, which permits us to say that God is not 'one *despite* being triune', but that God is 'one precisely *because* He is triune'. This is a passage that requires moving from necessity to liberty. Human reason is called to make this jump, as it achieves itself through its insertion into the rhythmic pulsation of the intra-Trinitarian

---

[50] *Adversos Macedonianos*, (GNO III/1) 109, 7–15.

relations of mutual glorification. For the life of the three divine Persons is in fact nothing other than an eternal gift of Glory of One to the Other, that is, a gift of Self that becomes the foundation and affirmation of the infinite and absolute value of Self in and through the Other. The Trinity in itself is a mystery of adoration and praise, which can only be known in adoration and praise.

Once the ultimate foundation of being, thanks to co-relativity, has been recognized as a personal and relational mystery, the cognitive act in general, and the theological one in particular, becomes an act of praise, a latreutic act, which can be compared to the *writing* of an icon. As the icon is not the mystery that it represents, so too our concepts and our theological doctrines are not the mystery to which they refer. At the same time however, as the icon permits one to enter into relation, through the act of worship, with the divine mystery, so too should theology place one in relation and communion with the Mystery of the One and Triune God, whose being is *koinonia* and relation. Thus, from a perspective of Trinitarian ontology, the apophatic dimension is a fundamental element of theology, not due to any presumed inadequacy of human reason, but due to the relational and personal depth of being. For this reason, one can say that without a sense of the divine transcendence, there is no authentic theology, and at the same time, that all theology that merits the name must maintain the proper contours of Greek apophatic theology.

# Conclusion: Rethinking Faith and Reason

There are important consequences that derive from this, on the levels of ontology, gnoseology and epistemology, which should be taken into account in the current discussions of the relationship between faith and reason. God has his *Logos* from all eternity, who is God himself, and not only an intermediary. God cannot go against himself, and cannot go against the *Logos*. This *Logos* is only accessible through the self-gift that God offers to man. The *Logos* is given to us in an act of the Father's free will, which Gregory expresses in his theology in the role of the *energies* in approaching God. It is impossible to approach Him alone, with one's own forces. At the same time however, this infinite distance also reveals the infinite value of human reason, which is marked by liberty and which permits relation, with God and among men.

For if a word were exclusively mine, it would not be useful for communication: in order to create communion, to be efficacious, it must be at once mine and another's. The true *logos* is, then, that which permits relation, with reality and with persons. For this reason it is tied to love, in so far as communication itself is an act of union, in which something of oneself is placed in communion. In fact, received and given love is required to communicate important words. Intelligence is thus reinterpreted as the capacity to recognize relation, because gift enjoys a radical anteriority. For God, who is irreducible to any concept in so far as He is supersubstantial, enters into relation with me and desires to have a word in common with me, a word that cannot be anything other than Himself.

Thus man too, created in the image and likeness of God, discovers that he is capable of relation through the intelligence and the will. In this manner one can even recognize him as capable, in a certain way, of *con*-creating being, since the foundation of being is itself relational. When man studies, when he forms relations, when he loves, he *is* more, and the world *is* more. When this does not happen, both man and the world suffer.

From this perspective, psychology and sociology, which are disciplines classically considered to be non-metaphysical, appear to jump to the ontological level, and they acquire a metaphysical status even more elevated than other disciplines, due to their relational depth.[51] In the same way, the ethical perspective cannot be misunderstood as an external imposition, but becomes a dimension that is intrinsic to being itself, which is now entirely marked by liberty.

Being is conceived, in its depths, as free, eternal and dynamic relation, which surpasses the animosity between mine and yours, between faith and reason, between existence and essence. For if the foundation of being is personal being and relation, self-gift is not a loss, but it is instead the only path to find oneself and exist in fullness. It is thus that faith, i.e. to know through the other, is no longer a lower degree of knowledge. In fact, the deepest dimension of being can only be reached through relation, because this deeper dimension *is* relation. In this perspective, love cannot be reduced to the subjective dimension, but must be read in its metaphysical depth, thanks to the Christian inseparability of *Logos* and Gift.

One can resolve the oscillation between existentialism and essentialism in this way, something that has marked both the twentieth century and the entire history of human thought. This oscillation has led on the one hand to both relativism and subjectivism, and on the other to totalitarianism and conservatism. The tragic opposition between the individual's reason and the necessary dependence on extrinsic nature or law is resolved in the Trinitarian dimension, which unites essence and existence in the connection of intelligence and will through relation and person.

The value of person itself as received in the domain of Christian thought is founded on this depth of relation, which is ontological, and not only psychological, sociological or juridical. The study of Patristic solutions

---

[51] For this point, the first chapter, 'Sociologia e Teologia', in P. Donati, *La Matrice Teologica della Società*, Rome: Rubbettino 2010, pp. 3–36, appears particularly interesting.

could offer valid suggestions and a basis on which to confront the terrible and fascinating problems that we face in present times.

However, this requires theology to be reinterpreted from the perspective of the theology of the image, in order to manifest its iconic dimension: apophatism prevents the Mystery from being reduced to the conceptual level, but at the same time, the mystery must be communicated, that is, it must be stylized in such a way as to lead to relation. This is just like the role of icons, which do not substitute Christ or the Trinity, but which are born of a vital relation with Them, and which lead to Them. The victory of Orthodoxy against iconoclasm thus acquires an essential role for human thought, for every man. For the iconic conception of theology should be extended to every science and to human cognitive activity as a whole. In particular, this approach would permit rethinking the relationship between philosophy and theology, in the spirit of uniting without confusing and distinguishing without separating, as is characteristic of Chalcedonian expression. If the foundation of being is relation and communion, every authentic approach to the truth can only be made in relation and communion.

The doctrine of the Fathers of the Church thus naturally permits a path for responding to the despair of contemporary relativism and the pathologies that it induces. In order to realize this task, however, we must contemplate Mary: her silent love can be the most luminous icon of Trinitarian ontology, in the harmony of logical word, which is the expression of her free obedience, and the ontological Word, received in her womb and received again in her arms as Mother of Christ at the foot of the Cross. Apophatism shows all its force in that *Let it be*, which silently sustains the world out of nothing, in the transfiguration of life and person in the pure relation of mother and Son, which introduces every man into the Mystery of the Father and Son, at the root of Being and Love.

# 10

# The Lord and Giver of Life: A 'Barthian' Defense of the *Filioque*

## Bruce McCormack

*'... we have consistently followed the rule, which we regard*
*as basic, that statements about the divine modes of being in*
*themselves* cannot be different in content *from those that are to be*
*made about their reality in revelation.'*[1]

## Introduction

Even those who make the most fundamental decisions with respect to truly profound questions are not always in a position to understand all the possible implications which might follow upon those decisions. Only with time, through repeated testing of the ramifications of the decisions that really matter, does it become possible to see further than, shall we say, the dogmatic geniuses who made them.

The statement above does not yet reflect a truly basic decision. But it certainly points in the direction of a basic decision. On the surface, the meaning of the statement is that nothing can be said about the immanent Trinity which does not find its basis in the divine economy, and the reason

---

[1] K. Barth, *CD* I/1, p. 479 (emphasis mine).

this is so is because the immanent Trinity and the economic Trinity do not differ in content. The explanation for the 'rule' however, does not yet appear here – certainly not in its fullness. The most basic decision would be the one which provided that explanation, and the only possible form it could take – if the 'rule' were to be consistently upheld – would consist in making the eternal act in which God has His being from everlasting to everlasting to be the act of election, *not* (as classically) a necessary act of Self-constitution as triune which is *abstracted from* the gracious relation to human beings established in the covenant of grace. For the 'rule' to be adequate to the reality of God, there could be no 'in Himself' which is not already a 'for us'. There could be no state of existence on the part of the Logos *asarkos* above and prior to the eternal act in which He is given the *determination* to become incarnate in time. There could be no talk of the Spirit as the act of a communion between the Father and the Son which is not also, and at the same time, the act of turning towards the world in creative and redeeming power.

The problem is that Barth *did* speak of the Spirit (in good Augustinian fashion) as the 'act of communion' between the Father and the Son.[2] And he *did* speak of the Logos *asarkos* on occasion in abstraction from the determination to become incarnate in time. So he was not consistent with his own rule; and yet, it is equally clear that he was not aware of the inconsistency – and that is a point of no small importance. For what it means is that there are possible conclusions to be drawn from a more consistent application of the rule which Barth himself did not envision but which he clearly was seeking.

As exhibit A in a proof that Barth wanted something more, something which even he could not fully express, I would draw the reader's attention to the fact that a great stone fell into the otherwise calm pool that is the *Church Dogmatics* with Barth's radical revision of the doctrine of election in *CD* II/2. With that revision, a shift took place from a concentration upon the doctrine of revelation (and with that, the need to elaborate a theological epistemology) to a concentration upon Christology (and with that, the need to elaborate a theological ontology). Another way to put it would be to say that Barth's theology only now became truly 'Christocentric'. The formal (structural) requirements of a doctrine of the Word as the starting point for theological reflection upon a host of doctrinal issues gave way to a starting point in the narrated history of Jesus Christ, and with that a shift occurred

---

[2] Barth, *CD* I/1, p. 470: The Holy Spirit 'is the common element, or, better, the fellowship, the act of communion, of the Father and the Son. He is the act in which the Father is the Father of the Son or the Speaker of the Word and the Son is the Son of the Father or the Word of the Speaker.' Barth continues here to appeal to the Augustinian characterization of the Spirit as 'the *vinculum pacis* (Eph.4:3), the *amor*, the *caritas*, the mutual *donum* between the Father and the Son ...'.

from a concentration upon the situation of believers addressed by the Word in their 'here and now' to a concentration upon the 'there and then' of Jesus of Nazareth.[3]

It is worth noting here that the contents of the first three part-volumes of the *Church Dogmatics* (I/1–II/1) can be mapped quite easily onto the contents of the parallel paragraphs in the Göttingen Dogmatics. Anyone who has carried out a close comparison of these two versions of the same material will recognize that such development as has occurred between them consists only in a 'deepening and application'[4] of what Barth had already said. But that is not true of II/2, nor of any of the doctrines treated in volume III. The material elaboration of those doctrines is quite new and fresh. All of that, I would suggest, is the result of the Christological concentration which emerges with II/2.

Development of a different order occurs at the point at which Barth's Christological concentration turns to the problem of Christology itself. At this point, Barth abandons altogether the traditional Protestant ordering of topics along the lines provided by the *loci communes* approach and opts for

---

[3] Hans Urs von Balthasar deserves credit for being among the very first (if not the first) to put his finger upon this development. 'As Barth continued to publish succeeding volumes of the *Church Dogmatics*, he gradually and without fanfare, but no less inexorably, replaced the central notion of "the Word of God" with that of "Jesus Christ, God and man"'. See von Balthasar, *The Theology of Karl Barth: Exposition and Interpretation*, San Francisco: Communio Books/Ignatius Press 1992, p. 114. The only thing missed by von Balthasar – and missed because Barth had yet to write his doctrine of reconciliation when von Balthasar's book appeared in 1951 – is the new preoccupation with history. Those German interpreters possessed of a close acquaintance with the doctrine of reconciliation, however, saw the development quite clearly. Consider the following: 'Originally, Barth's doctrine of the Trinity was 'bound up with the concept of revelation, in the strict sense of God's self-revelation which is grounded in God's trinitarian self-unfolding'…. But as the *Church Dogmatics* evolved, the emphasis shifted away from the inner structure of revelation towards the history of Jesus and, in particular, the cross. And in stressing the 'displacement' between Father and Son at the cross, Barth increasingly intensified the divine plurality.' See I. U. Dalferth, 'The Eschatological Roots of the Doctrine of the Trinity', in Ch. Schwöbel, (ed.), *Trinitarian Theology Today*, Edinburgh: T & T Clark 1995, pp.149–50.

[4] Karl Barth, *How I Changed My Mind*, Edinburgh: The Saint Andrew Press 1966, p. 42: 'If I now attempt to judge how far I have actually changed in these last ten years [i.e. 1928–1938] with regard to my work, then it seems possible to put the case in a formula: I have been occupied approximately equally with the *deepening* and *application* of that knowledge which, in its main channels, I had gained before. Both these developments have, of course, gone forward at the same time.' Now it is quite true that Barth immediately went on to say that 'The *deepening* consisted in this: in these years I have had to rid myself of the last remnants of a philosophical, i.e. anthropological (in America one says 'humanistic' or 'naturalistic') foundation and exposition of Christian doctrine.' But if it were true that Barth had exchanged one foundation for another, a stronger word than 'deepening' would be required to explain it. But it is not true, as I have tried to show elsewhere. See B. L. McCormack, *Karl Barth's Critically Realistic Dialectical Theology: Its Genesis and Development, 1909–1936*, Oxford: Clarendon Press 1995, pp. 421–41.

a completely new architectonic which applies to the doctrine of reconciliation as a stand-alone mini-dogmatics unto itself.[5] Why did it come to this? Because here, for the first time, the category of history really came into its own in Barth's theology. Seen in the light of Barth's later Christology, the doctrine of Trinity elaborated in I/1 has to be subjected to critical scrutiny. After all, the problem of the Trinity was understood at that time as the problem of 'the knowledge…of the unsublateable [*unaufhebbare*] subjectivity of God in His revelation.'[6] But Barth himself was never able to return to thorough re-working of his doctrine of the Trinity. For that reason, I say that he was seeking something more. His later Christology pointed beyond his earlier attainments.

I have already discussed several times the changes in Barth's Christology between I/2 and IV/1.[7] I have also sought to reconstruct Barth's doctrine of the Trinity in the light of his later Christology.[8] What I would like to do here is to focus attention on Barth's pneumatology – and especially upon his defence of the *Filioque* as mandated by the economy of God. My guiding question will be: would Barth's defence be rendered even stronger than it already is by the employment of a pneumatology which arises more naturally from my reconstruction of his earlier doctrine of the Trinity? Or, seen from another angle, if his pneumatology were rendered less susceptible to criticism, would his critique of the Eastern understanding of the Spirit's procession from the Father alone be even more convincing?

In what follows, I will begin with a brief exposition of Barth's understanding of the *Filioque*, as well as the reasons he gives for defending it. I will then proceed to an outline of the major options in the doctrine of the Trinity after Barth. Most of them were developed, at least in part, in terms of a critique of Barth's doctrine in *CD* I/1. But none of them considered the

---

[5] On the disposition of the material in volume IV of the *Church Dogmatics*, see E. Jüngel, 'Einführung in Leben und Werk Karl Barths' in ibid., *Barth-Studien*, Zürich-Köln: Benziger Verlag-Gütersloher Verlagshaus 1982), p. 55. Jüngel rightly judges volume IV to be 'at one and the same time, a great recapitulation but also a revision of the whole of Barth's theology.' See ibid.,p.53.

[6] K. Barth, *Unterricht in der christlichen Religion*, I, *Erster Band: Prolegomena, 1924*, Hannelotte Reiffen (ed.), Zürich: TVZ 1985, p. 120; cf. ibid., *CD* I/1, p. 348, *Leitsatz*.

[7] See B. L. McCormack, 'Karl Barth's Historicized Christology: Just How "Chalcedonian" Is It?' in ibid., *Orthodox and Modern*, Grand Rapids: Baker Academic 2008), pp. 201–33; ibid., 'Divine Impassibility or Simply Divine Constancy? Implications of Barth's Later Christology for Debates over Impassibility', in J. F. Keating and T. J. White (eds), *Divine Impassibility and the Mystery of Human Suffering*, Grand Rapids: Eerdmans 2009, pp. 150–86; ibid., 'Karl Barth's Version of an 'Analogy of Being': A Dialectical No and Yes to Roman Catholicism' in T. J. White (ed.), *The Analogy of Being: Invention of the Anti-Christ or the Wisdom of God?*, Grand Rapids: Eerdmans, 2010.

[8] B. L. McCormack, 'The Doctrine of the Trinity After Barth: An Attempt to Reconstruct Barth's Doctrine in Light of His Later Christology', in *The Doctrine of the Trinity After Barth*, M. Habets and Ph. Tolliday (eds), Eugene, OR: Cascade Books, 2011, pp. 87–118.

possibility that Barth's later Christology might have mandated a revision of his earlier treatment of the Trinity, or the fact that such a revision would differ in important ways from their own proposals. In a third section, I will briefly outline my own reconstruction of Barth's doctrine of the Trinity. A fourth section will be devoted to an examination of a concept of election adequate to ground this reconstruction. In a fifth and final section, I will return to the question of the *Filioque* and offer my own defence of its importance for Christian theology.

# Barth's Understanding and Defence of the *Filioque*

Karl Barth's basic model for comprehending the Trinity is well-known, though the full significance of it is not always appreciated. The basic understanding is that the triune God is a single divine Subject in three 'modes of being'. A *single* Subject: here already lay the guarantee that the *Filioque*, as taken up by Barth, could not possibly lead to the notion of a 'double procession'. Barth does not understand the 'persons' as distinct centres of consciousness and agency; as a consequence he simply *cannot* understand the procession of the Spirit as rising from 'persons' defined in this way. So the traditional Western view which understood the Spirit as having two sources, two 'principles' of origin consisting in two distinct 'persons', had to be set aside. And yet Barth's departure from the Western conception at this decisive point does not enable him to embrace the traditional Eastern conception either, in spite of his Eastern-like emphasis upon something akin to the monarchy of the Father.

From whom, then, does the Spirit proceed? A way forward to an answer may be found if we bear in mind that, for Barth, there can be no final distinction between the being of God and God's 'modes of being'. God simply *is* His 'modes of being'. There is no shared being or 'essence' *if* that is taken to refer to something lying behind or beneath these modes. The Godhead of God is *the being of the one divine Subject in the three modes of Father, Son and Spirit*; one God three times, an eternal repetition in eternity.[9] Given that this is so, the choice which is sometimes presented in discussions of the *Filioque* in Barth's theology between *either* a procession from the 'persons' of the Father and the Son on the one hand *or* a procession from the 'common being' of the Father and Son is, or at least can be, misleading.[10]

---

[9] Barth, *CD* I/1, p.350.
[10] David Guretzki has expressed himself in this way. 'Rather than speaking of a double procession of the Spirit from the modes of being (or hypostases) of the Father and Son, Barth

For Barth, 'procession' is from the one divine *Subject* precisely in His first two modes of being, not from a 'common being' which is somehow distinguishable from those 'modes of being'.[11] What has happened here is that the logic of divine *subjectivity* has supplanted the ancient logic of substance metaphysics by which the choice between essence and 'persons' was traditionally made possible. Indeed, a fundamental distinction between essence and persons has been closed down, so that the divine 'essence' is being equated directly with the one Subject in His three modes of being.[12]

What is at stake in all this for Barth is, initially at least, the identity of the Spirit as *the Spirit of the Son*: 'If the Spirit is … the Spirit of the Son only in revelation and for faith, if He is only the Spirit of the Father in eternity, i.e. in His true and original reality, then the fellowship of the Spirit between God and man is without objective ground or content.'[13] Barth is clearly looking for the 'objective ground' in God's eternal being for the relation of God and the human in time. That is a point to which we will return. But it is important to note that he expresses this desire in terms of the identity of the Spirit *in eternity* as 'the Spirit of the Son'. If the Spirit is 'the Spirit of the Son' only in time and not also in eternity, then the Spirit has another, a different identity in eternity. And so Barth says that if there is no '*relatio origines* between the Son and the Spirit', then the Spirit can only be called the Spirit of the Son 'improperly' – i.e. 'not in the way that the Son is called the Son of the Father.'[14] The meaning is clear: if the Spirit is truly the Spirit of the Son *already in eternity*, then that must be because the Son too stands in a relation of 'origin' to the Spirit.

But this also has implications for the identity *of the Father*, and it is at this point that we cut most deeply into the problem Barth is seeking to resolve. If the One from whom the Spirit proceeds is not the Father of the Son *in the act* of breathing forth the Spirit, then He has another identity (indeed His *proper* identity) above and prior to 'becoming' Father. This

---

sought to preserve in this matter a delicate dialectic balance between the essence (*Sein*) and the Persons (*Seinsweisen*) of the Trinity without giving ontological priority to one or the other.' See Guretzki, *Karl Barth on the Filioque*, Farnham, UK: Ashgate 2009, p. 185; cf. p. 181. That is *almost* true – but the proposed dialectic between being and modes of being requires a distinction between them that does not exist in Barth. Having said this, I should note that this is an extremely impressive book – and the only thing like it in English.

[11] Barth, *CD* I/1, p. 474: '… the procession is not from the one essence of God as such but from another mode of being or other modes of being of this one essence.'

[12] Barth would later put it this way: 'For Godhead, divine nature, divine essence, does not exist and is not actual in and for itself. Even Godhead exists only in and with the existence of Father, Son and Holy Ghost, only as the common predicate of this triune Subject in its modes of existence.… The Godhead as such has no existence. It is not real. It has no being or activity.' See Barth, *CD* IV/2, p.65.

[13] Barth, *CD* I/1, p. 481.

[14] Barth, *CD* I/1, p. 482.

means further that the begetting of the Son must *logically* be prior to the procession of the Spirit. If that is the case, then the procession of the Spirit from the one divine Subject is a procession from the one divine Subject *in His first two modes of being*. That is what is ultimately at stake for Barth in the debate over the *Filioque*. Barth puts it this way: 'Even the oneness of God the Father is called into question if implicitly He is not already the origin of the Spirit as the Father of the Son, the origin of the Spirit from Him being a second function along with His fatherhood.'[15] To secure this oneness or Self-identity, Barth reads the logic of begetting back into the very depths of the Godness of God, so that the one divine Subject is never not already *Father*.[16]

It is because Barth is committed to the notion that God is *Father* even as He breathes forth the Spirit that he cannot even be satisfied with the addition of the phrase *dia tou huiou* to the basic Eastern affirmation that the Spirit proceeds *ek tou patros*. For the *dia* was never intended to say that the Spirit also proceeds *from* the Son. It was understood only as 'a continuation or extension or prolongation of the procession of the Spirit from the Father.... The Son is a mediating principle, the Father alone being *aitia* or principle in the strict sense of the Word.'[17] Whatever else may be said with regard to the validity of Barth's own understanding of the procession, he is right in thinking that an irreducible difference still exists between his own understanding of the procession of the Spirit and that of the Eastern churches.

So how does Barth justify all of this *economically*? His rule, it may be recalled, is that statements about the divine modes of being in themselves cannot be different in content from those that are to be made about their reality in revelation.'[18] That rule will have been observed only where it is the case that 'All our statements concerning what is called the immanent Trinity

---

[15] Barth, *CD* I/1, ibid. It should be noted that I have altered Bromiley's translation here at one point. I have translated *Einheit* as 'oneness' rather than 'unity' (though the German word embraces both meanings) because Barth's concern with the identity of the Father with Himself in breathing forth the Spirit does not come to expression in the word 'unity'. Again, what is at stake here is the *logical* priority of the begetting of the Son over the breathing forth of the Spirit, in order to secure the fatherhood (and sonship) of the One who breathes forth the Spirit; cf. Barth, *KD* I/1, p. 506. I should add that logical priority has to do with how we humans must think of things. It is not to be taken as suggesting an ontological priority of the Father and Son over the Spirit, since we are speaking of an eternal event which allows for no metaphysical gap to be introduced between the one divine Subject in His first two modes of being and the one divine Subject in His third mode of being. Such a conclusion is the necessary consequence of thinking of triunity in God in terms of an eternal repetition in eternity.

[16] Jürgen Moltmann's belief that Barth works consistently with an 'Absolute Subject' crashes on the rocks of this claim. See Moltmann, *The Trinity and the Kingdom*, San Francisco: Harper & Row 1981.

[17] Barth, *CD* I/1, p. 482.

[18] See above, n.1.

have been reached simply as confirmations or underlinings or, materially, as the indispensable premises of the economic Trinity.'[19] What, then, is the economic root of Barth's understanding of the procession of the Spirit?

The answer has to do, not surprisingly, with the content of Barth's doctrine of revelation.[20] From the Göttingen Dogmatics on through CD I/1, Barth understood the work of the Spirit to consist pre-eminently in making effective the Word addressed to the human individual by God in Christ. Since at this time revelation was made to be the event in which reconciliation was made effective, the *act* of making effectual was given a prominence which it might not have had if reconciliation had been understood as an already effective reality prior to the Spirit's work (as would be the case later). Indeed, Barth understood election at this time as an altogether this-worldly activity of the Spirit in granting or withholding faith in the event of revelation. Given further that faith, for Barth, is never the secure possession of the individual, given that the granting or withholding of it by God is an event which is repeated throughout the Christian life, election and rejection were related to each other in a wholly dynamic process *in this world* which knows of no end, no final equilibrium.[21] All of this, I would like to suggest, contributed to seeking in the *eternal* Spirit the ground of this element in Barth's revelatory actualism and this element alone; and he found it in the act of communion between Father and Son.

But this also led quite directly to one of the more significant weaknesses in Barth's doctrine of the Trinity, namely the reduction of the Spirit to the 'act of communion' between Father and Son.[22] If the triune God is one

---

[19] Barth, CD I/1, p. 479.

[20] Guretzki has pointed instead to the *structural* feature of Barth's early theology as the root of Barth's understanding of the *Filioque*; see Guretzki, *Karl Barth on the Filioque*, pp. 84–90. He holds that Barth's defence of the unity of the three forms of the Word of God by means of an analogy to the unity-in-differentiation of the triune God played a decisive role in his subsequent elaboration of the doctrine of the Trinity. The analogy is this: as preaching (the third form of the Word) proceeds in time from Christ and Scripture (the first two forms), so also the Spirit proceeds eternally from the Father and the Son; see Barth, *Unterricht in der christlichen Religion*, I, *Prolegomena*, 1924, Hannelotte Reiffen (ed.), Zürich: TVZ 1985, p.19. There is something to this claim; certainly, it may well have been the element of thought which put Barth onto the path which culminated in his affirmation of the *Filioque*. But it overlooks, it seems to me, the importance of the content of Barth's doctrine of revelation and his appeal in *CD* I/1 especially to the nature of the Spirit's work in the economy as the material root of the *Filioque*.

[21] For more on the doctrine of election in the Göttingen Dogmatics, see McCormack, *Karl Barth's Critically Realistic Dialectical Theology*, pp. 371–4.

[22] For consideration of the problems surrounding Barth's attempt to derive the Trinity from the formal logic of his concept of revelation, see my 'The Trinity After Barth', pp. 7–14. I will not enter into these problems here but simply stipulate my agreement with the following statement made by Wolfhart Pannenberg: 'Barth believed that he had found a way out of the problems by deriving the trinity of Father, Son and Spirit from the concept of revelation, or, more

divine Subject three times, then the treatment of the third mode of being ought to have made clear the way in which that one Subject was fully a *Subject* in that third mode. But it is not at all clear that the depiction of the Spirit as the 'love' between Father and Son or as the 'act' of their communion achieves this aim.[23] That is something that would have to be rectified at a later point, and when it was, it would not be the result of simply adding some more robust statements about the Spirit. No, the basic model would itself have to be revised – but revised in such a way that the original insights where the *Filioque* is concerned were preserved.

# The Doctrine of the Trinity after Barth

In the last years of Barth's life, German-speaking theologians (both Protestant and Catholic) were already searching for ways to take Barth's rule with greater seriousness than, it was thought, he himself had been able to take it. In the process, the 'rule' was subjected to considerable radicalization and formalization.

The formalization occurred through Karl Rahner's re-casting of the rule. As he famously put it: 'The "economic" Trinity is the "immanent Trinity" and the "immanent Trinity" is the "economic" Trinity.'[24] I call this a formalization because, as a stand-alone formula, it gave no advice with regard to how it was to be applied. One had to possess a close knowledge of Rahner's work in order to know how he himself meant it to be taken.[25]

The radicalization, on the other hand, took different forms. That the economy of God had to provide the basis for any discussion of the immanent Trinity was clear to all. Differences emerged as a consequence of how the economy itself was understood. In what did the history of revelation and/ or salvation (as the case may be) consist? What was its decisive moment(s)?

---

precisely, from the statement that 'God reveals Himself as the Lord, ' which, when grammatically analyzed into its three components – subject, object, and predicate – leads us to the three modes of being of the self-revealing God. This is not the same, however, as basing the doctrine of the Trinity on the revelation of God as it is materially attested in the biblical writings. It is simply to derive the doctrine from the formal concept of a self-revealing God.' Pannenberg, *Systematic Theology*, I, Grand Rapids: Eerdmans 1991, pp. 303–4.

[23] This is a point well made by Robert Jenson: see Jenson, 'You Wonder Where the Spirit Went' in *Pro Ecclesia* 2/3 (1993) p. 302.

[24] K. Rahner, *The Trinity*, New York: The Seabury Press 1974, p. 22. It should be noted that this work first appeared in German in 1967.

[25] David Guretzki makes Rahner's rule responsible for the tendency of later theologians to collapse the immanent so completely into the economic Trinity that no role remains for the immanent Trinity; see Guretzki, *Karl Barth on the Filioque*, p. 191. Since Guretzki does not provide any examples, I will simply say that such a collapse is not true of Rahner himself or any of the three Protestant theologians under consideration here.

Rahner offered one answer. Post-Barthian Protestant theologians like Eberhard Jüngel, Jürgen Moltmann and Wolfhart Pannenberg provided others.[26]

It was Rahner who took the most important step, for it was he who, most impressively after Barth, made incarnation to be *proper* to the eternal Son. Behind this claim lay a question: does revelation tell us anything that is *specific* to the Son as such or is revelation somehow generic, true of what is common (and therefore essential) to all the persons of the Godhead without respect to their differentiation? The question had been forced upon him by traditional claims: '... starting from Augustine, and as opposed to the older tradition, it has been among theologians a more or less foregone conclusion that each of the divine persons (if God so freely decided) could have become man, so that the incarnation of precisely this person can tell us nothing about the peculiar features of *this* person within the divinity.'[27] In this view, though it is the Logos alone who exercises the 'hypostatic function'[28] of uniting Himself with human nature, it might just as well have been the Father or the Spirit had the triune God so willed. The problem with this is that it leaves us without any knowledge of the Logos as such. The incarnate life of the Logos is merely 'appropriated'[29] to Him; such appropriation does not entail, however, a real relation. The air of agnosticism which surrounds traditional teaching of the Trinity is easily comprehended in the light of this observation. That we know who God is, but not what He is, is certainly axiomatic for many.

Rahner's counter-thesis was that the concept of *Self*-revelation requires that knowledge be given of the divine person who does the revealing. Where knowledge of *this* divine person remains shrouded in mist even after revelation has (allegedly) occurred – as was the case in most traditional treatments of the Logos *asarkos* – there could be no Self-revelation. What traditional theology was left with, in order to bind the immanent Trinity to the economy, was the concept of *verbal inspiration* – and that alone.[30] We know that God is triune in and for Himself because He tells us He is.

---

[26] Whether in confirmation or reaction, all three drew inspiration from Barth. All three believed that any Christian theology worthy of the name ought to be *Offenbarungstheologie*. The differences had to do with the differing conceptions of revelation with which each worked. On this point see M. Muhrmann-Kahl, *'Mysterium Trinitatis'? Fallstudien zur Trinitätslehre in der evangelischen Dogmatik des 20. Jahrhunderts*, Berlin-New York: Walter de Gruyter 1997, p. 101. Thus the phrase 'post-Barthian' is not meant to suggest a departure but a continuation of many of Barth's themes in critically engaged forms.

[27] Rahner, *The Trinity*, p. 11.

[28] *The Trinity*, p. 86.

[29] *The Trinity*, p. 13.

[30] *The Trinity*, p. 39: 'For him who rejects our basic thesis, the Trinity can *only* be something which ... can be told about in purely conceptual statements, through a merely *verbal* revelation.'

The problem with this, quite obviously, is that the New Testament writers know nothing of an ontological Trinity, and therefore the attempt to build an ontological Trinity on the basis of their witness inevitably entailed a highly selective use of passages whose intent was quite different. No, in the absence of a concept of Self-revelation which understands the incarnation as *proper* to the second Person of the Trinity[31], there can be no adequate basis for a doctrine of the immanent Trinity.

Having taken this step, Rahner then made the 'missions' of the Son and the Spirit the starting point for reflection on the immanent Trinity. This was, as I say, an important step, and even those most critical of Rahner today will acknowledge the necessity of speaking of the immanent Trinity on the basis of the economy. But it also has to be said that there was much that was left undiscussed in Rahner's little book. For example, though Rahner came very close to identifying the missions of the Son and Spirit with the eternal processions (seeing them as *one* eternal activity with effects *ad intra* and *ad extra*), he did not say so explicitly. What had been said, however, accorded nicely with trends emerging in Protestant reflection upon the Trinity.

Already in his 1965 monograph on Barth's doctrine of the Trinity, Eberhard Jüngel had stressed that eternal election in Barth was a decision with ontological consequences. 'God's being-in-act was understood [by Barth] to mean that God is his decision. Decision sets in relation, for it is as such a setting-oneself-in-relation.... God's setting-himself-in-relation points in both an inward and outward direction at the same time. This is grounded in Barth's understanding of revelation as the self-interpretation of God in which God is his own "double." And so it is not surprising that this double structure of the one being of God also finds a place in the doctrine of election in the *Church Dogmatics*.'[32] The 'one being of God' is thus a 'being in correspondence'[33] – a correspondence between what God is in the economy and what God is in His eternal decision to be the God of the covenant. The importance of this observation lay in its stress upon election as the ontological basis for the correspondence of God with God or, expressed another way, of an identity of content in the relationship between the economic Trinity and the immanent Trinity.

As a consequence of his close study of Barth, Jüngel was well-positioned to greet Rahner's book on the Trinity with enthusiastic support when it appeared a decade later.[34] The one modification he wished to introduce

---

[31] *The Trinity*, p. 23.
[32] E. Jüngel, *God's Being Is in Becoming: The Trinitarian Being of God in the Theology of Karl Barth*, Grand Rapids: Eerdmans 2001, p. 83.
[33] Jüngel, *God's Being Is in Becoming*, ibid.
[34] Jüngel, 'Das Verhältnis von 'ökonomischer' und 'immanenter' Trinität: Erwägungen über eine biblische Begründung der Trinitätslehre – im Anschluß an und in Auseinandersetzung mit Karl Rahners Lehre vom dreifaltigen Gott als transzendentem Urgrund der Heilsgeschichte',

into Rahner's reformulation of Barth's rule had to do with the fact that he wanted, in his own theology, to take up his starting point *within* the economy in a specific event, namely God's experience of death on the cross.[35] What he had learned since writing his 'paraphrase' of Barth's doctrine of the Trinity was to give greater prominence to the fact that the *later* Barth 'interpreted the dogma of the true divinity of Jesus Christ so as to make clear that the deity of this Person is demonstrated precisely in lowliness, the true humanity of Jesus Christ in exaltation. Barth concluded from this that lowliness and this-worldliness cannot be excluded from the concept of the essence of God; rather, God has only been thought and understood in His divinity when He can be believed to have suffered death without ceasing to be God.'[36] This was not an insight which could be found in Jüngel's earlier monograph on Barth and it showed that, since writing it, he had come to a greater appreciation of developments which had occurred within the bounds of the *Church Dogmatics*.[37] The conclusion which Jüngel drew from all of this is that the economic root of the immanent Trinity (in its entirety) was to be found above all in the crucifixion, not in the 'history of salvation' more generally considered.[38]

Jürgen Moltmann too wanted to root the doctrine of the immanent Trinity in the divine economy. For him, too, the economic root of the immanent Trinity was to be found in the event of the cross. Unlike Jüngel, however, whose focus lay on the *unity* of the Father with the Son through God's act of identifying Himself with the crucified One, Moltmann's

---

in ibid., *Entspechungen: Gott – Wahrheit – Mensch*, Munich: Chr. Kaiser Verlag 1980, pp. 265–75.

[35] Dalferth, 'The Eschatological Roots of the Doctrine of the Trinity', p. 150: 'His [i.e. Jüngel's] own work on the Trinity starts from God's self-identification with the crucified on the cross, and he conceives its function as being to work out the identity of God's being-for-himself and his being-for-us in the person of Jesus Christ.'

[36] Jüngel, *Gott als Geheimnis der Welt: Zur Begründung der Theologie des Gekreuzigten im Streit zwischen Theismus und Atheismus*, 3rd revised edition, Tübingen: Mohr 1978, p. 134.

[37] An important document of Jüngel's learning process is to be found in his essay, '... keine Menschenlosigkeit Gottes ... Zur Theologie Karl Barths' in ibid., *Barth-Studien*, Zürich-Köln: Benziger Verlag and Gütersloher Verlagshaus 1982, pp. 332–47. Michael Murrmann-Kahl's comment on the use of the later Barth to critique the earlier volumes of the *Church Dogmatics* simply ignores the evident development that took place over the many years of its production. 'The selective nature of this procedure is obvious, when certain Christological or eschatological themes are held up as a normative self-revision on the part of Barth. In the process, it is no longer the total-context of the 'KD' that is reflected upon ... Obviously, this selective reception of Barth by these authors [he has in view Moltmann as well as Jüngel] gives the appearance of providing the justification they need in order to carry through their far-reaching revision under Barth's flag.' Muhrmann-Kahl, *'Mysterium Trinitatis'?*, p. 105. It is hard to avoid the suspicion that Murrmann-Kahl (ever the faithful student of Falk Wagner) did not want the later Barth to have engaged in any sort of retraction, so that he can be held fast to the weaknesses of his earlier doctrine of the Trinity and, on that basis, set aside.

[38] Jüngel, 'Das Verhältnis von 'ökonomischer' und 'immanenter' Trinität', pp. 267–9.

focused instead upon the 'separation' of the Father and the Son in the event of the cross which, in his rendering of it, allowed for their differentiation *as distinct subjects*. This then appeared to give him an economic basis for an understanding of divine persons in the immanent Trinity as three distinct subjects, the Spirit having been introduced as the subject who continues to bind together Father and Son in and through the experience of alienation and loss.

That Moltmann achieved his goal of establishing a basis for a trinity of distinct subjects through making the eternal Son *as such* the subject of death in God-abandonment was a problem, however – and it showed the limits of his project. Identified ontologically with the man Jesus, the Subject of death in God-abandonment ought to have been the God-human rather than simply 'God'. If that were the case, then the humanness of the experience might have been taken with full seriousness – as an event in God's own life, to be sure, but in all of its humanness. Instead, Moltmann immediately retreats from this identification and treats the 'Son' as a subject in His own right, without reference to His humanity. 'God', he says, 'is forsaken by God. If we take the relinquishment of the Father's name in Jesus' death cry seriously [i.e. "My God, my God, why have you forsaken me?"], then this is the breakdown of the relationship that constitutes the very life of the Trinity. If the Father forsakes the Son, then it is not merely the case that the Son lose his sonship; the Father loses His fatherhood as well. The love that binds the one to the other is transformed into a dividing curse.'[39] Obviously Moltmann needs to make this move in order to achieve his goal of an immanent Trinity composed of three distinct subjects. But with the abstraction of the Son from the man Jesus, the economic root of the immanent Trinity has been lost. Moltmann's account has about it the air of mythology. Still, his intention to move from the economy to the immanent Trinity places him in a line with Rahner and Jüngel.[40]

Wolfhart Pannenberg's quest for the economic root of the doctrine of the Trinity brought him quite close to Barth's later Christology. In fact, it is hard to avoid the suspicion that he had learned a good deal from Barth, though his tendency to engage only Barth's formal treatment of the Trinity in *CD* I/1 had the effect of concealing the debt.[41] To be sure, Pannenberg was convinced that the integrity and reliability of the narrated history of Jesus of Nazareth as attested in the NT writings could not simply be

---

[39] Moltmann, *The Trinity and the Kingdom*, p. 80.

[40] For Moltmann's affirmation of Rahner's 'rule', see ibid., *The Trinity and the Kingdom*, p. 160.

[41] Pannenberg, *Systematic Theology*, I, pp. 300–4; cf. Pannenberg, 'Die Subjektivität Gottes und die Trinitätslehre: Ein Beitrag zur Beziehung zwischen Karl Barth und der Philosophie Hegels' in ibid., *Grundfragen systematischer Theologie: Gesammelte Aufsätze*, II, Göttingen: Vandenhoeck & Ruprecht 1980, pp. 96–111.

taken for granted, as Barth tended to do; it had to be established through a responsible use of historical-critical methods of investigation. Still, it is Jesus' act of self-differentiation from and relating to the One He called Father that provides the economic basis for Pannenberg's doctrine of the Trinity. The economic root of the immanent Trinity is to be found in the obedience of the man Jesus to the will of the Father,[42] and this last named element especially does bring him close to Barth.

Still, differences remain. For Pannenberg, the self-distinction of the historical Jesus from the Father is 'constitutive' not only of His historical relation to the Father but also – and as a consequence – of His relation as eternal Son to the Father. The transition from the one to the other is effected in the following way: 'As the one who corresponds to the fatherhood of God, Jesus is the Son, and because the eternal God is revealed herein as Father everywhere only as He is so in relation to the Son, the Son shares his deity as the eternal counterpart of the Father.'[43] The thought here seems to be that if it is through the revelation which takes place in Jesus' obedience that God's rule is made effective – a rule that belongs to God essentially – then Jesus too must belong to God essentially: 'The eternal God cannot be directly thought of as from eternity related to a temporal and creaturely reality unless this [reality] is itself eternal, as a correlate of the eternal God, and thus loses its temporal and creaturely nature. A distinction has thus to be made between the relation of Jesus' to God's eternal deity ... and his human creaturely reality. This is the root of the differentiation between a divine and human aspect, or two "natures".'[44] The word 'aspect' in this last statement is decisive. Pannenberg is speaking of the man Jesus from two points of view, from the standpoint of his historical act of relating to God and from the standpoint of the eternal implications of that act for the eternal fatherhood of God, and therefore for the deity of Jesus.

At the end of the day, what makes Jesus' obedience constitutive of the eternal relation of the Son to the Father is Pannenberg's retroactive ontology, if I may put it that way.[45] This is not Barth's ontology, of course, and that is the root of the differences between them. Barth's ontology, as we

---

[42] Pannenberg, *Systematic Theology*, I, p. 304: 'To base the doctrine of the Trinity on the content of the revelation of God in Jesus Christ we must begin with the relation of Jesus to the Father as it came to expression in his message of the divine rule.' Cf. p.309: 'To establish the lordship of God is the chief content and primary goal of the mission of Jesus, and as his whole life is his mission, he shows Himself to be the Son who serves the will of the Father (cf. John 10:36ff.).

[43] Pannenberg, *Systematic Theology*, I, p. 310.

[44] I Pannenberg, *Systematic Theology*, I, p. 311.

[45] Stanley Grenz has spoken similarly of 'the retroactive power of the future on the past' in Pannenberg's thought. See Grenz, 'A Survey of the Literature' in C. E. Braaten and Ph. Clayton, (eds), *The Theology of Wolfhart Pannenberg*, Minneapolis: Augsburg Publishing House 1988, p. 30.

shall see, is rooted in a pre-temporal decision *for* this 'constitutive' activity in time. So what is *finally* constitutive of the triune being of God for him is God's *eternal election* – or, more adequately expressed, it is the ontological *anticipation* of the historical activity by which God is Self-constituted;[46] and that takes place in election.

Because Pannenberg makes the historical activity of Jesus as such to be constitutive of the eternal being of God as triune, he winds up with a trinity of three distinct subjects. Only three divine 'subjectivities',[47] he thinks, can do justice to taking the historical Jesus as the starting point for reflection. But of course, this means that divine unity can only be conceived along the lines of a 'joint working',[48] rather than a unity that might do greater justice to the biblical equation of the God and Father of our Lord Jesus Christ with the one God of Israel.

Our task now must be to show how the later Barth was able to reconcile the formal structure of his earlier doctrine of the Trinity (one divine Subject in three modes of being) with his new material starting-point in the humility and obedience of the man Jesus. It should be noted that Barth does not connect all the dots as I am about to do it. But the conceptual building-blocks for what I am about to say are all in place in *CD* IV/1 and IV/2.

# Barth's Later Christology as the Basis for a Revised 'Barthian' Doctrine of the Trinity

All the theologians just considered share with Barth the insistence that nothing be said of the immanent Trinity which does not find a basis in the economy. But none of them stopped to consider whether Barth's sporadic musings on the Trinity in *CD* IV/1 and his extensive reflections on the relation of the two 'natures' of Christ to His Person in IV/2 do not provide a basis for reconstructing his doctrine. My own view is that such a reconstruction is indeed possible – and superior to the alternatives chosen by these theologians.

The economic root of a reconstruction of Barth's doctrine of the immanent Trinity is to be found, as it was for Pannenberg, in the humility and obedience of the man Jesus. For Barth, however, unlike Pannenberg,

---

[46] Pannenberg is able to arrive at a notion of the pre-existence of the Son, however, from his starting-point in Jesus' relation to His Father which makes the final outcome of these two (in themselves quite different) ontologies to be similar. See Wolfhart Pannenberg, *Systematic Theology*, II, Grand Rapids: Eerdmans 1994, pp. 368–70.

[47] Pannenberg, *Systematic Theology*, I, p. 308.

[48] Pannenberg, *Systematic Theology*, I, p. 334; cf. p. 335: 'The unity of the essence may be found only in the concrete life of their relations'.

that humility and obedience reaches its goal in voluntary subjection to divine judgment, in a death in God-abandonment.

Now the key to making the history of Jesus the economic root of the doctrine of the immanent Trinity is to be found in Barth's cautious approval of an often forgotten sub-class of classically Protestant treatments of the Christological problem of a 'communication of attributes', namely the so-called *genus tapeinoticum* (or 'genus of humility'). The phrase *genus tapeinoticum* was devised in the late sixteenth or early seventeenth century as the logical corollary to traditional Lutheranism's *genus majestaticum* (the 'genus of majesty'). Together, they constituted the logical possibilities which arise on the soil of an assumed 'inter-penetration' or *perichoresis* of the two 'natures', as Martin Chemnitz had it.[49] Of these two logical possibilities, only the *genus majestaticum* was finally affirmed. The human nature of Christ, it was suggested, shares in the attributes of the divine majesty (such things as omnipotence, omniscience and omnipresence) as a consequence of the hypostatic union.[50] Thus human nature can be 'divinized' in the sense of obtaining a share in the divine attributes. But the additional thought was that divine nature cannot be humanized without ceasing to be divine. The divine nature cannot participate in human attributes (such as composition, contingency and becoming) or the experiences those attributes make possible (such as physical, emotional or spiritual suffering) with ceasing to be 'simple' and 'impassible'. So the *genus tapeinoticum* was rejected. It should be added that the old Reformed church rejected this possibility too and did so for much the same reasons.

It was this theologoumenon to which Barth now gave cautious approval.[51] I call his approval 'cautious' because he did not believe in a direct communion of the natures – and by volume IV, could not – since he did not affirm the substantialist understanding of the 'natures' which had made Chemnitz' understanding of an inter-penetration of the natures possible in the first place.[52] Barth subscribed instead to an older tradition, in accordance with which the communication of attributes does not take place between the natures but is rather a communication of the predicates both 'natures' to the 'person of the union'. He explained this 'communication' in actualistic terms along the lines of a living correspondence of *wills* which enacted the singular history in which the unity of the God-human was realized. In any event, there is no room here for a substantial participation of either nature in the other.

Still, Barth himself did not explore the possibilities opened up by this

---

[49] M. Chemnitz, *The Two Natures in Christ*, Saint Louis: Concordia Publishing House 1971, p. 292.
[50] Chemnitz, *The Two Natures*, pp. 84–5.
[51] See Barth, *CD* IV/2, pp. 77–8, 84–5.
[52] Barth, *CD* IV/2, p. 79.

move. What is clear is that he wanted to make the Son of God to be, in a sense which always remained less than fully explained, the Subject of human suffering. In order for that commitment to be rendered meaningful, we need to take a final step which Barth did not, namely that of affirming that the Son or Logos related to the man Jesus in the mode of *receptivity*. All that came to Him in and through this human being was taken up into His Person.

Now as I see it, a reception by the Son of human predicates and the experiences they make possible requires that the 'person of the union' be understood as a 'composite person'. The thought is not a new one; it was affirmed by the Dyotheletes of the seventh and eighth centuries.[53] It also confirms another step that Barth most definitely did take, namely that of understanding the history of the divine Self-humiliation and the history of the exaltation of the royal human as one and the same history; not two histories which overlap each other as a second story sits on top of a first (as some distinctions of time and eternity would have it), not two histories which succeed each other as stages succeed each other, but one and the same history.[54] The divine 'personhood' of the Son is made concrete (and in that sense 'realized') in this singular history. And the 'personhood' of Jesus is, quite evidently, realized in this singular history. But these are not two 'persons' but one,[55] and their unity is guaranteed by the *receptivity* of the Son to the being-in-act of the man Jesus *as an act of ontic Self-concretization*. What we have before us is the ancient idea of the *an-* and *enhypostasia* of the human nature of Christ in the Person of the Logos – but an *an-* and *enhypostasia* once the 'natures' have been actualized by being rendered in terms of the category 'history'.[56]

Now what are the implications of this Christological train of thought for Barth's doctrine of the Trinity? Barth clearly wanted to find the ontological

---

[53] See, for example, St John of Damascus, *An Exact Exposition of the Orthodox Faith*, in ibid., *Writings*, Washington, DC: The Catholic University of America Press 1958, pp. 274–6.

[54] See, for example, Barth, *CD* IV/2, p. 106: 'What is it, then, that we have done? ... What has happened ... is that we have left no place for anything static at the broad centre of the traditional doctrine of the person of Christ – its development of the concepts of *unio*, *communio* and *communicatio* – or in the traditional doctrine of the two states.... [T]hinking and speaking in pure concepts of movement – we have re-translated that whole phenomenology into the sphere of a history. And we have done this because originally the theme of it, which here concerns us, is not a phenomenon, or a complex of phenomena, but a history. It is the history of God in his mode of existence as the Son, in whom He humbles Himself and becomes also the Son of Man Jesus of Nazareth ...'. Cf. p. 107: 'The Subject Jesus Christ is this history', or again, p. 113: '... it is a matter of the existence of Jesus Christ in the common *actualization* of divine and human essence.'

[55] And so Barth can speak of a 'direct unity of existence' of the Son of God with the man Jesus, and he says that this is brought about by the Son of God in that He causes 'His own divine existence to be the existence of the man Jesus'. Again, I would turn this around and say that the human existence of the man Jesus is His divine existence. The adjustment is slight but its consequence are momentous. See Barth, IV/2, p. 51.

[56] For Barth's treatment of the *anhypostasia*, see IV/2, pp. 49–50.

condition of the possibility of his later Christology in the eternal relations of the Trinity. More specifically, he wanted to find in God the Son an eternal ground of His humility and obedience in time:

> If the humility of Christ is not simply an attitude of the man Jesus of Nazareth, if it is the attitude of this man because ... there is a humility grounded in the being of God, then something else is grounded in the being of God Himself. For, according to the New Testament, it is the case that the humility of this man is an act of obedience.... If, then, God is in Christ, if what the man Jesus does is God's own work, this aspect of the self-emptying and self-humbling of Jesus Christ as an act of obedience cannot be alien to God. But in this case, we have to see here the other and inner side of the mystery of the divine nature of Christ and therefore of the nature of the one true God – that He Himself is also able and free to render obedience.[57]

What Barth has done here, in effect, is to make humility and obedience personal properties of God in His second mode of being: 'In itself and as such, then, humility is not alien to the nature of the true God, but supremely proper to Him *in His mode of being as the Son*',[58] and so: 'We have not only not to deny but actually to affirm and understand as essential to the being of God Himself an above and a below, a *prius* and a *posterius*, a superiority and a subordination.... His divine unity consists in the fact that in Himself He is both One who is obeyed and Another who obeys.'[59] Barth has taken here the same step which Rahner would later take, namely making the capacity for incarnation proper to the Son alone.

In doing so, he has also introduced greater plurality into the differentiation of the three modes of being. For it is no longer the case that these three modes are distinguished only as 'modes of origination'. It is also the case that they are distinguished by personal properties. We might flesh this out further by reference to the fact that the Spirit is the effective power of all that is done by the triune God *ad extra* (in creating and redeeming). I will explain the reasons for this in a moment. Suffice it here to say that the fact that the third mode of being is a mode of being of a definite *Subject* is maintained in this way. The 'personhood' of the Spirit is more clearly upheld here than was the case with Barth's reduction of the Spirit in *CD* I/1 to the act of communion between Father and Son.

Still, the structure of Barth's doctrine of the Trinity remains unchanged. It is still the case that what we have before us is a single Subject in three

---

[57] Barth, *CD* IV/1, p. 193.
[58] Barth, *CD* IV/2, p. 42 (emphasis mine).
[59] Barth, *CD* IV/2, p. 201.

modes of being. What has changed is simply the fact that we can now do a much better job of distinguishing these modes one from another.

# Election as the Divine Act of Self-Constitution

Barth's doctrine of election has become the subject of controversy in recent years.[60] What is not disputed is the fact that Barth understood election to be an eternal act of Self-determination. What is disputed is, rather, what he means when he says that Jesus Christ is the Subject and the object of election. My own view is that the more startling side of this thesis – that Jesus Christ is the Subject of election – is a claim whose meaning can only be addressed once it has been decided what is meant by the second half of the thesis. In any case, it is the second half we are concerned with here. What does it mean to say that Jesus Christ is the *object* of election? And what is the significance of the claim that this is an act of *Self*-determination? Is the 'determination' in question simply a decision to *do* something – to perform an action *ad extra* which has no ontological significance where God Himself is concerned? Or is the 'determination' in question an action of God directed first and foremost to His own *being*, an act with ontological significance?

Consider the following the passage:

> It is only the pride of man, making a god in its own image, that will not hear of a determination of divine essence in Jesus Christ. The presupposition of all earlier Christology has suffered from this pride – from the fathers to both Reformed and Lutheran orthodoxy. The presupposition was a Greek conception of God, according to which God was far too exalted for His address to man, His incarnation…to mean anything at all for Himself, or in any way to affect His Godhead. In other words, He was the prisoner of His own Godhead.[61]

Once Barth has said that the 'determination' in question is a determination of the divine *essence*, it seems to me that we have no choice but to understand election as a decision with ontological significance. Barth clearly treats the divine essence as plastic in nature,[62] i.e. as susceptible

---

[60] For a summary of the various contributions, see Bruce L. McCormack, 'Trinity and Election: A Progress Report', in A. van der Kooi, V. Küster and R. Reeling Brouwer, (eds), *Ontmoetingen: Tijdgenoten en getuigen*, Kampen: Kok 2009, pp. 14–35.

[61] Barth, *CD* IV/2, pp. 84–5.

[62] For a similar line of reflection, see C. Malabou, *The Future of Hegel: Plasticity, Temporality and Dialectic*, London and New York: Routledge 2005.

of a 'determination.' And given the content of election – namely that this 'determination' is *for* incarnation, for a uniting with the man Jesus (and in Him, with the *humanum* proper to all men and women[63]) – it becomes clear that Barth is using the word 'determination' much as the great Idealists did, in terms of *a relation which makes concrete*. In the absence of such a relation and the concreteness it realizes, we are dealing only with an idea, an abstraction which has no reality – even if it be named 'the triune God in and for Himself'.

What does all this mean for the relationship of election to triunity? If the divine essence is susceptible to a determination which makes concrete, then only two options are open to us. Either God's being was something complete in itself above and prior to giving His essence this determination or it wasn't. If the former is the case, then a determination of the divine essence would have to be productive of essential change. If the latter is the case, then the determination which makes concrete is simply the act of eternal Self-constitution. If the former is the case, then a metaphysical gap would have been opened between what God is in and for Himself and what He 'becomes' in relation to us. If the later is the case, the metaphysical gap would have been eliminated.[64] In my view, the only sensible option is to reject the thought of essential change, of a pre-temporal mutation in the being of God, and to affirm that the act of Self-constitution and the act of election are one and the same eternal event.

The net result of this series of reflections is that we would do well to see the 'command' of the Father which is treated by Barth as basic to the covenant of grace as generative. The 'command' simply is the eternal generation of the Son – as a mode of being in the one divine Subject in which He then 'obeys', it being understood that the language of 'command' and 'obedience' must remain irreducibly metaphorical, given that we are talking about a single Subject in three modes of being. Barth comes very close to saying precisely this in the following passage:

> In his mode of being as the Son, He fulfils the divine subordination, just as the Father in His mode of being as Father fulfils the divine superiority. In humility as the Son who complies, He is the same as the Father in majesty as the Father who disposes. He is the same in consequence (and obedience) as is the Father in origin. He is the same as the Son, i.e. as the self-posited God (the eternally begotten of the Father as dogma has it) as the Father is as the Self-positing God (the Father who eternally begets).

---

[63] Malabou, *The Future of Hegel*, p. 49.
[64] It was to protest against this metaphysical gap in Helmut Gollwitzer's doctrine of God that Eberhard Jüngel wrote his paraphrase of Barth's doctrine of the Trinity in 1965. See Jüngel, *God's Being Is in Becoming*, pp. 104–7, especially p. 107.

Moreover, in His humility and compliance as the Son, He has a supreme part in the majesty and disposing of the Father. The Father as the origin is never apart from Him as the consequence ...[65]

Barth comes very close here to an open confession that the eternal generation of the Son is willed activity. Certainly the language of Self-positing points in that direction. The Father is the 'origin' and the Son the 'consequence' of that activity. It remains true on this scheme that all that the Father has, He gives to the Son. The Son lacks nothing that is proper to the One divine Subject in all His modes of being, though He also has personal properties which distinguish this mode of being from the other two.

It remains only to say that if the Son undergoes no change of an ontic nature in becoming human, then the 'becoming' in time which results from His receptivity to all that comes to Him in and through His human 'nature' must already be the result of His eternal humility and obedience. He is already, in Himself, receptively disposed to that which is to come. Indeed, His eternal identity is constituted by this disposition, this act of looking forward. In so far, then, as He is already in eternity, by way of anticipation, that which He will become in time, namely Jesus Christ, His willed non-use of the omnipotent power He shares with the Father and the Spirit in time must correspond to a willed non-use of that power eternally. That, I think, is the final outcome of a strict application of the rule with which we began is concerned. This means that the Son acts everywhere and always, in creation and redemption, in the power of the Spirit. The Spirit is the effective power of Father and Son.

# The *Filioque* Revisited

Barth's defence of the *Filioque* in CD I/1 focused on the question of the identity of the God who breathes forth the Spirit. He wanted to say that the Father can only breathe forth the Spirit if He is already the Father of the Son, for the term 'Father' implies precisely this filial relation. But if the Father is the Father of the Son in breathing forth the Spirit, then the one divine Subject is Father *and Son* in this activity. It goes without saying, of course, that all these distinctions are logical in nature; there is no 'before' and 'after' in these activities.

What I would add to this thought is that the Holy Spirit is breathed forth to be the effective agent of all that is done by the triune God in relation to the world, creation and redemption. It will not do to speak of

---

[65] Barth, *CD* IV/1, p. 209.

the Spirit simply as the bond of love or the act of communion between Father and Son, though that also is true. But we can say much more than that. It is the Spirit who unites the man Jesus to the Word in the miraculous conception. It is the Spirit, poured out upon Jesus Christ which is the effective power by means of which He performs miracles, does His works of love, and suffers the passion of an impending withdrawal of the Father in His death. It is the Spirit who unites the man Jesus to the Word so that it may truly be said that God does what the man Jesus does. That is why being the effective agent of Father and Son in this world are personal properties of the Holy Spirit.

In the seventeenth century, the Puritan theologian John Owen held that the only active use of divine omnipotence on the part of the Word vis-à-vis His human nature lay in the assumption itself. All other works performed by Him were performed humanly, that is to say, in the power of the Spirit. 'The only singular immediate *act* of the person of the Son on the human nature was the *assumption* of it into subsistence with himself.'[66] This could be so, he thought, because the Spirit is the Spirit of the Son. 'The Holy Spirit is the *Spirit of the Son*, no less then the Spirit of the Father. He proceedeth from the Son, as from the Father.... And hence he is the immediate operator of all divine acts of the Son himself, even on His human nature. Whatever the Son of God wrought in, by, or upon human nature, he did it by the Holy Ghost, who is His Spirit, as He is the Spirit of the Father.'[67] The only correction I would offer to this is that I would not even make the assumption itself a direct work of the Son. I would say that all the Son's work is indirect, mediated by the Spirit who is at work in His human nature. But Owen is quite right to say: 'The Holy Ghost ... is the *immediate, peculiar, efficient cause* of all external divine operations.'[68]

That the Spirit proceeds from the Father *and the Son* is proof that all that the Spirit does, He does as the effective agent of the Son. Together with the Father, the Son breathes forth the Spirit with this precise goal in view, so that all that the Spirit does may rightly be said to have been done by the Son; the axiom *opera trinitatis ad extra sunt indivisa* still holds true. Nevertheless, being the effective agent of all that is done by the Father and the Son in relation to the world is the personal property of God in His third mode of being and in it alone.

Finally, the fact that the Son participates with the Father in breathing forth the Spirit is itself a sufficient warrant for the claim that the Son shares in all that the Father has. Breathing forth the Spirit to be the effective agent

---

[66] J. Owen, *Pneumatologia* in *The Works of John Owen*, III, Edinburgh: Banner of Truth Trust 1965, p. 160.

[67] Owen, *Pneumatologia*, p. 162.

[68] Owen, *Pneumatologia*, p. 161.

at work in and through His human nature is an act of majesty even as it takes place in humility and obedience. He breathes forth the Spirit to be the active agent who forms His human nature and unites Him to it. Does the logic of this description require that the Son be acting in this event as a Logos *asarkos* abstracted from the human nature to be assumed? It must be remembered that this event of Self-constitution takes place with a definite goal and purpose in view, so that even in breathing forth the Spirit, the Son is already, by inclination and disposition, that which He will become. When we hold election and triunity together in this way, it becomes impossible to think of the Son apart from the humanity He would assume. There is but one eternal event which is both election and Self-constitution.

# Conclusion

The preceding train of reflections is highly speculative in nature. It is a proposal for further thought. All my previous efforts in this area have never been intended to be anything more than that. When we speak of an eternal act of Self-constitution, we are quite obviously speaking of a mystery.

Barth himself was inclined to speak of the Father as the 'origin'. If we were to ask about the logical presupposition of this event where a Subject is concerned, Barth would be inclined, I think, to point simply to the Father. This brings him into line with John Zizioulas' more recent attempt to find in the Father the root of God's 'ontological freedom'.[69]

But I would also not be averse to appealing to Schelling's reflections on divine Self-constitution as a parable of the mystery I too am seeking to describe. Schelling certainly understood God to have the ground of His existence in Himself. To that extent, he had much in common with ancient philosophical and theological understandings of God. But: 'All philosophies say this; but they speak of this ground as of a mere concept without making it into something real [*reell*] and actual [*wirklich*]. This ground of his existence that God has in himself is not God considered absolutely, that is, in so far as he exists; for it is only the ground of his existence. It, the ground, is *nature* – in God, a being indeed inseparable, yet still distinct from him.'[70] The meaning of this remarkable statement is made clear when Schelling goes on to say, 'God has in himself an inner ground of his existence that ... precedes him in existence; but, precisely in this way, God is again the *prius* of the ground in so far as the ground, even as such, could not exist if God

[69] J. Zizioulas, *Being as Communion: Studies in Personhood and the Church*, Crestwood, NY: St Vladimir's Seminary Press 1985, pp. 41, 44.
[70] F. W. J. Schelling, *Philosophical Investigations into the Essence of Human Freedom*, Albany: State University of New York Press 2006, p. 27.

did not exist *actu*.'[71] What Schelling is here saying is that the inner *ground* of God's existence and His *existence* in act are given in the same moment. Indeed, the ground of God's existence could not itself be, were it not the case that God exists in act. How then does he describe this inner ground of God's existence? In terms of yearning: 'It is the yearning the eternal One feels to give birth to itself.'[72] Schelling can also describe this movement in trinitarian terms:

> But, corresponding to the yearning, which as the still dark ground is the first stirring of divine existence, an inner, reflexive representation is generated in God himself through which, since it can have no other object but God, God sees himself in an exact image of himself. This representation is the first in which God, considered as absolute, is realized [*verwirklicht*], although only in himself; this representation is with God in the beginning and is the God who is begotten in God himself. This representation is at the same time the understanding – the Word – of this yearning and the eternal spirit which, perceiving the word within itself and at the same time the infinite yearning, and impelled by the love that it itself is, proclaims the word so that the understanding and yearning together now become a freely creating and all-powerful will and build in the initial anarchy of nature as in its own element or instrument.[73]

Of course, all this can only be a parable. Schelling's problems – to which the foregoing reflections are his answers – are philosophical in nature, e.g. the subject-object problem, the relation of will and being, etc. The pantheistic overtones are a bit too strong for my taste, though I remain sympathetic. But I am not averse to thinking of the 'presupposition' of the divine act of Self-constitution in terms of 'yearning' or desire – a desire, I would say, to exist in a particular way that excludes other ways; to be concretely God, in other words.

Here I must stop. No doubt the reflections contained in this essay will awaken many new questions in readers. Many of them have, however, already been dealt with in previous essays and I would direct readers to those earlier essays.

---

[71] Schelling, *Philosophical Investigations*, p. 28.
[72] Schelling, *Philosophical Investigations*.
[73] Schelling, *Philosophical Investigations*, p. 30.

# 11

# The Scope of Rahner's Fundamental Axiom in the Patristic Perspective: A Dialogue of Systematic and Historical Theology

## Philipp Gabriel Renczes

The importance of the Rahnerian *Grundaxiom* in today's Trinitarian theology can hardly be exaggerated. The thesis in question, namely that 'the Economic Trinity is the Immanent Trinity and vice versa',[1] has been

---

[1] It appears that Karl Rahner publicly presented his 'Fundamental Axiom' as it is commonly referred to, for the first time in 'Kleine Bemerkungen zum dogmatischen Traktat "De trinitate"', *Universitas* [FS A. Stohr], I, Mainz: Grünewald 1960, pp. 130–50. This contribution to a Festschrift was published also in the same year in *Schriften zur Theologie*, IV, Einsiedeln: Benzinger 1960, pp. 103–33, [translated as: 'Remarks on the Dogmatic Treatise *"De Trinitate"'*, in *Theological Investigations* IV, *More Recent Writings*, Baltimore-London: Helicon Press-Darton, Longman & Todd, 1966, pp. 77–102], the usual source cited. Thereafter Karl Rahner returned regularly to this principle: cf. 'Der dreifaltige Gott als transzendenter Urgrund der Heilsgeschichte', in *Mysterium Salutis*, II, Einsiedeln: Benzinger

the object of much discussion since its publication in 1960. Among theologians, the correct relationship between 'immanent' and 'economic' Trinity has become a matter of basic constructive interest[2] and polemics,[3] which at this time allows for an at least provisional evaluation, to wit: the recip-

---

1967, pp. 317–401, [trans. *The Trinity*, New York: Herder, 1970], esp. pp. 328, 332, 336–7, 339, 344, 352, 370; *Sacramentum Mundi*, IV, (Freiburg: Herder, 1968), p. v. 'Trinität', p. 1011, [trans. 'Trinity divine', in *Sacramentum Mundi* VI, London: Burns & Oates, 1970, p. 298]; s. v. 'Trinitätstheologie', p. 1024 [trans. 'Trinity in theology', in *Sacramentum Mundi* VI, London: Burns & Oates, 1970, p. 304]. Without referring to it by name, the principle also figures in *Grundkurs des Glaubens*, Freiburg-Basel-Wien: Herder 1976, p. 142 [trans. *Foundations of Christian Faith. An introduction to the idea of Christianity*, London: Darton, Longman & Todd, 1984, p. 137].

[2] I cite a minimal representative sample of the relevant literature on this theme, a complete listing being out of the question: Yves Congar, 'Le moment "économique" et le moment "ontologique" dans la sacra doctrina (Révélation, Théologie, Somme Théologique)', in *Mélanges offerts a M.-D. Chenu*, (Bibliotheque Thomiste, 37), Paris: J. Vrin 1967; Lambert van der Heijden, *Karl Rahner, Darlegung und Kritik seiner Grundposition*, Einsiedeln: Johannes, 1973; E. Jüngel, 'Das Verhältnis von "ökonomischer" und "immanenter" Trinität. Erwägungen über eine biblische Begründung der Trinitätslehre in Anschluss an und in Auseinandersetzung mit Karl Rahners Lehre vom Dreifaltigen Gott als transzendenten Urgrund der Heilsgeschichte', in *Zeitschrift für Theologie und Kirche* 72 (1975) 353–64; Giovanni Blandino, 'La dottrina trinitaria di K. Rahner', in G. Blandino, (ed.), *Questioni dibattute di teologia*, II, Roma: Città Nuova 1978, pp. 187–237; P. Schoonenberg, 'Zur Trinitätslehre Karl Rahners', in E. Klinger and K. Wittstadt (eds), *Glaube im Prozess: Christsein nach dem II. Vatikanum für Karl Rahner*, Freiburg-Basel-Wien: Herder 1984, pp. 471–91; J. Wohlmuth, 'Zum Verhältnis von ökonomischer und immanenter Trinität: eine These', in *Zeitschrift für Katholische Theologie*, 110 (1988) pp. 139–62; W. Brändle, 'Immanente Trinität – ein "Denkmal der Kirchengeschichte"?: Überlegungen zu Karl Rahners Trinitätslehre', in *Kerygma und Dogma* 38 (1992) 185–98; M. González, *La relación entre Trinidad Económica e Immanente: El 'Axioma Fundamental' de K. Rahner y su recepción. Líneas para continuar la Reflexión*, Roma: Libreria Editrice PUL 1996; J. Bracken, 'Trinity: economic and immanent', in *Horizons* 25 (1998) 7–22; J. Prades, 'De la Trinidad económica a la Trinidad immanente', in RET 58 (1998) 285–344; E. Durand, 'L'autocommunication trinitaire: Concept clé de la *connexio mysteriorum* rahnérienne', in *Revue Thomiste* 102 (2002) 569–613; ibid., 'L'identité rahnérienne entre la Trinité économique et la Trinité immanente à l'épreuve de ses applications', in *Revue Thomiste* 103 (2003) 75–92; L. Ladaria, 'La teología trinitaria de Karl Rahner: Un balance de la discusión', in *Gregorianum*, 86 (2005) 276–307; G. Zarazaga, 'La communion trinitaria: la contribución de Karl Rahner', in *Estudios Trinitarios* 80 (2005) 263–90; M. Böhnke, 'Die Wahrheit der ökonomischen Trinität: Versuch über das Axiom der Identität von ökonomischer und immanenter Trinität in ökumenischer Absicht', in *Theologie und Glaube* 96 (2006) 262–89; D. W. Jowers, *The Trinitarian Axiom of Karl Rahner: The Economic Trinity is the Immanent Trinity and vice versa*, New York: EMP 2006; ibid., 'A test of Karl Rahner' s axiom, the Economic Trinity is the Immanent Trinity and vice versa', in *The Thomist* 70 (2006) 421–51.

[3] Among the best known critics of the Fundamental Axiom are H. U. von Balthasar, *Theodramatik*, III, *Die Handlung*, Einsiedeln: Johannes Verlag 1980, pp. 253–62; W. Kasper, *Der Gott Jesu Christi*, Mainz: Grünewald, 1982; B. Forte, *Teologia della Storia*, Cinisello-Balsamo 1991, pp. 54–5; G. Lafont, *Peut-On connaître Dieu en Jésus-Christ?*, (Cogitatio Fidei, 44), Paris: Cerf 1996; P. D. Molnar, *Divine Freedom and Doctrine of the Immanent Trinity*, London-New York: T&T Clark 2002.

rocal 'is' of the axiom, especially in the case of the 'vice versa', cannot be theologically upheld as a marker of univocal identity. In other words, the character of the immanent Trinity, as being absolutely gratuitous and free, has to be more clearly stated than the Rahnerian formulation manages to do. This perspective is reflected in the effort of the International Theological Commission in 1981 to reword the axiom: 'Hence the Fundamental Axiom of contemporary theology is expressed most correctly in the following formulation: the Trinity that manifests itself in the Economy of Salvation is the Immanent Trinity; [and] it is the Immanent Trinity that communicates itself freely and in unconditional gratuity in the Economy of Salvation.'[4]

# 'Immanent' and 'Economic' between 'Theologia Apophatica' and 'Theologia Cataphatica'

This 'yes, but' to the Rahnerian Fundamental Axiom insists upon greater precision in the determination of the relationship of immanent and economic Trinity; it has relied mainly on two lines of argument. One is 'incarnational', in the sense that the basic axiom in respect of the economic Trinity fails to take adequate account of the character of the real newness that consists of the fact of the incarnation of the second Person of the immanent Trinity.[5] The other 'transcendent' approach notes that the equation of immanent and economic Trinity obscures the absolute freedom of God, which is incompatible with any conclusive deduction from the historically contingent.[6] The two complementary arguments direct one's attention in my opinion to the recent renaissance of 'negative theology'. Stimulated by impulses

---

[4] 'Dunque l'assioma fondamentale della teologia odierna s'esprime molto correttamente nella formulazione seguente: la Trinita' che si manifesta nell'economia della salvezza è la Trinità immanente; è la Trinità immanente che si comunica liberamente e a titolo gratuito nell'economia della salvezza.' (Commissio Theologica Internationalis, *Desiderium et cognitio Dei. Theologia-Christologia-Anthropologia.* Quaestiones selectae. Altera series), in EV 8, 1981, pp. 366–7 (translation: Renczes).

[5] Cf. Walter Kasper, *Der Gott Jesu Christi*, Mainz: Grünewald 1982, p. 335 [trans. *The God of Jesus Christ*, London: SCM 1983, p. 275]. See also Luis Ladaria, *The Living and True God. The Mystery of the Trinity*, Miami: Convivium Press 2009, p. 62: 'Therefore, the identification between the economic Trinity and the immanent Trinity has to be understood in the sense that on the one hand, God gives himself to us and is revealed to us just as he is in himself, although he does it freely. In other words his being is not realized or perfected in this self-communication. On the other hand, God maintains his mystery in this revelation, and his greatest closeness will be the most direct manifestation of his highest greatness.'

[6] Ibid., p. 336 [276].

of contemporary philosophy,[7] negative theology has exercised a decisive influence on recent Christian thought.[8]

The attention to a greater clarity of expression in regard to the transcendental character of divine being (which of course especially characterizes the immanent Trinity over against the economic Trinity) is nevertheless paired with the effort at all costs to avoid throwing out the baby, i.e. the cataphatic side of authentic Christian theology, with the bath water. In the present case, 'throwing out the baby' means to work out the specificity of the immanent Trinity versus its economic revealedness in such a way that the validation of the *historia sacra*, definitively sealed by the immanent Trinity in Jesus Christ, could be made relative again and lodged in the realm of the contingent.

Thus one can detect in more recent approaches, such as that by Catherine LaCugna, a kind of apophatic-cataphatic going beyond the Rahnerian principle in its alternation between *theologia* and *economia*. In this case the pendulum – following the logic of the 'transcendentalization' of the immanent Trinity – swings definitively over to the side of a soteriology, with the result that the immanent Trinity disappears behind the economic Trinity. The immanent Trinity is left with the sole function of disclosing anthropology by way of the economy: the hidden Trinitarian God reveals Himself as the full realization of human potentiality.[9]

---

[7] Especially notable in this connection is Jacques Derrida, cf. *L'écriture et la différence*, Paris: Seuil, 1967; 'Comment NE pas parler. Dénégations', in *Psychè. Inventions de l'autre*, Paris: Galilée 1987, pp. 535–95; from another perspective (inasmuch as he makes no explicit references to traditional *Theologia Negativa*), see also E. Lévinas, cf. 'Le temps et l'autre', in J. Wahl, (ed.), *Le Choix, Le Monde, l'Existence*, (Cahiers du Collège Philosophique), Paris-Grenoble: B. Arthaud 1947, pp. 125–96. Cf. G. Vattimo, *Credere di credere*, Milano: Garzanti 1996 and Jean-Luc Marion, 'In the Name: How to Avoid Speaking of 'Negative Theology'', in J. D. Caputo and M. J. Scanlon (eds), *God, the Gift, and Postmodernism*, Bloomington, Indiana: University Press 1999, pp. 20–53, have exposed their thought in conjunction with the noted resurgence in the theological field and no doubt have further reinforced this development of systematic theology.

[8] See for instance Bruno Forte: 'The transcendence and 'beyondness' of *Deus in se* compared to *Deus pro nobis* can be noted in two directions: on the one hand, in the sense of *apophaticism*, that is the ineffability of the divine mystery which is totally 'other', even when totally become inner part of the human event, and on the other hand in the sense of eschatology' ('La trascendenza e l'ulteriorità del Dio in se rispetto al *Deus pro nobis* si lasciano cogliere in una duplice direzione: da una parte, nel senso dell'apofasi, dell'indicibilità del mistero divino totalmente altro, anche se fattosi totalmente dentro alla vicenda umana; dall'altra nel senso dell'escatologia [...], *Trinità come storia. Saggio sul Dio cristiano*, Cinisello Balsamo: Edizioni Paoline 1988, pp. 21–2 (translation: Renczes).

[9] This is the judgement of S. Grenz, claiming that C. LaCugna 'has lost any conception of God beyond the economy of salvation'; cf. *Rediscovering the Triune God: The Trinity in Contemporary Theology*, Minneapolis: Fortress 2004, p. 160. See also T. Weinandy, *The Father's Spirit of Sonship*, Edinburgh : T&T Clark 1995, pp. 123–36.

Already in Rahner, of course, one finds the 'anthropological' interest as prime motive for the formulation of the basic axiom, especially when he observes that the Trinity faded from the Christian consciousness in a process of alienation beginning with the eighteenth-century Enlightenment. As a theologian, he saw this development as closely connected with splitting the doctrine of God into the two tracts *De Deo Uno* and *De Deo Trino*.[10]

It may well have been this anthropological perspective, perceived as 'contemporary', 'modern' or in any case 'post-Enlightenment,' that has led to a noticeable tendency to treat the relevance of patristics for the issue of the reciprocity of immanent and economic Trinity rather haphazardly, or even as somehow suspect.[11] One delves into it quite selectively or polemically and often subjects it prematurely to modern perspectives and problematics.[12] This is at base a glaring anomaly, given the fact that we owe to the patristic era the introduction and definition of all those notions that are centrally connected with the fundamental Axiom, as well as the posing of the problem itself and its essential theological elaboration.

One can take the characterization of the theology of Augustine with respect to the fundamental Axiom as an exemplary case for this *status quaestionis* in systematic theology. Karl Rahner himself thought his axiom was quite un-Augustinian, on the presumption that the Latin bishop constructed his teaching on the Trinity starting from the inner life of the soul. Thus a speculative reflection on the human mind was made to do duty for the scriptural starting place of the connection between the economy of salvation and the immanent Trinity.[13] Walter Kasper maintains on the contrary that 'by means of this transcendental theological deduction, Rahner has renewed the essentials of Augustine's Trinitarian speculation.'[14] Characteristically,

---

[10] Cf. Karl Rahner, 'Bemerkungen zum dogmatischen Traktat "De Trinitate"', in *Schriften zur Theologie*, IV, Einsiedeln: Benzinger 1960, pp. 103–7, [trans: 'Remarks on the Dogmatic Treatise '*De Trinitate*', pp. 83–7]; ibid., 'Um das Geheimnis der Dreifaltigkeit', in *Schriften zur Theologie*, XII, Einsiedeln: Benzinger 1975, pp. 320–5.

[11] This is certainly not the case with the theological reflection of H. U. von Balthasar. In his criticism of Rahner's Fundamental Axiom, however, he contents himself, in regard to references to patristic theology, with a very compressed evocation of the theologoumenon of the *sacrum commercium*, which as such is indisputably patristic. Cf. *Theodramatik*, III, pp. 253–62.

[12] See M. R. Barnes, 'Augustine in Contemporary Trinitarian Theology', in *Theological Studies* 56 (1995) 237–50; see 241–2. See also D. Marmion, 'Trinity and Salvation: A Dialogue with Catherine LaCugna', in *Irish Theological Quarterly* 74 (2009) 115–29; see 121–3.

[13] Cf. K. Rahner, 'Bemerkungen zum dogmatischen Traktat "De Trinitate"', in *Schriften zur Theologie*, IV, Einsiedeln: Benzinger 1960, pp. 112–13 [trans: 'Remarks on the dogmatic treatise *De Trinitate*', pp. 84–5].

[14] W. Kasper, *Der Gott Jesu Christi*, p. 367 [transl. *The God of Jesus Christ*, p. 301]: 'Rahner mit dieser transzendentaltheologischen Deduktion das Wesentliche der augustinischen Trinitätsspekulation erneuert hat'.

neither author cites sources for his evaluation of Augustine's Trinitarian teaching.

The present contribution therefore undertakes the task of going back over the decisive stations that patristic theology set up on the narrow and slippery path towards an understanding of the proper relationship between the immanent and economic Trinity. It is done in the hope of making these precedents fruitful for the current discourse of systematic theology, in particular theological anthropology.[15]

The Cappadocians[16] figure largely in this endeavour, as do Augustine and Maximus the Confessor. A sort of patristic itinerary will be mapped out; it will indicate that the struggle for the proper theological presentation of the Christ event in patristic theology was articulated dynamically. The 'dynamism' in question indicates not so much a dialectic between East and West as a dialogue between Revelation and patristic Tradition, and thus attained a high level of reflection. The fruit of this process can undoubtedly make a contribution not only in critically countering possible one-sided understandings of the Fundamental Axiom, but also in advancing towards a greater precision in the determination of the relationship of immanent and economic Trinity.

# The Cappadocian Framing of Principle: The Systematic Distinction of 'Theologia' and 'Oikonomia' as Distinctive Mark of Christian Theology

By its own nature, the biblical revelation of the Old and New Testaments that grounds patristic theology gives witness primarily to God as creating and caring for his creatures. Yet there is an inherent awareness in this

---

[15] This essay can of course make use of investigations that have compared the Fundamental Axiom with the theology of the Cappadocians or Augustine. In regard to the Cappadocians, see especially J. D. Zizioulas, 'The Doctrine of the Holy Trinity: The Significance of the Cappadocian Contribution,' in Ch. Schwöbel (ed.), *Trinitarian Theology Today: Essays on Divine Being and Act*, Edinburgh: T&T Clark 1995, pp. 40–4. As to the relation between the Fundamental Axiom and Augustine, cf. D. C. Benner, 'Augustine and Karl Rahner on the Relationship between the Immanent Trinity and the Economic Trinity', in *International Journal of Systematic Theology* 9 (2007) 24–38. Our focus, unlike these studies, is on the interaction of continuity with increasing refinement in the patristic development, as this is of particular importance for a systematic utilization in the present.

[16] Among the three Cappadocians, Basil, Gregory of Nyssa and Gregory of Nazianzus, the overall resemblance in language and culture, especially in regard to the relation of theology and economy, allows us to present them together, even though divergent nuances are not to be denied.

witness of the unattainable otherness of 'the God of heaven',[17] living outside of time and space. At certain critical points, this is even spelled out: 'Even heaven and the highest heaven cannot contain you.' (1 Kings 8:27); 'Surely God is great, and we do not know him; the number of his years is unsearchable.' (Job 36:26).

These two strands of revelation of the one God famously come together in the story of the burning bush (Gen 3:14–15), where He is revealed as the one who 'makes' history, without ever being confined to that realm. The unnamed God comes forth as the one who dealt with the ancestors and was now to be known by name, but a name that is and remains ineffable.

The message of the Old Testament, that God's abiding inaccessibility is part and parcel of his activity in history, gets dramatically radicalized in the New Testament. The eternal Word becomes flesh, the incarnation of God comes to completion in his resurrection and ascension into heaven, so that the risen One become Man is present within the gathering of the community as one who 'lives in inaccessible light' (1 Tim 6:16).

## The Mystery of God beyond all Revelation

This revelation grounds the necessity of a theological (especially Christological) distinction between God's eternal being and his temporal acts; as early as Origen, one finds the paired concepts of *theologia* and *oikonomia*.[18] While the latter refers to the Logos becoming man, the former considers the Logos in respect of his inner-godly existence. Here one has the groundwork for the terminology and content of Rahner's Fundamental Axiom, which with the differentiation between the *Deus in se* and the *Deus ad nos* insists in the first place on the corresponding exchange between the two.

To meet the challenge of the neo-Arian Eunomius, who adopted the Gnostic idea that the human being disposes of a basic and all-encompassing knowledge of God, the Cappadocians made precise the extent of what *theologia* and *oikonomia* must mean. They identified the first with God's nature/essence (οὐσία) and the second with God's (saving) action (ἐνέργεια), and went on to couple this distinction with the concepts of 'cataphatic' and 'apophatic' theology. As humans we have at our disposition a conceptual knowledge of God to the extent that He has revealed himself for our salvation (*oikonomia* = cataphatic propositions that concern God's activities) as well as a presentiment of the mystery of God that can only be formulated in negatives ('unconceptual' 'inaccessible') and that refers to

---

[17] 'אלהי השמים (Elohe-haschamaiim)', cf. e.g. Gen 24,7, 2 Chr 36, 23.

[18] Cf. B. Studer, 'Theologia – Oikonomia. Zu einem traditionellen Thema in Augustins De Trinitate', in *Studia Anselmiana* 124 (1997) 575–600, p. 577.

His own being (*theologia* = apophatic statements that concern the nature/essence of God).[19] The classical formulation of this insight is in Letter 234 of Basil:

> We say that we know the greatness of God, His power, His wisdom, His goodness, His providence by which He takes care of us and the justness of His judgment; but not His very essence. (...) we say that we know our God from His operations, but do not undertake to approach near to His essence. His operations come down to us, but His essence remains beyond our reach.[20]

Having reached this point, it makes sense to bring out how thoroughly Karl Rahner's theology fits into the horizon of this biblical-patristic perspective:

> One can only speak correctly of God when he is conceived of as the infinite. [...] We could call him (if we wished to give such a title to what is) the nameless, that which is other than all finite things; the infinite: but we should not thereby have given him a name, merely said that he has none. We have understood the designation 'nameless' only when we recognized it as radically and primordially different in its uniqueness from all other designations. [...] For how should one name the nameless, sovereign beloved, which relegates us to our finitude, except as 'holy', and what could we call holy if not this? Or to what does the name 'holy' belong more primordially than to the infinite Whither of receptive love which before this incomprehensible and inexpressible being becomes trembling adoration? In transcendence therefore is found, in the form of the aloof and distant which rules unruled, the nameless being which is infinitely holy. This we call mystery, or rather, the holy mystery, to recall more expressly that freedom is transcendent with regard to knowledge.[21]

---

[19] In the light of all the quotations that Giulio Maspero himself reports in his article *energeia* to illustrate the notion of *energeia* in Gregory of Nyssa – quotations which all without exception serve to mark the distinction of *energeia* from *ousia* or *nature* – the formula that he then chooses to characterize the term remains surprisingly ambivalent: 'The discourse on ἐνέργεια is thus linked, for Gregory, to apophatism, which in turn is at the service of the correct formulation of the Trinitarian doctrine.' See G. Maspero, 'Energy', in L. F. Mateo-Seco & G. Maspero (eds), *The Brill Dictionary of Gregory of Nyssa*, Leiden-Boston: Brill, 2010, 258–62, at 258–59.

[20] Basil of Caesarea, *Letter* 234, Yves *Courtonne, Saint Basile. Lettres*, III, Paris: Les Belles *Lettres* 1966, p. 42 [trans. *NPNF*, 2nd *series*, 8, 274]: Καὶ γὰρ τὴν μεγαλειότητα τοῦ Θεοῦ εἰδέναι λέγομεν καὶ τὴν δύναμιν καὶ τὴν σοφίαν καὶ τὴν ἀγαθότητα καὶ τὴν πρόνοιαν ᾗ ἐπιμελεῖται ἡμῶν καὶ τὸ δίκαιον αὐτοῦ τῆς κρίσεως, οὐκ αὐτὴν τὴν οὐσίαν. (...) Ἡμεῖς δὲ ἐκ μὲν τῶν ἐνεργειῶν γνωρίζειν λέγομεν τὸν Θεὸν ἡμῶν, τῇ δὲ οὐσίᾳ αὐτῇ προσεγγίζειν οὐχ ὑπισχνούμεθα. Αἱ μὲν γὰρ ἐνέργειαι αὐτοῦ πρὸς ἡμᾶς καταβαίνουσιν, ἡ δὲ οὐσία αὐτοῦ μένει ἀπρόσιτος.

[21] K. Rahner, *Schriften zur Theologie*, IV, pp. 70; 73 [trans. 'The Concept of Mystery in

Precisely in light of this theology of mystery, then, Karl Rahner sees his identification of the immanent Trinity with the Trinity in the economy of salvation as 'favoured by the doctrine of the Greek Fathers',[22] even though his reference to the latter remains rather cursory.

As we undertake our further investigations here in comparative mode, let us highlight two items of convergence with patristic theology that stand out in this last citation and that serve as typical of Rahner's theology:

1   As is only consistent with the biblical content, the central focus of theological interest remains that of reckoning with the fact of divine action for the human being. Thus, for the Cappadocians, the 'energies' of God signified the metaphysical warrants of an anti-Aristotelian conviction of divine providence and redemption, warrants that characterize God as primarily 'dynamic.' For Karl Rahner, the sense of the Fundamental Axiom, does not lie in the communication of an objectifiable knowledge of God, but in making the case for the possibility of an understanding of God wherein ungraspable transcendence occurs as affirming, loving freedom.[23] In both theologies it becomes apparent that it would be wrong to think that the immanent and economic Trinity would stand fixed and stationary before the human intellect like a diptych, the two panels of which form a whole in a kind of systematic construction. Divinity is dynamic identity.

2   The prominence of the dynamism of God suggests concentrating likewise on the dynamism of human knowing, again in contrast to a static, objectifiable concept. Although the human being does not grasp God as such, he perceives in his existence a dynamism – ἐνεργείαι in the Cappadocians, the human act of openness to transcendence in Karl Rahner – that leads him in a kind of conversion movement to God, who had first performed this movement in the other direction, towards the human being.

# The Mystery of God and the Trinitarian Persons

Let us return to the Cappadocians. Aside from fixing more precisely the general terminology of the epistemological tension between God's being

---

Catholic Theology', pp. 50–1, 53].

[22] 'durch die Lehre der griechischen Väter begünstigt', K. Rahner, *Schriften zur Theologie*, IV, p. 96 [trans. 'The Concept of Mystery in Catholic Theology', p. 70].

[23] Cf. K. Rahner, *Grundkurs des Glaubens*, p. 74 [trans. *Foundations of Christian Faith*, pp. 65–6].

and action, the most pertinent theological achievement of the three Church Fathers was to guarantee that this tension would not lead to a confusion regarding the understanding of the distinction of the three divine hypostases within the one divine Being. The characterization as divine persons rests exclusively on the relations that exist within the one divine essence; such relations are in no case to be understood as the comprehension of separate subjects in respect of their actions (ἐνέργεια):

> Even where many people engage in the same activity (ἐνέργεια), each one does his own task specifically and does not share another's individual action with those who are engaged in the same undertaking (...) Since among human beings the action of each individual in the same undertaking is distinct, one properly speaks of many individuals, each of them being separated from the others by one's individuality and the corresponding specific character of one's action. Regarding the divine nature, on the other hand, we have not learned in a similar fashion that the Father accomplishes something by himself, in which the Son is not involved, or again that the Son operates individually without the Spirit. On the contrary, we have learnt that every operation which extends from God to the created realm and is named according to our variable conceptions of it, has its origin from (ἐκ) the Father, and proceeds through (διὰ) the Son, and is brought to completion in (ἐν) the Holy Spirit. For this reason the designation of this activity (ἐνέργεια) is not split up into the multiplicity of agents, as the participation of each (divine person) in everything is not specific and individual. Whatever comes to pass, whether within the sphere of God's foreknowledge on our behalf, or in regard to the disposition and preservation of the universe, comes to pass by the action of the three, yet what does come to pass is not three things. [24]

A paradoxical insight seems to follow from an examination of this text.

---

[24] Gregory of Nyssa, *Ad Ablabium*, (GNO III/1) 47, 11–48; [trans. Renczes]: ὅτι ἄνθρωποι μέν, κἂν μιᾶς ὦσιν ἐνεργείας οἱ πλείονες, καθ᾽ ἑαυτὸν ἕκαστος ἀποτεταγμένως ἐνεργεῖ τὸ προκείμενον, οὐδὲν ἐπικοινωνῶν ἐν τῇ καθ᾽ ἑαυτὸν ἐνεργείᾳ πρὸς τοὺς τὸ ἴσον ἐπιτηδεύοντας· (...) οὐκοῦν ἐν μὲν τοῖς ἀνθρώποις, ἐπειδὴ διακεκριμένη ἐστὶν ἡ ἐν τοῖς αὐτοῖς ἐπιτηδεύμασιν ἑκάστου ἐνέργεια, κυρίως πολλοὶ ὀνομάζονται, ἑκάστου αὐτῶν εἰς ἰδίαν περιγραφὴν κατὰ τὸ ἰδιότροπον τῆς ἐνεργείας ἀποτεμνομένου τῶν ἄλλων· ἐπὶ δὲ τῆς θείας φύσεως οὐχ οὕτως ἐμάθομεν ὅτι ὁ πατὴρ ποιεῖ τι καθ᾽ ἑαυτόν, οὗ μὴ συνεφάπτεται ὁ υἱός, ἢ πάλιν ὁ υἱὸς ἰδιαζόντως ἐνεργεῖ τι χωρὶς τοῦ πνεύματος, ἀλλὰ πᾶσα ἐνέργεια ἡ θεόθεν ἐπὶ τὴν κτίσιν διήκουσα καὶ κατὰ τὰς πολυτρόπους ἐννοίας ὀνομαζομένη ἐκ πατρὸς ἀφορμᾶται καὶ διὰ τοῦ υἱοῦ πρόεισι καὶ ἐν τῷ πνεύματι τῷ ἁγίῳ τελειοῦται. διὰ τοῦτο εἰς τὸ πλῆθος τῶν ἐνεργούντων τὸ ὄνομα τῆς ἐνεργείας οὐ διασχίζεται, ὅτι οὐκ ἀποτεταγμένη ἑκάστου καὶ ἰδιάζουσά ἐστιν ἡ περί τι σπουδή· ἀλλ᾽ ὅπερ ἂν γίνηται τῶν εἴτε εἰς τὴν ἡμετέραν πρόνοιαν φθανόντων εἴτε πρὸς τὴν τοῦ παντὸς οἰκονομίαν καὶ σύστασιν, διὰ τῶν τριῶν μὲν γίνεται, οὐ μὴν τρία ἐστὶ τὰ γινόμενα.

At first glance, it constitutes for us today an impressive anticipation or confirmation of the Rahnerian Fundamental Axiom. In one of its basic thrusts, it is indeed that; i.e. that it is theologically impossible to divide up and allocate immanent Trinitarian being and its revealed activity *ad extra* according to the order of 'being.' With a more exact analysis, however, the passage turns out to be, *ante litteram*, a frontal countermanoevre to the Fundamental Axiom.

To be sure, the Cappadocians do uphold the following proposition: just as the indivisible unity in the divine being (οὐσία) allows for the personal distinction of the three persons, so there is also for each person of the Trinity a definite describable role with respect to God's action in the unity of such action *ad extra* (ἐνέργεια). God's economy meets up with the creature in 'enhypostasized' ('in-person') form. Most explicitly by means of preposi-tions (ἐκ-διά-ἐν), the passage just quoted introduces a standard language that refers the one economy in any given case to one of the three divine persons. It is here that the closest approximation of Rahnerian theology to the Cappadocian teaching is evident; after all, the Jesuit polemicizes with evident determination against an occidental, in Rahner's view (post-) Augustinian, idea of an inner-Trinitarian exchangeability of the divine roles and actions.[25]

Yet this insight leads the Cappadocians, in a further step, to take a turn that is little less than dramatic when compared to the Fundamental Axiom. While the access of the human person (by way of specific actions of a divine Person) to the knowledge of the one God or to a divine Person does not permit deductions as to the transcendent being of God (neither does the Fundamental Axiom, which never envisages the transcendent being of God as such), in the same way the economic reality of the Trinity that imparts itself to the human being cannot reveal the core and fullness of meaning of the hypostasized inner-Trinitarian persons. The Trinity of God himself and his way of knowing himself can only be known by God. In other words: no revelation in the economy is able to give us full direct access to the structure of the innertrinitarian life (*theologia*).

Thus for example Basil notes, presumably against the Messalians, that even though in baptism 'we are born out of the Spirit and become Spirit ourselves',[26] this would not make any pneumatological essential identity available to us:

---

[25] K. Rahner, *Schriften zur Theologie*, IV, pp. 97; 106; 118–19; 'Remarks on the Dogmatic Treatise "*De Trinitate*"', in *Theological Investigations*, IV, Baltimore: Helicon Press 1966, pp. 80 and 91. For a critique of this appraisal, cf. François Bourassa, 'Théologie trinitaire chez saint Augustin', in *Gregorianum* 58, 675–725; D. Brenner, 'Augustine and Karl Rahner on the Relationship between the Immanent Trinity and the Economic Trinity', in *International Journal of Systematic Theology* 9 (2007) 24–38.

[26] St. Basil, *De baptismo*, I, 2, 20, (SCh 357, pp. 168, 16–17) [trans. Renczes]: ἐκ τοῦ πνεύματος

This spirit, however, does not trace back to the great Glory of the Holy Spirit which is inaccessible to human intelligence, but can be perceived – even though only in an obscure way – in the diversity of the spiritual gifts which God through Christ bestows upon each singular person by an activity (ἐνέργεια) and to the benefit of all, similar to other expressible realities.[27]

The critical view has been expressed in relation to the Cappadocians that, influenced by Neo-Platonism, they make too sharp a distinction between the works and the essence of God. This would have opened a door to downgrading the economic Trinity as a 'non-essential' appearance of the Triune Godhead. In particular they are charged with having executed a neo-Platonic equation of 'essence' and '(self)-knowledge' that no longer appears so convincing: does the divine essence have to remain inaccessible to human knowing, just because we admittedly cannot experience it as God does?[28] Against this view, however, one must once more take into account that the Cappadocian apophasis comes ultimately not from Neo-Platonism[29] but from the biblical witness.[30]

Actually, given the current state of 'Rahner reception' with its 'reserve' towards the Fundamental Axiom, there appears a prima facie affinity with the Cappadocian theology. Precisely the dynamism of the meeting of God and humanity, which we have observed as leitmotiv of Cappadocian and Rahnerian theology, should not find its rationale only in anthropology (by means of a kind of 'eschatological proviso' affecting human

---

γεννωμένους, πνεῦμα. The authenticity of this work, which has been challenged in the past, can be deemed probable in the wake of recent investigations; cf. J. Pauli, 'Basilius von Cäsarea', in S. Döpp and W. Geerlings (eds), *Lexikon der Antiken Christlichen Literatur*, Freiburg-Basel-Wien: Herder 2002, p. 116.

[27] Basil of Caesarea, *De baptismo*, I, 2, 20, (SCh 357, 168, pp. 18–23) [trans. Renczes]: πνεῦμα δὲ οὐ κατὰ τὴν μεγάλην καὶ ἀκατάληπτον ἀνθρωπίνῃ διανοίᾳ δόξαν τοῦ ἁγίου Πνεύματος, ἀλλὰ τὴν ἐν τῇ διαιρέσει τῶν τοῦ Θεοῦ διὰ τοῦ Χριστοῦ αὐτοῦ χαρισμάτων ἑκάστῳ πρὸς τὸ συμφέρον, καὶ ἐνεργείᾳ τούτων ἁπάντων αἰνιγματωδῶς θεωρουμένην, καὶ ἐν ἄλλοις δὲ ῥητοῖς ὁμοίως

[28] Cf. J.-M. Garrigues, 'L'énergie divine et la grâce chez Maxime le Confesseur', in *Istina* 19 (1974) 272–96, p. 281.

[29] The primarily biblical and less philosophical mode of thought of the Cappadocians emerges most clearly in more recent research. Cf. e.g. K. Corrigan, 'Οὐσία and ὑπόστασις" in the Trinitarian Theology of the Cappadocian Fathers: Basil and Gregory of Nyssa', in *Zeitschrift für Antikes Christentum* 12 (2008) 114–34.

[30] In the light of Cappadocian theology, one can see in the New Testament a fine but unmissable line that marks off, within the comprehension of the Godhead, the innertrinitarian self-knowledge from the knowledge which Revelation makes available to humanity: cf. Mt 11, 27: 'All things have been handed over to me by my Father. No one knows the Son except the Father, and no one knows the Father except the Son and anyone to whom the Son wishes to reveal him.'

knowledge), but should be understood primarily as a pointer to God's transcendence.

In the Fathers, in fact, the unsearchableness of God was understood not so much as a finding about the human being's limited intellectual reach and more as the *Deus semper maior*. All the same, such insight into the limitless God does not lead man in the Cappadocians' treatment to a stagnant resignation[31] or recoil, but, at least in the interpretation of Gregory of Nyssa, to a receptive dynamic of unlimited growth towards God in the form of *epectasis*:[32]

> Participation in the divine good is such that it makes the one in whom it occurs ever greater and more capacious than before, providing the receiver an increase in size and strength, in such a way that this nourished beneficiary continues growing without ever ceasing to augment.[33]

It appears that the 'growth character' of the anthropological pole has a much more emphatic shaping in the Cappadocian approach than in Karl Rahner's theology. In my opinion, it is this that gives the decisive impulse for the further development of patristic theology in the matter of the relation between the *Deus in se* and the *Deus ad nos*. This further patristic development can certainly be seen, I think, as a more explicit unfolding of the interpretative possibilities of the interplay between *theologia* and *oikonomia*. A departure from the basic position of the Cappadocians, however, it is not.

---

[31] Gregory of Nyssa, *In Canticum Canticorum*, Hom. 12, (GNO VI) 369–70: ἀλλὰ περιαιρεῖται τὸ τῆς λύπης θέριστρον διὰ τοῦ μαθεῖν ὅτι τὸ ἀεὶ προκόπτειν ἐν τῷ ζητεῖν καὶ τὸ μηδέποτε τῆς ἀνόδου παύεσθαι τοῦτό ἐστιν ἡ ἀληθὴς τοῦ ποθουμένου ἀπόλαυσις τῆς πάντοτε πληρουμένης ἐπιθυμίας ἑτέραν ἐπιθυμίαν τοῦ ὑπερκειμένου γεννώσης. ['But the veil of sadness is lifted when learning that progressing in the research and never standing still in the ascent is the very enjoyment of the One desired by a desire which is always filled with the generation of another desire of what is superior (sc. to the already found)' (trans. Renczes)].

[32] For a more detailed examination of this term, see J. Daniélou, *Platonisme et Théologie mystique*, Paris: Aubier, 1944, pp. 309–26; L. F. Mateo-Seco, 'Epectasis', in *The Brill Dictionary of Gregory of Nyssa*, pp. 263–8.

[33] Gregory of Nyssa, *De anima et resurrectione*, (PG 46, 105B), [trans. Renczes]: Τοιαύτη γὰρ ἡ τοῦ θείου ἀγαθοῦ μετουσία, ὥστε μείζονα καὶ δεκτικώτερον ποιεῖν τὸν ἐν ᾧ γίνεται, ἐκ δυνάμεως καὶ μεγέθους προσθήκην ἀναλαμβανομένη τῷ δεχομένῳ, ὡς ἂν αὔξεσθαι τὸν τρεφόμενον, καὶ μὴ λήγειν ποτὲ τῆς αὐξήσεως.

# The 'Dynamization' in Augustine of the Biblical-Patristic Fundamental Position

Augustine indubitably takes a central place in our investigation, in so far as the above diagnosed alienation between the theology of the Church Fathers and systematic theology in the present also after Karl Rahner is especially laid at his feet.[34] As is recognized, Karl Rahner's criticism of the Western take on Trinitarian theology, as the origin of which he identified Augustine, is ultimately indebted to a polarizing schema of Théodore de Régnon.[35] De Régnon believed he could perceive a shifting of the theological accentuation in the geographical transition from East to West: whereas in the East one starts from the Trinity of persons, whose unity is guaranteed by the Father as origin, in the West since Augustine what stands at the centre of Trinitarian theology is the one divine essence, to which the three personal ways of subsistence belong.[36] As a consequence Rahner sees in the West a depersonalization of the Trinity; Augustine's 'psychological doctrine of the Trinity' would be its most distinctive example.

In the meantime de Régnon's perspective has been largely discredited; de Régnon himself appears to uphold it only in part.[37] In comparison, recent investigations are working out more and more clearly the intellectual commonality that Augustine shares with the Cappadocians: theology as the strenuous task of plumbing the possibilities of human discourse on God, under the conviction of God's absolute transcendence.[38]

---

[34] Cf. M. R. Barnes, 'Augustine in Contemporary Trinitarian Theology', in *Theological Studies* 56 (1995) 237–50. The article quotes as examples Bertrand de Margérie, Catherine Mowry LaCugna, David Brown, James P. Mackey, John O'Donnell and Jürgen Moltmann (pp. 238–9).
[35] Cf. E. Hill, 'Karl Rahner's Remarks on the Dogmatic Treatise De Trinitate and St. Augustine', in *Augustinian Studies* 2 (1971) 67–80.
[36] For a schematic presentation of de Régnon's pattern, cf. W. Kasper, *Der Gott Jesu Christi*, Mainz: Grünewald 1982, p. 361 [trans. *The God of Jesus Christ*, London: SCM 1983, pp. 296–7].
[37] Cf. M. R. Barnes, 'De Régnon Reconsidered', in *Augustinian Studies* 26 (1995) 51–79.
[38] Cf. J.-L. Marion, *Au lieu de soi. L'approche de Saint Augustin*, (Epiméthée), Paris: Presse Universitaire Française 2008; P. van Geest, *Stellig maar onzeker. Augustinus' benadering van God*, Budel: Damon 2007.

# The Dynamic of the 'Interiority-Exteriority' Dialectic as Expression of Apophatic-Cataphatic Communication of the Trinitarian God

Within this Cappadocian framework of a Christian negative theology,[39] Augustine develops a concept of revelation characterized by the dynamic of the God-man relationship: revelation means God's approach to man, which is only to be understood against the background of the Augustinian concept of freedom. Hence the causality of action is seen as anchored in the basic acts of willing (*velle*) and loving (*amor/caritas*) of the self-realization of their being that is proper to persons.[40] If God makes himself available to man to know, then this happens in an encounter of the willing and loving divine freedom with human freedom that responds to it with willing and loving. In other words, God's essence reveals itself as loving and helping Person and can be known by the human person not only objectively, but subjectively affirmed and accepted with trusting and loving.

## *Interioritas*

The space where God's making himself known to man takes place is referred to in Augustine's preferred terminology as *interioritas*, inwardness. It is the centre of man's personhood, in so far as it is here that the person's own being and acting come together. Interiority as such is outside the realm of verifiable visibility and for this very reason is closest to the invisible divine essence. Thus God can still communicate himself to man authentically, i.e. in a manner that comes closest to the intimate life of God. That is still the case even though human interiority as a consequence of the Fall has become a place of weakness and neediness:

---

[39] Paradigmatically, two famous Augustinian exclamations can be revoked here: 'Putas quid est Deus? Putas qualis est Deus? Quidquid finxeris, non est; quidquid cogitatione comprehenderis, non est'. 'You wonder: What is God? How is God ? – All that you can figure, He is not. All that you embrace with your thought, He is not.', *s.* XXI, 2, PL 38, 143 [trans: Renczes]; 'Quid ergo dicamus, fratres, de Deo? Si enim quod vis dicere, si cepisti, non est Deus: si comprehendere potuisti, aliud pro Deo comprehendisti. Si quasi comprehendere potuisti, cogitatione tua te decepisti. Hoc ergo non est, si comprehendisti: si autem hoc est, non comprehendisti.' 'What then shall we say of God, brothers? In fact, if you have understood what you want to say, it is not God. If you were able to grasp something, you have grasped a different reality in lieu of God. If you seem to have grasped him to some extent, you are deceiving yourself with the help of your imagination. So that precisely is not God, what you have understood and if he is that, you have not understood., *s.* LII, 6, 16, PL 38, 366 [trans: Renczes].

[40] Cf. Marianne Djuth, 'Will', in A. D. Fitzgerald (ed.), *Augustine through the Ages*, Grand Rapids-Cambridge: Eerdmans 1999, pp. 881–5, pp. 883–4.

*For lo, God is helping me,* though the Ziphites among whom I am hiding do not know it. If they too were to set God before their eyes, they would discover how God helps me. All the saints are helped by God, but within themselves, where no one sees. Just as the wicked endure fierce inner torment from their consciences, so do God-fearing persons find in their consciences immense joy, for, as the apostle claims: *Our boast is this: the witness of our own conscience* (2 Cor 1:12). Such people take pride in this, but within themselves, not in the showy outward prosperity of the Ziphites. Accordingly they testify here, '*Lo, God is helping me.*'[41]

Hence Augustine can describe grace as a 'hidden communion' (*occulta communicatio*), ultimately corresponding to the 'hiddenness' of God:

We read, indeed, of those being justified in Christ who believe in Him, by reason of the secret communion and inspiration of that spiritual grace which makes everyone who cleaves to the Lord one spirit with Him.[42]

Yet Augustine does not leave it at the description of the apophatic element that still exists even in the economy of salvation. The field of action of God's discrete grace that affects the human being expands, issues forth from the human inwardness and crosses into the human witnessing of divine efficacy. This movement, which can be described as a process of becoming aware and making known, is also altogether due to grace; that is, it can only be caused by the continuation of the very divine action within. The experienced knowing of the action of God in one's own self is once again a special gift of grace; it is distinguishable from the original action of grace and should be acknowledged as a further stage of the (economic) self-gift of God.

In the above cited commentary of Augustine to Psalm 53, 'Lo, God is helping me', this further step is recognized. As another example of a more extended sort one can cite the intention of the *Confessiones*, read as giving

---

[41] *En Ps.*, 53, 8, (CCL 39), Turnhout: Brepols 1956, pp. 662–3 [trans. M. Boulding, *Works of Saint Augustine: A Translation for the 21st Century*, III/17, New York: New City Press 2001, p. 49]: *Ecce enim Deus adiuvat me. Et ipsi nesciunt inter quos lateo. Si autem et ipsi ponerent Deum ante conspectum sum, invenirent quemadmodum me adiuvat Deus. Omnes enim sancti adiuvantur a Deo, sed intus ubi nemo videt. Quomodo enim magna est poena impiorum conscientia, sic magnum gaudium piorum ipsa conscientia. Nam gloria nostra haec est, ait apostolus, testimonium conscientiae nostrae. In hac gloriatur iste intus, non in flore Ziphaeorum foris, qui modo ait: Ecce enim Deus adiuvat me.*

[42] *Pecc. mer.*, I. 10, 17–20, (CSEL 60), Vienna-Lipsia: F. Temspky & G. Freytag 1913, p. 12, [NPNF, 8, Grand Rapids: Eerdmans 1971, p. 19]: *Nempe legimus iustificari in Christo qui credunt in eum propter occultam communicationem et inspirationem gratiae spiritalis, qua quisquis haeret Domino unus spiritus est.*

an account of the mysterious collaboration of the divine 'prevenient' inner grace and the not merely apparent but real human activation:

> Late have I loved you, beauty so old and so new: late have I loved you. And see, you were within and I was in the external world and sought you there, and in my unlovely state I plunged into those lovely created things which you made. You were with me, and I was not with you. The lovely things kept me far from you, though if they did not have their existence in you, they had no existence at all. You called and cried out loud and shattered my deafness. You were radiant and resplendent, you put to flight my blindness. You were fragrant, and I drew in my breath and now pant after you. I tasted you, and I feel but hunger and thirst for you. You touched me, and I am set on fire to attain the peace which is yours.[43]

## *Sacramentum-exemplum and Spiritus bis datus*

The dynamism of the revelation that takes place in man in the crossing over from interiority to exteriority manifests itself on the side of God in the economic missions of the Trinitarian Persons, the Son and the Holy Spirit, as they show up in time. In this context, Augustine works out the pairing of the concepts of *sacramentum* and *exemplum* regarding the sending of the second Person of the Trinity, while in the case of the Holy Spirit he reflects on the duality of before and after, i.e. the sending of the Spirit before and after the glorification of Christ.

To express adequately what the encounter of man with Christ amounts to, only the pairing of *sacramentum-exemplum* suffices. For in fact both 'sacrament' and 'example' are Christological 'effective signs', and hence not to be taken as simple *signa* whose function is to refer to something else[44]. The efficacy of the sacrament (*sacramentum*) concerns the inner man and can signify an already realized state, though invisible. The visible efficacy of example (*exemplum*), meanwhile, aims at the outer man and points to

---

[43] *Conf.*, 10, 27, 38, (CCL 27), Turnhout: Brepols 1981, p. 175 [trans. H. Chadwick, Saint Augustine Confessions, Oxford: Oxford University Press 1991, p. 201]: Sero te amavi, pulchritudo tam antiqua et tam nova, sero te amavi! Et ecce intus eras et ego foris et ibi te quaerebam et in ista formosa, quae fecisti, deformis inruebam. Mecum eras, et tecum non eram. Ea me tenebant longe a te, quae si in te non essent, non essent. Vocasti et clamasti et rupisti surdidatem mean, coruscasti, splenduisti et fuagasti caecitatem meam, flagrasti, et duxi spiritum et anhelo tibi, gustavi et esurio et sitio, tetigisti me, et exarsi in pacem tuam.

[44] Cf. *doc. c.* 2.1.1: 'from this it will be easy to understand what I am calling signs; those things, that is, which are used in order to signify something else', CCL 32 (Turnhout: Brepols, 1962), 7 [trans. E. Hill, *Works of Saint Augustine: A Translation for the 21st Century*, vol. I/11 (New York: New City Press, 1996), 107]: Ex quo intelligitur quid appellem signa, res eas videlicet quae ad significandum aliquid adhibentur.

an eschatological destination.[45] In this light, Augustine comprehends the crucifixion of Christ and his resurrection not only as events that affect and transform the inner man, but also as models for the concrete mode of existence of the human person, who can accept his own biological end as an imitation of the death of Christ, with the hope thereby engendered of the resurrection of the body.

In other words, in the economic undertakings of the Son, the dialectic of the apophatic and the cataphatic is once more made intentionally complicated in terms of salvation history. The hidden has already taken place and nevertheless maintains its inaccessibility, while the visible is still hoping for its definitive realization, although it is accessible to all.

The Holy Spirit, for his part, as Augustine observes in the Old and New Testaments, was already given before he was sent on Pentecost: 'If the Holy Spirit had not been given at all before, what were the prophets filled with when they spoke?'[46] The case of Jesus' disciples serves in still another way to make the point clear that the Spirit is not given only to one who did not have Him, but also to one who already possesses Him: 'he was given twice.'[47] Augustine again makes sense of this through a dynamic growth, in this case of the gift of the Spirit itself, that corresponds to the crossing over from hiddenness to being revealed.

We are therefore to understand that he who loves has already the Holy Spirit, and by what he has becomes worthy of a fuller possession, that by having the more he may love the more. Already, therefore, the disciples had that Holy Spirit whom the Lord promised, for without Him they could not call Him Lord; but they had Him not as yet in the way promised by the Lord. Accordingly they both had, and had Him not, inasmuch as they had Him not as yet to the same extent as He was afterwards to be possessed. They had Him, therefore in a more limited sense: He was yet to be given them in an ampler measure. They had Him in a hidden way and they were yet to receive Him in a way that was manifest; for his present possession also had a bearing on that fuller gift of the Holy Spirit that they might come to a conscious knowledge of what they had.[48]

---

[45] Cf. R. Dodaro, '*Sacramentum Christi*: Augustine on the Christology of Pelagius', in *Studia Patristica* 27 (1993) 274–80; L. Gioia, *The Theological Epistemology of Augustine's De Trinitate,* Oxford: Oxford University Press 2008, p. 99.

[46] *Trin.*, 4, 29, (CCL 50), Turnhout: Brepols 1968, pp. 200–1 [trans: E. Hill, *Works of Saint Augustine: A Translation for the 21st Century*, I/5, New York: New City Press 1991, p. 183]: Si enim antea spiritus sanctus non dabatur, quo impleti prophetae locuti sunt cum aperte scriptura dicat.

[47] Ibid: bis datus est.

[48] *Io. eu. tr.*, 74, 2, (CCCL 36), Turnhout: Brepols 1954, p. 513 [trans: NPNF, 7, Grand Rapids: Eerdmans 1978, p. 334]: Restat ergo ut intellegamus Spiritum sanctum habere qui diligit, et habendo mereri ut plus habeat, et plus habendo plus diligat. Iam itaque habebant Spiritum discipuli, quem Dominus promittebat, sine quo eum Dominum non dicebant ; nec tamen eum

# 'Grace' as Expression of the Christo-Pneumatological Connectedness of Theology and Economy

In the course of the above noted clarifications, grace (*gratia*) becomes ever more prominent as a key concept that forms a theo-anthropological arc and as it were presents itself as a broker between *theologia* and *oikonomia*. One can see with Augustine's help how *gratia*, of which the second and third Persons of the Trinity are the donors (economic Trinity), at the same time indicates them as its bearers (immanent Trinity). Theological considerations such as this will prove themselves capable, it seems, of supplying support (*ante litteram*) to the Rahnerian Fundamental Axiom.

On the face of it, one needs to admit, it appears that the distinction that Augustine proposes between an eternal *generatio/processio* and a temporal *missio*[49] of the second and third Persons of the Trinity rather suggests the contrary: indeed, the Latin Father stresses that, in relation to Jesus Christ, grace characterizes only the status of the incarnate Son of God and expressly does not have to do with the relationship of the Son eternally begotten of the Father:

> Christ's being the only-begotten, equal for the Father, is not of grace, but of nature; but the assumption of human nature into the personal unity of the only-begotten is not of nature, but of grace, as the Gospel acknowledges when it says, 'And the child grew, and became strong, being filled with wisdom, and the grace of God was in him.'[50]

It is easy to see how this affirmation unfolds exactly along the axis drawn by the Cappadocians concerning the ungraspable reality of God: the manifest grace of the incarnate Son of God does not do away with the transcendence of his eternal divine sonship in consubstantiality with the Father and the Holy Spirit. This observation has its importance and must be kept in mind, precisely also in view of statements like that offered by Edmund Hill, that 'the sendings of the Son and of the Holy Spirit reveal their eternal processions from the Father and thus reveal the inner Trinitarian mystery

---

adhuc habebant, sicut eum Dominus promittebat. Et habebant ergo, et non habebant, qui quantum habendus erat eis amplius. Habebant occulte, accepturi fuerant manifeste ; quia et hoc ad maius donum sancti Spiritus pertinebat, ut eis innotesceret quod habebant.

[49] Cf. *Trin.*, 2, 9.

[50] *Io. eu. tr.*, 74, 3, (CCL 36), Turnhout: Brepols 1954, p. 514 [trans: NPNF, 7, Grand Rapids: Eerdmans 1978, p. 334]: Quod enim est unigenitus aequalis Patri, non est gratiae, sed naturae ; quod autem in unitatem personae unigeniti assumptus est homo, gratiae est, non naturae, confitente evangelio atque dicente: *Puer autem crescebat et confortabatur plenus sapientia, et gratia Dei erat in illo.* Cf. also Augustin, *Praed. Sanct.*, 31; *Ser.*, 153,14; *Trin.*, 15, 46.

of God.'[51] It is essential here to recognize how Augustine's theology is substantially more nuanced, I might even say 'more Cappadocian': 'Just as his being born (the generation) means for the Son his being from the Father, so his being sent (mission) means his being known from him. And just as for the Holy Spirit his being the gift of God means his proceeding from the Father, so his being sent means his being known to proceed from him.'[52] If the Church Father constructs an analogy between *processio* and *missio*, this can only concern their relationality qua *relations*. Saying this, the bishop of Hippo indirectly but firmly rejects the view that the *missio* would permit reasoning back to conclusions about the nature of the *processio*.

Even so, a closer consideration also clarifies that the Augustinian theology of grace does once again cast light on the conception of the relationality that characterizes analogically both the *missiones* as well as the *processiones*. Thereby it points (in a pre-Rahnerian way, one might be tempted to say) to the possibility of piercing the obscurity around the mutual relations of the inner-Trinitarian Persons by way of the connections characteristic of the mediating Trinitarian Persons. One can describe this illumination from two points of view.

## *Gratia praeveniens* marks God as *Deus ad nos* and *Deus in se*

In the quest for the ultimate motive of the incarnation of Jesus Christ, the teacher from Hippo comes to the conclusion that this can only be God's grace:

> I mean, what greater grace could have shone upon us from God, than that having his only-begotten Son, he should make him a Son of man, and thus in exchange make the Son of man into the Son of God? Look for merit there, look for a cause, look for justice; and see whether you can find anything but grace.[53]

Here, it is clear, grace acts as *gratia praeveniens*. This makes clear that the starting point of any relationship between God and man is anchored in

---

[51] E. Hill, *The Mystery of the Trinity*, London 1985, p. 89.

[52] *Trin.*, 4, 29, (CCL 50), Turnhout: Brepols 1968, p. 199 [trans: E. Hill, *Works of Saint Augustine: A Translation for the 21st Century*, I/5, New York: New City Press 1991, p. 174: Sicut enim natum esse est filio *a patre* esse, ita mitti est filio cognosci quod ab illo sit. Et sicut spiritui sancto *donum dei* esse est *a patre* procedere, ita mitti est cognosci quod ab illo procedat.

[53] *Ser.*, 185, 3, (PL 38, 999A), [trans: E. Hill, *Works of Saint Augustine: A Translation for the 21st Century*, III/6, New York: New City Press 1993, pp. 22–23]: Nam quae major gratia Dei nobis potuit illucescere, quam ut habens unigenitum Filium, faceret eum hominis filium, atque ita vicissim hominis filium faceret Dei Filium? Quaere meritum, quaere justitiam; et vide utrum invenias nisi gratiam.

God's initiative. In actual fact, of course, the very awareness of the existence of such a relationship can only be due to grace.[54] The question as to the condition of the possibility of a relationship between man and God then finds its answer in the prearrangement from above of divine activity and human receptivity.

In addition, the more Augustine has to nail down the framing of the grace question in this way against Pelagian tendencies, so much the more does its teleological content (*causa finalis*) come to the fore against the backdrop of a thought structure that had predominantly considered the causality of grace in terms of its origin (*causa efficiens*):

> Nor could we pass from being among the things that originated to eternal things, unless the eternal allied himself to us in our originated condition, and so provided us with a bridge to his eternity. (...) There you have what the Son of God has been sent for.[55]

God's economy is the unfolding of a plan that has its place in eternity, where the inner-Trinitarian relations are at home. In this sense one can indeed draw the conclusion that the purposefulness of the economy evokes the mission of the Son. In this delving into a deeper understanding of the history of salvation, one observes the characteristic construction of a bifocal view, looking at its origin (*ab eo quod*) and its purpose (*ad quod*), while according priority to the latter. There is a parallel to this, not to be overlooked, in the late Augustine's shaping of the doctrine of predestination. There too the issue of grace as *gratia praeveniens* is related both to the situation of the *initium fidei*, i.e. the origin of the God-man-relationship, and also to its goal – where the latter is strikingly of greater weight. Accordingly, the whole conception of predestination looks to the *missio* of Jesus Christ. Its significance can and must be decoded from the combination of the two directions of view (origin and goal), but in the process the persuasiveness of the analogy between Christ and every human being derives from the goal:

---

[54] Cf. the famous liminal reflection of the *Confessiones*: 'Grant me Lord to know and understand which comes first – to call upon you or to praise you, and whether knowing you precedes calling upon you. (...) You have been preached to us. My faith, Lord, calls upon you. It is your gift to me.', *Conf.*, 1, 1, 1, (CCL 27), Turnhout: Brepols 1981, p. 1 [trans. H. Chadwick, *Saint Augustine Confessions*, Oxford: Oxford University Press 1991, p. 3]: Da mihi, domine, scire et intellegere, utrum sit prius invocare te an laudare te et scire te prius sit an invocare te. (...) praedicatus enim es nobis. Invocat te, domine, fides mea, quam dedisti mihi.

[55] *Trin.*, 4, 18, 24–19, 25, (CCL 50, pp. 192–3), [trans: Hill, *Works of Saint Augustine*, pp. 170–1]: nec ab eo quod orti sumus ad aeterna transire possemus nisi aeterno per ortum nostrum nobis sociato ad aeternitatem ipsius traiceremus. (...) Ecce ad quod missus est *filius dei*.

Each human being becomes a Christian from the beginning of his faith by the same grace by which that man became Christ from his beginning. Each person is reborn by the Spirit by whom he was born. The same Spirit produced in us the forgiveness of sins who brought it about that he had no sin. God certainly foreknew that he was going to do these things. God certainly foresaw that he would do these things. This, then, is the predestination of the saints which was seen most clearly in the Holy One of all holy ones. (…)

That elevation of human nature was predestined, an elevation so great and so lofty and supreme, that it had no higher point to which it might be raised, just as the divinity itself had no point to which it might descend lower for us that than the assumed nature of man along with the weakness of the flesh up to the death of the cross. Just as, then, that one was predestined to be our head, so we many have been predestined to be his members. [56]

If we now turn from the consideration of the second Person of the Trinity to that of the role and Person of the Holy Spirit, our observations may take a parallel course. The Spirit's *missio* can take place only after the resurrection of Christ, since only then does the gift of himself actually include the effect that accords with the goal of the sending, that is, the fulfilment of the will of Christ, which was to enable human beings to be bound up with his divine nature as well. 'He wanted them (sc. the disciples), rather, to have a divine affection, and in this way to turn them from being under the spell of the flesh to being spiritual, which a person cannot become except by the gift of the Holy Spirit.'[57] It seems indeed that the identification of the goal of the *missio* and Person is realized the most clearly and closely with the Holy Spirit:

Nothing is more excellent than this gift of God. This alone is what distinguishes between the sons of the eternal kingdom and the sons of eternal

---

[56] *Praed. Sanct.*, 15,31, (PL 44, 982C–983A), [trans: R. Teske, *Works of Saint Augustine: A Translation for the 21st Century*, I/26, New York: New City Press 1999, pp. 174–5]: Ea gratia fit ab initio fidei suae homo quicumque christianus, qua gratia homo ille ab initio suo factus est Christus: de ipso Spiritu et hic renatus, de quo est ille natus; eodem Spiritu fit in nobis remissio peccatorum, quo Spiritu factum est ut nullum haberet ille peccatum. Haec se Deus esse facturum profecto praescivit. Ipsa est igitur praedestinatio sanctorum, quae in Sancto sanctorum maxime claruit. (…) Praedestinata est ista naturae humanae tanta et tam celsa et summa subvectio, ut quo attolleretur altius, non haberet, sicut pro nobis ipsa divinitas quo usque se deponeret humilius, non habuit, quam suscepta natura hominis cum infirmitate carnis usque ad mortem crucis. Sicut ergo praedestinatus est ille unus, ut caput nostrum esset: ita multi praedestinati sumus, ut membra eius essemus.

[57] *Ser.*, 270, 2, (PL 38, 1238C) [trans: Hill, *Works of Saint Augustine*, p. 289]: Volebat autem eos affectum potius habere divinum, atque ita de carnalibus facere spirituales; quod non fit homo nisi dono Spiritus Sancti.

perdition. (...) This is the reason why it is most apposite that the Holy Spirit, while being God, should also be called the gift of God. And this gift, surely, is distinctively to be understood as being the charity which brings us through to God, without which no other gift of God at all can bring us through to God.[58]

## *Gratia* clarifies the complementary-representative dimension of the teleological relationship between Son and Spirit

It has become almost commonplace to criticize the *doctor gratiae* for simply placing the Christological and the pneumatological elements of his theology of grace alongside each other with no attempt to coordinate them. A classic example would be Volker H. Drecoll's view: 'The anomaly that stands out the most in the various directions of Augustine's writings on grace is the difference between Christological argumentation on the one hand and pneumatological accentuation on the other.'[59]

It is true that the respective christocentric[60] or pneumatocentric[61] interpretations of Augustine's theology of grace should not be understood as incompatible alternatives, Basil Studer maintains, but rather as mutually complementary, against the background of the joinedness of the divine Persons in the Trinity: 'Augustine is more interested in the similarity and unity of Father, Son and Holy Spirit than in what is proper to each.'[62] This allows Studer to go so far as to recognize 'a unitarian tendency in Augustine's concept of the Trinity that carries over to the *ad extra* operations of the three divine persons.'[63]

Without overtly saying so, this claim by Basil Studer leads directly back again to the Cappadocian tradition, which in my view is a theological plus.

---

[58] *Trin.*, 15, 18, 32, (CCL 50A, pp. 507–8), [trans: Hill, *Works of Saint Augustine*, p. 421]: Nullum est isto dei dono excellentius. Solum est quod dividit inter filios regni aeterni et filios perditionis aeternae. (...) Quocirca rectissime spiritus sanctus, cum sit deus, vocatur etiam donum dei. Quod donum proprie quid nisi caritas intellegenda est quae perducit ad deum et sine qua quodlibet aliud dei donum non perducit ad deum.

[59] Cf. V. H. Drecoll, 'Gnade', in *Augustinus Lexikon*, 3/fasc. 1/2, pp. 182–241, 234. Cf. G. Philips, *L'influence du Christ-Chef sur son Corps mystique, in Augustinus Magister*. Congrès International Augustinien, Paris 21–4 septembre 1954, vol. 2, Paris: Études Augustiniennes 1954, p. 812; G. Rémy, 'La théologie de la mediation selon saint Augustin. Son actualité', in *Revue Thomiste* 91,4 (1991) 621.

[60] G. Rémy, *Le Christ médiateur dans l'oeuvre de Saint Augustin*, Paris: H. Champion 1979; G. Madec, *Le Christ de saint Augustin: la patrie et la voie*, Paris: Desclée 2001.

[61] J. J. Verhees, *God in beweging. Een onderzoek naar de pneumatologie van Augustinus*, Wageningen: H. Veenman & Zoonen 1968.

[62] B. Studer, *Augustinus. Eine Einführung*, Paderborn: Ferdinand Schönigh 2005, p. 186.

[63] Ibid, 187, comment. in *Trin.*, 4,30.

But also in my view a decisive aspect of the conceptual content of *missio* gets lost in the process. This concept serves in Augustinian thinking as well to sharpen awareness of the distinction between (a) God the Father as font of every mission and (b) God in his economic co-communication with and in the Son and Spirit. Applied to the context of grace, this means that *gratia dei* denotes the grace of God that is imparted by God and has its origin in God (the Father), but is always mediated through the Son and the Spirit. To speak of a *gratia patris*, thus isolating the gift of grace from the mediating missions of the Son and the Holy Spirit, is in my opinion imprecise and in the end misleading.

In this respect I hold that it is much more in line with Augustinian theology to bring out the complementarity in the transmitting of grace that the missions of the second and third Persons display. What does it mean, this phenomenon in Augustine's writings of naming the 'agents of the mediation of grace' separately, now Christ and another time the Holy Spirit? It actually points to a structural characteristic of grace itself that blocks a one-sided Christological or pneumatological reading: Grace, in so far as it is *gratia praeveniens*, is also *gratia pro-veniens*, i.e. it is existentially both *for* (Latin: *pro*) someone other and *in place of* (Latin also: *pro*) another, aiming at the goal of divine-human unification.

Numerous passages in the Augustinian corpus document this twofold *pro* dimension of the *gratia Christi* in relation to the human being. The Son takes the place of the human being where man has become incapable of acting in accordance with the final goal in view. In line with this same principle he then gives his own divine being to the being of man. In the form of sacrifice, being-existentially-*for* becomes reality:

> Why be surprised that Christ died, although Christ committed no sin whatsoever? He wanted to pay back for you what he didn't owe himself, in order to deliver you from debt. (...) The Lord, the only-begotten Word, took on for you what he would offer for you. But he took it on for you from nowhere else but from you, because he did not have in himself anything to die for you with. You didn't have anything to live by, and he didn't have anything to die with. What a marvellous exchange! Live by what is his, because he died with what is yours.[64]

---

[64] *Ser.*, 265D (= *s. Morin* 17), pp. 4–7, *Miscellanea agostiniana,* Rom: Polyglottis Vaticanis 1930, pp. 661, 664 [trans: Hill, *Works of Saint Augustine: A Translation for the 21st Century,* III/7, New York: New City Press 1993, p. 289]: Quid mararis quia mortuus est Christus, cum omnino non peccaverti Christus? Reddere pro te voluit quod non debebat, ut te a debito liberaret. (...) Dominus autem, unigenitum Verbum, assumpsit pro te, quod offerret pro te. Assumpsi autem pro te, non nisi ex te : quia unde moreretur pro te, non habebat in se. Nec tu habebas unde viveres, nec ille unde moreretur. O magna mutatio! Vive de ipsius, quia de tuo mortuus est.

What I might call the 'pro-existential principle,' that manifests itself in the gift of grace, since it takes the place of the other, comes into play in the very salvation-history relation of Son and Spirit:

> What He (namely Jesus Christ) is saying is this: 'I am sending you a gift which will make you spiritual, the gift, that is, of the Holy Spirit. But you cannot become spiritual unless you stop being spellbound by the flesh. Now you will stop being under the spell of the flesh, if the form of flesh is removed from your eyes, so that the form of God may be inserted in your hearts".[65]

It seems possible to me to construct an arc from the pro-existential dimension of the imparting of grace in the economy of salvation (which connects the Son with the Spirit) to the Augustinian theology of the immanent relationship between Son and Spirit. After all, Augustine does see the basis for the pro-existential action on the part of the Son and the Spirit (the *missiones*) in the inner-Trinitarian relationship between Father and Son, Father and Spirit:

> – 'The reason why the Son is said to have been sent by the Father is simply that the one is the Father and the other the Son.'[66]
> – 'Being the gift of God means the Holy Spirit's proceeding from the Father, as being sent means his being known to proceed from him'[67]

In the end, this pro-existential principle for designating within the economy the relation of the Son with the Holy Spirit leads to the well-known inference, 'We have found that the Holy Spirit also proceeds from the Son.'[68] In the very generation of the Son, the Son receives from the Father the pro-existential being. Basically, it is impossible in the framework of Augustinian thinking to suppose that this 'for,' this 'being in place of' that the Son has received from the Father, does not bear also on the inner-Trinitarian relation of the Son to the Spirit:

---

[65] *Ser.*, 270, 2, (PL 38, 1238C), [trans: Hill, *Works of Saint Augustine*, p.289]: Hoc ergo ait: Mitto vobis donum, quo efficiamini spirituales; donum scilicet Spiritus sancti. Spirituales autem fieri non poteritis, nisi carnales esse destiteritis. Carnales vero esse desistetis, si forma carnis a vestries oculis auferatur, ut forma Dei vestries cordibus inseratur.

[66] *Trin.*, 4, 20, 27, (CCL 50, p. 195), [trans: Hill, *Works of Saint Augustine*, p. 172]: Secundum hoc missus *a patre* filius dicitur quia ille pater est, ille filius.

[67] *Trin.*, 4, 20, 29, (CCL 50, p. 199), [trans: Hill, p. 174]: Spiritui sancto *donum dei* esse est *a patre* procedere, ita mitti est cognosci quod ab illo procedat.

[68] *Trin.*, 15, 17, 29, (CCL 50A, p. 503), [trans: Hill, p. 419]: et de filio spiritus sanctus procedere reperitur.

It is not without point that in this triade only the Son is called the Word of God, and only the Holy Spirit is called the gift of God, and only the Father is called the one from whom the Word is born and from whom the Holy Spirit principally proceeds. I added 'principally' because we have found that the Holy Spirit also proceeds from the Son. But this too was given the Son by the Father (not given to him when he already existed and did not yet have it), but whatever the Father gave to his only-begotten Word he gave by begetting him. He so begot him then that their common gift would proceed from him too.[69]

# The Dynamization in Maximus of the Biblical-Patristic Fundamental Position

With Maximus the Confessor we come to an author whose theological legacy, a 'highpoint of patristic thought,'[70] is distinguished by its function of synthesis.[71] This quality makes it especially appealing to turn to his thinking in respect to our theme. One may legitimately hypothesize that Maximus would take up and work out in exemplary fashion the basic patristic concern that the Cappadocians problematized: the relation of *theologia* and *oikonomia*. If so, his work would lend itself most helpfully to a confrontation with Karl Rahner's thesis.

In fact it is not difficult to retrieve that 'dynamization of the basic Cappadocian framing of the question' that we have already discovered in Augustine, only now in the form of epistemological-metaphysical principles of a more developed cast. Once more the conception of grace – the Augustinian *gratia* will appear here centrally in its eastern formulation as divinization (*theosis*) – will be the key criterion. By this means the Rahnerian Fundamental Axiom receives support in its profound intuition, while at the same time, more clearly than in the reflection on Augustine, its limitation becomes obvious.

---

[69] Ibid, pp. 503–4: Et tamen non frustra in hace trinitate non dicitur verbum dei nisi filius, nec donum dei nisi spiritus sanctus, nec de quo genitum est verbum et de quo procedit principaliter spiritus sanctus nisi deus pater. Ideo autem addidi, principaliter, quia et de filio spiritus sanctus procedere reperitur. Sed hoc quoque illi pater dedit (non iam exsistenti et non dum habenti), sed quidquid unigenito verbo dedit gignendo dedit. Sic ergo eum genuit ut etiam de illo donum commune procederet.

[70] A. Grillmeier, *Le Christ dans la tradition chrétienne*, II, 1, *Le Concile de Chalcédoine (451) Réception et opposition (451–513)*, (Cogitatio Fidei, 154), Paris: Cerf 1990, p. 31.

[71] Cf. P. G. Renczes, *L'agir de Dieu et liberté de l'homme*, (Cogitatio Fidei, 229), Paris: Cerf 2003, pp. 13–18.

# The Dialectic of 'Being' and 'Having' as expression of apophatic-cataphatic communication in the Trinitarian God.

Building on the thought of the Cappadocians and of Dionysius the Areopagite, Maximus works with a layered meaning of apophatic theology that is derived ultimately from a fundamental distinction. On the one hand, *apophasis* means a definitive rejection of any claim to grasp God himself in discourse. On the other, it is a method of knowing that aims at a dynamic progress in knowledge through dialectical interaction with the *kataphasis* that corresponds to it. Apophasis, therefore, serves to avoid agnosticism and anthropomorphism.

In the final analysis, the first, radical, sense of speechlessness (apophasis) can only be asserted as a basic principle asymptotically. It must nevertheless always be at work, according to Maximus, for otherwise you will fall into some kind of rationalism as soon as you make any statements at all about God:

> We are speechless before the sublime teaching about the Logos, for He cannot be expressed in words or conceived in thought. Although he is beyond being and nothing can participate in him in any way, nor is he any of the totality of things that can be known in relation to other things, nevertheless we affirm that the one Logos is many *logoi* and the many *logoi* are One.[72]

And the Confessor goes on to develop a cosmology of the *logoi*. On the basis of a synoptic reading of John's Logos-Christology (John 1:1) and Paul's Logos-Creation theology (Col 1:15–16), he portrays the *logoi* as created bearers of divine ideas to which God through creation and providence imparts his intentions. In particular God invites man to learn how to know and implement these goals by reason of their connection with the second Person of the Trinity, in a dynamic process of interchange of faith and reason. Against this background, apophasis in its second meaning serves to articulate the ontological link of the created with the uncreated in the interchange with the cataphatic mode. In other words: all Godtalk, limited as it always necessarily is by the infinite mysteriousness of God

---

[72] *Amb. Io.*, 7, (PG 91, 1081C), [trans: P. Blowers, R. Wilkens, *On the Cosmic Mystery of Jesus Christ. Selected Writings by Maximus the Confessor,* Crestwood: St. Vladimir's Seminary Press 2003, p. 57]: Ὑπεξηρημένης οὖν τῆς ἄκρας καὶ ἀποφατικῆς τοῦ λόγου θεολογίας, καθ᾽ ἣν οὔτε λέγεται, οὔτε νοεῖται, οὔτεἔστι τὸ σύνολόν τι τῶν ἄλλῳ συνεγνωσμένων, ὡς ὑπερούσιος οὐδὲ ὑπό τινος οὐδαμῶς καθ᾽ ὁτιοῦν μετέχεται,πολλοὶ λόγοι ὁ εἷς λόγοςἐστι, καὶ εἷς οἱ πολλοί.

(apophasis in its first meaning), structures itself ontologically in the ongoing dialectic of kataphasis and apophasis (here in its second meaning):

> But if it is possible for man, in a wonderful way superior to his nature, in the course of this life to achieve the highest measure of virtue and knowledge and wisdom and to obtain thus the knowledge of divine realities, then all this is realized in form of type (sc. cataphatic) and the image of archetypes (sc. apophatic). In fact, every truth that we now hold as such is type, and at the same time it is shadow and image of the Higher Logos. This Logos, the creator of the everything, is present in everyone, in so far one's present and future is concerned; he is considered in type and in truth, and as such he is and appears, because he is beyond the present and future of type and of truth, to the extent that there is nothing opposed to him, and that nothing alongside him can be considered.[73]

Here we have the Cappadocian division of the inaccessible *Deus in se* from the revealed *Deus ad nos* translated into a more precise fixing of the relationship. We can make no statements at all about the transcendent God himself. Even the label 'Theologia' as logical-ontological designation of the '*Deus in se*' halts before or below the absolute transcendence of God, and this is all the more the case in regard to the conceptuality of the 'immanent Trinity' expressed in dogma.

What is more: even the revealed *Deus ad nos* of the economy remains mysterious, anything but comprehensively intelligible, and is only approachable in the combination of the cataphatic and the apophatic. That the human being can, nevertheless, approach God with the help of the cataphatic and the apophatic is due in the last analysis only because of the initiative of God, God who as mystery does not keep a passive-uninterested distance from man, but condescends to human being: the divine Logos that embraces the human '*ratio*', and in an intriguing interplay of concealing and revealing, furnishes it with orientation in the experience of reality:

> In an ineffable way (sc. the Logos), for our sake, hid himself in the *logoi* of things and according to analogy is shown by every visible thing, as if it were a letter to be interpreted: (the Logos) remains completely whole in

---

[73] *Amb. Io.*, 37, (PG 91, 1296C), [trans: Renczes]: Ὡς δ' ἂν ὑπερφυῶς τε καὶ ὑψηλῶς δυνατόν ἐστι κατα τὸν αἰῶνα τοῦτον τῷ ἀνθρώπῳ τὸ ἀκρότατον φθάσαντεςμέτρον τῆς ἀρητῆς καὶ τῆς γνώσεως καὶ τῆς σο'ας περιγενέσθαι τὴντῶν θείων ἐπιστήμην, ἐν τύπῳ καὶ εἰκόνι τῶν ἀρχετύπων ἐστί. Τύπος γάρ ἐστιν ὡς ἀληθῶς πᾶσα παρ' ἡμῶν νυ῀ν εἶναι νομιζομένη ἀλήθεια, καὶ σκιὰ τοῦ μείζονος λόγου καὶ εἰκών. Ὁ ἐν ὅλοις κατὰ τὸ παρὸν πρὸς τὸ μέλλον καὶ τῶν ὅλων ποιητικὸς λόγος κατανοούμενος ἐστιν ὡς ἐν τύπῳ καὶ ἀληθείᾳ, καὶ ὦν καὶ φαινόμενος, ὡς ὑπὲρ τὸ παρὸν καὶ τὸ μέλλον ὦν, και, ὑπὲρ τύπον καὶ ἀλήθειαν, τῷ μηδὲν ἔχειν ἀντικείμενον συνθεωρούμενον.

his fullness in the totality of things and complete, found as fully integral and not diminished in singular things, because it is unchangeable and always the same in the changeable things, simple and not composed in the composed things, without beginning in the things subject to a beginning, the invisible in the visible, the intangible in the tangible. For our sake He accepted to become flesh and to be expressed with letters, syllables and voices, so that as a consequence of all this He would little by little reunite us to himself inasmuch we follow Him, unified in the Spirit, having been led to ascend to the simple notion concerning Him that is without relation to anything, just as much as he spread himself out to us because of His compassion for us, we will contract ourselves in union with Him.[74]

Thus Maximus actually finds the definitive guarantee for the union of transcendence and contingency not in creation, but in the mystery of the incarnation of the eternal Logos in history. The incarnation, though ultimately withdrawn apophatically from any rational purchase, has become ontological reality and thereby the foundation of any and all kataphasis as the fulfilled condition of its possibility.

The incarnation provides a definitive clarification for two factors that condition created being. Their explanation uncovers also the paradoxical relationship between them, and shows that they represent an application of the multi-layeredness of the concept of apophasis that we alluded to above:

1　Any divinization of created being, as it took place in principle in the incarnation of Jesus Christ, is not explainable naturally. Divinization is a new state of 'being,' to which a new 'having' corresponds, that is only ascribable to God's action:

It is not possible that divinization is realized according to the potential of things that belong to us naturally; in fact, divinization does not belong to the things that depend on us. Effectively there is no principle in our nature that is supernatural: divinization, of which we do not possess the

---

[74] *Amb. Io.*, 33, *(PG 91, 1285D–1288A), [trans: Renczes]:* τοῖς τῶν ὄντων ἑαυτὸν δι᾽ ἑκάστου τῶν ὁρωμένων ὡς διά τινων γραμμάτων ὑποσημαίνεται, ὅλος ἐν ὅλοις ἅμα πληρέστατος, καὶ τὸ καθ᾽ ἕκαστον ὁλόκληρος, ὅλος καὶ ἀνελάττωτος, ἐν τοῖ˜ς διαφόροις ὁ ἀδιάφορος καὶ ὡσαύτως ἀεὶ ἔχων, ἐν τοῖς συνθέτοις ὁ ἁπλοῦς καὶ ἀσύνθετος, καὶ ἐν τοῖς ὑπὸ ἀρχὴν ὁ ἄναρχος, καὶ ὁ ἀόρατος ἐν τοῖς ὁρωμένοις, καὶ τοῖς ἁπτοῖς ὁ ἀναφής· ἢ ὅτι δι᾽ ἡμᾶς, τοὺς παχεῖς τὴν διάνοιαν, σωματωθῆναί τε δι᾽ ἡμᾶς καὶ γράμμασι καὶ συλλαβαῖς καὶ φωναῖς τυπωθῆναι κατεδέξαντο, ἵνα ἐκ πάντων τούτων ἡμᾶς ἑπομένους αὐτῷ κατὰ βραχὺ πρὸς ἑαυτὸν συναγάγῃ, ἑνοποιηθέντας τῷ πνεύματι, και, εἰς τὴν ἁπλῆν περὶ αὐτοῦ καὶ ἄσχετον ἔννοιαν ἀναγάγοι, τοσοῦ˜τον ἡμᾶς δι᾽ ἑαυτὸν πρὸς ἕνωσιν ἑαυτοῦ συστείλας, ὅσον αὐτὸς δι᾽ ἡμᾶ˜ς ἑαυτὸν συγκαταβάσεως λόγῳ διέστειλεν.

potential according to our nature, is therefore not an actualization of our potential, but only of divine power.[75]

2   This receptive 'having' in the creaturely 'being,' however, adapts itself in such a way that the 'being' can be understood not just as (an active) realization of (a passive) potency, as an Aristotelian notion of being would have it; beyond that it also includes a form of (active-passive) self-surpassing of one's own being. This derives not exclusively, but yet also, from one's own being, given that divinization never comes to pass against or without the natural being. Consequently creaturely being in its dynamic is no longer expressible in the bipolar schema of potency and act, but must be described generally in a triple dimensionality of being:

Those who try to seek to understand divine things say that there are three ways (namely of being): One observes that the whole reason of the entire origins of rational beings comprehends the reason of 'being', that of 'being-well' and that of 'being-always'. The first reason of 'being' is given to all beings according essence, the second, that of 'being-well' is given to all that move by self spontaneity according to free choice and the third reason, that of 'being-always' is conferred by grace; and they say that the first reason contains the potential, the second the operation, and the third the rest. The reason of 'being', which by nature possesses only the potential towards actualization absolutely cannot possess this same actualization in its fullness outside of free choice; the reason of 'being-well', which possesses only the actualization of the natural potential at the level of its free choice, absolutely cannot possess this potential in its fullness outside of nature; and that of 'being-always', which completely circumscribes that which is before it, that is, the potential of the first (reason) and the actualization of the second (reason), absolutely does not exist by nature according to the potential in the beings, nor does it follow at all the necessity of the will of free choice.[76]

---

[75] *Th. Pol.*, 1, (PG 91, 33C), [trans: Renczes]: Οὐκ ἔστι δὲ τω ̔ν παρ᾿ ἡμῶν κατὰ δύναμιν γίνεσθαι πεφυκότων ἡ θέωσί, οὐκ οὖσα τῶν ἐφ᾿ ἡμῖν· οὐδεὶς γὰρ ἐν τῇ φύσει, τῶν ὑπὲρ φύσιν λόγος.῎Αρα τῆς ἡμῶν οὐκ ἔστι δυνάμεως πρᾶξι, ἡ θέωσις ἧς οὐκ ἔχομεν κατὰ φύσιν τὴν δύναμιν· ἀλλὰ μόνης τῆς θεία ̈ δυνάμεως

[76] *Amb. Io.*, 65, (PG 91, 1392A–B), [trans: Renczes]: Τρεῖς γάρ φασι τρόπους οἱ τῶν θείων ἐπιστήμονες.῾Οσύμπας τῆς ὅλης τῶν λογικῶν οὐσιῶν γενέσεως ἔχων θεωρεῖται ο λόγος τὸν τοῦ εἶ ναι, τὸν του ̔ εὖ εἶναι, καὶ τὸν τοῦ ἀεὶ εἶναι, καὶ τὸν μὲν τοῦ εἶναι πρῶτον κατ᾿ οὐσίαν δεδωρῆσθαι τοῖς οὖσι, τὸν δὲ τοῦ εἶναι δεύτερον δεδόσθαι κατὰ προαίρεσιν αὐτοῖς ὡς αὐτοκινήτοις, τὸν δὲ τοῦ ἀεὶ εἶναι τρίτον αὐτοῖς κατὰ χάριν πεφιλοτιμῆσθαι. Καὶ τὸν μὲν πρῶτον δυνάμεως, τὸν δὲ δεύτερον ἐνεργείας, τὸν δὲ τρίτον ἀργίας εἶναι περιεκτικόν. Οἶον ὁ μὲν του ̔ εἶναι λόγος μόνη φυσικῶς ἔχων τὴν πρὸς ἐνέργειαν δύναμιν, αὐτὴν πληρεστάτην δίχα τη ̔ς προαιρέσεως τὴν ἐνέρ- γειαν ἔχειν οὐ δύναται παντελῶς· ὁ δὲ τοῦ εὖ εἶναι αὐτὴν μόνην γνωμικῶς ἔχων τῆς τῆς φυσικῆς

To put it another way, in the economy of salvation man receives a new divine being (apophatic), toward which his own dynamic being naturally tends (cataphatic): a miraculous supernatural transaction that turns out to be congenial, since it lights upon a basic receptivity on the part of human nature to be transcended by divine grace.

Two principles are here finally discerned, which can contribute positively to a greater precision of the Fundamental Axiom of Rahnerian provenance:

a) Economic Trinity is *not* simply the same as Immanent Trinity and vice versa; instead the Economic Trinity shows itself in the human being transformed by grace as the Immanent Trinity, and vice versa.

Like Dionysius the Areopagite, Maximus displays a considerable reserve, as we have just seen, towards all statements about God that deal with what He is:

The divine, in fact, cannot be comprehended through any word or thought, so that not even when we predicate of it that it *is*, do we affirm its *being-itself*. Being, in fact, comes from God, but God is not being. In fact He is above being itself, and beyond anything that is said or conceived, in a specific or simple way.[77]

Of course, Rahner's Fundamental Axiom presupposes an analogy of being, but that does not seem sufficient to clear up the reservations of Maximus (which admittedly can only have an '*ante-litteram*-status') to its formulation. After all, it aims at identification of Economic and Immanent Trinity in *being*. According to Maximus, being as such, when it comes to God, is only expressible in terms of the economy, that is, in the realm of the relation of God to the created world. To be sure, cases of surmounting the economic Trinity to find hints or traces of the beyond can be discovered *in the human being* qua object of divine grace. Maximus even expresses this with a pointedness that the Fundamental Axiom itself does not dare to put in words:

They say that God and man are examples one for the other and that as much God made himself human because of his love for man, so is

---

δυνάμεως τὴν ἐνέργειαν, αὐτὴν ὁλόκληρον τὴν δύναμιν τὸ σύνολον χωρὶς οὐκ ἔχει τῆς φύσεως· ὁ δὲ τοῦ ἀεὶεἶναι τῶν πρὸ αὐτοῦ καθ'ὅλου περιγράφων, τοῦ μὲν τὴν δύναμιν, του˜ δὲ τὴν ἐνέργειαν, οὔτε φυσικω˜ς κατὰ δύναμιν τοι˜ς οὖσιν ἐνυπάρχει παντελω˜ς, οὔτε μὴν ἐξάναγκης τὸ παράπαν θελήσει προαιρέσεως ἕπεται.

[77] *Amb. Io.*, 10, (PG 91, 1180D), [trans: Renczes]: Ἀνεπίδεκτον γὰρ παντὸς λόγου καὶ νοήματος τὸ Θεῖόν ἐστι, καθ'ὃ οὔτε κατηγοροῦντες αὐτοῦ τοῦ εἶναι λέγομεν αὐτὸ εἶναι. Ὑπὲρ γάρ ἐστι καὶ αὐτοῦ τοῦ εἶναι, τοῦ τε πῶς καὶ ἁπλῶς λεγομένου τε καὶ νοουμένου.

man made capable by God to be divinized in love. Again they say that man accesses, thanks to God, knowledge of the unknown as much as he (namely man) manifests God, who is invisible, by means of his virtues.[78]

At the level of being, what can be juxtaposed is actually not that between God's being (Cappadocians: οὐσία) and God's action (ἐνέργεια), which according to Maximus are both ultimately simple and coincide with one another. The two terms that allow for approximation are on the one hand man's being as formed through the action of God and on the other God's (inner) Trinitarian Self, in so far it is accessible to the human logos. For God lets himself be known because and to the extent that He has transformed, is transforming and will transform the human being. Hence all statements about God must be understood as the effect of a dynamic in the economy of salvation of the human being, clearly all a matter of God's gracious initiative. Certainly, this dynamic is not God in His transcendence, even if it shows Him effectively. One might almost say: the divinized human being is mediator between Economic and Immanent Trinity.

Does Maximus go beyond Augustine? First of all, it seems that – not unlike Augustine – the Confessor's main point was to keep the principle of grace consistently in mind (and not to defend the superiority of negative theology over affirmative theology, as is often claimed).[79] All the same, it is appropriate to notice the advance over Augustine that is perceptible in respect of the greater clarity with which the difference from the Rahnerian formulation stands out. This difference can be described as both limitation and expansion of the Fundamental Axiom: limitation, in that the human being cannot claim to be able to know the Economic and the Immanent Trinity in the dynamic relation of one to the other (not to mention the relation between the divine work and the divine being), but only as it offers itself to man as gift. Only in accord with and by means of grace does the Immanent Trinity bestow itself in the Economic Trinity and vice versa.

At the same time the Fundamental Axiom undergoes in Maximus a decisive extension, in so far as man himself in this grace-filled process of giving and receiving is expressly drawn in as active partner. It is not only the

---

[78] *Amb. Io.*, 10, (PG 91, 1113B-C), [trans: Renczes]: Φασὶ γὰρ ἀλλήλων εἶναι παραδείγματα τὸν Θεὸν καὶ τὸν Θεὸν καὶ τὸν ἄνθρωπον, καὶ τοσοῦτον τῷˏ ἀνθρώπῳ τὸν Θεὸν διὰ ˋλανθρωπίαν ἀνθρωπίζεσθαι, ὅσον ὁ ἄνθρωπος ἑαυτὸν τῷ Θεῷ δι᾽ ἀγάπης δυνηθεὶς ἀπεθέωσε, καὶ τοσοῦτον ὑπὸ Θεοῦ τὸν ἄνθρωπον κατὰ νοῦν ἁρπάζεσθαι πρὸς τὸ γνωστόν, ὅσον ὁ ἄνθρωπος τὸν ἀόρατον φύσει Θεὸν διὰ τωˏˋν ἀρετῶν ἐφανέρωσεν.

[79] Dirk Westerkamp, to be sure, is of the opinion that 'the movement of knowing implies in its interminability the continuing priority of negative theology,' in *Via Negativa. Sprache und Methode der negativen Theologie,* (München: Wilhelm Fink 2006, p. 44. I believe that I have shown contrariwise that in terms of method, i.e. for Maximus at the level of being, there always exists for the Confessor a dialectic in the strict sense between apophasis and kataphasis, allowing neither of the poles to claim a preeminence.

case that the Economic Trinity bestows itself by grace as Immanent Trinity and hence also the other way around, but according to the Confessor it is also true that God enables human beings to show Him, the Economic Trinity, as Immanent Trinity – in this and in the reverse relationship to each other:

> But who transgresses the natural contemplation, having left behind all which is caused, in order to reach out for the Cause itself by means of apophatic theology, has died to his previous state, since he no longer moves in the realm of created things, but has directed his movement towards the Creator of everything. He (namely Jesus Christ) now says about death, which (i.e. before this new state) meant the negation of everything, that 'they will not taste it' (Mark 9:1), i.e. all those who are on a par with the apostles in regard to virtue, will not suffer death before the transfigured Lord will reveal himself, not more as one, by which something is affirmed through a positive statement in regards to his being, but as one who shows the concealment of the inaccessible divinity through negative theology. [80]

b) Immanent Trinity is not identifiable with Economic Trinity as such, but the logic of finality is the same in the proportion that is revealed of the Immanent to the Economic Trinity: the logic of truth and love.

Maximus is aware of the danger that the divine and human realms of being might go separate ways as a result of the Cappadocian distinction between οὐσία and ἐνέργεια. The end result might well be the subjection of the history of salvation to a metaphysics reminiscent of the Aristotelian 'unmoved mover'. In his view, the incarnation definitively opened up the ontological perspective of a valid distinction between God's transcendental essence and his historical revelation, but not in a backward-looking sense, that would challenge the essential difference between man and the Creator God. Rather, the incarnation frees up a forward-looking glance to uncover God's intentionality, correlating both God's self and his communication with creation which comes about dynamically – until the eschatological realization of their union:

---

[80] *Qu. D.*, 190, (CCSG 10), Turnhout: Brepols 1982, p. 182 [trans: Renczes]: ἀλλὰ καὶ ὁ περάσας τὴν φυσικὴν θεωρίαν καὶ πάντα τὰ αἰτιατὰ καταλιπὼν καὶ εἰς τὸν αἴτιον ἐλθὼν διὰ τῆς θεολογικῆ˜ς ἀποφάσεως, καί, οὗτος ἔθανεν τῇ προτέρᾳ καταστάσει, μηκέτι ἐν τοῖς πεποιημένοις κινούμενός ἀλλ᾽ ἐν τῷ ποιητῇ τῶν ὅλων μεταβιβάσας τὴν κίνησιν - περὶ οὖν τοῦ κατὰ ἀφαίρεσιν πάντων γινομένου θανάτου λέγει ὅτι οὐ μὴ γεύσονται αὐτου, τουτέστιν οὐ μὴ πάθωσιν αὐτὸν οἱ τῶν ἀποστόλων κατ᾽ ἀρετὴν ἰσοστάσιοι, ἕως οὗ μεταμορφωθεὶς ὁ κύριος παραδείξει ἑαυτὸν μηκέτι καταφασκόμενον ἐκ τῆς τῶν ὄντων θέσεως, ἀλλὰ τῇ κατὰ ἀπόφασιν θεολογίᾳ παραδεικνὺς τὸ ἀπρόσιτον τῆς θεότητος κρύφον.

The divine apostle Paul says that we do not know the Word but in part. Yet, the great evangelist John claims to have seen his glory: 'We have seen his glory' he says 'the glory as of the Father's only Son, full of grace and truth.' How is it then that Paul says he has never known the Word of God, if only in part?

The Word is only known, somehow, from its activity. For knowledge of the Word from his essence and hypostasis is inaccessible to angels and men alike, and nobody is in possession of this knowledge, whatsoever. But St John having been introduced to the accomplished reason of the Incarnation of the Word dwelling among men, declares that he has seen the glory of the Word in the Flesh, that is to say, he contemplated the reason, that is the goal because of which God became man, full of grace and truth. For the Son was not filled with grace in his divine nature, being consubstantial with the Father, but because He took the nature of man in the economy and he was made consubstantial with us. He became full of grace for us who are in need of grace, so that we can continuously receive the same grace from his completeness, in correspondence to our progress.[81]

This soteriological perspective of the Confessor shifts the teleological dimension of the relationship of God and man into the centre of theological investigation. It suggests a curious corollary, one last thing that needs to be addressed. The modern criticism of Rahner's Fundamental Axiom for the most part zeroes in on the vice versa of the formula, relying therefore on the ultimately philosophical difficulty of trying to derive the particular (the Economy of salvation) from the universal (the Transcendent God). By contrast, the underlying thrust of the argumentation in the case of Maximus goes right in the opposite direction: in actuality only the *Logic* of the *Deus in se* makes sense of revelation for us. To put it another way: a *theological* verification of the Fundamental Axiom takes place only in the vice versa that has its origin unequivocally in the initiative of the Immanent Trinity.

---

[81] *Th. Oec.*, II, 76, (PG 90, 1160C–1161A), [trans: Renczes]: Ο μὲν θεῖος Ἀπόστολος Παῦλος, τὴν τοῦ Λόγου γνῶσιν, ἐκ μέρους ἔφη γινώσκειν. Ὁ δὲ μέγας εὐαγγελιστὴς Ἰωάννης τεθεᾶσθαι λέγει τὴν αὐτοῦ δόξαν. Ἐθεασάμεθα γὰρ, φησὶν, τὴν δόξαν αὐτοῦ, δόξαν ὡς Μονογενοῦς παρὰ Πατρὸς, πλήρης χάριτος καὶ ἀληθείας.Καὶ μήποτε ὁ μὲν ἅγιος Παῦλος τὴν ὡς Θεοῦ Λόγου γνῶσιν ἐκ μέρους ἔφη γινώκειν. Ἐκ γὰρ τῶν ἐνεργειῶν, ποσῶς μόνον γινώσκεται. Ἡ γὰρ ἐπ᾽ αὐτῷ κατ᾽ οὐσίαν τε καὶ ὑπόστασιν γνῶσις, ὁμοίως πᾶσιν ἀγγέλοις τε καὶ ἀνθρώποις, καθέστηκεν ἄβατος, κατ᾽ οὐδὲν οὐδενὶ γινωσκομένη· ὁ δὲ ἅγιος Ἰωάννης, τελειονὼς ἐν ἀνθρώποις, τὸν τῆς ἐνανθρωπήσεως τοῦ Λόγου μυηθεὶς λόγον, τὴν ὡς σάρκα Λόγου δόξαν ἔφη τεθεᾶσθαι· τουτέστι, τὸν λόγον, ἤγουν τὸν σκοπόν, καθ᾽ ὃν ὁ Θεός γέγονεν ἄνθρωπος, πλήρη χάριτος ἐθεάσατο, καὶ ἀληθείας. Οὐ γὰρ καθ᾽ ὃ κατ᾽ οὐσίαν Θεὸς, καὶ τῷ Θεῷ Πατρὶ ὁμοούσιος ὁ Μονογενὴς κεχαρίτωται, ἀλλὰ καθ᾽ ὃ φύσει κατ᾽ οἰκονομίαν γέγονεν, ἄνθρωπος καὶ ἡμῖν ὁμοούσιος, δι᾽ ἡμᾶς καχαρίτωται τοὺς χρήζοντας χάριτος· καὶ ἐκ τοῦ πληρώματος αὐτοῦ διαπαντὸς κατὰ πᾶσαν ἡμῶν προκοπὴν τὴν ἀναλογοῦσαν δεχομένους χάριν.

Therefore the correspondence of the thesis set forth in the first clause of the Fundamental Axiom with the reality, that is the truth, of the agreement of the Economic with the Immanent Trinity, can, in the perspective of the Confessor, only be the object of amazed acceptance and hence remains outside the realm of the verifiable.

# Conclusion

The initial hypothesis of this research was that too great a distance between historical and systematic theology affected the original presentation of the Fundamental Axiom itself, but also its critical reception in the intervening years. In the course of subsequent reflections, it turned out that Karl Rahner's intuitive association of his thesis with Greek thought proved simultaneously true and false, while his polarization with respect to Augustinian theology has not held up. Even though these historical inexactitudes affect theology down to the present day, what seems to be a great deal more significant at the end of this investigation is the discovery of a remarkably vital antecedent re-confirmation on the part of patristic theology of an important preoccupation of the Fundamental Axiom, namely the grounding of the claim of a foundational connection of the doctrines of the Trinity and of grace. It is puzzling, to say the least, to realize that the Fundamental Axiom itself has stayed put almost entirely within treatments of the doctrine of God, while Karl Rahner's theology of grace, at least as utilized by other theologians, serves primarily for philosophical-anthropological reflection. The Cappadocians, and particularly Augustine and Maximus, give testimony of a theological anthropology which takes seriously the conviction that Trinity and humankind have entered into a union such that soteriology becomes doxology (Walter Kasper), but doxology of the Trinitarian God is also, in fact, an eschatological feast for all who are invited.

# 12

# Trinity and Understanding: Hermeneutic Insights

## Andrzej Wiercinski

## Understanding Differently: Shrouded in the Mystery

One of the fundamental hermeneutic insights of the Trinity is the possibility of experiencing God in *different* ways. Thinking about the Trinity helps us to glimpse the meaning of God the Father, Son and Holy Spirit and their communitarian interest (in the deepest sense of *inter-esse*) in transforming their inner-Trinitarian life and the history of creation into the universal history of salvation. Laden with mystery, Trinity clearly endorses the plurivocity of meaning and therefore calls for multiple interpretations. Since the triune God manifests himself to his creature, it means that he wants to be understood in his inner-Trinitarian life. In a powerful dialectic of question and answer, we can experience a profound divine logic, which can be seen in the history of Christian dogmatics. This history can be symbolically described as a movement towards the condensation of meaning, which in turn calls for decondensation in order to grasp the multiplicity of the possible perspectives to be recapitulated again in the form of a condensed singular interpretation. Welcoming this circularity and clearly endorsing the plurivocity of meaning, hermeneutics presents itself as a philosophical reflection not only on what needs to be understood, but on the understanding of understanding. It is a philosophical deliberation on what is happening to us when we understand. Any theological reflection cannot escape the hermeneutic circle between the Biblical revelation and the context in which this revelation originally came to life and still comes to life in being interpreted. The understanding of the Trinity is the privileged subject of theological hermeneutics, since it thematizes the tension between unity and diversity, the One and the Many as revealed in the mystery of the divine inner life of the infinite omniscient Creator.

This disclosure contains an infinite depth, which corresponds to God's infinite mind. As such, it is an invitation to the infinite task of interpretation. Since the Bible is an infinite revelation, it opens up a horizon of infinite possibilities for understanding. Theological hermeneutics fully embraces those infinite possibilities for interpretation, while understanding the Christian life as a living response to the living God. In that hermeneutic horizon we situate ourselves as the participants in a conversation in which we not only engage the other in order to be understood but allow the subject matter, in this case Scripture, to raise questions. We can go even further by saying that in that non-methodological disclosure of divine truth we allow Scripture to question us. In our hermeneutic gesture of openness we accept the divine claim to validity and the fact that this disclosure has something to say to us with many possible consequences, including the free recognition of the imperative to change our lives. If to understand a question means to ask it, we need to encounter the mystery of the Trinity in the context of being questioned by God, who in his eschatological-historical self-disclosure as the Trinity invites us to participate in a conversation, which is His own mode of being.

# The Inner Life of the Trinity as a Mode of Understanding: The Interpenetration of Invocation and Donation of the Holy Spirit

God's self-manifestation in the events of Incarnation and the Pentecost recapitulates the revelation of the inner-Trinitarian mystery. Our deepening awareness of the Holy Spirit within ourselves enables us to see things differently, to understand differently, to remember that what needs to be comprehended is not a historical record of God's self-revelation, but a living reality. By understanding that God speaks to each one of us directly, we confirm that our belief and faith in God make this experience a reality. The Holy Spirit is the outpouring of a plenitude of love from the Trinity. This outpouring does not diminish the plentitude; on the contrary, the *processio* out of the Trinity is grounded in the inner-Trinitarian passage from the one to the other and from the two to the one. This processual explanation of the Holy Spirit helps us to see His truly mediating character, which allows him to be the same and different in the constantly changing inter-Trinitarian manifestations without instrumentalizing any of the relations for any particular purpose .

As the interpreter of the Trinity, the Holy Spirit will lead all people of all time to the whole truth. The role of the Holy Spirit is not as much of a 'giver' of the 'proper' interpretation. The Holy Spirit *is* himself the interpretation of the Trinity. The responsibility of the Holy Spirit within the Trinity can be seen in its horizon of meaning. *Re-spondeo* captures the essence of the communicative performance: the persons of the Trinity are in a constant dialogue. This main characteristic of the inner communicative dynamic is disclosed to us in the events of Incarnation and the Pentecost. The Holy Spirit *is* the understanding of the Trinity and as such is an invitation to understanding.

The history of Christianity can be seen as a continuous attempt to find the human expression of the relationship between the Father, the Son and the Holy Spirit, as we profess the Creed. The baptism in the name of the Holy Trinity and every subsequent sign of the cross are the powerful recollection of the rootedness of our life in the primordial relationship between the divine persons. The inclusion into the divine reinterprets our very life as the relationship, which embraces all our being, and thus consecrates us in the name of the Trintiy. Thus, in the sign of the cross, there is a powerful proclamation of faith that generates faith.

The Gospel's passage from the Last Supper speaks of Christ, who promises His disciples to pray to the Father for another Paraclete (ἄλλον παράκλητον) who will remain with them forever (Jn. 14:16). In Eph. 1:13, we encounter 'the Spirit of the promise, the Holy': τῷ πνεύματι τῆς ἐπαγγελίας τῷ ἁγίῳ. This promised Paraclete is God himself who comes to live with and in His people. He is a true epiphany of Trinity.

The recorded event of Pentecost (Acts 2.1-13) can be seen as the beginning of the Church (*der Anfang der Kirche*) and the Church of the beginning (*die Kirche des Anfangs*). The acting of the apostles has its origin in the gift of the Spirit himself. The account of Pentecost confirms that the new divine breath upon humanity in the form of the Holy Spirit as the new and powerful self-communication of God belongs to the dialogue between the Trinity and creation. It involves everything created, human beings and the whole cosmos, with its history and culture. The Trinity as communication between the divine persons discloses itself by sending the Holy Spirit God's plan towards humanity. This plan can be seen as a communion, which is the mode of Trinitarian life. This profound mystery of divine inner life is communicated to us through the incarnated Word. In the Word, the access to the unspeakable reality of God is given to us. The inner life of Trinity reveals to us the essential traits of the mode of understanding. It is a transgression of one's own personal way of thinking and acting towards a communitarian sensitivity. The multiple languages at Pentecost promote the plurivocity of understanding as manifested and foregrounded in the unity of the Spirit. It is an invitation to what hermeneutics calls 'understanding differently', not in the sense of an essential disbelief in absolute truth, but as a fundamental conviction in the plurivocity of understanding and the demise of a singular world-view.

Gen. 11.1–9 tells us that in Babel everyone spoke the same language. The dispersion of languages as symbolically depicted in the Tower of Babel made it impossible for people to understand one another. It stopped their common growing in wisdom. The poetics of Prov. 8.22–31 further personalizes Wisdom as the Lady created by God before the creation of the world to communicate God's love towards His creation and reveal His divine nature. Personalized Wisdom is an anticipation of the Holy Spirit. Wisdom is, on the one hand, intimately involved with God, and is the mode of communicating his divine nature. On the other hand, Wisdom is needed to discern God's unity in His self-manifestation to the created world. As emanated from the triune God, Wisdom is superior over all things created due to her origin, as begotten by God at the beginning. At the same time, Wisdom is most visible to us and invites us to reflect on the eternal quality of her relationship to the Creator.[1] Her attributes signalize that the essence of the relationship with God is not merely the intellectual capacity of analyzing the accumulated data but the willingness to participate in the original experience of God in his threefold unity.

At Pentecost, the diversity of languages no longer impedes communication between people. However, it is essential to discern that the reason for overcoming the linguistic impediment is the empowerment to understand what is proclaimed in the name and the praise of God. This empowerment happens as the gift of the Holy Spirit in order to create the inter-human union in the world permeated by God's presence, which goes beyond the boundaries of languages. The Holy Spirit helps us to understand not just Jesus' words, but guides us toward a personal experience of the intimacy of God himself. What we discover is not an infinite solitude, but a communion of life given (*actio*) and received (*passio*) in an everlasting dialogue between the Father, the So and the Holy Spirit.

From a hermeneutic perspective, it is important to note the threefold use in Jn. 16.12–15 of the verb ἀναγγελῶ (future active indicative, first person singular, to announce in detail, to declare, rehearse, report, show, speak, tell). The promised Spirit will announce the future and disclose the things to come (v. 13). The Spirit will proclaim what He has received from Christ (v. 14). The third time the verb is used to repeat the disclosure of that which the Spirit has received from Christ (v. 15), but with an important

---

[1] *De Veritate* 4, 1: 'We say that God creates by means of His wisdom predicated essentially; hence, His wisdom can be called a medium between God and creature. Yet, this very wisdom is God.'

accentuation of the unity between the Father and the Son: πάντα ὅσα ἔχει
ὁ πατὴρ ἐμά ἐστιν. This threefold usage indicates a critical discernment
of belonging: everything which belongs to the Father belongs to the Son,
because the Father and the Son belong to each other. The communitarian
notion of belonging to the Father and the Son is grounded in their personal
primordial unity.

The mission of the Holy Spirit, to take what is of Christ and to disclose
it to us, indicates a special relationship between Christ and the Holy Spirit.[2]
He will 'take it of mine', says Christ: ἐκ τοῦ ἐμοῦ λήψεται (v 14). This taking
what is of Christ indicates a profoundly personal contact with Him. Christ
willingly accepts something to be disclosed of him by the Holy Spirit. It
happens in the spirit of glorification of Christ: ἐκεῖνος ἐμὲ δοξάσει (v. 14).
In fact, the reason for this revealing is the glorification of Christ. Since He
lives in this primordial unity with the Father, the disclosure of the Son is
also the glorification of the Father. And it is happening through the Holy
Spirit, who is by no means a stranger to the communion of the Father and
the Son. The increasing glory of God is this progressive revelation of the
Trinity. Here we deal with two increases: δοξάσει indicates that the Holy
Spirit will render Christ glorious to us; and the other increase deals with
the further disclosure of the inner life of the Trinity. By glorifying Christ
(and the Father in their divine unity) in the disclosure to the world, the
Holy Spirit overcomes a one-sided relationship with regard to the external
mission. Christ is essentially present in the representation of the Holy Spirit,
who will take something of Christ and reveal it to the world. Christ will be
there in the action of the Holy Spirit, and the Holy Spirit will disclose the
Son in a very particular way. The art of disclosure in the Holy Spirit will
serve the presentation of Christ (and the Father) in full glory. Therefore, the
art of disclosure, which we can call the art of the happening of truth, is not
incidental to the mission of the Holy Spirit. In fact, it is so essential to the
task of the disclosure of truth that it needs to be seen as belonging to the
very Being of the Holy Spirit and thus as the expression of the inner life of
God in his inner-Trinitarian communion.

This disclosure of the truth of the Trinity as an emanation of the
intensity of the relationship between the divine persons is the experience of
an increase in Being. It emanates as an overflow. By revealing the fullness
of life as the overflow, it presents itself as superabundance. Therefore the
disclosure does not decrease the richness of the mystery of the Trinity, but
rather contributes to the revelation of the fullness in its superabundance.
By revealing the inner life of the Trinity, the Holy Spirit contributes to the
increase in Being, hence increasing truth and meaning. This increase is not

---

[2] See John R. W. Stott, *The Message of Acts: The Spirit, the Church and the World* (Leicester:
InterVarsity Press, 1990).

in the sense of adding something that was not there before. But what is genuinely new is the event of disclosure itself. If the prevailing reason for that disclosure of which Christ speaks in the Gospel is his own glorification, then being glorified in the world is an increase in the glory, not necessarily in the sense of the quantity, but definitely in the aspect of its lived intensity. It indicates that the disclosure of the mystery of the Trinity is not happening primarily for any other external reason, but because of the immanent intense relationship between the persons of the Trinity. In fact, the mission of the Holy Spirit can be seen not only as the externalization of divine life, but as the task of bringing the external world to participate in the inner life of the Trinity.

The proclamation of the things received from Christ needs to be seen as the promise of the continuation of Christ's mission to the world.[3] If we understand Incarnation as the superior event of divine self-manifestation, the task of the Holy Spirit will be to interpret the meaning of this divine self-manifestation in its *Wirkungsgeschichte*, in the light of Christ's Death and Resurrection. Therefore this interpretative task needs to be understood as a search for a deeper meaning, which might have been undisclosed to Christ's disciples also due to the lack of historical distance. With the guidance of the Paraclete, the inspired disciples of Christ will be empowered (*ermächtigt*) to understand Jesus' teaching on God in the light of the succeeding events of His personal history and the history of the lives of his followers.

At Pentecost, the fact that the Apostles speak different languages does not hinder their being understood. In fact, everyone understands the message in his own tongue. It means that no individual language is able to express the whole of the 'one' message which is sent by the Holy Spirit. We need to understand this message in a variety of languages and in a variety of ways. The hermeneutic criterion for the discernment of the plurivocity of understanding comes from the effusion of the Holy Spirit.

The revelation of the essentiality of the plurivocity of understanding at the Pentecost is, at the same time, the opening of the horizon of understanding.[4] On the one hand, it is a speculative opening in the sense of getting a deeper insight into the very nature of understanding. On the other hand, it is a spatial widening of the horizon of understanding. By overcoming the historical, cultural and religious barriers, this new outpouring of divine energy into the created world, we are reminded of the universality of hermeneutics. It is, in its essence, the call to understanding. And this universal

---

[3] See Robert S. Coleman, 'The Promise of the Holy Spirit for the Great Commission', *Evangelical Review of Theology* 16 (1992): 271–83.
[4] See John Habgood, *Varieties of Unbelief* (London: Darton, Longman & Todd, 2000) and Curtis Chang, *Engaging Unbelief: A Captivating Strategy from Augustine and Aquinas* (Downers Grove, Ill.: InterVarsity, 2000).

task of understanding questions the common expression of universality as connected with the number 12. In fact, Luke broadens the horizon by going beyond the number 12: 'We are Parthians, Medes, and Elamites, inhabitants of Mesopotamia, Judea and Cappadocia, Pontus and Asia, Phrygia and Pamphylia, Egypt and the districts of Libya near Cyrene, as well as travellers from Rome, both Jews and converts to Judaism, Cretans and Arabs, yet we hear them speaking in our own tongues of the mighty acts of God.' Luke goes beyond the familiar geographical horizons of Asia and northwest Africa by welcoming the habitants of islands (Cretans) and mainland (Arabs). He embraces the strange Western world as represented by the Romans and extends the gesture of hospitality toward the Jews and proselytes.

The appearance of tongues as of fire can be seen as a powerful self-manifestation of God, as the expression of Trinity's logic of self-giving. It is a self-communication of God, who cares about His people and will not leave them bereaved and comfortless as ὑμᾶς ὀρφανούς (Jn. 14.18). The relationship between God's manifestation on the Sinai and the Pentecost is of particular hermeneutic interest. The understanding of God's revelation is happening here in the vivid memory of the marvellous experience of Sinai. The flame of the Holy Spirit burns but does not destroy. The fire of the Holy Spirit reminds us of the bush that burned without being consumed (cf. Exod. 3.2). As an eloquent sign of the Holy Spirit, whose burning is the paradigm for purification, this flame brings about profound transformation. The passion for understanding, which is at heart of the hermeneutic task has its powerful transformative character. Both 'tongues' as signifiers of the mission of proclamation and witness to God's call and 'fire' as the expression of God's power to renew the face of the earth become in the junction as 'tongues of fire' a new paradigm for the mission from the Pentecost as inter-preted in the light of the past salvific history of the covenant with Jahwe as the empowerment to prophesying by the outpouring of the divine Spirit (Acts 2.17; Joel 3.1–5).[5]

As a sign of the awareness of the interpretative task of the Christian community in her *statu missionis*, the 'tongue' presents truth and love of God. Therefore language receives in the event of Pentecost a new dimension as a communicative tool in truth and love. Thinking, speaking and action of people filled with the Holy Spirit contribute to the edification of their real community as the visible sign of overcoming the symbolic historical impediments from the Tower of Babel. Language is not only the tool of communication between people talking to each other and understanding the diverse dialects, but becomes the mode of communication with God. As a house of God, language is the house of a human being, invited by the Spirit to participation in the inner life of Trinity. We could say that the Holy

---

[5] See Luz Iglesias, 'Mission: A Paradigm from Pentecost', *MJTM* 6 (2003; 2005): 9–17.

Spirit is the language we speak and truly *are*. With the invitation to the life in God, we can understand Trinity from now on as our homeland, and the Holy Spirit as God's Spirit of Truth and Love is our mother tongue. Within this Trinitarian paradigm, we can share our new homeland with everyone, and yet speak our own language while being understood by others.

# The Philosophical Discourse on the Theological Insight: *Verbum Interius*

The philosophical world has been profoundly surprised to learn that revolutionary discovery regarding the nature of language is not of philosophical but specifically theological provenance.[6] In an opening statement of 'Language and Verbum', in part three of *Truth and Method*, 'The Ontological Shift of Hermeneutics Guided by Language', Gadamer explains: 'There is, however, an idea that is not Greek which does more justice to the being of language, and so prevented the forgetfulness of language in Western thought from being complete. This is the Christian idea of *Incarnation*.'[7] Since the human relationship between thinking and speaking corresponds, despite its imperfections, to the divine relationship within the Trinity, a deeper understanding of how language connects to the world can be understood by seriously engaging Augustine's doctrine of the *verbum interius*. Gadamer summarizes the universal aspect of his language-oriented hermeneutics as the *verbum interius* by shifting the accent from the word as the subject of the philosophy of language to the inner word, the core of Augustine's teaching on the Trinity.[8] Taking into consideration Gadamer's understanding of Augustine's *verbum interius*, it is instructive to see the importance of the preferred translation of *logos* as *verbum* and not as *ratio*. Following further Gadamer's claim that the universality of hermeneutics consists in the *verbum interius*, an insight Gadamer learned from Augustine's *De Trinitate*, the notion of *verbum* transcends all its particular manifestations in any given language.[9] By identifying the task of theology

---

[6] See Andrzej Wiercinski, 'The Hermeneutic Retrieval of a Theological Insight: *Verbum Interius*', in ibid., ed., *Between the Human and the Divine: Philosophical and Theological Hermeneutics* (Toronto: The Hermeneutic Press, 2002), 1–23.

[7] Hans-Georg Gadamer, *Truth and Method*, trans. Joel Weinsheimer and Donald G. Marshall, 2nd rev. ed. (New York: Continuum, 2000), 418. See also Petra Plieger, *Sprache im Gespräch. Studien zum hermeneutischen Sprachverständnis bei Hans-Georg Gadamer* (Wien: WUV, 2000), 187–92.

[8] See Jean Grondin, *Introduction to Philosophical Hermeneutics*, trans. Joel Weinsheimer (New Haven, Conn.: Yale University Press, 1994), XIV.

[9] See John Arthos, *The Inner Word in Gadamer's Hermeneutics* (Notre Dame, Ind.: University

as grasping the independent personal existence of Christ within this sameness of Being, Gadamer emphasizes that the human analogue to Christ is the mental word, the *verbum intellectus*: 'The inner mental word is just as consubstantial with thought as is God the Son with God the Father.'[10] In God, there is no distinction between His thinking and the expressed thought. There is an identity between the Creator and His *verbum mentis*.

By criticizing the prevailing instrumental relationship to things, which, since Plato, reduced language to a tool for thinking and communicating, Gadamer rediscovers the fundamentally ontological connection between words and things and redefines language as the medium of hermeneutic experience. Through language the world is disclosed to us and our understanding of the world is happening in the dynamic interplay of revealing and concealing. The genius of the theological reflection on the Trinity with the speculative insight into the inner-Trinitarian life of God, and, in particular, the Christian notion of Incarnation, allow for disclosing the essential mystery of language. Gadamer is not a theologian and is not particularly concerned with the theological implications of the speculative teaching on the Trinity, similarly to Heidegger, who is not really interested either in disclosing the Christian belief (*orthodoxy* – ὀρθοδοξία), or in the particular way of living the faith in the Christian community (*orthopraxis* – ὀρθοπραξις), but in the primordiality of Christian life experience, which serves him as a methodological *Zugriff* of factual life and as a formal indication of primordial temporality.[11] For Gadamer, the Christian conceptual resources from the medieval interpretations of the Trinity shed light on philosophical problems, particularly illuminating language and history. However, what is not to be underestimated is the fact that both Augustine and Aquinas who serve as the inspiration for Gadamer's reflection, develop their respective philosophies of language not primarily because of engaging the philosophical sources of Aristotle and Neoplatonism, but because of their profound Trinitarian and particularly Christological interests, which shapes their understanding of the ontological relationship between words and things.

Gadamer compares the relation between the *verbum mentis* and thought

---

of Notre Dame Press, 2009). See further, Mirela Oliva, *Das innere Verbum in Gadamers Hermeneutik* (Tübingen: Mohr Siebeck, 2009).

[10] Gadamer, *Truth and Method*, 420.

[11] See Andrzej Wiercinski, *Hermeneutics between Philosophy and Theology: The Imperative To Think the Incommensurable* (Münster: LIT Verlag, 2010) and his 'Heidegger's Atheology: The Possibility of Unbelief', in Sean McGrath and Andrzej Wiercinski, eds, *A Companion to Heidegger's 'Phenomenology of Religious Life'* (Amsterdam: Rodopi, 2010), 151–80. See further Sean J. McGrath, *The Early Heidegger and Medieval Philosophy: Phenomenology for the Godforsaken* (Washington, D. C.: Catholic University of America Press, 2006) and his *Heidegger: A (Very) Critical Introduction* (Grand Rapids, Mich.: Eerdmans, 2008).

to the consubstantial relation between the Father and the Son. As the Father and the Son are of the same substance, language and human thought are of primordial unity, also essentially one. The essential unity does not mean, however, that the elements are not distinguishable. Oneness does not mean sameness. Gadamer stresses the unity of human thinking and speaking.[12] By rejecting the priority of thinking over speaking, he stresses that language is not a mere communicative tool, something that can be added to thought. Being appreciative of Augustine's contributions to the notion of the *verbum*, Gadamer clarifies that the *verbum interius* is not the Greek *logos*, the dialogue that the soul conducts with itself. Gadamer stresses that the universality of *verbum* lies in transcending all particular manifestations of it in any particular language. What he finds illuminating in Augustine is the idea that the Word, as the second person of the Trinity, progresses from the Father (as Son) and becomes Incarnate. However, the Incarnation does not deprive God the Father of virtually anything. On the contrary, Incarnation of the Word is an appropriate and faithful expression of the divine nature.[13] In fact, the Word Incarnate reveals the Father, but, as Aquinas says, 'the eternally generated Word has manifested Him to Himself. Consequently, the name word does not belong to the Son merely in so far as He is Incarnate.'[14]

Gadamer honours also Aquinas' contribution to the Christian notion of the *verbum*, which is essentially based on the Prologue to John's Gospel systematically elaborated with reference to Aristotle.[15] Gadamer realizes that for Aquinas, *logos* and *verbum* do not completely coincide. By emphasizing in the process of word formation the ontological character of an event, it is important to see the relationship of the inner word to a possible externalization, neither related to a particular language, nor to an ambiguous procession of a word from memory, but to a process of thinking the subject matter through to the end which Aquinas calls '*forma excogitata*'. In following Aquinas, Gadamer stresses the processual character of the word, which proceeds *per modum egredientis*, thus achieving the perfection of thought.

For Aquinas, the Neoplatonic idea of emanation, of flowing out without diminishing its source, serves as an analogy for the procession within the

---

[12] See Andrzej Wiercinski, 'Die ursprüngliche Zugehörigkeit von Denken und Sprechen', in Andrzej Przylebski, ed., *Das Erbe Gadamers* (Frankfurt a. M.: Peter Lang, 2006), 65–83.

[13] See Andrzej Wiercinski, 'Inkarnation als die Ermächtigung des Differenzdenkens: Das Logosverständnis und die permanente Herausforderung zur Interpretation', in Christian Schaller, Michael Schulz and Rudolf Voderholzer, eds, *Mittler und Befreier: Die christologische Dimension der Theologie* (Freiburg i. Br.: Herder, 2008), 162–204.

[14] *De Veritate*, 4, 1.

[15] See Bernard Lonergan, *Verbum: Word and Idea in Aquinas*, eds Frederick E. Crowe and Robert M. Doran (Toronto: Lonergan Research Institute, Toronto, 1997).

Trinity, and for the procession of the word.[16] The Father is not lessened or deprived when he generates the Son.[17] Aquinas' treatment of *verbum interius* in *De Veritate*, is an example of a fruitful symbiosis of the Neoplatonic endeavour to describe God as a divine mind with the properly Christian reflection on human being as *imago Dei* and resemblance of the Trinity.[18] Aquinas emphasizes the importance of the analogy between the human concept and divine *Verbum* for finding the proper language to speak about God: 'Our intellectual word, which enables us to speak about the divine Word by a kind of resemblance, is that at which our intellectual operation terminates. This is the object of understanding, which is called the conception of the intellect.'[19] We can call the divine word a word because of its resemblance to the inner word.[20] In expressing human thinking,

---

[16] *De Veritate*, 4, 1: 'Now, because the vocal word is expressed by means of a body, such a word cannot be predicated of God except metaphorically, that is, only in the sense in which creatures or their motions, being produced by God, are said to be His word inasmuch as they are signs of the divine intellect as effects are signs of their cause. For the same reason, the word which has an image of the vocal word cannot be properly predicated of God, but only metaphorically. Consequently, His ideas of things to be made are called the Word of God only metaphorically.'

[17] 'In the process of emanation, that from which something flows, the One, is not deprived or depleted. The same is true of the birth of the Son from the Father, who does not use up anything of himself but takes something to himself. And this is likewise true of the mental emergence that takes place in the process of thought, speaking to oneself. This kind of production is at the same time a total remaining within oneself. If it can be said of the divine relationship between word and intellect that the word originates not partially but wholly (*totaliter*) in the intellect, then it is true also that one word originates *totaliter* from another, i.e. has its origin in the mind like the deduction of a conclusion from the premises (*ut conclusio ex principiis*). Thus the process and emergence of thought is not a process of change (*motus*), not a transition from potentiality into action, but an emergence *ut actus ex actu*. The word is not formed only after the act of knowledge has been completed in Scholastic terms, after the intellect has been informed by the species; it is the act of knowledge itself. Thus the word is simultaneous with this forming (*formatio*) of the intellect. Thus we can see how the creation of the word came to be viewed as a true image of the Trinity. It is a true *generatio*, a true birth, even though, of course, there is no receptive part to go with a generating one. It is precisely the intellectual nature of the generation of the word.' Gadamer, *Truth and Method*, 422–3.

[18] Andrzej Wiercinski, *Philosophizing with Gustav Siewerth: A New German Edition with Facing Translation of 'Das Sein als Gleichnis Gottes'/'Being as Likeness of God,' And A Study, 'From Metaphor and Indication to Icon: The Centrality of the Notion of Verbum in Hans-Georg Gadamer, Bernard Lonergan and Gustav Siewerth'* (Konstanz: Verlag Gustav Siewerth Gesellschaft, 2005).

[19] *De Veritate* 4, 2.

[20] *De Veritate* 4, 1: 'We give names to things according to the manner in which we receive our knowledge from things … Consequently, since the exterior word is sensible, it is more known to us than the interior word; hence, according to the application of the term, the vocal word is meant before the interior word, even though the interior word is naturally prior, being the efficient and final cause of the exterior… The interior word is that which is expressed by the exterior. Moreover, the exterior word signifies that which is understood, not the act of understanding nor the habit or faculty as the objects of understanding, unless the habit and the

the inner word reflects the finiteness of our understanding, which has a discursive character. Our comprehension is a process of an inner dialogue in which the human mind draws what it thinks on the subject matter out of itself, and present it to itself as if in an inner dialogue. In this sense human thinking can be rightly called 'speaking to oneself'. This inner unity of thinking and speaking to oneself corresponds to the Trinitarian mystery of Incarnation.

The *verbum interius*, also called by Aquinas the principal word, tends towards manifestation. As it is true that the manifestation of something happens through a word that is vocally expressed, there is a manifestation to oneself, as in a case of a *soliloquium*, which is mediated by the *verbum cordis*. For Aquinas, the concept as a representation of on object does mediate understanding and signification.[21] He refers to the concept 'by which our intellect understands a thing distinct from itself originates from another and represents another'.[22] The concept represents an object due to its formal principle by directing the intellect to its object. Therefore the concept is the *intentio intellectus*, that directs an intellect to an object of understanding. For Aquinas, another term for the concept or *intentio intellectus* is *verbum mentis*. He occasionally uses the term *verbum cordis* or *verbum interius*, which is an image of the vocal word.[23]

By calling the concept a *verbum*, Aquinas makes a clear reference to the second person of the Trinity as expressed in the Prologue to John's Gospel. This – maybe one of the most profound doctrinal statements in the New Testament – relates the mystery of the beginning of the world to the

---

faculty are themselves the things that are understood. Consequently, the interior word is what is understood interiorly.'

[21] *De Veritate* 4, 1: 'A medium can be understood in two ways. First, it can be understood as being a medium between the two terms of a motion, as pale is a medium between white and black in a process of blackening or whitening. Second, it can be understood as existing between what is active and what is passive, as the instrument of the artist is a medium between the artist and his work. In fact, anything by which the artist acts is a medium in this sense. It is in this second sense, too, that the Son is a medium between the creating Father and the creature created through the Word. The Son, however, is not a medium between God creating and the creature created, for the Word is also God creating. Hence, just as the Son is not a creature, so also He is not the Father.'

[22] 'Huiusmodi ergo conceptio, sive verbum, qua intellectus noster intelligit rem aliam a se, ab alio exoritur, et aliud repraesentat.' *De Pot.* 8.1. Cf. *In Sent.*, d. 2, q. 1, a. 3, c.; d. 8, q. 2, a. 1d, ad 1.

[23] John O'Callaghan shifts the importance of Aquinas' *verbum mentis* into the properly theological context. 'It has the theological purpose of providing nothing more than an image or metaphor for talking about man, made in the image and likeness of God as Trinity.' John O'Callaghan, '*Verbum Mentis*: Philosophical or Theological Doctrine in Aquinas?' *Proceedings of the American Catholic Philosophical Association* 74 (2000): 103–19. See also his *Thomist Realism and the Linguistic Turn: Toward a More Perfect Form of Existence* (Notre Dame, Ind.: University of Notre Dame Press, 2003).

Incarnation: Ἐν ἀρχῇ ἦν ὁ λόγος, καὶ ὁ λόγος ἦν πρὸς τὸν θεόν, καὶ θεὸς ἦν ὁ λόγος. In the Latin translation, the Divine Logos in God becomes *verbum, qui caro factum est*. All processions within the Trinity are the expressions of the one eternal divine act. The mystery of the procession of *verbum* from God inspires philosophers to interpret analogically the formation of a concept or *verbum interius* in the human intellect. The process within the Trinity can be seen as a pattern for the processual character of human thinking. Hermeneutically interesting successiveness characteristic of the discursiveness of human thought emphasizes that thinking is not a temporal relation but a mental process, an *emanatio intellectualis*.

The analogy of bringing something to language and becoming incarnate as the Word is the expression of the inner life of the Trinity and discloses the mystery of language. Similarly to the divine procession within the Trinity, the coming to language of something is not a diminishment of the Being of that particular being (*das Sein des Seienden – esse entium*), but an actualization of it, its coming to subsistence.[24] With Gadamer we can say that 'the true Being of things becomes accessible precisely in their linguistic appearance.'[25]

*Actus signatus*, what a statement says, and *actus exercitus*, the enactment (*Vollzug*) of what has been understood, constitute the dynamics of understanding. In *actus exercitus*, the expression of the inner meaning is fully realized; *actus exercitus* goes beyond what is expressed in words, and embraces also the application of what has been said and understood. Meaning is not only communicated in what is said, but also in how it is expressed, what Heidegger calls 'formal indication'.[26] The inner word requires a multiplicity of external words: 'The production of words is a remaining with self, not a change, a move from potency to act, but a procession of act from act. In forming a word, the mind is not directed towards its own reflection: There is no reflection when the word is formed, for the word is not expressing the mind but the thing intended. The starting point for the formation of the word is the substantive content (the species) that fills the mind.'[27] As the inner unity of thinking and speaking, the inner word shows the direct and spontaneous character of thinking. The word

---

[24] See Andrzej Wiercinski, *Inspired Metaphysics? Gustav Siewerth's Hermeneutic Reading of the Onto-Theological Tradition* (Toronto: The Hermeneutic Press, 2003).

[25] Hans-Georg Gadamer, 'The Nature of Things and the Language of Things', in ibid., *Philosophical Hermeneutics*, trans. and ed. David E. Linge (Berkeley, Calif.: University of California Press, 1976), 77.

[26] Cf. Martin Heidegger, *Logik: Die Frage nach der Wahrheit*, GA21, ed. Walter Biemel (Frankfurt a.M.: Vittorio Klostermann, 1976), 410. The propositions about *Dasein* only indicate *Dasein*. The young Heidegger, concerned with facticity, turned his phenomenological interest toward pre-theoretical experience, which he calls '*faktische Lebenserfahrung*'. Formal indication was Heidegger's answer to Husserl's theoreticization of factual life.

[27] Gadamer, *Truth and Method*, 426.

is not an articulation of the human mind's reflection upon itself, but a *similitudo rei*. That which is externalized in language is already word before it is uttered. The inner word is pre-reflective; it expresses a thing that has been thought.

With his deep fascination for Augustine's account of the *verbum interius*, Gadamer clarifies the understanding of language with words being not just tools at our disposal for describing reality, but as, in fact ontologically connected to things. Similarly to the Word, as the second person of the Trinity, who as the Son proceeds from the Father and becomes the incarnated Word, thus allowing us to access the mystery of the Trinity, the human word makes it possible to see the true Being of things (*das Sein des Seienden*) in their linguistic appearance. The other element of similarity refers to the idea that the incarnated Word of God takes nothing away from God the Father. By analogy, coming to language does not diminish the Being of a thing, but is, in fact, an actualization of the possibility for being. The word is not exhausted by its linguistic expression, since the unsaid also belongs to what is said. Gadamer's understanding of the word goes beyond significative function to word as an enactment of thinking (*Vollzug des Denkens*). As such, it is never a final word, for thinking is always thinking further: there is always more to be said. The processual character of language makes it possible for Gadamer to think of *Dasein*'s finitude in relation to divine infinity: 'Christology prepares the way for a new philosophy of man, which mediates in a new way between the mind of man in its finitude and the divine infinity.'[28] *Verbum* mediates between the human and the divine. The essential point here is that the procession from the *verbum interius* to the *verbum exterius* is not a movement through space, but a procession in time, an ecstatic self-transcendence. Scholastic Trinitarian theology offers a figure for understanding the emergence of the word as the procession from act to act (*ut actus ex actu, et non ut actus ex potentia*).

Without engaging in the details of Gadamer's endorsement of Trinitarian theology for the rediscovery of the truth of language, we can definitely emphasize that Augustine's and Aquinas' philosophy of language and philosophy of mind are profoundly indebted to their theology, in particular to their deep Trinitarian and Christological thinking. It is exactly this intellectual heritage which helps us to situate the question of the ontological relation between things and words in the proximity of theological thinking.

---

[28] Ibid., 428.

# Conclusion: In Praise of Thinking the Self-Revealing Triune God

As the Arian heresy stimulated the crystallization of the speculative notion of the Trinity, the attempt to delineate the understanding of the Trinity within the confines of a solemn definition perpetuated the negativity of a dogmatic perception of the 'captive mind' as the enemy of freedom of expression and the prison of human spirit. The dogmatically interpreted Scripture lost for many its genuine hospitable character as the realm of trust and freedom, respect and reverence. Dogmatics became, therefore, a big Non-sense (*das Unwort*), both an ugly but also an unwanted word.

However, the task of thinking the Trinity is definitely one of the most exciting intellectual enterprises. Already starting from the address of the ontological status of Christ as the second person of the Trinity, we discover the potential for disclosing and expressing God in an absolutely unique way. This Christological approach to the mystery of the Trinity serves as the key context for understanding not only the concept of the divine immutability, but also of the relationship between the Creator God and his creation. The obedience of Christ as demonstrated in the event of Incarnation opens up a new horizon of the disclosure of the Trinitarian God. This Christological-Incarnational revelation along with the kenotic nature of God's self-manifestation in the event of the Cross and Resurrection calls into question the notion of the divine immutability. In fact, the divine kenosis indicates a profound movement and indeed a transformation in God not as imposed on Him by the logic of creation, but as accepted by his own disinterested self-giving in the event of Incarnation, which, in turn, is understood not as the enfleshment and external radicalization of the divine power but as the kenosis of the intra-Trinitarian life of love. This Trinitarian event of the intra-Trinitarian self-giving is the very condition of the possibility of God's externalization. In other words, the intra-Trinitarian dynamics of life, which is love, is the paradigm of any externalization of God in his kenotic expression from creation through the Incarnation, and the Cross. God's intra-Trinitarian disinterestedness calls him to kenosis in order to exteriorize a liveliness within the Trinity, which in a divine superabundance becomes the heritage of the whole humanity. The complexity of life of the Incarnated God is a revelation of the Trinity under the particular aspect of kenotic obedience. The hermeneutic circle seems clear: the privileged access to the mystery of the Trinity is the mystery of the Incarnated God. But thinking the mystery of the Trinity is, in turn, the condition of the possibility of thinking of the supreme expression of God's kenotic self-manifestation in the Incarnation, and finally the event of the Cross and Resurrection of Christ.

Holding on to the two-nature distinction, Christ's suffering, which occurs in His human nature, does not necessarily imply a univocal suffering in the Trinitarian God. An enduring and incommensurable difference between the Creator God and his creature prevents the logical necessity of the suffering of the whole Trinity. However, if we accept the fact that God's nature is intrinsically interpersonal, then we must open up a horizon of a possible acceptance of being personally affected by Christ's suffering by the whole Trinity in their mutual interpersonal relations. The mystery of the Trinity is the essential identity of God as a personal *communio*. God, in His deepest reality is not a solitude, but a *communio* of life and love and therefore this community can not remain immune to the pain and suffering in the history of its externalization. The community of the Father, the Son and the Holy Spirit is the prototype of the human community with the concept of the intimate indwelling, περιχώρεσις, as the structural axis.[29] If we are further inclined to call the fatherhood and the sonship in the Holy Spirit a family, in truth a divine family, then thinking about the Trinity also discloses something essential about the family. It is a discovery of a profoundly engaging and dynamic relation, which out of the lived love shares its own spirit of love with others and invites them to the participation in the eternal feast of love.

By implementing the ontological difference between the Creator God and his creature, the Creation can be interpreted as a participation in the role of the Son as image and expression of the Father within the Trinity. Creation can be seen as God's own gift to himself: coming out of the Non-Being (*ex nihilo – Nichts*) and yet empowered to Being by God. What is striking here is the fact that God remains not unaffected by His own decision (*Entschluss*). The transformation in God is substantiated by his own inner-Trinitarian event of love. This transformation we can interpret in the sense of an increase in Being.

The postmodern challenge inspires us to argue uncompromisingly for a genuine theological thinking. It is a thinking which thinks the truth of God and Being and strives to reach back into the essential ground from which all thinking emerges. Hermeneutics situates theological systematics in a critical relation to the history of theological thinking. It reminds us of the historically conditioned character of understanding. We are always histori-cally situated and live with the deep conviction in the plurality of writing the history of theological thinking. Hermeneutically speaking, we will never have one 'true' history of theology. The task of a theologian is to combine a hermeneutic commitment to both theological speculation and historical

---

[29] 'Die trinitarische gegenseitige Durchdringung (perichoresis) ist der grundlegende und höchste Archetyp des Lebens als Gemeinschaft, wo Einheit und Unterschiedlichkeit völlig und gleichzeitig zum Ausdruck kommen'. Gisbert Greshake, *Der dreieine Gott: Eine trinita-rische Theologie* (Freiburg i. Br.: Herder, 2001), 189. See also Oliver D. Crisp, 'Problems with Perichoresis', *Tyndale Bulletin* 56, no. 1 (2005): 119–40.

engagement. In that sense, there is no systematic theological thinking deprived of the critical engagement with the past. Particularly, in the age of a jittery search for a 'non-metaphysical' and 'non-dogmatic' theology, we can experience some profound difficulties with the theological task, which are in my understanding largely related to a mistrust in hermeneutics, preventing the adequate address of that which needs to be thought.[30] We can speak of the *Not*, in a similar way to Gadamer's attempt to discover anew the inherent potential of language. Theological hermeneutics is not a method of interpreting the event of faith, but it thematizes an ontological relationship between an interpreter and that which needs to be interpreted. It engages the complexity of a personal act of believing in the Greek sens of πιστεύειν and Latin *credere*, which embraces both aspects of faith: holding for true *(das Für-wahr-halten, geglaubter Glaube, fides quae creditur)*, and the active pursuit of trusting *(glaubender Glaube, fides qua creditur)*. Our personal faith relates our very life to the Trinity as the source and the summit *(fons et culmen)* of all mysteries.

If we understand the postmodern age as the flourishing of religious pluralism, philosophical scepticism and cultural relativism, we need to address a question of 'dogmatism' of systematic theology. Is it necessarily for systematic theology to be orthodoxic? Orthodoxic or orthopractic? Or maybe just instructive and supportive in the realm of right-living on the way to individual self-perfection? We would need to ask further about the specific traits of systematic theology.[31] Historically confronted with the secularization and pluralization of Western society, which undoubtedly contributes to the much hated relativism, some versions of theology vehemently oppose the attitude of resignation regarding absolute truth. However, the history of Christianity, which profoundly shapes Western culture, is the symphony of voices constituting the tradition we have now. Hermeneutics calls for the discernment of truth in history, which cannot happen without acknowledging the cultural contributions and enduring presence of traditions, including those substantially different from our own. It is the hermeneutic gesture of hospitality and welcoming the other as the possible disclosure of that which is undisclosed to us. It is particularly urgent where, despite being conscious of the plurivocal horizon of meaning, we still stubbornly declare that we have the *one and only* interpretation.

Goethe extends his powerful inspirational invitation to everyone:

---

[30] See Jeffrey W. Robbins, *In Search of a Non-Dogmatic Theology* (Aurora, Colo.: Davies Group Publishers, 2004); see also his *Between Faith and Thought: An Essay on the Onto-theological Condition* (Charlottesville, Va.: University of Virginia Press, 2003). Robbins' non-dogmatic theology is a post-critical affirmation of the traditional theological pattern of *fides quaerens intellectum* and transformed religious and theological sensibility.

[31] See Thomas Ruster, *Der verwechselbare Gott: Theologie nach der Entflechtung von Christentum und Religion* (Freiburg i.Br.: Herder, 2003).

'Whatever you think you can do or believe you can do, begin it. Action has magic, grace and power in it.' The hermeneutic task is to discern the meaning of action, which is distinguishable from its occurrence as a particular spatiotemporal event. Every reading of action and of text requires interpretation. This leads us to the insight that no theoretical expertise will make us masters of understanding. Instead, hermeneutics repeats a call to search for understanding by interpreting always anew while being conscious of the operative force of a tradition we have now. Understanding, then, is an act of *Wirkungsgeschichte*, which conditions us as we are conscious of being influenced by the course of history. Doing theological hermeneutics in the context of the much celebrated 'theology without God', 'a God without Being', 'a religion without religion', means a conscious participation in the interpretative understanding of the dynamics of the event of faith in the triune God.[32] The theological task concerns our understanding of the image of God as revealed by Him and the implication of this revelation for our life. This understanding happens as a creative interaction between the perception of God and the perception of the world we live in.

Doing theology cannot in fact be separated from doing the history of theology and philosophy, since it is essential to be aware of the extent to which tradition and language fashion us as lingual beings. Tradition shapes and informs our very being and understanding. With regard to the hermeneutics of the Trinity, we need to theologize about the mystery of the inner life of God by trying to understand all preceding theological questions and answers and to situate ourselves in a dialogue with the theological tradition to disclose the mystery of Trinity in its speculative richness. We gain our insight into the mystery of the the Trinity by way of doing a theological exegesis of God's self-manifestation in the Scripture. This is a powerful hermeneutic experience of searching for understanding of God's mystery by engaging His Word and, at the same time, of allowing the biblical texts to reshape our previous understanding, while offering the referential language for our theological enterprise. The hermeneutic *plaidoyer* for not holding to the distinction between philosophers, theologians and exegetes speaks loudly for *theological exegesis* and *biblical theology*, which further a theological insight. It is also a constant reminder that doing theological hermeneutics advances our understanding of the triune God by critically interpreting His Word, which forms and transforms us, who listen.

As in the case of the ancient Greek word φάρμακον, there is no single translation, which would capture the play of its signification. Since the Greek word – as a poison transformed, through the Socratic *logos*, into

---

[32] Frank T. Birtel, ed., *Reasoned Faith: Essays on the Interplay of Faith and Reason* (New York: Crossroad, 1993) and Patrick Glynn, *God: The Evidence: The Reconciliation of Faith and Reason in a Postsecular World* (Rocklin, Ca.: Prima Publishing, 1997).

a cathartic power to awaken the soul to the truth – is overdetermined, the very notion of signification gets overloaded. Here we touch upon the hermeneutic problem of overdetermination. It is not a simple question of translating the Greek word into a modern language. The overdetermination of the word opens up the possible horizons of interpretation and situates the philosophical and theological discourse in the realm of ambiguity. The question remains if this ambiguity needs to be dogmatically dismissed as an infertile equivocity, vagueness, fuzziness and deceptiveness. If δοκέω means to think, then dogmatics is truly the matter of thinking; in truth, a special concentration and intensity of thinking, since it relates the human mind to its origin. It needs to overcome a fearsome apologetics in the sense of avoiding or combating the erroneous opinions of the individual thinkers. Maybe we can even see the interpretative ambiguity and an apparent doctrinal laxity as a counteraction to the poison of simplification, as an *antidotum* (ἀντίδοτον) to the levelling democratic reductionist tendencies of our time, and most of all as an endorsement of the plurivocity of understanding in the unity of the Spirit.

In the process of translation and interpretation, we realize that by choosing only one of the meanings we do injustice to that which is translated, somehow annihilating the original plurivocal meaning. The translation and interpretation are then not necessarily incorrect, but are definitely incomplete. In theological thinking we are not less incomplete. Every interpretative translation is both violent and impotent, as Derrida tells us.[33] The sense of dissatisfaction leaves us somewhere between happily acceptance and bitter rejection.

---

[33] See Jacques Derrida, *Dissemination*, trans. Barbara Johnson (Chicago: University of Chicago Press, 1981).

# 13

# Trinitarian Theology: Notes Towards a Supreme Phenomenology

## Kevin Hart

### A Little Dialogue

*A:* On the face of it, and for a very clear reason, it seems that there can be no phenomenology of the Trinity. Phenomenology is the study of τὰ φαινόμενα, the things that display themselves to us, and God does not manifest Himself as Triune in any of the usual ways that philosophy countenances. We may speak of a phenomenology of the holy, but God as Trinity falls outside 'religious experience'.

*B:* We must be careful not to place phenomenology and philosophy on one side of a line with theology on the other side. Phenomenology can be practised in theology as well as in philosophy, literary criticism and other disciplines. That's one thing I wanted to say. Here's another: God certainly makes Himself known, for any child can work out through the light of natural reason that there is a God.

*A:* Even if we accept this view, underscored by Vatican I, this natural light is of no help in grasping God as Triune. *That* God is and *what* God is are entirely different. We're not talking about a phenomenology of God, which is demanding enough, but of God as Trinity.

*B:* And yet God seems to have revealed Himself as Trinity to certain beloved souls as a special grace, and presumably they at least could examine this Trinitarian indwelling in a phenomenological manner. Think of Hildegard of Bingen's vision of the Trinity as described in her *Scivias*, for example, or Teresa of Ávila's entry into the innermost mansion, home of the Trinity, as described in her *The Interior Castle*, and think too of the many testimonies over several centuries and from different lands about the experience of Trinitarian indwelling.[1]

*A:* Remember that Teresa speaks there of seeing the Trinity in an 'intellectual vision'.[2] We would need to know just what that is.

*B:* Indeed, and what people mean when they speak of the *imago trinitatis*.

*A:* You're not talking, are you, of triads such as memory, understanding and will that Augustine entertains and finally rejects in the final book of *De Trinitate* but that continue far into the Middle Ages?[3]

*B:* Not necessarily: the image may not be psychological in that way. It might even be social. But I would want to keep the *imago trinitatis*, since it may well be a part of what people mean by the experience of Trinitarian indwelling.

*A:* We would be dealing with a peculiar sort of experience, neither sensual nor intellectual; the Trinity would come to the soul *modus sine modo* and consequently not be able to be constituted – restored, made present – or described. Intentionality does not seem to be able to capture this sort of manifestation.

*B:* Remember Scheler's warning not to set up 'too narrowly exclusive a concept of 'experience' – to equate the whole of experience with one particular kind of experience'?[4]

*A:* Or even two or three kinds ...

*B:* Perhaps the Triune God discloses Himself otherwise, and we should look to non-intentional phenomenology. Or maybe we should look to a phenomenology of counter-intentionality, of reception instead of constitution.

*A:* These are radical suggestions, and require detailed discussion. Let's put them to one side for the moment. Perhaps there are other things that need to be said in a preliminary way about a phenomenology of the Trinity.

---

[1] See A. Hunt, *The Trinity: Insights from the Mystics,* Collegeville, MN: Liturgical Press 2010). See Hildegard of Bingen, *Scivias,* New York: Paulist Press 1990, pp. 161–2, and St Teresa of Ávila, 'The Interior Mansion', in *The Complete Works of Saint Teresa of Ávila,* London: Sheed and Ward 1978, II, Seventh Mansion, chapters 1–3. One might mention John of the Cross and Elizabeth of the Trinity as two people who have testified to some extent of Trinitarian indwelling.

[2] St Teresa, *Interior Castle,* II, p. 331.

[3] See Augustine, *The Trinity,* X, 4, Brooklyn, NY: New City Press 1991.

[4] M. Scheler, *On the Eternal in Man,* Hamden: Archon Books 1972, p. 255.

*B:* Yes there are: in addition to the witness of contemplatives and, if you like, mystics, we have the testimony of the New Testament, especially the Gospels. The basis of our understanding of God as Triune is there, in the layer of Scripture known as *Frükatholizismus*. It is in and through Jesus of Nazareth that the Father and the Spirit are revealed, though, to be sure, not right away. Jesus' first followers had little or no understanding of the Holy Spirit as divine. For that we have to wait until the revised version of the Nicean Creed in 381 and the confession of Chalcedon in 451.

*A:* When you relate Scripture and the Trinity, I assume that you are not relying on the 'Comma Johanneum' (1 Jn. 5.7)! If we exclude that little addition to Scripture, your suggestion has potentially more weight than what you have said about the testimony of the mystics, for it's a matter of general rather than specific revelation. And there may well be more evidence than you think for an early affirmation of the divinity of the Spirit, although, to be sure, none of it is completely decisive. Think of Paul in I Cor. 3.16, Rom. 5.5 or Rom. 8.11 or many another verse in that layer of *Frükatholizismus*. So your suggestion certainly calls for further deliberation, especially with respect to its phenomenological ground. Let's add it to the ideas you've already proposed.

*B:* In a quite different key, it might also be noted that not all phenomena display themselves properly or fully when we come across them, and this is why we need phenomenology in the first place. It is the gentle art of nudging phenomena by performing the ἐποχή and adopting the transcendental attitude so that they manifest themselves as they are. Could it not be so with the Triune God? Could it be that God as Trinity hides from us only at first, and that we can train ourselves to perceive the Trinity?[5]

*A:* To see if this is so, we need to work out if the Triune God is like other phenomena, even saturated phenomena. I can consider the walnut tree outside my window, aspects of which are certainly hidden from me at any one time; and the same is true, in more complex ways, for my experience of anxiety or fatigue, a memory of a friend, my childhood, my death, a fantasy of a Betazoid or my sense of my lived body. I can perform eidetic and transcendental reductions, and in each case get a fuller, clearer sense of each of these phenomena. There will always be aspects that are absent from me, though: phenomenology is not the study of presence but of presence and absence.

*B:* Is it the absence of the Trinity that bothers you?

*A:* No, it's not that. It's rather that no matter what attitude I adopt I simply cannot perceive the Triune God. I can strive to approach God by

---

[5] On the issue of perceiving God (though not necessarily the Triune life of God), see W. P. Alston, *Perceiving God: The Epistemology of Religious Experience*, Ithaca: Cornell University Press 1991.

using my intellect but God gives Himself to me as Trinity only by revelation or by a special grace. I may appeal to my graced knowledge of God as Triune but even then I cannot perceive the Trinitarian relations. I may say with Augustine, *vero vides trinitatem si caritatem vides*, if I truly see love, I see the Trinity; but if I see genuine Christian love it does not make the Trinity, and exclusively the Trinity, manifest to me, for I also hold that if I truly see love then I see Christ.[6] To be sure, Christ does not act or exist independently of the Father and the Holy Spirit, but it seems possible to have an appearance of Christ that is not also a manifestation of the Trinity. In short, I cannot find the εἶδος of the God who is both one and three. If I adopt a noetic attitude towards the Trinity, I can make various noeses by intending love, fear, longing and so on, but cannot find any fulfilment by my acts. I must finally accept that the Christian God is not a phenomenon but a holy mystery.

*B:* I don't think it was ever in question that we were dealing with an object or even being in the usual sense of the word, *ens commune*.

*A:* No, but it now seems that the theme of our discussion is no more than a category mistake. The Triune God is not a phenomenon and therefore not open to phenomenology. I cannot pretend to see Him in the way I see essences. All the things I listed a moment ago – the walnut tree, anxiety, fatigue, a memory and so on – are transcendent to my consciousness, and in order to examine them as phenomena I must render them immanent. Yet God's mode of transcendence is singular; it cannot be rendered immanent. Husserl recognized this fact in *Ideas* I: 'extra-worldly 'divine' being. . . would obviously transcend not merely the world but 'absolute' consciousness. It would therefore be *an 'absolute' in the sense totally different from that in which consciousness is an absolute*, just as it would be *something transcendent in a sense totally different from that in which the world is something transcendent.'*[7]

*B:* If Rahner's Trinitarian theorem is correct, and the immanent Trinity *is* the economic Trinity, then surely we do have historical phenomena of the Triune God.[8]

*A:* I'm not sure that the economic Trinity presents itself as a phenomenon, though.

*B:* Three objections come to mind. First, even if the Triune God is not a phenomenon, isn't it possible for the all-powerful God to phenomenalize Himself as Trinity?

*A:* Perhaps in a certain way in so far as Jesus Christ is the Second Person of the Trinity and always one with the Father and the Holy Spirit. We need

[6] Augustine, *The Trinity*, VIII, 12.
[7] E. Husserl, *Ideas Pertaining to a Pure Phenomenology and to a Phenomenological Philosophy*, I: *General Introduction to a Pure Phenomenology*, Dordrecht: Kluwer Academic Publishers 1998, p. 134.
[8] See K. Rahner, *The Trinity*, London: Burns and Oates 1975.

to draw a couple of distinctions, though. We don't want to confuse phenomenalizing with representation. There are beautiful artworks of the Trinity in S. Apollinare in Classe, in the Museum im Prediger in Schwäbisch-Gmünd, and of course there is El Greco's painting of the Trinity in the Prado; but these are human representations and not divine phenomenalizations. The pictorial vision of the Trinity in the now lost *Rupertsberg Scivias* has a stronger claim on us in that way, but we simply do not know who drew it and why. What Hildegard actually saw may mark a *limit* of manifestation or even a theophany of the Trinity, namely that we see only Christ. We also need to keep appropriation in mind: we tend to figure the divine *personæ* in terms of what is proper to each one, according to the divine missions, yet the Trinity in and of itself always works as one. Anyway, this suggestion returns us to the auditions and visions of the mystics, so let us place the question with the one you made earlier. What else were you thinking?

*B:* Obviously the Trinity will not appear on an intentional horizon set by ordinary perception, for the Father and Holy Spirit are without form; besides, as you say, we need always to remember that the *personæ* are constituted by subsistent relations. We speak analogically when we speak in 'person' language about God. But I wanted to draw attention to intentional relations such as hope, and love and faith. One can pray to the Trinity, and those intentional rapports would be in play then.

*A:* I see you are not urging a non-intentional phenomenology as the one and only way to approach the Trinity. Can you have both? Anyway, let's keep your question on ice and return to it. I think you had another objection.

*B:* Yes, your quotations from Husserl do not represent all that he says about God, not even in *Ideas* I. He says that we cannot take 'the immanence of God in absolute consciousness. . . as immanence in the sense of being as a mental process' (117). Yet it does not follow from this statement that there are not 'within the absolute stream of consciousness and its infinities, modes in which transcendencies are made known other than the constituting of physical realities as unities of harmonious appearances' (117).

*A:* I hadn't forgotten that passage; it's an idea that Husserl doesn't develop.

*B:* My point is that there could be, even for Husserl, a way in which the divine could be in human consciousness that cannot be picked up by our intentionality. He tells us that 'ultimately there would also have to be intuitional manifestations to which a theoretical thinking might conform, so that by following them rationally it might make intelligible the unitary rule of the supposed theological principle.' (117). This is what Husserl had in mind when he said to Dorion Cairns and Eugen Fink that 'Only when the nature of a transcendental consciousness is understood, can the transcendence of God be understood. Thus all religion has been naïve and therefore unintelligible, but in the phenomenological attitude the naïve theses of religion receive not only intelligibility, but also a certain validity.'[9] A door has been opened a little, only to be quickly closed: 'But none of that concerns us here any further,' Husserl flatly says, and then immediately adds, 'Our immediate aim is not theology but phenomenology.' (117). What, though, if our aim *were* theology, or more precisely phenomenological theology? Would it be possible to keep the door open, and what would we see if we looked through it?

*A:* Every now and then Husserl himself gave us an idea of what we might see through the open door, at least if we use the lenses he ground for himself. Ethical-religious questions, he thought, were the very last ones that phenomenology kept in reserve to be answered; they needed all the resources that could possibly be mustered, for they were even more demanding than those that pressed on him when developing his phenomenology of time.[10] He was not attracted to confessional issues, he said, and so we find no comments on soteriology or eschatology or Christology, only speculations on the existence of God; and God, he came to think (as a private view), is the horizon of all possible horizons, the end to which all reality is ordered, the monad of all monads, that can look into each and every consciousness.[11] Without a doubt, this is a God of the philosophers, not of the theologians; moreover, even though Husserl had converted from Judaism to Lutheran Christianity, this God is not conceived as Triune.

*B:* We've said nothing at all about Heidegger, Merleau-Ponty, or any other phenomenologist, including the recent ones who are deeply interested in Christianity: Emmanuel Falque, Jean-Yves Lacoste and Jean-Luc Marion, for example. We've barely touched on Max Scheler's *Vom Ewigen im Menschen* (1921), which Heidegger castigates as giving 'the impression that phenomenology is something "for becoming Catholic"'.[12] And Michel Henry invokes the Father and the Son in his enstatic phenomenology. Shouldn't we discuss him at least?

*A:* We've surely come up with quite enough in one conversation, and non-intentional phenomenology has already been asterisked for attention. Let's pause for a while.

---

[9] D. Cairns, *Conversations with Husserl and Fink,* The Hague: Martinus Nijhoff 1976, p. 47.

[10] Cairns, *Conversations with Husserl and Fink,* p. 47.

[11] E. Husserl, *The Basic Problems of Phenomenology: From the Lectures, Winter Semester, 1910–1911,* Dordrecht: Springer 2006, pp. 177–8.

[12] See M. Heidegger, *Phenomenology of Intuition and Expression: Theory of Philosophical Concept Formation,* London: Continuum 2010, p. 23.

# *Ideas I–V*

Let's gather together the ideas generated by the discussion between *A* and *B*, noting that they are both orthodox Christian voices. No credence is given to Unitarianism or Tritheism, for example: the Mormon conception of God as three distinct heavenly persons who share the one purpose is not entertained. Neither *A* nor *B* seems to be a modalist; for each of them God is one being and three *personæ*. In short, they affirm the Nicean Creed in its final form and the confession of Chalcedon that *B* mentions. Neither seems bothered by the *Filioque*, and so that important issue must be left to one side. Nor does either *A* or *B* raise the question of charismatic experience of the Holy Spirit. Let's leave it for another time. Finally, *A* and *B* are mostly intrigued by Husserlian phenomenology, while not discounting other approaches; and this emphasis shall be retained in the interest of economy.

*A* and *B* leave us with five more or less disconnected ideas: (1) A phenomenology of the Trinity could be proposed if and only if God phenomenalizes Himself as Triune; (2) It would have to use the intentional rapports of faith, hope and charity; (3) Such a phenomenology would have to attend to reception instead of constitution; (4) If there is a phenomenology of the Trinity, it would have to be non-intentional; and (5) A phenomenology of the Trinity would have its ground in the New Testament revelation of Jesus as the Christ. I shall briefly consider each in turn.

1. Like many others, *A* and *B* fail to draw some important distinctions, and I shall start by doing what they do not; for we need to be aware of differences between a theophany, a manifestation, a revelation and a vision (or audition). A manifestation gives an aspect of a phenomenon; it is given, and can be sought by attending to it. While some aspects of it will be absent from one's view, they can be co-intended: no one is surprised to find that a laptop has a back when one is focused on its screen. A revelation, however, cannot be sought, except perhaps in prayer, but must be given by grace; it may re-veil as well as reveal and so retain a mystery. Revelations may be general (Scripture) or specific (individual visions and auditions). St Augustine distinguishes three species of visions – intellectual, imaginative and perceptual – and St Teresa follows him.[13] What is given is given according to a particular 'region of being', as phenomenologists say, and has varying levels of *Evidenz*, self-evidence.

It is possible for God to disclose Himself as Trinity in several ways for example in Scripture, in preaching, in imagination and in auditions. None of these manifestations needs to be full or complete: there is no full exhibition of the Trinity in the New Testament, as *B* realizes. God could also show

---

[13] See Augustine, *Literal Commentary on Genesis*, in *On Genesis*, XII. 15–16 (The Works of Saint Augustine 1/13), Brooklyn, NY: New City Press 2002; St Teresa, *Life*, chapter 27.

Himself by way of the triads that *A* and *B* put to one side, and even though the liturgy displays and enacts the economic Trinity's plan of salvation one might hesitate to say that the Trinity is fully phenomenalized there. A theophany, however, is a sensuous appearing of an aspect of God, such as the voice in the burning bush in Exod. 3.4–6; and while there are a number of testimonies to theophanies there are very few, if any, that involve God as Trinity. There are also limits to the ways in which the divine *personæ* display themselves, for the Father and the Holy Spirit are without form, and the Father is hidden from sight. 'No man hath seen God at any time' we are told in Jn. 1.18 (KJV), 'the only begotten Son, which is in the bosom of the Father, he hath declared *Him*' [θεὸν οὐδεὶς ἑώρακεν πώποτε· μονογενὴς θεὸς ὁ ὢν εἰς τὸν κόλπον τοῦ πατρὸς ἐκεῖνος ἐξηγήσατο]. This verse poses a problem for any showing of God as Trinity: the Father is forever hidden from earthly sight and we know His nature (as compassionate, forgiving, just, loving and so on) only through the testimony of Jesus. This view is supported by 1 Tim. 6.16 where we are told, 'no man hath seen, nor can see' the Father. Of course, there are passages from the Tanakh that are in apparent tension with this view: 'I the LORD will make myself known … in a vision', we read in Num. 12.6. More starkly, in Exod. 33.11 we are told, 'And the LORD spake unto Moses face to face, as a man speaketh unto his friend.'[14] Most problematically of all in Gen. 18.1–2 we hear of Abraham: 'And the Lord appeared unto him in the plains of Mamre: and he sat in the tent door in the heat of the day: And he lift up his eyes and looked, and, lo, three men stood by him.' In the first two passages God is said to have manifested Himself but not in a Trinitarian fashion. A Christian committed to the revealed truth of John and Timothy would have to say that God the Father might have spoken in the vision and talked with Moses without appearing visibly before him, or could argue that if anyone has been seen, it would be Christ or an angel.

Only in the final passage is there a possibility of a theophany of the Trinity, though many centuries before any dogmatic definition that God is Triune. If God is Triune, it will be said by way of objection, He was so from eternity and the date of the dogmatic determination does not matter in the least. Nonetheless, if 'three men' are seen, even if as in Andrei Rublev's beautiful fifteenth-century icon, it is unlikely that Genesis can be relating a theophany of the Trinity. For mainstream Christians believe that the Trinity is simple and cannot be divided into three separate beings. The Trinitarian relations are distinctions, not divisions; and the Trinitarian life is perichoresis. Ephrem the Syrian observes the three men are angels and that God 'alighted upon one of them' and that 'when the two departed to

---

[14] On the singular status of Moses, see Augustine, *Letters 100–155*, (The Works of Saint Augustine), Hyde Park, NY: New City Press 2003, 147.32.

go to Sodom, that one through whom God was speaking remained.'[15] The image is of unity, not Trinity. Similarly, at the very end of the *Paradiso* Dante seeks to evoke the Trinity as '*tre colori e d'una contenenza*' [three colours and of one dimension] (*Paradiso* XXXIII, 117), which does not render the phenomenon of the Trinity so much as the impossibility of such a rendering. Christians will say that Abraham may have seen Christ and two angels but not the Father, Son and Holy Spirit. Indeed, in Christianity it is more than enough that we have Christ as a phenomenon. He is, as St Gregory Nazianzus said, ὁ Λόγος παχύνεται, the condensed Word, and as St Bernard of Clairvaux said, *Verbum abbreviatum*, the abbreviated Word: all that we need to know of God for our salvation.[16] To these should be added Julian of Norwich's remark, 'for wher Jhesu appirith the blessed trinitie is vnderstood,' and the observation of the father of *ressourcement*, Henri de Lubac: 'The mystery of the Trinity, which sheds light on the mystery of human existence, is wholly contained in the mystery of Christ.'[17] Even Hildegard's vision of the man – if it is a man – in sapphire blue is of a human figure and two concentric circles: we see the human in the Trinity, and perhaps what is exhibited is that the Trinity is one with humanity through the incarnation of Christ. If we have Christ we also have the Trinity, though not as phenomenon. So we should devote our energies to a phenomenology of the Christ while believing in the Trinity and praying to Father, Son and Holy Spirit.

2. It is certainly possible to pray to God as Trinity, and when this happens one prays in faith, hope and love, among other intentional rapports. In prayer, awe or thankfulness or wonder prompts us to reduction, and so we become aware of how we comport ourselves to God. Faith, here, is different from belief; it is the *fides qua* and not the *fides quæ*. It is directed to the Trinity in which one believes, regardless of whether or not there is a Triune God. Christians will say that they *are* addressing the Triune God and the same deity is hearing them and will answer their prayers in one way or another. They may even speak of experiencing the Trinity in the sense of being aware of Trinitarian indwelling, the *sensus amoris*. To these remarks a phenomenologist would add that 'experience' is not the living through of particular events external to consciousness but rather, as Husserl says, 'the

---

[15] *The Armenian Commentary on Genesis Attributed to Ephrem the Syrian*, I, Louvain: Peeters 1998, p. 97.

[16] See for example Gregory of Nazianzus, *On Epiphany*, (PG 35, 313b) and Bernard of Clairvaux, *On the Eve of the Lord's Birth*, I.1, in *Sermons for Advent and the Christmas Season*, Kalamazoo: Cistercian Publicans 2007. Both have Rom. 9.28 in mind.

[17] H. de Lubac, *The Christian Faith: An Essay on the Structure of the Apostle's Creed*, San Francisco: Ignatius Press 1986, p. 15. Julian of Norwich anticipates the claim. See *A Book of Showings to the Anchoress Julian of Norwich*, II, Toronto: Pontifical Institute of Mediaeval Studies 1978, p. 295.

relevant acts of perceiving, judging etc, with their variable sense-material, their interpretative content, their assertive character, etc'.[18] Experience, for phenomenology, is therefore given to us by way of intentional acts; we live through them but they do not appear to us as objectified events. When we study prayer in phenomenology we can always show that the intentional rapports appear concretely on a horizon, and we can thereby analyze any noetic engagement with the Triune God. Yet we cannot usually say whether our intentions are fulfilled. I may find that I have more and more profiles of the deity, learned through meditation on Scripture or from reading Theology or from the experience of a life of prayer. However, unless I have mystical illumination, or even a vague awareness of the Trinity, I shall not have a proper fulfilment of any intention, and maybe not even then. Not even Karl Rahner's 'transcendental experience' of the Holy Spirit gives us a satisfactory fulfilment of an intention.[19] I might have awareness of Christ, such as the one to which St Teresa of Ávila testifies in her autobiography, but not of the Trinity, even though I may firmly believe that Christ is the second person of the Trinity and that He does not manifest Himself without the other divine persons being present in some way.[20]

3. When we pray to the Trinity, we do not constitute the Triune God as phenomenon; we dispose ourselves so that we receive Him as mystery. We do not bring God into presence; we enter into His presence, which may be quite different from human modes of presence. The Triune God is not an object or a being, nor strictly being itself but rather *ipsum esse subsistens omnibus modis indeterminatum*, to use Aquinas' fine expression, that is, wholly undetermined subsistent 'to be' itself.[21] God is an absolutely singular *event*, and doubtless His Triune nature is an index of that singularity. If I engage in ἐποχή and reduction in an attempt to figure the Trinity as phenomenon, I may find a noesis but I cannot find a noema, what my intentional act aims at, since the Trinity exceeds human thought, as much in the transcendental attitude as in the natural attitude. I can think of the unity of God and I can think of Jesus Christ, but the Triune nature of God transcends any mental act I might perform. One might say that I pray to God believing that He is Triune, and not to the Trinity as such. However, none of this blockage on my part prevents the Triune God from giving Himself to me or to anyone. I may receive the Trinity in a pre-predicative manner, and the Trinity may dwell within me. In some ways phenomenology is a mode of *contemplatio*: it trains us in essential seeing, what Husserl calls *Wesenserschauung*. Of course, in Christianity *contemplatio* is directed to

---

[18] E. Husserl, *Logical Investigations*, II, London: Routledge and Kegan Paul 1970, p. 540.
[19] See K. Rahner, 'Experience of the Holy Spirit', in ibid., *Theological Investigations*, 18, New York: Crossroad Publishers 1963.
[20] *The Life of Teresa of Ávila by Herself*, London: Penguin, 1957, pp. 187–8.
[21] Thomas Aquinas, STh, I, q.11, a.4, resp.

the Triune God who transcends the world, while phenomenology teaches us only how to look behind the world, at the constituting activity of transcendental consciousness, and to grasp as knowledge what can be rendered immanent. When we look inwards at the Trinity dwelling there, however, we do not find pure consciousness; instead, we find that which exceeds consciousness and that, so Christians believe, gazes at us. The Trinity enters us *modus sine modo*, as St Bernard says about the reception of the Word.[22] We cannot experience God, for God is not a thing, as Husserl recognized. (He is no-thing-ness, as Eckhart says.) Nonetheless, Husserl added, 'God would be 'experienced' in each *belief* that believes originally-teleologically in the perceptual value of that which lies in the direction of each absolute ought and which engages itself for this perpetual meaning.' [my emphasis].[23] We live through the intentional act of belief, though Husserl would remind us that we have suspended any affirmation or denial of the object of belief.

4. There is reason, then, to think that if the Trinity dwells within us, or at least in some good souls, we would need a non-intentional phenomenology in order to say anything about this indwelling. This idea of relating the divine and the non-intentional seems to be what Husserl was thinking in *Ideas* I, when he evokes the possibility of there being 'within the absolute stream of consciousness and its infinities, modes in which transcendencies are made known other than the constituting of physical realities as unities of harmonious appearances' (117). If we think of God within the natural attitude, He is outside or beyond the world, or He may be deep within the soul. 'Inside' and 'outside', 'above' and 'beyond', and all other expressions like them, are mundane descriptors. They bespeak worldly attitudes, even if they appeal to the supernatural. The Abrahamic religions, as practised by the theologically untutored, are beleaguered by the supernatural attitude as much as by the natural attitude. The latter is the default acknowledgement of the positive sciences as being able to explain phenomena as existing irrespective of consciousness; and the former is the naïve view that creedal statements are theses about two worlds, one heavenly and one earthly, both of which exist as entities without reference to consciousness. It is only when we pass from the natural or supernatural attitude to the transcendental attitude that the statements of Christianity or any religion become intelligible. Moreover, Husserl says, they also receive thereby 'a certain validity'.[24]

---

[22] See Bernard of Clairvaux, *On the Song of Songs*, IV, *Sermon* 74. II. 5, Kalamazoo, MI: Cistercian Publications 1980.

[23] Husserl, A V 21, 128a. I quote James G. Hart's translation of the passage in his 'A Précis of Husserlian Phenomenological Theology', in S. W. Laycock, J. G. Hart (eds), *Essays in Phenomenological Theology*, Albany: State University of New York Press, 1986, p. 148. More generally, see A. A. Bello, *The Divine in Husserl and Other Explorations*, in *Analecta Husserliana* XCVIII, Dordrecht: Springer 2009.

[24] Carins, *Conversations with Husserl and Fink*, p. 47.

We may honour the ἐποχή and reduction without committing ourselves to the mentalist account of the human subject that Husserl endorses. We may have learned, that is, from Heidegger or Merleau-Ponty or others who have succeeded them. In ecstatic phenomenology, what is important is that we step back or aside from the natural and supernatural attitudes in order to see the ways in which our intentional relations with phenomena are concretely embedded on a horizon. Yet in enstatic phenomenology, where the transcendence of the ego is not a concern, we do no such thing.

An enstatic phenomenology of the Trinity would begin by acknowledging something like what Descartes observed in the third Meditation: 'in some way I have in me the notion of the infinite earlier than the finite – to wit, the notion of God before that of myself' [Latin (1641): *ac proinde priorem quodammodo in me esse perceptionem infiniti quàm finiti, hoc est Dei quàm meî ipsius*; French (1647): *partant que j'ai en quelque façon premièrement en moi la notion de l'infini, que du fini, c'est-à-dire de Dieu, que de moi-même*].[25] Now Husserl thought that by the time Descartes began the third Meditation he had lost the transcendental attitude and returned to scholastic ways of thinking. And to be sure Husserl's remark in *Ideas* I is at best a distant harmonic of Descartes' point. Husserl alludes to the stream of consciousness 'and *its* infinities' [my emphasis] while Descartes identifies the infinite in himself. So Husserl's case for God is teleological, and Descartes' is not. Let us leave Husserl for the moment, and look more closely at Descartes. Why should he wish to correlate the notion of infinity and God? To find an answer we must go back to St Gregory of Nyssa's reformulation of the received idea of God in his *Contra Eunomium*. Eunomius of Cyzicus, an Arian bishop with a powerful philosophical mind, had argued against the divinity of Christ by pointing out that God is unbegotten but that, as the Nicene Creed asserts, Christ is begotten and therefore cannot be divine. Gregory argued against this view that only the Father is unbegotten, not all the divine *personæ*, for no one word can describe the divine essence, least of all an unbiblical one, and the determining trait of Godhood is infinite goodness; indeed, it is this rethinking of the notion of God that makes the doctrine of the Trinity defensible for the Pro-Nicene party, which included Gregory and the other Cappadocian fathers.[26]

Were Descartes merely making the argument that the concept of infinity is prior to the concept of finitude, he would not necessarily be saying anything at all about the existence of God. To do that, he must reply on Gregory's redefining of God as infinite; and of course the account of God's

---

[25] Descartes, 'Meditation III' in *The Philosophical Works of Descartes*, I, Cambridge: Cambridge University Press 1931, p. 166.
[26] See St Gregory of Nyssa, *Contra Eunomium*, (Nicene and Post-Nicene Fathers, 2nd Series), Peabody, MA: Hendrinkson Publishers 1994, I, p. 673, II, pp. 554–7.

infinity is also the justification for the divinity of the Son and the Holy Spirit. Descartes is committed to prove the existence of God in the third Meditation, and has nothing to say about His Triune nature, and Husserl does not evoke the Trinity in his remarks on God in *Ideas* I or, as far as I know, anywhere. Yet a phenomenologist who is aware of Gregory's arguments in *Contra Eunomium* may well wish to contend that the Triune God dwells behind or before intentional consciousness. Can intentional consciousness direct itself towards this God? Yes, in prayer; but of course the Trinity cannot be conceived as an object embedded on an intentional horizon. God overflows all horizons.

5. The final suggestion takes us away from philosophy and to the New Testament. It is proposed that a phenomenology of the Trinity would have its ground in the revelation of Jesus as the Christ in the New Testament. To discuss the entire stratum of *Frükatholizismus* or proto-Catholicism, or even a fair bit of it, is beyond the limits of a short essay. Many texts could be cited to indicate the intimacy, even the unity, of Jesus and the Father; others can be cited with historical-critical reservations about the claim of unity of the Father, the Son, and the Holy Spirit. There is Matt. 3.16–17: when John baptizes Jesus 'the heavens were opened unto him, and he saw the Spirit of God descending like a dove, and lighting upon him; And lo a voice from heaven, saying, This is my beloved Son, in whom I am well pleased.' Yet an adoptionist Christology could also make use of this passage, and 'Spirit of God' need not imply a Trinitarian person in this context. Later in Matthew we hear the great commission: 'Go ye therefore, and teach all nations, baptizing them in the name of the Father, and of the Son, and of the Holy Ghost' (Matt. 28.19). The verse bespeaks a liturgical practice among early Christians that is at least consonant with the dogmatic definition of the Trinity, for the parataxis may be taken to imply equality between Father, Son and Holy Spirit. In the Gospels, then, Jesus is presented as the one by whom the Father and the Holy Spirit are made manifest. Whether they are disclosed as Trinity is not decisive in the Gospel but calls for the intense Christological and Trinitarian debates that were formally resolved, if not accepted by all parties, in 381.

The Gospels afford us a means by which we can begin a phenomenology of the Christ. We can study the phenomena of His practices of eating and preaching, how He brings forth sin and forgiveness as phenomena, his phenomenology of proper relations with the Father (by way of the βασιλεία), the phenomenon of His death and the saturated phenomenon of His bodily resurrection. We also can recognize that He engages in a phenomenology of His own, for Jesus performs a ἐποχή and reduction of his own: not along the lines of Husserl or anyone who learned from him but in a quite different manner. We see Jesus perpetually confronted with a version of the natural attitude, 'the world', in its various forms (αἰών, κόσμος, *mundum, orbis terrarum, imperium mundi*) and responding by leading his audience (and us) back to something that has a prior claim on us, the βασιλεία or Kingdom. The good arrangement and harmony of κόσμος must be led back to a better arrangement and harmony in which the Father is regarded as absolute, not His creation or anything in it. The power of *imperium mundi* must be bracketed for us to see what is radically prior to it, the loving rule of the Father. It is in passing from the everyday attitudes to human existence, including religious existence, to the Kingdom of the Father that we draw close to God and to our original and primary engagement with life as created beings. Self-interest at the level of the individual, the family and the State is set aside, and we are enjoined to be compassionate towards one another, even when this appears to go against the rules and regulations of religious practice, as in the parable of the Good Samaritan (Luke 10.25–37).

What we see here is a different mode of phenomenality from the one to which Husserl alerted us. For Husserl, writing in 1925, the ἐποχή switches off the allure of natural objects and psyches, and 'reduces all that to its phenomenality and takes its own position not in the world, but in the subjectivity for which the world is experienced ... pure subjectivity'.[27] Three years later, lecturing in Amsterdam, he adds, 'Accordingly, phenomenality, as a characteristic that specifically belongs to appearing and to the thing that appears, would, if understood in this broadened sense of the term, be the fundamental characteristic of the mental.'[28] However, if we pass from phenomenology as practised within philosophy to phenomenology within theology, things change. We see in the New Testament that Jesus is a phenomenon, to be sure, but He is also the phenomenality of God, the singular mode in which God gives Himself to us. The Christian God is not abstract but is one with Jesus of Nazareth. So Jesus is the one by whose light we see the Kingdom of the Father, and when we look back in belief from the dogmatic definition of God as Triune we can grasp that He is the phenomenality of the Triune God. Yet how do we see Jesus as the Christ? The same belief will require us to say: by the light of the Holy Spirit, who is another phenomenality of the same deity. A Christian might venture to say that Husserl is not the father of phenomenology; he supplied a vocabulary and an approach to it in the field of modern philosophy, but what he discovered had long been around, although in another mode. Husserl purifies phenomenology, he does not inaugurate it; and in theology, at least, we need to wean ourselves from the mentalist account of it that he offers.

---

[27] E. Husserl, *Phenomenological Psychology: Lectures, Summer Semester, 1925*, The Hague: Martinus Nijhoff 1977, p. 179.
[28] Husserl, 'The Amsterdam Lectures' in ibid., *Psychological and Transcendental Phenomenology and the Confrontation with Heidegger (1927–1931)*, Th. Sheehan and R. E. Palmer (ed. and trans.), (Collected Works, VI), Dordrecht: Kluwer Academic Publishers 1997, p. 218.

After these initial responses to the five ideas thrown out by the conversation between *A* and *B*, I propose to say a little more about two of them, 4 and 5: the view that the Triune God dwells within us in a non-intentional manner, and the claim that Jesus is the phenomenality of God.

# 'They will get it straight one day at Montpellier'

Michel Henry has long argued for a non-intentional phenomenology of God, that is, that God is immanent in human being. Seen negatively, his position seeks to reverse the phenomenology of Husserl and Heidegger; and seen positively, it draws from the Gospel of John, Meister Eckhart's homilies and J. G. Fichte's *Die Anweisung zum Seligen Leben* (1806). Put very briefly, Henry rejects the Husserlian and Sartrean account of the transcendence of the ego and, with it, the doctrine that phenomenology is governed by intentionality. On the traditional understanding of phenomenology, human being, whether intentional consciousness or *Dasein*, is directed to the world. Intentional phenomenology regards each thing as becoming manifest by the shining of being or, for Husserl, consciousness. There is a split, then, between the phenomenon and phenomenality or, as Henry likes to put it, between what is deemed to be true and the truth itself.[29] It is Henry's view that this split, this 'ontological monism', in which all being must be subject to the transcendence of the ego, and in which mundane visibility is privileged, hides a prior immanence of subjectivity.[30] It is a movement of losing interiority that has been coming upon the West since Galileo, with only a minor tradition, including Fichte, Schopenhauer and Nietzsche, to contest it.[31] 'What, then, is a truth that differs in no way from what is true?' he asks. And his answer is 'If truth is manifestation grasped in its phenomenological purity – phenomenality and not the phenomenon – then what is phenomenalized is phenomenality itself.' (25). All transcendence ultimately relies on a prior immanence in human subjectivity.

It follows for Henry that God is not a being or being itself, and is certainly not subject to intentional analysis. Christian belief in God is not a question of sincerely affirming creedal statements in the existence or saving acts of a transcendent being (or being as transcendent) but of acknowledging the priority of Life and bringing one's life into strict conformity with

---

[29] See M. Henry, *I am the Truth: Toward a Philosophy of Christianity*, Stanford: Stanford University Press 2003, p. 24. For more generally on Henry, see my essay 'Inward Life' in Jeffrey Hanson (ed.), *Michel Henry: The Affects of Thought*, London: Continuum, forthcoming.
[30] See Henry, *The Essence of Manifestation*, Dordrecht: Kluwer 1973, p. 74.
[31] See Henry, *The Genealogy of Psychoanalysis*, Stanford: Stanford University Press 1993.

it. One does this by rejecting the lure of the world, its commitment to exteriority, representation and production, and by living life as an individual, working with creative force, and in the light of subjectivity.[32] God, therefore, is Life, pure self-revelation, and we are 'livings'.[33] We experience God in the auto-affection of Life: its *pathos* and its self-development. This may bring comfort to process theologians, although it does not mean that God is an epiphenomenon of human or animal life. 'The relation between the Ipseity of absolute Life and the me of each living being implies no reciprocity,' we are assured: 'God could just as well live eternally in his Son and the latter in his Father without any other living being ever coming to Life.' (129). This is an echo of Aquinas's account of the asymmetry of Creator and creation, in which our relations with God are real, *relatio realis,* but God's relations with us are unreal, *relatio rationis tantum:* we depend on God for our existence but He does not depend on us for His.[34] Nonetheless, this God does not create *ex nihilo*, for Life is an endless process, Henry believes, and so orthodox Christians will be wary of Henry and regard him, with good reason, as a modern Gnostic.[35]

One will therefore not look to Henry for a Trinitarian understanding of God, even though he proposes to offer a discourse converging on 'une philosophie du christianisme,' as the subtitle of *C'est moi la vérité* (1996) proclaims. His philosophy of the faith is biniterian rather than Trinitarian, answering to Semi-Arianism and not to orthodox Christianity. For Henry, the Father gives birth to the 'Arch-Son' who is '"consubstantial" with the Father' – the scare quotes around 'consubstantial' should be noted – and we, in conforming ourselves to His self-revelation, become sons of God as well. We are truly born not when we enter the world as children but when we enter Life.[36] As Henry stresses: *'no man is the son of man, or of any woman either, but only of God'*. (70). Relying heavily on the fourth gospel, especially the 'Farewell Discourse', and setting the synoptic gospels and the Pauline epistles to one side, Henry dwells on verses such as 'And he that seeth me seeth him that sent me.' (Jn. 12.45) and would seem to follow C. H. Dodd's reading of the fourth gospel as having a Hellenistic pneumatology.[37] Instead of seeing the Holy Spirit in all its vibrant activity as

---

[32] See Henry, *Du Communisme au capitalisme: Théorie d'une catastrophe*, Paris: Éditions Odile Jacob 1990, p. 29.

[33] Although he nowhere mentions her, Henry would be close to Hildegard in her affirmation of God as life. See her *Symphonia: A Critical Edition of the Symphonia Armonie Celestium Revelationum*, Ithaca: Cornell University Press 1988, p. 143.

[34] See Aquinas, STh, I, q.13 a.7, c; I, q.28, a.1, ad 3; I, q.45 a.3, *De Potentia*, I, q. 3, 3, and *Truth*, I, q.4 a.5, resp.

[35] See Henry, *I am the Truth*, p. 62.

[36] Henry, *I am the Truth*, p. 109.

[37] See C. H. Dodd, *The Interpretation of the Fourth Gospel*, Cambridge: Cambridge University Press 1953, esp. p. 222.

presented in Acts 2.1–4, we are pointed to the 'reciprocal phenomenological interiority of Father and Son' and informed that it is 'phenomenological in its very essence, being nothing other than the mode in which phenomenality originally phenomenalizes itself – as the original phenomenality that is Life' (91). When Henry admits 'The Spirit blows where it will' (232) we are not told if this is a divine person, and in the absence of any Trinitarian framework we have no reason to think that Henry thinks it is.

Now one may well take Henry's binitarianism as a caution for developing any phenomenology of the Christian God along enstatic lines. At the same time, one might ask if this account could be reformulated so that it is an adequate 'philosophy of Christianity', one that acknowledges the Triune God, or indeed could be rethought more radically so that it is a part of Christian theology? Let us follow this thread for a moment. We might say with Henry that God is radically immanent in each of us, pure phenomenality, truth that is also what is true, Life itself. Immanence here does not imply any restriction of God's power; it merely indicates that transcendence, the world, emerges out of immanence and relies upon it. Henry proposes that the Father generates the Arch-Son, the Christ, and while we may find his way of articulating this teaching somewhat odd, and perhaps indebted to Eckhart, there is no reason immediately to deem it unorthodox: the generation of the Son is a mystery.[38] Could one also add, as Henry does not, that the Holy Spirit proceeds from the Father and the Son (or perhaps, as the Greek and Russian Orthodox teach, simply from the Father)? The difference between generation and procession is profoundly obscure at best, and perhaps this obscurity has a positive function: to deter philosophers from attempting to offer too full an account of Trinity solely by the light of natural reason or transcendental consciousness. In terms of Henry's enstatic phenomenology, however, there would be no philosophical reason to posit or even countenance the Holy Spirit: God the Father would be regarded as pure phenomenality, and we would participate in this radical Life by resisting the allure of 'the world'. Henry goes further than this, as already noted, and acknowledges the life of the Arch-Son. And yet, strictly speaking, Henry does not need to posit even the sacrifice of the Son for his phenomenology to become a religious discourse. If God is radically immanent in each of us, pure phenomenality that phenomenalizes itself through the *sensus amoris*, say, then Henry does not actually require the mediation of the Son. All he needs is the dyad of Life and living. Not only is Henry's 'philosophy of Christianity' not Trinitarian, but also it does not need, in its own terms, to involve the historical Jesus at all. A Christ who comes to us more surely from Neoplatonism than from the New Testament will suffice perfectly well.

---

[38] See Henry, *I am the Truth*, p. 57.

# The Phenomenalities of the Trinity

Not to accept Henry's enstatic phenomenology of Christianity is not thereby to reject his insights into immanence. It is only to indicate that his phenomenology will be of no help in describing the Triune nature of God or rendering it present to consciousness or *Dasein*. Finally, then, let us return to the one remaining possibility that *A* and *B* canvassed in their introductory dialogue, the view that I have refined through preliminary discussion to be that Jesus is the phenomenality of God.

On this understanding, 'God' when used generally is a purely abstract notion, although in Christianity it is concrete because the words and acts of Jesus of Nazareth, and the Church's continuing reflection on Him, disclose the Triune God. From the viewpoint of phenomenology, it cannot be said that Jesus actually renders God present as a matter of historical fact, for phenomenology establishes and proves nothing. Considered within philosophy, phenomenology can speak of this manifestation only as an eidetic possibility. If it has been experienced, it can be posited as existent in some way; and so it can be regarded as a possible phenomenon.[39] It can be said, even without faith, that in His parables, in his teaching of the Lord's Prayer and in His acts as testified in the Gospels, Jesus makes the Father manifest as possibility. He is not shown visually but by way of the right relationship that we human beings may have with Him. This relationship is what Jesus calls βασιλεία or Kingdom. By ἐποχή and reduction in the telling of the parables, Jesus leads us to the proper relationship with the Father, and if we make a theme of this movement we may see the basileiac reduction as having two moments: κένωσις, whereby one withdraws from 'the world', and ἐπέκτασις, whereby one stretches into the endless possibilities of the Kingdom. Each could be explored in considerable detail, for the preaching of the βασιλεία leads to the Cross, while the Resurrection is the vindication that this preaching is the right relationship with the Father. Jesus shows us by word and example that the Lord God of Israel is our Father, and he shows us that the relationship that He enjoys is of such intimacy and union that He is the Son of this Father. In this sense, we may speak of Jesus as the phenomenality of God: He is the light by which we see a relation with the Father made manifest, as open to us in the βασιλεία. If we ask ourselves, though, how we are open to see the radiance of the Father in Jesus of Nazareth, we would have to say that there is another phenomenality at issue, a light by which the phenomenon of Jesus *as the Christ* is made visible. A Christian would not hesitate to say that this is the Holy Spirit, or more exactly the Father in and through the Holy Spirit. Each Trinitarian person illuminates the others in ways appropriate to each.

---

[39] See Scheler, *On the Eternal in Man*, p. 255.

Inevitably, this representative Christian would be speaking from the perspective of faith while regarding the New Testament as a decisive prompt to that faith. No phenomenology can neutrally identify God as Triune; that is, no phenomenology within the limits of philosophy can have anything to say about the Trinity. However, the same discipline also teaches us not to concede that philosophy, as a historical discourse, has the right to establish the final meaning of any experience or non-experience. If we regard phenomenology as a mode of thinking that participates in theology, then it can let us see what would be needed in order to propose a phenomenology of the Triune God. Even here, though, there are very strict limits to what can be achieved. The New Testament presents us with the manifestation of Jesus as the Christ, and normative belief assures us that there is no Christ without the Trinity. When we see Christ we see the Father, as John can testify when he has Jesus saying to Philip, 'he that hath seen me hath seen the Father' (Jn. 14.9). Normative Christianity may add that it is the Holy Spirit who enables this perception: God the Son reveals God the Father through God the Holy Spirit. Far from static, this relationship is entirely dynamic, for the Son is always being born as Son, the Father is always 'fathering-forth', as Gerard Manley Hopkins says, and the Holy Spirit is always inspiring the love of Christ and His Father.[40] However it is conceived, and in whatever degree of detail it is proposed, this last step will be labelled construction, not description. Jesus constitutes the approach of the Father in the Kingdom in Husserl's sense of rendering Him present to us: not through immanent mental acts but by our experience of Jesus's parables and acts. *Evidenz* for this presence occurs only through the conversion that Jesus asks of us, a conversion that takes place in a leading back from world to Kingdom. For it is life in the Kingdom that is the transcendental attitude for Christianity, an attitude that is also eschatological in that our hope, through Christ, is in the Kingdom coming in its fullness. To the extent that the phenomenon and phenomenality do not perfectly coincide we do not have absolute certainty of the truths of Christianity; and in this life such coincidence is not possible. We live in faith, not knowledge, even when animated or consoled by the *sensus amoris*.

Part of this faith is in the agency of the Holy Spirit and in the acknowledgment of the divinity of the Holy Spirit. We may say, as we have done, that there is liturgical evidence for the equality of the three divine *personæ* (Matt. 28.19), but this is a biblical statement, not anything given directly to intuition. Some might wish then to say that we can propose a phenomenology of non-experience in order to discuss the Trinity, and to some extent this is true. What we will gain, however, is a phenomenology of anticipation

---

[40] See G. M. Hopkins, 'Pied Beauty', in ibid., *Poems*, 3rd edition, London: Oxford University Press 1948, p. 74.

of when God shall be all in all. Others might add that we need a phenomenology of mystery, a discourse on how the mysterious displays itself, and
they would be right. In the end, the project of a phenomenology of the
Trinity has clear limits: the Trinity discloses itself only in the phenomenon
of the Christ, and phenomenology can follow this manifestation only eideti-
cally until an act of faith is made. Only then may one even talk of having a
partial fulfilment of one's intentional relationship with the Trinity through
the *sensus amoris*. It is probably given only to the saints. So phenomenology
can still be used in theology, but as a way of clarification and constitution
that is determined by a broader seeing that is neither that of the natural
attitude nor (for the thoughtful) that of the supernatural attitude. Even
here, phenomenology can focus with confidence only on the Christ as given
to us in the words of Scripture, preaching and the Eucharist. It is a phenomenology of the Christ, in the objective and subjective senses of the genitive,
which needs to be undertaken. The one would tell us how Jesus renders His
Father manifest though a study of all that Scripture shows Him doing and
suffering; and the other would show us how Jesus asks us to turn from the
world to the Kingdom, even though the Cross is implicit in the preaching
of the Kingdom. That would be the true supreme phenomenology.

# PART FOUR

# Anthropological Paradigms

# 14

# Trinity as 'Communio'

## Gisbert Greshake

## Towards a Communio-conception

### The primacy of the 'One'

In search of the ultimate reason for the long and complex post-Nicene disputes in the areas of Christology and Trinitarian theology, one would agree with Roland Kany who notes 'that ancient philosophy had no concept that could satisfactorily express the union between unicity and difference or the one and the multiple as required in the realm of dogmatic theology.'[1] The thought of the ancients was heavily influenced by the primacy given to the concept of the One. The Neoplatonic philosopher, Proclos, expresses this in the classical formulas: 'All Multiplicity is subordinate to the One "and" all Multiplicity participates in one way or another in the One.'[2] The supreme One and similarly the unique and most intimate essence of each being is thereby defined by the fact that it excludes all multiplicity, all difference and thus also all relationality and communication. In contrast to this stands the many and multifarious Individual, that by reason of its origin and its end is to be considered 'non essential', and ultimately, 'unreal'.

This focus on the One is not based on theoretical considerations; it is instead closely linked with man's concrete and existential quest for the immutable and the 'constant' in the midst of all transformation and change. This is because everything that involves multiplicity and variety also undergoes change: things are either in one way or another, combined with one or the other, always forming new variations and differentiations, even

[1] R. Kany, 'Via caritatis. Von Augustins Suche nach Gott', in: G. Augustin and Kl. Krämer (eds) *Gott denken und bezeugen*. FS W. Kasper, Freiburg-Basel-Wien: Herder 2008, p. 151.
[2] Cited in K. Ruh, *Geschichte der abendländischen Mystik*, Bd I, München 1990, p. 50.

contradictions that all come into conflict with man's desire for stability and a lasting home. In the long run, the main reason for the primacy given the One and the universal is man's great need for an ultimate sense of security, stability and order sought in the One, the immutable monads/universal beings, far from the confusing, often contradictory and chaotic variety in life and the world. Hence the priority given to the concept of the One from antiquity which states: the more something is One, the more it rejects and eliminates multiplicity, reducing the many to One or subordinating it to the One.

Within this prescribed horizon it initially proved difficult to conceive a threefold differentiated God based on his radical auto-revelation in the incarnation of the Logos and the sending of the spirit. Though the 'threeness' was not completely absorbed by the primacy of the 'oneness', it nevertheless remained substantially weakened by it. The tension between these two currents has led to the well-known variety of contrasting and conflicting positions formed in the Trinitarian reflections of early Christianity: either the Son and the Spirit were understood as the *ousia* of the Father, thus subordinated to Him (subordinationism) or they were considered only as manifestations of the Godhead (modalism). The first possibility was the preferred option in eastern theology, the second by those in the west. The east proceeded from the multiplicity of the persons but tended to place the Son and the Spirit after the Father – 'source' and 'origin' of the Trinity (not temporally, but ontologically, i.e. in accordance with the divine being); the west instead took as its starting point, the one divine nature, in which the Father, Son and Spirit are seen 'then' (again not temporally, but ontologically understood) as final determinations of the divine nature. Even though these characterizations are gross oversimplifications and generalizations, they nevertheless identify the problems resulting from the clash of the ancient concept of the One with faith in a Trinitarian God.

It was in principle clarified in Nicea that the difference of persons in God (the hypostaseis) did not lie on the level *beneath* the divine being (*ousia*), but that rather the differences were *identical* to it. In other words: in Nicea, it was clearly determined that there is a difference of persons within the One divine being and nature (in the one *ousia*). This also implied that the divine *ousia* is a framework of *plural* personal relations, thus different, but all absolutely of equal standing, paving the way for the primacy of the Personal and personal relations over and above the primacy of the substance, the universal and the One. However, these initial insights, with all they implied, came to be generally accepted only after a long and laborious process. Even there, where faith and theology long since validated the Trinitarian concept, the notion of the One still persistently sought to come forward into the limelight.

That new difficulties keep coming up was and is due to the absolutely revolutionary nature of the perspectives opened up by the Trinitarian faith that contradicted and strove to replace the then prevalent horizons of thought restricted to the primacy of the One. J. D. Zizioulas rightfully formulates it thus:

> When within the Greek and specifically Aristotelian onthology the term 'hypostasis' is no longer understood to mean 'substance' but rather 'person' in describing that reality which makes a being what it is, we are indeed standing *before a revolution*. Since the hypostasis (*sub-stantia* = that which constitutes the ultimate fundament) is conceived as referring not to the *ousia* (universal, immutable being) but rather to the person, consequently the ontological question will be answered not with reference to that which is in itself (a being confined to and determined by the limits of its own very existence) but rather to a being that through its extasis transcends these limitations by the movement of *communio*.... Since 'hypostasis' is identified with personhood and not with substance, the being *is itself* and only *wholly itself* not by virtue of its 'self-existence' but rather by virtue of being in Communio.[3]

What exactly is meant by communio here?

# The Concept of *Communio*

Communio is a term gleaned from the world of our human experience that like every other term can be applied to God only analogically, i.e. according to a certain similarity, while recognizing therein an even greater dissimilarity. Let us take a look at the literary history of this concept and the body of experiences that forms it.[4]

Contrary to common assumption, Communio has nothing to do with the linguistic root '*unio*' as if Communio were the sum of '*cum* ' + '*unio*', with the resulting meaning being, 'union with one another'. Far from it! Communio, from its linguistic origin has instead two connotations. First of all, it refers to the indogermanic root – 'mun', which means entrenchment, dike or embankment (in Latin, *moenia* = city wall). People who are '*in communione*', find themselves together behind a common embankment, i.e. they are joined in a common existential reality, which ties them together to a life in common, in which each person is dependent on the other. Seen in this

---

[3] J. D. Zizioulas, 'Human capacity and human incapacity. A theological exploration of personhood', in: *Scotish Journal of Theology* 28 (1975) 409. Similarly, Kl. Hemmerle, *Glauben – wie geht das?*, Freiburg-Basel-Wien: Herder 1978, p. 147.

[4] Cf., H. U. v. Balthasar, 'Communio – Ein Programm', in IkaZ 1 (1972) 4nn; R. Kress, 'Church as Communio', in: *Jurist* 36 (1976) 129n; G. Greshake, 'Der Ursprung der Kommunikationsidee', in *Communicatio Soc.*, 35 (2002) 3–26.

way, Communio designates the 'part-*taking* in a third common reality, i.e. in a common Lebensraum and other common goods, and *Communicatio* accordingly means the shared-*giving* of these 'bona'.

Secondly, (Com-)munio points to the root – 'mun' with the Latin equivalent being *munus* = task, service, as well as gift or present. Whoever lives in communion, puts himself at the service of another, hands on to this other a gift that shapes and forms him such that out of the giver and the receiver of communication, a third is constituted: the communio that is shared together.

The following is therefore common to both graphic linguistic associations: Communio is the process of a mediation; many individuals become a unity that is imparted and reciprocated; the unity resulting from communication has its 'contrary' – multiplicity and variety – not outside itself, but within; the unity of the Communio is therefore the enduring unity of many that are different. This comes to exist by the fact that the many partake of one and the same reality, be it a something pre-existent (a common environment of life behind the *moenia*), be it a reality that is common in so far as it is communally realized by the giving and receiving it entails. In whichever forms it may appear, Communio means mediation of identity and difference, of the particular and the universal. That which differentiates, that is different, the strange or foreign, is drawn to unity by partaking in and/or the shared giving of a common reality, without thereby losing the element of their differences.

This is exactly what sets the term 'Communio' apart from another very closely related term: 'community'. Community is rather associated with the static being-together of different persons. On the other hand, however, Communio is a thoroughly dynamic term, which stresses the very event of the mediation of the particular with the many, the part with the whole, the different with the identical. In all this, the Latin word *communio* corresponds very precisely to the Greek word κοινωνία (*koinonia*), that means both communion in itself (*communio*) as well as the realisation of this communion (*communicatio*).

Reality and concept of κοινωνία (*communio/communicatio*) are not foreign to ancient thinking. Apart from the theory of friendship that can be found for instance in Aristoteles, the Koinonia, in consonance with the primacy held by the One in ancient thinking, consists therein that the One and the universal shares of itself by a gradual weakening of itself towards the constitution of the many.[5] This results in the secondary position taken

---

[5] One of the most important Platonic axioms says: *Bonum est communicativum*, i.e. The Good is communicative, shares of itself, overflows. This principle is however understood within the context of the debate over the relationship between the One and the Multiple. In other words, it seeks to answer the following question: how can there exist the multiple beyond the divine Oneness? The answer: the One overflows into nothingness, just as light from a candle does not remain with itself but overflows into the darkness. In this way, from the immutable absolute

by the category of relation, relationality, appearing last on Aristoteles' list of categories. This is because relationality necessarily requires multiplicity, at least two who are in relation to each other and in any variable of reciprocity. True, real being in ancient thinking therefore excludes relationship; true and real being here means 'being-in-itself' and 'being-for-itself'. True being is -precisely put – substantial being. Thus it is clear that given its origin, *Communio/Communicatio* is in antiquity a thoroughly secondary mode of reality.

Now, on the other hand, the new experience of God in the New Testament from within century-long theological reflections has led to a new understanding of reality, and thereby also of *Communio*. For if God in Himself is not the one immutable Monad, but Life that shares of itself, relationality, *Communio*, then, that which for Aristotle is the least and the most insignificant part of being i.e. 'relation', is therefore the true nature of all beings. Being is relationality, to-be-with, being-with-others, 'interconnectedness', in short: *Communio*.

## Historical Insights

As we have already seen, the council of Nicea represents a tremendously important stage in this new discovery. By the statement that the Son is equal in nature to the Father, '*homoousios*', a new understanding of the divine is set in motion. A transcendental Monad is no longer the ultimate reference point of all reality, but a God, who is both unity as well as including personal differences within, a God, who is at once a 'relational unity'[6] and realizing in himself (as *actus purus*) *Communio/Communicatio*.[7] As Novatian puts it, the divine substance is a '*communio substantiae*',[8] hinting

---

Monads, by means of a gradual differentiated communicated sharing of itself, the subordinated multiplicity is constituted. This in turn, each according to the degree of 'being' possessed, can also communicate its being further downwards. Here, *Communio/Communicatio* occurs not actually between equals, but is rather constituted in a superior-versus-subordinate kind of relationship.
[6] Cf., I. U. Dalferth, *Jenseits von Mythos und Logos*, (QD 142), Freiburg-Basel-Wien: Herder 1993, p. 95: In Trintarian dogma [it had to do with] the replacing of the undifferentiated Platonic Monads and their hierarchically subordinated hypostases with a relational Unity.
[7] Cf. P. Hünermann, *Jesus Christus, Gottes Wort in der Zeit*, Münster Aschendorff 1994, p. 145: 'By this, the Greek concept of God is corrected. The communication in God Himself is accepted, because only so can God be conceived as one who could share his own Logos with the world.' As a fact, it is only on the basis of a relational God can it be understood that God himself enters into the relationality of history. On the contrary, based on Arian presuppositions, a real self-communication of God was not conceivable. Only a God who is in Himself communicative can communicate His own very self. (Original text, final sentence: Nur ein in sich ,kommunikativer' Gott kann *sich als er selbst* kommunizieren.)
[8] Novatian, *De Trin*, 27,6; 31,20 (CC 4,64.78).

possibly at a personal as well as 'communicative understanding of the *Unitas substantiae*'.[9] In this way the supremacy given the one substance in theological thinking gives way to a more personal, communication-oriented thinking. A 'person-centered' take on the horizon of thought and human experience would displace the cosmocentric thinking of antiquity.

This initial revolutionary thinking and understanding in the early church of God and being was continued in the Middle Ages. This was why, for instance, Wilhelm v. Auxerre could describe the Trinity as '*perfecta communicatio*'.[10] Richard of St Victor applies the Neo-platonic axiom '*Bonum est communicativum sui* 'and gives a Trinitarian theological twist to it when he writes: 'If we assume only one person in the true divinity, as well as only one substance, then this would obviously have no one with whom to share (communicare) the infinite abundance of its fullness.'[11] It is however proper of love 'not to want to have anything that one cannot communicate (*communicare*).'[12] Thus there must be a highly interpersonal communication in God.

Progress in this line of theological reflection is found in Bonaventure and Thomas Aquinas. Bonaventura understands the Trinitarian God as 'that unit, which remains one in several; [and this form of oneness] is higher than that which can guarantee its oneness, only in one person.'[13] For this very reason, 'the divine nature due to its simplicity can be communicated and can *be* in several.'[14] Valid here is a norm from the theory of communication: 'The simpler something is, the more communicable it is';[15] and the reverse is also valid: the more communicable (regarding the differences) something is, the greater the unity it attains. And as the second rule, Bonaventure adds: Where the most perfect Act is, [meant is the *actus purus* of being], there should also be the most perfect communication.'[16] In other words, perfection in Being, Being-as-real, is in the long run identical to Communio and Communicatio.

In this regard, Thomas Aquinas expresses a thought of defining importance for the following era, and which before him had never been so radically expressed when he says that in God, the persons are constituted by the very same divine relations: Personhood in God is a subsistent relation

---

[9] See: J. Werbick, *Trinitätslehre*, in Th. Schneider (ed.), *Handbuch der Dogmatik*, II, Düsseldorf: Pamos, pp. 481–576, here: p. 495.

[10] For this, see J. Arnold, '*Perfecta Communicatio*'. *Die Trinitätstheologie Wilhelm v. Auxerres*, Münster; Aschendorff 1995, esp. pp. 118n.

[11] Richard v. St Victor, *Die Dreieinigkeit*, III,4, Einsiedeln: Johannes Verlag 1980, p. 87.

[12] III, 6.

[13] Bonaventura, *De Myst.Trin.*, 2,2,6 (Quaracchi V, 64b).

[14] Bonaventura, *I Sent.*, 2,2c (Quaracchi I, 54a).

[15] K. Obenauer, *Summa actualitas. Zum Verhältnis von Einheit und Verschiedenheit in der Dreieinigkeitslehre des heiligen Bonaventura*, Frankfurt u.a.: Pater Lang 1996, p. 48.

[16] Bonaventura, I *Sent.*, 8,2,1ad 1 (Quaracchi 1, 166a).

and thus communication. Before the time of St Thomas of Aquinas, this thought was considered impossible. This was because – it was assumed – 'relation is just an (accidental!) connection between one independent being and another, thus from one towards the other; how can it then be that the relation is constitutive of the being of the Related and even logically precedes them?'[17] Thomas solves this problem, by identifying the being of the relations with the divine substance, and so inversely identifies the divine substance with the *Communio* of absolutely relationally understood persons.[18] The one divine substance is the one ongoing communication of different persons, who within the very structure of the *Communio*. acquire, retain and perfect their uniqueness.

This novel understanding of the being was so new and unexpected with respect to the earlier understanding that it would become generally accepted only gradually into Christian faith and thinking. That still holds true today. Even when faith and theology emphasize and clearly validate Trinitarian thinking, the unity concept (*Einheitsidee*) keeps coming to the forefront, particularly in the transcendental theological (and philosophical) formulations of modernity. The change came only after the First World War, with personalistic and dialogical thought.[19] This new way of thinking soon showed that the world of the personal followed categories and logic other than the world of things and substances. In this sense, due to the numerous initiatives and ideas of the past, and also because of the many biblical references in favour, many theologians today (though not all) accept a clearly communicative view of the triune God, even if their opinions differ in specific areas: to name only a few: Hans Urs von Balthasar, Walter Kasper, Klaus Hemmerle, Jürgen Moltmann, Wolfhart Pannenberg, Piero Coda, Gonzalo J. Zarazaga and Gisbert Greshake. In the following paragraphs I shall briefly present some rather systematic reflections from my past Trinitarian studies.

---

[17] H. Chr. Schmidbaur, *Personarum Trinitas. Die trinitarische Gotteslehre des heiligen Thomas von Aquin*, St. Ottilien: EOS 1995, p. 388.

[18] Cf. I Sent., 9,2,2: 'Pater est sua essentia et communicat suam essentiam Filio'. Here we see a deficiency in Thomistic and thereby western theological thinking: even when the Trinity was understood as a process of self-communication, it remained under the primacy of the Father and understanding it as a reciprocal, interpersonal self-communication was not seen in the same way nor accorded the same importance. This step was taken only in Trinitarian theology of our times. For this, see G. Greshake, *Der dreieine Gott. Eine trinitarische Theologie*, Freiburg-Basel-Wien: Herder [5]2007, pp. 182–90.

[19] The most important characteristics of this development are noted down in Greshake, *Der dreieine Gott*, pp. 150–71. Bibliographical references are contained there.

# God is *Communio*

## *Communio* as a Term of Mediation

The formulation 'God is the *Communio* of three persons' could be thoroughly misunderstood if one were to associate with it the community of three independent self-sufficient persons, who come together, to a certain extent 'adding up' to a kind of 'community-of-Gods.' This is naturally not what is intended. Here, our human experience should not be projected onto God. For us, community results when independent persons enter into relation with one another, yet in this state of communion remain independent. The same is not so in God. In God, there are not originally three, who subsequently out of their self-subsisting states enter into relation with one another. Rather, the unity of God transcends all comprehension, an original relational unity of love, in which the three persons mutually transmit the divine life and in this exchange prove both their distinctiveness as well as, and above all, their oneness. Unity of relationality, of love, and not unity of the substance or a collectivity: that is the new Christian unity concept, which gains ground in the light of the Revelation of the triune God.

Gaining ground at the same time is also the fact that mankind, affected by the chaos of the many, of confusion and of dispersion, profoundly seeks such unity. When humanity desires unity, harmony, peace and concordance, it does not at all seek the unity typical of a monad or a substance, a system or a collective, that considering itself as the 'one and only' aims a removing and cancelling out all differences, conflicts and tensions. No, in the long run, what is desired is the unity of pure love, a love 'that in being no other that itself, is in itself relation and community'.[20] Therefore the Trinitarian God is an ongoing mediation of three persons who live their common divine life in perfected love, a process which we have already named *Communio*. This word, as opposed to the static concept of a (stable, motionless) 'community', refers instead to a process (*actus purus*), in which the different persons, by the mutual giving of their lives and attaining hence a common existence, realize by means of their very distinctiveness the most perfect unity. *Communio* is thus – as already noted – a unity, which has its contrary, i.e. multiplicity, not outside itself, but within: the unity of *Communio* is that very unity which implies communication by distinct persons who maintain their distinctiveness. It is the mediation of identity and difference: of differentness, which tends towards unity, and of unity, which is in itself the very interaction of the many, in this case the three persons in God.

---

[20] Kl. Hemmerle, *Gemeinschaft als Bild Gottes*, (WW 5), Freiburg-Basel-Wien: Herder 1996, p. 91.

In a Trinitarian theological context, the great Cappadocian theologians of the fourth century already saw things in this light. They phrased it this way: The life of God is to a certain extent a kind of 'pulsating' in accordance with which 'from Unity comes Trinity, and from Trinity comes Unity'.[21] This was later taken up in the theological concept of the Perichoresis (reciprocal encompassing and interpenetration).[22] Perichoresis is originally a word, which comes from the world of dancing (to dance around). One dances around the other, the other dances around the one. Applied to the Trinity, this would mean, metaphorically speaking: the three divine persons are in such communion with each other that they can be presented only as 'common dancers' in one dance: the Son is completely in the Father and with the Father, the Father wholly in the Son and with the Son, and both have their unity by the bond of the Spirit. Thus they dance the one common dance of the divine life. That which belongs to the one, belongs also the other, what one has, the other also possess, what one does, it is done together with the others and in the others. Only in so far as the Father, Son and Spirit are in each other, and are 'no other' as the mutual relationship and a 'being-in-each-other' (*Ineinandersein*), is the one, same and indivisible divine nature in them and they are themselves in it.'[23]

This corresponds to the pronouncement made in the Gospel of John which speaks in its Prologue of an atemporal relation of intimate love of the Son for the Father: He is 'God the only Son, who is close to the Father's heart, who has made him known.' (1,18).[24] And because love is so penetrating, Jesus can say: 'whatever the Father does, the Son does likewise.' (5,19) and: the disciples should know and understand 'that the Father is in me and I am in the Father' (10,38). Accordingly, Jesus himself speaks to the Father: 'All mine are yours, and yours are mine.' (17,10). In this way, Jesus and the Father are by perichoresis completely one. Similarly, the Spirit operates according to what is characteristic to Him and distinguishes Him, not separately from the others since He 'comes from the Father' (15,26) and will – Jesus says – 'take what is mine and declare it to you'. (16,14). In brief:

---

[21] Gregor v. Nazianz, *Carmina Theol.*, I, 1,3 (PG 37, p. 413).

[22] For this cf. G. Greshake, *Perichorese*, in: LThK ³VIII, 31–3 (+ bibliography).

[23] Hemmerle, *Gemeinschaft als Bild Gottes*, p. 91. Very well formulated by M. Böhnke, *Einheit in Mehrursprünglichkeit*, Würzburg: Echter 2000, p. 154 following Kl. Hemmerle: 'One's own is in the other, the other in one's own, but one's own is not the other's. As one's own shares of itself with the other and thereby perfects itself, so is the relationship between one's own and the other in so far as as proceeding from what is proper to the one, originally the very same as the other and is also the very same original relationship in so far as it also proceeds from the other. (original text: "Das Eigene ist im Anderen, das Andere im Eigenen, aber das Eigene ist nicht das Andere. Indem das Eigene sich ins Andere gibt und darin sein Eigenes vollzieht, ist es die Beziehung von Eigenem und Anderem, wie sie vom Eigenen ursprünglich ausgeht, das Andere ist gleich ursprünglich dieselbe Beziehung, wie sie gegenläufig vom Anderen ausgeht.")'

[24] (The translated Bible texts are taken from the New Revised Standard Version – NRSV).

never is only one divine Person at work. Despite or, better still, precisely because of their difference they are radically united and are reciprocally interpenetrated.

All of these are statements of faith. However, in view of experiences made in interpersonal relationships, these statements are verifiable. In this sense, Thomas Aquinas says the following in a phenomenological reflection on human love: 'Since love transforms the lover into the beloved, it allows the lover access to the intimate sphere of the beloved (and vice versa), such that nothing belonging to the beloved is excluded in the union with the lover ...'.[25] Love thus joins the lover and the beloved, although they are different persons, into an inseparable and indivisible unit. However, among human beings there remains the difference between the uniting act or reali-zation of love and the being of the lovers that yet remains independent each of the other. This is because even if the lover in the realization of their love become 'one flesh', i.e. completely one, they remain nevertheless outside the actual realizations of their love, two separate, distinct individuals. This 'must' be different in God, since there is no difference between act and being: in and through the love which exists between the divine persons, there is realized both the most perfect distinction of persons (because love demands the difference between lovers) as well as the most sublime unity (mutual interpenetration).

In other words: the persons in God are so strongly identified by such a 'being in-relation' that this reality both differentiates between them as well unites them. What is proper to each divine person, their 'uniqueness', that which identifies them as 'Father', 'Son', or 'Holy Spirit' (covered in more detail in section two), comes from the usual relational structure of *Communio* and is nothing 'exclusive', setting one apart from the other, in the sense of 'separating, isolating'. Instead, the 'uniqueness' proper to each person is possessed in such a way as to be shared through that person with the others, and so the distinguishing traits of all form the one fullness of the divine life

This idea becomes clearer when we take the human body as an example. Each organ, each member, has its own peculiar function: for instance, the lung is responsible for supplying oxygen to the body. But this peculiarity is such only in so far as it affects the whole of the body. In the long run, every part of the body is finally supplied with vital oxygen by the lung: the special or peculiar becomes common within the organism. Seen from the other angle, the identifying trait of the lung would cease to exist were it not made possible and sustained by the whole of the body. This organic life of a body is but a poor picture for (inter)personal life and action: what one has as unique is possessed as destined for the other(s) as well as – for the

---

[25] Thomas v. Aquin, *III Sent.*, 27, 1, 1 ad 4.

most part – received from them (in the case with humans: from parents, education, environment, society). What we can recognize starting from our creatural reality reaches its fullness in contemplation of the triune God: the profound significance of being and reality, can be discovered in God as the most radical relatedness, Being in relation, the sharing-ones-own-with-another. Yes, in the final analysis, the true significance of such a relationship was to become evident, and only perfectly so, with the knowledge of a Trinitarian God.

## 'God is love'

Once again we have clarified what the revolution in the understanding of being entails: the faith in the Trinitarian God changes the whole under-standing of reality. At the forefront, we do not have the oneness of the substance, the being in itself and for itself, nor is the focus on being as a collectivity, in which all differences are churned together. Instead, from a Trinitarian God a decisive paradigm on the world of relationality of the person is opened up which helps in understanding reality without losing one's bearing. Being-in-relation reveals itself then as the most profound nature of reality. The most sublime and actual reality both in the creatural as well as within the divine existence is Being-with-one another, *Communio*.

As can be demonstrated by human experience, Being-in-itself and Being-with-one-another are not actually opposites, and do not stand in an inverse relationship to each other in the sense of: the more I am me, the less I am dependent on and ordered towards another. No, both are directly propor-tional: I am all the more myself when I am the you for others, and am in relation with them and vice versa. I thus have no need to fear that my 'me' is endangered if I enter into relationships. If it really has to do with personal relations (and not with immature hanging on to another, or an escape into a symbiosis with others, similar to the primal infant symbiosis at the mother's breast), it is then that I directly realize my actual, mature and personal self in relationships. However, within the creatural dimension, and so among humans, a lasting difference remains between Being oneself (or Being-in-itself) and Being-for-others, between Being-in-substance and Being-in-relations. But if both are in principle directly proportional to each other, then it is at least initially to be understood and would not appear a contradiction that the persons in God are more truly so by the very fact that they are absolutely from and for the other and so constitute the inseparably one Godhead. From this perspective, Being-one and Being-three in God do not at all contradict themselves. God is as much one as he is an inseparable, personal – better still: interpersonal – relational structure. The one divine nature exists only in the dynamic living exchange between Father, Son and Spirit; like the orthodox tradition says – it is the 'content of the three persons in God,'[26] that, in which the life of the three takes place. Each of the divine persons is completely for the other and from the other, in strict reciprocity, giving and receiving at the very same time. The persons in God have thus no self-existence apart from each other. Instead, what they are, they are such only in Being-from-others, Being-with-others and Being-for-others.

Only from the above does the well-known saying from the New Testament come to be seen in its full significance: 'God is love' (1 Jn 4:16). If the one God is Love, then the three Persons are the nodal points between which the rhythm of love is played out: giving – receiving – giving back, and in this giving back: a leading back to a unity. As H. U. v. Balthasar succinctly points out, all three persons are thereby 'one and the same Love in three ways of being that are necessary, so that Love, the most sublime selfless Love may exist'.[27] The one God is the drama of love that is enacted between three Persons: Loving, Being-loved, Loving-together-with-others (Lieben, Geliebtwerden, Mitlieben).[28]

The question may be posed why in God there are only three Persons that exist in exchange of life and love. Why not four, five...? Even if we cannot and never will fully grasp the nature of the eternal God, and therefore are dependent on the fact of his Self-revelation as three Persons, there remains the possibility by means of careful reflection of drawing close to the mystery of God from afar.

In answer to this question, a path had already been indicated by the great theologian of the Middle Ages, Richard of St Victor: if God is perfect love, then there is need of two equal partners; we know this basically from our human experience. But love between two can not yet constitute the highest form of love. For this to occur, Loving in itself and Being loved, i.e. reciprocal love, must yet again open up to include a third. He writes:

Where two ... embrace each other in reciprocal love and each in this reciprocal love experiences sublime joy, the summit of this joy lies precisely in the most intimate love of the other and vice versa: the summit of the joy of the one lies in the love of the other. However, as long as one loves to

---

[26] J.-V. Leb, V. Bel, 'Dumitru Staniloae', in P. Neuner, G. Wenz (eds), *Theologen des 20. Jahrhunderts*, Darmstadt: WBG 2002, p. 151.

[27] H. U. von Balthasar, 'Einleitung zu Richard v. St Victor', in Richard von St Victor, *Die Dreieinigkeit*, Einsiedeln: Johannes Verlag 1980, p. 20.

[28] The same content is formulated in his own way by E. Jüngel, *Gott als Geheimnis der Welt*, Tübingen: Mohr 1978, pp. 449nn: 'God possesses himself and only so in the fact that He gives of Himself. Thus in giving of Himself, He possesses Himself. That is how he is. His self-possession is the event, is the story of a self-giving.... Like this story, He is God, in fact, this story of love is "God himself".' (Original text: 'Gott hat sich selbst so und nur so, dass er sich verschenkt. So aber, sich verschenkend, hat er sich. So ist er. Seine Selbsthabe ist das Geschehen, ist die Geschichte eines Sich-Verschenkens.... Als diese Geschichte ist er Gott, ja diese Geschichte der Liebe ist "Gott selbst".')

the exclusion of the other, he remains the sole possessor of his joy, and the same applies to the other. As long as they do not have a love common to both, the best of the joy of each can not not be held in common. For each to communicate in their joy, there is need for a common beloved.[29]

We can thus further sharpen Richard's line of thought: human experience shows that the exclusive love between two always threatens to turn into a dual egoism. Each enjoys himself in and through the other. The other is to a certain extent solely a means and reflection of one's own narcissism. Only by the common relationship, the common overflowing into a third that receives that which each experiences and shares, can the egoistic threat to love be broken. This third can – above all – be a person (the child of both, a common friend, a common relationship with God), or it could also be a common occupation, a common hobby, common aims. Whatever the case may be, it is only with respect to a 'third' and in relation to it can the 'I' and the 'You' be constituted in the common 'We'. It is for this reason that the fundamental element of true love is not the dialogic aspect, the 'I-you' relationship, but rather the I-You-He(She/it) relationship, in other words, the trialogic dimension.

This phenomenology of love taken from human experience is certainly not proof that the same would apply to God. Rather, it offers a graphic help towards understanding the 'trialogic-Trinitarian' nature of God, or in other words, the understanding of God as *Communio*.

## The Different Persons in God

The phenomenological approach discussed above also helps deepen our understanding of the differences as well as the distinguishing qualities of the Persons in God. First, the Holy Spirit as the 'third' could be plausibly underestood as having the peculiar characteristic of being the bond of unity between the Father and the Son forming a 'we', as well as the Factor that enables the Love that is in God to overflow the 'I' and the 'You': primarily in God himself, then also into creation and into our hearts ('the spirit of the Lord has filled the world ...': Wis. 1.7; 'God's love has been poured into our hearts through the Holy Spirit': Rom. 5.5). God is, in the Spirit, the Third, who unites and spurs on to overflow, and is as such truly 'Love'.

Since the fullness of God who is Love is to be found in the Holy Spirit, 'Spirit' is not only the name of the third Person, but also the ultimate description of God. We see this in Jn 4.24: 'God is Spirit'. For this reason the Holy Spirit retreats behind the 'We' of the Father and the Son (as in Jn

---

[29] Richard von St Victor, *De Trin.*, III, 11, 14, 15. [The author of this article in the German original says: 'The translation above, with some exceptions, follows von Balthasar', (Richard von St Victor, *Die Dreieinigkeit*, pp. 95, 100n).

17.21ff) because he is the guarantor of this 'We' and is only fully expressed when the possibilities to be opened up by the 'We' are reflected upon.

In relation to the Holy Spirit, the Father is in the 'rhythm of love,' the Originating-Gift (*Ur-Gabe*), the inconceivably profound mystery of Self-giving. For this reason he is the reason and fundament of the divine *Communio* as a continuing act of love. By the fact that the distinguishing characteristic of the Father is that he possesses the divine life as a Self-giving, this goes to show that his identity also is determined in relation to the other Persons, for only in the acceptance does the offered Gift really become a Gift. Only in relation to and from the others is the Father, Father.

The characteristic unique to the Son in this 'rhythm of love' is in His 'Being in receiving' (H. U. von Balthasar). He receives His divine being from the Father; that this gift in Him, through Him, comes to be an 'other', distinct from the Father, is acquired by this being-an-other, a distinct form and a radical expression of its potentialities; in the Son, the Gift becomes in a certain sense emphatic, expressive, explicit. In the same way as the Son receives His self from the Father, so does He enable this gift to achieve its end: He thankfully receives it and returns it, thereby constituting the Father as Father. However, together with the Father, He gives the gift of divine life and love to the Spirit who, as we saw, unites in Himself the Father and the Son and makes their love overflow.

All these determinations that seek to identify the specific unique characteristics of each Person are backed up by Scripture. More important, though, than a detailed analysis is the fact that each Person, in His own very uniqueness, possesses His divine life from and in relation to the others. Each Person is such within a context of giving and receiving, in which the most sublime Being, God, is shown as *Communio*, as Being-with, and each is Person seen as nodal points in the network of Love. In the final analysis, this does not need to be proven or justified. More important is the central idea that God is *Communio*/community, relationship, love, life that gives of itself.

## Prospects

This image of God that is brought to light in the fundamental experience of the Christian New Testament and that opens up a new perspective on reality has had an immensely influential history. Kant's statement that nothing of practical use can be taken from the doctrine of the Trinity[30] has thereby been shown to be wrong. If the most sublime being that exists is Being-with, reciprocal sharing, interconnectedness, in brief: *Communio*, then a new

---

[30] I. Kant, *Der Streit der Fakultäten*, (WW IX), Darmstadt 1971, p. 303.

direction is being given to man who is described in Scripture as 'image of God'; creation is newly understood (in terms of interconnectedness); the very end of the individual and world history is newly determined. This points towards the fact that all that is in the world, ultimately through the ministry of the church as *sacramentum unitatis*, is to become one, as God himself is one, such that all creation may be prepared to partake for ever in the life of the communional God. Thus, the understanding of God as *Communio* is a new key towards understanding the whole of reality.

An ordinary Indian from near Lake Titicaca in Peru with whom I struck up a conversation about God and other mundane issues expressed these concepts in the following way: 'God is *Communio*, hence we have to become *Communio*!' I consider this sentence one of the best formulated axioms of the Christian faith that I know of. These brief allusions made here should suffice.[31] However, they illustrate in some way the statements of Klaus Hemmerle:

> The 'revolution' in the image and concept of God brought about by faith in … the triune God can hardly be measured. Even our very consciousness as Christians is not yet completely penetrated by it. That God is in all respects communication, overflowing life, that He is as much self-sufficient beatitude as he is pure reciprocal self-giving, all this radically overturns the human concept of God; it also affects our under-standing of ourselves, our understanding of the world.[32]

---

[31] Rich, concrete material regarding the practical consequences of the Trinitarian faith under the heading *communio* can be found in Greshake, Gott.`

[32] Hemmerle, *Glauben – wie geht das?*, p. 147.

# 15

# Becoming a Person and the Trinity

## Stefan Oster

*'The present is the point at which time touches eternity'*
C.S. LEWIS[1]

## Personhood as Existential Self-perfection

Following the well-known definition of Boethius, the person is an undivided substance of a rational nature. This definition has had a broad influence throughout its history along with its share of criticism. 'Substance' sounds static, whereas the Person is a dynamic and especially relational being, a Being-in-relation. In an early essay (first published 1966) 'Zum Personverständnis in der Theologie', Joseph Ratzinger wrote that for a Christian understanding of the person, Boethius' definition was 'wholly insufficient'[2] since Boethius' concept remained completely 'on the level of the Greek substance-oriented thinking.'[3] Ratzinger approvingly mentions someone else struggling with the concept of the person, Richard of St Victor,

---

[1] C. S. Lewis, *The Screwtape Letters*, Macmillan: London 1944, p. 76 ('Denn die Gegenwart ist der Punkt, an dem Zeit und Ewigkeit sich berühren.' C. S. Lewis, *Dienstanweisungen für einen Unterteufel*, Moers, 2003, p. 73.)
[2] Now available in: J. Ratzinger/Benedikt XVI., *Dogma und Verkündigung*, Donauwörth: Wewel Verlag 2005, pp. 201–19, here: p. 212.
[3] Ratzinger/Benedikt XVI., *Dogma und Verkündigung*, p. 213.

whose understanding of the person as '*spiritualis naturae incommunicabilis existentia*, the incommunicably proper existence of a spiritual nature',[4] contrasts with Boethius in so far as it highlights the existential dimension and is not essentialist or substance-based.

In my opinion, this appears to be a one-sided appraisal of Boethius' thinking. First, his approach to the question on the right relationships and understanding of person, substance, subsistence and nature are clearly seen in his work '*Contra Eutychem et Nestorium*' in the midst of the Christological controversy. Secondly, he actually does not only contemplate the substance on the level of the essence (*ousia*) but sees it instead on the level of subsistence, specifically on that of being, and hence in Ratzinger's own words, on the level of existence.[5] In Boethius, therefore, substance is not understood only as static being, but also as the fulfilment, the subsisting, the 'being itself' according to the manner of 'being substance', of 'existing'. The Boethian concept of the person is therefore not simply static but is also open to a dynamic understanding. Nevertheless, Ratzinger's objection is to a certain extent still justified in that while the dynamic character of personhood can be found in Boethius, the dimension of relationship, of relationality is hardly present.

A deepening with respect to the concept of relationality is to be found in St Thomas Aquinas, not to mention the fact that he is also the suspected protagonist of both rationalistic thinking on the one hand, and static-hierarchical substance-ontological thinking on the other. The unfounded nature of these suspicions have been demonstrated in the twentieth century by Etienne Gilson in particular, and with him other researchers on St Thomas who agree on the fact that the essential, original and central aspect to Thomas' *Metaphysics* is his experience of being, in which created *esse* is determined as pure actuality, as the fullness of act (*actus actuum*), as the perfection of all perfections (*perfection omnium perfectionum*),[6] as absolute perfection because it is the overflowing, gratuitous gift of God. Being is the 'likeness to the divine goodness'[7] and therefore equally a *completum et simplex, sed non subsistens*.[8] It is everything, it is overflowing fullness, since all proceeds from it;[9] but it is equally nothing, since it does not subsist in

---

[4] Ratzinger/Benedikt XVI., *Dogma und Verkündigung*.

[5] Cited from: A. M. Boethius, *Die Theologischen Traktate*, (PhB, 397), Hamburg: Felix Meiner Verlag 1988, p. 79: 'Die Individuen aber subsistieren nicht nur, sondern sind auch Substanzen, denn sie selbst bedürfen der Akzidenzien nicht, um zu sein.' (The individuals do not only subsist, but rather are also substances, for in themselves they do not need accidents in order to be.)

[6] *De Pot.*, 7, 2, 2 ad 9.

[7] 'Esse est similitudo divinae bonitatis': *De veritate,* q. 22, a. 2, ad. 2.

[8] *De Pot.*, 1, 1.

[9] STh I-II, q. 2, a. 5, ad 2 'ipsum esse praehabet in se omnia subsequentia'.

its own self; it can in no way be conceived as a material or spiritual reality on an intermediate plane between creator and creation. In truth, it is pure gift and pure giving all at once, pure loving that from itself obtains for the other its subsistence as self-perfection and existence in its own self: creation as a divine act is giving of being, giving of creative personal love (*'creare autem est dare esse'*)[10] that in the creation of the created intended for its own sake, bestows on it the gift of being. Hence, *subsistence* as finite, created being implies 'being that is received' and consequently 'existence owing to another.' Each creature perfects itself according to its being when it is more itself, when it becomes more of what it is and can be, when it better realizes that which it has received, in other words, its very self and also *what* it is.[11] According to Thomas Aquinas, it is the substance in so far as it subsists, that which actually receives being[12] and which consequently actually *is* or 'has being'.[13] Understood in this way, substance is the primary venue of God's faithfulness, the giver of all being; it is that creatural reality that is gifted with being so that it may precisely *be* this being.

# Self-Perfection Through Loving Perception/ Cognition/Intellection

If selfhood is not just a static reality but an ongoing realization, then in finite beings this realization is necessarily performed in time. In this sense, selfhood is in certain respects always a becoming, i.e. in successful cases a self-realization. That the process is successful must be taken into consideration, since for finite beings their own self-realization or self-constitution can fail. In the case of failure, we would have a becoming that does not lead to a more profound integration of selfhood but instead to disintegration. The reasons for this in finite beings can be due to external causes in a world in which all interests cannot be equally satisfied. However, particularly in the case of a finite freedom, the reasons could come from within: the human being can through his own fault lose his way and progressively become less

---

[10] 1 *Sent* 37, 1, 1; *In De Div Nom.* 4, 3 'universaliter autem omnes substantias creat, *dans eis esse*'.

[11] In 3 *Sent* 6, 1, 1: 'ratio substantiae est, quod per se subsistat'; STh I, 45, 4: 'illi enim proprie convenit esse, quod habet esse; et per hoc est subsistens in suo esse'. For speculative re-enactment of the created being's finitude to finite substance see: F. Ulrich, *Homo abyssus. Das Wagnis der Seinsfrage*, Einsiedeln: Johannes Verlag 1998.

[12] The substance is the 'proprium susceptivum eius quod est esse' (*ScG* II, 52).

[13] *In Met.*, 12,1 (2419): 'ens dicitur quasi *esse habens*, hoc autem solum est substantia, *quae subsistit*'; vgl. STh 1, 29, 2: 'substantia … secundum enim quod per se existit et non in alio vocatur „subsistentia": illa enim subsistere dicimus, quae non in alio, sed in se ipsis existunt.'

of who he truly is and could be. He can jeopardize his 'being oneself' (= Subsistieren) and become an alienated person who loses himself in the long run.

The focus of our reflection will now be successful self-realization. We assume with Thomas that each being receives its being and therein its very self as a gift. We likewise assume this reception of being, in terms of a *creatio continua*, to be an ongoing event especially with respect to living beings. Therefore self-realization is at once always a reception of self, a continual self-acceptance from the hands of the loving Giver. Self acceptance for the human being is realized however in his essential perfections or, according to St Thomas, 'in his natural operationes'. The human being is a rational animal and – as seen in Boethius – the rational nature of an undivided Subsistence. Traditionally, the operatio peculiar to man had always been assumed to be knowledge by means of his *intellectus*. It is the intellectus that according to St Thomas makes humans human.[14] The operatio proper to him is therefore *intellegere*, the act of knowing.[15] For this reason, the human soul is not only just an anima, but an *anima intellectiva*, that has as its most determining and configuring trait its capacity to know. Unique in the knowing rational soul is its ability to know not just something or the 'particular' but rather basically everything. Man is open to all that is in the world; he can by dissociating himself from all the rest objectify them in order to ask: what is that? He is not instinct-bound like an animal, but is capable of assuming an objective attitude, in keeping with his nature, towards what is known. This attitude is then appropriate to reality when the known is met, not necessarily in the context of something desired, but rather with the disposition to letting the known reveal itself. When one encounters the world, things or others with this attitude in which the known is not primarily considered as being 'for me' but rather 'in itself' in its own dignity and freedom, the known is by this very act of knowing set free. This attitude in encountering the known is based on the realization that things observed each exist independently of the observer. Only then can he know things from the perspective of their own existence, experience or read them from within. For this reason St. Thomas says – even if what he says is perhaps etymologically incorrect, but thematically pertinent – that intellegere is quasi an *intus leggere*, an inwards reading.[16] Whoever in knowing, remaining merely on the superficial level, one whose relation to the known is desire-motivated and does not first set the thing known free, in its own self-existence, does not possess nor

---

[14] 'Intellectus a quo homo est id quod est' (*in Met.*, 1, 1, 1–5).

[15] *ScG* II, 79, similarly: *ScG* II, 60; 73; 76. Naturally, Thomas here follows in the Aristotelian tradition; cf. Nikomachische Ethik, 1098 a: 'Wir nehmen nun an, dass die dem Menschen eigentümliche Leistung ist: ein Tätigsein der Seele gemäß dem rationalen Element oder jedenfalls nicht ohne dieses.' (cited according to the translation by F. Dirlmeier, Stuttgart 1983, p. 17).

[16] STh II–II, q. 8, a. 1: 'dicitur enim intellegere quasi intus legere.'

know things in the same way as one who, in knowing people and things, welcomes them and, facilitated by the resulting relationship, enters into communication with them. Only in maintaining a certain distance, one that is truly liberating and acknowledging, can knowledge as such be so deepened as to render possible the union with the known, postulated by St Thomas. He says, in fact, that in the process of knowing, the perceiving intellect in a certain sense *becomes* the known/perceived: the *intellectus* fully actualized (in act) *is* ultimately the known.[17] St Thomas sees the relationship established in knowing as a reality so intimate that he describes it using the imagery of marriage and the offspring resulting from it. The interior word formulated thereafter within the knower, externalized in the word, is a child/ offspring of this generative, cognitive process.[18] Now, when the soul is in a certain sense everything, as St Thomas in line with Aristotle affirms, since it is open to all finite reality that exists and can be known, then it can in this same sense by the unitive nature of knowledge become everything.[19]

In Thomas Aquinas, selfhood is explicitly seen as intimately ordered towards the *actus* or *operatio* of a being. This operatio in a finite being can be essentially considered as self-expression and self-communication. This is so since, according to St Thomas, each substance exists for and because of its specific operatio. [20] This operatio though has not only to do with accidents but rather with the subsisting substance itself. The accidents are just the

---

[17] STh I, q. 87, a. 1, ad 3: 'intellectus in actu est intellectum in actu'; *ScG* I, 48: 'secundum enim hoc intellectus perfectus est quod intelligit; quod quidem est per hoc quod est unum cum quod intelligitur.'

[18] Cf. *Comp. Theo.*, 34: 'quando igitur intellectus intelligit aliud a se, *res* intellecta est sicut *pater* verbi in intellectu concepti: ipse autem intellectus magis gerit similitudinem *matris*, cuius est, ut *in ea fit conceptio*. Quando intellectus intelligit seipsum, verbum conceptum comparatur ad intelligentem sicut *proles* ad *patrem*.'

[19] Cf. *Ver.*, 1,1 the *anima humana* is seen here 'quodamodo omnia'. STh q. I, a. 14, ad 1 'dicendum quod in deo perfectissime est scientia. ad cuius evidentiam, considerandum est quod cognoscentia a non cognoscentibus in hoc distinguuntur, quia non cognoscentia nihil habent nisi formam suam tantum; sed cognoscens natum est habere formam etiam rei alterius, nam species cogniti est in cognoscente. unde manifestum est quod natura rei non cognoscentis est magis coarctata et limitata, natura autem rerum cognoscentium habet maiorem amplitudinem et extensionem. propter quod dicit philosophus, iii de anima, quod anima est quodammodo omnia. coarctatio autem formae est per materiam. unde et supra diximus quod formae, secundum quod sunt magis immateriales, secundum hoc magis accedunt ad quandam infinitatem. patet igitur quod immaterialitas alicuius rei est ratio quod sit cognoscitiva; et secundum modum immaterialitatis est modus cognitionis. unde in ii de anima dicitur quod plantae non cognoscunt, propter suam materialitatem. sensus autem cognoscitivus est, quia receptivus est specierum sine materia, et intellectus adhuc magis cognoscitivus, quia magis separatus est a materia et immixtus, ut dicitur in iii de anima. unde, cum deus sit in summo immaterialitatis, ut ex superioribus patet, sequitur quod ipse sit in summo cognitionis.'

[20] Cf. *ScG* I, 45: 'omnis substantia est propter suam operationem'; *ScG* III, 113 'quaelibet res est propter suam operationem' *In De Cael* 2, 4 'unumquodque quod habet propriam operationem, est propter suam operationem.'

means in and through which this self-expression is realized or perfected.[21] The specific operation of a substance therefore reveals the being as realized in its selfhood. In so far one realizes an operatio proper to him, he is who he can be and becomes ever progressively more so. For this, I believe it necessary to understand St Thomas' concept of self-perfection of the person through his *propria operatio*, in other words, his intellegere from a more wholistic perspective, and more explicitly, as a loving knowledge. The will as love is the basic appetive capacity (*Grundvermögen*)[22] that following the example of God's gratuitious generosity sets the things of the world free and therefore reaches out to them precisely in their otherliness and differentness.

When the will as love goes beyond the mere desire for selfish possession in order to enter into the logic of a tension towards the other for the other's own sake, only then can this capacity permeate and transform knowledge. On the other hand, too, such an act of knowledge has an effect on the capacity to love because it knows in a new and different way, since it has been transformed by the other: metanoia. Love transforms the capacity of knowledge into a reality that truly comes to dwell alongside the other as an other, converting it into a capacity wholly imbued with the dimension of reception, acceptance, a certain neediness that lets the other exist as such, in order to be truly and fittingly known.

A biblical example that makes this clear is the account of the Good Samaritan (Lk. 10.25–35). The Samaritan did not acknowledge the wounded person only from his own perspective in view of his planned actions. He lets the other exist in his otherliness. Movivated by love, he perceives the wounded not from a self-oriented perspective but rather in an other-oriented manner. For this, he becomes a neighbour to the wounded. Loving knowledge leads to another type of behaviour and to a more profound relational experience to others. The Samaritan here acts as one who lovingly knows; he acts wholeheartedly, we might say, in an integral manner, backed up by his whole self. In a certain sense we can say he not only gives his consideration, his time and energy to the other, but something much more: himself. Loving knowledge demands total selfgiving. The one who loves is totally with the other or completely present in what he is concerned with at the moment. He is completely dedicated.

In so far as he knows, loves and acts, he becomes the neighbour to the other, as we see in the biblical texts, and simultaneously through such action more profoundly himself. He not only becomes a neighbour to the other (from the other's point of view), rather he is himself – from his own perspective – now made into the neighbour of the other.

---

[21] *ScG* III, 42 'operatio substantiam sequitur'; III *Sent* 28, 1, 1 'agere non est accidentium, sed substantiarum.'

[22] Cf. *ScG* I, 91 'omnis affectionis principium est amor.' STh I–II, q. 27, a. 4 'dicendum quod nulla alia passio animae est quae non praesupponat aliquem amorem.'

In loving knowledge and action, community is experienced anew. In this community, the lover discovers himself in his self-relationship as one newly constituted by the other. He steadily becomes more of whom he is capable of being, a lover or, in a deeper sense, the person as God sees him.

Now this means that the more profoundly one's actions are rooted in his loving knowledge, the more complete and wholesome his actions will be; the more intense his self-dedication, so much more integrated and reliable will his actions be; the more a respondent he becomes, the more open and receptive his heart – biblically speaking – will become. Philosophically speaking, one could say that his actions are no longer simply 'accidental'; his volitive and intellectual capacities are not just externalized accidents but are instead reciprocally integrated and complemented in the deepest recesses of the person's heart. The actions of such a person become substantial in the positive sense of the word. He lives from within; he is a trustworthy person, a person who reliably responds to his enviroment, remaining true to himself, to the things, persons and situations around him, to which he always responds wholeheartedly, from the profound centre of his very self. One can therefore say in certain respects that the more a human being knows, loves and acts integrally out of this centre, the more the location/focal point from which his actions originate is transfered from the purely accidental or the superficial periphery of his self to its very centre. Colloquially speaking, we describe such a person as being authentic; we say that he is genuine, that in him the external and the internal are a harmonic whole. He appears to be completely himself. We also say, he lives, loves and acts wholeheartedly. At the same time with such people, one senses that they are free, that – precisely because they are with themselves in the positive sense – they are capable of taking in their stride the real distance that separates them from the other. It is only this positive distance which makes it possible to turn freely towards the other with the already described completeness and entirety, and not out of a negative dependence that stems from a previous subliminal enduring attachment to the other or one that only artifically admits a certain distance (and hence only apparent) in order to control the extent of his self-giving to the other.

## Selfness from Subsistence and Relation

We see how, starting from Boethius and on through St Thomas, a relational understanding of the person can be developed, one that does not have to do away with the category of the susbtance but instead transforms and deepens it. Following this insight, let us take a step further: we saw that the human being through loving knowledge and knowingly loving becomes more and more himself. These actions unite him; in other words, we could guess that such a human being is united within himself. We understand that he is a more profound person, one who through self-perfective knowing and loving becomes more and more himself. If then we were to observe this self-perfection from the perspective of our initial problem, namely the relationship between substance and relation, we then see how the understanding of a new kind of relationship is opened up here. We have already seen that for Boethius, and even more so for St Thomas, it is possible and even necessary to consider not so much the static nature of substance as its existential and dynamic dimension. The substance subsists: that is to say it perfects its selfhood, its being-in-itself. We then went on to see that this self-perfection could be best considered as the subsisting of the person. The being that in the deepest sense subsists, rooted in itself, that is the person.[23] Taking a step further, we saw that this is qualitatively realized in its most perfect form in the person who lovingly knows and knowingly loves, in the person who is integrated and wholesome. Wherever a person does what he does wholeheartedly, it is there that his personhood is fully realized. In other words: there, he is also a Substance in the best and most profound way.

Here, however, two ontologically seemingly different categories are now mutually penetrated: the category of substance and that of relation. If the integral person perfects himself as such when he knowingly loves, he is then on the one hand wholly himself, subsisting in himself; simultaneously, he is on the other hand completely present for the other, or in that reality that is loved. In being-with-another (relation), the person is wholly established in himself. This can best be shown in such actions in which the person is oblivious of self – for instance in the intense dedication and concentration during a game or music, a loving meeting, a deep conversation. The person is completely present in the thing at hand or with the person, but yet at the same time he is quite oblivious of himself. He is not paying particular attention to what he is doing at the moment nor on the effect he has on the other or anything of the kind. He is simply a respondent, a listener, an observer, one who re-acts. He is immersed in what is at hand and lets himself be led along by the issue, the conversation, by the other person. And yet, in the midst of all this, he is completely himself, he acts, speaks and behaves as himself: the action is the passion and vice versa. If we were to ask ourselves in which moment of our lives we were ourselves the most, at the most authentic, real, then we would normally name such experiences of self obliviousness. In this sense, one can say: there where creation comes to its perfection, that is to say in an integral and intact personhood, in loving

---

[23] For this reason, St Thomas considers the person as the most perfect of all natures: 'persona significat id quod est perfectissimum in tota natura, scilicet subsistens in rationali natura', STh I, q. 29, a. 3.

knowledge and knowing love, there exists selfhood as a manner of being-in-relation; there the person is a *relatio subsistens*.[24]

# The Unity Between Selfhood and Self-becoming and the Experience of Temporality

We were able to tell by the example of the merciful Samaritan that the helper becomes a neighbour to the wounded by doing what is necessary. The one that turns out to be needy meets the other up front, in a certain sense from the future. He is the one who comes up to the Samaritan. The Samaritan welcomes this rapprochement, he frankly and expectantly receives him. At the same time, however, he behaves as who he always has been, as one who in this concrete situation brings all he has into the game, and with it the being that he has become, his origin, memory, all that he usually brings along with him. He puts all this completely to use. He throws himself into the balance and proves to be one that is and can be completely at the service of the other. The same also applies to the person in need. He also opens himself up to the other coming up to him; he does this with all that he has ever been.

Origin and future, the past and the expected are disclosed here for one another; they are perfected in the reciprocal being-with-another and come together in the experience of being-present. In this manner, the Samaritan is completely present, he is in an acting, a living presence and reveal. Being-present is here a profound realization of selfhood and self-becoming. In this manner of selfhood, the temporal ecstasies opening up to each other, create a space for the present. The future and the past disclose to each other a living presence/dynamic present and reveal the present as a space in time that is living and self-completing. The living presence understood in this sense, is no static extrinsically measurable period but rather a dynamic space in time in which the future and the past are revealed to one another and serve each other. In the human person, who acts as himself in this manner through loving knowledge and by knowingly loving, the unity of being and becoming is realized in the present as living presence (*lebendige Gegenwart*). The human being is at the same time, then, himself; he becomes more and more himself and perfects this since he does not cling to himself, close up in himself, but instead lets go, gives up and forgets himself. Here, living presence and time-duration occur within a solely extrinsically

---

[24] St Thomas uses this expression in order to describe the inner-Trinitarian persons: *relationes subsistentes*. Cf. 'persona igitur divina significat relationem ut subsistentem,' STh I, q. 29, a. 4.

computable temporality, or in the historical structure of a future that due to the punctual and therefore non-existent present, immediately falls irrevocably into the past. Here, the human being is himself, he leaves behind the torn and overstretched condition of temporality which he is accustomed to, given his urgent need to come to terms with his past or out of fear, to protect himself from the future, to mention just two examples of how we relate to historical, measurable time. But a child, for instance, that in its self-evident existence, playing and oblivious of itself, conquers its world under the protective care of loving parents, does not have measured time, nor fragmented time, nor does it have a history in an extrinsic sense. It is simply there, and its existence (*Dasein*) is its becoming. It is in the middle of time and has – because it lacks chronological time – all the time in the world: it lives in the present.

## Personal Selfhood and Trinity

I believe that human existence seen in this light presents us with the phenomenom we seek when we search for fully perfected humankind or personhood. The loving Knower and the knowing Lover in perfecting such selfhood fully realizes himself. When such a person acts, he shares of himself, he is dedicated to the thing or other person at hand, he gives himself. He does not just give anything but himself. He does not just do something, but rather gives himself.[25] This expression makes explicit the fact that the lover in the concrete historical situation does not act only in the universal sense as 'human' but instead as 'Peter' or 'Monica', in other words, as a singular, unique person and not just as a universal interchangeable human being.

Here also the difference between nature and person is seen. The lover acts from within and through his nature (his natural humanity), even then, he acts in a special way as a unique historical person. When one really knows and acts as a person in love, this concrete act in a certain point in time and history can be realized only by this person; the action is holistic and at the same time unique. I consider this aspect as particularly important when we delve deeper into the question of the relationship between Trinitarian theology and personal self-perfection. The loving person transcends his mere nature and acts in and through his nature, above all, as a distinctive self. On the other hand, the following also holds: the less one loves, the more his works and acts become interchangeable, only human acts in the universal sense. These acts no longer bear the transcending marks of

---

[25] Cf. K. Rahner, *Grundkurs des Glaubens*, Freiburg-Basel-Wien, Herder 1976, p. 101: 'In der wirklichen Freiheit meint das Subjekt immer sich selbst, versteht und setzt sich selbst, tut es letztlich nicht etwas, sondern sich selbst.' (In true freedom, the subject always means itself, it understands and presents itself. It does not in fact do 'something' but rather 'itself'.)

significant personal distinctiveness, uniqueness and responsive commitment (*antwortenden Verbindlichkeit*), but instead fluctuate between the two extremes of predictability and arbitrariness. I believe that this relation between person and nature that comes to light in delving into the the loving self-perfection of the person allows us an insight into the relationship of human personality as an image of the Trinitarian God. Out of various answers to the question if in creatures a trace of the Trinity ought necessarily be found, Thomas Aquinas states: 'in all creatures there is found the trace of the Trinity, inasmuch as in every creature are found some things which are necessarily reduced to the divine Persons as to their cause. For every creature subsists in its own being, and has a form, whereby it is determined to a species, and has relation to something else. Therefore as it is a created substance (*substantia*), it represents the cause and principle, and so in that manner it shows the Person of the Father, Who is the 'principle from no principle'. Since it has a form and species, it represents the Word in the same way as the form of the thing made by art arises from the conception (*conceptio*) of the craftsman. Since it has relation of order, it represents the Holy Ghost, inasmuch as He is love, because the order of the effect to something else is from the will of the Creator.'[26]

I would like to take up the hint given by St Thomas, building also on what up until now has already been said. As our point of departure is the assumption that man is most similar to God when he in the aforementioned manner (loving and knowing) realizes his personhood. This is more especially so then, when this loving-knowing relationship is directed to God. The human being is called to love God with his whole heart, his whole soul, his whole strength and all his mind (Mk 12.30). If we were then to apply the Thomistic description of the trace of the Trinitarian God present in creatures to the human person, the structural similarities and perfections of the human person ought to become more evident, the Trinitarian characteristics would be more clearly outlined; more still: it is precisely in the intact and well-realized form of personality that all this would most clearly be seen. I believe this is the case as will be shortly demonstrated. St Thomas sees the dimension of the father in the original creatural existence, that is to say, as a creature that subsists in its own

---

[26] STh I, q. 45, a. 7: 'sed in creaturis omnibus invenitur repraesentatio trinitatis per modum vestigii, inquantum in qualibet creatura inveniuntur aliqua quae necesse est reducere in divinas personas sicut in causam. Quaelibet enim creatura subsistit in suo esse, et habet formam per quam determinatur ad speciem, et habet ordinem ad aliquid aliud. Secundum igitur quod est quaedam substantia creata, repraesentat causam et principium, et sic demonstrat personam patris, qui est principium non de principio. Secundum autem quod habet quandam formam et speciem, repraesentat verbum; secundum quod forma artificiati est ex conceptione artificis. Secundum autem quod habet ordinem, repraesentat spiritum sanctum, inquantum est amor, quia ordo effectus ad aliquid alterum est ex voluntate creantis.'

being, always subsistent, already present due to a source that points to an unoriginated origin (*principium non de principio*). In order to understand better this being subsistent, I would approach it from the perspective of having been, in order to bring into play the element of creatural temporality. The creatural being is simply there, it is a given reality; it is already a given in itself, and always anew out of this given source, it stirs again and again into (future) action. The human person adds to this action what is peculiar to him, what and who he always was; he always carries his orginality, his provenance with him. Through his acts he bears witness to his originality, his provenance. It is for this reason that the dimension of creatural originality with respect to to the Trinity could be seen in the analogy of the person of the Father from whom all proceeds, especially the Son and the Spirit.

The question now is towards what end the human being's perfection is realized; what is the aim of his actions? Phrased in temporal terms: what is his future? In consonance with the Bible, we can draw attention to two moments that show us the Son as a future figure: first, the Son is He who, coming from the future, meets the loving person face to face in the person of the other. (Mt. 25.40: 'as you did it to one of the least of these my brethren, you did it to me.') Secondly, the figure of the son is also that with which the believer is increasingly identified as he becomes more similar to the Son through loving self-perfection. As a common saying known in ancient anthropology goes: 'become who you are.' If a Christian should ask who or what he ought to become, the Bible would answer he should become more and more like Christ; the son of God should take form in him (Gal. 4.19). For this Paul says, 'it is no longer I who live, but Christ who lives in me' (Gal. 2.20). The author of the letter to the Ephesians extends this Christ-becoming to the comunity: 'until we all attain to the unity of the faith and of the knowledge of the Son of God, to mature manhood, to the measure of the stature of the fulness of Christ' (Eph. 4.13). In analogy to the way of Jesus Himself, the redeemed persons' identification with Christ is also an eschatological event since it implies the ultimate perfection: 'But our citizenship is in heaven, and it is from there that we are expecting a Saviour, the Lord Jesus Christ. He will transform the body of our humiliation that it may be conformed to the body of his glory, by the power that also enables him to make all things subject to himself.' (Phil. 3.20–21 *NRSV*)[27]. In Trinitarian analogical terms one could also say: we come from the Father, we are originally with the Father and go on towards the Son in so far as we become more similar

---

[27] Cf. The profound and comprehensive paper by H. Rahner, 'Die Gottesgeburt. Die Lehre der Kirchenväter von der Geburt Christi aus dem Herzen der Kirche und der Gläubigen', in: ibid., *Symbole der Kirche. Die Ekklesiologie der Väter*, Salzburg 1964, pp. 13–87.

to Him. In my opinion, this insight can be brought into harmony with the earlier cited text of St. Thomas since he links the *forma substantialis*, the form-image of the creature with the Son who is the image, Word and expression of the Father. The difference between a non-personal creature and a person is precisely seen in that the similarity to the Son is not merely analogically linked to the typical natural form (a human being) as such, but rather goes beyond that to end up in the concrete individual Person (*this* human being) who as a unique person constantly grows in similarity to Christ, because Christ takes form in him. The simultaneaous consequence of this for the person is that he discovers in the encounter with and accompaniement of Christ, his own profile – he becomes himself. Similarity with Christ does not imply negation of one's own selfhood. When Paul says that it is not he who lives, but rather Christ who lives in him (Gal. 2.20), he does not mean to say that Paul as a concrete person disappears; rather he intends saying that his most primal personhood is more completely realized. In the encounter with Christ, Paul becomes more himself. He becomes the profiled *Gestalt* that only he in and through the relation with Christ can become. This taking-*Gestalt* occurs above all as we have seen in the loving-knowing person. We have also seen that to the extent that the person is capable of loving, in that same measure would he be able to live in a present in which his origin and future join to give rise to a concrete existence as a perfected being. This third dimension of the present in Trinitarian analogy can be identified as the dimension of the Holy Spirit. We proceed from the Father in the Spirit, and in the Spirit we become more similar to the Son. In the presence of the Holy Spirit we fully realize ourselves as human beings who remain themselves in being with others and thereby fully possess themselves. It is thus that we fully become what we always have been. Therefore, in proceeding from the unoriginated origin, presently tending in the Spirit towards him to whom we are more and more conformed, we *are* an image of the Triune.

## Trinitarian Inversion

Occupying a key position in the above analysis is the dimension that from a Trinitarian perspective I consider as offering an analogy to the Spirit of God. How is this key position to be justified, considered now from the perspective of the Trinity in whom the Spirit proceeds from the Son and the Father; in whom, strictly speaking observed from the inner-Trinitarian processes implies in the creature a temporarily posterior presence for which the aforementioned Spirit would belong to the dimension of the future? An initial hint towards an answer can be found in the cited excerpt from St Thomas, where he shows the Spirit as represented by the order existing in every creature and the ordering of one towards the other based on the will of the Creator who is love in the Holy Spirit. [28]

If the person in his self-perfection (in the sense of self-becoming) is ordered towards the other, the You and the reality of an encounter, then the origin of a true ordering towards, as we have seen, is love, that turns towards the other and in receiving, sets the other free in its/his selfhood. Humanly and temporarily speaking, this loving setting-free precedes the unitive knowledge. Josef Pieper calls this unitive-knowing contemplation, and describes its content: 'just as for the realization of contemplation which is the beholding of a loved one requires not an intellectual but rather an immediate harmonic existential relation to reality, the world and oneself, in the same way the act of free dedication cannot be expected unless it equally grows from a profoundly rooted disposition of an all-encompassing acceptance, one that can only be described as love.'[29] Together with St Thomas, Pieper does not see love wholly as an acknowledging-appreciative observation, as contemplation in itself (and therefore in a certain sense as perfection); rather love is a prerequisite for such being-perfected.[30] If the person during his life is to become who he is meant to be, implying the aquiring of a more defined *Gestalt* to which he is destined; and if this taking on a defined form is only to succeed through the encounter with an other to himself, and further through the ever more intense knowing union with Christ, then that which orders the person towards this encounter with the other and with Christ is again love. In an analogical reference to the Trinity: the Spirit is the bond of love that unites the Father and the Son. Analogically, too, the Spirit is in the human person the inner venue in and through which the person out of his origin (i.e. from the Father) would arrive at whom he can be, becoming whom he truly is (Son/child of the Father).

A second important hint can be seen in what Hans Urs von Balthasar called the Trinitarian Inversion.[31] For Balthasar, the concept of mission predominates his understanding of the relationship between the Father and the Son. According to him, even though the Son from time immemorial received the mission from the Father to the world, this sending is also a

---

[28] STh I, q. 45, a. 7: 'quaelibet enim creatura ... habet ordinem ad aliquid aliud. secundum autem quod habet ordinem, repraesentat spiritum sanctum, inquantum est amor, quia ordo effectus ad aliquid alterum est ex voluntate creantis.'

[29] J. Pieper, *Kulturphilosophische Schriften*, (Werke, 6), Hamburg: Felix Meiner 1998, p. 232 (cursive by author): 'Wie nämlich das Gelingen der Kontemplation, da sie Anschauen des Geliebten ist, ein bestimmtes, nicht intellektuelles, sondern unmittelbares, *daseinshaftes Verhältnis zur Realität*, eine existentielle Übereinstimmung des Menschen mit der Welt und mit sich selbst *voraussetzt*, genauso ebenso ist der Akt des freien Hingebens nicht erwartbar, es sei denn, er wachse gleichfalls hervor aus dem Wurzelgrund einer umfassenden Bejahung, für die sich schwer eine andere Bezeichnung finden lässt als wiederum der Name "Liebe".'

[30] STh I–II, q. 3, a. 4: 'essentia beatitudinis in actu intellectus consistit.'

[31] Cf. H. U. von Balthasar, *Theodramatik*, II/2, Einsiedeln: Johannes Verlag 1978, pp. 167–75.

command. A command demands obedience and 'obedience implies not being the one commanding,' but rather being at the disposal of another. As long as such a being-at-another's-disposal of Jesus is as primary as his 'I'-consciousness, his incarnation whilst possibly free and voluntary, would still not be the result of something that is self-sought. In the free acceptance of the sending/mission, the obedient Son can be wholly one with the freely sending Father; there where the difference between commanding and obeying appears, only the Holy Spirit can strike the mediating balance between the Father and the Son.'[32] Balthasar goes on to draw attention to the biblical event of the Incarnation: in the Incarnation, the Son places himself at disposal. He is conceived by His mother through the power, the action of the Holy Spirit. The Spirit is in this event the active party, the procreator; the Son is instead the one at the disposal of the other, conceived, gestated, born, taking on a human *Gestalt*. With respect to the incarnation, one can affirm that the action of the Holy Spirit precedes the being-at-another's-disposal and the taking on a form of the Son in the human being. In this, Balthasar corrects the Thomistic emphasis that accentuates the Son as a pre-existent creator,[33] in and through whom all is created (see Jn. 1.3 or Col. 1.16), and therefore in a certain sense, coming *non ordine temporis, sed naturae et intellectus* before the Spirit. Balthasar, together with Walter Kasper, considers this accentuation one-sided.[34] Placing the emphasis on the being-at-another's-disposal of the Son evidenced in the Incarnation, he accentuates less the dimension of co-creator while bringing more to the

---

[32] Balthasar, *Theodramatik*, pp. 167n.: 'Gehorsam besagt: nicht selber verfügen, sondern sich verfügen lassen. Sofern nun ein solches Sich-verfügen-lassen Jesu ebenso ursprünglich ist, wie sein Ich-Bewusstsein, kann schon sein Menschwerden zwar ein freies und freiwilliges sein, aber nicht das Ergebnis eines Selbstverfügens. In der Freiheit des Bejahens der Sendung kann der gehorchende Sohn völlig eins sein mit dem frei sendenden Vater; aber wo die Differenz zwischen Verfügen und Gehorchen aufscheint, tritt notwendig auch eine ausgleichende Vermittlung zwischen Vater und Sohn auf, die nur dem Heiligen Geist zukommen kann.'

[33] Vgl. STh I, q. 45, a. 6, ad 2: 'dicendum quod, sicut natura divina, licet sit communis tribus personis, ordine tamen quodam eis convenit, inquantum filius accipit naturam divinam a patre, et spiritus sanctus ab utroque; ita etiam et virtus creandi, licet sit communis tribus personis, ordine tamen quodam eis convenit; nam filius habet eam a patre, et spiritus sanctus ab utroque. unde creatorem esse attribuitur patri, ut ei qui non habet virtutem creandi ab alio. de filio autem dicitur per quem omnia facta sunt, inquantum habet eandem virtutem, sed ab alio, nam haec praepositio per solet denotare causam mediam, sive principium de principio. sed spiritui sancto, qui habet eandem virtutem ab utroque, attribuitur quod dominando gubernet, et vivificet quae sunt creata a patre per filium. potest etiam huius attributionis communis ratio accipi ex appropriatione essentialium attributorum. nam, sicut supra dictum est, patri appropriatur potentia, quae maxime manifestatur in creatione, et ideo attribuitur patri creatorem esse. filio autem appropriatur sapientia, per quam agens per intellectum operatur, *et ideo dicitur de filio, per quem omnia facta sunt.* spiritui sancto autem appropriatur bonitas, ad quam pertinet gubernatio deducens res in debitos fines, et vivificatio, nam vita in interiori quodam motu consistit, primum autem movens est finis et bonitas.'

[34] Balthasar, *Theodramatik*, II/2, p. 170.

limelight the dimesion of the sending as Saviour. It must however also be noted that for Balthasar this disposition of being-at-another's-disposal by the Son in no way implies mere passivity but 'is instead a form of action that – humanly speaking – demands more self-possesion and engagement from the subject than the execution of personally formulated resolutions and the realization of personal objectives.' In this respect also, taking into consideration his Incarnation and humanity, the Son is a *'product of the Spirit'* obtained *ex Maria virgine*, even though the Spirit is within the Trinity the product of the combined spiration of the Father and the Son.'[35] This is how Kasper formulates the same content: The Spirit is thereby the personified freedom of Love in God as well as the creative principle that so sanctifies the man Jesus that He is capacitated, by means of his freely given obedience and his dedication to be the incarnated answer to Gods self-communication.'[36]

Later on, with respect to the resurrected and ascended Lord, Balthasar and Kasper both take up this Trinitarian inversion in its original form: 'in the consuming oblation till death, the Spirit is set free; it is loosened from the bonds of its particular, historical form, a reason for which the death and resurrection of Jesus equally implies the coming of the Holy Spirit.'[37] This means the Son is and remains eternally He, who together with the Father expirate the Spirit (*Filioque*); but he is also the one who with respect to the work of salvation, in freedom[38] places himself at the disposal of the Spirit.

I believe von Balthasar and Kaspar present this issue convincingly so I will not delve further into this issue here, but will instead try to see how it can help in our theme concerning the Trinitarian explanation of an anthropology of the person (trinitarisch erläuterten personalen Anthropologie). It is central to the question under study to see the leading role the Spirit plays in the Incarnation and humanity of Jesus, up until the point where the Lord, lifted up and dying on the cross, reveals who he is. Let us keep this inversion in mind for when we shall explain the concept of personal self-perfection. I have mentioned that the human being by the act of full personal self-perfection fully realizes his selfhood and self-becoming as one. The successful selfhood *is* a kind of self-becoming. And searching for the answer to the question about the end, the final aim of this self-becoming, we found it together with the Bible to be in the form of the Son of the Father.

---

[35] Balthasar, *Theodramatik*, II/2, pp. 170n.

[36] W. Kasper, *Jesus der Christus*, Mainz: Mathias Grünewald Verlag 1975, p. 298 (italics by author).

[37] Kasper, *Jesus der Christus*: 'In der sich bis in den Tod hinein verzehrenden Hingabe wird der Geist sozusagen frei; er wird von seiner partikulären geschichtlichen Gesalt entbunden, weshalb Tod und Auferstehung Jesu zugleich das Kommen des Geistes vermitteln'.

[38] Kasper places special emphasis on this moment of freedom between the Father and the Son in the Spirit. Cf. Kasper, *Jesus der Christus*, pp. 298–300.

Christ also, as Son of God, attains the perfection of his sending/mission –
in Johannine terms – through his elevation, his glorification as seen by the
Evangelist in his crucifixion: here is made evident who the Son is, and that
He lives in the most profound sense, out of love. Only here does he expirate
the Spirit (Jn 19.30) in the sense of a total handing over, something not as
fully realized before the self-giving on the cross: 'Now he said this about
the Spirit, which believers in him were to receive; for as yet there was no
Spirit, because Jesus was not yet glorified.' (Jn 7.39). Mark's Gospel also
presents us with the cry of the centurion who at the foot of the cross, saw
and believed: 'Truly this man was God's Son!' (Mk 15.39).

Crucifixion is therefore a perfection of Mission and a last demonstration
of his gift of love. If we were to observe Christ's earthly life on a timeline,
one could say that who He truly is, in his case is also revealed most clearly
from the future, in His death on the cross. He went this way in the Spirit
of the Father and on the cross; he gives the world the Spirit. In a certain
sense, He dispenses the spirit so that the faithful can henceforth go in the
Spirit, and in and through His presence become more similar to the Son.
I am of the opinion that the Trinitarian Inversion observed by Balthasar
and Kasper and seen in this light is not only of significance with respect to
God's Incarnation, but also helps towards a more profound understanding
of the 'incarnation' of humankind, or better put: the 'personalization' of the
human being, his identification with or assimilation in Christ. The human
being is then perfected as its own self when he lives in the Holy Spirit,
becoming who he has always been: child of the Father. Salvation is already
underway because the Spirit our guarantee, pledge, a first instalment (2 Cor.
1.22; 2 Cor. 5.5, Eph. 1.14) of our promised salvation, has already been
given us since we ought to be journeying already in the Spirit. However,
salvation in the fullest sense is not yet attained, because even though we are
already children of God, full identification and oneness with Him will only
become a reality at the fullness of time, at Christ's coming (1 Jn 3.2).

All that has been previously said can be summarized thus: the human
being subsists in his knowing-loving self-perfection in so far as he is with
and for the other. He is ever more himself in the same measure as he gives
of himself. In this act, his inner sanctuary is not his actual 'I' consciousness,
nor is it a closed 'I' concept out of which life is objectivized, mastered and
controlled. His 'I' consciousness has in the loving selflessness of the person
descended instead as it were into that place called the 'heart' in biblical
language. This is the place I intend showing as the real locus of personal
self-realization. If the loving Knower is really an authentic person, he would
at the moment of this personal self-perfection appear primarily as a relating
self and not as a static 'I' reference point. He is himself in his relation to
other and therein relates similarly to his own self. In this we are touching on
a profound insight by Søren Kierkegaard in 'Krankheit zum Tode': the self
is a relationship that relates to itself or is that which in relationships relates

the relationship with itself; the self is not the relationship but rather the relationship that relates to itself.'[39] In addition to what we have developed up until now, we could add: the more selfless and loving the person, the more naturally he would live in and out of this self-relationship, the more profound is his presence, he is wholly present. He is freed from the self-encapsulating 'I' fixation and opens up to the equanimous, loving manner of existence of one who becomes in so far as he simply 'is'. He lives out of his integrating, unitive centre, that is already always given. With some caution (since it does not actually have to do with a static reality but rather an alive, dynamic process) this manner of existence in its analogies could also be graphically illustrated:

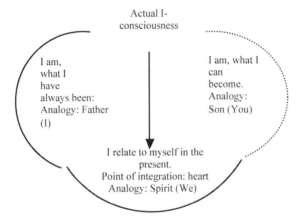

This understanding of the correlation existing between personal self-perfection and the Trinitarian relations in my opinion allows for a deeper insight into the manner according to which human nature from the Christian perspective perfects itself. It becomes however more evident how essential is the belief, not only in God but specifically in a *triune* God, whose image in man is not only the triad of Augustinian origin – *memoria, intellectus, voluntas* – but above all in the human being's entire and also temporally extensive self-perfection as humans.[40]

The sketch illustrates the perfection of a calm, freed, lovingly knowing being as far as this is possible under the condition of a temporary existence. It also shows that in an analogous sense every individual human being can

---

[39] S. Kierkegaard, *Die Krankheit zum Tode*, (Ges. Werke, Abt. 24/25), Düsseldorf/Köln, 1985, p. 8.

[40] In my opinion, the model is also capable of explaining malformations in personal self-realization something that we cannot dwell upon given the limited space available to us. Cf. more in-depth studies in: S. Oster, *Person und Transsubstantiation. Mensch-sein, Kirche-sein und Eucharistie – eine ontologische Zusammenschau*, Freiburg-Basel-Wien: Herder 2010.

be said to be in himself an 'I-you', himself as an other that he already is or could become. He encounters himself ever anew in his loving outpouring of self into the other. He experiences himself therein each time anew becoming who he always has been or could become. In the other, he himself becomes as it were the other, in order to remain and become fully himself. Taking a step further, one would say that the unitive Heart-dimension is analogous to the We-dimension in which the 'I' of the 'have been' and the 'you' of the 'being an other' find their uniting centre. In a certain analogous sense, the individual human being is already in himself an 'I-you-we'.[41] The human being of the redemeed existence is in an analogous sense an equanimous, not-fixated loving 'We-form of freedom'.[42]

Unredeemed existence therefore would be a self-perfection that never succeeded in completing the selfless descent of the actual 'I' consciousness into the relational Heart-dimension. In such a case, the 'I' consciousness clings on to itself according to the 'I' = 'I' schema, simply so as not to have to face nor ever dare this selfless descent. As a consequence, it will incline towards not identifying itself with that which is perfected in free, equanimous, actual self-relatedness, because it is already gratefully accustomed to receiving self as a gift. It will rather be inclined to identifying itself in an objectifying way with its 'having been': I am what I have always had and now have. Or it will be inclined to look towards a yet pending and imaginary future just so as not to be nor have to accept what it is or has been. Analogously, Kierkegaard conceives these discrepancies in the self as forms of despair: 'one despairs in being oneself' or 'one despairs in not being oneself.'[43]

# Liberated Freedom as a We-form and a Personal Dwelling of the Triune God

Now the above sketch is admittedly still considerably lacking: it still does without the other as an 'other' that in lovingly knowing and knowingly loving functions as the orienting personal correlate in the self-perfection of the individual. Love and knowledge are in view of the other and if as a

---

[41] I owe these reflections (the individual as I-You-We) – including its linguistic formulation – in a special way to F. Ulrich, who has done much to show through innumerable nuances the successful and unsuccessful forms of selfhood that are conceivable therein; cf. *Gabe und Vergebung. Ein Beitrag zur biblischen Ontologie*, Freiburg: 2006; ibid., *Logo-Tokos. Der Mensch und das Wort*, Freiburg: Johannes Verlag 2003, esp. pp. 507–693.

[42] F. Ulrich, *Gegenwart der Freiheit*, Einsiedeln: Johannes Verlag 1974, pp. 124–7.

[43] S. Kierkegaard, *Die Krankheit zum Tode*, (Ges. Werke, Abt. 24/25), Düsseldorf/Köln, 1985, p. 8.

knower, within the context of love, I am at the same time known and loved, the experience of the We-form is made. Lovers or friends speak of 'our relationship', 'our friendship', 'our love' like a kind of third party that unites and binds both partners. They express this relationship in mostly atmospheric and/or spatial categories because they have the impression that they live *within* these realities and are contained by them in a similar manner to the weather that surrounds us. We speak of warmth or coldness in the relationship, of tensions and harmony; we also speak of inner nearness and distance, and of oneness and division in order to describe the quality of such experiences. In mature trusting relationships, the partners sense each from his own perspective the quality, the condition of this relationship in which they find themselves. But they speak of a third party, in which both feel at home even though both know that this third party, namely the relationship itself, is produced by them and without them would not exist. On the other hand they experience the fact that such a relationship in which they live and find themselves cannot simply be produced through objectifying means. It is created, it occurs, it develops and grows in a mysterious way also all by itself. Now and then, lovers contemplate full of wonder at the miracle and gift of their friendship. They experience each other therein, while on the other hand being themselves co-originators of the same. In some way, the relationship was always there; on the other hand, it results only from the interaction of the partners. If that inner mysterious relationship – in so far as not being materially attainable – of both partners is actually love that takes pleasure in the other and first wishes the other to be(come) oneself, then the lovers would have the experience of the fact that the mystery of unity grows and both become ever more similar one to the other, while at the same time, each becomes more him- or herself, acquiring a distinctive unique profile in view of the partner. Becoming-one with the other and the respective unique self-realization, considered in the context of love that acknowledges the other as an 'other', does not imply a contradiction but rather presents two aspects of the same experience. The partners therefore constitute a We-form that one can once more illustrate graphically; again with the hint that what is tried here, is to give at least from the structural perspective a certain (still inadequate) form to what it essentially a non-tangible reality.

The personal relationship of one to the other allows both partners of the relationship a certain kind of reciprocal indwelling, since each of the two is not a static encapsulated 'I'='I' but rather lives in an equanimous self-relatedness, in which he, in the manner of being-with-the-other, is wholly himself, and at the same time allowing room in himself for the other, realizing together with the other his self-perfection. When this encounter occurs in the context of a reciprocal trusting relationship, each partner in the relationship dwells equally in the other as well as in himself. In this way, from below upwards, so to speak, the we-spatiality of unfettered Being-with-another opens up the We-form of freedom. This is on the one hand the

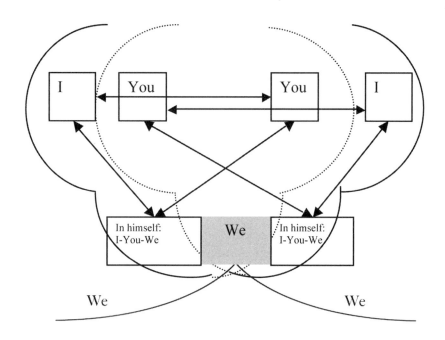

heart of this dynamic relationship. It develops from within outwards, but is on the other hand, as a fully realized relationship, a kind of expanded, secure space for relationships.

If the partners of the relationship are not equals, as in the pedagogic relationship, or if one of the partners is more relationally stronger, while the other is more taciturn, then the unitive 'we' will be more clearly nurtured and carried along by the relational strength of the stronger partner, and by his intra-subjective (not inter-subjective) We-form which he actually is, as seen above. The strength of the partner more capable of loving distinguishes itself in being capable of ultimately weakening itself in so far as it dares more, trusts, risks more, is more committed – becoming consequently more vulnerable. Whosoever takes another to heart, an other that is initially not open but closed up in himself or rejecting, such a person nurtures the We-form out of his strength of love much more than the taciturn or reserved partner. The We-form lives more deeply from the loving capacity of the former. This supports and carries along the reserved, 'I'='I' self-relationship of the other and thereby the whole relationship – and this up until the other is ready for self-giving, opening up to a new, more mature and mutual We-form.

Now we know also of the phenomenon that there are people who are so charismatic and fundamental for others that out of their holistic We-form – in other words, their all-encompassing capacity of love – they offer a fundamental originating model for a whole community of people. Many let themselves be touched by this great capacity for love in the one person and therein they develop their own capacity for love, opening up to a growing, holistic We-form. For instance, the charisma of founders of a congregation belongs here. Out of their capacity for love, an holistic communal We-form grows that is shaped originally and carried along by the personality of the founder and has its origin in him or her. Above, we saw that the Spirit of God is the interior centre of intra- as well as inter-personal relationships. It already exists, since on the one hand, lovers bring it into existence in so far as they through their reciprocal openess and giving open themselves to this Spirit and create room for Him.

The lovers who create room for the Spirit are therefore those who respond to and have always responded to the call and touch of the Spirit. People who live in the presence of the Spirit and whose lives are conformed accordingly, these are the new people. They are the ones who shape the church and ever anew contribute towards the growth of the church as a big We-form of freedom, manifesting itself as the dwelling place of God. If, however, we were to seek its origin, who then would be the original illuminating model of the church, who has lived in the deepest and most intimate relationship with the Spirit of God, then the above reflection would lead us to the Mother of Jesus. She is the quintessential created answer to the call of the Spirit and is thereby the holistic We-form that contains all those in the church who follow in the response to the call of the Spirit. One can therefore say: every real answer of the church to the Holy Spirit has its root in this original We-form and is carried along by it. Fruitfulness in the church implies all activity through which God's ever present Spirit is borne out of love, is nutured from this all-encompassing and all-containing anwer, her 'yes'. She is the holy, created person, who in a way unlike any other creature owes everything to the Unoriginated paternal origin and brings forth in the presence and fruitfulness of the Spirit Him who would be the future salvation for her and all her humans. In her is finally to be seen the indwelling of the Trinitarian God in the human being. And that the human being is in his self-perfection, past, present and future, the image of the triune God.

# 16

# Social Trinitarianism and its Critics

## Kathryn Tanner

Use of a social analogy for the Trinity is common in early Christian thought, particularly in the East. For example, the relationship of origin that holds between the equally divine first and second persons of the Trinity can be illuminated by the way a human father generates an equally human son.[1] The unity of nature among the three persons of the Trinity is something like the common human nature shared by three human beings.[2] And the fact that no one doubts Adam and Abel had the same human nature despite their different origins – without and with a human father – helps explain the idea that the unbegotten Father and the begotten Son have the same divine nature.[3]

But it becomes commonplace in Christian theology to prefer a social analogy for the Trinity, over the psychological ones stemming from Augustine, or the analogies with inanimate processes (light and water) that always accompanied social ones in the early Christian East, only after the late nineteenth century.[4] One reason for this development is surely the modern shift in the meaning of the term 'person' employed in the

---

[1] See, for example, Gregory Nazianzen, 'Fourth Theological Oration', section 20, in *Nicene and Post-Nicene Fathers*, Second Series, vol. 7, Grand Rapids, Michigan: Eerdmans 1983, p. 316.

[2] See, for example, Gregory of Nyssa, 'On Not Three Gods', in *Nicene and Post-Nicene Fathers*, Peabody, Massachusetts: Hendrickson 1994, p. 331

[3] See, for example, Gregory of Nyssa, 'Against Eunomius', III, 3, in *Nicene and Post-Nicene Fathers*, Second Series, vol. 5, Peabody, Massachusetts: Hendrickson 1994, p. 143.

[4] For a good treatment of this modern trend, with attention to major theologians up to the mid-twentieth century, see C. Welch, *In this Name: The Doctrine of the Trinity in*

Latin-derived formula summing up the parameters for proper discussion of the Trinity laid down by the ecumenical councils: 'three persons in one substance.' While having a range of associations, including 'mask', 'role' and 'function,' 'persona' at the time of the ecumenical councils was arguably a technical term used simply to uphold the permanent distinctions among whatever there were three of in the Trinity. Without having any firm definition transferred to theological use, 'persona' could serve as the equivalent of 'hypostases' in the Greek version of same formula; and, like the latter term's (again rather indefinite) sense of individual subsistence, suggested little, therefore, in the way of the 'personal'. 'Person' in modern usage, however, suggests nothing but the personal: for example, the distinctive centre of consciousness, thought and intentional agency that constitutes one's human 'self'. Modern people are naturally inclined to substitute that sort of meaning of 'person' within the Trinitarian formula. Modern theologians try to make a virtue of that fact by drawing out the way in which such a substitution could become a helpful primary analogy for the Trinity. Individual persons are obviously distinct, but they are also social beings, gaining their identities from the relations they have with other persons in human society. While firmly undergirding the distinctness of the three persons of the Trinity, the modern sense of 'person' could therefore also perhaps suggest how the three persons are one: through the intensity of their personal relationships or the manner in which they form an interpersonal community.

The social analogy of the Trinity has the added benefit for these theologians of making clear the biblical roots of the doctrine and its relevance to Christian life – both in dispute in the modern period. For example, even if the idea of the Bible as a source of revealed propositions or deposit of faith has fallen into disrepute with the rise of modern biblical criticism, the gospels still seem to be narrating some sort of relationship of personal community or fellowship between Jesus and the one He calls Father: in those biblical stories Jesus prays to the Father, works to align His will with the Father, strives to carry out the mission upon which He suggests His Father in heaven has sent him, and so on. The Trinity often seemed a speculative theological abstraction of little importance to Christian worship and community life in much of Christian theology after the Enlightenment.[5] But now, using a social analogy for the Trinity, the personal relations or community that Christians form with one another and with the persons of the Trinity for the sake of the world – for example, the way that Christians

---

*Contemporary Theology*, New York: Charles Scribner's Sons 1952, pp. 29–34, 78–85, 95–100, 108–13, 252–72.

[5] Schleiermacher's purported relegation of the Trinity to a near appendix of *The Christian Faith*, Philadelphia: Fortress 1976, because of its lack of direct connection with Christian experience, is often cited as the paradigm of this trend.

pray together to the Father through the power of the Spirit in the name of the Son for help as a community in serving the mission of the triune God within the world – has its foundation in the very life of triune God which is itself something like an interpersonal form of communion.

This latter fact – that the Trinity gains practical significance when understood according to a social analogy – is very much stressed in contemporary theologies concerned with the social and political implications of Christian belief and commitment. In contemporary theology, the espousal of social Trinitarianism, an account of the Trinity in primarily social terms, is what allows the Trinity to be enlisted so readily to give Christian grounds of support for particular socio-political judgments. John Zizioulas, Jürgen Moltmann, Leonardo Boff and Catherine LaCugna are among the most important names in this regard.[6] Thus for Zizioulas the primacy of the category of person over substance in Trinitarian theology highlights the freedom of human persons from biological necessity and counters the individualism of modern society by suggesting that even divine persons are what they are only in community. For Moltmann, Trinitarianism breaks through the way in which monotheism legitimizes authoritarian rule by a single holder of exclusive power such as a monarch, and thereby allows humans to assume their freedom both under God and in human society. Because the persons of the Trinity are united to one another in their personal and social character, the Trinity makes clear that human beings are not isolated individuals but persons with social responsibilities, and that human relationships are to take the form not of lordship, but of a fellowship without privileges and without subordinates. For Boff, human community, which follows the pattern of the social Trinity, is to be an open rather than an exclusive one, in which all persons are able to participate fully, and have their differences respected. For LaCugna, the personal and social community of the Trinity refutes the male ideal of autonomy or determination of oneself apart from relations with others, replaces hierarchical social relations with ones of mutuality and reciprocity, and maintains the equal dignity of all. This specific form of contemporary social Trinitarianism, in which political and social judgments come to the fore, is the subject of my critique in what follows.[7]

Although theological judgments here seem quite simple – for example, if the persons of the Trinity are equal to one another then human beings should be too – figuring out the socio-political lessons of the

---

[6] See J. Zizioulas, *Being as Communion*, Crestwood, New York: St Vladimir's Seminary Press, 1993; J. Moltmann, *The Trinity and the Kingdom,* New York: Harper Collins, 1991; L. Boff, Trinity and Society, Maryknoll, New York: Orbis 1988; C. LaCugna, *God For Us,* New York: Harper Collins 1991.
[7] An expanded version of this critique can be found in chapter five, 'Politics' of my *Christ the Key*, Cambridge and New York: Cambridge University Press 2010.

Trinity is a fraught task, full of complexities and perils. I systematically explore these complexities and perils, and conclude that it would be better to steer one's immediate attention away from the Trinity when trying to determine the proper character of human relations in Christian terms. Christology, I suggest, is the far more direct and less misleading avenue to take when making socio-political judgments on Christian grounds.

# Inflated Claims for the Trinity

My first caveat concerns inflated claims made for the Trinity in contemporary political theology. Many contemporary theologies overestimate the progressive political potential of the Trinity. Monotheism, it is alleged, supports monolithic identities and authoritarian forms of government in which power is held exclusively by a single leader or group. An internally diverse triune God, in which persons share equally with one another, avoids these dangers. Or so the story goes.[8]

Overlooked in such a simple contrast between the political implications of monotheism and Trinitarianism are the complexities of such theological claims (can monotheism and Trinitarianism, for example, be this easily distinguished?), their fluidity of sense (can't monotheism or Trinitarianism mean many different things?) and the possible variety of the political purposes that each might serve. To limit myself to the last consideration for the moment: monotheism need not be all that bad in its political implications. Of course it can suggest rule by one: one God, one lord – meaning one human lord. But monotheism can also suggest (particularly when understood to deny that divinity is a general category of things) that no one shares in divinity and therefore that no one can stand in as God's representative: 'no lord but God'.

Trinitarianism, moreover, is not often – to say the least – historically associated with an egalitarian politics and respect for diversity within community. Trinitarian thinking arose in tandem with Christian support for an increasingly centralized Roman imperial rule, once Christianity became the state religion under the Emperor Constantine. Indeed, the major theological arguments in favour of imperial rule were not at all obviously monotheistic but presumed a diversity of divine principles or powers. Thus Eusebius, in probably the most famous of these, his 'Oration in Praise of the Emperor Constantine', argues that the emperor has near absolute authority to govern the whole known human world as the agent and representative of

---

[8] See E. Peterson, *Der Monotheismus als Politisches Problem*, Leipzig: Jakob Hegner 1935; Moltmann, *Trinity and the Kingdom*, pp. 192–202; Boff, *Trinity and Society*, pp. 20–4.

the Word – a second divine principle – who rules the cosmos from on high at the supreme God's request.[9]

Behind this poor historical showing lies the ambiguous socio-political potential of Trinitarian theology itself. Many aspects of classical Trinitarianism seem on the face of it at least politically awkward. Contrary to respect for difference, for example, divine persons are equal to one another because in some very strong sense they are the same. Short of tritheism, it is difficult to argue that divine persons are different from one another in the way human persons properly are – able to go their separate ways, distinguished by their own particular projects and interests, never in exactly the same place at the same time, distinct individuals sharing a common humanity in a general sense, but not the same one humanity in the way the divine persons are the same one and indivisible divine being or substance, and so on. Taken as an indication of proper human sociability, here it seems is humanity subsumed by community with others. (Perhaps for this reason most advocates of a Trinitarian social or political program err, to my mind, in the direction of a very strong communitarianism; that is much of the point of looking to the Trinity for social guidance.) The common theological view that divine persons are constituted by their relations, along with the idea of their indivisibility in being and act, is simply hard to square with a politics that would like to foster the agency of persons traditionally effaced in relations with dominant members of society – women, racial or ethnic minorities, those over-identified with social roles in which their own needs and wants are given short shrift. Moreover, the order among divine persons, no matter how complex, tends to differentiate persons by their unsubstitutable functions or places. The Holy Spirit, for example, has to go third in the liturgically favoured, biblically derived formula, 'Father, Son, and Holy Spirit'. The order among divine persons is therefore ripe for justification of human hierarchy. It easily supports fixed social roles and the idea that people are equal despite the disparity of their assignment to such roles. And so on.

The turn to the economic Trinity – the Trinity's working for us in the world as the New Testament recounts – is no help on this score, although lots of politically progressive Trinitarian theologian seem to think it is. New Testament accounts of Jesus' relations with the one He calls Father are much more subordinationalist in flavour than accounts of the so-called immanent Trinity usually are: Jesus prays to the Father, subordinates His will to the Father, defers to the Father, seems ignorant on occasion of what only the Father knows, etc. (see, for example, Jn 14.28; Mk 13.32; Mk 10.18; Lk. 18.18; Mt. 19.16). This sort of hierarchical relation between Son

---

[9] Eusebius of Caesarea, 'Oration in Praise of the Emperor Constantine', in *Nicene and Post-Nicene Fathers*, vol. 1, New York: Christian Literature Co., 1890.

and Father, a relationship of inferior to superior, very obviously suggests the propriety of human hierarchy.

Finally, the inclusion of gendered imagery in classical characterizations of the relationships among the persons of the Trinity themselves and in their workings for the world has enormously problematic social and political ramifications. The pervasive Father-Son language of the New Testament in particular always holds the potential for rendering women second-class citizens of the church or effacing their contributions altogether. Granted, Father-Son language is always given a quite limited theological rationale in classical Trinitarian theology. The point is very much not to import gender into God. That is quite explicitly denied: 'The divine is neither male nor female (for how could such a thing be contemplated in divinity ...?'[10] The significance of the imagery is quite often limited simply to the idea that the one comes from the other and is of the very same substance with it, equal to it and not other than it. The intent is to distinguish the second person from a creature that also comes from God but is not equal to God. 'Making' language therefore trumps 'kinship' language when the Father's relations with the world are at issue: the Father does not act like a Father exactly in creating the world; the Father makes the world and does not beget it from his own substance. The gendered imagery in classical Trinitarianism is always played off, moreover, against other forms of biblical imagery of a quite impersonal sort – light and water imagery, for example. Paired with these other images, the meaning of Father-Son imagery is therefore often quite abstract, not specific to its gendered character. No one set of biblical images, furthermore, is privileged; they mutually modify one another in their theological import.[11] For example, light imagery is usually considered far better than Father-Son imagery in conveying the inseparable, indivisible character of the two. But whatever the theological intent, the rhetorical punch of the language in practice is another thing altogether; and nothing erases the sorry history in which the importance of such language has been magnified out of all proportion, in defiance of these quite circumscribed understandings of its theological point.

Granted too that in classical Trinitarian thinking this is a Father who acts like a mother: He births or begets the Son. The term used to sum up the activity remains gendered male (probably for one reason because

---

[10] Gregory of Nyssa, *Commentary on the Song of Songs*, cited by V. Harrison, 'Male and Female in Cappadocian Theology', *Journal of Theological Studies* 41 (1990) 441; see also Gregory Nazianzen, *Fifth Theological Oration* (31.7), cited and discussed by Harrison, 'Male and Female', pp. 456–7.

[11] For a clear expression of this principle, see Gregory of Nyssa, *Against Eunomius*, Book 8, sections 4–5, in *Nicene and Post-Nicene Fathers*, Second Series, vol. 5, Peabody, Massachusetts: Hendrickson 1994, pp. 204–10.

'father' is the dominant gendered term in the New Testament), but the activity itself seems much more in keeping with what only women can do: give birth. Notwithstanding the ancient biological theory in which the father is responsible for the substance of the child – the mother being a mere container for what the father contributes – what is of theological interest here is the way the Son issues immediately out of the Father like a child being birthed from its mother. Birth as the primary metaphor for developing whatever the Father is doing in relation to the Son is therefore quite strong – for example, in Hilary of Poitiers.[12] One might even say, following Ps. 120.3, as Hilary does, that the Son is begotten of the Father's womb.[13] And Jesus' mother, Mary, an actual woman, consequently becomes a prime analogy, since her birthing, like the Father's birthing of the Son, happens in the absence of any contribution by a sexual partner: the Son – the second person of the Trinity – has only a Father in the way the Son incarnate had only a mother.[14]

This sort of gender-bending use of imagery associated with both sexes – a Father with a womb – might very well present the best hope for avoiding the theological reinforcement of male privilege. Gendered imagery is 'exceeded' in a 'baffling of gender literalism'.[15] 'Roles are reversed, fused, inverted: no one is simply who they seem to be. More accurately, everyone is *more than* they seem to be ... the Father and the Spirit are more than one gender can convey.'[16] However, nothing stops talk of a Father with a womb from simply erasing the contribution of real women by usurping their place: a man can do everything now! The genders are not being bent here in a strictly reciprocal way. The Father is not simply more than any one gender – male or female – can convey, but is already as Father everything that the other gender ordinarily suggests. The divine Father may act in the way a human mother does; and a human mother – Mary – may give birth in a close parallel to the way the divine Father gives rise to the Son. But the genders are still clearly distinguished by ranking them across the division of human and divine. Women generally and Mary in particular may be privileged over men as the closest analogue on the human plane to divine generation, but they are nevertheless bested on a divine level by what only a Father is said to do. Quite commonly, moreover, the use of both paternal and maternal language merely reinforces gender stereotyping. The Father

---

[12] See Hilary of Poitiers, *On the Trinity*, VI, 9, 35; IX, 36 in *Nicene and Post-Nicene Fathers*, Second Series, vol. 9, Peabody, Massachusetts: Hendrickson 1994, pp. 100, 111, 167.

[13] Hilary, *On the Trinity*, XII, 8, pp. 219–20.

[14] Hilary, *On the Trinity*, XII, 50, p. 231.

[15] J. M. Soskice, 'Trinity and Feminism', in S. F. Parson (ed.), *The Cambridge Companion to Feminist Theology*, Cambridge: Cambridge University Press 2002, p. 146.

[16] S. A. Harvey, 'Feminine Imagery for the Divine: the Holy Spirit, the Odes of Solomon, and Early Syriac Tradition', in *St Vladimir's Theological Quarterly* 37/2–3 (1993) 114.

is also a Mother because he is nurturing and compassionate and slow to anger, following, e.g. Isa. 49.15; 66:.13.[17]

One might try to avoid gendered imagery altogether. But even when absolutely equal Trinitarian persons of unassigned gender are made the basis for political conclusions, the essential relatedness of those persons easily leads to heterosexism. The importance of differences between male and female for the identity of human persons can simply be presumed and substituted within a Trinitarian account of the essential relatedness of persons to suggest that the identity of a woman depends on her relationship to a male counterpart.[18]

Clearly, then, Trinitarianism can be every bit as socially and politically dangerous as monotheism. Everything depends on how that Trinitarianism (or monotheism) is understood and applied. The only Trinitarianism that is clearly more politically progressive than (some forms of) monotheism is Trinitarianism within a very specific range of interpretations and modes of application. Those lauding the political merits of Trinitarianism over strict monotheism eventually make clear that this holds only for Trinitarianism when properly understood and employed – in other words, for the sort of Trinitarianism they are actively trying to construct. What these theologians are trying to do, indeed, is systematically modify as many of the politically problematic aspects of classical Trinitarianism as they can.

Thus Moltmann and Miroslav Volf argue that the persons of the Trinity are not simply constituted by their relations without remainder.[19] Following Moltmann, politically progressive Trinitarian theologians, such as Leonardo Boff, downplay irreversible orders among the Trinitarian persons in favour of perfectly reciprocal perichoretic relations – relations of indwelling – among them: the Father is in the Son just as the Son is in the Father, etc. It is these perichoretic relations that do the heavy lifting. The reversibility of those relations, rather than identity of substance, is what accounts for the *equality* of the persons. And they come to replace politically problematic

---

[17] See, for example, Boff, *Trinity and Society*, p. 171.

[18] M. Volf, *Exclusion and Embrace*, Nashville, Tennessee: Abingdon 1996, p. 187. Volf moves illegitimately here from a necessity of conceptual reference (from the fact that one term is defined with reference to another) to a necessary relation of fact (women must actually be related to men, e.g. married to them, in order to be themselves). The logical slippage involved becomes readily apparent when one considers other cases where terms are defined with reference to one another but where it would be absurd to infer a requirement of actual intertwined lives of intimacy: heterosexuality, for example, develops as a concept in relation to homosexuality, and so on.

[19] For example, M. Volf, '"The Trinity is Our Social Program": The Doctrine of the Trinity and the Shape of Social Engagement' in *Modern Theology* 14/3 (1998) 410; Moltmann, *Trinity and the Kingdom*, pp. 172–4.

alternatives, such as identity of substance, as the basis for the Trinity's unity.[20]

The theological merits of these politically progressive theologies hinge on how good the arguments are for such theological moves. One argument in their favour is simply the fact that these moves support a progressive politics, and I have no interest in denying the importance of that. But this political consideration hardly overrides the many problematic features of the sort of Trinitarianism typically advanced. Inexplicably to my mind, for example, no one has adequately addressed how the heavy load that perfectly reciprocal perichoresis carries in these theologies is compatible with their equally strong emphasis on the biblical economy, in which Jesus seems clearly to be acting in a non-mutual relation of subordination to the Father (e.g. the Son prays to the Father, but the Father does not pray to the Son; the Son does the will of the Father, but the Father does not do the will of the Son, etc). In other words, not all the relations among the persons of the Trinity in the biblical narration of them seem even close to being reciprocal ones, in which the persons can change places with one another, and little explanation is offered for this; that fact is for the most part just ignored.[21]

The very heavy emphasis on perfectly reciprocal relations among the members of the Trinity and severe downplaying of any idea of their fixed positions in an order (for example, the persons are often now said to be all equally origins of one another, even if they are always properly named in the order Father, Son, and Holy Spirit[22]) seem, moreover, hard to reconcile with the usual ways of making clear that the persons are distinct from one another. The most common way in the history of theology is to talk about their being related to one another in some non-interchangeable way – the Father is related to the Son as the one begetting Him but in doing so he is specifically the Father and not the Son – and to make a distinction on that basis between communicable or shareable properties (what all the persons exhibit qua divine) and incommunicable ones (when the Father gives the Son everything in begetting Him that does not include the character of being Father).[23] Most politically progressive theologies simply start from the assumption of distinct persons, taking this for granted as a feature of the biblical witness, and go on to talk about the unity of the Trinity on that basis: as a function of how closely related the persons are to one another. But if the relationships they have with one another allow for no distinctions

---

[20] See, for example, Boff, *Trinity and Society*, p. 84; and Zizioulas, *Being as Communion*, p. 134.
[21] See Boff, *Trinity and Society*, pp. 138–9, where every biblically narrated relationship among the persons is said to involve their being in one another.
[22] Boff, *Trinity and Society*, pp. 138–9.
[23] See Boff, *Trinity and Society*, 88–9, for an explicit rejection of the latter.

among them, it is hard to see how such a starting assumption helps. Their relations work to undercut the distinctiveness of the persons that is simply assumed at the start and there is no remaining way to shore it up.

Other moves made by politically progressive Trinitarian theologians suggest, to the contrary, that the persons of the Trinity are *too* distinct from one another. Moltmann, for example, maintains that the existence of the persons of the Trinity is distinct from their relations.[24] It is simply impossible, Moltmann maintains, for persons to be their relations, in the way an Augustinian or Thomistic account of Trinitarian persons as subsistent relations would have it. But this is simply to give the Trinitarian term 'person' (a rather ill-defined placeholder for whatever there might be three of in the Trinity) the modern sense of 'human person' and then insist on taking it quite literally. It is impossible for human beings to enter into relationships unless they already exist; we have to exist before we can relate to other people. Or, to make the distinction between existence and manner of existence perhaps more properly (as Moltmann himself does in a later article), we can be said to exist because of certain relationships – in virtue, say, of being born of a particular mother and father, whatever the characters we come to have by way of subsequent ones.[25] But why assume any of this must hold for divine persons?

Quite a bit more argument than Moltmann offers would be necessary to justify the use of a modern sense of 'person' here, with implications diverging so markedly from previous uses of personal language in Trinitarian theology. Personal terms have long been employed to talk about the persons of the Trinity: Father and Son are the prime examples. But (as Boff, *pace* Moltmann, properly points out in support of the use of the modern sense of person to discuss the three) that is to suggest the very constitution of such persons in and through their relations with one another: there is no Father without this Son and no Son without this Father.[26] The point was to highlight their essential or constitutive relationality; personal language was certainly not used to distinguish the existence of a person of the Trinity from the *way* it exists in relation to another.

Taken literally, the argument clearly suggests tritheism. The persons of the Trinity become very much like human persons; and therefore the Trinity itself becomes a collection – tightly interwoven to be sure – of distinct persons on a very close – too close – analogy to a society of human persons.

---

[24] Moltmann, *Trinity and the Kingdom*, p. 172.
[25] Moltmann, 'Theological Proposals towards a Resolution of the *Filioque* Controversy' in L. Vischer (ed.), *Spirit of God, Spirit of Christ*, London: SPCK 1981, pp. 164–73.
[26] Boff, *Trinity and Society*, pp. 88–9, 115–16.

# From God to Humans

No matter how close the similarities between human and divine persons, differences always remain – God is not us – and this sets up the major problem for theologies that want to base conclusions about human relationships on the Trinity. The chief complication is how to move from a discussion of God to human relationships, given those differences.[27] How exactly, in short, does a description of the Trinity apply to us? Three more specific problems arise here.

First of all, the differences between God and us suggest we do not understand very well what we mean when using ordinary language to speak of the Trinity. What the Trinity is saying about human relations becomes unclear, because the meaning of the terms used to talk about the Trinity is unclear. Divine persons are equal to one another, but in what sense? The persons are in one another but what does 'in' mean here? Divine persons are distinguished from one another by the character of their relations but who understands exactly what that character is? So Hilary can say: 'Begetting is the secret of the Father and the Son. If anyone is convinced of the weakness of his intelligence through failing to understand this mystery ... he will undoubtedly be even more downcast to learn that I am in the same state of ignorance.'[28] What indeed does even the language of 'person' suggest, if with Augustine we have to say that 'the formula three persons was coined, not in order to give a complete explanation by means of it, but in order that we might not be obliged to remain silent.'[29] Because God is not very comprehensible to us, and certainly not fully so, discussion of the Trinity, all by itself, seems of little help in better understanding human relationships: what is difficult to understand – the proper character of human society – is explicated with reference to what is surely only more obscure – the character of divine community.

The second problem is that much of what is said about the Trinity simply does not seem directly applicable to humans. The differences between God and humans stand in the way. Many of these differences that prevent a direct application have to do with the essential finitude of human beings. Human society could therefore take on the very character of the Trinity in these respects in which they differ only if people were no longer human. So, for example, it seems bound up with their essential finitude that human

---

[27] See M. Volf, *After Our Likeness*, Grand Rapids, Michigan: Eerdmans 1998, pp. 191–200; and his 'Trinity is our Social Program', pp. 403–7.

[28] Hilary, *On the Trinity*, II, 2, p. 55, following the more felicitous translation in Boff, *Trinity and Society*, p. 174.

[29] Augustine, *On the Trinity*, V, 9 in *Nicene and Post-Nicene Fathers*, vol. 3, Grand Rapids Michigan: Eerdmans 1956, p. 92, following the more felicitous translation in Boff, *Trinity and Society*, p. 143.

persons can only metaphorically speaking be in one another, if that means having overlapping subjectivities in the way the persons of the Trinity do.[30] Because all the other members of the Trinity are in that person, when one person of the Trinity acts the others are necessarily acting too. Clearly this does not hold for human persons: I may enter empathetically into the one I love, but that does not mean I act when my beloved does.

Divine persons, moreover, seem much more relational than human beings. Human persons can never be as closely tied to their relations with others as persons in the Trinity are commonly thought to be; and that is the case even were one to think (as I do not) that it is proper to make a real distinction between the existence and character of Trinitarian persons.[31] Thus it would be very unusual to suggest that Trinitarian persons temporally precede the relations among themselves that make them what they are, in the way this happens in human relations. Human beings have no character to begin with as that is decisively shaped by what happens to them later; I therefore exist prior to those relationships with duplicitous significant others, for example, that end up making me a bitter, distrustful old person.

Character, moreover, in human beings is not as bound up with actual relations with others. I can be defined by certain general relational capacities before (and whatever the way in which) these capacities are actualized in my relationships. For example, my character might be constituted by the tendency to be suspicious before, and whether or not my relations with others give me good grounds to be that way. For much the same reasons, the character formed in me in virtue of my relations with others remains even when the relations that gave rise to it end: for example, my character remains despite the deaths of the people and communities who have contributed most to it. The relational characteristics of Trinitarian persons, to the contrary, are much more tightly a function of actual relationships: the Father, for example, is not defined as someone with the general capacity to beget someone or other, but as the Father who is and remains such only in begetting this Son.[32]

Furthermore, the character of a human person takes different forms in the course of relations with different people. I always have the capacity to be more or other than I am right now: I have the capacity, for example, to be enormously engaging and incredibly funny (unlike now); and the capacity to be hateful when made the brunt of ridicule, and therefore to know a human person in her relations with you is to know her only incompletely. Theologians generally do not want to say anything quite

---

[30] Volf, *After Our Likeness*, pp. 209, 211.
[31] See T. Weinandy, *Does God Suffer?*, Notre Dame, Indiana: University of Notre Dame Press 2000, pp. 115, 119, 128, 134–5, 140, 207–8.
[32] See Gilles Emery, 'Essentialism or Personalism in the Treatise on God in Saint Thomas Aquinas?' in *The Thomist* 64 (2000) 551–3.

like that of the Trinity: Trinitarian persons are fully themselves in their relations with one another and with us; Trinitarian persons are not in themselves, for example, other than the persons they show themselves to be to us.

Moreover, despite their intense relationality, Trinitarian persons remain irreducibly distinct from one another in ways that human beings cannot imitate. Father and Son remain absolutely different from one another in the Trinity, so to speak, because, unlike the case of human fathers and sons, here the Father has never been a Son – the Father is always Father – and the Son never becomes a Father – the Son is always Son. The terms Father and Son in the Trinity do not, in short, indicate general capacities which a variety of individuals might exhibit, but are person-defining properties. In the human case, I am different from my mother in that I am my mother's daughter but I can also become like my mother by becoming the mother of a daughter myself; and therefore in being different from my mother I am not absolutely different from her. The human relations that distinguish people never simply define them and therefore one can lose the way one has been identified by virtue of those relations (one's identity as a daughter, say, once one's mother has been dead for thirty years) and take on others (the identity of a mother to one's own daughter) while remaining oneself. But persons of the Trinity are too tied to their specific relationship, for example, of being Father and Son, to do this. They are too absolutely what they are – Son or Father – and too absolutely distinct from one another in such a relationship for that to be possible.

Indeed, in the Trinity relations of tremendous intensity never threaten the individuality of the persons in the way relations like that threaten to blur the identities of human beings. Unlike the case of Trinitarian persons, the finitude of humans seems to require the policing of boundaries between themselves and others that break off relationships. I will never be my own person unless I can break away from the incredibly intense relationship I have with my mother. In the Trinity, to the contrary, the persons are absolutely different from one another in the very intensity of the relationships they have with one another. It is because the relationship is so intense for them both, so to speak, that the Father can only be a Father and the Son only a Son.

Finally, human finitude also seems to entail that humans give of themselves so that others may gain in ways that often bring loss to themselves. In the case of Trinitarian persons, in contrast, their perfect equality is usually thought to involve giving without loss and receiving without increase. The first person of the Trinity does not give all of itself to the second at any cost to itself; and the second does not receive from the first what is not already its own.

One could argue, as I have done elsewhere, that loss in giving to others on the human plane is a function of a world in disarray and not a necessary consequence of simple finitude.[33] It is possible in principle for the world to be arranged in ways that make giving to others a benefit to oneself. But this simply brings us to the third problem: direct translation of the Trinity into a social programme is problematic because, unlike the peaceful and perfectly loving mutuality of the Trinity, human society is full of suffering, conflict and sin. Turned into a recommendation for social relations, the Trinity seems unrealistic, hopelessly naïve, and for that reason perhaps even politically dangerous. To a world of violent, corrupt and selfish people, the Trinity seems to offer only the feeble plaint, 'Why can't we all just get along?'

So how is the gap between the Trinity and sinful, finite human persons to be bridged in ways that allow us to see its implications for human community? One strategy for bridging the gap is to supplement the move down from the Trinity when envisioning human society, with a move up from below.[34] In other words, given what one knows about human beings, one can figure out the extent to which human relations might imitate Trinitarian ones. The Trinity tells us what human relations should ideally be like. The understanding of humans as creatures and sinners tells us of what sort of approximation of the ideal we are in fact capable. The danger of such a strategy is that the Trinity fails to do any work. It does not add anything to what we already know about the real possibilities for human community, given the human limits and failings we live under.

The other major strategy for closing the gap looks to the economic Trinity for help.[35] One does not have to bring an account of the Trinity together with what one knows about the limits of human life to figure out how human relationships could come to approximate Trinitarian ones. The economic Trinity – how the Trinity acts in saving us – instead makes that clear, because what one finds in the economic Trinity itself is the Trinity brought closer to what humans are capable of. For example, in the economy the Trinity appears as a dialogical fellowship of love and mutual service between Jesus and the one he calls Father – the kind of relationship that human beings could imitate because it is one in keeping with their finitude – in contrast, say, to perfectly mutual indwelling or perichoresis.

The same goes for sin. The economic Trinity is the Trinity entering a world of sin and death. Apart from any theological speculation, the economic Trinity itself therefore gives a clue as to how Trinitarian relations should be lived out in a world of sin. For example, those relations have the broken and sorrowful character of a Father losing his own Son by way of a death undergone for the sake of others.

---

[33] See my *Economy of Grace*, Minneapolis, Minnesota: Fortress Press 2005.
[34] Volf, *After Our Likeness*, p. 200; and his 'Trinity is our Social Program': pp. 405–6.
[35] See Moltmann, *Trinity and the Kingdom*; and LaCugna, *God for Us*.

However, the same sort of problem that beset the previous strategy resurfaces here. The closer Trinitarian relations seem to human ones in the economy, the less the Trinity seems to offer advice about how to move beyond what we already expect of human life, given human limits and failings. The Trinity simply confirms what we already know and solidifies our chastened hopes under the circumstances. We all have some sense of what dialogical relations of loving fellowship are like. We all know about the way death severs relationships and about how obedience to a good cause often comes at the price of sacrifice in troubled times. And the Trinity offers us nothing more.

# Do We Model Ourselves on the Trinity or Participate in It?

My own strategy for closing the gap also looks to what the Trinity is doing for us – what is happening in the life of Christ, in short – to answer the question of how the Trinity applies to human life. The Trinity itself enters our world to close the gap, but not (as the previous strategy suggested) by presenting us with a form of the Trinity we can imitate; the Trinity does not close the gap by making itself over in a human image of community in which we can imitate dialogical fellowship, say. Instead, in Christ the Trinity enters our world to work over human life in its image, through the incorporation of the human within the divine Trinitarian life. By joining us to those relations. Christ gives us the very relations of Father, Son and Spirit for our own. By becoming incarnate, the second person of he Trinity takes the humanity joined to it into its own relations with Father and Spirit, and therefore in Christ we are shown what the Trinity looks like when it includes the human, and what humanity looks like when it is included in the Trinity's own movements – the character of a human life with others when it takes a Trinitarian form, as that is displayed in Jesus' own human life.

The gap between divine and human is not closed here by making the two similar to one another, but by joining the two very different things – humanity and divinity – into one via Christ, via incarnation. Trinitarian relations need not be like human relations in order for humans to be taken up in this way into them, and therefore the problematic trade-off mentioned earlier is avoided: The more Trinitarian relations seem close in character to human ones (and therefore relations that human beings could imitate), the less the Trinity tells you anything you did not already know about them. Gone, too, is the basis for hope in the idea that Trinitarian relations are sufficiently close to human ones to be imitated by us. Now hope is fuelled by how *different* the Trinitarian relations, in which we are to be incorporated, are from anything with which they are familiar under the constraints of finitude and sin. The difference between the Trinity and us now holds out hope for a radical improvement of the human condition. The Trinity is not brought down to our level as a model for us to imitate; our hope is that we might one day be raised up to its level.

Finitude is no longer a problem either. Finitude does not make Trinitarian relations inaccessible to us, since human relations come to image Trinitarian ones as they are swept up into them and not as they become like them in and of themselves. Human relations need not somehow become more than human themselves in order thereby to approximate the Trinity. Human relations, which remain fully human, only image the Trinity as they are joined up with its own life. Humans do not attain the heights of Trinitarian relations by reproducing them in and of themselves, by mimicking them, in other words, but by being taken up into them as the very creatures they are. They come to share a divine form of existence, not their own by nature, by becoming attached to it.

The usual strategy of looking to the economy – the Trinity at work in the world – seems stuck on the idea that the Trinity appears to us in the economy as a model for our imitation because it fails to follow the economic workings of the Trinity all the way down to their impact on us. In other words, that strategy stops with relations among Trinitarian persons in the economy – for example, the Son incarnate doing the will of the Father – and makes them a model for human ones rather than following through on what the economy of the Trinity itself is suggesting about human relations. Jesus' life, in short, exhibits not just the sort of relations that humans, in the image of the Son, are to have with Father and Spirit – relations of worshipful dedication to the Father's mission, empowered by the Spirit – but in his relations with other people Jesus also shows how those relations with Father and Spirit are to work themselves out in community with other people. If one wants to know how a Trinitarian life impacts on one's relations with other people, this second part of the story is very obviously the place to look: Jesus' relations with other people constitute the sort of human relations that the economy of the Trinity itself specifies; Jesus' way of life towards other people as we share in it *is* the Trinitarian form of human social life.

It is not at all clear, however, that Jesus' relations with other people are Trinitarian by following the Trinitarian pattern of his relations with Father and Spirit. The human being Jesus relates to Father and Spirit in much the way the second person of the Trinity does. Because Jesus *is* the second person of the Trinity, He retains as a human being the same sort of relations with Father and Spirit that He has as the second person of the Trinity. This is a very direct translation of Trinitarian relations into a human form. But none of that is true for Jesus' relations with other people; they are simply not the direct translation of Trinitarian relations into a human form in the same way.

Indeed, if one takes into account the whole story of the economy – both parts of it – and avoids isolated attention to what is narrated about the relationships among the Trinitarian persons, it is not at all apparent that the one side establishes the pattern for the other: Jesus' relations with Father and Spirit do not appear in any obvious way to be the model for His relations with other human beings in the story. Rather than establish the pattern for human relationships, Jesus' relations with Father and Spirit are – quite obviously – the sort of relations that it is appropriate for humans to have with Father and Spirit. One is to worship the Father following the precedent of Jesus' own prayers, carry out the will of the Father as human beings filled up with, empowered by, the Holy Spirit as Jesus was, which means working for the wellbeing of others like Jesus did, and so on. But why think one will relate to other humans in the process in anything like the way one is relating here to Father and Spirit?

Let me make the same rather obvious point in the light of the way we are incorporated within the Trinitarian life by being joined to Christ. When humans are incorporated into the Trinity through Christ, different people are not spread out across the Trinity to take on its pattern; instead, we all enter at the same point, we all become identified with the same Trinitarian person, members of the one Son, sons by the grace of the Holy Spirit, and move as a whole, as one body, with the second person of the Trinity in its movements within the dynamic life of the Trinity. The Trinity does not therefore in any obvious way establish the internal structure of human community, the unity of the Trinity being what makes human society one, the diversity of the persons establishing its internal complexity. Instead, the one divine Son and the one divine Spirit are what make human society one; we are one, as the Pauline texts suggest, because we all have the same Spirit and because we are all members of the one Son. And the diversity of this human community is internal to the one Spirit and one Son, so to speak; the diversity is a diversity of gifts of the Spirit and of that one Son's bodily members. Rather than establishing the pattern of unity and diversity in human community, the Trinity establishes more what that one united but diverse body of spirit-filled sons by grace does, how it moves; the whole body of Christians moves together in the way any single human being, united to Christ's own life, follows a Trinitarian dynamic.

There are of course New Testament passages that suggest the unity between Son and Father is what unity in human community is to be like: Jesus asks his Father 'that they may be one as we are one' (Jn 17.11, 22). Rather than read these passages as some brief for understanding the unity of human persons on an analogy with unity among persons of the Trinity, one can, however, take them to be indicating simply the centrality of Christ, and of his relations with the Father, for our relations with the Father. That is, Christ is one with the Father, perfectly doing the Father's will, and we should all be one by being one with the Father as Jesus is, united in doing the Father's will in the way Jesus does.

The way Jesus images in a human form the relations among Father, Son and Spirit has an effect, of course, on his relations with other people: Jesus relates to other people in highly unusual ways, which have everything to do with his relations to Father and Spirit. The way the persons of the Trinity relate to one another over the course of Jesus' life, relations among the divine persons in which we are to share by being united with Christ in the Spirit, bring with them changed relations among human beings. The Son is sent by the Father into the world and, empowered by the Spirit, to carry out a mission that brings him into relationship with us. A life empowered by the Spirit in service to the mission of the Father for the world means that Jesus is with and for us, and that we, in turn, are to be with and for one another, in the way that mission specifies.

The character of that mission, as Jesus' own way of life makes clear, is to inaugurate a life-brimming, spirit-filled community of human beings akin to Jesus in their relations with God: the mission means bringing in the kingdom or new community that accords with Jesus' own healing, reconciling and life-giving relations with others. This way of being is what the Trinitarian relations as they show themselves in the economy – Jesus' praying to the Father and serving the will of the Father in the power of the Spirit – amount to in human relational terms. Jesus' relations with Father and Spirit make His whole life one of worshipful, praise-filled faithful service to the Father's mission of bringing in the kingdom; that is to be the character of our lives too, both in and out of church, as we come to share Jesus' life. We are to participate in the Father's mission for the world, mediating the life-giving Spirit of Christ, through union with Him. Glorified, worked over into Christ's image, so as to take on his shape in relations with other human beings, we are to form the citizens or members of a new kingdom or community with Christ as both the director and forerunner of the sort of new lives we are to lead together.

The question then becomes what the kingdom has to do with the Trinity that works to bring it about. To what extent is the kingdom, in other words, not just the consequence of a Trinitarian life like Jesus' in relation to Father and Spirit, bound up, part and parcel of it for that reason, but also reflective of the Trinity's own character? A lot depends here on exactly what one thinks the kingdom is like. I would venture that the kingdom is like the Trinity in that both are supremely life-affirming for all their members, organized to bring about the utmost flourishing of all. Both are paradigmatic instances of what I have called elsewhere a community of mutual fulfilment in which the good of one becomes the good for all.[36] The

---

[36] Tanner, *Economy of Grace*.

Trinity is coming to us to give us the sort of life-giving relations of mutual flourishing that the Trinity itself enjoys.

There is an analogy, then, with the Trinity, but not a very specific one. What one gets out of the Trinity here for an understanding of the kingdom one might also find by treating any number of other theological topics: the incarnation, for example. The incarnation too – but in a significantly different manner from what one finds in the Trinity – sets up a kinship, in this case between humanity and divinity, a community of now mutual fulfilment in that the human is to benefit from what the divine already enjoys. In some ways, indeed, the incarnation is a better model for the sort of human community or kingdom to be set up: when every human being becomes one in Christ this overrides in a significant sense forms of already established kinship that would otherwise keep people apart; this is an unnatural community, one might say, in much the way human and divinity in Christ are an unnatural community, made up of what is naturally disparate and dissimilar. More like the relationship between humanity and divinity in Christ than the Trinity, this is a community of previously diverse persons brought together only by something different from them that they all share: Christ.

# 17

# Trinitarian Theology and Spirituality: Retrieving William of St Thierry for Contemporary Theology

## David Tracy

## Towards a Trinitarian Theology Centred on Love

As many theologians have observed, the separation of theology from spirituality has been the great tragedy of both theology and spirituality.[1] Moreover, Pierre Hadot, distinguished scholar of ancient Western philosophy, argued that most modern philosophers do not even notice that they consistently misread ancient philosophical texts – Platonist, Aristotelian, Stoic,

---

[1] M. A. McIntosh, *Mystical Theology*, Oxford: Blackwell Publishers 1998, esp. pp. 39–90.

Epicurean, academic-sceptical alike.[2] Moderns misread the ancients because they have lost the ability to relate philosophical theory to a way of life. For all the ancient philosophers, theory (in the compartments of logic, physics, ethics) was always on behalf of a way of life. Every day an ancient philosopher would practise the spiritual exercises of his or her school (e.g. the Platonist Hypatia, the Stoic Marcus Aurelius, the Epicurean Lucretius) to assure that one's way of life and one's theory were indivisible.

In the medieval period, many theologians and philosophers moved to the university. In many ways, of course, this move from the rural monasteries or the urban canonries (e.g. the Victorines) to the urban universities was a boon for theology: greater clarity and precision; a drive to system; a more differentiated theoretical and practical consciousness. By the thirteenth century, many more theoretically inclined, scholastic university theologians (e.g. Thomas Aquinas) distinguished but did not separate theory and way of life, theology and philosophy, theology and spirituality, but they did highlight theories in their intellectualist, university emphases. Bonaventure was a partial exception since some of his works were situated in the new scholastic emphasis of the University of Paris where he taught, as did Thomas Aquinas. Other theological works of Bonaventure (e.g. the classic *Itinerarium*) were written in a more directly spiritual way reminiscent of the great spiritual theologies of the twelfth century. In the fourteenth century, however, the division between theology and spirituality became a separation: implicitly in the brilliant logic and conceptualist theology of Duns Scotus; explicitly in William of Occam and the nominalists who, however much they admirably wanted theology to be more related to spiritual experience, in fact separated even more strongly theology and spirituality (in theological nominalism) and, yet more fatally for theology and philosophy alike, word (*nomen*) was now separated from its traditional reference to reality in an increasingly influential epistemological nominalism. By the fifteenth and sixteenth centuries, neither the humanists of the Renaissance nor the Protestant Reformers could bear the nominalist – and more generally the Scholastic – stranglehold of theology. The humanists (e.g. Erasmus and Ficino) produced theologies with affinities to the humanist theological works of the twelfth century. The Reformers produced works at times reminiscent of the spiritual theologies of experience of the twelfth century. For example, both Martin Luther and John Calvin greatly admired Bernard of Clairvaux's theology of experience.

The modern philosophical division of theory and way of life would have been as unintelligible to most ancient philosophers as it is to contemporary Buddhist thinkers in Asia. Two centuries before the nominalists, however, monastic, mystical and humanist theologians in the twelfth

---

[2] P. Hadot, *Philosophy as a Way of Life*, Arnold I. Davidson (ed.), Oxford: Blackwell 1995.

century presciently feared the emerging separation of theology and spirituality, philosophy and way of life. Bernard of Clairvaux, that colossus who
bestrode the entire twelfth century, seemed, with all his formidable energies
and convictions, to be everywhere at once. Bernard with his monastic vision
and his complex, indeed sometimes deeply troubling, personality interfered
in secular and monastic affairs alike: Bernard dominated his era as much
as Athanasius of Alexandria had dominated his. Like Athanasius, Bernard
was restless, energetic, brilliant, unyielding, often intransigent and inflexible
about new ways of thinking (e.g. Abelard). Bernard of Clairvaux was a
rhetorician of exceptional fluency and, at times, a poet of genius. To read
Bernard's paradoxical life[3] (as often outside his monastery as within it) is
to find a character both serene and pugnacious. Bernard's genuine greatness
can scarcely be doubted. But like many larger than life figures, the great
theologian of love also seemed to possess a surprising talent for unchecked
anger and rage: his unjust attacks on Cluny; his preaching for the disastrous
Second Crusade (which as he later acknowledged was a resounding failure);
his relentless attacks on Peter Abelard (whose dialectical method, with
an increasing rhetorical fierceness proportionate to his equally increasing
failure to understand Abelard's actual dialectical method, Bernard hounded
until their reconciliation at Cluny). Moreover, as the historian of theology
Willemien Otten reminds us,[4] the famous twelfth-century Renaissance
included not only the new monastic theologies of experience and love of
Bernard and William of St Thierry. Nor did it include only harbingers of
the great Scholastics of the following century. Rather, as Otten persuasively argues, the twelfth-century Renaissance was a humanist renaissance
in a new world enacting humanist poetry, philosophy and theology alike
(William of Conches, Alan of Lille, Peter Abelard, Héloïse d'Argenteuil).
This humanist theology was a whole new mode of theologizing: neither
merely a signal of the emerging triumph of Scholastic theology nor
only a profoundly visionary theology like that of Hildegard of Bingen,
nor only a monastic theology of experience and love (themselves partially
humanistic in the emphasis on experience [ut experiar] for theology and their
possible connections to the love poetry of the troubadours of Provence).
The explicitly new humanist theologies were based on a humanist recovery
of conversatio and a central affirmation of the intellectual and affective
dignity of a humanity construed as in conversation with both natura and
God. The twelfth-century Renaissance was a century of rich diversity in
forms of theology: monastic, mystical, emerging Scholastic, humanist.

---

[3] On the controversy on his person, see A. H. Bredero, Between Cult and History, Grand
Rapids: Eerdmans 1996. On his theology, see Etienne Gilson, The Mystical Theology of St
Bernard, New York: Sheed & Ward, 1940.
[4] W. Otten, From Paradise to Paradigm: a Study of Twelfth-Century Humanism, Leiden: Brill
2004, pp. 1–78.

Although my focus here is on the greatest of the monastic theologians, William of St Thierry, one must always remember that his theology too was only one fragment in the twelfth-century mosaic. Between them, the two Cistercian friends, Bernard of Clairvaux and William of St Thierry, largely defined twelfth-century monastic theology.

Bernard's many admirers (among them Bonaventure, Martin Luther and John Calvin) sensed that in Bernard's work and person, theology and spirituality were never separated. For all his controversial actions, Bernard made major and enduring contributions to theology, indeed to Western culture as a whole. First, Bernard's theological turn to experience was both needed and prescient. Second, by placing love, not reason, as the central reality for the Christian theologian to try first to experience (*ut experiar*) and then to understand (*ut intelligam*), Bernard appropriated and re-thought Augustine's love emphasis anew for the twelfth-century love-obsessed age.

William of Thierry took up both these Bernardine themes, transformed them and worked them into a highly original theology of the Trinity grounded in an experienced spirituality of the interrelationship of love and reason for a new Trinitarian theology – an existential direction from which many philosophers and theologians may learn even today. This was a reasoned, speculative theology grounded in an experience of divine love as articulated in three stages of the theologian's spiritual and intellectual journey. In his unique Trinitarian theology, William expressed a theology of deeply interdependent love-knowledge made possible *through* Christ *in* the gift of love of the Holy Spirit, the *unitas Spiritus*. Many later theologians – from William's contemporary Richard of St. Victor to Bonaventure to Blaise Pascal, Friedrich Schleiermacher, Karl Rahner, Hans Urs von Balthasar and the later work of Bernard Lonergan, would also follow a love-centred direction for theology, a few even a Trinitarian theology centred in love. William of St Thierry formulated a linked theological and spiritual way to clarify how the New Testament's deepest belief 'God is Love'[5] is the first Christian way of saying God is One God in three divine Persons.

# Reason Transformed by Faith and Love

William of St Thierry lacked Bernard's genius for a rhetorical and passionately poetic way to articulate the singular richness of the experience of faith become love. And yet William too held that faith was a new and richer form of reason. William learned from Bernard to make theology more experiential

---

[5] D. Tracy, 'God as Infinite Love: A Roman Catholic Perspective,' in J. Levin and S. G. Post (eds), *Divine Love: Perspectives from the World's Religious Traditions*, West Conshohocken: Templeton Press 2010, pp. 131–54.

and more love-centred. However, William more than compensated for his lack of Bernard's poetic-rhetorical genius by becoming a more careful, methodical and systematic theologian than Bernard ever was. William, like Bernard and their common mentor Augustine, insisted that love drives knowledge, not the reverse; that our *affectus* (dispositions, affects, feelings) was as important for a theologian to analyze as reason; that faith transforms reason into a new *ratio fidei*;[6] that eventually faith becomes love and evokes the most expansive and rich forms of this transformed reason: meditation and contemplation. At the end (stage three) love and reason alike are transformed together into loving wisdom (*sapientia*). For William, therefore, a spirituality and theological analysis of the experience of love was needed in order to develop an adequate Trinitarian theology grounded in the experience of love fully interdependent with the many forms of reason.

For William, a spirituality of love demanded a new Trinitarian theology as much as a Trinitarian theology needed a spirituality embedded in the graced experience of divine love. William's major spiritual works (*The Nature and Dignity of Love, Commentary on the Song of Songs, Mirror of Faith*, the *Golden Epistle*)[7] focus principally upon the new spirituality of divine love through describing various stages of a lifelong ascetical-mystical spiritual journey. By contrast, in his more speculative theological works (especially the *Enigma of Faith*), William produces a methodical, systematic speculative Trinitarian theology correlative to the spiritual journey described in his other works. William's speculative theology is logically coherent, speculatively and dialectically daring, especially in the *Enigma of Faith*. William's theology is designed not only to allow an experience of divine love (the *Mirror of Faith* emphasizes *ut experiar*). In the companion work, the *Enigma of Faith*, William developed a strict Trinitarian theology of *ut intelligam*.[8] The *Enigma* emphasizes a strict Trinitarian theology of *ut intelligam*. William's full Trinitarian theology analyzes the radical interdependence, harmony, almost unity of love and reason with love as primary.

---

[6] William of St. Thierry, *Speculum fidei*, in *Deux Traités sur la Foi: Le Miroir de la foi; L'Énigme de la foi*, Paris: Vrin 1959: 'Rationalitas enim, sicut dictum est, in seipsa inquieta et improba, ubi ratiocinandi habet facultatem, fidem sepius aggreditur, etsi non studio contradicendi sed natura ratiocinandi; non ut illi velit occurrere sed quasi illam sibi concurrere. Nam sicut solet agere in rebus humanis humana ratio, quasi per mediam credendi necessitatem irrumpere nititur in rerum divinarum cognitionem; set tamquam aliunde ascendens, offendit, impingit, labitur, donec revertatur ad ostium fidei; ad eum qui dixit: *Ego sum ostium*, et humiliata sub jugo divine auctoritatis, quanto humilius tanto securius ingrediatur. Sed in aliis non sentit temptationem negligentie magnitudo, in aliis rationis hebetudo in aliis illuminate fidei concepta certitudo.' (p. 50, Par. 31)

[7] *De nature et dignitate amoris*, (PL 184, 379–408); *Expositio super Cantica Canticorum*, (PL 180, 475–546); *Speculum fidei*, (PL 180, 365–87); *Aenigma fidei*, (PL 180, 397–440); *Epistola ad Fratres de Monte Dei [Epistola aurea]*, (PL 184, 307–54).

[8] See his *Aenigma fidei*.

One of the extraordinary conversations in the history of Christian theology and Christian spirituality (like the conversation of Gregory of Nyssa and his sister Macrina on her deathbed; like the mystical conversation of Augustine and Monica in the garden at Ostia) was the days-long conversation in the infirmary at Clairvaux between Bernard and William on the Song of Songs. In reading their two quite distinct commentaries on that favorite text of all mystical theologians from Origen onwards, one senses both the profound similarities of Bernard and William (theology must be grounded in an experienced life of graced love) and their profound differences. The poetic-rhetorical language of Bernard moves to heights of rich expression worthy of Gregory of Nyssa or the Friedrich Schleiermacher of the *Speeches* or the John Henry Newman of the *Plain and Parochial Sermons*. The more careful, more philosophical and speculative language of William moves to a slower rhythm more like Gregory of Nyssa's *Contra Eunomium*, Schleiermacher's *Glaubenslehre* or Newman's *Grammar of Assent*. Whatever happened in the conversation of Bernard and William in the infirmary in those precious few days when illness freed both monks to share their thoughts on divine love, each of them thereafter seemed liberated to write two of the greatest commentaries on the Song of Songs in the entire history of Christian mystical writings on the Song.

Both Bernard and William developed profound spiritual theologies. Only William, however, developed a Trinitarian theology appropriate to what both had discovered in the experience of divine love in the Song of Songs.[9] One way to clarify how this shared experience of divine love also became, in William, an original theology of the Trinity, is to focus first on faith, because for William faith, decisively and uniquely, transforms both reason and love only to be transformed itself by pure love united to contemplative reason.

Like many medieval theologians, William held to a distinction between the *imago Dei* and the *similitudo Dei* (based on a literal reading of the Genesis 'Let us make human beings in our image and likeness').[10] For William the *imago Dei* in us is damaged but not lost. As human beings we retain what the *imago* gives each person as pure gift: an openness to and capacity for God. We never entirely lose the *imago Dei*. After the fall, however, human beings have lost the *similitudo Dei*. Like Adam and Eve before us, all human beings since the Fall have lost Eden. They must now take refuge as best they can in the disturbing, fragmented *regio dissimili-*

---

[9] A. Matter, *The Voice of My Beloved: The Song of Songs in Western Medieval Christianity*, Philadelphia: University of Pennsylvania Press 1990.

[10] See D. N. Bell, *The Image and Likeness: the Augustinian Spirituality of William of Saint Thierry*, Kalamazoo: Cistercian Publications 1984 and O. Brooke, *Studies in Monastic Theology*, Kalamazoo: Cistercian Publications 1980.

*tudinis*, an arresting metaphor which William found in both Origen and Augustine.

Both our intellects and our wills have been wounded by our inherited and personal sin. We wander aimlessly in the labyrinth of the *regio dissimilitudinis*. Through God's grace we are still open to God through the *imago Dei* in our souls (Augustine's *memoria, intellectus, voluntas*).[11] The human question to itself is unavoidable: how can we fallen ones recover the *similitudo Dei* to ensure the proper functioning of our wounded reason and our misdirected desire?

The answer for William, as for the Christian tradition in general, lies in first acknowledging we are certainly not self-authored nor can we cure ourselves. We are finite creatures of the creator-God. We are also fallen creatures who are saved through Christ in the Spirit as the scripture, the liturgy and the prayers of ordinary Christians manifest. We are saved only through God's redeeming grace given to us through the birth, teaching, ministry, death and resurrection of Jesus the Christ, true God (the Second Person of the Trinity, the eternal Son of the eternal Father) and true man (the Word made flesh and like us in all things save sin).

William shared in much of the Christian humanistic optimism of his age: we have never lost the *imago Dei*; all creation including nature and body is good; we possess free will; in our reason is an infinite desire to know and by that fact is still open to knowing God; our desire to know and all our other desires are grounded in desire for the Good. In sum, for William we have never lost our openness to and capacity for God (our *imago Dei*): our reason, our freedom of will, our human dignity are intact. This is William's form of a pervasive twelfth-century optimism shared with his considerably more optimistic and more fully humanistic colleagues (Alan of Lille, William of Conches, Peter Abelard) in that exciting age of Renaissance.

However, unlike the more optimistic and humanistic thinkers of his day, especially Abelard, William's humanism was far more mitigated or perhaps, more nuanced. William never abandoned Augustine's basic theological anthropology on our fallen state. At the same time, William never conceived our fallen state in the radical terms of Luther, Calvin, Jansen or the later Augustine himself. Like twelfth-century thinkers in general, William never speaks such Augustinian language as that we humans are so fallen that we are a *massa damnata*. William never uses the most anti-humanistic of all Augustine's later, rather desperate teachings against the Pelagians: double predestination. In sum, William was never the kind of radical, pessimistic late Augustinian that John Calvin or Cornelius Jansen became. William always enunciated and consistently defended the human dignity of a reason

---

[11] Augustine, *De Trinitate*, (*PL* 42, 819–1098), esp. XI, 10–XII, 19.

open to God. He always defended free will. But William was never a full-fledged optimistic humanist. Even after William began to read and learned from Origen, he never swerved into full-fledged humanism. Origen was far more optimistic in his anthropology than not only the later Augustine but even the mature Augustine (e.g. in *The Confessions*) ever was. William did indeed drink deeply at Origen's well: most deeply in William's later use of Origen's three stages of the spiritual journey.[12] Even then, however, William maintained the more Augustinian rather than Greek portrait of humanity, the more tragic-realistic humanism of the mature (not the late) Augustine. Abelard's more optimistic and humanistic reading of the use of dialectic in theology, in so far as William understood it (see below), frightened him to the depths of his Augustinian soul.

Like Thomas Aquinas and Bonaventure in the following century, William learned more from Augustine than from any other prior theologian. However, either consciously or unconsciously, William as a child of the more optimistic and more humanistic twelfth-century Renaissance, articulated a basically Augustinian anthropology but never with the profoundly pessimistic turn of the later Augustine. For William, free will is more lucidly analyzed and defended than it was in Augustine: for William, when we receive gift-grace of the self-manifestation of God in the Word made flesh, we also receive the gift of faith which we freely accept or reject. Faith therefore is both grace from God attendant to the grace of the revelation of the Incarnate Word itself and an action of our own genuine free will. In principle, William agreed with the ancient tradition: God created us without ourselves (we are not self-authored; we are finite creatures of a loving Infinite Creator) but chooses not to save us without our consent (we are justified by Christ's grace through faith; we are sanctified through the work of the Holy Spirit working in us and with us).

Faith, therefore, is the decisive, unique, irreplaceable moment for the beginning of the full healing of the *imago Dei* in us and an ever deepening spiritual restoration of the *similitudo Dei* in us by our graced and free journey of sanctification. Faith is the all-important necessary beginning of that restoration. Without faith, our reason, otherwise strong, struggles in vain to reach God and cannot even acknowledge its own limit. Without faith, our desire sinks into vanity, our loves attach themselves not to God's Infinite Love and others (the neighbour) in love for each other through our pure love of God. Rather, we stumble with our restless, disoriented, confused desires. We move in the dark with our loves dragging us along by their energy and weight (*amor meus, pondus meum*)[13] after another

---

[12] William of St Thierry, *Epistola ad Fratres de Monte Dei [Epistola aurea]* in *La Lettera D'Oro [Italian and Latin]*, Florence: G. C. Sansoni Editore Nuova 1983.

[13] Augustine, *Confessions*, XIII, 9.10.

foolishly loved improper object (fame, money, power). Even proper objects of love become distorted: every person becomes an object, every desire is unconsciously trapped in its own deluded self-love not a subject for our love; so we cannot even love ourselves truly; every other person is not allowed to be an other but only a target for my possession; nature is there to be used merely as our instrument not as a proper object of our awe and love; God is loved, if at all, only for our own possible merit, not for the pure love of God in godself. Like all the Cistercians, especially Aelred of Rievaulx, William cherished the grace of friendship. But he also knew that even the great gift of friendship could be tempted to live only for itself (*egoisme à deux*) rather than being, as it is constituted to be, a further healing of our natural egotism and a further sanctifying of our journey with our friends to friendship with God.

Without faith, the soul (senses, intellect, will-desire) is an unfathomable and harrowing mystery to itself. At crucial points William's anthropology seems less twelfth-century Renaissance, i.e. straight-forwardly optimistic and humanistic, than Augustinian and tragic in orientation. Nevertheless, tragic humanism is also one of the classical forms of Western orientation.[14] William's passionate insistence that we are a complete mystery to ourselves resonates not only with the famous portrait of Pascal on the human state as tragically-humanistically constituted by both '*grandeur et misère.*' At times, in reading William, one hears echoes of what is to come: Nietzsche's unsettling question to all optimistic humanists in the preface to his *Genealogy of Morals*: 'We are unknown to ourselves, we knowers – and with good reason. We have never sought ourselves – how could it happen that we should ever *find* ourselves ... who are we really? ... Each is furthest from himself applies to all eternity.'[15] For myself, it is William's combination of a tragically humanistic portrait of our situation combined with his enormous capacity to show a way forward to healing, to a pure love of God and neighbour to a contemplative wisdom. It is that tragic humanistic spirituality, once transformed into more contemporary terms, which gives me more hope for a way forward in our theological time: a time that shares the rich diversity of theologies of the twelfth century but not the optimism nor the relatively untroubled, non-tragic humanism of the fully admirable, if too optimistic about reason's powers, Abelard and William of Conches.

For William, faith comes first as an external force.[16] Faith happens to us; it is not our own achievement. Faith is first external to us, touching us from outside and calling us to freely accept its truth. At the beginning,

---

[14] Augustine's anthropology can be read as a classical Christian tragic humanism. See D. Tracy, 'A Trouble Conflict: the Two Selves in Augustine' (forthcoming).

[15] F. Nietzsche, *On the Genealogy of Morals*, New York: Random House 1967, p. 15.

[16] William, *Speculum fidei*, in *Deux Traités sur la Foi*, p. 48, par. 27.

faith is healing but mostly exterior; it is not yet interior to us. This first faith – 'simple faith', William names it – is nevertheless, for all Christians, including intellectual élites like William himself, the decisive beginning of our later understanding of ourselves and all reality, especially, of course, the reality of God and all things related to God, the object of theology. Indeed, as William acutely declares: the first strictly theological discovery of faith is grace. The first discovery of faith is, therefore, that it happens to us by means of some Other – not self – Power, some external force which faith as faith can acknowledge as God's own force, God's gift, grace, Other-Power touching us. Faith happens to us either suddenly as in Paul's conversion or more likely gradually as, through faith, we learn to understand ourselves, reality and God anew and to love God and all others as other, not only the friend but the neighbour, even the enemy.

After William's 'conversion' to the monastic life, first Benedictine, then Cistercian, along with a love for the Carthusians to whom his last text, the famous *Epistola Aurea*[17] is addressed, his understanding and experience of faith is deepened beyond 'simple faith' in the first place through the carefully structured ascetic, liturgical and prayerful practices of the monastic life. Indeed, the greatest part of William's last text, the *Golden Epistle*, discusses the nature and necessity of asceticism for novices to the monastery. United to monastic ascetical practices for interiorizing faith are the sacraments, especially the Eucharist, where at times, reason can become contemplative joy in the eucharistic presence of God, meditative communal and private prayers, and meditative readings (*lectio divina*) of the Scripture.[18]

Faith becomes less external and more internal as these spiritual practices take hold. Faith frees the understanding (*intellectus*) to discern spiritual realities. Gradually the spiritual novice learns to read the scriptures morally and spiritually to make their treasures his own. At this point, a second stage of the relationship of faith and reason quite naturally takes hold in the rhythm of the spiritual journey

William calls this second stage of reason's spiritualizing journey *ratio fidei*: i.e. faith in its creative power of illumination transforms ordinary reason – natural reason – into a new, richer form of reason than natural reason on its own possesses. William calls this transformed reason *ratio fidei*.

William's concept of *ratio fidei* is different from what he understands (mostly incorrectly) as Abelard's more humanist and more rational optimistic position on faith and reason for theology (on which see section 3 below). More surprisingly, William's *ratio fidei* is also different from

---

[17] In the famous *Epistola aurea*.
[18] Although William is best know as a Cistercian, it must be remembered that he was a Benedictine for fifteen years and learned the Lectio Divina there.

Anselm's earlier position on theology as *fides quaerens intellectum*.[19] The differences of content between the theologies of Anselm and William are less important than their important differences in method. For Anselm, as much as for William, the theological journey begins in faith. However, for Anselm, theology proper begins as faith seeks understanding (*fides quaerens intellectum*) through all the instruments of natural reason (dialogue, dialectic, logic).

Anselm insists, unlike William of St Thierry and in this case, more like William of Conches and Abelard, on the importance of the defence and extensive use of dialectic, logic and dialogue (reason in its natural form) in theology. Anselm also encourages (here far more like William of St Thierry than like William of Conches or Abelard) the theological acknowledgment that reason is employed in theology within the encompassing context of meditative prayers and readings as well as contemplative reason, *sapientia* as distinct from *scientia*. As the endless conflict of interpretations on the famous 'ontological argument' in Anselm demonstrates, the full complexity of Anselm's position on theology as *fides quaerens intellectum* is a major and difficult hermeneutical task – far more difficult than it at first seems. On the one hand, Anselm accords a full theological role to *intellectus*, i.e. to logic, metaphysics and dialectic. For example, the so-called ontological argument[20] and all Anselm's other arguments are indeed genuine arguments and to be judged as such. Anselm's logical and dialectical arguments can, in principle, be abstracted from his larger text and judged strictly as arguments as they are in Thomas Aquinas, Bonaventure, Descartes, Kant, Hegel, Hartshorne and many other philosophers, especially the analytical and process philosophers of today.

Anselm may have accepted William's later formulation but he himself does not speak of a new kind of transformed reason (*ratio fidei*) which theology, unlike philosophy, employs. On the other hand, Anselm's arguments, again in all his theological texts, including the *Monologia* and the *Proslogian*, are situated within an encompassing context of Benedictine prayer (often textually included), meditation and contemplation, as such interpreters as Anselm Stolz, Karl Barth and many other theological interpreters have insisted. Unlike either William of St Thierry on the one hand or William of St. Thierry on the other, Anselm's theological model (like Augustine's before him) of *fides quaerens intellectum* is not nearly as clear as it first seems and still does to many interpreters. Perhaps both William of St Thierry and Peter Abelard sense the latent ambiguity in Anselm's formulation of *fides*

---

[19] *St. Anselm's Proslogion*, London: Oxford University Press 1965. See also G. R. Evans, *Anselm*, Wilton: Morehouse-Barlow 1989, pp. 37–49.
[20] J. H. Hick and A. C. McGill, *The Many-faceted Argument*, NY Macmillan 1967 and *L'Argomento Ontologico*, M. M. Olivetti (ed.), *Archivio di filosofia*, LVIII (1990).

*quaerens intellectum* and decided for clearer theological models. Whatever the case may be, that magnificent theologian and philosopher, Anselm of Canterbury, did not provide a model for William of St Thierry in his different use of reason in theology: for William reason's principal but not sole use in theology was as *ratio fidei*.

William's theological method is notably different from Anselm's. Natural or ordinary reason is no longer accorded the high place it had in Anselm, although William continues to use logic and dialectic when he needs them. Reason, for William, has been so transformed by faith that it now functions as a more-than-natural reason. In that sense, for William, ordinary reason (e.g. logic, dialectic, dialogue) will continue to be used by the theologian when needed but will not define the more expanded range of reason opened by faith. For William, *ratio* has now been transfigured into a richer *ratio fidei*. *Ratio fidei* therefore elicits new rational powers of discernment of spiritual realities (in the scripture, the liturgy, the prayers of all Christians), new hermeneutical possibilities of meditative reading, ultimately discerned to be new speculative, contemplative reasoning. William's new *ratio fidei* is ultimately discerned to be driven by the love which faith itself becomes in the second stage.

In the second stage of William's spiritual and intellectual journey, *ratio fidei* yields to what might be named (although William himself does not so name it) *ratio amoris*.[21] This final transformation of reason culminates in what William, transforming Gregory the Great, famously claimed: '*Amor ipse intellectus est.*' With the power of *ratio fidei*, the intellect (*intellectus, ratio*) can now discover that it itself is inexorably driven by a deeper desire than even its powerful, indeed unrestricted desire to know: the desire for the Good, i.e. the authentic love of God.

In sum, for William, *fides* produces *ratio fidei*. *Ratio fidei* discerns spiritual realities. A key example of William's use of *ratio fidei* is his insistence that philosophical categories like 'person' and 'substance' cannot be directly applied to the mystery of the Trinity, traditionally three persons in one substance. William did use Boethius'[22] second definition of person rather than Boethius' more widely used first definition (*subsistens distinctum in natura intellectuali*) but he changed it into a more theological Trinitarian category. *Ratio fidei*, for William, can and should transform philosophical

---

[21] William of St Thierry, *Speculum fidei* in *Deux Traités sur la Foi*: 'Tu ergo, o fidelis anima, cum in fide tua nature [*sic*] tripidanti ingeruntur occultiora mysteria; aude et dic, non studio occurrendi, sed amore sequendi. *Quomodo fiunt isa?* Questio tua oratio tua sit, amor sit, pietas sit, et humile desiderium; non in sublimibus scrutans Dei majestatem, sed in salutaribus Dei salutarium nostrorum quaerens salutem....' (p. 62, par. 46)

[22] See the excellent discussion of Henry Chadwick in *Boethius, The Consolations of Music, Logic, Theology, and Philosophy*, Oxford: Oxford University Press 1981, pp. 190–203 on the two definitions of person in Boethius.

categories into theological categories. In contemporary theological terms, William's *ratio fidei* has more affinity to an *analogia fidei* (Karl Barth) or an *analogia caritatis* (Hans Urs von Balthasar) than to an *analogia entis* (Boethius, Thomas Aquinas, Karl Rahner). William's use of his map for the spiritual journey in three stages is consistent. In the second stage, *ratio fidei* progresses through its spiritual exercises and becomes meditative, for example, by meditating on sensual images of the life of Christ in the gospels (here like the future use of images in Ignatius Loyola). As the soul moves to its third stage of deeper love and understanding, *ratio fidei* yields to its own transformation into *ratio amoris*. Thus begins the final stage of the journey within which contemplative wisdom (the gift of the Spirit's love) harmonizes and integrates reason and love in the soul. In this final stage of its journey, *ratio fidei* becomes more speculative, more contemplative. *Scientia* yields to *sapientia*. *Sapientia* is the wisdom-love that can now be tasted (*sapiens*). When faith was an external force in stage one it touched the soul. Now that faith has been so interiorized by its journey through all three stages it has become a pure love of God. Love-reason now tastes (*sapiens*) its new-found pure love and contemplative reason (*sapientia*). Rarely have the 'spiritual senses' first enunciated by Origen been so well employed as in William's sensual description of the soul's journey from faith touching the soul to the soul tasting love and reason, now united in *sapientia*.

At this point of contemplative wisdom, William retrieves and gives even deeper meaning to Gregory the Great's aphorism, '*Amor ipse notitia est*,'[23] which William reformulates as '*Amor ipse intellectus est*.' The meaning of '*Amor ipse intellectus est*' can be fully understood, however, only by recalling William's version of the three stages of the spiritual-theological life. In stages one and two, the searching soul moves from simple faith to *ratio fidei*, akin to ancient Christian *gnosis* in Clement of Alexandria and Origen.[24] Just as faith transforms reason into *ratio fidei*, so too faith, as it becomes more and more interior to the self, yields to love. As the spiritual life continues, faith working through love becomes pure love, delight in God for Godself. Pure love continues to expand and continues to transform reason to prepare for the reception of a new form of loving contemplation made possible by the gift of the Holy Spirit as the *unitas Spiritus* of the Trinity itself to the soul. Just as natural reason has been sublated into *ratio fidei*, *ratio fidei* is sublated into love (*ratio amoris*). Pure love itself has been

---

[23] For an analysis of Gregory the Great on love and knowledge, see B. McGinn, *Growth of Mysticism: Gregory the Great through the 12th Century*, New York: Crossroad 1994, pp. 34–80. Gregory's *amor ipsit notitia est* is a major motif in both Gregory's *Moralia on Job* and the *Expostiones in Canticum Canticorum, In Librum Primum Regum*, ed. Patrick Verbraken (CC 144).

[24] See the discussion of William's relationship to ancient Christian gnosis in L. Bouyer, *The Cistercian Heritage*, Westminster: The Newman Press 1958, pp. 120–4.

sublated by the Spirit into the grace of the *unitas Spiritus*. This gift-grace of the Spirit allows the soul, now restored not only as *similitudo Dei* but as *imago Trinitatis*, to participate *in* the Spirit and therefore in the inner life of the Trinity itself. In the Trinity, the Spirit is the eternal bond of love of Father and Son. Moreover, through their eternal, divine, loving relationships the Father, Son and Spirit are not merely united and harmonized but are one through the bond of the Spirit who is Love. The Trinitarian constant of Love is manifested in the Spirit who lovingly relates the Loving Father and the Beloved Son.

## Amor Ipse Intellectus Est

As with Bernard, love is primary for William. Unlike Bernard, whose brilliant style is more poetic-rhetorical than dialectical and whose theological-spiritual interests are more directly pastoral-affective than speculative, William methodically works out the relationship of reason and love. William reached a unique and still underappreciated understanding of how, in effect, the New Testament proclamation 'God is Love' means God is Triune.

For William, love, like understanding-knowledge, begins with faith. As with reason, so with desire-love: we live, as Adam did after the fall, in a *regio dissimilitudinis* of our confused minds and our disordered desires. Our problem in this labyrinthine region is harrowing: we find ourselves in a space of colliding acts of understanding and desire where the differences are so marked that anarchy prevails in both our reason and our will. The harder we try to escape this region of ever-increasing dissimilarities, the more we find ourselves sinking as if in quicksand. Sometimes we think we see, mirage-like, a possible door out, e.g. through love of another, that often proves to be another dissimilarity, e.g. we do not really love the other as other but want only to possess her/him.

William's unyielding portrait of our lostness in the *regio dissimilitudinis* can, at times, remind one of Franz Kafka's *Das Schloss*:[25] in the radical confusion of constant dissimilarities in our fallen state there is, we believe, a door of relief, one in fact constructed only for me, but that door is now and forever closed upon me. Our own powers are delusory. We possess, like Kafka's K., a knowledge incapable of understanding its own limits. Our natural desire for the Good finds itself trapped by false loves, insatiable desires, infinite hunger for release from the region of dissimilarity. However, what we seem unable to admit to ourselves, with our own powers of reason and love alone, there is no exit.

---

[25] Kafka, *Das Schloss*, Frankfurt am Main: Fischer Taschenbuch 1981.

Not only are we weary, wandering and unable to understand ourselves. We are also unable to love properly. Our knowledge cannot reach God. We are an insoluble puzzle to ourselves. Our *affectus* (feeling, dispositions, loves) cannot rightly love God or others (the neighbours) or even the self. As Augustine taught William, our sin-laden affections possess a downward gravity to attractions to false loves. Our sin-laden minds can become, as another Augustinian, Martin Luther, memorably said, a factory for manufacturing idols. Our loves, restless, wandering, confused, self-deluding, flail about with false love after false love only to become more and more trapped in themselves.

In these portraits of bleak, tragic reality in our lives in the fallen *regio dissimilitudinis*, William challenged the humanistic optimism of his day as much as Augustine had challenged his fellow Platonists, and Freud would later challenge his optimistic colleagues in psychology by his terrifying portrait of the reality of the Unconscious.[26]

As with knowledge, so too can love be liberated to its true course only by grace and the spiritual journey. We recover our *similitudo Dei* by grace and by a graced commitment to undertaking the stages of the spiritual life. We slowly convalesce through ascetical, liturgical, meditative and finally contemplative love. At last we sense again the presence of a healed *imago Dei* and a sanctified *similitudo Dei* by which we can at last begin to understand and love God properly and love every neighbour. As a final result of our spiritual and intellectual journey, we learn to answer the earlier, once desperate question all tragic realists share with Augustine, Pascal, Nietzsche and Kafka: Who am I?

God's loving, justifying grace answers that otherwise unanswerable question. Grace comes to us through Christ and faith in him. We receive that gift free *through* the Incarnate Word *in* the Spirit. The will and its affections, like the understanding they drive forward, begin to heal as they are strengthened and focused by this simple faith. Faith, originally an exterior power, works as strongly in the will as it does in the understanding. Faith redirects the affections, the soul's weight upward to the flame of love. In the first stage of healing following God's gift of faith, love is guided by *ratio fidei* to learn to read the Scriptures more meditatively, more interiorly. For example, we learn to understand one of William's most frequently cited texts: 'We can love because God first loved us' (1 Jn 4.16).

The new *ratio fidei* helps not only our understanding but also heals our drives, desires, affections. Love makes us understand and love the scriptures, the liturgy, ancient theological texts. For William, an attentive, loving faith helps us become attuned (Heidegger's *Befindlichkeit*) to the scriptures,

---

[26] On the terrifying character of Freud's unconscious, see J. Lacan, *Écrits*, New York: W.W. Norton & Co. 2006, pp. 671–746.

the liturgy, the community, the texts of the earlier great theologians. The writings and persons of the Fathers, the Mothers, the Teachers of the early church are central for William: above all the great Augustine as well as in the later texts of William, the more optimistic Greek fathers – Origen on the three stages of the soul and Gregory of Nyssa on the relationship of soul and body.[27]

As with the earlier spiritual traditions in Christianity, East and West, William held that faith, as it became more and more interior and personally appropriated, purified the mind by evoking a more spiritual reading and meditation of the scriptures and purified the will by embracing the monastic ascetical practices of poverty, obedience and chastity. For William, ascetical practices were not unnatural at all as the critics of the monks charged. For him, asceticism was as natural to the converted monk as constant and often painful practice was for the athlete or the musician. These ascetical practices were hallowed by the traditional spiritual understanding (from Dionysius the Areopagite) of the soul's movement from purification (or purgation) to illumination (meditation) to union (loving contemplation).

In the first stage of William's spiritual journey, therefore, the soul – both mind and will – is purified until it is gradually re-formed and trans-formed into a consciously loving soul delighting in God's presence. At the limit of stage one the soul moves from this first purificatory stage. Then, in stage two, the soul's senses and affections are further healed and sanctified through grace and spiritual practice.

In the second stage, love guides reason even more than reason guides love. The relationship of love and knowledge becomes deeply harmonized with every step taken forward in the meditative practices of stage two. Now the soul is capable of meditative readings of Scripture and meditative prayers. The soul now finds itself in loving conversation with God now loved rightly, i.e. purely for God's own sake. In this second stage, faith now works through love. Indeed, in a foretaste of the afterlife, faith becomes love.

In stage two, the soul now heals its damaged but not lost *imago dei*, i.e. its openness to, capability of, desire for a Loving God). The soul thereby steadily departs from the region of dissimilarity to find a graced personal recovery of its *similitudo Dei*. The soul then reaches a purified meditative understanding more and more imbued with a purified, even pure love. In stage one, love is guided by *ratio fidei*. In stage two, *fides* itself becomes love so that reason in turn is now guided by a purified love.

The soul never leaves the region of dissimilarity completely in this life since one will always need to fight against never-ending temptations and distractions. As Peter Brown observes about Augustine after his conversion,

---

[27] Gregory of Nyssa, *De Hominis Officio*, (PG 44, 123–256).

William of St Thierry remained a convalescent, not completely cured.[28] Nevertheless, in stage two, the soul now finds itself in a new open space. One might even say that for William, the soul now begins to find its love and understanding more and more harmonized and united into an ever-expanding loving knowledge and understanding love. The soul begins to live in a *regio similitudinis*. The soul's capacity for and openness to God (the *imago*) is no longer merely a pre-unconscious unconscious trace of an unknown presence in the *memoria*. The soul is now somewhere else:[29] through the grace always informing its spiritual efforts, the soul touches and brings to consciousness the loving presence of God in flashes of eternity.

In the second stage, the soul now moves naturally through its spiritual practices. The soul's love is now purified enough to experience a pure love of delight in the presence of God and unselfish love for the other as other at transient moments. Like most Eastern spiritual traditions (the Hindu guru, the Zen Master, the Taoist sage), the Christian monastic traditions believed in the need for a spiritual director to instruct and guide any person undertaking a spiritual journey.[30] William named this need for a director the 'obedience of necessity' appropriate to the early stages of the novice's inward journey.

In stage two the obedience of necessity spontaneously yields to an obedience of *caritas*. Once faith has been transformed by grace and graced spiritual exercises into an ever more pure love of God and neighbour, an obedience of love takes over from an earlier obedience of necessity in a way reminiscent of his mentor's (Augustine) famous saying, '*Ama et fac quod vis*.' Freely, spontaneously, easily, the soul now lives no longer through duty and command but through love alone, 'an obedience of charity'. William's position here is sound not only spiritually and theologically but psychologically as well. As William James, the great psychologist of religion insisted, the 'saint' does the good with ease and spontaneity.[31] For James, the saint performs good, loving acts spontaneously, easily, naturally. When the rest of us perform our good acts for our neighbours, we do so more out of duty

---

[28] P. Brown, *Augustine of Hippo: A Biography*, Berkeley: University of California Press 2000, pp. 108–125.

[29] William, *Aenigma fidei* in *Deux Traités sur la Foi*: 'Amat autem locutio sive inquisitio de Deo, humiles ac simplices in paupertate spiritus Deum queretes, quos ad inquirendum non curiositas agit, sed pietas trahit. Amat loqui non verbis precipitationis et alienis; sed ipsis quibus semetipsum et Patrem et Spiritum sanctum manifestavit mundo Verbum Dei ipso locutionis caractere, quo fidem Trinitatis propagaverunt in mundo homines Dei.' (pp. 132, 134, par. 48)

[30] (Sr) Donald Corcoran, 'Spiritual Guidance', in B. McGinn, J. Meyendorff and J. Leclercq, *Christian Spirituality: Origins to the Twelfth Century*, New York: Crossroad 1992, pp. 444–52.

[31] W. James, *The Varieties of Religious Experience*, Garden City: Doubleday & Co. 1978, pp. 261–370.

than spontaneous love. We non-saints live by one or another obedience of necessity; the saints by an 'obedience of *caritas*'.[32]

In the third stage of the spiritual journey, a person begins to understand what the tradition named *unio*.[33] For William, in the third stage of union, the soul understands and experiences its *imago* and *similitudo* as an *imago* of the Trinity itself (*imago Trinitatis*). At this final stage, the soul finds that it consciously and lovingly participates in the Love who is God, i.e. the loving God who is the Trinity. This new loving wisdom is made possible through the special sanctifying grace of the Holy Spirit, the *unitas Spiritus* that allows the soul to live *in spiritu*. Analogous to the manner in which faith's major theological discovery in stage one was the reality of grace through Christ, in stage three, love's major theological discovery is the reality of the love who is the tri-personal God in the Holy Spirit in its new gift-grace to the soul of *unitas Spiritus*.[34] At the last the soul discovers as fully as possible in this life the Spirit's presence through a retreating, echoing sound of the thunder heard in the soul's transient moments of eternity and the lightning flashes of divine love experienced even in this life by the soul. Only then does the self know that its *imago Dei* is not only the *imago* constituted by an openness to and capacity for God, but something totally unexpected: the soul is *imago Trinitatis*. William's theology of mysticism (*unio*)[35] is also theology of the Trinity. At this final stage, the soul feels and understands a harmony of love and knowledge so profound that they can almost seem one: love-knowledge is knowledge-love.

William ingeniously names the final grace *unitas Spiritus*. In discerning the Spirit's presence in us, we understand as deeply as we finite beings can *in* the Spirit, God's Triune presence. We understand, as Paul insisted, through a mirror in an enigma.

In William's *Commentary on the Song of Songs* as well as in the final section of his last work, the *Golden Epistle*, William presents most firmly his new Trinitarian spirituality of the Spirit. Only one who has gone through all three stages of the spiritual life culminating in the extraordinary grace of the *unitas Spiritus* has experienced God's love powerfully enough to begin to understand the greatest of all revealed mysteries: the Trinity.

---

[32] William, *Aenigma fidei* in *Deux Traités sur la Foi*, pp. 130, 132, pars. 45–7.

[33] Thus William can conclude the *L'Énigme de la foi* with this remarkable sentence: 'Sed ideo solus sufficit quia separari a Patre et Filio non potest, cum quibus inseparabiliter facit cuncta que facit.' (p. 178, par. 100)

[34] *Aenigma fidei* in *Deux Traités sur la Foi*: 'Cum ergo sit Spiritus sanctus spiritus Patris et Filii, et ab utroque procedat, sitque caritas et unitas amborum; manifestum est, quod non sit aliquis duorum, quo uterque conjungitur, quo genitus a gignente diligitur, genitoremque suum diligit, ut sint non participatione aliena sed propria essentia, nec alterius dono sed suo proprio *servantes unitatem spiritus in vinculo pacis*.' (p. 176, par. 98)

[35] For William's theology of mysticism as a spirit-centred mysticism, see McGinn, *Growth of Mysticism*, pp. 225–75.

William insists on a theology of the experience of love as ultimately an experience of the Spirit – a theology grounded in living '*in Spiritu*.' In one of his most impressive theological insights, William wrote two complementary theses inspired by St Paul's famous 'We see now as through a mirror in an enigma but then we shall see God face to face' (1 Cor. 13.12). William designed the first treatise, the *Mirror of Faith*, to show the contours of a theology and spirituality of love in the Spirit. In the second companion treatise, the *Enigma of Faith*, William articulated his Trinitarian theology as the necessary theological expression of the spirituality of love expressed in the *Mirror of Faith*, the *Commentary on the Song of Songs*, in the *Golden Epistle*, as well as earlier in *The Nature and Dignity of Love* and almost everywhere in the twelve volumes we possess of his work.

As the *Mirror* and the *Enigma* demonstrate, for William there can be no separation of theology and spirituality. Only the theologian who is spiritual will be able to help the Christian community to begin to understand as far as our finite minds are able the ultimate mystery of Christian faith: God is Love; God is Triune. Some mystical theologians may reach the point of experiencing the triune God in moments of contemplation, in contemplative prayer, in spontaneous outbursts of pure love for both God and neighbour. Mystical theologians feel-understand our union *per Christum in Spiritu* as *imago Trinitatis* through the *unitas Spiritus* that envelops the soul in the stage of union. William daringly proposes that the soul, by the grace of the *unitas Spiritus*, experiences its participation in the loving union of the Trinity's own inner self. In the Trinity the Holy Spirit *is* the unity-harmony-communion of the Father and the Son. Thus the soul now experiences and begins to understand the inner life of the Trinity as an inner life of love. Each person of the Trinity, for William as for the earlier Christian tradition,[36] can be described as a distinct because related person: the Father is origin and source; the Son as Son comes forth from the Father as Son and Eternal Word; the Spirit, as the eternal procession (as in breathing) of Father and Son is the *unitas* uniting all three persons in mutual love. Precisely as loving relationships the Father, Son and Spirit are distinct persons; as love through the eternal bond of the Spirit, the Trinity is One God – Trinity in Unity – the uniquely Christian Trinitarian monotheism.

William claims that, in the third stage of the spiritual journey, love and knowledge are so harmonized and unified through the grace of union which is the *unitas Spiritus* that the loving-knowing sanctified soul actually experiences a participation in the loving, harmonious unity of the Trinity's inner life.

---

[36] Bernard Lonergan's *De Deo Trino*, II, *Pars Systematica*, Rome: Pontifica Universitatis Gregorianae 1964, pp. 152–205.

William's theological daring here is amazing: Our contact in faith with the Incarnate Word (stage one) becomes ever more purified, interior and meditative (stage two) until this life of intensifying union with God expands to become, in an amazing claim, our experienced participation in the internal life of love of God's own Trinitarian self.[37] In the Trinity, the Spirit is the unity of love. In us the final grace of our life through Christ in the Spirit is no less than a radical deified participation in the Trinity's own inner life through the *unitas Spiritus* given to us as grace in the final moment of our graced spiritual journey. At this moment, William found further spiritual and theological meaning in one of his favourite New Testament texts, 'We love because God first loved us.' How does the soul know this? The soul knows that love through Christ in the Spirit. How does the soul interiorize this knowledge? Ultimately, the soul's final knowledge-love is the loving contemplation of God's own inner Trinitarian life made possible in the ultimate stage of union made real by the *unitas Spiritus* Itself.

The gift mystically experienced as *unitas-Spiritus* in the union with God allows the soul to experience and finitely begin to understand a Trinitarian theology grounded in the Trinity's own life, the source of all life. The First Letter of John was entirely accurate: God is Love. The early councils and theologians were equally accurate: through Christ in the Spirit we now know the Ultimate Mystery: God is Trinity-in-Unity. William's enduring contribution to the Trinitarian theology is his claim that a *full* Trinitarian theology should be a mystical theology of union and a mystical theology should be a Trinitarian mysticism. Deification is as real to William as it has traditionally been for all Eastern theologians. William's full optimism on humanity is now clear: the final dignity of the human being is his/her divinization. We can not only can have conversation with God; we can live lovingly, conversationally in God.

Thanks to William's fascinating account of the soul's three-staged spiritual journey, in part a synthesis of Augustine and Origen, our theological knowledge (understood as saturated by love) is now capable of a deeper theological understanding of the Trinity as the central mystery. For that very reason, our deeper knowledge of the Trinity is not an explanation, much less a proof, of the Trinity but a more deeply understood because more purely loved deeply apophatic insight into the ultimate mystery of the Real, God as Trinity as real, as mystery. Our love is the love of desire-possession-desire:

---

[37] William, *Speculum fidei* in *Deux Traités sur la Foi*: 'O ergo, quem nemo querit vere, et non invenit, quippe cum ipsa veritas te querendi in conscientia querentis non suspectum jam habeat responsum, aliquatenus invente veritatis, inveni nos, ut inveniamus te; veni in nos, ut eamus in te, et vivamus in te, quia vere non est volentis, neque currentis, sed tui miserentis. Tu prior inspira, ut credamus; tu conforta, ut speremus; tu provoca et accende, ut amemus; totumque de nobis tuum sit, ut bene nobis in te sit, *in quo vivimus, movemur et sumus.*' (pp. 88, 90, par. 78)

never-ending. Furthermore, in the stage of union, William's description of the rhythm of our desire-love suggests certain affinities to Gregory of Nyssa's notion of *epektasis*:[38] every new participation in God increases but never fulfills the desire of the soul. For Gregory of Nyssa, even in the life to come hereafter, *epektasis* never ends.

# Conclusion: The Contributions and Limits of William of St Thierry to Trinitarian Theology for Contemporary Trinitarian Theology

For William, as for any Christian theologian, the mystery of the Trinity always remains mystery. Even with its highest cataphatic name for God – God is Love – theology remains apophatic. Trinitarian theology enhances and enriches our understanding of the mystery of God which is no less than the ultimate mystery of the Ultimate Reality which as one-in-three is the source, sustainer and end of all reality. The Triune God's Infinite Incomprehensibility is not only a comment on our finite limits to know. God's Infinite Incomprehensibility is even more a comment on the fully positive Incomprehensibility of God's Infinite, Triune Godhead. As Dionysius of Areopagite demonstrates,[39] beyond our best cataphatic as well as our most apophatic knowledge of God lies a mystical experience of God. William wants to reflect theologically upon that mystical experience of God as Triune far more than Dionysius did. For William, the theologian through the very mystical experience can now not only experience but reflect on the possibility of a Trinitarian mystical theology of union which Dionysius phenomenologically described, as the next theological step beyond Dionysius after a mystical experience of God. Here too William's daring and originality are remarkable.

Christianity is a trinitarian monotheism: the Triune God is One Nature (*ousia, substantia*) in Three Persons (*hypostases, prosopa, personae*). For William, through the spiritual journey, the *memoria* in our wounded but intact *imago dei* (the traces of God in our unconscious) have become fully conscious as a pure love leading to a new illuminated knowledge of

---

[38] For Gregory of Nyssa's teaching, *epektasis* (always striving for those things which still lie ahead) is symbolized by Moses' constant attempt to rise higher; see his *Life of Moses*, New York: Paulist Press 1978, pp. 111–20.

[39] This is the primary reason that Dionysius wrote a 'Mystical Theology' (pp. 33–42) as a concluding text after his famous cataphatic and apophatic analyses of 'The Divine Names' (pp. 47–132); see *The Complete Works of Pseudo-Dionysius*, Mahwah: Paulist Press 1987.

ourselves as a restored *similitudo Dei,* because ultimately an unexpected *imago Trinitatis.* That, for William, is who we are; that is our ultimate dignity as human beings. In fact, that is how we finally discover what is most deeply human about a human being--our participation in God's own inner life of love and intelligence-in-act. Beyond William's earlier tragic humanism, that amazingly optimistic Trinitarian vision of who we are – an *imago Trinitatis* – is William's final vision of Christian humanism.

Like many (most?) theologians and unlike William of St Thierry, I am not a mystic.[40] Nevertheless, that unhappy fact does not disallow my presuming to read William's texts, both theological and mystical. Theologians who are not mystics impoverish their theological thinking and their spiritual lives alike by hesitating to read and interpret the classic mystical theologies. Interpretations are needed of such texts by all theologians. As Hans-Georg Gadamer rightly insists, our intellectual and spiritual interiorization-application of the truth we grasp in our hermeneutic efforts are necessary for interpretation itself. In my judgment, this hermeneutical key is also applicable to non-mystics interpreting mystical texts. As William James argued, non-mystics (like James himself) should read mystical texts.[41] They they could learn at least this much: something more than modern rational persons ordinarily think possible may be the case. For the psychological James, the mystics may well have been in touch with wider and deeper aspects of consciousness and the pre-conscious beneath and outside the usual rather narrow limits of ordinary rational consciousness. Jacques Lacan, unlike his maestro, Sigmund Freud, shared James' fascination with and hermeneutical appropriation of mystical texts as a possible entry into the Freudian unconscious, for example, in his analysis of mystical *jouissance* in Teresa of Avila.[42] Julia Kristeva, linguist, philosopher and psychoanalyst, has also made important contemporary analyses of love-mysticism (in, for example, Bernard of Clairvaux and Teresa of Avila although not yet in William of St Thierry).[43] Given this wide interest in mystical texts by so many secular thinkers, it is disconcerting to find so few Trinitarian theologians addressing William of St Thierry who was, after all, not a mystic but a first-rate, mystical theologian. Presumably this theological *gran rifiuto* to mystical theologies is another illustration of the lingering toxic effect of the now centuries-old separation of theology and spirituality. Surely it is long past time for that separation to end. Trinitarian theology needs to recover

---

[40] Perhaps the main difficulty here lies in the fact that 'mysticism' and therefore 'mystic' remain essentially contested concepts. See McGinn, *Foundations of Mysticism,* pp. 165–343.

[41] James, *The Varieties,* pp. 370–418.

[42] J. Lacan, *Feminine Sexuality,* New York: W.W. Norton & Co. 1982, pp. 137–49.

[43] J. Kristeva, *Histoires d'amour,* Paris: Denoel 1983 and her forthcoming study of Teresa of Avila.

its link to spirituality as much as all Christian spirituality needs to recover its ultimately Trinitarian nature.

Most of us are not only not mystics but also not poets. The analogy of poetry and mysticism deserves reflection by all theologians hesitant to interpret mystical texts as an aid to their Trinitrian theologies. Most people, whether educated or not, instinctively and, when educated in reading poetry, intelligently respond to all great poetry. We have learned to internalize the poem's rhythms, its tone and sensibility, above all its singular vision; this is similar to what happens in William's stage two. After learning to appreciate poetry by careful study,[44] we find ourselves both experientially and intellectually ever more deeply grateful for those poems that have become, often without premeditation, a part of their very lives. As T. S. Eliot suggested in his great modern Christian poem, *Four Quartets*,[45] all experiences of human love, the beauty of nature, reading poetry, listening to music, seeing paintings are one and all 'hints and guesses; hints followed by guesses' of a realm of meaning beyond ordinary consciousness. As a Christian poet, Eliot also added to this list a line of poetry William of St Thierry would have applauded: 'And the hint half-guessed, the gift half-understood is Incarnation.' In the final stage of interiorizing of any great work of art, every person knows this truth of Eliot's claim about certain experiences of all art, here music: 'Or music heard so deeply/ That it is not heard at all, but you are the music/ While the music lasts.'[46] If we non-poets can learn to love and understand great poetry, as most theologians do, then we can also, without the experience of being a mystic oneself, learn from mystical theological texts like those of William of St Thierry. At a minimum, such texts should help Trinitarian theologians to find new ways to unite anew spirituality and theology.

In postmodern culture many philosophers and theologians have become more open to poetry as well as to mystical and prophetic religious modes of thinking, and not only modes of feeling. Modern culture, except for the Romantics, has had far narrower criteria of what is rationally possible. Enlightenment thinkers, e.g. Kant, would allow art or mysticism to count cognitively. In modern philosophy, for example, Kant's criteria of the conditions of possibility of rational knowledge allowed in the *Third Critique* a role (still largely related to feeling, not knowledge) for experiences of the

---

[44] The text suggests only the initial steps of learning to appreciate poetry; to interpret it adequately is of course a complex operation. For the fuller complexity of interpretation, see P. Ricoeur, *Interpretation Theory: Discourse and the Surplus of Meaning*, Fort Worth: TCU Press, 1976.

[45] T. S. Eliot, 'The Dry Salvages', in *Four Quartets*, London: Faber and Faber Ltd., 1944, pp. 23–31.

[46] Eliot, 'The Dry Salvages', p. 30 (ll. 214–17).

beautiful and the sublime.[47] However, Kant's modern sublime, in contrast
to postmodern understandings of the sublime like that of Jean-François
Lyotard,[48] became, at the end, reason's self-fascinated experience of its
own remarkable powers in the presence of such awe-ful experiences as
the Alps or the ocean. Only in postmodern philosophy and theology do
Kierkegaard's dialectical arguments for a positive understanding of the
category 'The Impossible'[49] flourish in a manner directly analogous to
the positive notion of God's Incomprehensibility discussed above. Some
postmodern philosophers[50] (Derrida, Levinas, Deleuze) have allowed art,
especially poetry, to challenge their philosophy intellectually, not merely to
provide it with 'feeling' as the moderns did.

Every Trinitarian theologian, I suggest, can read and learn from William's
classic texts: a love-focused, participatory mystical theology of the Trinity
that is simultaneously a Trinitarian mysticism, spirituality. In meditating on
William's Trinitarian theology, the reader's own desire stretches (*epektasis*)
while the reader's understanding is deepened both cataphatically (Love
is God's highest name) and apophatically (the mystery of the Trinity has
been enriched by theological understanding to become even more richly
apophatic).

Any reader of William's texts can sense the magnet-like attraction of
his highly spiritual Trinitarian theology. A reader gradually begins to sense
how faithful William was to his oft-repeated aphorism: 'To believe in Christ
is to go to Christ by loving Him.' Every practitioner of theology (that
almost impossible discipline) also knows the truth of another aphorism
of William, 'Love apprehends more by its ignorance than knowledge does
by its [apophatic] ignorance because love rejoices to fade away into what
God is.'[51]

Reading a theologian like William of St Thierry is both disheartening
and encouraging for any contemporary theologian living in the wake of the
disastrous centuries-old separation of theology and spirituality along with
the modern separation of philosophy and a way of life. That separation
may have begun with a valuable distinction between theological theory and
spiritual practice when mainline theology moved out of the monasteries

---

[47] I. Kant, *Critique of Judgment*, New York: Macmillan Publishing Co. 1951, pp. 82–181.

[48] J.-F. Lyotard, *Rudiments païens: genre dissertatif,* Paris: Union Générale d'Editions 1977, p. 176.

[49] See the essays in Martin J. Matustik and Merold Westphal, (eds), *Kierkegaard in Post/Modernity*, Bloomington: Indiana University Press 1995.

[50] J. Derrida, *Acts of Literature*, London: Routledge 1992; G. Deleuze, *Francis Bacon: the Logic of Sensation,* Minneapolis: University of Minnesota 2003. On Levinas: the influence of Russian literature on his work is profound; the influence of Maurice Blanchot on Levinas's later work (and vice versa) is also profound.

[51] As quoted in McGinn, *Growth of Mysticism*, p. 233.

into the universities of the cities. But within a century the distinction deteriorated into a separation.

William believed in the distinction. He feared and opposed the separation. In fact William's own early education was in the new emerging dialectical methods, possibly at Laon with Anselm of Laon, and if not then at a similar school at Rheims.[52] William's early conversion to a vocation away from the secular world to the monastery emancipated him to become one of the last and probably the greatest of monastic theologians. William lived 'before the [scholastic] revolution' preferred the *douceur de vivre* of an earlier theology, the theology of the early church, especially his great model for theology, Augustine of Hippo. For several of William's theological colleagues – William of Conches, Gilbert de la Porrée, Peter Abelard, Alain of Lille – the new intellectual methods produced, as noted above, a new more humanistic theology: more optimistic about reason's role to forge an open *conversatio* among God, nature and humanity within which the new rational tools of dialectic, logic and dialogue can be employed without restriction.

Near the end of the theologically rich and pluralistic twelfth century, much theology became more urban, more intellectualist, more Scholastic. Both monastic theologies and humanistic theologizing seemed to enter a twilight zone. By the thirteenth century, in the triumph of Scholastic theologies in the new universities, both these modes of theology were largely maginalized: monastic theologies to the monasteries; humanistic theologies to memory. In the fourteenth and fifteenth centuries, moreover, theology became more conceptualist rather than intellectualist, first with that genius of logic, Duns Scotus, and after Scotus with the refined logic and dialectics of the nominalists. Jean Leclerq,[53] the leading twentieth-century historian of monastic theology, ironically called the dominance of the Scholastic method in Catholic theology from the thirteenth century until Vatican II, the 'long interruption' in Catholic theology.

Leclerq exaggerates but has a legitimate point. To describe Scholastic theology as a mere interruption in the history of theology ignores the fact that the thirteenth-century great Scholastics made many enduring intellectual contributions to all theology: lucid definitions; intellectually refined *quaestiones*; the careful use of the rediscovered (through the Arabs) logic and dialectic of Aristotle; the new dialectic of authorities set forth in the *Sic et Non* use of Abelard; the purifying intellectualist thrust of the Scholastic drive to system, first in *Sentences* like those of Peter Lombard and then,

---

[52] There is still a debate among specialists on which cathedral school William attended to learn dialectics, logic and grammar before his conversion to the monastic life.

[53] J. Leclerq, *The Love of Learning and the Desire for God: A Study of Monastic Culture*, New York: Fordham University Press 1961.

in the mid-thirteenth century, the arrival of the cathedral-like magnificent *Summae* of Thomas Aquinas and several others.

The great Scholastics, unlike their neo-Scholastic successors, were thinkers of the first order producing theologies of the first order. Thomas and Bonaventure distinguished but did not separate theory and practice (way of life), theology and spirituality. As professors representing the new mendicant, not monastic, orders in the new University of Paris, Thomas and Bonaventure were as mendicants in the world, not monastics withdrawn from the world, intellectually and spiritually at home in the world of the university. Both struggled against the separation of faith and reason among the thinkers in the liberal arts faculty of the University of Paris, Bonaventure far more angrily than the equally determined Thomas.

But even Thomas was alarmed enough by the separation of faith and reason, and therefore also of spirituality and theology-philosophy, to call his work against the professors in the liberal arts faculty (especially the radical Aristotelian Siger of Brabant) *Contra Murmurantes*. Bonaventure is exemplary in his age by systematically attempting to keep theology and spirituality together in the new intellectual situation. Thomas, too, in his hymns and in the strong undertow of a wisdom spirituality in all his texts, worked hard to keep the distinction between spirituality and theology a distinction, not a separation. What, however, did Thomas mean in the amazing words he is quoted as saying near the end of his too short life: 'Compared to what I have now experienced, all that I have written is as straw. I shall write no more'? Indeed, he did not; the great *Summa* is unfinished. Did some powerful mystical experience silence the Scholastic perfection of Thomas' theology? Thomas' Dominican intellectualist spirituality was always real. Indeed, that wisdom spirituality was a strong spiritual undertow in all his extraordinary work. At the end, however, it was apparently not enough for Thomas compared to the mystical experience he underwent near the end of this life when he was both badly overworked and seriously ill. A 'Cleopatra's nose' in the history is the unavoidable question: what kind of new theology would this genius have produced if he had lived beyond his brief forty-nine years? Might Thomas have begun a new theology grounded in his new mystical experience? The 'silence of St. Thomas' haunts theology to this day. Neither Thomas nor Bonaventura knew William of St Thierry's Trinitarian theology. For one thing, the new mendicant orders, the Franciscans (Bonaventura) and the Dominicans (Thomas) were not monastic but committed to living in the world through contemplation-in-action through preaching,[54] works of charity and justice, and university teaching.

---

[54] The new mendicant spiritualities differed between themselves: the Franciscans with emphasis on affective spirituality (Bonaventure) and the Dominicans with emphasis on intellectualist spirituality (Thomas Aquinas).

Furthermore, a strange fate had overtaken the texts of William of St Thierry by the time of Bonaventure and Thomas. His theology was either largely unknown outside the monasteries or, even within the monasteries, his works were often listed as works by Bernard of Clairvaux. Even the one work that continued to be read down through the centuries, William's *Golden Epistle* (*Epistola Aurea*) was cited, e.g. by Bonaventure, as a work of Bernard of Clairvaux. William, the supreme monastic Trinitarian theologian and supreme mystical theologian of the Spirit, was not part of the canon of theological classics until in the early twentieth century when some scholars, especially Déchanet, rediscovered some texts of William as William's not Bernard's.[55] Since that time, William's texts continue to be critically edited and variously interpreted by scholars. Until recently, William is hardly mentioned in any histories of the Trinity. When William's work on the Trinity is mentioned at all, it is often hurriedly interpreted, i.e. misinterpreted. Moreover, in histories of spirituality before the twentieth century William's texts were noted – but usually as texts of Bernard. During the early to mid-twentieth century when William's work was finally being retrieved as his work, an even more important discovery of a whole new genre of medieval theology was also being retrieved: neither the Scholastic nor the monastic theologies of the medieval period but the recently named genre of 'lay theology',[56] especially the texts of the now, at last, classical women mystics of the period. Some medieval women theologians are more affective mystics (e.g. Angela of Foligno); some more intellectualist mystics (Marguerite of Porete); some resided in monasteries (e.g. Hildegard of Bingen); some in béguinages (e.g. Hadewych). All are now irreplaceable figures in the canon of theological and spiritual classics.

The medieval mystical theologians are now read along with William and the Victorines to demonstrate a crucial fact that needs constant repetition: theology without spirituality is too thin; spirituality without theology is too soft. On the whole, modern Enlightenment culture had little use for spirituality and even less for mysticism. The Enlightenment had many achievements: its more democratic political theories and practices, its endorsement of tolerance and pluralism, its crucial development of critical methods to unmask all obscurantism and tyranny, whether in church or state. At the same time the dark side of Enlightenment thought has been clarified thanks to postmodern thinkers. The Enlightenment continued and strengthened the separations already present in Western culture since the fourteenth century nominalist crisis. The Enlightenment, in effect,

---

[55] J.-M. Déchanet, *Aux sources de la spiritualité de Guillaume de Saint-Thierry*, Bruges: Éditions Charles Beyaer 1940; Id., *Guillaume de Saint Thierry: L'homme et son oeuvre*, Bruges, Charles Beyaert 1942.
[56] For new lay theology, see Bernard McGinn, *Flowering of Mysticism: Men and Women in the New Mysticism (1200–1350)*, New York: Crossroad 1998.

not merely continued but reified and enforced the now familiar modern separations: theory from practice (philosophical theory separated from a philosophical way of life, unimaginable to an ancient philosopher); theology separated from personal and spiritual experience (unintelligible to a monastic or to a lay mystical theologian); the separation of form and content (the moderns privileged the form of propositional definitions arrived at through logical and dialectical method; other forms – narrative, symbolic, poetic, aphoristic – were marginalized to *belles lettres*). The final separation of emotion and thought, feeling and thought was the separation which both Bernard and William saw emerging in their culture and presciently feared as causing, if continued, a benighted future for theology: the separation of love from theological and philosophical theories of love; the separation of *affectus* (feelings, affects, dispositions, passions) from *intellectus*, culminating in the separation of spiritual experience from theological understanding.

We still live in the ruins produced by those fourteenth-century nominalist separations. Fortunately, postmodern culture, unlike the more narrow Enlightenment regime of Western modernity, is far more welcoming to difference, especially the now valued differences of all those marginalized and rejected by modern culture, including mystics, prophets and visionaries. Indeed, the very word 'mystical', as Michel de Certeau argues,[57] was once a familiar and honoured adjective but became in the modern, centralizing seventeenth century a dismissive noun. A mystic was outside the centre – strange, bizarre, unnerving to the majority. 'Mystic' as a noun was used especially for women mystics like Jeanne-Marie Bouvier de la Motte-Guyon. Moreover, modern neo-Scholastic theologians in the seventeenth and eighteenth centuries, as Michael Buckley has persuasively argued,[58] abandoned theology's roots in communal, especially liturgical experience as well as in more personal spiritual practices. Modern neo-Scholastic and modern Cartesian theologies soon drifted into a vague attempt to function as modern semi-philosophies attempting to prove through modern rationality one or another item of traditional theology. In fact the neo-Scholastics of the seventeenth through to the mid-twentieth century became obsessed with certainty in contradiction to what Thomas Aquinas considered theology's chief intellectual task: not certainty but some partial, analogous but real understanding of the great mysteries of faith. The neo-Scholastics reduced the earlier Scholastic exercises in analogous understanding to mere corollaries of theology proper, i.e. the kind of question worth considering only after the theologian had established 'certainty' through the 'proofs' of scripture, counciliar or magisterium definitions, earlier accepted theologies,

---

[57] M. de Certeau, *La fable mystique*, I, *XVIe–SVIIe siècle,* Paris: Gallimard 1987.
[58] M. Buckley, *At the Origins of Modern Atheism,* New Haven: Yale University Press 1987.

etc. As Bernard Lonergan[59] once remarked: the modern neo-Scholastics believed in clear and distinct ideas and very few of them. Whatever its confusions and exaggerations, postmodernism is proving a boon to theology. On the whole, postmodern thinkers reject modernity's separations: theory from practice, content from form; *affectus* from *intellectus*; spirituality from theology; philosophical theory from a philosophical way of life.

Many contemporary philosophers and theologians now read the mystics and artists with new eyes. There is a now widely recognized need for plural forms to express theological content. Contemporary theology also now acknowledges that theology should analyze and articulate both reason and *affectus* as Augustine always insisted. Among the texts and persons ripe for retrieval in this new cultural postmodern situation are the theological and spiritual texts, including mystical texts, on Christian love: love both as relationship and love as postmodern excess.

William took the theology of the Trinity and gave it a new focus and form: love was the harmonizing focus for both spirituality and Trinitarian theology. The meditative contemplative form of William's Trinitarian theology still seems unused by many contemporary Trinitarian theologians. Is contemporary Trinitarian theology condemned to stay in a modern model of theology, purely intellectualist, even conceptualist? When will the lay mystical Trinitarian theologies, the early Greek Trinitrian theologies, the monastic Trinitarian theologies begin to play a proper role as possible models for contemporary Trinitarian theology?

# Two Criticisms of William of St Thierry and Some Suggestions for His Contributions in Contemporary Trinitarian Theology

In any major thinker there are always limits and critical problems. So it is with William of St Thierry's spirituality and theology. First, the spirituality: William's account of the three stages of the spiritual journey to the experience of *unitas Spiritus* is, as I have argued above, profound and illuminating for any honest seeker, not only for William's fellow monks and mystics. However, too often William's journey is directed only to monks. This is especially true of his most widely read work, the *Golden Epistle*. William seems to leave the rest of his readers (non-monks) with some heavy work of translation to apply his monastic suggestions to their own lives in the world. Perhaps this is an inevitable problem in reading any monastic

---

[59] B. Lonergan, *Method in Theology*, New York: Herder and Herder 1972, esp. pp. 267–355.

writing for any reader (like myself) lacking a calling to the monastic life. Reading William's texts (sometimes lucid, sometimes obscure, sometimes orderly, sometimes digressive) is, I have argued in this essay, well worth the effort for every theologian. As Hans-Georg Gadamer reminds us,[60] every interpretation includes application, most clearly in law and preaching. In William's meditative reading of the scriptures, the reader learns that careful reading can also be a spiritual exercise. To learn to read a biblical or theological text well is to be able to translate it for one's own interior development dependent on one's present receptivity: *quidquid recipitur in modo recipientis recipitur*. Like the monastic texts of Theravada Buddhism, William's texts need translation for non-monks unlike the texts written for lay Buddhists (not only monks) in the more open and inclusive form of Buddhism, Mahayana Buddhism. Unlike Christian texts written for all thinking persons, like Thomas Aquinas' *Summa Contra Gentiles* or William's own *On the Nature of Body and Soul*, most monastic texts in all traditions need an extra effort of translation from the monastery to the world. A hermeneutical translation is by no means impossible. Thoughtful readers can understand William's theological-spiritual texts as long as they are intellectually and spiritually receptive to mystical-theological writings. But the extra effort of translating and interpreting William's monastic texts from their original monastic context is necessary. The monastery is not the world. However, good thoughts and practices, like good persons, cross all borders.

My second criticism of William is not occasioned by his monastic setting. Before this more substantial theological criticism, however, first a summary of William's singular and eminently retrievable achievements. William's contribution to Trinitarian theology is twofold. First, William made his theology explicitly and directly related to his spirituality. William of St Thierry shows one way forward for contemporary Trinitarian theologians endeavouring to join their intellectual and spiritual tasks. William's lesson is an important one: a theologian's theoretical efforts in Trinitarian theology should be informed by spiritual practice, whether that practice be inchoate or, like William's, explicit, direct and methodical: the three stages harmonizing faith, love and reason. Reading William, one can be more alert to the limits of one's own journey and own intellectual development.

Second, William enacted an alternative focus for understanding the Trinity, regarding pure love as *unitas Spiritus*, rather than retaining Augustine's primary focus in his *De Trinitate* on intelligence-in-act. Here is the crucial difference William's Trinitarian theology makes. By shifting the principal focus from reason to love-*affectus*, William provided new intellectual and spiritual resources for all Trinitarian theologies, even modern 'social'

---

[60] H.-G. Gadamer, *Wahrheit und Methode*, Tübingen: J. C. B. Mohr 1965, pp. 290–324.

models of the Trinity. The desire to know, intellectuals too easily forget, is a desire (*desiderium, affectus*). The desire to know is ultimately anchored in and is driven by the greatest of all desires, the desire for the Good. We desire to know because we desire the good of truth. The desire for the Good, in turn, is best understood for Christians as both the desire for the spiritually and theologically as eventualizing in the pure personal love of God itself grounded in the mystical grace of *unitas Spiritus* which harmonizes reason and love, senses and mind, soul and body.

William did not shift his focus from intelligence to love without also analyzing understanding. As we have argued above, at every stage of the journey William shows the always/already interdependence of love and knowledge. Intelligence and love *are* eternally one in the Infinite Trinity. In human life and theology, love and understanding-knowledge are radically united in us by contemplative love, even though they always remain partial and participatory in us finite beings. Human beings, as humans, desire ever greater spiritual and intellectual harmony by rediscovering their *similitudo Dei* and *imago Trinitatis*. Through grace human beings participate in the Trinitarian life of love and understanding. We participate as finite beings. The Infinite God *is* that life. Human understanding of the Trinity, however far it may reach at the level of contemplative wisdom, remains and will always remain a finite apophatic understanding of the Incomprehensible Triune God. Karl Rahner argued that this apophatic understanding of God's Infinite Incomprehensibility will still be in force in the Beatific Vision. Human desire for the Good, however purified into a pure love of God for God's own sake, will never be fully satisfied. Desire for the good will always desire more in satisfaction of its desire. As Gregory of Nyssa speculated in his fascinating interpretation of St Paul's *epektasis*, human beings will always be engaged in a constant process of desire-possession-desire – even in the hereafter! By its very deepening, human knowledge increases its apophatic sense not only of the negative, finite limits of our knowledge but also of God's positive Incomprehensibility. Human desire for the Good, by the purifying powers that allow it to become pure contemplative love for a God who is love, lives forever a life of contemplative *apophases* and loving (*epektasis*).

For William, the constant deepening of faith and then love and the expansion of reason is the kind of reason needed by theologians, especially theologians of the Trinity. William's position remains, I believe, a profound contribution to how to approach a Trinitarian theology by understanding that faith and love so transform reason that reason itself can move past dialectic and all other exercises in ordinary reason to meditation and contemplation.

Nevertheless, in my judgment, William could also have and perhaps should have spent more effort in understanding ordinary reason, beginning with Augustine's classic analysis of intelligence-in-act in *De Trinitate*. If

William had studied Augustine on intelligence-in-act more thoroughly than he seems to have done, then he could also have understood the dialectic and logic used more extensively by Anselm as well as William's own more humanistic contemporaries. Dialectic and logic, after all, are also exercises of intelligence-in-act. Transformed reason (*ratio fidei*) need not lessen the need for ordinary reason. Without weakening his own distinct position or the need in theology for a transformed reason, William could have affirmed a theological development of reason by his more humanistic theological contemporaries as also a *conversatio* among humans, nature and God within which conversation, logic and dialectic function quite well when they function freely. It is puzzling why William found the *conversatio* model of Abelard and others so threatening to his own model of *ratio fidei*. William possessed an exemplary knowledge of Augustine as witnessed to in his early works as well as in his continued fidelity to Augustine even in his later works, where Origen becomes a real influence on William's formulation of the stages of reason and love from an animal to a rational to a spiritual state. William seemed not to have noticed that he also had at his intellectual disposal, in Augustine's own brilliant analysis in *De Trinitate*, a refined understanding of intelligence-in-act with far more precision, clarity and depth than he himself usually accorded ordinary reflective reason as intelligence-in-act. William knew and used the old and new tools of reason: dialectic, logic, rhetoric, dialogue. Unlike Augustine, however, William does not enact a discussion of the power of reason as intelligence-in-act in both acts of direct understanding issuing intelligently, not automatically, in concepts and acts of reflective understanding intelligently issuing (not emanating through some vague necessity) in judgments.

As Thomas Aquinas will later argue, Augustine's reflective analysis of intelligence-in-act yielding acts of concept and judgment was at the heart of Augustine's so-called psychological analogy. With his sharper Aristotelian tools, which Augustine lacked,[61] Aquinas could demonstrate how Augustine's intelligence-in-act was metaphysically act-act. Even granted these limits in the analysis of ordinary reason, William was not a fideist. He clearly respected the dialectical, rhetorical and logical uses of reason. He used them throughout his life when he found them useful. However, William believed that his notion of *ratio fidei*, of 'natural reason', almost always provided for theology a new form of transformed reason that sublated and held under under its aegis all uses of 'natural' or ordinary reason like dialectic. As we have seen above, William's position on the theological sense of 'natural' reason in fact was more restrictive than Anselm's earlier notion of *intellectus* in his mode of theology as *fides quaerens intellectum*. Anselm's position on faith and reason would return, in highly refined, complex

---

[61] P. Verdeyen, *La théologie mystique de Guillaume de Saint-Thierry*, Paris: FAC-éditions 1990.

and distinct forms, in the thirteenth century. In his own use of reason in theology, William seemed to fear – sometimes obsessively – what he construed as the excessive role assigned to reason by William of Conches, Gilbert de la Porrée and Abelard. Doubtless these more humanistic theologians sometimes erred on the side of what later centuries called rationalism. But their basic rational model of reasoned *conversatio* was not rationalist, despite the fears of Bernard and William.

A much needed future theological task for Trinitarian theology, I suggest, is a newly thought-through union of the intelligence-in-act analyses in the Trinitarian theologies of Augustine and Aquinas with the love-in-act analyses in the Trinitarian theologies of William, Richard of St Victor and Bonaventure. Through such a dual approach the interdependence of love-knowledge, of *affectus-intellectus* would find its full actuality in a new Trinitarian theology based on the interdependence of reason and love with love as the primary drive: the desire to know is grounded ultimately in the desire for the Good. Such a union for love and knowledge for a new Trinitarian theology and spirituality remains a difficult but possible future task for all Trinitarian theologians who know the more intellectualist approaches to a Trinitarian theology of Augustine and Aquinas as well as the more love-centred and spiritual-experience grounded Trinitarian theologies of William of St Thierry and Bonaventure.

It seems a fair surmise that William of St. Thierry would have been fully capable of such a further development in his own Trinitarian theology if he had given more sustained attention in his description of stage one to his mentor Augustine's analysis of intelligence-in-act. If he had, perhaps William would also have spared us the one major stain on his record: his rush to judgment, his almost obstinate refusal to provide a more judicious assessment of the more intellectualist but not necessarily rationalist positions of William of Conches, Gilbert de la Porrée and, above all, Peter Abelard. Perhaps the unfortunate clash between William and Abelard was inevitable – as inevitable as other theological clashes in the modern period between Luis de Molino and Domingo Bañez, Karl Barth and Paul Tillich, Hans Urs von Balthasar and Karl Rahner. Rationalism was Abelard's temptation but his theology was humanistic rather than rationalist. Fideism was William's temptation but his theology was spiritual rather than fideistic.

Finally, my analysis of the Trinitarian theology of William of St Thierry should not end on a negative note. We all always need greater theological balance in one form or another. At central moments in the history of theology, a balance of reason and faith, intelligence and love, experience and critique, *affectus* and *intellectus* have often split apart into clashes, often fierce, between different theological models.

In the welcome pluralism of theologies in the twelfth century as in our own, one hopes for theologies that will prove *diversa sed non adversa*. But theologians too are 'human all too human': differences all too quickly can become intractable oppositions. We still need both critical theologies in the tradition of Abelard and experiential theologies in the tradition of William. One often learns best from a theological tradition different from one's own, as I have tried in this essay to learn from and appropriate as much as I can of the spiritually profound, the intellectually sharp and the magnetic attraction of William of St Thierry's Trinitrian theology and spirituality.

In William, a Trinitarian theology should be mystical; a mystical theology should be Trinitarian. All contemporary Trinitarian theologians should consider anew how, by studying the complex and profound Trinitarian theology of William of St Thierry, they too may discover some extremely fruitful suggestions on how to relate in explicit, stage by stage terms Trinitarian theory to experience, *affectus* to *intellectus*; Trinitarian spirituality to Trinitarian theology. It is also not so difficult to imagine some further expansion by some future theologian of William's Trinitarian theology which will be achieved by adding some more critical uses of reason in theology in the mode of Abelard and modern critical theology: a difficult task but not, in principle, an impossible one when theology moves past its present impasse where *diversa sed non adversa* theologies seem utopian. Let the final words be William of St Thierry's as central clues for contemporary Trinitarian theology:

> *Amor ipse intellectus est.*
> *Amor noster est Spiritus.*

# PART FIVE

# New Systematic Perspective

# 18

# How does God enter into Theology? Reasons for the Centrality of Trinitarian Discourse in Christian Dogmatics

## Robert J. Woźniak

It is well known that Trinitarian theology has undergone recently a thorough reconstruction and renovation.[1] The first result of such renewal is the new location Trinitarian theology has achieved in the whole structure of Christian theology. In the present – as it was until the high medieval period – the Trinity is placed in the very centre of theological endeavour. 'If a universe – affirms Leupp – may be defined as innumerable realities shaped by and answering to a primary organizing principle, then the Christian conviction of God as triune is the centre of the theological

---

[1] Cf. S. Grenz, *Rediscovering the Triune God. The Trinity in Contemporary Theology*, Minneapolis: Fortress Press 2004; V. Holzer, 'Le renouveau de la théologie trinitaire au XXe siècle', in V. Holzer and E. Durand, *Les sources du renouveau de la théologie trinitaire au XXe siècle*, (Cogitatio Fidei, 266), Paris: Cerf 2008, pp. 9–16; P. Coda, 'Le renouveau de la théologie trinitaire au XXe siècle: le fait et les enjeux' in Holzer and Durand, *Les sources du renouveau de la théologie trinitaire*, pp. 19–31.

universe.'[2] One can ask: *why is it this way?* In my opinion, the time has come to reflect more about the theo-*onto*-logical roots of the decision to put the meditation on the Trinity at the centre of theological universe.[3] What are the reasons that justify such centrality?

The present article is aimed at exposing and describing some of the basic waves of the above-mentioned renewal in modern theology as far as they have caused the 'coming back'[4] of Trinitarian theology to the centre of Christian thinking. There were the concrete new theological projects of accessing the mystery of God's inner life in twentieth-century theology which can be used as a solid ground for our purpose. I think especially about the Trinitarian propositions of Karl Barth (1900–1968), Karl Rahner (1904–1984) and Bernard Lonergan (1904–1984). They are directly responsible for the renovation of Trinitarian consciousness after its eclipse in late modern theology.[5] Each of the authors represents highly developed Trinitarian theologies saturated by the new technical solutions of old issues in Trinitarian systematics and placed in the modern philosophical sensibility. Both Barth and Rahner alike have contributed to this area of theological studies. Their discoveries, propositions and solutions have

---

[2] R. T. Leupp, *Renewal of Trinitarian Theology: Themes, Patterns and Exploration*, Downers Grove: IVP Academic, 2008, p. 19.

[3] The issue of centrality of Trinitarian Theology we are adressing here has to be distinguished from the question of the location of *De Deo Trino* in dogmatics. What I am intending to do is to show the fundamental character of Trinitarian faith for the whole body of dogmatics. On the location of the Trinitarian treatise, cf. O. Bayer, 'Die Mitte am Ende. Der Ort der Trinitätslehre in der Dogmatik', in M. Welker and M. Volf, *Der Lebendige Gott als Trinität*. FS J. Moltmann, München: Gütersloher Verlagshaus 2006, pp. 114–22.

[4] Contemporary historical research constantly discovers new proofs of the past centrality of Trinitarian theology in Christian theology. Among important works one can enumerate K. Anatolios, *Athanasius: the Coherence of his Thought*, (Routledge Early Church Monogrpahs), London-New York: Routledge 2004; G. Emery, *La Trinité créatrice. Trinité et création dans les commentaires aux Sentences de Thomas d'Aquin et de ses précurseurs Albert Le Grand et Bonaventure*, (Bibliothèque Thomiste), Paris: Vrin 2002; ibid., *The Trinitarian Theology of Saint Thomas Aquinas*, Oxford: Oxford University Press 2010; R. J. Woźniak, *Primitas et plenitudo. Dios Padre na la teología trinitaria de San Buenaventura*, (Teológica 117), Pamplona: Eunsa 2007; P. Kärkkäinen (ed.), *Trinitarian Theology in the Medieval West*, (Schriften der Luther-Agricola-Gesellschaft, 61), Helsinki: Luther-Agricola Society 2007 and R. L. Friedman, *Medieval Trinitarian Thought from Aquinas to Ockham*, Cambridge: Cambridge University Press, 2010. These studies show that the Trinity appeared in ancient and medieval theology as the absolute centre of thological reflection, which oriented all other systematic doctrinal insights. Nonetheless, it was contemporary theology which attempted to justify systematically such a centrality. It seems that the major eclipse of Trinitarian theology after the Middle Ages was due to the *frammentazione* of the dogmatic corpus. Modern theology is characterized by a strong intent at defragmentization; cf. G. Lorizio and S. Muratore (eds), *La frammentazione del sapere teologico*. Atti del Convegno Lateranense del 6–7 dicembre 1996, Cinisello Balsamo: Edizioni San Paolo, 1998.

[5] Leupp, *Rediscovering the Triune God*, pp. 6–32.

helped very much to encounter once again the whole truth of Trinitarian faith of the Church in its totality and theoretical-existential beauty. One can admit – and it is my personal main thesis and argument here – that Trinitarian theologies of Barth, Rahner and Lonergan – taking into account all their limitations and failures – refocused all of the theological themes and issues in the Trinitarian mystery. The description of the manner in which it was achieved is the aim of this article.

In short: what I am trying to show and explain in the following presentation are the reasons for the centrality of Trinitarian truth in the theological and practical life of Christians as we can discover them arising from the new theological sensibility that appeared in European theology in the twentieth century. The plan of my investigation is as follow. I will start chronologically with a consideration of Barth's emphasis on the unity between Trinitarian theology and the event of revelation. Then I will move to the analysis of Rahner's *Grundaxiom* as the basic principle of the identity between *theology* and *economy*. After a description of the meaning of Barth, Rahner and Lonergan for the issue I am addressing, I will try to show the basic Christological ground of the centrality of Trinitarian theology (functional Christology). At the end of the argument I will sketch my own proposition of how to explain and ground theologically the centrality of the Trinity in a Christian theological and practical worldview.

# Trinity and Revelation: Karl Barth's Approach

Barth's Trinitarian theology belongs to one of the most interesting and stimulating chapters of the global history of this theological discipline. It was Barth who awakened the renewed interest in the Trinity in the Christian theology of various denominations.[6] The nucleus of Barth's approach to the Trinity has a formal character. His Trinitarianism is developed as an inner moment of the foundational reflection on the basis of theology as a discipline. For Barth, the Trinity is indissolubly connected with the event of revelation which consists in the unique base of Christian theology and its possibility.[7] Theology is Trinitarian or it is not Christian theology at all.

---

[6] As a matter of fact he was doing this out of a catholic influence; cf. B. McCormack, 'The Doctrine of the Trinity After Barth: An Attempt to Reconstruct Barth's Doctrine in the Light of His Later Christology', in M. Habets and P. Tolliday, (eds), *Trinity After Barth*, Eugene, OR: Cascade Books, 2010, forthcoming.

[7] It leads to direct although *impilicit* affirmation of the unity of immanent and economic Trinity; cf. E. Durand, '"Trinité immanent" et "Trinité économique" selon Karl Barth. Déclinaisons de la distinction et son dépassement (Aufhebung)', in *Revue des sciences philosophiques et théologiques* 90/3 (2006) 453–78, 'Entre "Trinité immanente" et "Trinité économique" existe

For the author of *Kirchlische Dogmatik* the starting point of his reflection is always God's speech: *Deus dixit*.[8] On this point, Barth shares with Saint Bonaventure[9] the conviction that somehow theology is already always the matter of God who speaks, who revels Himself to humans.[10] In this way God is not only the quasi-object of theology but its subject as well. This is why Saint Bonaventure insists on the identity of Scripture and theology: *sacra Scriptura quam theologia dicitur*.[11] Theology is the very speech of God, His auto-presentation. Only God knows Himself, only He can share with humans His own knowledge about Himself making in this way His inaccessibility and hiddeness accessible and visible.[12] Theology is a function of God's *self*-manifestation and *self*-revelation. The act of God revealing Himself, the divine act of giving Himself to be known and recognized, is the radical and unavoidable ground of theology. It flows directly from Barth's conviction that 'God is known by God and by God alone.' (*Gott wird durch Gott, Gott wird nur durch Gott erkannt*).[13]

Why does such communication imply God's triunity? Why does revelation in its Christian sense have to be considered as Trinitarian? Basically, it is because of the Trinitarian structure of divine self-presentation in the Holy Scripture,[14] which is said to be the written Word of God (*das geschriebene Wort Gottes*)[15] which attests to the revelation.[16] It is the Bible which directs our gaze into the mystery of God's Word as the highest expression of the divine subject (divine *Ich*) revealing himself:

---

une triple relation, selon laquelle la "Trinité immanent" est le fondement (*Grund*), la possibilité (*Möglichkeit*) et le prototype (*Urbild*) de la "Trinité économique"'.

[8] It is true from the very beginning of the theological production of Barth. Such a point of departure can be met already in his first attempt at Christian dogmatic which we can find in his early lectures in Gottingen; cf. K. Barth, *Unterricht in der christlichen Religion*, I, *Prolegomena*, (KBG, 17) Zurich: Thelogische Verlag 1985, pp. 53–82. On the origin and meaning of this phrase in early Barth, cf. B. McCormack, *Karl Barth's Critical Realistic Dialectical Theology: Its Genesis and Development 1909–1936*, Oxford: Clarendon Press 1997, pp. 337–46.

[9] As a matter of fact Barth has dedicated a lot of attention to Saint Bonaventure's *Breviloquium*; cf. K. Barth, *Theology of John Calvin*, Grand Rapids: Eerdmans 1995, p. 27.

[10] Cf. E. Falque, *Saint Bonaventure et l'entrée de Dieu en théologie*, (Études de philosophie médiévale), Paris: Vrin 2002.

[11] Bonaventure, *Brev.*, Prol., (V, 26a).

[12] H. Bouillard, *Karl Barth*, III, *Parole de Dieu et existence humaine*, (Théologie), Paris: Aubier 1957, p. 185.

[13] Barth, *CD* II/I, p. 179 (*KD* II/I, pp. 200nn.)

[14] Barth, *CD* I/1, p. 298 (*KD* I/1, p. 314): 'Thus it is God Himself, it is the same God in unimpaired unity, who according to the biblical understanding of revelation is the revealing God and the event of revelation and its effect on man', and 'It is only – but very truly – by observing the unity and the differentiation of God (*Einheit und Verschiedenheit*) in His biblically attested revelation that we are set before the problem of the doctrine of Trinity.'

[15] Barth, *CD* I/1, pp. 99–111 (*KD* I/1, pp. 101–13).

[16] Barth, *CD* I/1, p. 307 (*KD* I/1, p. 324).

According to Scripture – writes Barth – God's revelation is God's own direct speech which is not to be distinguished from the act of speaking (*nicht zu unterscheiden von dem Akt dieses Redens*) and therefore is not to be distinguished from God Himself, from the divine I (*von dem göttlichen Ich*) which confronts man in this act in which it says Thou to him. Revelation is *Dei loquentis persona*. From the standpoint of the comprehensive concept of God's Word it must be said that here in God's revelation God's Word is identical with God Himself (*ist Gottes Wort identisch mit Gott selbst*).[17]

The cited text shows the realism of Barth's identification between God's being and act on the one hand and God's Word on the other.[18] When God speaks, His speaking is identical with His being. As a matter of fact God's speech is God Himself: 'if we are dealing with his revelation, we are dealing with God himself.'[19] The identification of God's being (*Gott selbst*) and his Word (*Gottes Wort*) makes space for further assumptions.

Barth's Trinitarianism in its inner stress on the event of revelation places the Trinity at the very heart of theology because it is a revelation which consists in the ground (Barth says *die Wurzel*, root) of human speech about God and to God (theology). We can think and talk about God because *Deus dixit*. For Barth *Deus dixit* is already always the basic event of revelation – although indirectly[20] – the Trinitarian statement. In this way Barth's approach could be labelled a formal one because of its inherent epistemological-foundational character. Barth as heir of a protestant anti-philosophical tradition does not need any ontological proof of the Trinitarian structure of Christian faith. His theological epistemology mediated in the personalism of the revelatory *Deus dixit* conducts him freely and spontaneously towards the basic Trinitarian ingredient of every single theological statement. The existence of a theological statement which is not at the same time a Trinitarian articulation of the mystery of God is – from the perspective of Barth's doctrine of revelation as the ground of theology – impossible. As far as theology is based on revelation, its every single statement is a Trinitarian one and has to be read in a Trinitarian way.[21]

---

[17] Barth, *CD* I/1, p. 304 (*KD* I/1, p. 320).

[18] Barth, *CD* I/1, p. 296 (*KD* I/1, p. 312).

[19] Barth, *CD* I/1, p. 311 (*KD* I/1, pp. 328–9).

[20] Barth, *CD* I/1, p. 308–9 (*KD* I/1, pp. 325–6): 'The statement or statements about God's Trinity cannot claim to be directly identical (*direct identisch zu sein*) with the statement about revelation or with revelation itself' and 'to call revelation the root of the doctrine of the Trinity is also to say that the statement or statements about the Trinity of God purport to be indirectly, though not directly, identical (*nicht direct, aber indirect identisch sein*) with the statement about revelation.'

[21] Barth, *Unterricht*, I, p. 105: 'Der Inhalt der Offenbarung ist Gott allein, Gott ganz, Gott selber'.

Barth's basic Trinitarian conviction is expressed in the decision to place his doctrine of the Trinity in the very centre of the *prolegomena* to his dogmatics. For Barth the prolegomena to dogmatics is 'the attempt to give an explicit account of the particular way of knowledge taken in the dogmatics, or as we might also say, of the particular point from which we are to look, think and judge (*gesehen, gedacht und geurteilt*) in dogmatics.'[22] In other words, the prolegomena to the science 'consists decisively in discussions and expositions of how knowledge is attendant in it (*wie es in der betreffenden Wissenschaft zum Wissen kommt*).'[23] Let us put it this way: the prolegomena to dogmatics is explication of the theological way to knowledge.

The Trinity occupies the privileged place in such an understood prolegomena. It guarantees the proper place of Trinitarian thinking in the whole body of theology. Trinity appears in it not as one of the topics, but as the essential one. It appears because of the very nature of theology itself, which is founded on the event of revelation. And the event of revelation is strictly a Trinitarian one. 'The crucial question for the concept of revelation, that of the God who reveals Himself, cannot be answered apart from the answer to this question given in the doctrine of the Trinity. The doctrine of the Trinity is itself the answer that must be given here.'[24]

One has to acknowledge that the placement of Trinitarian theology in the prolegomena to the dogmatics is Barth's fundamental and original idea.[25] It results in an innovative methodology and shapes the fundamental structure of his insight into the mystery of Trinitarian life. In reality such a decision unifies the methodological and material dimensions of theology. The medium of such unification is Trinitarian theology itself:

> In giving this doctrine a place of prominence, our concern cannot be merely that it have this place externally but rather that its content be decisive and controlling for the whole of dogmatics (*daß ihr Gehalt für die ganze Dogmatik entscheidend und beherrschend werde*). The problem of the Trinity has met us in the question put to the Bible about revelation. When we ask: Who is the self-revealing God (*wer ist der sich offenbarende Gott*), the Bible answers in such a way that we have to reflect on the triunity of God (*Dreieinigkeit Gottes*). The two other questions: What does this God do and what does he effect? (*was tut und was wirkt dieser Gott*) are also answered primarily, as we have seen, by new answers to the first question: Who is He (*Wer ist Er*)?[26]

---

[22] Barth *CD* I/1, p. 25 (*KD* I/1, p. 24).

[23] Barth *CD* I/1, p. 25 (*KD* I/1, p. 24).

[24] Barth, *CD* I/1, 312 (*KD* I/1, 330).

[25] Barth, *CD* I/1, p. 300 (*KD* I/1, 316).

[26] Barth, *CD* I/1, p. 303 (*KD* I/1, 319).

The Trinity is a true base of theological thinking. Barth describes its influence on the totality of theological issues using two concepts: Trinitarian theology is decisive, and it controls the whole of dogmatics. We can state that it is Trinitarian theology which decides the inner shape of Christian dogmatics. The 'problem of the Trinity' (*das Problem der Trinitätslehre*) shapes Christian dogmatics. It is the very nucleus of the theological universe, its innate (because of revelation) form.

The decisiveness of Trinitarian theology in dogmatics gives to it, on the other hand, the controlling role over the totality of concrete solutions and affirmations. In Barth's view, there are three main questions/issues in dogmatics: who is God, what does he do, and what does he effect/achieve? Trinitarian theology is the answer to all these three basic theological questions. What directly proceeds from such a perspective is the fact that Christian dogmatics is focused for Barth on the one problem, namely the problem of God in his revelation. The questions of divine acting (both as *Tun* and *Wirkung*) are reduced and synthesized in one basic '*who is God?*' Divine simplicity requires us to think about God's deeds in the horizon of His eternal being, but it requires us also to think about every single theological/dogmatical question from within a Trinitarian perspective. Trinitarian theology is radically normative. 'The criticism and correction of Church proclamation' – affirms Barth – 'must be done today, as it was then, in the form of a developing doctrine of the Trinity.'[27]

In this way, Barth locates himself once again in the line of the greatest theologians who have always admitted that the unique problem[28] of theology is God and the mystery of his salvific revelation. Theology is simply about God (*theo*-logia).[29] For Barth, it means that it is about God who presented Himself (revealed Himself) to us in His absolute freedom

---

[27] Barth, *CD* I/1, p. 311 (*KD*, I/1, 328).

[28] For some specification and useful distinctions in understanding what is *subiectum* and *obiectum* of the science, cf. J.-F. Courtine, *Suarez et le système de la métaphysique*, (Épiméthée), Paris: PUF 1990, pp. 10nn.

[29] Cf. for instance Thomas Aquinas and his deliberations on the problem of the *subiectum* of theology in STh I, q. 1, a. 7, resp.: Deus est subiectum huius scientiae (*theology*). Sic enim se habet subiectum ad scientiam, sicut obiectum ad potentiam vel habitum. Proprie autem illud assignatur obiectum alicuius potentiae vel habitus, sub cuius ratione omnia referuntur ad potentiam vel habitum, sicut homo et lapis referuntur ad visum inquantum sunt colorata, unde coloratum est proprium obiectum visus. Omnia autem pertractantur in sacra doctrina sub ratione Dei, vel quia sunt ipse Deus; vel quia habent ordinem ad Deum, ut ad principium et finem. Unde sequitur quod Deus vere sit subiectum huius scientiae. Quod etiam manifestum fit ex principiis huius scientiae, quae sunt articuli fidei, quae est de Deo, idem autem est subiectum principiorum et totius scientiae, cum tota scientia virtute contineatur in principiis. Quidam vero, attendentes ad ea quae in ista scientia tractantur, et non ad rationem secundum quam considerantur, assignaverunt aliter subiectum huius scientiae, vel res et signa; vel opera reparationis; vel totum Christum, idest caput et membra. De omnibus enim istis tractatur in ista scientia, sed secundum ordinem ad Deum.

as He really is: Father, Son and Holy Spirit. Trinity is the central point of theology because *sacra doctrina* is grounded in the very event and structure of revelation as the theological *factum*.[30] And revelation is a Trinitarian act. In virtue of this, every single theological statement being grounded in the revelation has to be – at least *implicite* – Trinitarian.

# Rahner and Lonergan: Trinity and Onto-epistemological Realism of the Event of Grace

What interests us here is the *identity thesis* which forms the main part of Rahner's basic Trinitarian assumption (*Grundaxiom*) if not its absolute centre and crucial ingredient. Even if it is not an original Rahner discovery,[31] it becomes – in the very precise formulation proposed by a German theologian – a very nucleus of his Trinitarian proposition. Trinitarian theology for Rahner can be said to be the meditation on the unity and identity of the different orders.

What is the base of Rahner's thinking about Trinity? First we have to affirm after Rahner that theology of the Trinity has to be drawn back once again to its historical horizon.[32] By this Rahner means two basic things. The first is the articulation of the historical roots of the possibility of our knowing the Trinity. We know something about God's very inner life only because it happened in our world and in our human historical time. The second basic thing is that the doctrine of the Trinity has to be revitalized. It is solidly Rahner's conviction that during the centuries Trinitarian theology

---

[30] Cf. B. Bourgine, *L'herméneutique théologique de Karl Barth. Exégèse et dogmatique dans le quatrième volume de la 'Kirchliche Dogmatik'*, (Bibliotheca Ephemeridum Theologicarum Lovaniensium), Leuven: Peeters 2003, pp. 165–261.

[31] The interpenetration of eternity and history is one of the most basic topics of Christian theology from its beginning (Irenaeus, Clement, Origen); cf. G. Maspero, 'La teologia della storia di Gregorio di Nissa', in *Excerpta e dissertationibus in Sacra Theologia*, University of Navarra, 45 (2003) 383–451; G. Richter, *Oikonomia. Der Gebrauch des Wortes Oikonomia im Neuen Testament, bei den Kirchenvätern und in der theologischen Literatur bis ins 20. Jahrhundert*, (Arbeiten zur Kirchengeschichte, 90), Tübingen: Walter de Gruyter 2005.

[32] Rahner, *Trinity*, New York: Herder and Herder 2001 (ibid., 'Der dreifaltige Gott als Transcendenter Urgrund der Heilsgeschichte', in J. Feiner and M. Löhrer, *Mysterium Salutis. Grundriss Heilsgechichtlischer Dogmatik*, II, Einsiedeln-Zürich-Köln: Benzinger Verlag 1967). Cf. Rahner's critical remarks on the psychological theory of the Trinity in K. Rahner, *Foundations of Christian Faith. An Introduction to the Idea of Christianity*, New York: Crossroad 1978, p. 135; and R. Jenson, *Systematic Theology*, I, *Trinity*, Oxford: Oxford University Press 2001, p. 112.

was isolated from its existential and liturgical context.[33] Instead of being conceived as a crucial soteriological statement and reality in Christianity, it was reduced to being merely a sophisticated doctrine, a logical-theological syllogism. Such a methodological approach led directly to the point of an unnatural separation and to a far-reaching separation between different treatises of dogmatic theology.[34] The result was a decentralization and fragmentation of catholic dogmatics as such. The first fruit of such a procedure was the strict separation of *De Deo Uno* and *De Deo Trino*. It was followed by the disappearance of Trinitarian consciousness not only from theology but also from popular piety.[35]

Saying this, let us turn to Rahner's central thesis. We can find it in various formulations. The classical one is from his *Der dreifaltige Gott als transzendenter Urgrund der Heilsgeschichte*. It states:

> The basic thesis (*Grundaxiom*) which establishes this connection between the treatises and presents the Trinity as a mystery of salvation (in its reality and not merely as a doctrine) might be formulated as follows: The economic Trinity is the immanent Trinity and the immanent Trinity is the economic Trinity.[36]

The very heart of this *Grundaxiom* is – as we noted above – the identity thesis. The Trinity of the history of salvation *is* the real, immanent Trinity. God appeared among us as He really is in His inner Trinitarian life. Rahner intends to establish with his *Grundaxiom* the ultimate theological foundation[37] for the possible realistic reading of the history of salvation. There is a very strong will in Rahner's theology to maintain the firm conviction of the theological tradition of the Church which always claimed the *akoluthia*[38] between theo-logy (God's inner reality) and the mystery of dispensation (His soteriological involvement in human history). Rahner maintains such *akoluthia*, stressing the unity and continuity of its subject: God in His inner life and God in His economical actuation is the same God. In order to save us and come to us, God does not use any kind of

---

[33] Rahner, *Trinity*, pp. 10–15 ('Der dreifaltige Gott', pp. 319–23).

[34] Rahner, *Trinity*, pp. 15–21 ('Der dreifaltige Gott', pp. 323–7).

[35] K. Rahner, 'Remarks on the dogmatic treatise "De Trinitate"', in K. Rahner, *Theological Investigation*, IV, *More Recent Writings*, Baltimore-London: Helicon Press-Darton, Longman and Todd 1966, p. 79.

[36] Rahner, *Trinity*, pp. 21–2 ('Der dreifaltige Gott', pp. 327–9, here esp. p. 328).

[37] K. Kilby, *Karl Rahner: Theology and Philosophy*, London-New York: Routledge 2004, pp. 70nn.

[38] On the topic of *akoluthia* as a theological (especially Trinitarian) concept, cf. H. Drobner, 'Fuentes y métodos filosóficos de Gregorio de Nisa', in *Teología y vida* 43 (2002) 205–15.

intermediary beings, He comes Himself as He is in His eternal life; He 'appears in immediacy'.[39]

In the process of interpreting Rahner's *Grundaxiom* one ought to avoid some possible hermeneutics of identity thesis.[40] According to the reading of Denis W. Jowers, the interpretations that should be omitted are: trivially obvious identity, absolute identity, copy theory and merely *de facto* theory.[41] The true meaning of the thesis can be reached at some point between very strict (absolute) ontological identity and merely theo-metaphorical or moral relation theory (identity of manifestation only). There is a real relation or correspondence between God's inner Trinitarian life and His self-manifestation in history (time and place). Jowers describes this relation from the *genetic* viewpoint: 'the immanent constitution of the Trinity forms a kind of *a priori* law for the divine self-communication *ad extra* such that the structure of the latter cannot but correspond to the structure of the former.'[42] In other words: for Rahner there is no equivalency or identity between *is* from the first part of the basic axiom and *is* from the second part (*vice versa*).[43] Nonetheless there is identity between the immanent and the economic Trinity.

The correspondence between the orders of Trinitarian life and its economic self-manifestation reveals its truth, meaning and nature in Rahner's theology of grace. Basically, Rahner's Trinitarian theology is grounded in his comprehension of the nature of sanctifying grace.[44] This is the economy of grace which dictates the necessity of correspondence of the immanent and the economic Trinity:

> Twofold mediation by Word and Spirit (as shown even more clearly in the history of the self-revealing self-communication) is not a mediation on the plane of the created, where God would not be imparted really as

---

[39] Rahner, *Foundations*, p. 136.

[40] Rahner's *Grundaxiom* has given rise to very serious theological debate; cf. S. Cichon-Brandmaier, *Ökonomische und immanente Trinität. Eine Vergleich der Konzeptionen Karl Rahners und Hans Urs von Balthasar*, Regensburg: Pustet 2008, pp. 78–92. One has to admit that even if von Balthasar was opposed to the Grundaxiom, his theology shares with Rahner´s identical premises, namely strong conviction of the reality of God's involvement in the history of the world. On Balthasar´s theology of the relations between immanent and economic Trinity, see: Cichon-Brandmaier, *Ökonomische und immanente Trinität*, pp. 186–99.

[41] D. W. Jowers, *The Trinitarian Axiom of Karl Rahner. The Economic Trinity is the Immanent Trinity and vice versa*, Lewiston: Mellen Press 2006, pp. 88nn.

[42] Jowers, *Trinitarian Axiom*, pp. 89–90.

[43] L. F. Ladaria, 'La teologia trinitaria de Karl Rahner. Un balance de la discussion', in *Gregorianum* 86 (2005) 283.

[44] J. P. Galvin, 'The Invitation of Grace', in L. J. O'Donovan, *A World of Grace: An Introduction to the Themes and Foundations of Karl Rahner's Theology*, Washington D.C.: Georgetown University Press 1995, pp. 64–75, esp. p. 67.

Himself. According to the testimony of faith, the salvific self-communication of God is really threefold, and a Sabelian view of the economy
of salvation is false. And again the modes of being whereby God comes
to us are not created intermediaries or powers of this world. Such a
basically Arian view of God's gift would eliminate all real self-communication and reduce the eschatological event of salvation in Christ to
the level of a series of provisional and incomplete mediations, such as
prophets and servants of the Lord, angelic powers or descending emanations of the Gnostic or Neoplatonic type. Thus the real communication,
divine in nature, which takes place in the dimension of salvation, must
also *be* a real communication in God's own immanent life. The 'trinity' of
the relationship of God to us in the order of the grace of Christ is nothing
other than the reality of God as it is in itself: a 'Trinity of persons'.[45]

The quotation represents some kind of different formulation of *Grundaxiom*.
This time it implies the open (*explicite*) treatment of the theological origin
of Rahner's Trinitarian thinking. From this point of view the necessity of
the historical and soteriological understanding of the actual meaning of
*Grundaxiom* is confirmed. Rahner explains here the fundamental motive,
which is at the same time the basic structure of Christian thinking and
action, which led him to the formulation of his basic thesis. This is obviously
the real communication of God in uncreated grace. The basic statement of
Christianity is the self-communication of God to humans. God really gives
Himself to his creature as He is in His eternal life. What Rahner seeks
to prevent in his *Grundaxiom* is the integrity of the basic grammar of
Christianity constituted by the strong conviction of soteriological realism.[46]
'In the Trinity in the economy and history of salvation and revelation we
have already experienced the immanent Trinity as it is in itself.'[47] This is
really God who saves us giving us a share in His own mystery.[48]
    What interests us here is the interconnection of Trinitarian theology
and a soteriologically orientated theology of grace. Rahner's *Grundaxiom*
establishes mutual correspondence between them. The Trinitarian theology
is the very heart of the event of grace. On the other hand, the reality of
grace and its theological treatment (the dogmatic treatise on grace) is part
of Trinitarian speculation. In this way, Rahner achieves the fusion of two
great poles and camps of Christian theology. The inner mystery of God is
the real centre of the mystery of salvation, which occurs as the *inhabitatio*

---

[45] Rahner, 'Remarks on dogmatic treatise', pp. 97–8.
[46] Cf. R. J. Woźniak, 'Metafiyzka i Trójca. Teo-ontologia trynitarna między apofatyką i
katafatyką', in ibid., *Metafizyka i teologia. Debata u podstaw*, (Myśl Teologiczna, 62),
Krakow: WAM 2008, pp. 270–304.
[47] Rahner, *Foundations*, p. 137.
[48] Rahner, *Trinity*, p. 36 ('Der dreifaltige Gott', p. 338).

*Dei* (which is already always Trinitarian *inhabitatio*)[49] in man transformed by divine grace. At the same time divine *inhabitatio* is grounded in free self-communication (*Selbstmitteilung*) of divine life.

All these theoretical affirmations help Rahner to bring once again the Trinity to the very heart of the Christian doctrine of salvation. Trinity is not any more mere speculation separated from the everyday life of man. It becomes its very centre. Precisely the existential potential and meaning of the Trinitarian mystery as the reality told in Christian dogmatics resituates it into the very heart of the whole body of Christian doctrine.

I mean by this that the unification of the theological and economical perspectives in Rahner produces a far reaching centralization of dogmatics itself. If the self-manifestation and self-donation of the immanent Trinity is the real centre of the history of salvation, dogmatics and theology as such receive a new and robust unity. Trinity enters into theology not as a theorem of speculative reason. It appears as the theme in theology in virtue of the real God's threefold self-dispensation as the Father, Son and the Holy Spirit.[50] God appears in theology (therefore we can know Him) because He appeared already in the world and in human interiority as the event of sanctifying grace mediated and operated in the historical coming of Christ-Logos-Son and Pneuma:[51]

---

[49] Rahner, *Trinity*, p. 36, note 34 ('Der dreifaltige Gott', p. 338). Rahner's explanation of this is as follow: 'It follows as a formal axiom that if the distinction present in something communicated by God exists *only* on the creature's side, then there is no *self*-communication of God in the strict sense. If, on the other hand, there is a real *self*-communication with a real distinction in that which is communicated as such, hence with a real distinction "for us", then God must "in Himself" carry this distinction. [...] Hence we may say that if revelation (a) testifies to a real *self*-communication and (b) explains this self-communication as containing distinctions "for us", that is, considers it as mediated, of a mediation that is not merely created (which would do away with the character of a real self-communication), then it affirms *ipso facto* a distinction and mediation in God as He is in Himself'. Cf. Rahner, *Trinity*, pp. 99–101.

[50] Rahner, *Foundations*, p. 136: 'In so far as the modes of God's presence for us as Spirit, Son and Father do not signify the same modes of presence, in so far as there really are true and real differences in the modes of presence for us, these three modes of presence for us are to be strictly distinguished. Father, Son-Logos and Spirit are first of all not the same "for us". But insofar as these modes of presence of one and the same God for us may not nullify the real self-communication of God as the one and only and same God, the three modes o presence of one and the same God must belong to Him as one and the same God, they must belong to Him in Himself and for Himself.'

[51] Rahner, *Trinity*, p. 55 ('Der dreifaltige Gott', p. 352): 'Concepts of dogma as such, in their 'logical' explanation, always refer back to the origin from which they come: the experience of faith which assures us that the incomprehensible God is really, as He is in Himself, given to us in the (for us) twofold reality of Christ and his Spirit, and which forbids us to think of this (for us) double reality (the way in which God's self-communication comes to us) in a modalistic way, as merely the result of a mental distinction deriving from our intelligence. For this would do away with the self-communication of God; it would no longer let God come to us as He is in Himself; thus modalism and Arianism belong together.'

The Trinity itself is with us; – affirms Rahner – it is not merely given to us because revelation offers us statements about it. Rather these statements are made to us because the reality of which they speak is bestowed upon *us*. They are made because the grace we have received and the glory we expect cannot wholly become manifest if we are not told about this mystery.[52]

In the background of the fusion of the traditional orders of Christian theological reflection into one organic structure, Rahner observes inseparable togetherness of existential and noetic-epistemic dimensions of Christian being. The order of knowing and thinking (the epistemic dimension of Trinitarian theology) is based in the existential-ontological reality of *inhabitatio* (the reality of Trinitarian-shaped self-donation of God to His creatures in *gratia increata*).[53] Divine Trinitarian self-donation is already always *conditio sine qua non* of knowing Trinity. We come to know God only because he is present inside our transformed *humanity*. Following Rahner, and adding a little bit to his own theory, we can affirm that Trinitarian theology occupies the very heart of Christian dogmatic first of all because it is God Himself who transforms our understanding by His indwelling in the transformed person. First there is 'the *reality* of God bestowed on us', then comes the transformation of human understanding.[54] The unity of an existential (ontological or *quasi*-formal) and epistemic moment of *inhabitation* leads directly to the discovery of what is at stake in *Grundaxiom*.

If the history of salvation is to present its serious character, one has to acknowledge that the Trinitarian event we are considering now is a *free*[55] gift grounded in the very life of God. God comes to the world as He really is in Himself. The seriousness and realism of this coming oblige theology to treat the whole created reality in the light of the free event of the Trinitarian life which happens among us. From such a standpoint the Rahnerian reason for the centrality of the Trinity in Christian theology is simple: the very fact of transforming *inhabitation*, in all its seriousness and definitiveness, requires that theology ought to be always about the Trinity as mystery in itself and mystery for us.[56] The factual unity of *in itself* and *for us* gives theology its inner form (its *logos*) which is the centre-structured mediation

---

[52] Rahner, *Trinity*, p. 39 ('Der dreifaltige Gott', p. 340).

[53] Cf. J.-B. Lecuit, *Quand Dieu habite en l'homme. Pour une approche dialogale de l'inhabitation trinitaire*, (Cogitatio Fidei, 271), Paris: Cerf 2010, pp. 23–78.

[54] Cf. M. de França Miranda, *O mistério de Deus em nossa vida: a doutrina trinitária de K. Rahner*, São Paulo: Loyola 1975, p. 109.

[55] Rahner, *Trinity*, p. 36 ('Der dreifaltige Gott', p. 338).

[56] Rahner, *Foundations*, p. 136.

of God's Trinitarian being. Thus the Trinity is the main centre of theological architectonics and its inner grammar.[57]

There is very interesting clarification and further development of Rahner's intuition in Bernard Lonergan's *Trinitarian mimetic theory*, as Robert McDoran calls it. Lonergan's four-point hypothesis states that:

> there are four real divine relations, really identical with the divine substance, and therefore there are four very special modes that ground the external imitation of the divine substance. Next, there are four absolutely supernatural realities, which are never found uninformed, namely the secondary act of existence of the incarnation, sanctifying grace, the habit of charity, and the light of glory. It would not be inappropriate, therefore, to say that the secondary act of existence of the incarnation is a created participation of paternity, and so has a special relation to the Son; that sanctifying grace is a participation of active spiration, and so has a special relation to the Holy Spirit; that the habit of charity is a participation of passive spiration, and so has a special relation to the Father and the Son; and that the light of glory is a participation of sonship, and so in a most perfect way brings the children of adoption back to the Father.[58]

What is interesting here is a very detailed enumaration and further explication of the relation between the intra-Trinitarian order of processions and the reality of grace which is seen as the Trinitarian reality. Divine grace is grounded in the eternal event of divine communication of being. Such grounding allows grace to be a real participation in divine life which is offered and given to human beings by a free act of God, the Trinity. We have to deal here with a creative exploration inside the very structure of the life of grace in its relation with its origin in the Trinity. Lonergan's analytical realism of the event of grace is a kind of specification of Rahner's general theory of Trinitarian identity of immanence and economy

---

[57] This point of view is grounded very deeply in Rahner's proper transcendental ontology. The first premise of this is the strong correlation and mutual dependence between the question of God and the question of being. It is certainly Rahnerian's ontology which presupposes the open inclusion of finite and infinite being (without ontological or metaphysical univocal identification) and the overlapping nature of philosophical (metaphysical) and theological inquiries (cf. K. Rahner, *Geist in Welt*, Karl Rahner Sämtliche Werke 2, Freiburg-Basel-Wien: Herder 1996, p. 229). This kind of meta-premise (which shares obviously some fundamental thomistic convictions) opens the way to direct theological formulation of the free and gracious mutual relation of theology and economy of dispensation, grace and nature. Cf. P. Eppe, *Karl Rahner zwischen Philosophie und Theologie: Aufbruch oder Abbruch?*, (Pontes, 42), Münster: LIT Verlag 2008, pp. 99, 114, 127nn.

[58] B. Lonergan, *The Triune God: Systematics*, (BLW), Toronto: University of Toronto Press 2009, pp. 471–3.

(*Grudaxiom*). Lonergan's hypothesis shows the realism and extension of Rahner's fundamental Trinitarian presuposition.

# Towards Linguistic Articulation of the Dogmatic Centrality of the Trinity

We have considered three basic propositions of Barth, Rahner and Lonergan. They have to be treated together, never separately. Barth's argument shows that the centrality of Trinitarian thinking in theology is based on the very event of revelation which is radically the Trinitarian reality. According to Rahner's *Grundaxiom*, the serious and adequate treatment of Christianity's essence demands acceptance of basic onto-epistemological realism which claims the *identity* between God's inner life as a Trinity and His involvement in human history. Lonergan's theology of a four-point hypothesis shows the degree of reality of such involvment: it is determined by a strong relation between the immanent Trinitarian process or event of life-giving communication/production and the economical dispensation of God for his human creatures.

But there could be another reason for the centrality of Trinitarian theology in the Christian theological and practical world. It comes directly from the theological consideration of language, which is at the centre of the modern philosophical project. The nineteenth and twentieth centuries brought with them the discovery of the philosophical-ontological reality of language. For the first time in the history of human speculation we managed to grasp the deeper understanding of the nature of human speech. It was made possible by such thinkers as *Gottlob Frege* (1848–1925), *Johann Georg Hamman* (1730–1788), *Martin Heidegger*'s (1889–1976) phenomenological existentialism and a new analytical school of philosophy represented in a very special way by its symbolic thinker *Ludwig Wittgenstein* (1889–1951).[59] These thinkers gave theology reach material for its own description of language. I would even say that the contemporary philosophy of language has fortunately reminded us of the importance of acts of speech for theology itself.

Nonetheless, one has to admit that the theological discovery of language is not a fruit of the modern turn to language. Theology was interested in language from its very beginning.[60] It is this way because theology is a

---

[59] M. Morris, *An Introduction to the Philosophy of Language*, Cambridge: Cambridge University Press 2007.
[60] Cf. the fruits of contemporary historical research in the field of language: M. Canévet, *Grégoire de Nysse et l'herméneutique biblique: étude des rapports entre le langage et la connaissance de Dieu*, Paris: Etudes augustiniennes 1983; D. Scot, *Theology Of The Gap:*

linguistic exercise by its very nature. As such, it is always an uncompleted and impossible project of speaking out God in human words. Theology's first task is speaking out Anselms's *id quo maius cogitari nequit*.[61] Christian theology was aware of this from its scriptural roots. In virtue of this, language was and has to be in the very centre of theological projects from its very beginnings. The problem of language is in itself a theological issue. This is true not only from the methodological perspective but, first of all, from the material one. Language is the topic of theology. Theology is already always a linguistic project and because of this language itself has to be one of the main subjects of direct reflection in theology.

In order to understand the last statement one has to point to the very nature of language itself. What is the truth of language? What is its very being? What is its real essence? To answer these questions let us turn to Martin Heidegger's philosophy of language. Heidegger has answered these questions in a very simple way: the very essence of speech is the speech of essence itself.[62] Language is the ontological economy of being which tends to its outer manifestation in a human being. Before language speaks about something, it always speaks about the nature of being as such: language is the house of being (*das Haus des Sein*).[63] The natural goal of language is not to say this or that but to make manifest – present and open – the very truth of being itself. Through human speech the hidden reality of being is constantly made visible (*aletheia*). Language itself speaks (*das Sprechen der Sprache*)[64] or brings its own essence to the linguistic evidence.[65] The being of beings makes itself present and visible in human speech: it reveals itself, it communicates itself, it gives itself. Speech and language are revelations of being: 'the essential being of language is Saying as Showing' (*das wesende der Sprache ist die Sage als die Zeige*).[66]

Language is a means of communication of being. In the very act of speech, which always is an act of communication, human beings disclose (*a priori* or *transcendentally*) their structure of being-in-the-relation. Language reveals the truth of a human being which is always *mit-sein* and being-for the-other. Such disclosure is fundamentally communicational in the original sense of this idea which is 'making of community'. Human speech is the event which

*Cappadocian Language Theory And The Trinitarian Controversy* (American University Studies Series VII, Theology and Religion), Franfurt: Peter Lang 2005; M. Ludlow, *Gregory of Nyssa: ancient and (post)modern*, Oxford: Oxford University Press 2007, pp. 234–46, 268–79; A. Robinson, *God and the World of Signs: Trinity, Evolution, and the Metaphysical Semiotics of C. S. Peirce*, (Philosophical Studies in Science and Religion, 2), Leiden: Brill, 2010.
[61] Anselm of Canterbury, *Proslogion*, III. 2.
[62] M. Heidegger, *Unterwegs zur Sprache*, (GA 12), Franfurt: Klostermann 1985, p. 186.
[63] M. Heidegger, *Holzwege*, (GA 5), Franfurt: Klostermann 1977, p. 310.
[64] Heidegger, *Unterwegs*, p. 243.
[65] Heidegger, *Unterwegs*, p. 236.
[66] Heidegger, *Unterwegs*, p. 254.

builds up the relations between human beings (community). The very act of speech reveals the communal character of a person, its ontological tension toward the other. The linguistic being reveals in its speaking its communal nature: being is communion.[67]

The theo-logical nature of language has to do primarily with God's saving auto-communication[68] which happens in the event of incarnate Logos. Revealing Himself, God communicates Himself; the revelation is the fundamental communication of life and truth in words and deeds (*verbis gestique*).[69] Revelation in words presupposes the communicational nature of human speech and – what is even more important and basic – it constitutes it[70] and saves it.[71]

Language is already always constitued in the very event of intra-Trinitarian communication of divine being which is an analogically linguistic act. Communication which takes place in divine revelation is based in the intra-Trinitarian, ontological communication of divine being (love and life). The linguistic inner-Trinitarian logic of communication conditions revelation itself: every single divine communication *ad extra* is a free prolongation of

---

[67] J. Zizioulas, *Being as Communion: Studies in Personhood and the Church*, Crestwood: New York, 1997, pp. 27–66, 83–9.

[68] On the topic of the relation between *communio* and communication, cf. B. J. Hilberath, *Communio. Ideal oder Zerrbild von Kommunikation?*, (*Questiones disputatae*), Freiburg-Basel-Wien: Herder 1999; B. Nitsche, *Von der Communio zur Kommunikativen Theologie. FS Bernd-Jochen Hilberath*, Berlin-Münster-Wien-Zürich-London: LIT Verlag 2008.

[69] Second Vatican Council, *Dei Verbum* 2: 'Placuit Deo in sua bonitate et sapientia Seipsum revelare et notum facere sacramentum voluntatis suae (cf. Eph. 1.9), quo homines per Christum, Verbum carnem factum, in Spiritu Sancto accessum habent ad Patrem et divinae naturae consortes efficiuntur (cf. Eph. 2.18; 2 Petr. 1.4). Hac itaque revelatione Deus invisibilis (cf. Col. 1.15; 1 Tim. 1.17) ex abundantia caritatis suae homines tamquam amicos alloquitur (cf. Exod. 33.11; Io 15.14–15) et cum eis conversatur (cf. Bar. 3.38), ut eos ad societatem Secum invitet in eamque suscipiat. Haec revelationis oeconomia fit gestis verbisque intrinsece inter se connexis, ita ut opera, in historia salutis a Deo patrata, doctrinam et res verbis significatas manifestent ac corroborent, verba autem opera proclament et mysterium in eis contentum elucident. Intima autem per hanc revelationem tam de Deo quam de hominis salute veritas nobis in Christo illucescit, qui mediator simul et plenitudo totius revelationis exsistit.'

[70] The idea of the divine origin of language was forged in modern philosophy *explicite* by Hamann; cf. G. Ward, *Barth, Derrida and the Language of Theology*, Cambridge: Cambridge University Press 1995, pp. 35–53; J. R. Betz, *After Enlightenment: Hamann as Post-Secular Visionary*, (Illuminations: Theory & Religion), Oxford: Blackwell 2008, pp. 141–64; M. N. Forster, *After Herder: Philosophy of Language in the German Tradition*, Oxford: Oxford University Press 2010, pp. 9–332.

[71] C. Cunningham, 'Language. Wittgenstein After Theology', in J. Milbank, C. Picstock and G. Ward, *Radical Orthodoxy. A New Theology*, (Radical Orthodoxy), London-New York: Routledge 1999, p. 86. Cunningham's insight seems to be related to J. Milbank's theological concept of language: cf. J. Milbank, *The Word Made Strange: Theology. Language, Culture*, (Challenges in Modern Theology), Oxford: Blackwell 1997, pp. 84–122 ('The Linguistic Turn as the Theological Turn').

intra-Trinitarian communication. God is the act of speech.[72] The Christian tradition approached intra-Trinitarian *communicatio* as the linguistic act. The generation of the Son is the act of speech: the Son's proper personal character is described metaphorically by the notion of *logos*. The generation of the Son can not be separated from the spiration of the Holy Spirit (*pneuma*). The divine paternal arche of being (*Pater*) generates the Word (*logos*) and spirates the Spirit (*pneuma*). Although these are two different acts of the Father (*generatio* and *spiratio*) there is a strong relation and interdependence between them. The analogy to human speech is more than obvious here: every single act of speaking involves a kind of *spiratio*. Speaking (which is the act of the Father) produces both word (*logos*) and breath (*pneuma*).[73] In this sense, the psychological analogy is a linguistic analogy.[74]

From this point of view, language – as such and not in its particular forms – was thought of as a possible medium of divine revelation. It was thought and prefigured and ontologically grounded in the very eternal event of generation of the Son and spiration of the Spirit. This Trinitarian origin makes it, in its very nature, the fudamental tool of the communication-shaped analogy on the image of the eternal Trinity conceived as the eternal act of ontological-existential-linguistic communication of divine love and life.

We are now at the point where it is possible to make explicit the main core of the argument. If language is already always constituted in the very

---

[72] Ch. Schwöbel, *Gott im Gespräch. Studien zur theologischen Gegenwartsdeutung*, Mohr Siebeck: Tübingen, 2010.

[73] There is an essential connection between logos and pneuma, which received in Christianity the particular form of the doctrine of *Filioque*. This catholic doctrine expresses the fundamental idea of the organic unity of the inner structure of God's actuation in itself. But there is a problem: *Filioque* explains only one way of interdependence of *logos* and *penuma*; actually there is no Spirit without the Son's participation in the act of spiration). What can we say about the opposite way of this first relation of *logos* to *pneuma*? Namely: what is the relation of *pneuma* to *logos*? Does the Spirit participate in some way in the very moment of generation of the logos by the Father? Giving the positive answer to this question one has to remember that such pneumatological participation can not be productive, as it is in the case of the participation of logos in spiration of the Spirit. T. Weinandy speaks about 'presence' of the Holy Spirit in the act of generation ('the Son is begotten by the Father in the Spirit …'). His idea looks theologically probable because of the eternal and timeless nature of Trinitarian life. There is no time when the Holy Spirit is not spirated by the Father and the Son. It proceeds from this that he has to be present in the atemporal moment of generation and in some sense both productive acts of the Father (*generatio* and *spiratio*) are simultaneous and in spite of a notional difference are in some sense familiar. Cf. Th. Weinandy, *The Father's Spirit of Sonship. Reconceiving the Trinity*, Edinburgh: T&T Clark 1995, esp. pp. 17–23.

[74] On the novelty of Augustine's Trinitarian thought based on the psychological analogy, cf. R. Kany, *Augustinus Trinitätsdenken. Bilanz, Kritik und Weiterführung der modernen Forschung zu 'De trinitate'*, Mohr Siebeck, Tübingen 2007, pp. 475–534.

event of Trinitarian communication of divine being, theology as a very particular act of speech is always (at least *implicite*) Trinitarian. The centrality of the Trinity in Christian theology is grounded in the linguistic nature of Christian theology.[75] Obviously this does not mean any possibility of transcendental and *a priori* deduction of the Trinitarian truth from the language. It confirms rather the radically Trinitarian nature and structure of theology in Christianity. Christian theology is the act of speech which wells out from the event of revelation which is based in the divine Trinitarian being. Theology from the Christian standpoint is the linguistic participation in Trinitarian *communio* and *communicatio* of thinking and loving.[76] Both of these acts – thinking and loving – are by their very nature linguistic and expressive acts.[77] Given that 'theologically interpreted, communication presupposes the category of communion, and not the other way round',[78] we can affirm that the Trinitarian event is the ground of communication process in its linguistic metastructure. It allows us to make an assumption according to which 'the specific Trinitarian language is part and parcel of the gift of the triune God's very self'[79] and 'the incorporation of created persons into personal communion with the uncreated Trinity'.[80] To do theology in a Christian way always implies and produces awareness of the Trinitarian nature of the linguistic game.

What I intend to say abides in the very direct connection with the previously described argumentation. God enters into theology, into our speech and language, because He forms the very foundation of the possibility of such speech in His revelation/manifestation (Barth) and because He is the very ontological ground of the new existence of the theologian, who thinks and speaks (theo-*logy*) about God. We can admit even more: namely that God is the very ground of such thinking and speaking (Rahner and

---

[75] The dispute on the nature of language constituted one of the most important chapters in the history of Trinitarian theology; cf. B. Studer, 'Der theologiegeschichtliche Hintergrund der Epinoiai-Lehre Gregors von Nyssa', in L. Kafikova, S. Douglas and J. Zachhuber (eds), *Gregory of Nyssa: Contra Eunomium II*, (Vigiliae Christianae, Supplements, 82), Leiden: Brill 2004, pp. 21–49 and M. del Cogliano, *Basil of Caesarea's Anti-Eunomian Theory of Names. Christian Theology and Late-Antique Philosophy in the Fourth-Century Trinitarian Controversy*, (Vigiliae Christianae, Supplements, 103), Leiden: Brill 2010.

[76] Cf.: G. Greshake, *Der Dreieine Gott. Eine trinitarische Theologie*, Herder, Feiburg-Basel-Wien 1997.

[77] J.-L. Marion, *Ce qui ne se dit pas – l'apophase du discours amoureux*, in ibid., *Le visible et le révélé*, (Philosophie et théologie), Paris: Cerf 2005, pp. 119–42.

[78] A. J. Torrance, *Persons in Communion: Trinitarian Description and Human Patricipation*, T&T Clark, Edinburgh 1996, p. 4.

[79] P. M. Collins, *The Trinity. A Guide for the Perplexed*, Continuum, London-New York 2008, pp. 92–3.

[80] A. DiNoia, 'Knowing and Naming the Triune God: The Grammar of Trinitarian confession', in A. F. Kimel (ed.), *Speaking the Christian God: The Holy Trinity and the Challenge of Feminism*, Eerdmans, Grand Rapids 1992.

Lonergan).[81] Both situations are openly Trinitarian and linguistic at the same time. Because of this, there is a direct parallelism and connection between revelation as a Trinitarian linguistic act and theology as an exercise of speech.

Finally one has to recognize and underline the Christological-pneumatological focus and starting point of linguistic centrality. The basic structure of the *logos* of theo-logy is Christological and pneumatological at the same time. The Trinitarian character of language of theo-logy is due to the Christological-pneumatological constellation of revelation. It means that the Trinitarian origin and character of language is made present and explicit only through Christ and the Holy Spirit. The Christ-event is bound to language: it is basically a linguistic event. The linguistic nature of the Christ event is the fruit of the direct operation of the Holy Spirit, from whom proceeds humanity of the incarnated Son in its linguistic dimension as well.

It was James K. A. Smith whose theological theory of language visualized the recently Christological constitution of theology as a linguistic project.[82] His argument is taken from the mystery of the Incarnation, which is understood as the strong version of the ancient idea of participation.[83] Thanks to the Incarnation of the eternal *logos*, God can participate in created reality and – as already pointed out by Saint Athanasius – created reality can participate in divinity. The Incarnation as participation grounds the Christian concept of language as well. Christ's human speech – because of His humanity which expresses itself in and through language – participates in the very speech of God: human words can analogically express divine *logos* because they belong to the unity of the divine incarnated person. In virtue of the mystery of Incarnation, language functions as the Incarnation.[84] This argument helps Smith to refuse some postmodern postulates to 'avoid speaking' (Derrida)[85] and to establish a new apologetic agenda for grounding the possibility of Christian theology. Smith's description of the Christological ground of language works perfectly only in the broader Trinitarian perspective. His Christological theory of language could be taken as the preamble of its more organic, Trinitarian vision. If Incarnation is for Smith the condition of the

---

[81] The approaches of Barth, Rahner and Lonergan seem to be very similar to Gregory of Nyssa's theory of *logophasis*. We can describe it shortly with M. Laird: '*Logophasis* is the consummation of Gregory's apophatic theology. Because of the incarnating dynamic of the Word, those who are united with the Word become vehicles of the Word, transforming those who see and hear them by the power of the Word in their deeds and discourse'; M. Laird, 'Logophasis' in L. F. Mateo-Seco and G. Maspero, *The Brill Dictionary of Gregory of Nyssa*, (Vigilae Christianae, Supplements, 99), Leiden: Brill 2010, p. 456.

[82] J. K. A. Smith, *Speech and Theology. Language and the Logic of Incarnation*, (Radical Orthodoxy), London-New York: Routledge 2002.

[83] Smith, *Speech and Theology*, pp. 170–81.

[84] Smith, *Speech and Theology*, p. 125.

[85] Smith, *Speech and Theology*, p. 3.

possibility of language at all, one has to admit that such a condition is itself conditioned by Trinitarian life which is presupposed by Incarnation and Christology. The Christian conception of Incarnation loses its meaning and content without its Trinitarian horizon. Incarnation can not be understood – as Aquinas reminds us[86] – without prior taking into account the mystery of the Trinity. Smith's theory of Christological justification of logos of theology, if it is true, has to presuppose Trinity. If it does so, it helps to grasp the necessarily incarnational logic of the Trinitarian event of speech. The lesson we can learn from Smith's linguistic theory is that a Trinitarian explanation of language and theology must obviously implicate Christology. The theological consideration of Christ (both His person and work, His deeds and words) can be defined as a theological science about the divine communicative word (Christ is the divine, intra-Trinitarian logos): Christology in its Trinitarian openness is the only true theological theory of language we have.

To complete this organic Trinitarian comprehension of language one has to acknowledge the pnematological structure of Christology: there is an organic unity between Logos and Spirit economy. According to tradition, it is the Holy Spirit who is the living *milieu* in which Christ pronounces His words. It is the Holy Spirit also who exegetes these words and gives them their vitality across the human-ecclesial history. This life-giving work of the Spirit is the basis of theology itself.

Only in this case can the full meaning of the Christian view of language be disclosed: language, which is essential in theo-logy, is presented as a Christological and pneumatological 'entity' of Trinitarian nature. This is why we can assume the Trinitarian character of theology as linguistic practice. This is also the fundamental reason for the centrality of the Trinitarian mystery in the entire *corpus* of Christian theology.

# Christocentrism and Trinito-centrism

All of the above mentioned propositions, the *formal* (Barth), *material* (Rahner and Lonergan) and *linguistic*, presume – as I have already indicated – the Christological foundation. God enters theology in

---

[86] STh I, q. 2: Quia igitur principalis intentio huius sacrae doctrinae est Dei cognitionem tradere, et non solum secundum quod in se est, sed etiam secundum quod est principium rerum et finis earum, et specialiter rationalis creaturae, ut ex dictis est manifestum; ad huius doctrinae expositionem intendentes, primo tractabimus de Deo; secundo, de motu rationalis creaturae in Deum; tertio, de Christo, qui, secundum quod homo, via est nobis tendendi in Deum. Cf. R. A. te Velde, *Aquinas on God: the 'divine science' of the Summa theologiae*, Aldershot: Ashgate 2006, pp. 11–18.

Christ who, as the incarnated divine speech (*logos*), is the plenitude of revelation and absolute redeemer of human kind. It is only in His person where two different moments of Christian truth come together to form the unique base for the Christian theological worldview. The economical moment (revelation and salvation, manifestation and grace or, better, revelation as salvation) and theological moment (God as Revealer and revelation, God as Saviour and salvation) are two really distinct sides of the same reality. Because of this Christological foundation of Trinitarian centrality, Christian theology is said to be Christocentric. How can this fundamental Christocentricity be justified with the centrality of Trinitarian theology?

In my book on Bonaventure's Trinitarian theology I proposed the new coherent lecture of Saint Bonaventure's theology of the first person of the Trinity.[87] My argument there was mainly about how to conciliate the strict Christocentrism of Bonaventure's theological system with his firm conviction of the radically important and foundational character of the mystery of the Father, which is, as a matter of fact, the creative development of some hitherto unedited chapters of the Greek's model of the Trinity. I proposed to recognize a two-centre structure of Bonaventure's theology. According to it one can distinguish the absolute centrality of the Father and functional centrality of the Son. The second one is in function of the first one. Bonaventure's Christocentrism grounded in the middle place of the Son in Trinitarian architectonics is functional. Christ, the incarnated logos, is in the centre of theology in order to be the vehicle of the human mind (*mens*) towards ultimate mystery of the Father who begets the Son and together with him spirates the Holy Spirit. Bonaventure's theology is grounded and structured on the mystery of the holy Trinity. It is the Trinitarian mystery which shapes all the particular issues in his theological system. Such a Trinitarian configuration is possible only in virtue of the Christ-event. In it the Trinitarian mystery is opened in the middle of the world and dwells among human beings communicating itself. Christ reveals the Father visualizing Him among his chosen ones and He sends, together with His Father, the Holy Spirit. The presentation of the Father in His one incarnated person and sending the Holy Spirit are essentially salvific acts of Christ the Son.

Saint Bonaventure's systematic achievement should be recognized as paradigmatical for the relation between Christocentrism and Trinitocentrism. It locates Christology in the broader contest of Trinitarian faith and, on the other hand, it mantains the unique place of Christ for our knowledge and participation in the mystery. There is no access to the divine, Trinitarian reality without Christ, the incarnate Son of the Father. The entire and integral event of Christ is directed towards Trinitarian reality and

---

[87] Woźniak, *Primitas et plenitudo*, esp. pp. 176–81.

grounded in it.[88] As we are now able to consider, Christocentrism does not exclude the centrality of the Trinity but renders it possible. It is because of Christ as the Son (Christ in His personal relation to his personal, paternal *arché*) that theology can be factually Trinitarian. God enters theology via His own co-equal Son incarnated in virtue of the power of the Holy Spirit. There is no Christology which is not simultaneously Spirit Christology and Trinitarian Christology. Ultimately it means that God enters theology as the Father of the Son who gives us himself in the power of His own Spirit. God the Father – revealed in the Son by the power of the Holy Spirit, as the first although indirect subject of theology and absolute ground of divine mystery – is the ultimate reason that both: God is Trinity (primarily in His own mystery and consequently in the economy for us) and theology – as real participation in the very *arché*-linguistic act of the Father´s eternal speach – is Trinitarian.

From such a Trinitarian-theoretical perspective, which is grounded in the mystery of divine *arché* (Father) who begets the logos (Son) and spirates the pneuma (Holy Spirit), flows the new vision of world and life[89] (which is often called Trinitarian ontology)[90] and new praxis.[91] But these are topics that deserve separate theological treatment.

---

[88] Cf. K. Tanner, *Christ the Key*, (Current Issues in Theology), Cambridge: Cambridge Univerity Press 2010, esp. pp. 140–206.

[89] Ch. Schwöbel, 'Die Trinitätslehre als Rahmentheorie des christlischen Glaubens. Vier Thesen zur Bedeutung der Trinität in den christlichen Dogmatik', in ibid., *Gott in Beziehung: Studien zur Dogmatik*, Tübingen: Mohr Siebeck 2002, p. 48.

[90] K. Hemmerle, *Thesen zu einer trinitarischen Ontologie*, Einsiedeln: Johannes Verlag 1976; cf. M. Knapp, 'Der trinitarische Gottesgedanke als Zentrum einer Theologie jenseits der Metaphysik? Eine theologische Auseinandersetzung mit Hegels Trinitätsverstandnis', in M. Knapp and Th. Kobusch (eds), *Religion-Metaphysik(kritik)-Theologie im Kontext der Moderne/Postmoderne*, Berlin-New York: Gruyter 2001, pp. 307–32. Knapp proposes – after Hegel – to understand Trinitarian theology as the basic theory in theology (a proper theological metaphysics).

[91] S. H. Webb, *The Gifting God: a Trinitarian Ethics of Excess*, Oxford: Oxford University Press 1996.

# 19

# Tam Pater nemo: Reflections on the Paternity of God*

## Luis F. Ladaria

*Tam Pater nemo*:[1] nobody is Father as God is. One cannot overemphasize the originality that the consideration of divine paternity introduces into the Christian message. It certainly has various echoes in different cultures and religions,[2] it is present in the Old Testament, but in the life and message of Jesus the idea acquires an unexpected originality and a new meaning. It is no longer a general idea of paternity founded in creation nor the election of a people that principally appears. The foundation of the Christian idea of God is the figure of Jesus, who addresses God in a unique and unrepeatable way as His Father. In this manner it can be seen, again in a unique and unrepeatable way, how it is the Son,[3] the Image and Word of God, who reveals His face to us in a definitive way, although He does not exhaust His mystery. One of the decisive ideas of Christianity is found in the paternity of God. The difference between the Old and New Testaments is quite notable on this point. If in the

---

* This is an English translation of the paper published before in Transversalités 2008 (107) 95–123.

[1] Tertullian, *De paenitentia*, 8, (CCL 1, 335): 'Quis ille nobis intelligendus pater? Deus scilicet : tam pater nemo, tam pius nemo.' The context refers to the divine mercy as it appears in the parable of the father and two sons (cf. Lk. 15.11–32).

[2] Cf. J. Masson, *Père de nos pères*, Rome: PUG 1988.

[3] This idea constitutes the fundamental orientation of the work of J. Ratzinger – Benedikt XVI, *Jesus von Nazaret*, I, *Von der Taufe im Jordan bis zur Verklärung*, Freiburg-Basel-Vienna: Herder 2007, esp. pp. 386–96.

first, in various contexts, the idea of God as Father appears 14 times, in the New Testament there are 261 references.[4] The Christian God is the Father of Jesus, who resurrected Him from the dead, to whom Jesus His Son and the Holy Spirit are united in an absolutely singular manner. It is a frequent occurrence in Paul that the terms 'God' and 'Father' are united (cf. 1 Cor. 8.6, Gal. 1.1, Eph. 6.23, 1 Thes. 1.1, 2 Thes. 1.1, Tit. 1.4). In many cases he underscores that God is 'our' Father, usually with a mention of Jesus in the same context (cf. Rom. 1.7, 1 Cor. 1.3, 2 Cor. 1.2, Gal. 1.4, Eph. 1.2, Phil. 1.2, Col. 1.1, 1 Thes. 1.3, 2 Thes. 1.2, 2 Tim. 1.2). There is also reference to the God and Father of our Lord Jesus Christ (cf. Eph. 1.3, Col. 1.3; also 1 Pet. 1.3). With the term 'Father', the idea of God acquires a new connotation and meaning. It is clear in the entire New Testament that divine paternity regarding Jesus is primary, and that it opens the path to paternity in respect to us. Since God is the Father of Jesus, God can also be, in His infinite condescension, our Father. These two dimensions of divine paternity have been revealed to us in the Son who became man. We know the first in so far as we have been called to adoptive filiation (cf. Mt. 6.9, Lk. 11.2, Gal. 4.4–6, Rom. 8.15, etc.). If in a first moment human paternity and filiation are the reference point for understanding the relation of Jesus with God, once the mystery that Christ reveals to us has been known, it is manifest that the name of 'Father' primarily and principally fits God, who is the only one to whom the title applies in all truth. This is manifest in certain passages of the New Testament: 'And call no man your father on earth, for you have one Father, who is in heaven' (Mt. 23.9); 'For this reason I bow my knees before the Father, from whom every family in heaven and on earth is named.' (Eph. 3.14–15). For it can only be affirmed of God that He is the 'Father of us all, who is above all and through all and in all' (Eph. 4.6). From the divine paternity in regard to Jesus, the NT moves to his disciples, and from there to a universal perspective.[5]

# The Gradual Discovery of Divine Paternity by the Christians of the First Centuries

Without a doubt this universal vision of divine paternity sketched out in the NT influences the relation between divine paternity and creation that will be established in the first centuries of theological reflection. In Clement of Rome we already find the union of the titles of Father and Creator:

---

[4] The density of the same is notably increased in the Johannine writings, around 140 times.
[5] I do not think it is necessary to clarify that in the New Testament, and the early centuries of Christianity, the use of 'God' was primarily in reference to the Father. It was precisely because of this paternity that they spoke of the divinity of the Son and the Holy Spirit.

Thus the humility and godly submission of so great and illustrious men have rendered not only us, but also all the generations before us, better; even as many as have received his oracles in fear and truth. Wherefore, having so many great and glorious examples set before us, let us turn again to the practice of that peace which from the beginning was the mark set before us; and let us look steadfastly to the Father and Creator of the universe ...[6]

The philosopher and martyr Justin also knows the idea of the universal paternity of God in relation to both creation and the generation of the only Son, to whom this name properly corresponds:

But to the Father of all, who is unbegotten, there is no name given. For by whatever name someone is called, he has as his elder the person who gives him the name. But these words – Father, and God, and Creator, and Lord and Master – are not names, but appellations derived from His good deeds and functions. And His Son, who alone is properly called Son, the Word who also was with Him and was begotten before the works, when at first He created and arranged all things by Him....[7]

The universal paternity and the generation of the Son through which everything has been made are two ideas that are close to each other in Justin's thought. The same God who is the Father of Jesus is also the Creator of the universe. Creation and salvation are united in the unity of the divine plan (cf. Eph. 1.3–10), and for this reason divine paternity has a universal perspective. It is not easy to determine which of this aspects has priority.[8] In any case, the theology of the early Christians used the idea of God's paternity to open up the universality of salvation before the

---

[6] 1 Clem., XIX 2–3 (Fuentes patrísticas 4, 96–97). Cf. all of n. XX which terminates with (XX 11, ib 98–9): 'The great Creator and Lord of the universe ordained that all things be maintained in peace and concord, pouring forth goodness on all and, in superabundance, on us who have taken refuge in his mercies by means of our Lord Jesus Christ.' Is this a distant reference to the mediation of Christ? On God as the Father of Jesus, cf. 1 Clem. VII 4 (80)? On the other hand, it should be noted that in the triadological texts, Clement speaks of God and not Father: cf. ib. I 3–2, 2 (70); 42, 2–3 (124); 46, 6 (130); 58, 2 (144). One can find more material on primitive Christian theology in E. Romero Pose, *Apuntes sobre Dios Padre en la teología primitiva*, in ibid., *Anotaciones sobre Dios uno y único*, Madrid 2007.
[7] Apology, II, 5 (6) 1–3 (SCh 507, 332–3). On more than a few occasions, Justin refers to God as the Father of everything (πάντων): Apol., I. 8, 2; 12, 9; 32, 10; 40, 7; 45, 1; 46, 5; Apol., II 10,6 (144; 156; 216; 234; 246; 252; 350). He also speaks of the Father τῶν ὅλων, in Apol., I 44, 2; 61, 3.10; 63. 11. 14. 15 (242, 290, 292, 296, 298), among others.
[8] Cf. Justin, *Dial. Tryph.*, 61, 3 (Marcovich, 175), The Word was engendered by the Father of the universe; ibid. 63, 3 (179), The God and Father of the universe Himself engendered His Son as man through a human womb.

restrictive attempts of the Gnostics and Marcion. In the beginning was the Word, the Son, who was always with the Father, who made all things through the Son.[9] Instead of speculations on the demiurge, the God of the Old Testament (YHWH), who, according to the Valentinians, created the world by obeying, without knowing it, to external impulses (of the Son and the Spirit), for the writers of the greater Church, it is clear that the God that the Israelites glorified, who was preached by the law and the prophets, is the Father of our Lord Jesus Christ.[10] His universal paternity is in an essential relationship with the love with which He created all things. Irenaeus expresses it in this way:

> Now this being is the Creator, who is, in respect of His love, the Father (*secundum dilectionem quidem Pater est*); but in respect of his power, He is Lord; and in respect of His wisdom, our Maker and Fashioner; by transgressing whose commandment we became His enemies. And therefore in the last times the Lord has restored us into friendship through His incarnation, having become 'the Mediator between God and men' (1 Tim. 2.5) propitiating indeed for us the Father against whom we had sinned, and consoling our disobedience by His own obedience; conferring also upon us the gift of communion with, and subjection to, our Maker.[11]

God the Creator, against whom men sinned at the beginning of time, is identified with the Father of Jesus. If He is our Lord because of His power, He is our Father because of His love. For the same reason that He is the only God, He is also the only Father.[12] With sin, man has not obeyed this commandment from the beginning. It is this same Creator and Father who has reconciled us through the incarnation of His Son, with respect to whom He is Father in a singular manner, having engendered Him. At the same time, it was the Son who gave us knowledge of and manifested Him as Father in a definitive manner.[13] The generation of the Son before the ages is the highest expression and realization of divine paternity. Nevertheless, because of the love with which this same Father of Jesus

---

[9] Irenaeus of Lyon, *Demons.*, 43 (SCh 406, 144–7).

[10] Irenaeus, *Adv. Haer.*, V 17, 2 (SCh 153, 226–7).

[11] Irenaeus of Lyon, *Adv. Haer.*, V 17, 1 (SCh 153, 220–4). A study on some elements of this passage can be found in D. Scordamaglia, *Il Padre nella teologia di Sant'Ireneo*, Rome: PUG 2004, pp. 21–3.

[12] Cf. Adv. Haer., II 28, 3 (SCh 294, 274–5)); in so far as He is Father by love, we too must love Him; cf. also *Demostr.*, 3 (SCh 406, 144–7); *Adv. Haer.*, IV 6,2 (SCh 100, 440–1).

[13] *Adv. Haer.*, IV 6, 6 (SCh 100, 448–449): 'For the Word already reveals the Creator God by creation, the Maker and Lord by the world (*Fabricatorem mundi Dominum*), the Artist by the work He made, and by the Son, the Father who engendered Him'; cf. also ib. II 30, 9 (SCh 294, 318–19).

creates His creatures, He is also the Father of the visible and invisible
worlds. Paternity is expressly tied to love, and not simply to the work of
creation. The Father is however also recognized as such only by believers,
since only they know the mystery of filial adoption. Faith in Christ
consequently opens us to an understanding of the universal paternity of
God, which is only known to believers. The two dimensions of divine
paternity are intimately united in any case.

For the early Christian writers, divine paternity is the most profound
dimension of the divine being, at least in His relation with us. Irenaeus,
in one of his most famous Trinitarian formulas, has shown us how the
definitive vision of God, which gives man eternal life, consists precisely in
seeing Him in his paternal condition, *paternaliter*:

> For man does not see God by his own powers; but when He pleases He
> is seen by men, by whom He wills, and when He wills, and as He wills.
> For God is powerful in all things, having been seen at that time indeed,
> prophetically (*profetice*) through the Spirit, and seen, too, adoptively
> (*adoptive*) through the Son; and He shall also be seen paternally (*pater-
> naliter*) in the kingdom of heaven, the Spirit truly preparing man in the
> Son of God, and the Son leading him to the Father, while the Father, too,
> confers the incorruptibility of eternal life [on him], which comes to each
> one from the fact of their seeing God.[14]

Irenaeus also speaks of the divine revelation and way of acting *paternaliter*
in another similar context: God will paternally grant that which no eye has
seen, nor ear heard, nor has it entered into the heart of man (cf. 1 Cor. 2.9).[15]
The fullness of eternal life will consequently consist in the communion with
God the Father, who in His Son and His Spirit makes us participants of
His very life. Paternity is not a secondary dimension of the divine being.
Neither creation nor salvation, in the indestructible unity of both aspects
of the divine work, cannot be explained without the action of the One who
is Father *secundum dilectionem*. If in creation already the love of God is
manifest, this is all the more true of salvation. The ideas of paternity and
love are already found together in the Bishop of Lyon. We will encounter
it again, however. We already saw how Tertullian indicated that the name
of Father is particularly proper for God.[16] This specific fittingness certainly

---

[14] Irenaeus, *Adv. Haer.*, IV 20,5 (SCh 100, 638–641). Cf. also the ascending rhythm of
*Demons.*, 5. 7 (SCh 406, 90–91–92–93); *Adv. Haer.*, IV 20, 2 (628–31): '... the Father's light
erupted in the flesh of our Lord, and then, by shining from his flesh, it came to us. And thus
man reached incorruptibility, since he was enveloped by the Father's light.'

[15] *Adv. Haer.*, V 36, 3 (SCh 153, 464–5): 'It is He who will paternally (*paternaliter*) grant these
goods that the eye has not seen ...'.

[16] Cf. n. 1.

includes the consideration of creation, but is not reduced to it. Merciful love is determining for the paternal condition.

If this divine paternity in relation to the economy of salvation clearly appears in a prominent position from the earliest times of the Church, it is more difficult to determine to what extent the foundation of this paternity was explicated in the domain of theology or of the immanent Trinity. In other words, the problem presents itself as to whether the paternity of God in relation to the Son that He engendered, above all in the strongest sense of the term, is essential, or if it came through His own free will. In his *Contra Noetum*, Hippolytus of Rome gives a general answer to this question: 'There is one God, who it fits to create, without birth, or passion, or death. He does everything as He wills, in the way He wills and when He wills'.[17] Is the generation of the Son an exception to this principle? Saint Justin expressly says that the rational power that constitutes the Son was engendered by the will of the Father (ἀπὸ τοῦ πατρὸς θελήσει).[18] The question of voluntariness is intimately tied to the eternity of God's paternal condition. The question remains unresolved in this period. For Tertullian, the Word, being engendered by creation, makes God his Father, and, in proceeding from Him, is made Son.[19] This work is not comprised of the real communication of the divinity to the engendered Son, and thus by God's real paternity. It is however clear at the same time that theological reflection had not managed to describe all the implications of divine paternity that would be accentuated throughout the centuries. Divine paternity, if it belongs to the divine being, must be real from the beginning, and cannot depend on the will in the same way that the creation of the world depends on it. Stating that God 'becomes' Father can also indicate that this condition does not necessarily belong to His being, and that it was only acquired in virtue of the economy of salvation that was freely realized.

Another aspect of the theology of the Father in ante-Nicene theology remains imprecise. In the preoccupation to maintain the monotheism inherited from the Old Testament and confirmed in the New Testament, it is not always clear that the communication of the divinity to the Son (and consequently to the Holy Spirit, although there are but few explicit references to Him in this context) is full and complete, that the Father gives the divinity with the same fullness with which He possesses it. Further, on numerous occasions, the contrary appears to be explicitly affirmed.

---

[17] Hippolytus, *Contra Noetum*, 8, 3 (Simonetti, 168–9).

[18] Justin, *Dial. Tryph.*, 61, 1 (Marcovich, 174). The same idea can be found in Theophilus of Antioch, *Ad Autolicum* 2, 22 (SCh 20, 154–5): 'When God decided to do all that He had deliberated, He engendered this Word outside, the first-born of all creatures.'

[19] Tertullian, *Adv. Prax.*, 7, 1 (Scarpat, 156): '[Sermo] exinde Patrem sibi faciens, de quo procedendo Filius factus est.'

Thus for Irenaeus the absolutely invisible Father is visible in the Son.[20] The Father is absolutely incommensurable, but the Son is his measure,[21] circumscribed and not unlimited as the Father is.[22] Tertullian appears also to suggest a descending gradation between the divine persons, although the common divinity is maintained without vacillation:

> For the Father is the entire substance, but the Son is a derivation and portion of the whole, as He himself acknowledges: *My Father is greater than I* (Jn 14.28). In the Psalm his inferiority is described as being *a little lower than the angels* (Ps. 8.6). Thus the Father is distinct from the Son, being greater than the Son, inasmuch as He who begets is one, and He who is begotten is another; He, too, who sends is one, and He who is sent is another; and He, again, who makes is one, and He through whom the thing is made is another.[23]

Tertullian's primary preoccupation is the affirmation of the personal distinction between the Father, Son and Holy Spirit. If the Father is greater than the Son, this distinction appears without any remaining doubts.

Origen particularly accentuates the pre-eminent position of the Father in respect to the other two persons. Only the Father is 'God in himself (αὐτοθεός)', while the Son and the Holy Spirit are 'Gods' in so far as He communicates the divinity by which He is God in Himself to them.[24] For Origen, the Son, the resplendence of the Light that the Father is, presents Himself to our mortal eyes in a more peaceful and sweet manner than the light itself, and thus makes us slowly capable of supporting it, raising us to be able to see it directly. The Alexandrian also made a large step forward in underscoring that God's paternity is eternal, since the Father has from all eternity been able to and desired to engender the Son, and it would be absurd to negate either the one or the other.[25] Attributing a beginning to the Son, Word and Wisdom of God is equivalent to offending the unbegotten

---

[20] *Adv. Haer.*, IV 6, 6 (SCh 100, 448–51): 'Finally, by the Word in person having become visible and palpable, the Father showed Himself, and if not all believed in Him in the same way, they did not any less see the Father in the Son: for the invisible Reality that they saw in the Son was the Father, and the visible Reality in which they saw the Father was the Son (*visibile autem Patris Filius*).'

[21] *Adv. Haer.*, IV 4, 2 (420–2): 'And he who said that the Father Himself, although He is incommensurable, is measured in the Son, expressed himself well'; cf. ib. 20, 1 (624).

[22] Cf. D. Scordamaglia, *Il Padre*, p. 231.

[23] *Adv. Prax.*, IX 2 (162).

[24] Cf. *In Joh. Ev.*, II 2, 17–18 (SCh 120, 216–19).

[25] *De Principiis*, I 2, 2 (SCh 252, 112): 'Where one will say that God could not have engendered this Wisdom before He engendered it ... or that He of course could have, but ... He did not want to. For both hypotheses are absurd and impious ... that one imagine that He progressed from powerlessness to power, or that, being able to, He neglected or deferred engendering Wisdom.'

Father, denying that He has always been Father.[26] 'The name of All-Powerful cannot be in God before that of Father, for it is by His Son that the Father is all-powerful.'[27] There is nothing in God anterior to his paternity. The title of Father is the most decisive one in God. It is not however evident whether for Origen paternity belongs to the divine nature. The eternal generation of the Son still depends on His free will. Because He is the Son of God's love (cf. Col. 1.13), we can call Him the Son of His will.[28] The generation of the Son is not perfectly distinguished from the salvific will of God; immanent Trinity and economy are not distinguished with sufficient precision. The paternity of God is not that which, ultimately, defines Him.

A definitive progress in this aspect will be made beginning from the Council of Nicaea and the following Arian controversies. One should first of all note that the Nicene Creed again joins 'God' and 'Father'. The only God is the Father of Jesus. All-powerfulness corresponds to Him in a special way, understood more in the concrete sense of effective dominion over the entire universe than as the abstract possibility of being able to do anything. With its Trinitarian structure, the Creed makes true paternity primarily refer to intra-Trinitarian relations. It is from the relation with Jesus that cosmic paternity is understood, and this second is clearly subordinated to the first. Athanasius of Alexandria will clearly indicate that the Father is such from all eternity, that the Son was engendered by Him eternally, independently from the function of salvific and cosmic mediation that He will assume in the economy. God the Father could be nothing without the wisdom and power that are proper to Him, and are personally identified with the Son.[29] The pre-existing Son did not come to existence for us, but we were created by Him.[30] Paternity pertains to the divine being essentially, to its nature, but this does not mean that the Son exists against the will of the Father:

> If the Son exists by nature and not by will, does this mean that He was not willed by the Father, that He exists without his will? The Son is absolutely willed by the Father ... Since, as his goodness did not begin by will, but He is not good without will or design at the same time ... so too, the existence of the Son, although it did not begin by will, is not involuntary or without consent. Because the Father loves his own

---

[26] *De Principiis*, I 2, 3 (116–17): 'He who attributes a beginning to the Word and Wisdom of God, does he not even more impiously ridicule the unbegotten Father, by refusing that He has always been Father, that He engendered a Word and had a Wisdom from all earlier times and ages ...'.

[27] *De Principiis*, I 2, 10 (134–5).

[28] Cf. *De Principiis*, IV 4, 1 (SCh 268, 402).

[29] Cf. *Contra Arianos*, I 19–20 (PG 26, 52–3)

[30] Cf. *Contra Arianos*, II 29–31 (PG 26, 208–13).

hypostasis the same way He loves the hypostasis of the Son, hypostasis that is proper to his essence.[31]

God cannot exist without being Father, He cannot exist without the Son, who is contemplated in the Father's divinity. He is God through Him, and there is only one God.[32] Paternity necessarily implicates the existence of the Son. Therefore the name of Father is that which belongs to God (the first person of the Trinity) most fittingly. This is far more so than *unbegotten*, which is not biblical and does not indicate his relation with the Son.[33] In this manner paternity necessarily belongs to the divine being;[34] further, in God paternity acquires a new plenitude and its full meaning.[35]

The ideas of Hilary of Poitiers on the divine paternity are particularly interesting and profound. In the face of the Arian doctrines, the Bishop of Poitiers considered it critical to give the names of Father and Son their full meaning. Only if the Father really engendered the Son from His substance do these names that the Gospel uses make sense.[36] Generation means that the Father communicates all that He is and all that He has to the Son, without undergoing any reduction on His part. It could be no other way if we take into account that the divine nature is completely simple, that all of God's being is life, and for this reason, it cannot be partially communicated. The divinity is communicated as it is had (*talis data est, qualis et habetur*).[37] God is thus total capacity for gift, and for this reason all subordinationism is to be excluded. God is thus only Father, with this name all that He is indicated: 'in "Father" there is however a name for his nature; but this Father is nothing but Father.'[38] He did not receive paternity from another, He possesses it in Himself from all eternity. Paternity in itself therefore belongs to the ultimate depths of the divine being. However, Hilary repeats and develops these ideas, adding the identification of paternity and love:

---

[31] *Contra Arianos*, III 66 (441). Cf. *Fides Damasi* (DH 71): 'Pater Filium genuit, non voluntate, nec necessitate, sed natura'; Conc. XI of Toledo (DH 526): 'quem [Filium] Deus Pater nec voluntate nec necessitate genuisse credendus est.'

[32] Cf. *Contra Arianos*, I 61.

[33] Cf. *Contra Arianos*, I 33–4 (80–1).

[34] *De decretis Nic. syn.*, 22 (Ath.Werke III/1,8).

[35] *Contra Arianos*, I, 21, 23 (60, 72).

[36] *Trin.*, II 3 (SCh 443, 278–9): '... depriving the Father of His fatherhood because they wish to strip the Son of His sonship. They take away the fatherhood by asserting that the Son is not a Son by nature; for a son is not of the nature of his father when begetter and begotten have not the same properties, and he is no son whose being is different from that of the father, and unlike it. Yet in what sense is God a Father (as He is), if He has not begotten in His Son that same substance and nature which are His own?'

[37] Cf. *Trin.*, VIII 43 (SCh 448, 448–9); Ambrosio de Milán, *De Fide*, V 2,36 (Opera, 15, 351): 'Sicut habet, sic dedit.'

[38] *Trin.*, II 6 (SCh 443, 226–87).

But God is incapable of being anything other than love, than Father, at every moment. Now he who loves knows no envy, and He who is Father cannot but be it entirely. For this name knows no division, so that one would be a father on one side and not be father on the other ... God is completely living in total unity, since He is not composed of pieces, but perfect in simplicity. Necessarily, according to His being Father, He is completely Father in regard to His whole self, for Him whom He engendered. The perfect generation of a Son, from all that He Himself is, gives Him the perfect quality of Father (*dum eum Patrem ex suis omnibus natiuitas Filii perfecta consummat*).[39]

This is undoubtedly a central text, not only for understanding the author's theology, but also for discerning the meaning of divine paternity in Christian thought. Paternity completely embraces God and is identified with the capacity for total loving gift; love and power are united.[40] This love of God excludes any envy that could impede a total gift of His nature to the Son.[41] The Father consequently communicates the full divinity to the Son because He is completely love and total self-gift. We should also retain another fundamental element of the quoted text, which will be amply reflected on throughout tradition: it is the generation of the Son that constitutes the Father as such, that which makes Him to be Father, and further, that which makes Him to be, and makes Him to be God. The Father is not more than what is in His relation to the Son (and, we should add, with the Holy Spirit). It is only by the generation of the Son that the Father is what He is, that the Father can be Father. The reciprocity of relations is essential for the divine being.[42] There is no unilateral dependence there. The

---

[39] *Trin.*, IX 61 (SCh 462, 140–3).

[40] *Trin.*, III 3 (SCh 442, 338–9): 'He engendered an only-begotten from that which was unbegotten in Himself, who was one, through His love and power, with He who was born of He who is everything that God is.'

[41] This same theme appears in other places: *Trin.*, VI 21 (SCh 248, 210–11): 'I also learned by my own birth that you were good, and because of that, I have confidence that you are not jealous (*invidum*) of your goods in reference to the birth of your only Son.' Cf. Also the hymn *Ante saecula*, (CSEL 65, 210). The lack of jealousy in God and the generation of the Son are also found in Gregory of Nazianzus, *Or.*, 25, 15 (SCh 284, 194–7); *Or.*, 2, 37 (SCh 247, 137–8); *Or.*, 23, 6 (SCh 270, 294–5); in Ambrose of Milan, *De Sp. Sancto*, III 16, 113 (CSEL 79, 198). Without direct reference to the Son, the lack of jealousy in God is already found in Irenaeus of Lyon, *Adv. Haer.*, IV 38, 3 (SCh 100, 952–3); V 24, 4 (SCh 153, 306–7): 'invidia enim aliena est a Deo.'

[42] On other occasions, however, Hilary refers to the 'achievement' of the Father through the Son, *Trin.*, VII 31 (SCh 448, 348–9): 'In confessing the Father it [the apostolic faith] confessed the Son, and in believing in the Son, it also believed in the Father, because the term of Father implies that of Son. There is no Father except because of a Son ... Thus, in confessing only one, there is not even one, because it is the Son who achieves the Father, and the birth of the Son comes from the Father (*In unius itaque confesssione non unus est, dum et Patrem consummat*

divine persons proceed one from the other, and the Father is the unique
source and origin of the divinity, but this does not imply an inferiority of
either the Son or the Holy Spirit. On the contrary, the Father's very capacity
of love and gift would be compromised. There is no degeneration of the
divine nature in generation.[43] If the primacy of the Father as origin and
principle must be clearly affirmed, one does not need to deduce a reduction
in the divinity of the Son or the Spirit. The Arians used Jesus' words in Jn
14.28: 'The Father is greater than I' in order to negate the Son's divinity.
The defenders of Nicene faith maintained that the Father is certainly greater
in so far as principle, but that, since He gives to the Son all that He is and
has, the latter is not lesser. As He receives from the Father, He always has
the fullness of the divinity.[44] Divine paternity in the Trinitarian sense is what
helps us understand cosmic paternity. Everything comes from the Father
who, through the Son, is the Creator of everything. While God's paternity
in relation to Jesus is based in the divine nature (*physis*), God's cosmic
paternity is based in his decision (*thesis*).[45]

The Cappadocians insisted in a similar way. For Basil, the Father is the
unique principle of the divinity and of all that exists,[46] but as soon as one
speaks of Father (the biblical term to be preferred to *unbegotten*), the idea
of the relation to the Son is already introduced.[47] It is precisely because
He is engendered by the Father that the Son must have the substance as
Him.[48] In response to Eunomius, who wanted to speak of *unbegotten*
and engendered, Basil reaffirms the pertinence of the biblical names of
Father and Son. It is in paternity, and not simply in the fact of not having
principle, that we encounter the most proper and definitive characteristic
of the first person of the Trinity. It is not only not having a principle that
characterizes Him, but his being the principle of the One who is God and
equal to Him, in personal distinction, without difference or diminution in

---

*Filius et Filii ex Patre nativitas est.*' For more information on this subject, see L. F. Ladaria,
*Dios Padre en Hilario de Poitiers*, in *Estudios Trinitarios* 24 (1990) 443, 479; '"... Patrem
consummat Filius". Un aspecto inédito de la teología trinitaria de Hilario de Poitiers', in
*Gregorianum* 81 (2000) 775–88.

[43] Cf., e.g., *Trin.*, III 22 (SCh 443, 376–7); V 20.39 (SCh 448, 132–3; 168–9); there are more
examples in Ladaria, *Dios Padre*, p. 454.

[44] Hilary, *Trin.*, IX 54–6 (SCh 462, 126–35); XI 12 (ibid. 316–17). Basil of Caesarea, *Contra
Eunomium*, I 24–5 (SCh 299, 256–63); the Father is greater in so far as cause and principle;
Gregory of Nazianzus, *Or.*, 30, 7 (SCh 250, 240–1); the Father is greater in reference to the
cause; the Son is equal in reference to nature. Augustine also echoes this tradition, *Trin.*, IV 20,
27 (CCL 50, 195). Nevertheless, Augustine insists more on the inferiority of the Son through
the Incarnation. The other cited authors also know this idea.

[45] Cf. among others, Athanasius, *Contra Arianos*, II 69 (PG 272–3).

[46] Cf. the texts cited in n. 43. of *De Sp. Sancto*, 16, 38 (SCh 17bis, 378).

[47] Cf. *Contra Eunomium*, I 5 (SCh 299, 176–7).

[48] Cf. *Contra Eunomium*, I 18 (234–9); II 9–10 (SCh 305, 36–41).

regard to the divinity.[49] The Father is the principle and cause of the Son as well as of the Holy Spirit, and in this sense they are the second and third; but divine nature is the same in all three, and from this perspective one should not speak of second or third.[50] The Trinitarian order and the full possession of the divinity for the Father, the Son and the Holy Spirit are not incompatibles but rather mutually require each other.

Gregory of Nazianzus also spoke numerous times of the Father as the unique principle of the divinity.[51] However, this does not eliminate, but rather presupposes, the full divinity of the Son. Negating it on the pretext of honouring the Father by affirming that none other shares his divine condition means, ultimately, depriving Him of his paternity:

> It is necessary neither to be so devoted to the Father as to rob Him of his fatherhood, for whose Father would He be, if the Son were separated and estranged from Him, by being ranked with the creation, (for an alien being, or one which is combined and confounded with His father and in this sense is the same, throws Him into confusion, and is not a son); nor to be so devoted to Christ, as to neglect to preserve both his sonship, (for whose son would He be, if His origin were not referred to the Father?) and the rank of the Father as origin, inasmuch as He is the Father and Generator. For He would be the origin of petty and unworthy beings, or rather the term would be used in a petty and unworthy sense, if He were not the origin of Godhead and goodness, which are contemplated in the Son and the Spirit.[52]

The honour of the Father is therefore joined with that of the Son and Spirit who come from Him. If one honours Him who is principle, one will honour those who proceed from Him, because He is principle of those who are like Him.[53] In virtue of the unique principle that the Father is, the unity of the

---

[49] Cf. *Contra Eunomium*, I 16 (230–1); II 23 (92–3): 'He who provides the principle (ἀρχὴν) of his being to another in a nature like his own is father, he is son who has received the principle of his being from another by generation.'

[50] *Contra Eunomium*, III 1 (SCh 305, 146–7): 'For, in the same way that the Son is second in relation to the Father in order, since He comes from Him, and the second in dignity, because the latter is his principle and cause (ἀρχὴ καὶ αἰτία), because He is his Father and that it is by the Son that God the Father is introduced; but He is no longer second in nature, because the divinity is unique in both of Them, as is also clear for the Holy Spirit …'. Cf. the entire passage (144–51). Basil only speaks of the Spirit as third in dignity in this context as a concession to his adversaries, using formulas of doubt.

[51] Cf. *Or.*, 2, 37 (SCh 247, 138–9); 20,7 (SCh 270, 70–3), etc.

[52] *Or.*, 2, 38 (SCh 247, 138–41); cf. similar ideas in 20,6 (SCh 270, 68–71); 23,7 (ib. 296–7).

[53] *Or.*, 23, 8 (SCh 270, 296–7): 'In accepting an intemporal, invisible and infinite principle of the divinity, I honour both the principle and the beings that depend on it … because He is the principle of things that are like Himself.'

Trinity is maintained, in that the Father, the Son and the Holy Spirit are united without separating or being confused.[54] The Father is Father in a singular way that has no comparison in this world: He is Father without conjugal union, of an only begotten Son; He is nothing but Father because before Him there is no son at all; He is completely Father, because He is completely from the Son; He is thus eternally, because He did not become Father after having come to be.[55] He is Father in the most proper sense.[56] This does not mean that his paternity is not free. There is no external constriction that conforms Him to the divine nature.[57]

The doctrine of divine relations that the Cappadocians began to formulate, and which had been implicitly present from the very beginnings of Christian reflection on God, were later, as is known, widely developed. In front of the accentuation of divine unity and the equal dignity of the three persons, Augustine did not forget that the Father is the origin and source of the divinity,[58] that the Son comes from the Father, and that the Holy Spirit also proceeds from Him *principaliter*.[59] At the same time, just as we cannot think of the Son without the Father, neither can the Father be without the Son, and consequently the mutual reference and the reciprocity of relation is fundamental for understanding divine paternity. Not only Oriental circles but also Occidental and Latin ones maintained the primacy of the Father as principle and source, at the same time maintaining the equality of the three divine persons, not despite the paternal origin, but precisely because of it. The Father engenders Him who is God like himself, He engenders the One who is the same reality, although not the same (*id* not *is*), as himself.[60] If the Father is He who engenders and the Son is the engendered, through the work of generation the Son, who is equal and co-eternal with the Father, subsists without temporal beginning, and without any reduction, in the

---

[54] Cf. *Or.*, 42, 15 (SCh 384, 82).

[55] *Or.*, 25, 16 (SCh 284, 196–197): 'The Father is truly father, and certainly far more truly that what occurs among us ... He is the only Father, because without conjugal union; He is the Son of but one Son, because He is the Father of the 'Only Son'; He is only Father, because there was no Son before Him, and He is entirely Father of the entirety of the Son ... He is Father from his beginning, because He does not become one later.' On the eternity of the Father-Son relation, cf. also *Or.*, 29,3 (SCh 250,182–3).

[56] *Or.*, 29, 5 (SCh 250,184–5): 'And He is Father in the proper sense, because He is not also the Son; likewise, the Son is such properly speaking, because He is not also the Father. In that which concerns us, these words are not said properly, because we are at once father and son ... and we become two beings ....'

[57] Cf. *Or.*, 29, 2. 7 (SCh 250, 180–1; 190–1).

[58] *Trin.*, IV 20, 29 (CCL 50, 200): 'totius divinitatis vel si melior dicitur deitatis principium Pater est.'

[59] *Trin.*, IV 20, 27 (195): 'Filius enim a Patre est, non Pater a Filio'; cf. *Trin.*, XV 17, 29 (503–4); 26, 47 (529); *In Joh. ev.*, 99,8 (CCL 36, 587).

[60] Cf. Agustín, *De fide et símbolo*, 5 (PL 40, 183).

same divinity.[61] The various Councils of Toledo used the formula of *fons et origo totius divinitatis* and insisted on the unity of the majesty and power, as well as on the fact that, although the Son is not without the Father nor the Father without the Son, that does not mean that the Father comes from the Son as the Son comes from the Father.[62] The equal dignity of the persons and the reciprocity of the mutual relations do not affect the order of the procession or the primacy of the Father, who is the unique principle.

High scholastics inherited these institutions, because God the Father is nothing but love, but infinite capacity of infinite communication. Saint Bonaventure accentuated this, speaking of the three divine persons with a clear allusion to the primacy of the Father:

> The most high good is most highly diffusive of itself ... through the most high communicability of the Good, that the Trinity, of the Father and of the Son and of the Holy Spirit, is necessary. Among whom it is necessary on account of most high goodness that there be a most high communicability, and from the most high communicability a most high consubstantiality, and from the most high consubstantiality a most high configurability, and from these a most high co-equality, and through this a most high co-eternity, and from all the aforesaid a most high co-intimacy, by which One is in the Other necessarily through a most high circumincession and One works with an Other through the omnimodal indivision of the Substance. For there is a most high communicability with the property of the Persons, a most high consubstantiality with the plurality of the hypostases, a most high configurability with discrete personality, a most high co-equality with order, a most high co-eternity with emanation, a most high co-intimacy with a sending-forth [*emissione*] ... For if there is a most high communication and true diffusion, there is a true origin and a true distinction; and because the whole is communicated, not the part; for that reason that which is given is what is had, and it is the whole; therefore the One emanating and the One producing, both are distinguished in properties, and are essentially one (*unum*).[63]

Following a line of thought that is known to us, Bonaventure insists here in the communicability of the divinity, which, as is sufficiently clear at

---

[61] Cf. III Council of Toledo (589 AD) (DH 470).

[62] Cf. Councils VI, XI and XVI (DH 490; 525–6; 568). The relative character of the persons, manifested in their names, is also accentuated; each of these names, although not always mentioning the persons, sometimes insinuates them (DH 332). On the development of these creeds, cf. J. Rico Pavés, 'Totius fons et origo divinitatis. La persona del Padre en los símbolos de fe de los concilios de Toledo (ss.V–VII)', in *Revista Española de Teología* 65 (2005) 173–95.

[63] Bonaventure, *Itinerarium mentis in Deum*, VI 2–3; cf. also *Breviloquium*, I 2, 3.

the end of the quoted text, has its origin in the Father. The greatest good, that He originally possesses, comes from Him; the consubstantiality and perfect equality of the persons, as well as their distinction, come from his communication. Since this communication is not partial but complete, we absolutely cannot think of a reduction of the divinity in the Son and the Holy Spirit. The divine processions do not lead to subordinationism or any type of reduction of the divinity. Although Bonaventure tends to see the most proper and specific characteristic of the first person in His being unbegotten rather than in paternity, he does not for this reason forget the fundamental role that belongs to the Father as principle (*origo*) of the entire divinity.

Saint Thomas, as is well known, will identify the Father with 'subsisting paternity'.[64] With this he has said what is most essential for us to approach the mystery of the first person of the Trinity. It is not only a property, but the very person.[65] It is therefore evident that we cannot consider Him independently of the Son at all, to whom He gives everything that He is and has, except paternity, just as He cannot be understood without his relation to the Holy Spirit. If by the fact of being the principle of the divinity we grant a certain primacy or *auctoritas* to the Father, this cannot be to the detriment of the equality of the persons.[66] Paternity itself would be affected.

There is a primacy of the Father in so far as principle, and an equality in the dignity of the three persons. Are these two opposed aspects, or are they mutually requiring? Tradition has seen their mutual implication, in such a way that the conviction in equal dignity of the persons came about when reflection on divine paternity was more explicitly developed. On the other hand, the doctrine of Trinitarian relations has kept from thinking of the Father while neglecting the other two persons of whom He is principle. The reciprocity of relations, contemplated with different accentuations throughout history, has avoided what could have become a unilaterality in the context of the doctrine of the divine processions. The relations of origin in this way do not imply either reduction in the dignity of the persons or subordination among them.

---

[64] STh I q. 33, a. 2: 'The proper name of a person delineates that which distinguishes them from all others ... Now, that which distinguishes the person of the Father from all others is paternity. For this reason the name Father, which expresses paternity, is the proper name of the person of the Father'; cf. also STh I q.40, a.4: the Father engenders the Son because He is Father, and not the reverse. He is not Father because He engenders.

[65] Cf. STh I q. 33, a. 2, ad.1.

[66] Cf. STh I q. 33, a. 1, ad 2.: 'attribuamus patri aliquid auctoritatis ratione principii, nihil tamen ad subiectionem vel minorationem quocumque modo pertinens, attribuimus filio vel spiritui sancto, ut vitetur omnis erroris occasio: we attribute a certain authority (*aliquid auctoritatis*) to the Father because of this principle, but nothing pertaining to subjugation or reduction of any sort do we attribute to the Son or the Holy Spirit.' Saint Thomas clarifies that principle means 'origin' and not 'priority' in this same context; ib. ad 3.

# Some Recent Interpretive Attempts

Some recent theological attempts, from the end of the twentieth century, seem to assume that the primacy of the Father as principle and origin of the divinity is incompatible with the complete equality in dignity of the three divine persons. This primacy would prohibit full equality, and thus the communion among Them. The two aspects that tradition has been united in underscoring, the fontal love of the Father and the totality of His gift to the Son and the Spirit, along with the reciprocity of relation, appear to some as impossible to maintain. Should we abandon or in some way complement the classical idea of Trinitarian processions in order to protect the equality of the three divine persons?[67]

Due to the influence that it has had and the debates that came from it, even within Catholic theology, the systematic proposition of W. Pannenberg merits attention. The New Testament, in the opinion of the German author, would have left the problem of the relation of the divinity of the Son and the Holy Spirit with the Father without a solution. Patristic authors understood that their divinity must be explicated beginning from the divinity of the Father. This would have been the path followed by Greek Patristics, which understood the Father as origin and source of the divinity.[68] Occidental theology, following the path set out by Augustine, would have interpreted the Son and the Spirit as expressions of the self-knowledge of the Father. It would have thus reduced these persons to the person of the Father, the unique subject of the divinity, while subordinating their divinity to that of the first person.[69] In his opinion, however, the doctrine of the Trinity should be based in the revelation of God in Jesus Christ that we find in the New Testament, and in particular in the relation of Jesus with the Father as expressed in the message about the Kingdom of God. The affirmations on Jesus' divinity presuppose His divine filiation and are based in this filial relation. Jesus is thus differentiated from the Father. From this differentiation, the Father and the Holy Spirit are also differentiated. This is the originality of the New Testament, since They do not appear distinct from God in the Old. The doctrine of the divine procession cannot be found developed in the New Testament, although, on the other hand, the relations between the divine persons belong to the eternal being of God, and are not only historical. They can however be described in other ways than with the

---

[67] One can find a vast panorama of recent theology of the Father in J. M. Rovira Belloso, 'La imagen de Dios como Padre en los últimos 40 años' in *Estudios Trinitarios* 39 (2005) 191–218.
[68] Our brief historical notes have done nothing but show that in fact Latin theology also maintained this same principle.
[69] Cf. W. Pannenberg, *Systematic Theology*, Grand Rapids: Eerdmans [Madrid 1992, 328–9]

classical concepts of the generation of the Son and the procession of the Holy Spirit.

The path that Pannenberg proposes, unlike the traditional one, is that of autodistinction or autodifferentiation that we have already alluded to. Jesus, in his preaching, recognizes His Father as God, His mission is at the service of the Father's glory, and He only lives in order to bring about the Kingdom of the Father among men. It is thus shown how the Son, in differentiating Himself from the Father, is thus leaving a place for His divinity. This autodifferentiation in respect to the Father constitutes his communion with the eternal God, unlike what occurred with the first man, Adam, who, desiring to be like God (cf. Gen. 3.5), separated himself from Him. Autodistinction is constitutive of the eternal Son in His relation with the Father. We could think that, just as Jesus autodistinguishes himself from the Father, so too the Father autodistinguishes himself from the Son, and that the relation of the two with the Spirit are based on a similar act.

The Father is, according to tradition, the origin of the Son and the Spirit, while being himself without principle. In this case, however, according to Pannenberg, one could not speak of a true reciprocity of relations between the divine persons. There would be a dependency of the Son and the Holy Spirit on the Father, but not the reverse. The Father is He who engenders and sends the Son, who thus depends on Him, but the Father does not depend on the Son. The relation would thus be irreversible. It is thus necessary to search for another path for formulating a dependence of the Father in respect to the Son (and the Holy Spirit), which can also be the foundation for a true reciprocity in Trinitarian relations. This foundation is found in that the Father gave all power to the Son (cf. Mt. 28.18), and He in turn will return it at the end of times according to 1 Cor. 15.24–28:

> In the gift and return of power from the Father to the Son, there appears a reciprocity of relations because the idea of generation is missing. The Father, in giving His power to the Son, causes his own reality to depend on the Son glorifying Him and from Him, completing His mission, making the dominion of the Father a reality. In this way the Father does not differentiate Himself only in engendering Him, but further, 'giving Him everything' to the point that His reign and divinity come to depend on the Son. Since the dominion, the Kingdom of the Father is not something so extrinsic to His divinity that the Father could continue being God without his Kingdom ... The world ... has its origin in the creative liberty of God, but, once it exists, it would be incompatible with the divinity for God not to have dominion over it.[70]

---

[70] Pannenberg, *Systematic Theology*, I, pp. [339–40].

The Holy Spirit also has his place in this mutual dependence of the three persons. The Father and the Son depend on the action of the Spirit who resurrects Jesus from the dead. We thus have a mutual dependence of the three, which Pannenberg sees expressed in the Gospel of John when he speaks of the glorification of the Son by the Spirit (cf. Jn 16.14). Pannenberg approves of the Augustinian idea of the Holy Spirit as love and bond of union of the Father and the Son because in this way it is manifest that the two first persons require the Spirit for their union. On the other hand, he rejects the idea of the procession of the Spirit from the Father and the Son, because, in this case again, the relations between the persons would be based on the relations of origin, which are limited by lacking the reciprocity to which we have already alluded:[71] 'The reciprocal autodifferentiation, in so far as it defines the relations between the three persons, does not permit that said relation be reduced to relations of origin, in the sense of traditional theology.'[72] One should also recall that the Father gives the Kingdom to the Son, and in this way He will be able to receive it from Him; the Son glorifies the Father, the Holy Spirit fills the Son and descends on Him, while glorifying the Son and the Father. These active relations of the three persons are important, and those of the Son and the Spirit in particular:

> One cannot deal with the active relations of the Son and the Spirit in respect to the Father, witnessed to by the Scripture, as if they were not constitutive of their respective identities, so as to think that it is only the relations of origin that constitute the persons. None of the active relations is secondary for the Son or the Spirit; they are all integral parts of the specificity of the Trinitarian persons and the communion that exists between them … Each of the persons cannot be reduced to a unique relation, as occidental theology in particular has attempted to do … Each of them is rather a nexus of various relations.[73]

This reciprocity is in relation to the autodistinction to which we have referred. Autodistinction shows the characteristics of each of the persons: the Son founds his divinity in the Father, at the same time distinguishing Himself from Him. The Spirit shows His divinity by recognizing and teaching to recognize the Son as Lord, and as Son of the Father. The Father autodistinguishes Himself from the Son and the Spirit as well, because the revelation of the divinity and power of the Father depends on the work of

---

[71] Pannenberg, *Systematic Theology*, I, pp. 343–4. P. notes at the same time (p. 344) that 'this is no obstacle for the origin of the Spirit being in the Father, from whom everything proceeds.' The divine processions are therefore not negated, but their importance is reduced.

[72] Pannenberg, *Systematic Theology*, I, pp. [347].

[73] Pannenberg, *Systematic Theology*, ib.

the Son (who returns the Kingdom to Him) and the Spirit (who glorifies Him). This does not however mean that the Father's monarchy disappears:

> From the reciprocity between the persons of the Trinity and their mutual dependence, not only in respect to their personal identity, but also in respect to divinity itself, the monarchy of the Father is in no way damaged. Quite the contrary: the Kingdom of the Father, his monarchy, is placed into creation through the work of the Son, and is perfected through the work of the Spirit ... That which the Son and the Spirit do is nothing but to be at the service of the Father's monarchy, of putting it into practice. Without the Son, however, the Father does not possess His Kingdom: He only has his monarchy by means of the Son and the Holy Spirit. This is true, not only in respect to the event of revelation, but, on the basis of the historical revelation of Jesus with the Father, we must also affirm it of the internal life of the Trinitarian God ... The monarchy of the Father is not the presupposition, but the result of the conjoined action of the three persons.[74]

As can be seen, Pannenberg is consistent in his insistence on the mutual dependence of the persons; the primacy of the Father is not presupposed to the action of the three, but is instead its result. It is only in this way that the Father is God. At the same time, he affirms that one cannot leave the question of God's relation to the world aside when dealing with the monarchy of the Father and the divinity of the triune God. Pannenberg notes at the same time that:

> The monarchy of the Father and knowledge of it are conditioned by the Son, so that it is absolutely necessary to include the economy of divine relation with the world in the question of the unity of the divine essence ... If the monarchy of the Father is not directly realized as such, except by means of the Son and the Spirit, the essence of the unity of the Kingdom of God will also be in said mediation.[75]

On various occasions he definitely expresses the need for a clear distinction between 'immanent' Trinity and 'economy'. The triune God does not need an historical process to come to be such; it is not necessary to await eschatological achievement for God to live in his fullness.[76] At the same time, however, he insists on the mutual implication of one and the other

---

[74] Pannenberg, *Systematic Theology*, I, pp. [352–3].
[75] Pannenberg, *Systematic Theology*, I, p. [534]; and already before, ibid., 'the question of the unity of the Trinitarian God cannot be clarified by looking only to the immanent Trinity.'
[76] Cf. Pannenberg, *Systematic Theology*, I, p. [358]; also pp. [359–60].

in terms that can raise difficulties: 'the eternal divinity of the Trinitarian God, like the truth of His revelation, nevertheless further entails their accreditation in history.'[77] One should develop an idea of God that is capable of including in one concept the highest aspects of the divine essence and the presence of God in the world, the eternal identity of God with Himself and the problematic situation of His truth throughout history. It will be the final consummation of this history that will decide on this truth.[78]

One can easily see that there are various points implicated in these propositions. For his fullness the Father requires, in the reciprocal dependence of the three persons that is achieved in mutual autodifferentiation, that the Son offers the Kingdom to Him at the end of time, as well as the glorification of the Spirit. Dominion over the world is in clear relationship with this Trinitarian reciprocity in mutual dependency. There is doubt, in the end, as to whether the interdependency of the persons does not in fact bring with it a certain dependency on the consummation of history itself, which 'decides on this truth'. The fact of the relativization of the primacy of the Father in so far as source and origin of the divinity, although there is certainly no negation of it, finishes by including with it a lack of clarity on the divine transcendence and the fullness of Trinitarian life from all eternity. The engagement of the Triune God with human history must certainly be affirmed, but if divine transcendence does not appear clearly, it calls into doubt the very signification of the presence of God in the world.[79] Is the perichoretic model sufficient to express divine unity, appearing as it does as an exchange of relations more than the primary fact of God's being?[80] In relation to what more directly regards our reflection, is it enough to see the relations between the persons as mutual autodistinction and, in particular, is it enough in relation to that which refers to the Father as complete love and gift of the fullness of being? Is mutual dependence a satisfactory concept? There has been no lack of reflections in Catholic theology that have accentuated that it is the mutual gift and offering of the persons that characterizes the relations in respect to each other, rather than reciprocal dependency. Nothing can reduce the Father's love of complete gift that engenders the Son and, with it, gives Him the fullness of the divinity.[81]

---

[77] Pannenberg, *Systematic Theology*, I, p. [359].

[78] Cf. Pannenberg, *Systematic Theology*, I, p. [360; also 424].

[79] Cf. Pannenberg, *Systematic Theology*, I, p. [631]; 'The treatment of this idea should show that one can think that the one God is so transcendent and at the same time so present in the history of salvation, that historical events mean something real for the identity of his eternal essence.'

[80] Cf. Pannenberg, *Systematic Theology*, I, pp. [361–2], which immediately follows the preceding text: 'It should also show if one can think of the concept of the divine essence as the synthetic composition of the relations between the Father, Son and Spirit, unlike the ontological idea of essence that Augustine felt obliged to presuppose.'

[81] The reflections of Schulz seems particularly important to me. M. Schulz, *Sein und*

Other than the ambiguities that can give rise to a confusion between the life of the immanent Trinity and the economy of salvation and the relations of the Trinity with history, this position has influenced difficulties in maintaining the traditional position of the Father as the origin and principle of the Trinity. In this sense, according to the position expressed by Greshake in his monumental work on the Trinity, the doctrine of procession and that of relations of origin constitute an obstacle for considering the Trinity as communion. According to him, one should accentuate that being is the 'event of communication',[82] and thus the divine essence is to be contemplated as the perichoretic unity of the three persons:

> Communio. This is the divine essence, divine nature, communio. It only exists in the exchange of the Father, Son and Spirit. Each of the persons exists ecstatically turned towards the others, and is in a correlative manner, in the measure that one gives and receives at once: The Father realizes his own being in so far as He gives Himself completely to the other who is the Son, and thus He 'only possesses' his divinity 'as given',[83] but it is precisely in this way that He receives from Him to be Father; the Son, in so far as He completely receives Himself from the Father and gives glory to Him; the Spirit, in so far as He receives Himself as the third from the relation of the Father and the Son and glorifies both of Them in turn. The three persons thus have no proper being in God as

---

Trinität. Systematische Erörterungen zur Religionsphilosophie G. W. F. Hegels im ontologiegeschichtlichen Rückblick auf J. Duns Scotus und I. Kant und die Hegel-Rezeption in der Seinsauslegung und Trinitätstheologie bei W. Pannenberg, E. Jüngel, K. Rahner und H. U. von Balthasar, St Ottilien: EOS 1997, pp. 423–505, 495–6: 'The Father is constituted in his autorelation through His paternity, which is reflected at the same time in the Son. As Father, He is generative and participatory gift of His essence to His Son, and not primarily autodifferentiation for His own benefit. One can think of nothing greater than the love of the Father who engenders ... and no added dependency in respect to the Son makes the Father's manner of gift (relation) grow in any way. The Father, so to say, does not need it. True love creates liberty and autonomy, but not relations of dependency. One therefore cannot speak of subordination of the Son ... The fact that the Father is origin is not to be understood as a property that configures His person, but it is the generative gift of the Father, paternity, to which the relation of filiation corresponds, that is considered and configuring of His person. With this, the reciprocal constitution of the persons has already been expressed.' Cf. also J. O'Donnell, 'Pannenberg's Doctrine of God' in Gregorianum 72 (1991) 73–98; J. A. Martínez Camino, 'Wechselseitige Selbstunterscheidung? Zur Trinitätslehre Wolfhart Pannenbergs', in H.-L. Ollig and O. J. Wierz (eds), Reflektierter Glaube, Egelsbach-Frankfurt/Main-München 1999; K. Vechtel, Trinität und Zukunft. Das Verhältnis zwischen Philosophie und Trinitätstheologie im Denken Wolfhart Pannenbergs, (Frankfurter Theologische Studien, 62), Frankfurt am Main: Knecht 2001, esp. pp. 224–37.

[82] G. Greshake, Der dreieine Gott. Eine trinitarische Theologie, Freiburg-Basel-Vienna: Herder 1997, p. 184.

[83] Reference to H.U. von Balthasar, Theologik, II, Wahrheit Gottes, Einsiedeln: Johannes Verlag 1985, p. 126.

one before the other, but only from the other, with the other and towards the other.[84]

The concept of gift used here appears much more adequate than that of autodistinction that we saw in Pannenberg. This use is certainly based on the idea of communion that he is trying to develop. God is life in the communion of persons, Greshake says, as well as at the same time the triune God is an event of interpersonal love.[85] If we desire, however, to ask ourselves what the origin of these persons is, we fall, according to the German author, into the same path without issue that would be produced in the classical conception if we were to ask what the origin of the Father is. The entire event of interpersonal love of God is innascible. The personal distinctions are an integral moment of the realization of the divine unity.[86] This unity, which is born of the weaving of the relations between the persons, does not come after the exchange of love that constitutes it. It is also a primary fact, a unity that is deeper than man can conceive.[87]

This concept does not correspond to the traditional one of processions. According to Greshake, plurality was traditionally viewed as a fall from an original unity, implying deficiency and reduction of being. Theology had been required to demonstrate that the plurality that comes from unity does not include a reduction. It insisted the divine persons have the same dignity, although there is an order between Them. In treating the constitution of the persons, however, although it avoids and even denies this, it falls into error with the temporal representation of a before and after. For this reason, according to Greshake, it is preferable to renounce the idea of processions, the constitution of the persons from a principle, and the idea of resulting relations. Although these concepts were necessary in the unitary perspective of other times, we now have other means, beginning from interpersonal celebration, for thinking of unity and Trinity.[88] This is not a reduction of unity, but the mode in which it is realized. God is the highest unity, because He consists in the exchange of the three persons. There is no more divine essence than that which is realized in the communion of the divine persons.[89] Certainly, the names of Father, Son and Spirit (of Them both) should indicate something. But they primarily refer to the economic Trinity. They can then be applied to the immanent Trinity in so far as the economy really shows us who God is, but the problem of the degree of correspondence between the history of salvation and divine life remains.

---

[84] Greshake, *Der dreieine Gott*, pp. 185–7.
[85] Cf. Greshake, *Der dreieine Gott*, pp. 188–9.
[86] Cf. Greshake, *Der dreieine Gott*, p. 189.
[87] Cf. Greshake, *Der dreieine Gott*, p. 191.
[88] Cf. Greshake, *Der dreieine Gott*, p. 195.
[89] Cf. Greshake, *Der dreieine Gott*, pp. 196–200.

Greshake refers to the fact that the relations between the Father and the Son in the profession of faith are not reducible to generation. No image is sufficient, they are all inadequate, so that for him it is necessary to use a variety of expressions.[90] On the other hand, like Pannenberg, Greshake thinks that the tradition was unilateral when it moved from the missions to the eternal processions while forgetting other aspects of the economy, such as the presence of the Spirit in Jesus, the mutual glorification of the persons, and so on. His conclusion is that the persons cannot be characterized from relations of origin alone: 'If the divine essence is literally love, that is, it *is* the perichoretic exchange of love, the difference between the persons needs to be determined precisely from this exchange'.[91]

From this principle he attempts to understand the characterization of the divine persons from certain foundations that are encountered in the history of salvation and analogies from creation. Concretely, in speaking of the Father, he underscores that there is an original gift (*Ur-Gabe*) in the rhythm of love that gives consistency to communion and maintains its unity. He warns, however, that this does not means returning to a genetic process, because this position of the Father in the centre is unthinkable if He is not in relation to the other persons. The love of the Father for the Son is from all eternity; the missions of the Son and the Spirit, and the end of creation towards which everything is directed, are some of the elements of the *historia salutis* that he accentuates. Among the creaturely analogies, he notes the person who takes the initiative and is the focalizing point for a community. Other analogies, into which we cannot enter here, characterize the Son and the Holy Spirit.[92] It cannot but cause some surprise that the analogy that is immediately suggested by the New Testament terminology of 'Father' and 'Son' is not enumerated. This is probably because it insinuates, his reading of tradition interpreting it in this sense, the genetic process which, as we saw, he attempts to exclude.[93] A question naturally arises: can one speak of divine paternity without the generation of the Son, and without taking into account the procession of the Holy Spirit as well?

---

[90] Cf. Greshake, *Der dreieine Gott*, pp. 201–3.

[91] Cf. Greshake, *Der dreieine Gott*, p. 205.

[92] Cf. Greshake, *Der dreieine Gott*, pp. 207–14.

[93] The considerations of Zarazaga, which are interesting from a number of perspectives, appear to be quite influenced by these reflections of Greshake. G. J. Zarazaga, *Dios es comunión. El nuevo paradigma trinitario*, Salamanca: Secretariado Trinitario 2004, pp. 307–11; on p. 309, n. 842, he affirms: 'That the Father is Father does not make of Him the principle, the root, and the cause of the divinity.' On p. 310–11 he adds: 'What the Father, Son and Holy Spirit manifest of their personal relations in the history of salvation is in fact that which we really "know". Innascibility, generation and spiration are on the other hand *possible*, analogical, modes of referring these relations to the immanent level. They should not add something "from outside" to that which was economically revealed to us.'

# Conclusion

If we dedicated so much space to the examination of the doctrine of these authors, it is because it is worthwhile to use that which is good and interesting in their efforts. It is worth integrating them into Trinitarian theology. The equality of the three persons is a fundamental element of Christian tradition. The teachings on the divine relations, and the doctrine of Saint Thomas on the divine person as subsisting relation in particular, served to support this essential aspect of the faith. For him, the teaching of the Father as principle and source of the entire divinity cannot be considered without tying it to His relations to the Son and the Holy Spirit. We have already seen how these two aspects were tied together in tradition. None of the divine persons, not even the Father, can be thought of as an absolute person, independently of the others. The Catechism of the Catholic Church itself (n. 221) has included the idea of the divine being as eternal exchange of love.[94] The ineffable communion of the three persons is the centre of the Trinitarian mystery. However, it is precisely because of this that we should ask whether maintaining these principles requires completely rejecting the great tradition of the generation of the Son and the procession of the Holy Spirit, which is further consecrated by the Nicene-Constantinople Creed. In the New Testament, God the Father is He from whom everything comes and to whom everything is directed, it is Him that Jesus obeys and He who constitutes His constant reference point, it is before Him the risen Jesus intercedes for us (cf. 1 Jn 2.1; Rom. 8.34; Heb. 7.25, 9.24). In the liturgy we habitually direct ourselves to the Father through the Son. We can ask if all these elements are done justice to with only a perichoretic conception of the divine unity, in so far as the Father's character of principle is not clearly affirmed. On the other hand, the foundation of divine unity has traditionally been seen in the fact that only the Father is the principle without principle.[95] This fact implies neither subordination nor inferiority of the other persons. As we have already seen, there is a reciprocity of divine relations according to the traditional conception, which is compatible with the fact that the position of each of them in the divine τάξις cannot change. We can actually ask ourselves if there is a better foundation of the equality of the three divine persons and their perfect communion than the love of the Father as source and origin, who is entirely gift and offering, and communi-

---

[94] Cf. also *Compendium*, n. 42.
[95] Cf. Hilary of Poitiers, *Syn.*, 60 (PL 10, 521B): 'Cum ergo unus Deus sit, duos innascibiles esse non possunt'; Thomas Aquinas, STh I q.33, a.4, ad 4: 'Ponere igitur duos innascibiles est ponere duos deos, et duas naturas divinas'; cf. also ibid. I 39,8. Gregory of Nazianzus, *Or.*, 42, 15 (SCh 384, 82): 'Union comes from the Father ("Ενωσις δὲ ὁ Πατήρ, literally: The Father is the union), from whom everything else comes and towards whom it returns.'

cates this fullness of love to the Son and the Spirit, while eliciting this same total gift in Them. The divine persons are more related to each other in the overflowing of love than in mutual dependency. The perfect communion of the persons and the primacy of the Father are mutually supporting. In my opinion, H. U. von Balthasar has expressed this very clearly:

> The human impossibility of thinking of God is the same thing as the impossibility of thinking of the Father, who has never been an omniscient and all-powerful person closed on Himself, but from all eternity He disappropriates Himself in His gift to the Son, and even this is not enough. With the Son and through Him, He gives himself to the Holy Spirit. That which is maintained in all of them is what is essentially divine: autodonation, from which we must start, which is only consummated in the Son and the Spirit in the mode of restitution to the person who gives himself *principaliter* (as Augustine says) to the Father, as well as to the Son in the measure that the Spirit owes Himself to the Son as well. However, the self-gift of the Father from all eternity, this fact, that goes beyond any possible memory or any possible thought, is the ultimate foundation for what God is, in an absolutely incomprehensible way, more than any finite concept can encapsulate: love, established absolutely, is that which is simply without principle and which communicates that property to all which, in determining his fullness, can be named as a property of God.[96]

The paradox of the affirmation of the primacy of the Father and the equality of the three persons does not degenerate into contradiction. It is in some way illuminated if we take into account that the generation of the Son and the procession of the Spirit are the highest expression of complete gift of the One who is only love, and consequently is capable of eliciting the equally radical offering of those to whom it gives Himself without measure. The reflection of the Christians of the first centuries on divine paternity was an enormous effort to delineate a decisive aspect of the originality of the Christian message. There is no more glorious name for God than that used by Jesus to invoke Him, and that we use as well in fidelity to his teaching. We must think that this name, always with the caution necessary when speaking of God, truly corresponds to a deep and mysterious reality. God the Father, originating love, capable of eliciting the same complete love in the Son and the Spirit who receive everything from Him as principle,[97] gives

---

[96] von Balthasar, *Theologik*, II, pp. 127–8.
[97] We will not enter into the problem of the procession of the Holy Spirit. It is clear in any case that He proceeds from the Father *principaliter*; cf. Augustine, *Trin.*, XV 17, 29; 26,47 (CCL 50A, 503–4; 529).

us a new key of interpretation, not only of God, but also of man and the world.[98] From the paternal love, from which the Son and the Spirit naturally proceed, all which exists, in complete liberty and gratuity, also comes. *Tam Pater nemo*.

---

[98] Saint Thomas, *STh* I q. 45, a. 6–7 the divine processions are the reason and cause of the production of creatures. Ibid., I *Sent.*, prol.: the temporal procession of creatures derives from the eternal procession of the persons.

# 20

# The Trinity through Paschal Eyes

## Anne Hunt

### Some Introductory Remarks

The flourishing of Trinitarian theology in recent years – to which this volume amply attests – has been prompted, *prima facie*, by a dissatisfaction with Trinitarian theology as traditionally fashioned. To modern eyes, the classical explication of the mystery seems strangely disconnected and oddly abstracted from the concrete events of salvation history – to such a degree as to require the rather strained strategy of appropriation. Moreover, Aquinas postulates that any of the divine three could have become incarnate.[1] All in all, the Trinity was left remote from Christian life and piety in the classical treatment.[2] From a methodological perspective, this flourishing has resulted from radical changes in theological method which, in turn,

---

[1] STh, III, a. 3, q. 5.

[2] Hence the comment by Karl Rahner SJ that psychological speculation in classical Trinitarian theology has 'the disadvantage that in the doctrine of the Trinity it does not really give enough weight to a starting point in the history of revelation and dogma which is within the historical and salvific experience of the Son and of the Spirit as the reality of the divine self-communication to us, so that we can understand from this historical experience what the doctrine of the divine Trinity really means. The psychological theory of the Trinity neglects the experience of the Trinity in the economy of salvation in favour of a seemingly almost gnostic speculation about what goes on in the inner life of God.' K. Rahner, *Foundations of Christian Faith: An Introduction to the Idea of Christianity*, (trans. William V. Dych), New York: Crossroad 1987, p. 135. As Karl Rahner noted, rather provocatively, it would seem that it would actually make

have been prompted by changes in the very milieu in which the theological mediation of the mysteries of faith is conducted. Theology, at least in the West, is now charged with the task of communicating in a distinctly empirically oriented culture. The contemporary milieu is far less amenable to classical philosophical approaches of a metaphysical kind. It is instead more experiential in mood and outlook. As a result, systematic theology, in order to serve the interests of Christian realism, has had to search for new methods and fresh expressions of its content.

In this new cultural context, some theologians have turned to what has been called the social model of the Trinity and its variants, including more politically attuned models, in order to bring out the existential relevance and meaning of the mystery. But, popular though such a perspective has certainly proved to be, approaching the mystery of the Trinity by way of the social model has itself proved problematic. The social model is arguably even more prone to the risk of projection than the classical approach. Without the rigorous philosophical frameworks that previously structured Trinitarian theology, the social Trinitarian model is dangerously inclined to confuse the ontological distinction between God and the human community. It has brought with it the risk of another kind of abstraction in Trinitarian theology. It can also drift away from the concrete events of salvation history. As such, it is no less susceptible to distortion. Indeed, it is liable to succumb to a crude anthropomorphism.[3]

In the same quest for new and fresh mediations of the meaning of the mystery of the Trinity, some theologians have returned to the actual events of salvation history, God's action in Jesus Christ, and particularly the paschal mystery of Jesus' death and resurrection, as communicated in the founding apostolic narrative. Here was to be found the grass-roots originating experience of Trinitarian faith. The paschal mystery is, after all, not just redemptive or salvific, but revelatory of God's own eternal being. To Christian faith, Jesus is 'the reflection of God's glory and the exact imprint of God's very being' (Heb. 1.3), just as 'he is the image of the invisible God' (Col. 1.15). It was precisely through their experience of the resurrection of Jesus, and within the post-resurrection shock waves that followed, that the early Christians came to acknowledge the three *dramatis personae* of Father, Son and Holy Spirit. This experience found expression in prayer, sacrament and worship, and eventually in Trinitarian doctrine. In this context, the

---

very little if any difference to the person in the pew were it to be announced from the pulpit that the doctrine of the Trinity was to be revoked.
[3] For challenging and sophisticated critiques of the social model of the Trinity, see K. Kilby, 'Perichoresis and Projection: Problems with Social Doctrines of the Trinity', *New Blackfriars* 81/956: pp. 432–45; M. Husbands, 'The Trinity is *Not* Our Social Program: Volf, Gregory of Nyssa and Barth', in D. J. Treier and D. Lauber (eds), *Trinitarian Theology for the Church: Scripture, Community, Worship*, Downers Grove, Ill: IVP Academic 2009, pp. 120–41.

paschal narrative affords an avenue for an ever-fresh exploration of the mystery of the Trinity, which can extend to a consideration of the divine persons as related and distinct, and include their hypostatic characteristics, their proper roles and distinctive missions.[4]

Admittedly, Thomistic scholar Matthew Levering, in his erudite exposition of Aquinas' Trinitarian theology, is very critical of the suggestion that the classical approach left Trinitarian theology remote from the actual events of Jesus paschal mystery.[5] Levering vigorously defends Thomas, appealing to Thomas' scriptural commentaries, especially the Commentary on John's Gospel. Now there is no doubting that Aquinas' entire theology is deeply imbued with and informed by his profoundly contemplative insights into the mystery of Jesus, as Jean-Pierre Torrell's fine study superbly demonstrates.[6] There is also no doubting that Aquinas recognized that the Trinity is revealed in Jesus' death and resurrection, as is clearly evident in his scriptural commentaries. But there is also no doubting that in the *Summa Theologiae*, Aquinas' magnum opus, Aquinas leaves the treatment of Jesus' death, descent and resurrection to a section under the rubric of redemption in the *tertia pars* of the *Summa Theologiae*, quite separate from his considerations of the mystery of the Trinity in the *prima pars*. In that treatment, Aquinas' emphasis is clearly on their redemptive rather than their revelatory aspect. As Levering agrees, the events of Jesus' paschal mystery are thus not obviously connected to an explication of the mystery of the Trinity.[7] Indeed, the movements of the paschal mystery are not obviously interconnected in the one mystery, but rather are treated almost independently from each other.[8] In his exposition of the mystery of the Trinity in the *prima pars* of his *Summa*, Aquinas begins with a consideration of the processions and the relationships of the divine persons *ad intra* and proceeds to their missions *ad extra*. Aquinas thus adopts the *via disciplinae*, not the *via inventionis*, the way of discovery. He begins with the supra-historical, intra-trinitarian processions, and moves from consideration of the immanent to the

---

[4] See S. Moore's highly imaginative and very plausible reconstruction of the disciples' experience, what he calls 'the grass-roots derivation of the mystery', in *The Fire and the Rose are One*, London: Darton, Longman and Todd 1980.

[5] M. Levering, *Scripture and Metaphysics: Aquinas and the Renewal of Trinitarian Theology*, (Challenges in Contemporary Theology), Oxford: Blackwell Publishing 2004, pp. 110–43.

[6] J.-P. Torrell, *Saint Thomas Aquinas*, vol. 2, *Spiritual Master*, (trans. Robert Royal), Washington DC: The Catholic University of America Press 2003.

[7] Levering, *Scripture and Metaphysics*, p. 111.

[8] Levering, in his defence of Aquinas, refers frequently to Aquinas' treatment of the paschal mystery. But Aquinas does not refer to the paschal mystery as such. He treats, in order, the passion, then the descent and then the resurrection, without explicitly bringing them together in the one mystery. The term, paschal mystery, is relatively new to Christian theology as such, having emerged in the liturgical renewal of the twentieth century and rising to some prominence in the Second Vatican Council.

economic realm. An understanding of the divine processions is expressed in terms of the Aristotelian categories of the intellect and will. In this way, Aquinas arrives at an analogy for the divine processions in terms of the acts of knowing and loving, which are proper to the Pure Act of being.[9] While the treatment of the mystery of the Trinity is metaphysically elegant and highly refined, it is remote from the biblical data concerning the actual events of salvation history. Only after a consideration of the processions and relations of the divine persons *ad intra* does Aquinas move to their missions *ad extra*. His consideration of the visible missions extends only to the incarnation and Pentecost. When Aquinas does treat Jesus' death and his resurrection in the *tertia pars*, his emphasis is on their redemptive effect, rather than their revelatory aspect.

The point here is not to denigrate Thomas' masterful explication. It is not to find fault in his approach. Nor is it to lend support to those contemporary theologians who disparage Thomas' explication, some with apparently little evidence of having grasped Thomas' monumental achievement. Our aim is rather to highlight the change in method, and the change in cultural milieu to which the change in method responds, and to highlight the methodological issues which are at play here. It is neither fair nor reasonable to expect Thomas' explication of the mystery to mediate meaning in a very different cultural milieu. Neither it is reasonable so to enshrine Thomas' contribution as to preclude the very possibility of further developments in explication of the mystery, such as recent decades evince, nor to dismiss them as naïve or second-rate or lacking in value.

In this article we propose to re-visit the insights into the mystery of the Trinity which have emerged when approached from the perspective of the paschal mystery as attested in the New Testament. In terms of method, such an approach is admittedly more akin to biblical theology than the directly dogmatic approaches to the mystery. It necessarily brings its own attendant challenges. It is less technical than critical exegetical approaches and lacks the terminological precision and conceptual clarity so meticulously forged in philosophically fashioned systematic approaches, such as that of the incomparable Thomas.

The New Testament itself is neither a theological treatise, nor is it an instance of inner-trinitarian metaphysics. It is written to give faithful testimony 'to what we have seen and heard' (Acts 4.20, 22.15; 1 Jn 1.1–3). What it offers is the founding narrative, based on the originating experience that so radically and profoundly altered the disciples' God-consciousness. In its own right, then, the New Testament account promises to each and every generation fresh insights into the mystery and the manner in which it is revealed.

---

[9] STh, I, a. 27.

# The Three Dramatis Personae in the Founding Paschal Testimony

We begin with the Lord Jesus. He stands at the centre of the paschal drama that unfolds in the course of the Easter triduum. The farewell discourses immediately preceding the passion narrative in John's gospel are replete with references to the mystery of God's triadic being and relationship to us: 'Believe me that I am in the Father and the Father is in me' (Jn 14.11); 'I will ask the Father, and He will give you another Advocate, to be with you forever. This is the Spirit of truth' (Jn 14.16–17); 'The word that you hear is not mine, but is from the Father who sent me' (Jn 14.24); 'The Advocate, the Holy Spirit, whom the Father will send in my name, will teach you everything, and remind you of all that I have said to you' (Jn 14.26); 'I am going to the Father' (Jn 14.28); 'I love the Father' (Jn 14.31); 'As the Father has loved me, so I have loved you; abide in my love' (Jn 15.9); 'I have called you friends, because I have made known to you everything that I have heard from my Father' (Jn 15.15); 'All that the Father has is mine' (Jn 16.15); 'As you, Father, are in me and I am in you, may they also be in us, so that the world may believe that you have sent me' (Jn 16.21); 'I am not alone, for the Father is with me' (Jn 16.32). The three *dramatis personae* are thus vividly depicted in John's farewell discourses, and the relation of mutual abiding in love of Father and Son particularly so.

Turning to the Synoptic accounts, in the garden of Gethsemane, just prior to Jesus' arrest, torture and death, Jesus, full of apprehension about what is to unfold, prays to the Father that, if it were possible, the hour might pass from him; 'Abba, Father, for you all things are possible; remove this cup from me; yet, not what I want, but what you want' (Mk 14.36; Mt. 27.39, 42; cf. Lk. 22.42). When arrested, He goes to His death like a lamb to the slaughter. He does not respond to violence with violence. Indeed, He rebukes the disciple who attacks the high priest's slave, cutting off his ear: 'Do you think that I cannot appeal to my Father, and He will at once send me more than twelve legions of angels?' (Mt. 26.53).

In his trial, he neither mounts a defence of his innocence nor counters the false accusations made against him. When he does speak, it is with a certain assuredness and authority. When Pontius Pilate, who is clearly perturbed (Mt. 27.14), asks him if he is the King of the Jews, Jesus replies, 'You say so' (Mt. 27.11; Mk 15.2; Lk. 23.3). Scorned, humiliated, abused by his captors, abandoned by his disciples, he goes meekly to his death: 'When he was abused, he did not return abuse; when he suffered, he did not threaten; but he entrusted himself to the one who judges justly' (1 Pet. 2.23). He is handed over for death by crucifixion, a method of execution most often inflicted on slaves, forbidden for Roman citizens, no matter how heinous their crimes. Thus he goes to his death, obedient even to dying the death of a slave: 'Let the same mind be in you that was in Christ Jesus, who, though He was in the form of God, did not regard equality with God as something to be exploited, but emptied himself, taking the form of a slave, being born in human likeness. And being found in human form, He humbled himself and became obedient to the point of death – even death on a cross' (Phil. 2.5–8). To one of the criminals crucified with him, the one who had rebuked the other for deriding Jesus, Jesus promises that He will join him in paradise (Lk. 23.43). Jesus prays for his executioners: 'Father, forgive them; for they do not know what they are doing' (Lk. 23.32).

In Mark's account of his passion and death, as in that of Matthew, Jesus, as death approaches, utters a cry of abandonment: 'Jesus cried out with a loud voice, 'Eloi, Eloi, lema sabachthani?' which means, 'My God, my God, why have you forsaken me?'' (Mk 15.34; Mt. 27.46). Then, He breathes His last and gives up His spirit (Mk 15.37; Mt. 27.50; Jn 19.30). The centurion, a pagan, looks at the dead Christ hanging on the cross, and, precisely then, perceives that He is the Son, thereby inviting all who have eyes also to see: 'Now when the centurion, who stood facing him, saw that in this way He breathed His last, he said, 'Truly this man was God's Son!'' (Mk 15.39; Mt. 27.54). It seems that, for Mark in particular, and similarly for Matthew who closely follows Mark in this regard, it is not Jesus' ability to come down from the cross (his captors' taunt, Mk 15.30) which turns out to be the manifestation of Jesus' identity as Son of God: it is rather His death. In Mark's account, the very manner in which Jesus died witnesses pre-eminently to the fact that He is the Son. For Mark, it is in His failure, in His death, that the very identity of Jesus as Son is disclosed.

Unlike the other Synoptic accounts, Luke's account of the passion and death makes *two* references to the Father in the passion narrative (Lk. 23.34, 23.46). Rather than a cry of abandonment (Mk 15.34; Mt. 27.46), Jesus cries out, 'Father, into your hands I commend my spirit' (Lk. 23.46). Having said this, Jesus then breathed His last. In Luke's account, death is precisely the moment par excellence for saying 'Father'. For Luke, it is as though the Son appears in the utter purity of his relationship to the Father precisely, and indeed only, in this moment when all else is lost. The dying Jesus gives himself over totally to Him whom He does not cease to call Father. For Luke, it is this perseverance in the invocation of the name of the Father, up to the moment of death, which bears witness to Jesus as Son of God. It is this totally stripped and pure invocation of the Father that is disclosive of who Jesus, the Son, really is. In Luke's account, then, Jesus' death discloses that Jesus' Sonship moves towards and culminates in a pure invocation of the Father, the symbol of which is death to absolutely any and every other reality.

Both Synoptic writers, Mark and Luke, thus clearly underline the link between Jesus' death and His divine Sonship. The two accounts point in the same direction: Jesus is Son, and pre-eminently so in his death, in his total self-yielding and unqualified self-offering, the culmination of a life of self-yielding and self-giving love. His death expresses a total self-giving, an unreserved kenosis and self-emptying. He dies to any identity other than that of the Son, Son of the Father. A similar message is conveyed when, in John's Gospel, Jesus promises: 'When you have lifted up the Son of Man, then you will realize that I am he, and that I do nothing on my own, but I speak these things as the Father instructed me' (Jn 8.28).

Jesus' kenosis goes to a further depth in his descent into hell. Admittedly, there are but few references to this mystery in the scriptures (1 Pet. 3.19, 4.6) or in the creeds. The Apostles' Creed simply avers that 'he descended into hell', with no elaboration. But if we are persuaded by Hans Urs von Balthasar, in the descent into hell Jesus' kenosis reaches its utmost limit and His mission its fullness. Balthasar would have us understand that the descent is not the victorious entry of the dead Jesus into the realm of the dead to free all those held captive since Adam's fall from grace. Rather, in the descent the crucified Jesus, in the utter defencelessness and weakness of love, enters into the loneliness and desolation of the sinner. Reduced to corpse-like silence and passivity, the dead Jesus sinks, like a cadaver into the grave, into the pit that is Godforsakenness. Far from being an active descent, it is instead an utterly passive 'sinking down'. In this way, the dead Jesus is in solidarity with us in the experience of death and Godforsakenness. Thus we proclaim in the words of the Divine Office for Holy Saturday, 'Today our Saviour has shattered the bars and burst the gates of death.'

The descent, this seeming loss of glory, is in fact the glory of the Lord. It is absolute glory because it is absolute love. This, as Balthasar contends, is the essential meaning of the descent: that, in and through it, God, out of love, gathers not only our experience of suffering and death, but our experience of being dead, of lostness and Godforsakenness, into God's triune life of love. This gathering up of our Godforsakenness into God is in fact only possible because God is Trinity. It is only because God is Trinity that God, while remaining God, is able to enter into our experience of Godforsakenness.

In the third movement of the paschal narrative, the Father raises Jesus to life in abundance: 'This Jesus whom you have killed, God has raised him up' (Acts 2.23–24, 32, 36; 3.15; 4.10; 5.30; 10.39–40; 13.28–31). In the resurrection, Jesus' total and unreserved gift of self, his self-giving self-yielding love, is again manifest. Having yielded Himself without reserve to the Father's will, the divine will, for our salvation, in this third movement He is raised to communion with God. Again, Jesus gives Himself and entirely but, in this movement, He yields Himself by unlimited and active receptivity. Here, His infinite merit is to receive, without limitation or reservation, the fullness of divinity and entry, now in His humanity, into communion with the Father. His death was total submission, a complete and utter self-surrender and self-gift. It prepared Him for the reception of the fullness of divinity. In and through His death and what seemed like total annihilation, Jesus opened Himself to the infinite gift of divine plenitude.

His resurrection reveals par excellence His receptivity and responsiveness to the Father and all that the Father has to give Him. The Father raises Him from the dead. In self-yielding love, the Son receives His being from the Father. His risen body shows forth for all eternity the wounds of His self-giving self-yielding love, proclaiming forever the paschal mystery of passing over in self-surrendering love from death to new life (Rev. 5.6).

In a post-resurrection encounter with Magdalene, she recognises Him only when He calls her by her name. She wants to hold Him, but He says to her, 'Do not hold on to me, because I have not yet ascended to the Father. But go to my brothers and say to them, I am ascending to my Father and your Father, to my God and your God' (Jn 20.17). Post-resurrection life is characterized by a new field of relationships and community. Again, the relationship with the Father is paramount. But, whereas before His references were to *His* Father, now, He stresses, His Father is *our* Father, His God *our* God (Jn 20.17). In this new realm, all are sons and daughters of our Father, sharing in Jesus' Sonship.

In an appearance to the assembled disciples, who were cowering behind closed doors in fear of the authorities, He says to them, 'Peace be with you.' He commissions the new community, which is established in and through His resurrection, and now united in mission. Jesus says to them again, 'Peace be with you. As the Father has sent me, so I send you.' (Jn 20.21). He does not leave them, however, without a Paraclete or Counsellor. A little later, he breathes on them and says to them, 'Receive the Holy Spirit' (Jn 20.22). The sharing in His Sonship, the promise of the Spirit and entry into communion with God's threefold being that was promised in the farewell discourses (Jn 14.20) now finds explicit expression in mission. His mission is now the disciples' mission. They share in His mission and, as for Him, the Spirit accompanies them in the exercise of that mission: 'As the Father has sent me, so I send you ... Receive the Holy Spirit' (Jn 20.21). The Father is the one who sends, Jesus the one who is sent, and, having come, commissions them and sends them the Spirit, the one who is received. The dominical instruction, prior to his departure and return to the Father, to make disciples and to baptize in the name of the Three (Mt. 28.19), attests to the early community's new sense of the identity of God revealed in Jesus' life, death and resurrection, and contains no hint of any inequality or hierarchy, indeed the contrary: 'Go therefore and make disciples of all nations, baptizing them in the name of the Father, and of the Son, and of the Holy Spirit' (Mt. 28.19).

Each movement of Jesus' paschal mystery, as described in the gospels, evinces a self-yielding and self-giving in love as characteristic of the Son. It is a love that insists on standing in the truth. It is a love that refuses to be anything but love, even when crucified, stumbling-block though it was to the Jews and foolishness to the Gentiles (1 Cor. 1.23). It is a love that creates community, a community that enters, in and through the Son, by sharing in His Sonship, into the community of Father, Son and Spirit. In His death, His descent into hell, His resurrection to new life, His return to the Father, Jesus yields Himself, and entirely, without hesitation, without reservation, with unqualified love, by unlimited and active receptivity, in utter transparency, to the Father and to all that the Father wishes.

The cross reveals that it is of the Son's very being to keep nothing for Himself but to yield everything to the Father. His death is the supreme act of His liberty. It is total submission, a complete and utter surrender and obedience without reserve to the divine will for our salvation. His descent manifests yet another dimension of His obedience, revealing the infinite expanse of their mutual love, an expanse that includes and surpasses all other possible separations, even the separation that is hell and Godforsakenness. His resurrection too reveals the Son's obedience to the divine will, at this point in the form of receptivity to the Father. In loving surrender and receptivity to the Father, the dead Jesus, stripped of everything, even of any active obedience, yields to being raised from the dead. At that point, when stripped of everything, His Sonship finds expression in pure receptivity to all that the Father has to give to Him. There, in His resurrection, the mystery of their threefold love is revealed in all its glory for those who have eyes to see: the Father who raises the Son, the Son who is raised, and the Holy Spirit, spirit of their self-surrendering abiding love.

Each movement of the paschal mystery thus attests to the mystery of Sonship as one of filial obedience and receptivity. It is pre-eminently in His obedience and receptivity that He is, and shows Himself to be, the Son. Both traits are essentially expressive of His personal identity as the Son, not merely some additional feature of the hypostatic identity of the Son, but constitutive of His identity as the Son, expressive of His divine Sonship and sovereign freedom as the Son. By no means a form of subservience or subordination of the Son in relation to the Father, to the contrary, His obedience to the Father is fully consonant with His sovereign freedom.

The Son's obedience and receptivity, as thus demonstrated in the economy, are effectively the expression within creation of Jesus' identity as the Son and of His relationship to the Father. They are the modality or kenotic translation of the Son's eternal self-surrendering love for the Father in the immanent Trinity. In other words, these traits are the translation, in the economy, of the Son's inner-trinitarian love for the Father. Their archetype is the eternal filial love of the Son in the Trinity, His receptivity and responsiveness to the Father and all that the Father has to give Him.

Turning attention now to the Father, it is disconcerting that throughout the course of Jesus' suffering, death and burial, and indeed in the day of His descent into hell, the Father does not intervene to protect His Son or save Him from His terrible ordeal. Indeed, the Father withdraws, without seeming to make the slightest saving gesture on Jesus' behalf, offering no assistance to Him and no resistance whatever to those who would destroy Him. Through Jesus' arrest, trial and torture, and right up to the last moment on the cross, the Father does not intervene to come to the aid of the one who finally has revealed Himself as Son. The Son goes to His death, derelict, abandoned by His disciples, with no one, not even His Father, to raise a hand in His defence or by way of protection or intervention. The Father withdraws and is silent.

Through His perseverance, Jesus is led to reveal the ultimate and primary character of His identity as Son. But His death, and particularly the cry of abandonment on the cross (Mk 15.34; Mt. 27.46), also reveals the mysterious face of fatherhood. Disconcerting though it is, it is precisely through the Father's abandonment that the Son is led to the perfection of filial relationship to the Father (and indeed to us). Abandonment by God becomes abandonment to God, and the Son's realisation and revelation of His divine sonship. His death is the passage, the passing over, symbolic of total surrender – even to the point of what seems like total annihilation – to the Father and rejection of any and every other identity.

The Father's abandonment of Jesus to His suffering and death reveals the Father's self-giving self-yielding love. In the Father's will for our salvation, He too holds back nothing, not even His beloved Son. The Father 'so loved the world that He gives the world His only Son' (Jn 3.16). The Father is He 'who did not spare His own Son but gave him up for all of us' (Rom. 8.32). The Father gives all that He has, and all that He is, for, in the perfection of divine being, what He is and what He has are one and the same. His love refuses to be anything but love, refuses to respond to violence with violence, and to resile from the truth. There is no question of payment of a ransom or redemption of a debt in the founding narrative. The Father does not impose suffering on His Son, nor demand suffering of Him. By no means does He take any delight or find any satisfaction in the Son's suffering. The Father suffers the death of His beloved Son. But He too does this out of sovereign freedom. No one takes His Son from Him. He yields His Son over to suffering and death, for us and for our salvation. This yielding of the Son is the supreme act of the Father's liberty. The self-surrender of the Son is thus perfectly complemented by the delivering up of the Son by the Father. Son and Father share, each in His own way, in a divine nature that is characterized by self-yielding love in sovereign freedom.

Thus it is that the Father does not intervene to save the Son from suffering and death. The Son dies and is buried and descends to the depths of hell, cut off from God, and, in that sense, Godforsaken. Again, the Father, out of love, allows His Son to sink into the depths of hell, into a separation from Him that surpasses every other separation in the cosmos, even the greatest possible separation of the human person from God. In this excess is found the separation of God from God, of the divine Father from the

divine Son. The passivity of the Son is matched and complemented, in its
own way, by the passivity of the Father. The Father allows Him to descend,
like a corpse into the grave, into the depths of hell.

Having yielded His Son to Godforsakenness, the Father then raises the
Son from the dead, highly exalting him and giving him 'the name that is
above every name' (Phil. 2.9). He raises Him to the plenitude of divinity,
in this too holding back nothing. In this way, the resurrection reveals the
utterly unreserved gift which the Father makes of Himself and all that is
His to the Son, holding back nothing. As Balthasar expresses it, the Father
makes Himself destitute in begetting the Son, while Bulgakov speaks of it
as a self-devastation. Here the identity of the Father is revealed in its glory.
He is the one who raises the Son from the dead, begetting Him to new life,
and begetting Him, in His humanity, to the fullness of divinity. Whereas the
cross and descent reveals that it is of the Son's very being to keep nothing
for Himself but to yield everything in the gift of self to the Father, the
resurrection reveals that it is of the Father's very being to keep nothing for
Himself and to yield everything in utterly unreserved gift of self to the Son.
In the fullness of the glorious light of the resurrection, fatherhood in God
thus emerges as the total self-giving and self-communication to the Son of
all that the Father has and is.

The Father's raising of the Son and begetting of Him to new life implies
that the person of the Father is characterized by unreserved self-giving
love. For the person of the Father self-giving love is manifest in paternity.
The Father emerges as the font of the divinity. He is the one from whom
all else comes, the one who begets, the Begetter of the Son. The mystery
of His person is that of paternity, begetting. The Father is total giving –
utterly without reserve – of all that He is and has to the Son. Moreover,
the sovereign spontaneity and freedom with which the Son shows Himself
in the post-resurrection appearances manifest not only the Son's sovereign
freedom, but also that of the Father. The Father who sends the Son and then
begets Him to new life, and the Son who obeys and receives from the Father,
both act by virtue of the same divine liberty of love.

The Father's paternity, His begetting action, is thus manifest as constitutive of His identity as the Father, expressive of His divine fatherhood
and freedom. Whereas the Son's obedience and receptivity is constitutive
of His identity as the Son, expressive of His divine Sonship and freedom,
the Father's paternity and unreserved self-giving in the begetting of the Son
is constitutive of His identity as the Father. The Son's obedience is by no
means a form of subservience or subordination of the Son in relation to the
Father. It is rather an expression of His sovereign liberty and love as the
divine Son, just as the Father's paternity is an expression of His sovereign
liberty and love as the divine Father.

Through paschal eyes, the resurrection thus emerges as a modality in
the realm of the economy of the eternal act of begetting, wherein the Son

receives His being from the Father and returns it to Him in love which is equally without reserve. While the Son's self-giving finds expression in the modality of obedience and receptivity, the Father's self-giving is expressed in the modality of paternity and benevolence. Fatherhood in God, as revealed in the paschal mystery, is the total giving of all that the Father is and has to the Son and, in and through Him, to the world. In giving His Son, for us and for our salvation, the Father gives Himself, albeit through the Son, and not directly. He gives the Son for the sake of the world, that all might be gathered into the one body of the Son and, in and through the Son, into the community of the divine Three.

Through the movements comprising Jesus' paschal mystery, the third divine person, the Holy Spirit emerges as the witness to and the fruit and personification of the mutual love of the Father and Son and of their love for creation. Indeed, the Holy Spirit emerges as the very love through which the paschal process becomes possible in the excess of its significance.

Jesus is conceived by the power of the Holy Spirit (Mt. 1.18, Lk. 1.35). The Spirit descends on Mary, and the Son becomes incarnate in her. Then begins the revelation of the mystery of God's threefold being as intimated in the Old Testament. In the incarnation, the Father sends the Son into the world in a new way, and the Spirit likewise. Prior to the commencement of his public ministry, Jesus is led into the desert by the Spirit (Mk 1.12). John the Baptist attests to having seen the Holy Spirit descend and remain on Jesus (Jn 1.32; cf. Mt. 3.13–17; Mk 1:9–11; Lk. 3.21–22). At the outset of his public ministry, Jesus, quoting from Isaiah, declares, 'The Spirit of the Lord is upon me' (Lk. 4.18). Jesus promises the Spirit to His disciples (Lk. 11.13; 12.12; 24.49) to direct and urge them in their mission to spread the Gospel after His departure from them.

Having guided Jesus through His life, the Holy Spirit accompanies Him in His arrest, trial, torture and death. It is the Holy Spirit who, as love, enables Jesus to enter with faithful endurance into the Father's withdrawal during Jesus' suffering and death. It is the Holy Spirit who, as love, enables the Father to surrender His beloved Son for us and for our salvation. The Spirit accompanies the Son in the descent into hell, holding open and bridging over the separation of Father and Son at this, their utmost point of separation, when God, in the person of God the Son, sinks to the realm of Godforsakenness. Indeed, the abandonment of the Son by the Father in the cross and descent is possible only because they are in each moment united in undying love by the Holy Spirit, who holds them in inseparable unity and, at the same time, irreducible distinction.

In the third movement of the paschal mystery, the Father raises the Son *in the Spirit*. While the Father takes the initiative in raising the Son, the resurrection of Jesus is accomplished in the powerful transfiguring action of the Spirit of God. Through the resurrection, the relationality of Father, Son and Spirit is thus revealed and enacted in creation. It is the Father who raises and glorifies the Son. It is the Son who is raised to new life and glory. It is the Holy Spirit who is the power of the resurrection, the operating power of God, not only instrument but milieu of the resurrection. It is in and through the Holy Spirit that the Son is raised to new life.

The Holy Spirit is the Spirit of the one who raised Jesus from the dead (Rom. 8.11). He is the spirit of the Father (Jn 14.16, Lk. 11.13, Mt. 10.20) and of the Son (Rom. 8.9, Gal. 4.6, Phil. 1.19). Indeed, it is in the Holy Spirit that the Father is Father, paternal person, and that the Son is Son, filial person. In them both and belonging to them both, it is in the Spirit that the Father begets the Son to new life, and it is in the Spirit that the Son is raised. The Spirit envelops and unites them, holding them in communion while in distinction from each other at each and every stage of the paschal drama.

Ascending to the Father, the Son sends the Spirit from the Father to the community (Jn 15.26, 16.7, 20.22). Following the return of the Son to the Father, the Father sends the Spirit in the name of the Son (Jn 14.26). The Spirit descends upon the community of disciples at Pentecost. The gift to the world of the Holy Spirit, the Paraclete, is made possible through the paschal mystery of Jesus' death, descent and resurrection. That the 'reunion' of the Father and the Son (now in his human nature) appears as the condition of the breathing forth of the Spirit into the world would seem clearly to imply the Son's involvement in that eternal emanation, in a filial way appropriate to His identity as Son. The Son's participation in the eternal procession of the Spirit from the Father is also implied in the free and unanimous consent of the Son and the Father to the salvific plan.

For the disciples, the Spirit is the one who identifies and confirms Jesus' identity: 'No one can say 'Jesus is Lord,' except by the Holy Spirit' (1 Cor. 12.3). The Holy Spirit is the spirit of truth (Jn 14.17; 15.26; 16.13). The Holy Spirit testifies on Jesus' behalf (Jn 15.26), teaches the disciples all things, and reminds them of all that Jesus said (Jn 14.26). The Holy Spirit enables them to 'interpret spiritual things in spiritual terms' (1 Cor. 2.13). It is the Spirit who 'will declare to you the things that are to come' (Jn 16.13). 'It is the Spirit that gives life' (Jn 6.63). 'Where the Spirit of the Lord is, there is freedom' (2 Cor. 3.17).

Giving freedom, providing testimony, ever self-effacing, the person of the Holy Spirit bears the qualities of gift, given, received and shared in love. The Spirit's mission is to mediate the presence of the risen Jesus, to interiorize the redemption wrought by Him, to animate the ecclesial structures established by Him and to complete what was begun in Him. Ultimately, the Spirit's mission is the incorporation of all humanity, and indeed the whole cosmos, in the Son. The Spirit moves all creation so that, in and through the Son, it may be fulfilled in the Father (1 Cor. 15.28; Eph. 1.10; Col. 1.19–20). In the realm of the economy, the Holy Spirit is thus the spirit of incorporation, for it is through the Holy Spirit that creation is incorporated into the person of Jesus Christ and shares in His eternal filial mystery. The self-emptying of the Holy Spirit, similarly born of sovereign freedom, is evinced in the Spirit's ever self-effacing witnessing to the Father and Son, ever pointing to them, and also in the Spirit's continuing presence in the Church, forming community and bestowing a variety of gifts for the building up of community. The Spirit's mission is characterized by unity in diversity, newness and creativity, ever bringing to birth the transfiguring power of God.

# The Trinity through Paschal Eyes

The paschal mystery of Jesus' passing from this world to the Father, realized in His death, descent, resurrection and ascension, reveals first and foremost the diversity and uniqueness of the divine persons: Father, Son and Holy Spirit. A strong sense of the differentiated Trinity of three distinct divine persons emerges when the mystery is approached in this way. God is revealed not as a homogenous undifferentiated divine subject, but as a dynamically threefold differentiated communion and communication of three persons, both within God's being and in relation to us.

This threefold differentiated communion and communication of three dramatis personae is manifest in a dynamic of activity and exchange. The whole paschal mystery unfolds in a dynamic reciprocal movement of self-surrender, of radical self-offering, mutual self-giving and self-yielding love of the Father, Son and Spirit. Each, in undying love and sovereign freedom, gives everything to the other and holds back nothing for Himself or from the other. As Balthasar summarizes it:

> Only in his holding-onto-nothing-for-Himself is God the Father at all; He pours forth His substance and generates the Son; and only in the holding-onto-nothing-for-Himself of what has been received does the Son show Himself to be of the same essence of the Father, and in this shared holding-onto-nothing-for-themselves are they one in the Spirit, who is, after all, the expression and personification of this holding-onto-nothing-for-himself of God and the eternal new beginning and eternal product of this ceaselessly flowing movement.[10]

At the very heart of it all is the decisive radically transformative event, the *sine qua non,* without which the paschal dynamic makes no sense, the resurrection. Through paschal eyes, it emerges with profound significance, firstly as a divine generation enacted in creation and, more profoundly still,

---

[10] *The Von Balthasar Reader,* M. Kehl and W. Löser (eds), (trans. Robert J. Daly and Fred Lawrence), Edinburgh: T&T Clark 1985, p. 27.

as the revelation of Trinitarian relationality in the economy. In and through the post-resurrection shock waves, the disciples recognize Jesus as Lord and God, the Father as author of this plan for our salvation, and the Holy Spirit as yet another divine power centre in their new God-consciousness, not merely a divine impersonal force but a distinct personal being, one in whom Father and Son are united in love.

The paschal event is grounded in the initiative of the Father and the Father's self-offering in the sending of His beloved Son into the world for us and for our salvation. The Father is He 'who did not spare His own Son but gave him up for all of us' (Rom. 8.32). In giving His Son to the world, the Father gives Himself. The Son, at each and every moment, responds in complete freedom and unqualified love in obedience and receptivity to the Father's self-gift to Him. The Spirit is objective witness to and personification of their love, poured out in abundance into our hearts (Rom. 5.5).

A strongly kenotic dynamic of self-giving, self-emptying love is evident at each point. The Father gives all that He is and has to the Son, holding back nothing. The Father is father by begetting and being for the Son. The Son is Son by being begotten from and being for the Father. The person of the Father is inconceivable independently of His begetting of the Son and of this utter bestowal and self-emptying in the person of the Son or Word. Likewise, the Son is inconceivable independently of the Father, because the Son is ever Father-ward, ever deferential to the Father, returning to the Father the gift of life and love given to Him by the Father. Their gift of themselves in, to and for each other in self-giving love is the Spirit, the love in which each has His being. Each is who He is by virtue of communion in and with the other. In this way, we glimpse the mystery of their mutual indwelling, the dynamic interpenetration, the divine perichoresis. The paschal event reveals that God is God in and through this mutual self-giving of the divine persons, a communion of persons that has its origin in the Father.

The missions of Son and Spirit are inextricably interconnected, inseparably interwoven. There is no sending of one without or independently of the other. The incarnation of the Son-Word occurs in and through the power of the Spirit. The Son-Word cannot be seen or recognized without the Spirit. Neither Spirit nor Son is subordinate to the other, nor to the Father, who emerges as source of the sendings, author of the salvific plan.

What is particularly striking is that the revelation, in and through the paschal mystery, that God is constituted by a kenotic self-giving and receiving between the three divine persons points to the paschal character not just of the person of the Son, but of the inner-trinitarian being *in se*. In the disclosure and enactment of Trinitarian relationality in precisely this way, there is, it appears, a certain paschal character in the eternal triune being of God. There is something analogous to the paschal movement of Jesus' passing over through death to new life that is attributable

– albeit analogically – to triune relationality and being. In other words, in its essential structure, the paschal mystery manifests, in a way that is appropriate to the economy, the eternal Trinitarian exchange, the divine perichoresis. The paschal event thus points to an eternal inner-trinitarian paschal dynamic which is anterior to the events of salvation history.[11] It is in this sense that Ghislain Lafont describes Jesus in his paschal mystery as 'le paradygme de la vie trinitaire.'[12]

The Augustinian-Thomistic strategy of appropriation, whereby substantial characteristics and roles are appropriated to the divine person, although they are not in fact 'proper', in a formal sense, to that person, is superfluous from this perspective.[13] So too is Aquinas' argument that any of the divine three could have become incarnate.[14] The mission of the Son, which He fulfils by His obedience and receptivity, is properly His own. It is not given to the Son accidentally, but as a modality of His eternal personal being. It is an expression of His person as the Son. The mission of the Spirit is similarly properly His own, by no means accidental to His person.[15]

As noted in the introduction, this method of approach to the mystery, more akin to biblical theology than more dogmatic approaches, does not pretend to match the terminological precision and the conceptual clarity of the classical philosophically fashioned approaches. It privileges a more basic experiential symbolism and engages more affectively laden categories of interpersonal relations. Thus the Father is font of the divinity, not by virtue of being unbegotten, but rather as the one who begets. The mystery of Sonship is one of filial obedience and receptivity in unswerving Fatherwardness. The Holy Spirit is the spirit, in person, of their abiding love. The Trinitarian perichoresis is one of a dynamic mutual abiding in self-giving love.[16]

This approach to the mystery of the Trinity challenges a number of notions in classical Trinitarian theology. Most notably, it challenges the notion in Latin theology whereby, following the psychological analogy, the first procession in the Trinity *ad intra* is explicated in terms of the Father

---

[11] I am most grateful to Ghislain Lafont for his profound insights in this regard. See G. Lafont, *Peut-on Connaître Dieu en Jésus Christ?*, (Cogitatio Fidei, 44), Paris: Les Éditions du Cerf, 1969. Lafont points to an understanding that it is indeed a *paschal* mystery *because* it is a Trinitarian mystery. See *Peut-on Connaître Dieu en Jésus Christ?*, p. 260.

[12] Lafont, *Peut-on Connaître Dieu en Jésus Christ?*, p. 234.

[13] For a classical explication of the strategy, see Aquinas, STh, I. a. 39, q. 7.

[14] STh, III. a. 3, q. 5.

[15] For a sophisticated treatment of the strategy of appropriations, see G. Emory, 'The Personal Mode of Trinitarian Action in Saint Thomas Aquinas', *The Thomist* 69 (2005) 31–77.

[16] It is interesting to observe that the Eucharistic prayers of the paschal liturgy in their portrayal of the divine Three show a more pronounced attention to the equality, consubstantial nature and unity of the three divine persons, which is understandable in the light of the anti-Arian Trinitarian controversies of the fourth and fifth centuries.

begetting the Son-Word by way of intelligence. Such a notion is foreign to the paschal perspective here presented, in that the Father accomplishes the begetting of the Son in love. Both processions, from the vantage point of the paschal mystery, are processions of love (Jn 3.35, 5.20, 10.17).

The paschal approach to the mystery also demands a refashioning of an understanding of the divine perfections as classically rendered. In contradistinction to Greek philosophical notions of immutability and impassibility, the divine perfections, seen through paschal eyes, are the perfections of self-giving, self-yielding, kenotic love. Divine omnipotence is manifest not as absolute power, but as the selfless self-emptying which is characteristic of love and which refuses to be anything but love. Divine sovereignty is manifest not in holding on to what is proper to Godself but in its self-surrender and a holding-onto-nothing-for-oneself. Divine freedom is the freedom of self-dispossession, a holding-back-of-nothing-for-oneself.

# This Development through Methodological Eyes

As Bernard Lonergan stated in lapidary terms, 'theology mediates between a cultural matrix and the significance and role of a religion in that matrix.'[17] Ultimately, it is cultural change which has prompted – indeed demanded – the development in recent years of a new theological method and style. The traditional Thomistic approach to Trinitarian theology had its understanding mediated through the psychological image, explicated in a highly theoretical way. But that approach to the mystery of the Trinity, albeit sophisticated and refined, is no longer disclosive or persuasive in a culture which is neither competent nor confident in the realm of classical metaphysics and which demands a more experiential and existentially meaningful explication. Thus it is that theology, in facing a new challenge in its task to affirm the realism of Christian faith, has turned to new means of mediation of meaning that are more apt to render meaning to contemporary consciousness. Without repudiating the classical approach, this approach to the mystery of the Trinity by way of the paschal mystery seeks to meet the genuine exigences of Christian faith and of contemporary culture. It effectively reworks the traditional metaphysically fashioned categories and renders traditional Trinitarian theology in more dynamic and relational terms. Metaphysically fashioned categories are thus replaced by psychologically fashioned categories. The divine persons are not explicated in a rather abstract ahistorical way as

---

[17] B. J. F. Lonergan, *Method in Theology*, Seabury: New York 1972, p. xi.

subsistent relations, but as dynamically interacting subjects. It is not that a counter-theology is thus established, nor that the validity of substance-based metaphysics is denied. Rather, this approach offers a complement to traditional Trinitarian theology that seeks to render meaning in a way that is adequate and appropriate in the contemporary context and consciousness.[18] It is actually the hegemony of the psychological image in the tradition that is being challenged in this approach, not its legitimacy or value. The paschal method and approach is justified to the degree that it prompts the conversion which the founding narrative prompted. Its efficacy is surely demonstrated in the remarkable reception that the theologies of Jürgen Moltmann and Hans Urs von Balthasar, fashioned in the light of the paschal mystery, have been accorded.

This approach to the mystery of the Trinity by means of a return to the founding narrative of Jesus' paschal mystery is by no means to be dismissed as a regression to an undifferentiated pre-critical naïve mode of thought. It is rather a post-critical symbolic construction that results in a dramatic incarnationally concrete rendering of the mystery which appeals to the contemporary more empirically oriented culture and sensibilities. Robert Doran's notion of psychic conversion, a distinctly psychological complement to Bernard Lonergan's framework of intellectual, moral and religious conversion, offers the possibility of a critical grounding for the development from a refined methodological perspective.[19] It does indeed seem that there is a kind of psychic conversion at work, a kind of conversion of the imagination, and with it a new horizon for Trinitarian reflection.[20] It is that new horizon, and the refashioning of Trinitarian theology which emerges from it, which we have sought to demonstrate and explain here.

---

[18] For a more detailed discussion of the relationship between the two approaches, see A. Hunt, 'Psychological Analogy and the Paschal Mystery in Trinitarian Theology', *Theological Studies* 59 (1998) 197–218.

[19] The most obvious systematic-theological relevance of expanding the foundations, by the addition of psychic conversion to Lonergan's scheme, Doran comments, 'is that symbolic categories and categories derived from authentic religious affectivity and sensibility can be employed in theology and even in systematics without any loss of rigour, since the base of these categories and the norms regarding their theological employment are found in interiorly differentiated consciousness.' R. M. Doran, *Theology and the Dialectics of History*, Toronto: University of Toronto Press 1990, pp. 440–1.

[20] See A. Hunt, *The Trinity and the Paschal Mystery*, (Collegeville MN: Liturgical Press, 1997) for a fuller study of the Trinity-paschal mystery interconnection, both in terms of its thematic gains as well as its methodological aspects.

# INDEX